Woolf
Studies
Annual

Volume 10, 2004

SPECIAL ISSUE
Virginia Woolf and Literary History
Part II

PACE UNIVERSITY PRESS • NEW YORK

Copyright © 2004 by
Pace University Press
41 Park Row, Rm. 1510
New York, NY 10038

All rights reserved
Printed in the United States of America

ISSN 1080-9317
ISBN 0-944473-67-9 (pbk: alk.ppr.)

Member

Council of Editors of Learned Journals

∞™ paper used in this publication meets the minimum requirements of American National Standard for Information Sciences–Permanence of Paper for Printed Library Materials, ANSI Z39.48–1984

Editor

Mark Hussey — *Pace University*

Editorial Board

Tuzyline Jita Allan — *Baruch College, CUNY*
Eileen Barrett — *California State University, Hayward*
Kathryn N. Benzel — *University of Nebraska-Kearney*
Pamela L. Caughie — *Loyola University Chicago*
Wayne K. Chapman — *Clemson University*
Patricia Cramer — *University of Connecticut, Stamford*
Beth Rigel Daugherty — *Otterbein College*
Anne Fernald — *DePauw University*
(Book Review Editor)
Sally Greene — *Independent Scholar*
Leslie Kathleen Hankins — *Cornell College*
Karen Kaivola — *Stetson University*
Jane Lilienfeld — *Lincoln University*
Toni A. H. McNaron — *University of Minnesota*
Patricia Moran — *University of California, Davis*
Vara Neverow — *Southern Connecticut State University*
Annette Oxindine — *Wright State University*
Beth Carole Rosenberg — *University of Nevada-Las Vegas*
Bonnie Kime Scott — *San Diego State University*

Consulting Editors

Nancy Topping Bazin — *Old Dominion University*
Morris Beja — *Ohio State University*
Louise DeSalvo — *Hunter College, CUNY*
Jane Marcus — *Distinguished Professor CCNY and CUNY Graduate Center*
Brenda R. Silver — *Dartmouth College*
Susan Squier — *Pennsylvania State University*
Peter Stansky — *Stanford University*
J. J. Wilson — *Sonoma State University*
Alex Zwerdling — *University of California, Berkeley*

Many thanks to readers for volume 10: Ann Gibaldi Campbell (Woodlands Acad., IL), Laura Davis (Kent SU), Georgia Johnston (St. Louis U), Barbara Lounsberry (U of Northern Iowa), Eleanor McNees (U of Denver), Jeanette McVicker (SUNY Fredonia), Diana Royer (Miami U, OH), Molly Abel Travis (Tulane U).

Woolf Studies Annual is indexed in the *American Humanities Index*, *ABELL* and the *MLA Bibliography*.

In Memoriam
Carolyn G. Heilbrun 1926-2003
Lucio Ruotolo 1927-2003

The Society of Authors has been appointed to act for the Virginia Woolf Estate. Inquiries concerning permissions should be addressed to:

Mr. Jeremy Crow
The Society of Authors
84 Drayton Gardens
London SW10 9SB

Phone: 020 7373 6642
Fax: 020 7373 5768

Email:
info@societyofauthors.org

URL: www.societyofauthors.org

Contents

Woolf Studies Annual

Volume 10, 2004

	viii	Abbreviations
Hans Walter Gabler	1	A Tale of Two Texts: Or, How One Might Edit Virginia Woolf's *To the Lighthouse*
Edward L. Bishop	31	Mind the Gap: The Spaces in *Jacob's Room*
Birgit Spengler	51	Michael Cunningham Rewriting Virginia Woolf: Pragmatist vs. Modernist Aesthetics
Carey Snyder	81	Woolf's Ethnographic Modernism: Self-Nativizing in *The Voyage Out*
Diane F. Gillespie	109	Virginia Woolf and the Curious Case of Berta Ruck

VIRGINIA WOOLF & LITERARY HISTORY: PART II
Edited by Jane Lilienfeld, Jeffrey Oxford, and Lisa Low

Jeanette McVicker	141	"Six Essays on London Life": A History of Dispersal. Part Two.
Patricia Cramer	173	*Vita Nuova*: Courtly Love and Lesbian Romance in *The Years*

Vara S. Neverow	203	The Return of the Great Goddess: Immortal Virginity, Sexual Autonomy and Lesbian Possibility in *Jacob's Room*
Meena Alexander	233	"The Shock of Sensation": On Reading *The Waves* as a Girl in India, and as a Woman in America
Mónica G. Ayuso	241	The Unlike[ly]Other: Borges and Woolf
Jane Lilienfeld	253	Shirking the Imperial Shadow: Virginia Woolf and Alice Munro
Beth Rigel Daugherty	275	Teaching Woolf/Woolf Teaching

GUIDE

	309	Guide to Library Special Collections

REVIEWS

Julia Briggs	325	*Editing Virginia Woolf: Interpreting the Modernist Text* James Haule and J.H. Stape, Eds.
Molly Hite	329	*Virginia Woolf and the Visible World* by Emily Dalgarno
Jen Shelton	334	*Virginia Woolf and the Discourse of Science: The Aesthetics of Astronomy* by Holly Henry
Molly Abel Travis	337	*Einstein's Wake: Relativity, Metaphor, and Modernist Literature* by Michael H. Whitworth
Harriet Blodgett	342	*Writing the Meal: Dinner in the Fiction of Early Twentieth-Century Women Writers* by Diane McGee
Helane Levine-Keating	345	*The Life and Work of Jane Ellen Harrison* by Annabel Robinson

Mónica G. Ayuso	350	*Invisible Work: Borges and Translation* by Efraín Kristal
Karen Levenback	353	*The Great War and the Language of Modernism* by Vincent Sherry
Shannon Forbes	357	*"Am I a Snob?" Modernism and the Novel* by Sean Latham
Vara Neverow	361	*From the Lighthouse to Monk's House: A Guidebook to Virginia Woolf's Literary Landscapes* by Katherine C. Hill-Miller; *Virginia Woolf's Women* by Vanessa Curtis
John Bicknell	368	*Before Bloomsbury: The 1890's Diaries of Three Kensington Ladies: Margaret Lushington, Stella Duckworth and Mildred Massingberd.* Anthony Curtis, Ed.
Diane Gillespie	371	*Modernist Women and Visual Cultures: Virginia Woolf, Vanessa Bell, Photography and Cinema* by Maggie Humm
Wayne Chapman	379	*A War of Individuals: Bloomsbury Attitudes to the Great War* by Jonathan Atkin
Janet M. Manson	383	*The International Theory of Leonard Woolf: A Study in Twentieth-Century Idealism* by Peter Wilson
Mark Hussey	386	*The Reception of Virginia Woolf in Europe.* Mary Ann Caws and Nicola Luckhurst, Eds.
Jeanette McVicker	392	*Step-Daughters of England: British Women Modernists and the National Imaginary* by Jane Garrity
Notes on Contributors	396	
Policy	399	

Abbreviations

AHH	*A Haunted House*
AROO	*A Room of One's Own*
BP	*Books and Portraits*
BTA	*Between the Acts*
CDB	*The Captain's Death Bed and Other Essays*
CE	*Collected Essays (4 vols.)*
CR1	*The Common Reader*
CR2	*The Common Reader, Second Series*
CSF	*The Complete Shorter Fiction*
D	*The Diary of Virginia Woolf (5 vols.)*
DM	*The Death of the Moth and Other Essays*
E	*The Essays of Virginia Woolf (6 Vols.)*
F	*Flush*
FR	*Freshwater*
GR	*Granite & Rainbow: Essays*
JR	*Jacob's Room*
L	*The Letters of Virginia Woolf (6 Vols.)*
M	*The Moment and Other Essays*
MEL	*Melymbrosia*
MOB	*Moments of Being*
MT	*Monday or Tuesday*
MD	*Mrs. Dalloway*
ND	*Night and Day*
O	*Orlando*
PA	*A Passionate Apprentice*
RF	*Roger Fry: A Biography*
TG	*Three Guineas*
TTL	*To the Lighthouse*
TW	*The Waves*
TY	*The Years*
VO	*The Voyage Out*

A Tale of Two Texts: Or, How One Might Edit Virginia Woolf's *To the Lighthouse*

Hans Walter Gabler

The Hogarth Press edition is our text, say the British readers, critics, editors. The Harcourt, Brace edition is ours, say the Americans. But it is the two editions together that are Virginia Woolf's public text of *To the Lighthouse*.[1] The doubling holds theoretical, critical and editorial challenges that the present article will explore.

The source materials for the novel, though not consistently preserved, are well defined. There is a complete holograph draft, and there are the first proofs from the Edinburgh printers, Clark & Clark, whom the Hogarth Press regularly employed. One set of these, marked up by Virginia Woolf herself, and a fragment of a second set, from page 273 to the end of the book, also marked up by her, have survived.[2] They were sent as printer's copy to Harcourt, Brace in New York. The set that carried the mark-up for the Hogarth Press edition, on the other hand, is no longer extant. That both main sets were identical, however—the preserved printer's copy for New York and the lost proof set used for a first round of corrections and revisions for the Hogarth Press edition—may be inferred from the significant textual identity in substantives as well as accidentals between the New York and London editions. More decisively, it is demonstrable from the close typographical congruence between the extant Clark & Clark first proofs and the Hogarth Press first edition. Unless text has been changed, or spacings have been adjusted by meticulous compositors, their line and page breaks fully coincide.

Since the novel's holograph draft survives,[3] the proofs make it possible, by retrospective exploration, to compare draft and revision states in terms of the structuring of the novel and the composition of its text. Although this would be

---

[1] Virginia Woolf, *To the Lighthouse*. Published by Leonard & Virginia Woolf at the Hogarth Press, 52 Tavistock Square, London, W.C., 1927 (E1); Virginia Woolf, *To the Lighthouse*. New York: Harcourt, Brace & Company, 1927 (A1).

[2] These are now housed in the Frances Hooper Collection, William Allan Neilson Library, Smith College, Northampton MA. The library's courtesy in supporting the research for the present investigation is gratefully acknowledged, as is the permission of the Society of Authors as the Literary Representative of the Estate of Virginia Woolf.

[3] It is item M31, in three parts, among the Virginia Woolf holdings in the Berg Collection, New York Public Library. It has been published in a transcript: Virginia Woolf, *To the Lighthouse*: The Original Holograph Draft, ed. Susan Dick, Toronto: University of Toronto Press, 1982.

a fascinating field to explore, I do not intend to do so here. Prospectively, the proofs document the textual point of departure towards the novel's public appearance. In the case of *To the Lighthouse*, this was a double appearance, manifested in the London and New York editions. These editions were published simultaneously—quite literally so, as they appeared on the same day, May 5, 1927, on both sides of the Atlantic. But, as is well known, they are not identical, since in a significant number of instances Virginia Woolf marked up the first proofs differently for each of them. She furthermore continued to revise the text for the Hogarth Press edition alone, making additional changes on Clark & Clark revised proofs; this final stage of revision has not before been clearly distinguished, but I shall argue for it below.

To the Lighthouse was thus given to the public in two distinct texts. In terms of their difference, the two first editions constitute two versions of the novel. In terms of their simultaneous appearance, these must be termed simultaneous versions. This is a new, or certainly an unaccustomed, category for the textual critic and editor, to whom versions are commonly consecutive. Versions as Siamese twins, simultaneous versions, have not been much reflected upon in textual scholarship. By contrast, criticism has in specific cases, such as those created by Virginia Woolf for a surprising number of her publications, sometimes at least shown itself aware of them—if only as an irritant. Yet such simultaneity holds a critical challenge. So it is under an angle of its critical implications, in the first place, that one should approach the text-critical as well as editorial problem of simultaneous versions.

From the outset, though, it is important to look at the problem from the perspective of textual materiality. In the case of *To the Lighthouse*, before the anomaly of the simultaneous versions takes effect, there is plentiful evidence of the normal identity, or else the simple difference, between the proofs and the published text. The *Lighthouse* proof text and the London and New York published texts are to a large extent identical. Where they differ, the proofs record a textual state that did not reach publication, while the British and American editions together manifest precisely the (one and only) public-text alternative to the pre-publication state. Simple acts of revision have created simple textual alternatives—or, looked at the other way round, the acts of revision have left textual alternatives altogether behind in the work's pre-publication state. To the extent that the two first editions of *To the Lighthouse* conform to such normality, they do so because the mark-up for revision (that is, the author's mark-up) on the two first-proof exemplars (basically identical in themselves) was identical. Nonetheless, however, the two editions present two distinct text versions of the novel. They do so because the mark-up of the proofs was not only identical; it also differed. Where it differed, we may distinguish three mark-up patterns.

Sometimes, the proof text was revised for the New York edition but left unchanged for the London edition; sometimes, the proof text was revised for the London edition but left unchanged for the New York edition; and sometimes, although the proof text was altered for both editions, it was revised differently for each.

From these three mark-up patterns, two reasons for the versional difference follow. The London and New York texts differ either because the proof text was doubly, and differently, over-written; or else, because it was only half over-written; the difference thereby created meant that one line of the transmission from the proof-text state to publication retained unaltered a reading changed in the other. The double alterations with a difference have the same effect as has the identical mark-up of the printer's copies for the New York and London editions: they leave the proof text altogether behind in the novel's pre-publication realm of existence. The double and divergent over-writing of the proofs might be termed the active cause of the versional distinction. On the other hand, the one-edition-only revisions also contribute to establishing the public texts' versional difference; but here, the difference arises because the proof text is not tracelessly over-written. Textual elements of the proof text thereby become public text. They do so, however, not because the work's text at the instances in question remains invariant, but because, paradoxically, it fails (as it were) to be touched and changed for either the one or the other of the two simultaneously published editions.

Taken in all, the situation is not easy to deal with. It is in fact impossible to contain it in terms of text-critical and editorial orthodoxies focused upon authorial intention. In terms of these orthodoxies, editors seek to establish an unambiguously perfected text—something that, as its circumstances of composition and transmission will suggest, is hard to determine for *To the Lighthouse*. The editorial aim so defined is posited, moreover, on the assumption of an authorial intention that is itself conceived of as directed towards an unambiguously perfected text. Implicit in this alliance between an intentionalist orientation and a teleology of the text is a notion of the closed text. This is a concept, however, that recent theories of literature and text would hesitate to uphold; as a matter of fact, it was the practice of Modernist writing in the twentieth century in particular that induced literary theory to question its viability. But if this is the case, how can textual criticism and editing take legitimate guidance from it? And how, specifically, could text-critical and editorial justice be done to a Modernist text in the light of a concept that literary theory has relinquished? The transmissional situation of the two simultaneous versions of *To the Lighthouse* should therefore not only suggest pragmatic non-intentionalist solutions to what is clearly a challenging editorial problem. To face its critical and theoretical implications may also lead, beyond pragmatics, to an adjustment of critical thinking and of the methodologies of criticism to both a Modernist sense of the literary text and to some fresh conceptualizations in terms of theories of literature. The acts of revision as they result in the simultaneous versions of *To the Lighthouse* may help to suggest fresh ways of thinking about the very notion of text, of textual processes, and of both the construction of, and the construction of meaning in, texts.

Examples should advance the argument. Let us begin with the (deceptively) easy cases of identical revision of the proof text for the London and New York editions.[4] Changes such as

```
     19.4      every footstep could be plainly heard and the sob of the
     [us]      =====  ========  =====  ==  =======  =====  ===  ===
     [eng]     =====  ========  =====  ==  =======  =====  ===  ===
     19.5      Swiss girl whose         father      was dying of cancer
     [us]      =====  ====  sobbing for her ======  who ===  =====  ==  ======
     [eng]     =====  ====  sobbing for her ======  who ===  =====  ==  ======
```
                                                          (A1,16; E1,19)

or:

```
     169.16    she    would never know what they were laughing at.
     [us]      they  =====  laugh         when she   was  not there.
     [eng]     they  =====  laugh         when she   was  not there.
```
                                                          (A1,164; E1,169)

or—a re-envisioning revision this—:

```
     117.1     "Is that Santa Sofia?"   "What's that?"
     [us]      ===  ====  =====  =======  "Is     that the Golden Horn?"
     [eng]     ===  ====  =====  =======  "Is     that the Golden Horn?"
```
                                                          (A1,112; E1,117)

suggest an uncomplicated process whose results almost automatically prompt an evaluation. A wish to perfect the text must have been at work: one might, if so inclined, pronounce the revised phrasings the better ones. With Virginia Woolf,

---

[4] In the collation printouts used as illustrations in this article, the base text is that of the first proofs. It carries their page.line numbering, which is close, or identical, to the page.line numbering of the British first edition. The collated texts are from the American [us] and British [eng] first editions. These are subjoined line by line in parallel to a base text line, with their variants only printed out. Text identity in the collated witnesses is marked by "==="; absence of text in any member of the collation is indicated by blank space. Where the collation display progresses numbered line by numbered line without parallel collation lines, the text in all three witnesses is identical. The symbol ¶ indicates a paragraph opening.

as with any author, it would indeed be as difficult to overlook the desire for improvement—however precarious in any given instance the determining of the appropriate criteria for evaluation might be—just as it would be foolish to close one's critical eye to writing and re-writing evidently intent on bettering the text. Yet we need to recognize that the critical attitude so taken is an author-centered one. It focuses on the author in control, and thus views the text and the given revision as the outcome of acts of writing realizing an authorial creative impulse.

Yet, if we consider especially the third example above: with only a slight shift in the interest of our inquiry, we may identify in the change a reading response to the text under re-vision. The proofs, by way of two loosely strung questions, textualize an imagined first view of Constantinople. Of the two questions, the second one is vague and undefined. At the same time, it holds a wealth of possibilities of what might be seen looking out over the city. It is therefore textually adequate in terms both of narrative and of character. But still: just what is it that the eye fastens on? If this is a question that the text's question "What's that?" elicits, it is a reading-response question. It appears that it was the author herself, re-reading for revision, who first read it as such, and that it acted on her for the moment as an extra-textual stimulus. It enticed her readerly imagination to envision what else, beside Santa Sofia, might meet the eye on first looking out over Istanbul. Hence, it was through the specification of a particular meaning—and therefore by way of a reader-response construction of the text read—that "Is that the Golden Horn?" got written in as a replacement question, narratively as appropriate as the question it superseded. What it loses in terms of a multiple potential to mean, it gains in terms of both the specificity of the vision, and the alacrity of the character narrated.

Our attention is thus drawn to revision as the outcome of acts of reading, and thus as the response of a creative imagination to potentials of meaning inherent in the text. Such a view of the acts and processes of revision is text-centered. It does not leave the author out of account but focuses on the revising author as reader. Author, author-as-reader, and reader are thereby placed at a common point of reference, which is language itself. For, writerly creativity notwithstanding, texts and their meanings are ultimately constituted in language, and it is in the nature of language and texts to have a potential for multiple meanings. Therefore, any response to the reading of a text by over-writing it in the interests of revision—rather like interpreting it in the interests of criticism—performs, in the very act of over-writing, only one of a potential multiplicity of re-textualizations.

Revision thus comes under a double control. In a secondary, because selective, respect, it is controlled by an author's intuition, intelligence, judgement and taste. But in a primary respect, it is controlled, since it is engendered, by the text's—the written, but as yet unrevised, text's—potentials to mean, and (indeed) to signify. To progress from a dominantly author-centered to a dominantly text-centered understanding of the nature of revision thus helps us not only to appreciate the author as reader even in the very acts of composition (and, incidentally, to remain undisturbed by instances of mis-revision: the critical evaluation as to bettering or worsening loses its relevance where the author can on occasion be just as good—meaning also: just as bad—a reader of the text as you and I). Above all, the shift to a dominantly text-centered understanding of revision also proves capable of avoiding a fixation on authorial intention when considering its acts and processes. In terms of a text-centered understanding, revision is recognized as being less the result of exclusively willed writerly decisions than of the playing of a text's potentials of meaning against one another. Revision releases, deepens, shifts, or suppresses these potentials in a tendentially limitless, and thus theoretically indeterminate series. Pragmatically, it is true, the theoretically indeterminate play of language and meaning is always determinately embodied in the revisions actually carried out. In practice, revision will thus be radically determinate, since as experienced, and documented, it tends to be unique, or at most successively singular. In the case of Virginia Woolf's reading response to her own writing in *To the Lighthouse* and other works, however, the documented revisions are simultaneously, and thus coexistently, double, or even multiple. Dealing even-handedly with that doubleness or multiplicity provides text-inherent openings to the text's potentials for meaning which a forcing of the simultaneous variation into hierarchies governed by imputedly overriding intentions would precisely foreclose. Thus text-inherently conceptualized, moreover, the authorial acts of re-visional reading may, in further consequence, be seen as initial steps toward their analogous continuation in the reading public's reading of the texts as well as in the (theoretically speaking, again limitless) analytical and re-interpretative performances of criticism.

To return, then, to readings from *To the Lighthouse* regarded in such light: in many cases, the double revision, or the half-revision, for that matter, is relatively unspectacular. Yet, freed from fretting over the question of which among alternative readings the text of *To the Lighthouse* should foreclose upon, we may find ourselves entertained, even thrilled by the play of equally possible alternatives. The American edition's revision against the proofs and the British edition,

A TALE OF TWO TEXTS *Gabler* 7

```
164.3      the square root of one thousand two hundred and fifty-three,
    [us]   === ====== ==== == === ======== === ======= === fifty-three.
    [eng]  === ====== ==== == === ======== === ======= === ============

164.4      which happened to be the number           on his railway
              ticket.
    [us]   That  was              === number, it seemed, == === watch.
    [eng]  ===== ======== == == === ======                == === =======
              =======
```

(A1,159; E1,164)

may, it is true, be no more than a gesture toward an American audience unfamiliar with the significance (if any) of memorizing the numbers on British railway tickets (though just what the cultural significance, if any, of numbers on American watches might be, then becomes the equivalent mystery). Similarly, the double-revision rendering of Mr. Bankes's mental image of Mrs. Ramsay at the other end of the telephone would, in its turn, seem to be simply that: a sketch with variant brush-strokes of essentially the same picture:

```
50.10      he thought of her at the end of the telephone
    [us]        He saw     === == === === == === line
    [eng]       He saw     === == === === == === line,

    [us]        very clearly Greek, straight,   blue-eyed.
    [eng]                    Greek, blue-eyed, straight-nosed.
```

(A1,47; E1, 50)

The decision, however, on the degree of sympathy or antipathy with which to read, and make readable, Charles Tansley is inevitably a more serious matter. It makes a difference—while the alternatives clearly both grow out of the text's potential—whether the New York edition reticently says of him:

> then what they complained of about Charles Tansley was that until he had turned the whole thing round and made it somehow reflect himself and disparage them—he was not satisfied. And he would go to picture galleries they said and he would ask one, did one like his tie? God knows, said Rose, one did not.(A1,16)

or whether the London edition sharply pronounces:

> ...and made it somehow reflect himself and disparage them, put them all on edge somehow with his acid way of peeling the flesh and blood off everything, he was not satisfied. And he would go to picture galleries, they said, and he would ask one...(E1,18)

What is more: while the double-revision sketch of Mrs. Ramsay at the other end of the telephone line was, either way, an invention made in the course of the revision, not an over-writing of antecedent text, the alternative renderings of Charles Tansley in the novel's simultaneous public versions each differently modify one common antecedent passage in the proofs:

> ...and made it somehow reflect himself, and made them all feel in the wrong somehow—if it was fine well; then, the farmers, he would say, wanted rain—he was not satisfied. And he would go to picture galleries—could one imagine him looking at pictures? — and he would ask one...(*Proofs*, 18)

What here may ultimately count for most, in critical terms, is our sharpened awareness of the play between the three variant characterizations that the text respectively realizes—in the proofs, the American edition, and the British edition. What we also sense at times is an excitement at the possibilities—or indeed needs—for re-writing that the text opens up in the re-reading toward revision. This is not only true when on occasion the reading of the proofs reveals a slip in stylistics that gets mended by one sure stroke, invariant in the two editions, as in the comment on Mr. Carmichael's success with the publication of his poems:

```
208.14      due,      people said, to the revival of
[us]        The war, ====== ===== had    revived their interest in
[eng]       The war, ====== ===== had    revived their interest in
            poetry owing to the war.
[us]        poetry.
[eng]       poetry.
```

(A1,202; E1,208)

It is also exemplified in the double reading response to what the proof text conveys of Lily Briscoe's sense of being caught up in one of those

```
246.3       habitual currents in which after a certain time
[us]        ======== ======== == ===== ===== = ======= ====
[eng]       ======== ========    ===== ===== = ======= ====
246.4       wisdom    forms,
[us]        experience forms  in the mind,
[eng]                  forms  experience in the mind,
```

(A1,237; E1,246)

This double rewriting of an initial attempt to articulate the dynamics of acquiring wisdom, and in the rewriting doubly to consider the reciprocity of experience and the mind, properly epitomizes that very reciprocity of the reading and writing processes in revision that we are here discussing.

If in this instance the variation is tripolar, it remains bipolar elsewhere. Revising the text for one but not the other of the editions in preparation need not mean more than that both the proof reading unaltered and its revision qualify as equally valid public realizations of the text for *To the Lighthouse*. It makes little difference, for example, whether "she sat in the window which opened on the terrace" as the proofs and the New York edition agree (A1,27), or simply "she sat in the window" as the London edition is content to phrase it (E1,29). Similarly, it is an even-handed alternative (in "Time Passes") whether, among the "usual tokens of divine bounty" which imagined visionaries pacing the beach might discern—such as "the sunset on the sea, the pallor of dawn, the moon rising, fishing-boats against the moon"–, the children, in whom this series of tokens culminates, should be engaged in one or two activities. The New York edition (again) follows the proofs in the doubling of "children making mud pies or pelting each other with handfuls of grass" (A1,201). According to the British text, they are merely "children pelting each other with handfuls of grass" (E1,207). The focus toward which this passage steers is anyhow not these tokens of divine bounty, but rather their antitheses of disharmony, "an ashen-coloured ship" or "a purplish stain upon the bland surface of the sea" signifying the upheavals in the order of nature in the times of war.

Even more importantly, the time passing under the reign of war unhinges the world of the novel and disjoins the lives of its characters. The telling of Prue's death in childbed gains poignancy from the juxtaposition of what "people said" in variant response to it:

```
205.19      ¶ (Prue            that summer in some illness connected
   [us]     ¶ [Prue Ramsay died ==== ====== == ==== ======= =========
   [eng]    ¶ [Prue Ramsay died ==== ====== == ==== ======= =========
205.20      with childbirth  died, which was indeed a tragedy, people
   [us]     ==== childbirth,      ===== === ====== = ======== ======
   [eng]    ==== childbirth,      ===== === ====== = ======== ======
205.21      said. Everything, they said, had promised so well.)
   [us]     said, everything, ==== ===== === ======== == well.]
   [eng]    =====             They said  nobody deserved happiness more.]
```

(A1,199; E1,205)

Throughout in the course of the revisions, one may observe several, and often subtle, re-readings of the characters. The ways in which they are told take a notable direction toward a greater reticence. While in "The Window," for example, the London text goes with the proofs in tracing Mr. Bankes's thoughts as he watches Cam: "it would have been pleasant if Cam had stuck a flower in his coat or clambered over his shoulder, as over her father's, to look at a picture of

Vesuvius in eruption" (E1,40), the phrase ", as over her father's," gets deleted for the New York edition (A1,37); as a result, Mr. Bankes stands, subtly, further apart from the intimacies of the Ramsay family circle in the American text than he does in the British one. The critical question is not of course which reading is more appropriate or right. What is important to recognize is that the variation between the public texts is expressive of just those fluctuations of intimate familiarity and polite distance between the Ramsays and their guests that characterizes the *Lighthouse* narrative as a whole. The inclusion of the phrase "as over her father's" is as fitting in terms of the novel's patterns of meaning as is its exclusion.

In other instances, the focusing of character, combined sometimes with an increased reticence in character portrayal achieved through revision, is more noticeably a feature of the British edition. In "The Lighthouse," for example, it is not "Just to please herself" (A1,281) that Cam would take a book from the shelf in the library, but, in the reading of the London text, "In a kind of trance" (E1,291). Just how his children see their father, and how the narrative itself sees Mr. Ramsay, becomes increasingly important, especially toward the end of the novel. That "he was not vain, nor a tyrant (these were the things they hated him most for) and did not wish to make you pity him" is what the proof text gives as Cam's sense of him. The parenthesis "(these were the things they hated him most for)" is identically deleted for both public texts. But thereafter, the British edition also ekes out his positive qualities. Cam now pronounces him "most lovable," "most wise;" and she does so, as well, without adding that he "did not wish to make you pity him." Consequently, the variation pattern looks as follows:

```
293.23      he was                                              not vain,
  [us]      == ===                                              === =====
  [eng]     == === most lovable, he was most wise; he was === vain
293.24      nor a tyrant   (these were the things they hated him
  [us]      === = ======
  [eng]     === = tyrant.
293.25      most for) and did not wish to make you pity him.
  [us]                    === === === ==== == ==== === ==== ====
  [eng]
```

(A1,282; E1,291)

It is in the course of the boat trip to the Lighthouse that Cam silently articulates these successively modulated feelings about her father. In terms of the construction of the novel, they echo and balance James's fiercer thoughts of rejection. These at the same time, however, also undergo revision. The writing even at this juncture, late in the novel, engages in composing by radically recomposing the character of James. But we would not be able to appreciate this fully, were it not for the survival of the proofs. The published texts only sparsely shadow James's inner turmoil that the proofs spell out in two adjacent passages. The first segment in question reads familiarly from the published texts as follows:

> But he pulled himself up. Whenever he...began hearing the rustle of some one coming, the tinkle of some one going, he became extremely sensitive to the presence of whoever might be in the room. It was his father now. The strain became acute.
>
> (A1,277; E1,286)

Virtually identical in both public versions, this passage replaces a paragraph of palpably greater urgency in the proofs:

> But he pulled himself up. Whenever he...began hearing the rustle of some one coming, the tinkle of some one going, or that laugh which ended with three separate "ahs", each less than the last, like drops wrung from the heart of merriment, it meant that he was drawing near the thing he did not want to think about (his mother), since it was terrible and horrible to think of her with his father near; it meant that something had started the sense of her, as still by opening a drawer in a cupboard or looking at a face—Rose's for instance—through one's fingers one could recover her absolutely for a moment. But it was horrible; the strain was acute.
>
> (*Proofs*, 286-287)

Behind the published texts' terse account of James's deliberate "ceas[ing] to think" under that strain, furthermore:

> But all the time he thought of her, he was conscious of his father following his thought, shadowing it, making it shiver and falter.
>   At last he ceased to think; there he sat with his hand on the tiller in the sun, staring at the Lighthouse,...
>
> (A1,278-9; E1,288)

the proofs provide an extended account of James's sense of his father after his mother's death. This is how the deleted paragraphs read in the basic wording of the proof typesetting (a few revisional corrections marked in before these paragraphs were deleted wholesale indicate that attempts at retouching preceded their complete removal):

> Now in London, now wherever they lived, they were surrounded by distortions; lamentations; and long speeches of violence; and old ladies like Mrs. Beckwith being kind, and bald men sipping tea and being clever while bread and butter

turned brown in the saucer, and there one twiddled one's thumbs in the heart of unreality, sitting in the background on a stool, and if in the middle of all this sighing and being clever some one sneezed or a dog was sick, nobody dared laugh. And the house grew darker, he thought, and turned the colour of dusty plush, and there were shrines in corners and nothing could be moved, and nothing could be broken. In the depths of the winter, or in those long twilight months which seemed interminable, his father, standing up very stiff and straight on a platform in the city (to get there they must dine early and drive eternally), proved conclusively (but they could none of them listen) how there is no God, one must be brave; for there is no God, he said, while rows and rows of the ugliest people in the world gaped up at him, in that greenish hall, hung with brown pictures of great men. If she had been there now, what would she have done? he wondered. Laughed? Even she might have found it difficult to tell the truth. He could only see her twitching her cloak round her, feeling the cold. But she was dead by that time. The war was beginning. Andrew was killed. Prue died. Still his father lectured. Even when his hall was full of fog, and only sprinkled with elderly women whose heads rose and fell, like hens sipping, as they listened and wrote down, about being brave, and there is no God, still he lectured.

Often they quarrelled among themselves afterwards, what could one say to him? How could one appease him? For he wanted praise. He wanted sympathy. He wanted them to go with him and listen to him, and to say how good it was; how it was the greatest success. Rose said it, forced herself to say it, but she said it wrongly and he was angry; he was depressed. And James himself wanted to say it, for he stood very straight and very stiff, facing that dismal group of people; one could not help admiring him; liking him; as he stood there doggedly sticking it out about God and being brave. So that sometimes James would have liked to say it himself; how he admired him; what a brain he had; and would have done so, only his father found him once with a book of his and sneered at him for "it wasn't the kind of thing to interest him", he said, whereupon James made a vow; he would never praise his father as long as he lived.

There he sat with his hand on the tiller in the sun, staring at the Lighthouse,...

(*Proofs*, 288-290)

To have these passages of Cam and James in silent contemplation of their father preserved in the proofs permits us, in critical terms, to assess how discerningly the characters were adjusted in revision, and especially so, it seems, for the concluding sections of the novel. In terms of the present argument, of course, Cam's warm views of her father, and James's control of his inner conflict of feelings toward his mother and father, as they sail with Mr. Ramsay to the Lighthouse, are identical in both public texts of the novel. The revisional changes take place between the proofs and the published text. Nonetheless, we have quoted these paragraphs, for they are perhaps the most remarkable passages of the book that were left behind at the pre-publication level of the text in the course of revision. Since they were so left behind, and hence are part neither of the British nor the American public text, it is true that they do not contribute to establishing the distinction between the simultaneous public versions of the novel. Yet comparing the paragraphs in proof against their revision as published helps us to appreciate the stringency of the text's multiple options to mean.

At one of the novel's crucial moments of composing and telling its characters, namely at the end of the "Window" section, such variant options are (again) pursued concurrently. This is when, after a day of fluctuating between irritation and affection, Mr. and Mrs. Ramsay are granted their moment of intimacy together. On the level of the plot, it is also the moment after which Mrs. Ramsay ceases to be the novel's living centre. Every reader will remember the end of the "Window" section, and in general terms also recall how the narrative here reaches its culmination. Specifically, however, the conclusion features significant versional differences that have seldom been highlighted as concurrent:

```
190.15                   he was watching her. She knew
190.16       that he was thinking . . . . . . . . . . . Will
190.18       you not tell me just for once that you love me?
190.19       He was thinking that, for he was roused, what with
190.21       . . . their having quarrelled about going to the
190.22       Lighthouse. But she could not do it; she could
190.23       not say it. Then, knowing that he was watching
190.24       her, instead of saying any thing she turned
190.25       . . . . . . . . . . . .and looked at him. And
190.26       as she looked at him she began to smile, for
190.27       though she had not said a word, he knew, of
190.28       course he knew, that she loved him. He could
191.1        not deny it. And smiling she looked out of the
191.2        window and said (thinking to herself, Nothing on
191.3        earth can equal this happiness) --
191.4          "Yes, you were right. It's going to be wet
191.5        to-morrow.  You won't be able to go."           And she
  [us]       tomorrow.   === ===== == ==== == ====           === ===
  [eng]      to-morrow." She had not said it, but he knew it. === ===
191.6        looked at him smiling. For she had triumphed
191.7        again.
  [us]       ====== She had not said it: yet he knew.
  [eng]      ======
```

(A1,185-6; E1,190-1)

It is possible to construct a scenario of successive stages of revision, and even to base this in part on the real circumstances and time scheme of the preparation of the book for publication. By the evidence of the mark-up on the proofs for the New York edition, the first modification of the end was apparently the simple addition to the final paragraph of the line "She had not said it: yet he knew." This carried with it two consequences: it shifted the chapter's final focus from Mrs. Ramsay to Mr. Ramsay; and it created a latent ambiguity: just what was it she had not said, yet he knew? Was it (as we were undoubtedly intended to understand) the words "I love you"; or was it perhaps, and somehow confusingly, the sentence just actually spoken: "You won't be able to go." Once the ambiguity was noted in the re-reading, it was that sentence—voicing, as it did moreover, the Mr. Ramsay note, rather than the Mrs. Ramsay one—that was recognized as dispensable, and removed. Slightly modified, the sentence first added at the end of the paragraph to the New York proofs was moved into its place: "She had not said it; but he knew it." It refers unambiguously to her silent declaration of love. And with much more force than at the pre-revision stage in the proofs, the chapter ends again as it originally did: "And she looked at him smiling.[5] For she had triumphed again."

The final shaping of the text thus in the British edition all the more incisively marks the end as Mrs. Ramsay's end. An orthodox one-text edition of the novel would, on the foundation of this argument, recognize the American text as in a transitional state of revision and establish its critical text according to the British first edition. In the reality of the novel's publication, however, the American and the British ending attain a simultaneous public presence. The critical insight which this leads to is that, according to the entire disposition of character and plot, either ending of the "Window" section is a real and a valid textual option for *To the Lighthouse*. We build our field of critical understanding between the positions that these two endings mark concurrently. The challenge to critical editing is to support and make perceptively possible such a critical approach.

To the Lighthouse deserves a study edition that does justice to its first publication in simultaneous versions. Such an edition's principles should be set out clearly and be consistently observed in establishing as well as in presenting the text. The principles should be evolved out of careful text-critical investigations and aimed at a concurrent presentation of the novel's versional texts. To make such a presentation readable as well as usable will require explanatory and analytical notes.

Textually speaking, the point of departure for establishing a critical text of *To the Lighthouse* is the basic text layer of the first proofs, provided by the set of these proofs typeset by Clark & Clark of Edinburgh for the Hogarth Press in London that was sent from London as printer's copy for the Harcourt, Brace & Company's New York edition.[6] These proofs are dated by date stamps between

---

[5] He is smiling, as well as she is, surely: the absence of a comma after "him" has that double effect.

[6] See above, note 2.

January 31 and February 12, 1927. The stages by which the novel's text reached the first proofs cannot be fully recovered. The point of origin for the composition was the extant draft manuscript. It was begun on August 6, 1925, and finished ("provisionally," as a diary entry of 28 September, 1926, comments) on September 16, 1926 (*D*3 111). Comparing the text in the proofs—set up from copy that must have reached Clark & Clark around mid-January, 1927—with that of the first draft reveals that the book underwent extensive revision before it reached the proof-stage state of the text. Evidence of this development is generally lacking. The book's middle section, "Time Passes," however, is documented at one intermediary point by a version of the chapter in typescript, datable to October, 1926, from which, at that stage, a translation was made into French.[7] Otherwise, all transitional documentation between draft and first proofs has been lost. But Virginia Woolf's diary entry of January 14, 1927, describes how the physical side of the process of revising looked to her, and how she went about it: "Since October 25th I have been revising & retyping (some parts 3 times over)" (*D*3 123). As a reference to her work on *To the Lighthouse*, this entry picks up on the more explicit note of November 23, 1926: "I am re-doing six pages of Lighthouse daily. This is not I think, so quick as Mrs D.: but then I find much of it very sketchy, & have to improvise on the typewriter. This I find much easier than re-writing in pen & ink" (*D*3 117).

Woolf was observing working habits evident elsewhere (if, for example, the pattern of progressive composition and revision of *Between the Acts* offers a reliable analogy, as preserved in the originals at the Berg Collection in the New York Public Library). The typing up of first drafts (done in pen and ink) in the manner indicated resulted in typescripts that look as if they were carried forward on a wave: stretches of pages consecutively and singly numbered alternate with stretches of sheets typed for a second or third time with identical page numbers. At such wave-crest moments in the accumulating typescript, the identically numbered pages can be identified as first, second, or third typings of the same, progressively revised passages of text.[8] From the cumulative revision typed out by Virginia Woolf herself, a further complete retyping was usually then prepared

---

[7] An account of the arrangements for the translation into French is given in Virginia Woolf, *To the Lighthouse*. Edited by Susan Dick. The Shakespeare Head Press Edition. Oxford: Blackwell Publishers, 1992; "Introduction," p. xxviii; Appendix C of this edition (pp. 212-229) gives a transcript of the typescript itself.

[8] For the surviving typescript pages of *Pointz Hall*—only late renamed *Between the Acts*–, I have come to these conclusions by undoing—virtually, if not physically—their rearrangement undertaken by a former curator of the Berg Collection. Future research into Virginia Woolf's working habits based systematically on the broad evidence in the archival holdings accessible on both sides of the Atlantic would seem greatly desirable.

professionally. This is likely to have been, and in the case of *To the Lighthouse* must have been, done in close parallel with Woolf's own typing. The diary entry for Friday, January 14, looks back on work accomplished on Virginia Woolf's part: "I have finished the final drudgery." Leonard is to be given the novel to read on the following Monday. That is, her professional typist may not have lagged behind her, if at all, by more than a day or two. Leonard in turn was not remiss in his reading: he pronounced the book a masterpiece by 23 January, and this tallies easily with the date stamp "31 January 1927" on the first gathering of the first proofs set in Edinburgh.

Presumably the Woolfs sent an un-marked-up carbon of the professional typescript to Donald Brace before the New York publishers agreed to publish the book. Virginia Woolf notes on February 12, 1927, that Brace was less enthusiastic than he had been about *Mrs Dalloway*; but, she adds, his "opinions refer to the rough copy, unrevised." However, if the typescript read by Brace was unrevised, there is no indication that it differed from Clark & Clark's printer's copy (which, one may presume, would have been the top copy of the same typescript). Apparently, Woolf did not go over the professional typescript at all but expected to revise in print. The Edinburgh consignment of the first proofs was imminent when she recorded Brace's reaction—or perhaps it had in part already begun to arrive, though the last proof gatherings, as we have mentioned, carry the date stamp of the very day of the diary entry, February 12: a Saturday. Woolf goes on to describe the task awaiting her: "I have to read To the L. tomorrow & Monday, straight through in print; straight through, owing to my curious methods, for the first time. I want to read largely & freely once: then to niggle over details" (*D3* 127).

This diary entry is quoted in the Shakespeare Head Press edition of *To the Lighthouse*, and indeed Susan Dick's "Introduction" to that edition also goes on to cite many, though not all, of the references in the diaries and letters to Woolf's reading and revising the proofs. In terms of relating the progress of revision to the book's production, however, further questions remain. Bibliographical facts and operations can be clarified that turn out to be not merely matters of bookmaking, but to relate to essentials of the text. One central question to be answered is just how the London edition of *To the Lighthouse* came to acquire its significant increase in unique changes over and above the state of shared revisions reached at the point when the extant set of proofs was sent off to New York, and thus also over and above the versional differences already thereby established. In terms of the routines of book production, one must assume that the further changes were made on revises. The routine of revises, however, is a stage that Susan Dick never allows for. Remaining either vague or silent on this issue, she nevertheless indirectly suggests that Virginia Woolf kept correcting the Hogarth Press exemplar of the one and only proof stage we still have a record of, by way of its Harcourt, Brace fellow set. But actually, the extent and substance of revisions in the Hogarth Press edition going beyond the New York edition is so rich as to be more easily accounted for if we assume that it accumulated successively in the first proofs as well as in revises. As to the notion of revises itself, it is true that the term never occurs as such in Virginia Woolf's diary entries. But this is probably because receiving and going through revises before giving the final go-ahead for printing was—and sometimes still is—a self-evident procedure in book production that hardly requires naming.

Unrecorded by Dick is a sentence from the diary entry of March 5: "Finishing, correcting the last proofs that is to say, of a book is always a screw." According to Dick's assumptions, what this would imply is that, while the extant first-proof set was sent to New York as Harcourt, Brace's printer's copy in late February, Virginia Woolf held on to the proofs for the London edition for another ten days or so, and continued to work on them until the early days of March. If so, she did not despatch the first proofs to Edinburgh until then. But it is equally possible that she returned the revised first proofs in their respective sets simultaneously to Harcourt, Brace for the New York edition and to Clark & Clark for the Hogarth Press publication. This would mean—the time schedule would have been tight, but not impossible—that on March 5 she was in fact reading revises and her diary would thus be speaking precisely and justly of "the last proofs."

An intriguing piece in the puzzle of putting together this sequence of events is provided by the fact that, on or around March 1, the concluding gatherings S to U(+) from another set of the first proofs were sent to New York (in two installments). Why would this have been desirable, or necessary? Textually speaking, this belated consignment instructs the printer to delete the long passage of James's thoughts, and to work in the changes in Cam's, about their father as they make the novel's culminating boat trip to the Lighthouse with him. In terms of character revision, as we have seen, these cuts and changes were momentous. In bibliographical terms, however, there was a thoroughly prosaic reason for the textual operation. It appears to have been suggested by a technical exigency. Its purpose, in terms of the London first edition, was to prevent an overflow of two pages of text into a new gathering and thus to contain the book within 320 pages, or a full twenty octavo (16-page) gatherings. It is quite conceivable that Clark & Clark warned Leonard and Virginia Woolf, as directors of the Hogarth Press, that to run the printing into another part-gathering with only two pages of text was extravagant. The point that it would mean a waste of paper, and an unnecessary cost, would certainly not have been lost on the careful Leonard Woolf. Such a warning, moreover, might have come with the return of the revises for final approval, when it was clear that the working-in of the revisions from the first proofs had not eliminated the overflow already apparent in those first proofs. The text changes that Virginia Woolf decided on in consequence were so significant—perhaps, in her opinion, even so happy—that it must have been important to her to incorporate them in the New York edition also, even though its typographical and bibliographical concerns were not affected. It would have been an advantage to take the sheets on which she marked up these further changes for New York from a remaining set of the first proofs, because the identical typesetting and pagination that the New York printers already had before them would help them to place these further instructions.

The inference, then, from the observable evidence is that the revises for the Hogarth Press edition were read in the first half of March, 1927. Accordingly, the date entered on the draft manuscript: "finished March 16th 192<6>7" carries full weight as witness of the fact. The diary entry of five days later, March 21, seems consequently to have been written as Woolf wound up the process of "finishing, correcting the last proofs that is to say, of [her] book:"

> Dear me, how lovely some parts of The Lighthouse are! Soft & pliable, & I think deep, & never a word wrong for a page at a time. This I feel about the dinner party, & the children in the boat; but not of Lily on the lawn. That I do not much like. But I like the end. (*D3* 132)

Receiving the revises with Virginia Woolf's *imprimatur* a few days after March 16 gave Clark & Clark some six to seven weeks to incorporate the final corrections, to print the edition, to have it bound and to distribute it to the trade. *To the Lighthouse* appeared on May 5, a date so significant that the Woolfs were surely aiming for it from the beginning of the entire production period, in January, on both sides of the Atlantic. May 5th was the day Julia Stephen died in 1895, and it is the epitaph for her mother that Virginia Woolf writes through Mrs. Ramsay, the imaginative centre of *To the Lighthouse*.[9]

---

[9] In a letter to her sister Vanessa Bell of May 15, 1927—that is, ten days after the date of publication—Virginia Woolf knows and mentions the book's exact number of pages: "Dearest, | No letter from you—But I see how it is–| Scene: after dinner: Nessa sewing: Duncan doing absolutely nothing. | *Nessa*: (throwing down her work) Christ! There's the Lighthouse! I've only got to page 86 and I see there are 320. Now I cant write to Virginia because she'll expect me to tell her what I think of it. | *Duncan* Well, I should just tell her that you think it a masterpiece. | *Nessa* But she's sure to find out—They always do. She'll want to know why I think its a masterpiece | *Duncan* Well Nessa, I'm afraid I cant help you, because I've only read 5 pages so far, and really I don't see much prospect of doing much reading this month, or next month, or indeed before Christmas" (*L3* 375-76). Page 86 of the first edition, which is as far as Vanessa is supposed to have read, seems intriguingly significant. It speaks of Lily Briscoe: "She took up once more her old painting

Ascertaining the recoverable facts and circumstances of the passage of *To the Lighthouse* from the first proofs through to the first editions, we have established the parameters for a critical edition in terms of the documents on which to base it. Textual criticism, in preparing the ground for the critical editing, has run half its course, and accomplished its first task. The second and remaining task lies in assessing the relative quality of the main witness texts themselves by applying text-related text-critical—that is, both bibliographical and critical—criteria and procedures. Would we be aiming for an orthodox critical edition on copy-text editing principles, a document text would also need to be selected, from among the extant witness texts, to serve as its copy-text. Since, however, our goal is rather to produce an edition that does justice to the existence of *To the Lighthouse* in two simultaneous public versions, the choice of a copy-text will not be a matter of overriding importance—though, as will be seen, the choice of a base text for the presentation of the two versions that we intend to propose will still require careful consideration.

For this enterprise, our first concern must be to establish each version on its own terms in a form of the highest possible authenticity. This means ascertaining how far, in every reading of words and punctuation, the witness for each of the novel's versions—that is the British first edition, on the one hand, and the American first edition, on the other hand—provides an authorial as well as a non-corrupt version text. Assessing the record of each version text in its respective first edition, so as to gain each version's genuine authorial text, means in turn stripping, from that record, the overlays both of house styling—most likely to occur in details of punctuation, spelling and typography—and of textual error.

Textual error may on occasion be inherited. It may have its origin in the proofs, from where it may descend to both, or only one, of the first editions. At 241.23, for instance, the proofs read "revivication" and this goes unobserved in the British tradition of the text until the Hogarth Press Uniform Edition of 1930 eventually corrects it; the New York first edition, by contrast, immediately recognizes this misprint and puts it right (A1,233). Or the origin of a textual error may even lie in the typescript that served as printer's copy for the Clark & Clark proofs. The proof phrasing of the second parenthetical passage in "Time Passes,"

---

position with the dim eyes and the absent-minded manner ... becoming once more under the power of that vision which she had seen clearly once and must now grope for among hedges and houses and mothers and children—her picture. It was a question, she remembered, how to connect this mass on the right hand with that on the left. ... But the danger was that ... the unity of the whole might be broken. She stopped ... she took the canvas lightly off the easel." With what greater emblematic succinctness in a letter could Vanessa's and Virginia's sisterhood in art, together with the figurative signification of Lily Briscoe and her painting for the novel, be expressed?

for example, looks deficient: "(One dark morning, Mr. Ramsay stumbling along a passage stretched his arms out, but Mrs. Ramsay having died rather suddenly the night before he stumbled along the passage stretching his arms out.)" A clause to end the sentence seems to be missing. This may be the typesetter's fault; or else, the typist already could have made the omission. Unfortunately, Woolf's two efforts to correct and revise this passage, attempted separately for the two versions, did not in either case fully succeed in mending the phrasing.[10]

Where textual error has been introduced in either of the first editions, a positive check to detect it against the proofs is generally only possible, or at any rate is a great deal easier, for the New York edition. Since the extant proofs which provided its printer's copy hold the record of every correction and revision actively made on them, any departure that the New York typesetters introduced is, if it is nothing else, house styling, mainly of punctuation and spelling; or it is a simple necessary correction of the proof text overlooked in the course of Woolf's own correcting and revising. But if it is neither house styling nor a simple correction, a departure without instruction in the setting of the New York first edition from the first-proof text must be assumed to be an outright textual error. To establish a text of the highest possible authenticity for the American version of *To the Lighthouse*, one would eliminate such textual errors; probably accept the occasional correction of proof-text errors; and decide on a policy of how to deal with the house stylings.

A policy regarding the house stylings should relate to the general notion that the American and British editions make public simultaneous versions of the novel. One main reason that we have put forward for terming them simultaneous is the fact that the editions were published on the same day. One logical consequence of our basing the idea of versional simultaneity on the simultaneity of these acts of publication is to respect the American guise of the New York edition, and especially so in matters of spelling and punctuation. In other words: the American edition, in significant ways, and especially at the textual surface of the so-called accidentals, derives its versional individuality from its not fulfilling authorial intention in these matters. To respect its American guise is thus, in terms of underlying tenets of editorial theory, a gesture toward translating a social theory of editing into editorial practice. This might even stretch, if the production context warranted it, to accepting American idiomatic equivalents in

---

[10] A1,194; E1,199-200. The only genuinely critical attempt, to my knowledge, to emend this persistent textual error has been made by Stella McNichol in her 1992 Penguin Books edition of *To the Lighthouse*. Julia Briggs mentions the instance in her perceptive critique of Woolf textual criticism, "Between the Texts: Virginia Woolf's Acts of Revision" (153).

words or phrases for English ones, even without the authority of an authorial instruction. The situation seems not to occur, however, in *To the Lighthouse*.[11]

The departures in the New York edition's wording from the text set in the first proofs, or Virginia Woolf's instructions for correction and revision on the extant exemplar of those proofs, can indeed with some confidence be identified as textual errors. The clearcut distinction is supported by the fact that, to the best of our knowledge, Woolf did not read revises on the American edition. She could thus not herself have made this change, for example, from "exaltation" to "exultation,"

```
171.13      the ring of exaltation  and melancholy in his voice:
   [us]     === ==== == exultation, === ========== == === ======
   [eng]    === ==== == ==========  === ========== == === ======
```

(A1,166; E1,171)

It is therefore entirely up to the editor to weigh the possibility of accepting "exultation" as the American version-text's emendation; or else to class it as a mistaken, if not unintelligent, guess at an intended reading, and consequently a textual error. Nor could Woolf have detected and amended mis-executions of her own revisional instructions that had resulted in textual errors in the American edition. One such instance is the strange compound "surface pool" on A1,266, where it is evident enough that the mark-up of the Harcourt, Brace printer's copy was deficient, and the American text should really have read as the English one: "surface of the pool" (E1,276). Another case is the syntactic conundrum in the American edition: "the great in birth receiving from her, some half grudgingly, half respect" (A1,17). The proof mark-up presented a two-fold problem. Woolf had neglected to delete the second "half" that she was replacing with "some" and at the same time, she had placed that "some" in an ambiguous position in the margin. The New York typesetters followed what they believed were their instructions, but the revised phrasing which the mark-up points to should be critically construed as "... receiving from her, half grudgingly, some respect."

The British text, however, has: "... receiving from her, half grudging, some respect" (E1,19): for "half grudgingly" it reads "half grudging." Is this a diver-

---

[11] But it is a pervasive phenomenon in transatlantic double publishing generally. Fredson Bowers may be remembered by some as protesting vigorously against what he saw as a malpractice in publishing to adjust everyday idiom ("gas" for "petrol" for example, or vice versa) when an English book was published in America, or an American one in England. What was anathema to the intentionalist could be taken in her stride by a post-intentionalist editor orientated, over and above intention, toward production and reception factors in the critical constitution of a text.

gent revision, or is it a textual error in the British edition? Seeing that before revision, the proof text at this point read: "the great in birth coming to her mind now and then, half grudgingly, half respectfully," is it safe to take the "grudging" of the British text as an authentically revised reading? Or might this, in turn, be a textual error in the British edition caused by an accidental curtailing of the proof's "grudgingly" in the process of dove-tailing the revision into the standing type? However, for the compound of changes before us, it would be text-critically unsound to accept one part—because it agrees with the evident revisional instructions for the American text—as a revision correctly carried out in print for the British edition, while rejecting another part—because it diverges from the American text—as a textual error. Grammatically, adverb and adjective are both possible in the given position, with only the subtlest shift in meaning, together with a perceptible modulation in rhythm and sound. The variance between "grudgingly" and "grudging" therefore constitutes a genuine versional difference between the American and the British text.

We have construed this example as a way of exploring how textual errors may be adjudicated in the British text. At the same time, what this experimental analysis highlights, is the greater difficulty of isolating them there at all. We possess no pre-publication witness against which to check the performance of the Edinburgh typesetters. The typescript from which they set up the text has not survived, nor has the exemplar of the first proofs hitherto been traced that Virginia Woolf marked up for the British edition in parallel to that for the American edition. Nor, thirdly, do the revises seem to have been preserved on which, as we have suggested, a further round of revisions was entered in addition to those made on the first proofs. In general terms, however, this lack of documentation is to some extent offset by the fact that, contingent upon the routine procedures of book production itself, repeated rounds of correction were performed on the British text. In the course of the marking-up of the first proofs, not only was the text revised, but Clark & Clark's typesetting was of course also corrected; and it was corrected a second time when the incorporation of the revisions from the first proofs was checked in the revises.

All this, naturally, did not guarantee an error-free text (typos like "revivication" remained undetected), but the repeated working-over heightens our expectation that the British text ought generally to be sound. If textual errors persist, even though isolating them is trickier than in the American edition, the presumption is also that they are rarer. Nonetheless, we encounter, for instance, the phrasing at E1,16.28-17.1: "...| like a Queen's raising from the mud a beggar's || dirty foot and washing, when she thus admonished |..."[12] We would argue

---

[12] The line breaks (|) and the page break between pages 16 and 17 (||) fall as indicated.

that these lines feature a textual error. To do so requires close bibliographical reasoning. The proofs have: "…| like a Queen's raising from the mud to wash a || beggar's dirty foot, when she thus admonished |…" (cf. A1,14). We assume that this should have been correctly revised to: "…| like a Queen's raising from the mud and washing || a beggar's dirty foot, when she thus admonished |…" To perform the revision he was instructed to make, the compositor needed to remove line 16.28, which is the bottom line of page 16, and line 17.1 from the standing type of the adjacent pages. To replace them, he would have arranged two new lines of type, and he would have partly used the broken-up type from the removed lines to do so. In the course of the operation, he would have had three strings of type of approximately equal length to juggle with and to distribute over the end of the one and the beginning of the next new line of type; The three units were "dirty foot," (in standing type), "a beggar's" and "and washing" and the latter two would appear to have been interchanged by mistake and put into each other's intended positions. The first edition's odd phrasing was the result.

The change effected produces a reading unique to the British edition. We believe it likely that this revision was made on the revises, and that this is the main reason that it was not identified as the textual error we assume it is, and thus not corrected before publication. In terms of the critical and bibliographic assessment of this passage and its textual error, the case would not be altered if the revision had been made on the first proofs. In this case, it is true that the revises would have offered an opportunity for checking that the revision had been correctly incorporated. Positive evidence, however, would be required that the opportunity was taken. It is a matter of principle of textual criticism and editing that a textual error passing under the authorial eye but left untouched in a round of correction cannot be considered as silently approved (and thus, by purely negative evidence, be regarded as no longer an error).

Oversights in correction, rather, are simply a fact of life in the transmission of texts. In the case of *To the Lighthouse*, indeed, these are not confined to easily detectable, and therefore in some sense trivial misprints. The persistent misnumbering of the sections in the final "Lighthouse" division of the novel, for instance, is perhaps the most serious failure to correct that both criticism and editing have to contend with. Going back to the Edinburgh proofs, it most immediately affects the British tradition of the text, where the "Lighthouse" division does not feature a section "2" until the Everyman edition of 1938 marks an additional section half-way between "1" and "3" and calls it "2." Whether this was inserted on authoritative instruction, however, is unknown. The American first edition, in contrast to both the Hogarth Press first and Uniform editions, notices straightaway that section "1" is irregularly followed immediately by a section "3" in the first proofs, without an intervening section "2." In restyling the section numbering from arabic to roman numerals, it simply calls "3" "ii" and renumbers all subsequent sections accordingly. Criticism may wish to resolve this crux by debating whether a segmentation into 13 or 14 parts is more appropriate to the "Lighthouse" division of the book. What we would not wish to assume, however, is that Virginia Woolf, in failing to adjust the numbering sequence in the course of her several corrective re-readings of *To the Lighthouse* before publication, sanctioned the chapter's lack of a section number, and/or a section, "2."

Despite a few textual errors and remaining misprints, the British edition of *To the Lighthouse* provides us with a thoroughly worked-over text. Its aggregate of correction and revision is appreciably higher than that of the American edition, and it remained under close authorial control throughout the period of the book's production. As regards the accidentals of spelling and punctuation, the Edinburgh typesetters' affinity to Virginia Woolf's own styling was close, and their house styling would have been the natural—meaning: the conventional—extension of her own conventions as a writer, as well as an amateur tradeswoman in the composing room. (As an aside it may be noted how aware of the technical consequences of her revisional instructions Virginia Woolf often shows herself to be. She will if she can accommodate her changes to the typesetters' need to shift type and typelines, helping them to limit the invasion into standing type to a minimum.) Both in terms of its textual substance, therefore, and of its British guise on the typographical surface, the Hogarth Press edition presents its own version of *To the Lighthouse*, distinctly individuated against the Harcourt, Brace edition. In the parlance of the intentionalist editors of old, it also, as it happens, provides the version of the text closest, overall, to the author's intention.[13]

The editorial challenge of *To the Lighthouse* is to design an edition that will convey both the fluidity of the revisional finishing of the book and the versional distinctiveness and individuality of the simultaneous British and American editions. One way to accomplish these aims in book form would be a facing-page text edition. This would utilize the parallel presentation to make the versional difference readable by the horizontal comparison of the two texts in juxtaposition. Antecedent states of readings for either text, or both, would be footnoted at the

[13] J.A. Lavin, however, gave original currency to the opposite view. "[W]ithout having Woolf's marked-up proofs to check against, [Lavin] mistakenly concluded that the American edition represented the latest and best state of the novel, 'superior to the one published in England by Mrs Woolf's own company' (187)," comments Julia Briggs (151). This is a nobly reticent assessment. It is true that Lavin worked under the handicap of assuming the proofs to be lost; they were at the time still in private repository. Yet systematic and critical collation, combined with the use he did make of diary and letters, should by sheer force of text-critical logic have led Lavin to truer conclusions about the textual situation, the lack of the physical evidence from the proofs notwithstanding.

bottom of the pages, as would any changes to the British text only—both corrections and revisions—that were made in British issues and editions after the first edition during Woolf's life-time. To each version, a small number of editorial emendations would lastly be necessary, and these, if not also footnoted, could be listed after the main facing-text block of the edition.

The essential aims of a two-version edition could, however, be accomplished less expansively in book form than through a relentless facing-page arrangement. The edition we are envisaging—while still featuring the three main presentational units described, namely the text page, its footnotes, and the appended matter—would challenge its readers by means of a dynamic and variable formatting of its continuous text pages. These would be more intricately arranged than plain reading-text pages. Mainly progressing as one text, and so emphasizing the novel's forward flow, they would divide down the middle for passages or paragraphs where only a visualization in parallel could adequately convey the divergence between the British and the American version. There would be two blocks of footnotes on the page. One would indicate the versional differences in any single words or phrases that were not displayed in parallel columns. The other would give the antecedent text from the proofs in cases where both versions were revised away from that text, whether identically or differently. Passages like the end of the novel's "Window" division might therefore be presented on the page in this edition as follows (where, at line 23, the text flow divides into two columns, the left-hand column represents the British text, and the right-hand column the American one):

    And what then? For she felt that he was still looking at her, but that his look had changed. He wanted something—wanted the thing she always found it so difficult to give him; wanted her to tell him that she loved him. And that, no, she could not do. He found talking so much easier than she did. He could say
5   things—she never could. So naturally it was always he that said the things, and then for some reason he would mind this suddenly, and would reproach her. A heartless woman he called her; she never told him that she loved him. But it was not so—it was not so. It was only that she never could say what she felt. Was there no crumb on his coat? Nothing she could do for him? Getting up she stood
10 at the window with the reddish-brown stocking in her hands, partly to turn away from him, partly because she did not mind looking now, with him watching, at the Lighthouse. For she knew that he had turned his head as she turned; he was watching her. She knew that he was thinking, You are more beautiful than ever. And she felt herself very beautiful. Will you not tell me just for once that you
15 love me? He was thinking that, for he was roused, what with Minta and his book, and its being the end of the day and their having quarrelled about going to the Lighthouse. But she could not do it; she could not say it. Then, knowing that he was watching her, instead of saying any thing she turned, holding her stocking, and looked at him. And as she looked at him she began to smile, for
20 though she had not said a word, he knew, of course he knew, that she loved him.

He could not deny it. And smiling she looked out of the window and said (thinking to herself, Nothing on earth can equal this happiness)–

"Yes, you were right. It's going to be wet to-morrow." She had not said it, but he knew it. And she looked at him smiling. For she had triumphed again.	"Yes, you were right. It's going to be wet tomorrow. You won't be able to go." And she looked at him smiling. For she had triumphed again. She had not said it: yet he knew.

11-12 did not mind looking now, with him watching, at the Lighthouse. For] remembered how beautiful it often is—the sea at night. But (p; us)

---

9 do for him?] do? (p) **24** to-morrow."] to-morrow. You won't be able to go." (p)

Similarly, a passage in mid-paragraph where a couple of sentences were deleted in revision for the American edition only might be presented thus:

Still, if every door in a house is left perpetually open, and no lockmaker in the whole of Scotland can mend a bolt, things must spoil. What was the use of flinging a green Cashmere shawl over the edge of a picture frame? In two weeks it would be the colour of pea soup. But it was the doors that annoyed her; every door was left open. She listened. The drawing-room door was open; the hall door was open; it sounded as if the bedroom doors were open; and certainly the window on the landing was open, for that she had opened herself.	Every

3-8 What ... every] STET (p)

These proposals for an editorial presentation of *To the Lighthouse* in its two simultaneous versions should be understood as a first sketch only, open to reconsideration and modification. The choice to footnote the versional variant at lines 11-12 of the first sample, for instance, has here been made mainly to illustrate that we envisage using both parallel passaging and footnoting to communicate the versional differences. Yet, weighing the variation critically, the editor might equally decide to parallel "did not mind looking now, with him watching, at the Lighthouse. For" against "remembered how beautiful it often is—the sea at night. But" in the same way as the end of the section is paralleled; or as is the deletion in the American edition, which the second sample exemplifies, and where the absence of text is immediately apparent from the blank right-hand column.

The second footnote block to the first sample records, with reference to line 9, that the published texts agree in reading "do for him?" against the proofs' "do?"–this therefore is a revision common to both versions. Next, with reference to line 24 of the left-hand column, the antecedent reading of the proofs is also reported. A look at the right-hand column of the text block will confirm that the American edition transmits the proof reading unchanged (except for the removal of one hyphen). This footnote entry therefore underscores the way in which the left-hand column, as it stands, is unique to the British edition's realization of the novel's text. Finally, the absence of footnoting in the case of the phrases, "She had not said it, but he knew it." of the British text, or "She had not said it: yet he knew." of the American one, implies that they have no antecedent reading in the proofs.

What the footnoting does not report at all is that, at line 9 "up" and at line 18 "any thing" in the first sample, the American text reads "up," and "any-thing"–that is to say, no space is given on the text pages to recording the variation in accidentals of the American edition. The text presentation in the edition here envisaged follows the accidence and styling of the British text, except in the right-hand (that is, the American-version) column where passages are displayed in parallel. This is where one might consider such an edition as in conflict with the rationale that we have here developed for it. For after all, we explicitly argued above for the autonomy of the American version of *To the Lighthouse* and maintained that this was due not least to its independent styling. On the other hand, however, we emphasized for the British edition that it had received repeated rounds of correction and revision, and altogether a constant general attention from author, publisher and printer cooperating on the book over an extended time-span. We thus recognized that it provided, by comparison, the more significantly and effectively worked-over of the novel's two texts. This should justify a decision to choose the British text as reference and base for the edition we propose, even as that edition sets out to enable its users and readers to experience Virginia Woolf's *To the Lighthouse* in the fluidity of its two simultaneous public versions of 1927.

A study edition of Virginia Woolf's novel *To the Lighthouse* as we have outlined it is not limited, in conception, to what it proposes to accomplish technically, in terms of text analysis, editorial discrimination and a function-oriented presentational surface. A command of the methods of textual criticism and the observance of precision and accuracy in editing, as well as of user demands in terms of presentation, while necessary, is not in itself sufficient when textual criticism and editing are properly understood as belonging among the foundational disciplines of literary scholarship and criticism. As such, they must be assessed in terms of their achievement, and according to how far they enable, and how much they contribute to, the critical endeavor.

An edition allows us to experience a text materially. A text edition that is based on the text- and work-related records of composition, revision and transmission conveys the dynamic quality of the text's materiality, which arises in its turn out of the generative potential of the creative processes of composition and variation. A text's dynamics of composition and variation are themselves always already played out in a field of force between writing and reading. Not only, therefore, is there a need for editions that render a text's range of variation accessible, in so far as it is possible for editions to do so, that is, as far as the texts and their variants survive in material records. It is equally essential that criticism in theory and method should recognise the nature of its own enterprise as a dialectic of reading and writing that constructs its discourse on the analogous discursive structure of its subject. The subject of literary criticism, the literary work, is always discursively structured in language. Its discursiveness plays itself out in that its text can always also be other. This is why revision is not accidental to it, but of its nature.[14] The option of revision is always inherent—which is also exactly why the literary text and work are interpretable. But to recognize whether, when and how a text's potential for revision has been realized, requires a material record of the processes of writing and reading through which works and their texts have been constituted, in form, in wording and in meaning.

The text of Virginia Woolf's *To the Lighthouse*, as we have seen, can always also be other: the novel's two simultaneous versions bear this out in very graphic terms. Thus, the character of Charles Tansley can be drawn both mildly ironically, and sharply; the children pictured as playing on the beach can be making mud pies as well as pelting each other with handfuls of grass, or they can only be pelting each other; perhaps, too, there can even be a "ring of exaltation and melancholy" quite as much as a "ring of exultation, and melancholy" in Mr. Ramsay's voice.[15] Moreover, in addition to speaking in alternative ways, the text can always also be other in alternatives of speaking or being silent. Mrs. Ramsay

---

[14] This is a central tenet in the laying of theoretical foundations for the study of revision by Roger Lüdeke in his *Wiederlesen. Revisionspraxis und Autorschaft bei Henry James*. (ZAA Studies: Language, Literature, Culture, no. 14.) Tübingen: Stauffenburg Verlag, 2002. Roger Lüdeke wrote the book as a dissertation under my direction, and he has taught me a wider understanding of authorial revision in literature.

[15] It is true that we have assessed "exultation" as a textual error in the American edition, for which reason it should not be accepted in a text-critically constituted text, conceived of as an authentic text, of the novel's American version. Nonetheless, this reading is testimony of a discerning reading of the first-proof text, resulting in a change that was assumed to be corrective. Hence, also the variation of "exultation," against "exaltation" goes to show that the text can always also be other.

can say or not say, for instance: "You won't be able to go." From exactly this passage, in which her saying or not saying these words distinguishes the simultaneous versions, we may find, indeed have found, a diachronic axis opening up into the text's pre-publication state. On this axis, the material record allows us to register the alternatives of silence or wording as operating between the absence, in the proofs, of text corresponding to the phrases: "She had not said it; yet he knew. / She had not said it, but he knew it." and the presence of these phrases in both the alternative wording and the alternative form (meaning here: the alternative placing) in the text's published versions. As to wording versus silence, reticence versus explicitness, the reverse situation occurs, for instance, with respect to a James outspokenly resentful of his father in the proof text, and an emotionally controlled James in the published text.

The evidence from this textual and text-critical analysis, reflected on such terms, establishes a point of vantage for criticism. *To the Lighthouse* may be seen to spring from, and at the same time, through its composition and revision, to generate, oppositions of silence versus speaking. In general terms, it is true, this thematic as well as structural duality can be understood simply from the novel's published text in either version. Insights can be deepened, furthermore, through a study of the material records as we have here described and analyzed them. Yet it is ultimately only through an edition, we would argue, that the reader and the critic, freed from any interposed discourse, but with the edited material record set directly before them, will be able to experience for themselves the processes of writing and revision of the work and its texts, and to assess their significance. And this is ultimately why textual study and the editorial enterprise critically matter.

Works Cited

Briggs, Julia. "Between the Texts: Virginia Woolf's Acts of Revision." *TEXT* 12 (1999): 143-165.

Lavin, J. A. "The First Editions of Virginia Woolf's To the Lighthouse." *Proof* 2 (1972): 185-211.

Woolf, Virginia. *The Diary of Virginia Woolf*. Ed. Anne Olivier Bell. 5 vols. London: Hogarth P, 1977-1984.

———. *The Letters of Virginia Woolf*. Ed. Nigel Nicolson and Joanne Trautmann. 6 vols. London: Hogarth P, 1975-80.

———. *To the Lighthouse*. London: Hogarth P, 1927.

———. *To the Lighthouse*. New York: Harcourt, Brace & Company, 1927.

———. *To the Lighthouse*. Edited by Susan Dick. The Shakespeare Head Press Edition. Oxford: Blackwell Publishers, 1992.

Mind the Gap: The Spaces in Jacob's Room
Edward L. Bishop

Classical pianist Alfred Brendel says, "I like the fact that 'listen' is an anagram of 'silent'. Silence is not something that is there before the music begins and after it stops. It is the essence of the music itself, the vital ingredient that makes it possible for the music to exist at all. It's wonderful when the audience is part of this productive silence" (Alvarez 53). He is speaking of piano concerts, but the same could be said of *Jacob's Room*. So much of the effect of this book depends upon the spatial silence, the white space of the gaps on the page. They are, to paraphrase Brendel, the essence of the text itself, the vital ingredient that makes it possible for the narrative to exist at all. And it is indeed wonderful when the audience is part of this productive silence. In *Mimesis*, Eric Auerbach talks about the narrative of the Bible and how the mind swarms into the dark spaces between the events that are lit up by the narration. The gaps, then, do not merely pace the reader, they allow her or his mind to move into the silence.[1] This is what happens, or at least can happen, in *Jacob's Room*.

Throughout her career Woolf was concerned by the conjunction of space and silence. At the end of 1921 as she was finishing the first draft of *Jacob's Room*, she concluded "A Glance at Turgenev" with the observation that in his stories Turgenev fuses his elements "in one moment of great intensity, though all round are the silent spaces" (*E3* 317). Two decades later, in a diary note on *The Years* she writes, "I think I see how I can bring in interludes—I mean spaces of silence" (*D4* 332; 17 July 1935). And in the *Pointz Hall* typescript she refers to "That feeling slipped between the space that separates one word from another; like a

---

[1] "Since so much in the story is dark and incomplete [... the reader's] effort to interpret it constantly finds something new to feed upon" (15). Auerbach is arguing that the styles of the *Iliad* and the Bible represent the two basic styles in Western literature of representing reality: "on the one hand [the *Iliad*] fully externalized description... all events in the foreground; on the other hand [the Bible], certain parts brought into high relief, others left obscure, abruptness, suggestive influence of the unexpressed" (23). See also pp. 9-11.

Auerbach is talking about elements of style, but as Roger Chartier insists, forms produce meaning, and with the early printings of the Bible the "visual articulation of the page" was a vexed issue. The sixteenth to the eighteenth centuries saw "the opening up of the page through the multiplication of paragraphs that broke the uninterrupted continuity of the text common in the Renaissance [...]. This textual segmentation (*découpage*) had fundamental implications when it was applied to sacred texts. The story of Locke's anxiety regarding the practice of dividing the text of the Bible into chapter and verse is well known. For him such a division presented a considerable risk of obliterating the powerful coherence of the word of God" (51-52).

blue flower between two stones" (36). The notion of silence as an essential element of Woolf's work has been recognized by Woolf critics for decades. Back in 1970 Harvena Richter argued that Woolf "approached this aspect of form in the same way as does an architect, painter, or composer—to use negative 'blank spaces' or 'intervals' in a positive way so as to make them contribute to subjective feeling" (229), and Richter drew attention to Woolf's comment that Sterne is a "forerunner of the moderns" because of his "interest in silence rather than in speech," which makes us "consult our own minds" (*CE* 1 98).[2] So gaps are essential, and if they are to be truly productive in engaging the audience they must be more than merely visual cues like paragraph indents. It is surprising, therefore, that while the linguistic text of *Jacob's Room* has been comparatively little altered through the various editions, the space breaks which are one of the most distinctive features of the book have been shrunk, paved over, and ignored altogether.

Students who want a machine-searchable text, or perhaps simply don't want to buy the book, can find *Jacob's Room* on the net at sites such as Project Gutenberg. The problem, however, is that in the online texts every paragraph is double-spaced and the space breaks Woolf wrote into her book are eliminated altogether. As Mark Hussey noted of the hypertext *Mrs. Dalloway* in "How Should One Read a Screen?" "the spaces on the page that contribute to the rhythmic context of the words on the page are insignificant, 'unreadable,' in effect, by the machine" (254).[3] But these days, when electronic texts are still in their infancy, we almost expect them to be flawed, and for most readers they are still things to be consulted, not read.[4] More interesting are the variations in the print editions, variations that have been there since 1923.

---

[2] Patricia Laurence's excellent *Reading of Silence* reproduces the black page from Sterne's *Tristram Shandy* and states, "Sterne's black page calls attention to the materiality of the text. Silences are marked. This forerunner of Woolf, with his modern interest in silence—the blank spaces, the white and black pages, the typography (asterisks, ellipses, dashes, parentheses)—illuminates the unsaid" (30). She only mentions *Jacob's Room* in passing, but the whole book provides a useful commentary on the silences of the gaps.

[3] Hussey reiterates the point that Woolf was "concerned not only with the sound of her words, but also with their visual display upon the page"; her use of space breaks all contributed "to the effort Woolf made to shape the *reading* of her fiction after about 1917—the date of her and Leonard's acquisition of the Hogarth Press and, not merely coincidentally I think, of her earliest experimental fictions" (253).

[4] John Thompson, writing in the introduction to *Books and Bibliography*, addresses this problem: "A year or so ago I searched the Web for copies of Rudyard Kipling's poem 'If.' There were many hundreds. I took the first eight hits my search engine produced: all eight were textually different. There is no answer to what a library, any library, should do faced with this digital tidal wave" (11).

The first English edition of *Jacob's Room* was published by the Hogarth Press—their first novel, and the largest production to date for the young publishing company—on October 27, 1922. Three months later, on February 8, 1923, in New York, Harcourt Brace brought out the American edition. There are very few changes to the linguistic text between the English and the American editions and these are for the most part variations in hyphenation and capitalization; they could have been made by a typesetter, and in any case none is substantive enough to give authority to the American text as an improvement over the English text. Woolf did no rewriting between editions.[5] Nevertheless, considerable variation *does* exist between the first British and the first American editions in the handling of the space breaks. In every chapter except chapter seven and the short final chapter there are more divisions in the English text, with the result that in the book as a whole the English edition has twenty-five more sections than the American edition: 148 as opposed to 123.[6] So how did this happen?

Woolf seems to have been a victim of Harcourt Brace's house style in page design. If you look at an English first edition you will see that many of the space breaks occur at the top or bottom of the page. In the American text no spaces are left at the top or bottom of the page; thus if a break in the English edition is due to occur at either point the American typesetters silently collapse it.[7] In fifteen of

---

[5] In preparing the text for the Shakespeare Head Edition I let inconsistencies between accepted spellings of the same word stand, such as *Flanders'* and *Flanders's*; and I did not make changes based on felicitous phrasing: the "smoothly sculptured" policeman on p.156, therefore, was not altered to "sculpted"; and I noted but did not change Woolf's idiosyncratic spelling of Van Gogh and Boulevard Raspail (*JR* 61, 206). In a letter to Jacques Raverat on 10 December 1922, she says, "Raspail was spelt wrong owing to Duncan and Vanessa, whom I consulted. A letter more or less means nothing to them" (*L2* 591-2). I did, however, correct three obvious misprints that appear in both 1E and 1A, and I included the two emendations that Woolf requested in the 4 October 1922 letter to Donald Brace quoted in Appendix A.

[6] Howard Harper, in *Between Language and Silence: The Novels of Virginia Woolf* (Louisiana State University Press, 1982), p. 88, n.3, notes that "Interesting patterns, almost musical in their rhythmic arrangement and in their effects, are involved in the distributions of chapters and sections in *Jacob's Room*," and argues that the twelve subdivisions in the first two chapters constitute a sort of base line from which the later chapters depart. My findings differ (he documents only eight lost sections between the first English and the first American editions, some of which in fact are there), but I am grateful to him for drawing attention to the differences in format between the first editions. I am also grateful to the Harry Ransom Humanities Research Center, U of Texas at Austin, for making the first editions of *Jacob's Room* available to me, and for the Andrew Mellon Fellowship which enabled me to study the texts.

[7] With *The Waves* on the other hand, the printers were actively attentive. J. H. Willis notes, "The managing director of R. & R. Clark, with the kind of attention to detail that

the cases this seems to be what happened. In another five instances the English text indicates only a small break at the top or bottom of its page, difficult for the typesetters to judge unless they compared it closely with a full page. Finally, there are five breaks clearly marked in the English edition that would not have fallen at the top or bottom of the page in the American edition, yet inexplicably do not make it into that edition.

There is another change: in the Hogarth edition there are four different sizes of breaks, ranging from one to four-line spaces, where in the Harcourt Brace edition they are all regularized as one-line spaces. Why should we care? Woolf herself did not seem concerned about the variations in the U.S. edition. She makes no note of these matters in the brief correspondence we have between her and Harcourt and Brace.[8]

Woolf could be casual about the fate of her texts once they made it into print, but in developing *Jacob's Room* she did care very much about the space breaks. When she began writing the novel in April of 1920 she had been setting Hope Mirrlees's *Paris: A Poem* (published May 1920), a complex text in which, as Julia Briggs points out, Mirrlees had "learned from Apollinaire, Cocteau and Reverdy that the placing of a line of poetry itself constituted a form of punctuation, and that the spaces on the page were a crucial part of a poem's rhythm."[9] Also, the year before she had hand-set T. S. Eliot's *Poems* (1919). So she was aware of the potential of space, but she did not use it immediately in the writing of *Jacob's Room*. At first Woolf divided her text only with numbered chapter divisions. After three months of writing she began using a row of 'x's to indicate subdivisions, and after six months she began to use space breaks in her manuscript book; thus the gaps, deliberate and considered, were part of the evolving shape of her novel.[10]

---

endeared him to the Woolfs, soon wrote back to Leonard in July 1931 explaining that while he had allowed a half-inch space in the seven places indicated in the text by their directions to 'leave larger space,' he believed there were other places where there were distinct breaks in the narrative, perhaps requiring two kinds of space (HP 575). He sought clarification before putting the text into page proofs" (198).

[8] See Appendix A.

[9] "'Printing Hope': Virginia Woolf, Hope Mirrlees, and the iconic imagery of 'Paris'." In press; I am grateful to Dr. Briggs for allowing me to read the typescript. J. H. Willis notes, "Their typesetting skill was tested at least twice[...]. T. S. Eliot's *Waste Land* (1923) required adroit spacing, and *Paris* (1920) by Hope Mirrlees was self-consciously modern in its typographical configuration, one line running vertically down the page (34).

[10] See my Introduction to Jacob's Room: *The Holograph Draft* p. xxi and *passim*.

MIND THE GAP

I will not weary the reader by analyzing all of the missing gaps, nor the nearly eighty instances where the English text has a space four times greater than that of the American text, but what I want to do below is draw attention to six pivotal moments in *Jacob's Room* and very briefly suggest how the absence of a space break, or even a variation in the size of the space break, can affect our response to the text. The argument here is not for a particular reading but for a modified practice: I believe critics of whatever theoretical persuasion, whether they are analyzing typography or investigating trauma, would find it productive to examine the first editions. For ease of access I have indicated the chapter and the page numbers in the first British, first American, and current Harcourt Brace paperback editions.

The conspiracy of hush and clean bottles

(12A, 13 HBJ)
She had her hand upon the garden gate.
    "The meat!" she exclaimed, striking the latch down.
She had forgotten the meat.
There was Rebecca at the window.

   The bareness of Mrs. Pearce's front room was fully displayed at ten o'clock at night when a powerful oil lamp stood on the middle of the table.

(15E)
She had her hand upon the garden gate.
    "The meat!" she exclaimed, striking the latch down.
She had forgotten the meat.
There was Rebecca at the window.

   The bareness of Mrs. Pearce's front room was fully displayed at ten o'clock at night when a powerful oil lamp stood on the middle of the table.

The first big (four-line) gap in the English text occurs after "There was Rebecca at the window." It comes shortly after the narrator's reflection "who shall deny that this blankness of mind, when combined with profusion, mother wit, old wives' tales [...] who shall deny that in these respects every woman is nicer than any man." Where the smaller gap in the American text allows the eye to skip easily into the next paragraph and Mrs. Pearce's front room, the large gap isolates

Rebecca in the window, situates her as an object of Betty's gaze, and distinguishes her from the minor characters we have already met or heard of—Mr. Connor who owns the yacht, Charles Steele the painter, Mr. Curnow who lost an eye. Thus we are expectant when Rebecca returns two pages later "bending over a spirit-lamp in the small room next door," the small flame of which burns quietly while the wind rushes outside. The two women murmur "over the spirit-lamp, plotting the eternal conspiracy of hush and clean bottles."

> (14A, 13 HBJ)
> "Good night, Rebecca" Mrs. Flanders murmured, and Rebecca called her ma'am, though they were conspirators plotting the eternal conspiracy of hush and clean bottles.
>
> Mrs. Flanders had left the lamp burning in the front room. There were her spectacles, her sewing; and a letter with the Scarborough postmark. She had not drawn the curtains either.

> (17-18E)
> "Good-night, Rebecca" Mrs. Flanders murmured, and Rebecca called her ma'am, though they were conspirators plotting the eternal conspiracy of hush and clean bottles.
>
> Mrs. Flanders had left the lamp burning in the front room. There were her spectacles, her sewing; and a letter with the Scarborough postmark. She had not drawn the curtains either.

The flame of female friendship, quietly subversive (it is a "conspiracy") assures the continuity of the household while the wind, associated with the male world of Captains and steamers, "rages" outside. The theme of female friendship will become important, and Woolf wanted to set off this intimate exchange over the spirit-lamp (which, interestingly, burns volatile liquid fuel to produce its quiet light). In the English text, the start of the scene is signalled by a two-line gap at "'I thought he'd never get off—such a hurricane'" (17E, 13A, 12HBJ). The scene still has resonance in the first American edition, but it is absorbed into the longer tri-partite scene of putting Archer to bed, Betty discussing the baby with Rebecca, and the narrator's description of the house after all have gone to sleep. We end with the famous image of the crab in the bucket (19E, 16A, 14 HBJ) and we lose the conspiracy of hush and clean bottles as a countervailing force to the confinements, and violence, of the male world.

What's the next thing to see in Scarborough?

(24A, 19HBJ)
But there was a time when none of this had any existence […]. Fix your eyes upon the lady's skirt […]. It changes; drapes her ankles—the nineties […].
 And now, what's the next thing to see in Scarborough?
 Mrs. Flanders sat on the raised circle of the Roman camp, patching Jacob's breeches[…].

(27E)
But there was a time when none of this had any existence […]. Fix your eyes upon the lady's skirt […]. It changes; drapes her ankles—the nineties […]. And now, what's the next thing to see in Scarborough?

 Mrs. Flanders sat on the raised circle of the Roman camp, patching Jacob's breeches […].

At the end of the well-known time-travel passage the narrator asks, "And now, what's the next thing to see in Scarborough?" In the first American edition the next line, "Mrs. Flanders sat on the raised circle of the Roman camp," immediately answers the question. The narrative gaze swivels from the Roman artefacts in the museum to Betty sitting at the Roman camp. But with the gap, and it is the largest, a four-line gap, the question hangs over the white space. The effect is subtly different now: the text instead of providing an answer for us asks us to speculate on our own. The gap is for us to fill in. The question takes us back to the imperative at the beginning of the interlude, "Fix your eyes upon the lady's skirt," and invites meditation on the palimpsestic quality of this historic town and of life itself. These are at once unique events, and rituals where the participants change but the actions remain the same. Thus when the line "Mrs. Flanders sat […]" comes after the gap it does so as a resumption of the narrative, not the answer to the question, and we see her now not as "the next thing to see in Scarborough" but as one of many figures through the ages who have "sat on the raised circle of the Roman camp." The spatial configuration is crucial: with the gap we continue our tunnelling into the past, without it we slip easily back into the unfolding present.

One word is sufficient. But if one cannot find it?

(117A, 71HBJ)
Then his mouth—but surely, of all futile occupations this of cataloguing features is the worst. One word is sufficient. But if one cannot find it?

"I like Jacob Flanders," wrote Clara Durrant in her diary. "He is so unworldly. He gives himself no airs, and one can say what one likes to him, though he's frightening because..."

(114E)
Then his mouth—but surely, of all futile occupations this of cataloguing features is the worst. One word is sufficient. But if one cannot find it?

"I like Jacob Flanders," wrote Clara Durrant in her diary. "He is so unworldly. He gives himself no airs, and one can say what one likes to him, though he's frightening because..."

Jacob's Room is filled with reflections on writing and the (im)possibility of capturing character. The narrator has been musing on Mrs. Durrant's phrase for Jacob ("distinguished-looking") and trying to apply it. In the English edition the reflection ends poised on the question, "But if one cannot find it?" followed by a large gap. The first American edition moves right on to Clara and her diary, where the concern is less for precision in language than for prescribed space: "Mr. Letts allows little space in his shilling diaries. Clara was not the one to encroach upon Wednesday." The point of the scene in the American text becomes the mild humor at Clara's expense ("But then, this is only a young woman's language") rather than, as in the English edition, the narrator's self-reflexive observation. It is a serious question—what indeed is the point of writing if one cannot find the right word, if perhaps it does not exist? This obsession with linguistic slippage dogs the narrator in her project throughout.

Whether she had a mind ... turning up Greek Street

(132A, 79HBJ)
But it did occur to Jacob, half-way through dinner, to wonder whether she had a mind.
They sat at a little table in the restaurant.
Florinda leant the points of her elbows on the table and held her chin in the cup of her hands.

(128E)
But it did occur to Jacob, half-way through dinner, to wonder whether she had a mind.

They sat at a little table in the restaurant.
Florinda leant the points of her elbows on the table and held her chin in the cup of her hands.

Here again the American text collapses a large gap. On the previous page Florinda has been wrestling with Shelley ("What on earth was it *about*?") and Jacob has been wrestling with chastity ("Whether or not she was a virgin seems a matter of no importance whatever. Unless, indeed, it is the only thing of any importance at all"). Then for Jacob a larger question looms, one that follows from what we've seen of Florinda's encounter with Shelley, not whether or not she's chaste but "whether she had a mind."

With the paragraph break Woolf has already shifted from the indeterminate space of authorial reflection to the scene at the restaurant (Jacob and Florinda are "half-way through dinner") but she more emphatically sets off her one-line paragraph. The gap renders Jacob's sudden apprehension of just how vacuous Florinda is. Between the manuscript and the published text Woolf made the decision to deny her narrator any access to Jacob's mind at all, and so rather than internal monologue it is the gaps that render the emotion. The white space is where Jacob's horror sinks in. Or where time stops, as it does in Greek street:

(158A, 94HBJ)
Then he saw her turning up Greek Street upon another man's arm.

The light from the arc lamp drenched him from head to toe. He stood for a minute motionless beneath it.

(152E)
Then he saw her turning up Greek Street upon another man's arm.

The light from the arc lamp drenched him from head to toe. He stood for a minute motionless beneath it.

Two chapters later we find Jacob still trying to rationalize his attraction to Florinda. He has come to terms with the fact that she is not chaste, but has convinced himself that she has an "inviolable fidelity." Then his delusion is violated by seeing her turning into Soho, up the notorious Greek Street, which a police commission in 1906 had called the worst street in the West End. (We might wonder what Jacob is doing in the area, but he sees her turning off Shaftesbury Avenue, a main thoroughfare, as he walks back to Bloomsbury from central London.) When the famous Italian libertine Giacomo Casanova (1725-98) came to London in 1763-4 he lived in Greek Street, and conceived a disastrous passion for an innocent-looking prostitute, Marianne Charpillon, who swindled him. Jacob is no Casanova but he is as devastated as the Italian was (who, like Jacob, knew better even as he slipped deeper into his obsession), and that sense of time standing still is rendered by the gap.

There is no break in the narrative, no shift in point of view or subject. There is in the American edition a one-line gap, but it is of course one of many. The four-line gap, on the other hand, imposes a moment of arrest upon the reader that corresponds to the blankness in Jacob's mind. Woolf's narrator tries in a series of similes—"as if a stone were ground to dust; as if white sparks flew from a livid whetstone which was his spine; as if the switchback railway, having swooped to the depths, fell, fell, fell"—to render what Jacob must feel. The passage turns to a reflection by the narrator on the impossibility of entering another's consciousness: "Whether we know what was in his mind is another question. Granted ten years' seniority and a difference of sex, fear of him comes first; this is swallowed up by a desire to help—overwhelming sense, reason, and the time of night [...]" (153E, 158A, 94HBJ), but the gap allows Woolf to have it both ways, at once rendering the emotion and then talking about the impossibility of capturing or articulating it.

Darkness drops like a knife

(300A, 175HBJ)
   Darkness drops like a knife over Greece.

"The guns?" said Betty Flanders, half asleep, getting out of bed and going to the window, which was decorated with a fringe of dark leaves.

(288E)
   Darkness drops like a knife over Greece.

"The guns?" said Betty Flanders, half asleep, getting out of bed and going to the window, which was decorated with a fringe of dark leaves.

As in the Greek Street passage, at the end of the book when war enters the text —the war that will kill Jacob—the four-line gap in the English edition leaves the line hanging, letting the ominousness of the metaphor (however clichéd the phrase "drops like a knife" might be) emerge fully. Similarly, at the end of chapter three the line, "Jacob Flanders, therefore, went up to Cambridge in October, 1906," which marks the beginning of the process that will lead Jacob to war, is set off by a four-line gap in the English edition, giving it a portentousness it does not have in the American volume. The editions that regularize the size of the gaps mute these effects, even if they do not obliterate them completely; they direct and foreclose the reader's response, rather than engage it. *Jacob's Room* is a novel full of fissures, ruptures, gaps, and chasms, and the intent of the novel is not just to tell the story of Jacob but to make us aware of these spaces.

Chasms in our ways

(161A, 96HBJ)
   As frequent as street corners in Holborn are these chasms in the continuity of our ways. Yet we keep straight on.
   Rose Shaw, talking in rather an emotional manner to Mr. Bowley at Mrs. Durrant's evening party a few nights back, said that life was wicked because a man called Jimmy refused to marry a woman called (if memory serves) Helen Aitken.

(155-6E)
   As frequent as street corners in Holborn are these chasms in the continuity of our ways. Yet we keep straight on.

   Rose Shaw, talking in rather an emotional manner to Mr. Bowley at Mrs. Durrant's evening party a few nights back, said that life was wicked because a man called Jimmy refused to marry a woman called (if memory serves) Helen Aitken.

At the end of chapter eight Woolf's narrator speaks of the chasms that exist in our daily lives, but which we remain unaware of and "keep straight on." This is the opposite of the cataclysmic rupture for Jacob in Greek Street. Here Woolf posits an encounter with an old busker on the street, whose tale, if you stop to talk to him instead of brushing by, will bring "you one winter's day to the Essex coast" and ultimately to the tropics, to "the verge of the marsh drinking rumpunch, an outcast from civilization." The first American edition closes over the gap and so the notion of the "chasm" is immediately reduced to the fact that someone named Jimmy has refused to marry someone called Helen, but in the

British edition the gap episode testifies to the contingency of life, where a single chance occurrence can take your life in a completely different direction. In *Jacob's Room* Woolf is seeking to articulate these fissures not only through the discourse but with the page design, and where the first British edition renders the chasms, too often the first American edition keeps straight on.

There are chasms in everyday life, and *Jacob's Room* makes us aware of those, but there is also the larger chasm underlying the novel: that of the Great War. I have spoken elsewhere of the freeze-frame effect of the narration in the novel (Bishop xx), and Susan Sontag in her recent *New Yorker* article, "Looking At War: Photography and Violence," argues that, "Non-stop imagery (television, streaming video, movies) surrounds us, but, when it comes to remembering, the photograph has the deeper bite. Memory freeze-frames; its basic unit is the single image." She goes on,

> In an era of information overload the photograph provides a quick way of apprehending something and a compact form for memorizing it. The photograph is like a quotation, or a maxim or proverb. Each of us mentally stocks hundreds of photographs, subject to instant recall. [...] Conscripted as part of journalism, images were expected to arrest attention, startle, surprise. As the old advertising slogan of *Paris Match*, founded in 1919, had it: 'The weight of words, the shock of photos.' (87)

The format is part of the memorializing impulse in *Jacob's Room*: the sections are like individual photographs; the book as a whole is like an album of snapshots. To remove or reduce the gaps then is not to alter something inconsequential, but to tamper with something that lies at the very core of the book.

Much has been made of the fluidity of Woolf's prose, but we are only now becoming aware of the fluidity of Woolf's texts. Woolf allowed both versions of *Jacob's Room* to stand, as she did some of the famous cruxes in her other novels (*To the Lighthouse* and *Mrs Dalloway*). And the issue is still with us: the current HBJ edition now incorporates most of the spaces but it does not give the variations in size; the Penguin text uses two sizes of gaps; the Oxford Classics edition provides the variation from one- to four-line gaps. The forthcoming Shakespeare Head Edition (2004) follows the page design of the first English edition and lists the variants from the first American edition. I would argue that readers in England and America, even though they may be reading the same words, are reading very different texts. And anyone who is reading a print edition is reading something radically different from those who are reading online editions. As textual studies of Woolf become more sophisticated we must be alert to more than the variations in the linguistic text: we must also mind the gaps.

Appendix A

May 26th 1922.
Donald Brace, Esq.
My dear Mr Brace,
    Many thanks for your letter of May 13th.
I much regret that I have been longer than I intended in sending you the manuscript of my new book. A long attack of influenza has delayed me in finishing the work, but it is now being typed, and I could count upon letting you have the manuscript by the end of July. It will be published here in October. Roughly speaking, it is about 60,000 words in length.

    With kind regards,
    Yours truly,
    [signed] Virginia Woolf

Aug. 31st 1922
    Dear Mr Harcourt,
    I am extremely sorry that you should have had the trouble of writing to me about the MS of my novel, Jacob's Room. My husband has written to explain that it was posted to you on July 31st. I hope that it may possibly have come to hand before this. I will send a corrected copy of the proofs at the earliest opportunity. Meanwhile, I am extremely sorry for the delay, & thank you sincerely for your courtesy in writing to me.

    Yours faithfully
    Virginia Woolf

4th Oct. 1922
Dear Mr Brace,
    Many thanks for your letter about my book Jacob's Room. I am greatly pleased that you should like it, & hope for both our sakes that it will find readers in America.

There are two slight misprints in the copies which the printer is sending you, &, as I have not been able to correct them before they were sent, I note them here:

page 14, line 16 for "colour" read "nature".

page 263, line 12, the words "Still, he went with them to Constantinople" should be in brackets.

The jacket, which is I think very effective, is from a design by Vanessa Bell (Mrs Clive Bell). If you wish to use it, we could arrange with her to send you, if necessary, the original drawing.

Yours sincerely,
Virginia Woolf

9 Oct. 1922
[Messrs?] Harcourt, Brace, & Co.

Gentlemen,
I enclose the agreement as to the publication of my book, Jacob's Room, duly signed.
Believe me,
Yours faithfully
Virginia Woolf

Feb. 23rd 1923
Dear Mr Brace,

I am much pleased to hear that <u>Jacob's Room</u> has been published, & feel sure that you have done your share in making the book attractive to the public. My copies have not yet arrived, but I do not like to wait to acknowledge your cheque for £20 in payment of the advance royalty, & the kind letter which accompanies it. I hope sincerely that the book will be well received in America. The sales here have been much better than we expected.

Yours faithfully
Virginia Woolf

D.C. Brace Esq.
18th Sept. 1923
My dear Mr Brace,

Many thanks for your letter, which I received yesterday. Of course, the sales of Jacob's Room are small, but a[t] the same time they are much better than I myself expected. Clive Bell, by the way, is writing something about it in the <u>Dial</u> which may serve to keep people interested.

I much look forward to sending you my next book, which will be of collected essays, but I do not think it would be wise to promise to have it ready by next spring.
October 1924 is, I fear, a more likely date. I find that a good deal of revision is needed to make the book at all readable, and this will take more time than I reckoned.

I am sorry that you are not able to publish Miss Mirrlees' book, but I am not altogether surprised. I have not read it, but judging by her first novel, she is not likely to be a popular writer, even over here.

My husband wishes to be remembered to you, and we both hope that you will give us the pleasure of seeing you whenever you are again in England.

      Believe me,
      your sincerely,
      Virginia Woolf

14th Feb. 1924
D. C. Brace, Esq.
Dear Mr Brace,

I must thank you for sending the forms for income return, which I have filled up and enclose. I must also acknowledge, with thanks, the receipt of your cheque for $89.51 on royalties for Jacob's Room.

      Believe me,
      yours sincerely,
      Virginia Woolf

Previously unpublished letters of Virginia Woolf: Copyright ©The Estate of Virginia Woolf 2004. Reproduced by permission of The Society of Authors as the Literary Representative of the Estate of Virginia Woolf. I am grateful to James Haule for bringing these letters to my attention.

Appendix B

The list below indicates the words introducing the sections following the gaps lost in the American edition. The first page number is the first Hogarth Press edition, the second is the first Harcourt Brace edition. The numbers in square brackets indicate the number of sections in each chapter for the English and the American editions respectively.

Chapter I [12/10]

page	17/13	"'I thought he'd never get off...'"
	18/14	"Mrs Flanders had left the lamp..."

Chapter II [12/10]

27/25	"Mrs. Flanders sat on the raised circle..."
28/25	"'That's an orchid...'"
36/35	"Wednesday was Captain Barfoot's day."

Chapter III [13/10]

48/47	"They say the sky is the same everywhere."
58/58	"'They're friends of my mother's,'..."
67/67	"The Moonlight Sonata tinkled away..."

Chapter IV [11/7]

78/78	"It is brewed by the earth itself."
89/91	"The rooks settled; the rooks rose."
90/92	"After six days of salt wind, rain,…"
94/95	"'When you are as old as I am…'"

Chapter V [6/4]

112/114	"'Yes; that should make him sit up,'…"
114/117	"'I like Jacob Flanders,' wrote Clara…"

Chapter VI [11/10]

129/132	"They sat at a little table…"

Chapter VII [10/10]

Chapter VIII [9/7]

156/161	"Rose Shaw, talking in rather…"
158/164	"He sat at the table reading the *Globe*."

Chapter IX [10/9]

169/175	"The fire burnt clear between two pillars…"

                    Chapter X [10/8]

189/197   "Now Jacob walked over to the window..."

193/200   "It was the middle of February."

                    Chapter XI [10/9]

210/218   "Edward Cruttendon, Jinny Carslake..."

                    Chapter XII [19/16]

230/240   "The evening air slightly moved..."

234/244   "'How very English!' Sandra laughed..."

235/245   "Though the opinion is unpopular..."

                    Chapter XIII [14/12]

276/288   "The gilt clock at Verrey's..."

279/291   "Even now poor Fanny Elmer was dealing..."

                    Chapter XIV [1/1]

Works Cited

Alvarez, A. "The Playful Pianist," *New Yorker*, 1 April 1996, 49-55.
Auerbach, Eric. *Mimesis: The Representation of Reality in Western Literature* trans. Willard Trask. Princeton: Princeton UP, 1971, 1953.
Bishop, Edward L. *Virginia Woolf's* Jacob's Room: *The Holograph Draft*. NY: Pace UP, 1998.
Chartier, Roger. "Labourers and Voyagers: From the Text to the Reader." In David Finkelstein and Alistair McCleery ed. *The Book History Reader*. London: Routledge, 2002. 47- 76.
Harper, Howard. *Between Language and Silence: The Novels of Virginia Woolf*. Louisiana State UP, 1982.
Hussey, Mark. "How Should One Read a Screen?" Pamela L. Caughie, ed. *Virginia Woolf in the Age of Mechanical Reproduction*. New York and London: Garland, 2000. 249—265.
Laurence, Patricia Ondek. *The Reading of Silence: Virginia Woolf in the English Tradition*. Stanford: Stanford UP, 1991.
Richter, Harvena. *The Inward Voyage*. Princeton: Princeton UP, 1970.
Sontag, Susan. "Looking At War: Photography and Violence." *New Yorker*, 9 December 2002, 82-98.
Thomson, John ed. *Books and Bibliography: Essays in Commemoration of Don McKenzie*. Wellington: Victoria UP, 2002.
Willis, J. H. *Leonard and Virginia Woolf as Publishers : The Hogarth Press, 1917-41*. Charlottesville and London: UP of Virginia, 1992.
Woolf, Virginia. *Jacob's Room*. London: Hogarth Press, 1922.
——. *Jacob's Room*. New York: Harcourt Brace, 1923.
——. *Jacob's Room*. New York: Harcourt, Harvest Book, n.d. [Reprint of the 1960 ed. which was published together with the author's *Waves* by Harcourt Brace & World]
——. *Jacob's Room*. Project Gutenberg. http://ibiblio.org/gutenberg/etext04/jcbrm10.txt. 6 August 2002; accessed 17 September 2003.
——. *POINTZ HALL: The Earlier and Later Typescripts of BETWEEN THE ACTS*. Edited, with introduction, annotations, and afterword by Mitchell A. Leaska. New York: University Publications, 1983.

Michael Cunningham Rewriting Virginia Woolf: Pragmatist vs. Modernist Aesthetics
Birgit Spengler

Literary interrelations between Michael Cunningham's 1998 Pulitzer Prize winning novel *The Hours* and Virginia Woolf's *Mrs. Dalloway* triggered an immediate interest in Cunningham's book, responses ranging from high praise— a "flattering homage to Virginia Woolf" (Urqhuart), "a fictional instrument of intricacy and remarkable beauty" (Eder), "a delicate, triumphant glance, an acknowledgement of Woolf that takes her into Cunningham's own territory" (Wood)—to accusations of a lack of originality (German critic Freund notably called Cunningham's method "Schwarzfahren in der Literaturgeschichte," literary fare-dodging). The fact that Cunningham utilizes the icon of modernism as a character in his novel and uses Woolf's tragic suicide as a crowd-puller has not contributed to a more unanimous evaluation of *The Hours* either. The success of a film version with a cast including Meryl Streep (Clarissa Vaughan), Nicole Kidman (Virginia Woolf) and Julianne Moore (Laura Brown), and director Stephen Daldry demonstrates that more than four years after its first publication, interest in *The Hours* has reached another climax.[1]

The suspicion that Cunningham utilizes Woolf not only to share in her fame but to participate in a wave of intertextual re-writings of famous novels is not far-fetched.[2] However, despite his affinities to a current literary fashion, Cunningham's "case" differs from the mainstream of intertextual practice. Thus, before judging his literary merits or crimes in comparison to Woolf, *The Hours* needs to be examined more closely to find out whether Cunningham is just clev-

---

[1] Both novel and film provide instances of "versioning" Woolf and participate in "a recognized and recognizable [cultural] pattern" (Silver xvi). As Silver has shown, the icon Virginia Woolf is a highly contested ground that occupies "multiple, contradictory sites [...] in our cultural discourses" (11). Every depiction of Woolf participates in this contest of meanings and no single version can possibly ever go without critique. By appropriating Woolf to discuss the status and meaning of creativity and art, *The Hours* focuses on an issue that was not only of vital importance to Woolf, but that is narrowly intertwined with her notions on gender and the canon. With regard to conflicting "versions" of Woolf, it is especially interesting to compare her filmic representation with that of Cunningham's novel.

[2] Lately, this fashion of re-writing has caused a scandal that culminated in a lawsuit. But since *The Wind Done Gone* it is once and for all clear: the practice of appropriating another author's body of thought, presenting it in a modified way and selling it as something new is poetic license. And who is to tell whose story it *originally* was anyway?

erly evoking and imitating Woolf to share in her fame or whether *The Hours* is a serious attempt at reinterpreting Woolf's notions on art and literature.[3]

Embodying such controversial issues as the nature and value of art, the division of fact and fiction—and thereby of classical notions of genre—, originality and imitation, intertextuality and the relations between modernism and contemporary literature, *The Hours* is a postmodern adaptation and extension of Woolf's concerns, an act of *writer-response* that establishes a pragmatist aesthetics.[4] Thus, in contrast to being just another product of a current literary fashion, Cunningham's novel is a complex examination of Woolf's oeuvre and its own status as a work of literature in postmodern times. From the beginning, Cunningham foregrounds his thematic concern, the juxtaposition and negotiation of purist and pragmatist concepts of art, as his novel's agenda.[5] In the course of the novel, he uses his fictional investigation of Woolf's aesthetics to position *The Hours* within an ongoing debate about the nature and effects of art.

In my analysis, I will examine the aesthetic concepts that underlie such works as *Mrs. Dalloway* and *To the Lighthouse* and demonstrate how Cunningham's reading of Woolf extends and transgresses her ideas. I will begin by briefly outlining structural parallels and general links between *The Hours*, *Mrs. Dalloway* and Virginia Woolf herself, and then demonstrate Cunningham's particular indebtedness to Woolf's aesthetic concerns and his development of them by juxtaposing Woolf's and Cunningham's "aesthetics."[6] The involvement of Cunningham's three main female characters with *Mrs. Dalloway*, namely in

---

[3] While the majority of early responses to the novel in the form of reviews emphasize the merits of Cunningham's book, scholarly reception of both novel and film tends to the critical, especially with regard to the depiction of Virginia Woolf. I will come back to scholars' reactions in my discussion of the film version of *The Hours*, as most of them refer to both novel and film and postdate the release of the film version. See "A Visual Hypertext" below.

[4] I am using the term "aesthetics" as referring to a concept, or, "philosophy" of art, including notions of what constitutes art, its content or subject matter, the artistic process, and the reception or "consumption" of a work of art as well as questions of form and style.

[5] The epigraphs from Jorge Luis Borges' poem "The Other Tiger" and Woolf's diary are statements about creativity and the imagination and focus attention on the novel's central theme and its status as a work of art and literary strategies. Cunningham chooses a postmodern as well as a modern writer's statement about the workings of the imagination and positions his novel within an ongoing debate about the meaning and functions of art. Besides Virginia Woolf, Borges—considered as the turning point of modernism, and an author who demonstrates the "difficulty, perhaps the unnecessity of writing original works of literature" (Barth 69)—is another, although less conspicuous influence on Cunningham's novel.

[6] Concerning Woolf's aesthetics I will necessarily limit my analysis to a short discussion of some aspects of her aesthetic notions. A full-length analysis of Woolf's aesthetic

terms of the content, production, and consumption of art, reflect the sectors in which Cunningham conspicuously demonstrates his indebtedness towards Woolf's aesthetics while simultaneously contributing elements of his own—i.e. elements that reveal a thoroughly pragmatic attitude—to his novel's overall concept of art. The film version provides another intertext that is investigated in relation to Cunningham's concept of art in *The Hours*. In my final section I will specify how far Cunningham shares not only in Woolf's aesthetics but also in postmodern literary concerns and how he employs his literary strategies to negotiate between both.

Mrs. Dalloway Revisited

Cunningham's involvement with Virginia Woolf and *Mrs. Dalloway* is obvious throughout *The Hours* and clearly foregrounded by its title: "The Hours" functioned as Woolf's working title for her fourth novel between March 1923 and October 1924. More importantly, the structure of *The Hours* mirrors that of Woolf's novel. Both are arranged in seemingly disparate strands of narrative that complement each other by means of recurring images and a common base of thoughts, problems and emotions.[7] Furthermore, Cunningham adds to this web of meanings and interrelations to *Mrs. Dalloway* by appropriating Woolf's leitmotifs and thematic concerns: birds, mirrors, flowers, clocks, kisses and waves/the sea are the most prominent images that Cunningham "borrows" from *Mrs. Dalloway*, while on a thematic level, the most obvious correspondences are the mutual concern with suicide and madness, life and death, art and creativity, identity, reality and fiction.

Apart from such general correspondences, each of *The Hours'* three strands of narrative establishes its own specific links to Woolf and *Mrs. Dalloway*. Each part presents a single day in the life of a middle-aged woman in the 1920s, 1940s and 1990s respectively. Two of these, Mrs. Dalloway and Mrs. Brown, are characters well known to readers of Woolf. Mrs. Dalloway, once a society hostess and wife of the English MP Richard Dalloway, is the nickname of Clarissa Vaughan, a lesbian editor who lives in New York City in the 1990s and prepares a party for her friend Richard, a homosexual writer dying of AIDS. The "Mrs. Dalloway" strand of *The Hours* naturally establishes the closest associations with *Mrs. Dalloway* and plays with the reader's expectations most obviously. It is an updat-

---

concerns would go beyond the scope of this article. As Cunningham's aesthetics, I understand the aesthetic concept such as can be deduced from *The Hours*.

[7] Woolf conceived of her novel in complementary oppositions such as "life & death, sanity & insanity" (*D2* 248) and invented the character of Septimus Warren Smith "to complete the character of Mrs. Dalloway" as she could not otherwise convey her "whole meaning about her" (*L5* 36).

ed version of Woolf's novel that modernizes and liberalizes its hypotext.[8] Cunningham's characters in contemporary New York City live out the hidden potential that Woolf's characters had to suppress in the London of the 1920s.[9]

Mrs. Brown, an ordinary woman whom one met in the train in Woolf's essay "Mr. Bennett and Mrs. Brown," is converted into Laura Brown, a housewife in Los Angeles in 1949 who desperately tries to be a good mother and wife while secretly longing for more freedom and a room of her own. Only by reading *Mrs. Dalloway* can Laura forget the limitations of her life. Although Mrs. Brown's indebtedness to Virginia Woolf is most prominent through her role as a reader of *Mrs. Dalloway*,[10] her last name emphasizes links to Woolf's essayistic work, in particular to her concepts of fiction and her ideas about women.

The third strand of narrative focuses on a day in the life of Virginia Woolf in Richmond in 1923, intensely working on her novel *Mrs. Dalloway*. The "Mrs. Woolf" episodes of *The Hours* are a well-investigated blend of fact and fiction in which every detail insinuates the historical Virginia Woolf, and, again, *Mrs. Dalloway*.[11] Historical details and fictional elements create a web of references to Woolf's novel, so that each thought and action of "Mrs. Woolf" adds to Cunningham's reading of *Mrs. Dalloway*. "Mrs. Woolf" functions as a fictional device that contributes to the novel's overall structure and impact at the same

---

[8] I use the term "hypotext" to signify the (literary) model from which the hypertext—a text of second degree—derives (compare Genette, 15ff). The plot of the "Mrs. Dalloway" strand of narrative runs parallel to those episodes in *Mrs. Dalloway* that are directly linked to Clarissa, and the most important characters are transformed into more up-to-date versions. Some characters such as Clarissa Dalloway and Hugh Whitbread have direct equivalents in *The Hours*, others bequeath characteristics to several characters. Traces of Peter Walsh can be found in Richard Worthington Brown as well as Louis Waters. On the other hand, Cunningham's characters often incorporate characteristics of more than just one character in *Mrs. Dalloway*: the "new" Sally is a conglomeration of Sally Seton and Richard Dalloway, whereas Richard Worthington Brown evokes Richard Dalloway, Peter Walsh and Septimus Warren Smith respectively.

[9] It should be noted that in both novels, Clarissa has bisexual potential and that most of her thoughts on the given day center on her "missed" opportunities: Clarissa Dalloway ponders Sally Seton's kiss and young Peter Walsh. Clarissa Vaughan is more concerned with her brief sexual relationship with Richard than with her long-term partner, Sally. Both Clarissas have chosen a stable relationship that promises security and leaves them room to breathe rather than more passionate relationships, but nevertheless they think longingly of the possible partners and the sexual choices they discarded. Clarissa Vaughan's "obsession" with Richard is particularly strongly singled out in the film version of *The Hours*. Clarissa Dalloway's homoerotic attraction to Sally Seton has been discussed by Abel, Boone, Bowlby, Henke, Tambling and Tomalin to name but a few.

[10] Here, the hypotext is present through extensive quotations.

[11] Cunningham's research on Woolf's life and work enabled him to depict a day in her life in 1923 that largely corresponds to what biographers would find plausible. From her

time as commenting on the text, thereby engendering a specific reading of Cunningham's novel and Woolf's literary oeuvre.

Woolfian Aesthetics

Frequent allusions to Woolf's essayistic work such as in the "Mrs. Brown" strand of narrative and a general thematic concern with artistic creation illuminate Cunningham's obligations towards Woolf's aesthetics. Thus, a brief look into the aesthetic notions that triggered *Mrs. Dalloway* is indispensable as a background for judging *The Hours*. It was in her essays which were "at all points intimately bound up with her work as a novelist and her thinking about women, politics and society" (Lee, "Essays" 91), that Woolf worked out her literary aesthetics as well as her thematic concerns and demonstrated most clearly her determined interest in "breaking down hierarchies, [and] validating ordinary lives" (ibid. 96).

In her essays of the 1920s, Woolf is preoccupied with questions concerning the nature of art and its relation to social structures. She criticizes contemporary concepts of what constitutes art and of what is the proper content of literature and demands changes in style, subject matter, and values, as well as an intellectual emancipation of women. According to Woolf, "the proper stuff of fiction is a little other than custom would have us believe it" ("Modern Fiction" 106). "'The proper stuff of fiction' does not exist, everything is the proper stuff of fiction, every feeling, every thought; every quality of brain and spirit is drawn upon, no perception comes amiss" (ibid. 110). Woolf perceives the task of the novelist of her day as creating "characters who are real" ("Mr. Bennett and Mrs. Brown" 76). However, the realists' "tools [...] are the wrong ones for us to use" as they lay too much "stress upon the fabric of things" (ibid. 82). Instead, a "modern" novelist should depict an "ordinary mind on an ordinary day" and its "myriad impressions—trivial, fantastic, evanescent, or engraved with the sharpness of steel" ("Modern Fiction" 106). To achieve this, to render human consciousness and to describe impressions on a mind, a new mode of writing is indispensable. Moreover, Woolf cautions her readers not to "take it for granted that life exists more fully in what is commonly thought big than in what is commonly thought

---

working habits, her eating problems, her relationships with Leonard, Vanessa, and the servants to her longing for London, Cunningham's "fiction" of Woolf can be sustained by Woolf's letters, diaries, and biographies in most points. Where historical details are concerned, Cunningham's depiction is almost faultless—even minor details such as Woolf's irritation with Marjorie Joad's voice rely on historical evidence. Naturally, the thoughts of Cunningham's Virginia Woolf on the given day remain fictional, even though Cunningham again uses historical sources as an orientation and inspiration.

small" (ibid. 107) and draws attention to the links between the criteria that "govern" the aesthetic canon and a patriarchal organization of society.

> And since a novel has this correspondence to real life, its values are to some extent those of real life. But it is obvious that the values of women differ very often from the values which have been made by the other sex; [...] Yet it is the masculine values that prevail. Speaking crudely, football and sports are "important"; the worship of fashion, the buying of clothes "trivial." And these values are inevitably transferred from life to fiction. This is an important book, the critic assumes, because it deals with war. This is an insignificant book because it deals with the feelings of women in a drawing-room. A scene in a battlefield is more important than a scene in a shop—everywhere and much more subtly the difference of value persists" (*AROO* 74).[12]

Insisting on a removal of the established hierarchy of values, Woolf's concept of art opens literature for everyday life and everyday experiences hitherto deemed "uninteresting" or "trivial." Women should "respect their own sense of values" and change "the subject matter of their novels" appropriately ("Women and Fiction" 146). The insistence on differences in values, the appreciation of the ordinary or the so-called trivial, and a concern with women's lives and experiences form an important part of Woolf's feminism[13] and shape her own art as well as her depiction of the artistic process in such novels as *Mrs. Dalloway* and *To the Lighthouse*. Woolf argues for a widening of traditional notions of art in terms of subject matter and style, but even more importantly with regard to *The Hours* she also depicts art in seemingly banal and common occupations. In *Mrs. Dalloway* and *To the Lighthouse* artistic creation is not restricted to painting or writing: housewives or shell-shock patients are engaged in creative processes that are likened to artistry. Thus, the concept of art that underlies *Mrs. Dalloway* and *To the Lighthouse*—and that is pivotal to *The Hours*—follows "two comple-

---

[12] Compare also "Women and Fiction": "[i]t is probable, however, that both in life and in art the values of a woman are not the values of a man. Thus, when a woman comes to write a novel, she will find that she is perpetually wishing to alter the established values—to make serious what appears insignificant to a man, and trivial what is to him important. And for that, of course, she will be criticized; for the critic of the opposite sex will be genuinely puzzled and surprised by an attempt to alter the current scale of values, and will see in it not merely a difference in view, but a view that is weak, or trivial, or sentimental, because it differs from his own" (146).

[13] This is not to say that this is the only way Woolf's feminism can be construed and interpreted. Laura Marcus has pointed out that Woolf's feminism is "not as clear-cut and consistent as many scholars [...] would have it" (214) and that Woolf has been used to support various perspectives in feminist debates (209-210). Bowlby considers multivalency as characteristic for Woolf's works and emphasizes that "the fixing of Woolf to one position rather than another is wholly counter to her strategies and perspectives" (cp. L. Marcus 239).

mentary ends: it argues for a widening of the aesthetic canon while simultaneously blurring distinctions between art and life" (Morgan 268).

The presentation of Clarissa's party in *Mrs. Dalloway* draws on this aspect of Woolf's aesthetic ideas. Despite critics' objections and her personal reservations toward her main character, Woolf maintained that her novel was an appropriate canvas to show life and the social system "at its most intense" (*D2* 248) and declared what happens to Mrs. Dalloway as important and significant.[14] Woolf's conviction that "the material conditions of life [...] dramatically affect her [a woman's] ability to produce art and the kind of art she makes" (Rosenman, *Room* 46) and her call for a reversal of traditional values, both foster an interpretation of Clarissa Dalloway as an artist figure—even if such a reading is not undisputed among critics.[15]

The preparations for the party and the value assigned to it in the novel underline its creative aspect. The party "is looked forward to as if it were a work of art to be created" (Holmesland 30): every item is arranged carefully to create its own premeditated effect. Clarissa is absorbed in the thoughts of her party all day and understands it as her tribute to life, her particular way of creating something meaningful, of overcoming isolation and loneliness:

> Here was So-and-so in South Kensington; some one up in Bayswater; and somebody else, say, in Mayfair. And she felt quite continuously a sense of their existence; and she felt what a waste; and she felt what a pity; and she felt if only they could be brought together; so she did it. And it was an offering; to com-

---

[14] For example, Woolf noted in her diary in reaction to her friend Lytton Strachey's critique of both the novel and the character of Clarissa Dalloway: "[...] I think there is some truth in it. For I remember the night at Rodmell when I decided to give it up, because I found Clarissa in some way tinselly. Then I invented her memories. But I think that some distaste persisted. Yet, again, that was true to my feelings for Kitty [Maxse], & one must dislike people in art without its mattering, unless it is true that some characters detract from the importance of what happens to them" (*D3* 32).

[15] While Showalter does not consider a reading of Clarissa's character justified "which celebrates her as a great artist whose medium is parties" (xliv), Rose sees the presentation of Clarissa as "at least partially analogous to an artist" (126). Caughie and Morgan regard Clarissa Dalloway and Mrs. Ramsay as artist figures who "create transient works of art out of social occasions and personal relationships" (Caughie 28). Holmesland, Howard, and Rosenman also stress the artistic aspects of Mrs. Dalloway's social efforts: "[I]n *Mrs. Dalloway*, the hostess is an artist," and "the lightly regarded sphere of women's social life" is reinterpreted "as the realm of legitimate art" (Rosenman, *Presence* 75). Littleton discusses Clarissa's artistry in a full-length article and maintains that she is "firmly established as a real artist, but one whose modes of creation destabilize not only traditional boundaries of art, but boundaries of personhood fundamental to English culture" (42). Cunningham foregrounds such aspects of Woolf's life and work that support an interpretation of Clarissa Dalloway as an artist figure. I will follow Cunningham's apparent reading of Woolf's oeuvre.

bine, to create; but to whom?
   An offering for the sake of offering, perhaps. Anyhow, it was her gift. (*MD* 133-134)

In the context of the novel, Clarissa's "gift" is valued highly. In contrast to domineering "conversion figures" such as Dr. Bradshaw and Miss Kilman,[16] Clarissa and her parties represent "the privacy of the soul" (*MD* 139) and personal freedom. The parties are an alternative to forced integration that is mainly male connoted in *Mrs. Dalloway*. They are "life, but life transformed," and draw the guests "out of the logic of the mundane" (Littleton 42) in a way similar to a work of literature or a successful work of art. Clarissa's parties function in the same way as a work of art and thereby blur formal differences between life and art.

In addition to *Mrs. Dalloway* and Woolf's essays, *To the Lighthouse* was clearly one of Cunningham's inspirations for *The Hours* as it contrasts traditional and unconventional artistic endeavors even more explicitly than Woolf's previous works. The episodes that center on Laura Brown establish particular parallels to Woolf's fifth novel. In *To the Lighthouse*, the painter Lily Briscoe compares the social art of a society hostess to painting, thinking that by drawing people together, Mrs. Ramsay is "making of the moment something permanent (as in another sphere Lily herself tried to make of the moment something permanent)" (176). Although compared to painting a picture or writing a novel Mrs. Ramsay's "art" seems evanescent, to Lily these endeavors are "little daily miracles, illuminations, matches struck in the dark" (ibid.) and they are remembered "almost like a work of art" (ibid. 175). Furthermore, in *To the Lighthouse* nicely arranged food or a well-cooked dinner are likened to the visual arts and are described as the outcomes of comparable artistic endeavors: Rose's fruit bowl is reminiscent of a still-life and matches Lily Briscoe's attempts to combine colors

---

[16] These figures stand for "domination and control" (Tambling 143), the imperial enterprise and its threat to individuality and freedom. In *Mrs. Dalloway* Woolf associates imperialism and repression with patriarchal power and male behavior. Both are discredited through Clarissa Dalloway's thoughts and the fate of Septimus Warren Smith: "Septimus's madness and suicide demonstrate [...] both the ferocity and the fragility of the patriarchal enterprise" (Gilbert and Gubar 25). Phillips, who explores Woolf's critical stance towards and condemnation of the Empire in detail, is less optimistic about the redeeming possibilities of Clarissa's social occasions and maintains that Woolf's main female character "is demolished by satire along with the rest of her world" (3), her superficiality being only occasionally alleviated by lucidity. I would suggest that even though Woolf was critical of her character Clarissa Dalloway, the artistic aspects of her social efforts are both acknowledged and appreciated in *Mrs. Dalloway*. In *The Hours*, the women characters' individuality and freedom are also threatened by demands made upon them that are linked to role expectations and social norms. For a further discussion see below.

and shapes to create a perfect picture (ibid. 118), the Boeuf en Daube is a "masterpiece" (ibid. 87) that intrigues by its taste as well as its visual qualities. The way Woolf establishes parallels between what is traditionally considered "art" and art in everyday life in *Mrs. Dalloway* and *To the Lighthouse* suggests that readers are "clearly expected to treat creativity in life (Mrs. Ramsay) and creative Art [sic] (Lily) as essentially the same impulse" (Marsh 143).[17]

Art and Life

The Hours supports an interpretation of Clarissa Dalloway, Mrs. Ramsay, and Rose as artist figures and presents a new generation of "artists in life." Clarissa Vaughan and Laura Brown are embarked on creative processes that resemble those of Clarissa Dalloway and Rose on the one hand and those of more traditional artist figures such as Lily Briscoe, the fictional Virginia Woolf and Richard Worthington Brown on the other. In the interplay of its three strands of narrative, *The Hours* addresses questions of what constitutes art and of what is appropriate subject matter for it and thus foregrounds a part of Woolf's aesthetics that is intricately linked to her feminism. Postulating an "egalitarian" concept of art that presents preparing a party, baking a cake and writing a novel as essentially the same impulse, Cunningham attempts to continue and radicalize Woolf's aesthetics with regard to the trivial and the contiguity of art and life. Furthermore, the likening of characters and the thoughts of Cunningham's fictional Mrs. Woolf concerning artistic creation and social efforts function as an interpretation of *Mrs. Dalloway* that implicitly denies objections to the concept of art that underlies Cunningham's reading of Woolf's oeuvre.

---

[17] Compare also Rosenman: "stressing unity and human relationships as essential to art, she [Woolf] links the party and the novel as comparable endeavors, exalting the hostess' role as a profoundly creative one" (*Presence* 75). Numerous critics have discussed Mrs. Ramsay as an artist figure. For example, Morgan discusses Mrs. Ramsay's art in terms of *tableaux vivants* or still-lives and stresses that both Mrs. Dalloway and Mrs. Ramsay create an art of the moment rather than "a final, tangible product" (269). As an "art of the moment," the women's art needs to be remembered to be of possible impact beyond the moment. Even though the "Time Passes" and "The Lighthouse" sections of *To the Lighthouse* suggest that Mrs. Ramsay succeeds only partially and temporarily in her attempts to shape life by creating social coherence and stable relationships, Ingram has pointed out that "both art and life are represented as art-forms which the artist creates in order to produce wholeness" (84-85) and that "painting-art" and "life-art" have "the same potential to perish" as well as "the same potential to endure" (93). Gillespie sees Mrs. Ramsay's art as a paradox, being on the one hand subject to change and perishable, but on the other hand regarded as transcending time by Lily and Mrs. Ramsay herself and remembered like a speech or a play. Laura Marcus has pointed out changes in critical attitudes towards Mrs. Ramsay and Mrs. Dalloway (227-228).

Like her predecessor in Woolf's novel, Cunningham's modern Mrs. Dalloway is involved with preparations for her party all day. Like Clarissa Dalloway, her walk through the city—both Clarissas are on an errand to buy flowers for the party—is scrupulously delineated. Moreover, Clarissa shares her literary predecessor's ambitions ("she will give Richard the best party she can manage," Cunningham 123) and her fears that the party could be a failure. Both novels draw parallels between the party and performance art by stressing the careful arrangement of items as if on a stage and the party as a situation of role enactment.[18] Finally, both Clarissas' understandings of their party resemble each other. The parties are respectively considered a "tribute to life," an "offering," a "gift" (Woolf, *MD* 134), and a celebration of life: "Here, then, is the party [...] It is, in fact, a party after all. It is a party for the not-yet-dead; for the relatively undamaged; for those who for mysterious reasons have the fortune to be alive. It is, in fact, great good fortune" (Cunningham 226). For both women facing death leads to a heightened sense of awareness and a more positive attitude towards life. Their parties become "a reminder of the intensity and joy of [...] life" (Showalter xlv).

However, despite general analogies, there is a major difference between the "old" and the "new" Clarissa. Cunningham's modern Mrs. Dalloway commands a higher degree of awareness, anticipates a possible critique of her way of life and her preoccupation with her party and meets these objections through her self-awareness and self-criticism. She explicitly intends "to create something temporal, even trivial, but perfect in its way" (Cunningham 123) and thereby refutes critics' objections against Woolf's Mrs. Dalloway who considered her heedless and trivial,[19] while simultaneously reinforcing her creative ambitions and her identification with her task. Cunningham's Mrs. Dalloway is well aware that she might be thought trivial, but she insists on the personal significance of the party and thereby emphasizes similarities between her own occupation and the work of a writer like the fictional Virginia Woolf or the painter Lily Briscoe.

---

[18] In the same way that Clarissa Dalloway enacts a certain role, has to draw "the parts [of her personality] together" (Woolf, *Mrs. Dalloway* 40), Richard Worthington Brown feels that he has to perform at the party to meet expectations: "There I am, a sick and crazy wreck reaching out with trembling hands to receive his little trophy. [...] I got a prize for my performance, you must know that. I got a prize for having AIDS and going nuts and being brave about it, it had nothing to do with my work" (Cunningham 62-63). Although Clarissa Vaughan assures Richard to the contrary it becomes clear that she, too, would have expected a certain performance of him: "She would confess [...] to how much she wanted him to come to her party and exhibit his devotion in front of her guests" (ibid. 203). Morgan and Holmesland stress the parallels between Mrs. Dalloway's party and performance art.

[19] For example, Showalter points out that "in view of what lies beyond the fairy-lights of her garden," Clarissa's anxieties "seem trivial" (xliv). Lytton Strachey considered

By implying and refuting a possible critique of his characters' art in *The Hours*, Cunningham objects to the criticism on Woolf's *Mrs. Dalloway* and explicitly justifies what her critics considered banal.

The idea of the party as a form of social art and an expression of "art in life" is strengthened in the two other strands of narrative of *The Hours*, especially by the fictional Virginia Woolf as she contemplates *Mrs. Dalloway*. Repeatedly, Mrs. Woolf ponders the correlation of life, art, and party that is established in *Mrs. Dalloway* and the "Mrs. Dalloway" strand of *The Hours*. For example, she compares her own work with a party that she is eager to join and envies the social art practiced by her mother, Julia Stephen, and her sister, Vanessa Bell.[20] Cunningham's Mrs. Woolf reassures the skeptical reader that "[t]here is true art in it, this command of tea and dinner tables" (Cunningham 83).[21] In numerous ways, the thoughts of Cunningham's fictional Virginia Woolf are related to *Mrs. Dalloway* and function as comments on both Woolf's novel and *The Hours*. They constitute *The Hours'* most explicit statements on "art" and "creativity" in everyday life and use a fictional representation of the famous writer as a mouthpiece of the novel's credo while simultaneously attempting to legitimize Cunningham's concept of art through Woolf's authority. However, due to Cunningham's research on Woolf's life, the "Mrs. Woolf" strand of *The Hours* also blurs the distinctions between fact and fiction and functions as Cunningham's main device for questioning traditional genre categories. The dichotomy between art and life—or fiction and fact—is thus not only questioned by the novel's subject matter, but also reflected on a meta-discursive level.

Mrs. Brown is occupied with a party on a smaller scale. It is her husband's birthday and Laura sets out to prepare a perfect evening with her family and to bake a perfect birthday cake. But although she tries desperately to fulfill her role

---

Clarissa Dalloway "disagreeable & limited" (*D3* 32) and Woolf herself feared that her character might be "tinselly" (ibid). See also note 14 above.

[20] Her "work is waiting for her and she is anxious to join it the way she might join a party that had already started downstairs, a party full of wit and beauty certainly but full, too, of something finer than wit or beauty; [...] a spark of profound celebration, of life itself, as silks rustle across polished floors and secrets are whispered under music" (31).

[21] Here, as almost everywhere in his fantasy of the famous writer, Cunningham sticks to the "facts" as much as possible. An autobiographical background to Woolf's oeuvre has been frequently suggested by biographers and critics. Woolf's diaries and autobiographical sketches as well as her husband's account of their life together give ample proof of her "party consciousness" and her admiration of the "social art" of her mother and some of her society friends. Compare, for example *D2* 250 and L. Woolf, *Downhill all the Way*: 101ff. Nevertheless, Woolf was generally highly critical of her Victorian heritage, including its forms of social life, an aspect Cunningham's rendering of Woolf does not take into account. Cunningham emphasizes those aspects of Woolf's personality that suit the overall concept of his novel.

as housewife and mother, Laura longs for more freedom and a room of her own to read *Mrs. Dalloway* undisturbed. In reflecting and problematizing art and creativity, the character Laura Brown has two important functions: in her role as an exemplary reader she demonstrates the possibilities and effects of literature—and of art more generally—and, due to social and historical circumstances, she reveals the difficulties confronted by a wife and mother in search of freedom and self-realization more than any of the other female characters. As mentioned above, both reading and female self-realization are topics that Woolf was always concerned with, in her fictional work, and, above all, in her essays. Accordingly, Cunningham uses the character Laura Brown to focus on yet another dimension of Woolf's aesthetics.

In the denouement of the novel, Laura, whose creative potential is restricted to the household, comes to realize the futility of her "creative" attempts and her limitations as a housewife without immediately having other options at hand. While unlike Clarissa Dalloway in London in the 1920s Laura is no longer content with the traditional female role, the life led by Clarissa Vaughan in 1990s New York is unimaginable in a suburban household during the late 1940s which reflects the family-centered ideology that Betty Friedan labeled "the feminine mystique." In order to survive and to live what will be taken for granted and considered almost bourgeois by Clarissa Vaughan, Laura has to overcome traditional role models and must go through a process Woolf described as killing "the angel in the house" in her essay "Professions for Women" (285-286).

Before Laura realizes that she must kill "the angel in the house," she tries to fulfill what she conceives of as her "wifely" and "motherly" "duties." Initially the birthday cake is only a possibility to compensate for her neglected duties, but Laura's emotional involvement demonstrates that the cake becomes the creative task that identifies her as yet another artist figure. Completely absorbed in her task of creating the perfect cake, Laura compares her own occupation with that of a writer, painter, or architect:

> She imagines making, out of the humblest materials, a cake with all the balance and authority of an urn or a house. The cake will speak of bounty and delight the way a good house speaks of comfort and safety. This, she thinks, is how artists or architects must feel (it's an awfully grand comparison, she knows, maybe a little foolish, but still), faced with canvas, with stone, with oil or wet cement. Wasn't a book like *Mrs. Dalloway* once just empty paper and a pot of ink? [...] At this moment, holding a bowl full of sifted flour in an orderly house under the California sky, she hopes to be as satisfied and as filled with anticipation as a writer putting down the first sentence, a builder beginning to draw the plans. (Cunningham 76-77)

Despite the ironic distance of the narratorial voice,[22] Laura's understanding of her birthday cake as a work of art is valid in the context of *The Hours* and it matches the concept of art in *Mrs. Dalloway* or *To the Lighthouse* as well as Woolf's demand for a reevaluation of aesthetic values and the women's sphere. Indeed, Woolf already draws the comparison between writing and architecture in "How Should One Read a Book?" where she describes writing a novel as "an attempt to make something as formed and controlled as a building: but words are more impalpable than bricks" (2). Furthermore, Laura's self-critical remarks have the same strategic function as those of Clarissa Vaughan described above. They anticipate possible objections against the novel's concept of art and her own high hopes and demonstrate her doubts concerning her own creativity. But as self-critique and self-doubt are characteristics shared by all "artist" characters in *The Hours*, they function as a means of identifying Laura and Clarissa Vaughan as artists rather than discrediting their endeavors.

What distinguishes Cunningham's from Woolf's artist figures is not the kind of art they create but their attitude towards their own creative efforts. Cunningham's "artists in life" are perfectly aware that they might be thought trivial—as indeed they may be—but they insist on the importance of their art as their own way towards self-realization. It is this degree of self-awareness and an almost defiant affirmation of the pragmatic value of their "art," regardless of its possible banality that suggest that Cunningham's artist figures are a "development" of Woolf's Mrs. Dalloway and Mrs. Ramsay. Whereas in *Mrs. Dalloway* art is depicted in occupations that may seem banal to critics, readers and even the author, Woolf's main female character does not explicitly reflect on or defend this triviality. In *The Hours* the awareness that the female characters' art might indeed be trivial does in no way decrease its value or appreciation.

The artist figures in *The Hours*, *Mrs. Dalloway* and *To the Lighthouse* insinuate that it is not the metier or the outcome of creative work that renders a person an "artist." Rather, it is the characters' striving for perfection, their ceaseless creative efforts, and above all, the emotional value assigned to their work that all "true" artists have in common. Establishing parallels between the creative efforts of Clarissa Vaughan, Laura Brown and the fictional Virginia Woolf, and insisting on their "art's" personal significance, *The Hours* forwards an egalitarian and pragmatic concept of art that recalls John Dewey's theory of art as aesthetic experience. Pointing out "the continuity of esthetic [sic] experience with normal processes of living" (Dewey 10), Dewey—and Cunningham—argue that it is the emotional intensity of the producer or perceiver of a work of art rather than the

---

[22] Woolf already uses irony to detach herself from her seemingly trivial female character in *Mrs. Dalloway* without discrediting her significance. Compare *D3* 32.

intrinsic values of an object that define "art." Dewey's concept is marked by a "privileging of aesthetic process over product" (Shusterman 25), a definition of art as "'a quality of experience'" (ibid.). Hence, it is not "[m]ere perfection in execution" (Dewey 47) but an intense emotional involvement that renders art art: "Craftsmanship to be artistic in the final sense must be 'loving;' it must care deeply for the subject matter upon which skill is exercised" (Dewey 47-48). Cunningham foregrounds the importance of emotional and experiential aspects of art not only in the portraits of his women characters, but also by explicitly juxtaposing Richard Worthington Brown's and Clarissa Vaughan's attitudes towards their surroundings. He emphasizes the poetic nature of the amateur's approach to life while mocking the detachment of the highly intellectual writer.

> She knows that a *poet* like Richard would move *sternly* through the same morning, *editing* it, dismissing incidental ugliness along with incidental beauty, seeking the *economic* and *historical truth* behind these old brick town houses [...] while she, Clarissa, simply enjoys without reason the houses, the church, the man, and the dog. It's childish, she knows. [...] Still, this indiscriminate love feels entirely serious to her, as if everything in the world is part of a vast, inscrutable intention and everything in the world has its own secret name, a name that cannot be conveyed in language but is simply the sight and feel of the thing itself. (Cunningham 12, italics mine)

An "experiential turn" (Shusterman 26) in defining art is latent in such novels as *Mrs. Dalloway* and *To the Lighthouse* and—according to the characters' awareness of the pragmatic value of their art—becomes prevalent in *The Hours*. Emotional intensity becomes a means of identifying Cunningham's artist figures as it characterizes all three women's attitudes toward their creations.

The women characters' identification with their work is so intense that it can even threaten their happiness and life. Cunningham's characters illustrate the tightrope walk between creativity and failure, sanity and madness, life and death that is a reiterative issue in Woolf's life and work. The assumption of a relation between mental instability and a special sensitivity, between artistic genius and madness that underlies many biographies about Woolf is taken up in *The Hours* and constitutes a significant trait of most artist figures in Cunningham's novel. The fact that both writer characters in *The Hours* have severe mental problems and even show the same symptoms—reflecting those described in Woolf's biographies—such as unbearable headaches, eating problems, sleeplessness, and hearing voices and birds singing in Greek, underlines Cunningham's attempt to liken their fates and to present a special sensitivity and an intense emotional relation to their works of art as characteristic of, but also as imminent threats to every artist's soul.

The characters' creative efforts are closely linked to their search for identity and self-fulfillment, functioning as a means of identification and the key for self-realization and happiness. However, the personal freedom that Woolf deemed necessary for self-realization is fragile. While Clarissa Dalloway and Clarissa Vaughan manage to negotiate between their "privacy of the soul" and demands made upon them, Laura Brown and Virginia Woolf are forced into roles they do not wish to play and vainly attempt to relate to the world according to their own wishes.[23] However, for these characters—and supposedly for the historical Virginia Woolf—it is again art that offers a possible escape. In depicting the effects and impact of art, i.e. what I previously termed the "consumption of art" aspect of *The Hours*, Cunningham again takes up and "re-forms" Woolf's ideas.

The Art of Reading

One way to overcome or at least to forget the limitations of everyday life in *The Hours* is by reading. Laura Brown is eager to read *Mrs. Dalloway* instead of doing housework or pampering her family. In the constellation of the novel, Laura functions as Cunningham's exemplary reader who demonstrates the possible impact of literature as well as enacting Woolf's concept of how one should read a book. Thus, besides reflecting the content and production of art aspects of *The Hours* like the "Mrs. Dalloway" and "Mrs. Woolf" strands of narrative, the "Mrs. Brown" episodes also demonstrate the "consumption of art" aspect of the novel.

For Laura reading is life's pleasure. Before her marriage, she was "Laura Zielski, the solitary girl, the incessant reader" (Cunningham 40). Now this girl "is gone, and here in her place is Laura Brown" (ibid.). However, "the incessant reader" is still a part of Laura's personality. The urge to go on reading becomes such a priority that Laura checks into a hotel—gets herself a room of her own—so that she may read for a few hours. While reading, Laura completely immerses herself in the novel, she "is trying to *lose* herself," or rather, "to *keep* herself by gaining entry into a parallel world" (Cunningham 37, italics mine), i.e. the world of literature and imagination. Her own world feels "more densely inhabited, more actual, because a character named Mrs. Dalloway is on her way to buy

---

[23] Even though Laura also tries to commit suicide, her attempt is thwarted. By leaving her family, she ultimately achieves the amount of personal freedom necessary for her to survive. In contrast, the fictional Virginia Woolf and Richard Worthington Brown choose to end their lives rather than endlessly wrestling with their inhibitions. By depicting both Septimus Warren Smith and Richard Worthington Brown as artist characters who fail, both Woolf and Cunningham do not limit their critique to the situation of women in society.

flowers" (ibid.). The clock on Laura's nightstand and her husband making noise in the kitchen are reminders of outer reality, of her duties and shortcomings.[24] The act of reading bridges the gap between outer reality and Laura's inner life.

The descriptions of Laura's feelings while reading are a tribute to *Mrs. Dalloway* as well as to Woolf's concept of reading and the importance she assigns to a reader. To Woolf, reading is no less an art than writing and "she thought of herself as a reader" (Lee, *Woolf* 408). Woolf's reading experiences clearly served as a model for Laura Brown's in *The Hours*. It is no coincidence that in her hotel room, the only place where she can read undisturbed, Laura imagines that Virginia Woolf "the drowned woman, the genius, might in death inhabit a place not unlike this one" (150), i.e. a place where one can go on reading as long as one wishes to:[25] "[s]ometimes I think heaven must be one continuous unexhausted reading. Its [sic] a *disembodied trance-like intense rapture* that used to seize me as a girl, and comes back now and again down here [Monk's House], with a violence that lays me low. Did I say I was flying? How then can I be low? Because, my dear Ethel, the state of reading consists in the *complete elimination of the ego*" (*L*5 319; italics mine with the exception of the word *ego*). According to Woolf, a good reader has to fully immerse him- or herself in a book, and therefore a reader must have a bold imagination and great sensibility as "[t]o read a novel is a difficult and complex art" ("How Should One Read a Book?" 3). "You must be capable not only of great fineness of imagination if you are going to make use of all that the novelist [...] gives you" (ibid.).

[24] Here, Bergson's time philosophy, influential in the way Woolf structured time in *Mrs. Dalloway*, resurfaces in *The Hours*. In *Mrs. Dalloway* the chiming of Big Ben does not only help to anchor the characters' experiences in space and time, and to provide a transition from one consciousness to another. External time (clock time) and "reality" are continuously juxtaposed to the characters' inner time (duration) and experiences. "The confrontation of the two kinds of time is [...] intimately connected with the major contrast in Virginia Woolf's fiction: surface reality versus inner life, analysis versus intuition, masculine versus feminine principle" (Hasler 152). In this sense, external time is associated with "male" connotated values, with domination and proportion, exemplified by the "[s]hredding and slicing, dividing and subdividing" of the clocks on Harley Street that "counselled submission, upheld authority, and pointed out in choruses the supreme advantages of a sense of proportion" (Woolf, *Mrs. Dalloway* 112). Furthermore, clocks serve as *memento mori* that remind Clarissa of how much she loves life and mark "the pulse of life itself" (Lee, *Novels* 114). In comparison to Woolf, Cunningham's references to time and clocks are more sporadic, less subtle, and less complex. Nevertheless his characters also experience the discrepancy between inner time and external time and time-clocks function as a leitmotif that connects the three strands of narrative. On the influence of Bergson's time philosophy on *Mrs. Dalloway* and the structuring function of the chiming of Big Ben see, for example, Morris, Showalter, Weber and Whitworth.

[25] In the film, Laura is suddenly engulfed by rushing water, which echoes the film's depiction of Woolf's suicide, and threatens to drown Laura, too.

Reading could be an escape and an addiction for Woolf (Lee, *Woolf* 401) and it is certainly both for Laura Brown. Woolf speculates that great writers "leave things open" and "can be read differently by each generation of readers" (Lee, *Woolf* 398). The reader has to respond to the book, let it settle and take new shape in his or her own imagination.[26]

Accordingly, Woolf values a reader's individual response more highly than the repetition of received opinions. Far from over-emphasizing the importance of the critic or being content to assign a writer and his or her texts a place in an ivory tower detached from real life, she stresses the importance of reading and the reader's involvement in constituting meaning. She refuses to accept a marginalization of the reader which is not a far cry from Riffaterre's assumption that "'readers make the literary event'" (Rabinowitz 606).[27]

However, Woolf's notions of an ideal reader are not only illustrated by Laura's response to reading *Mrs. Dalloway*, but they reflect Cunningham's own involvement with Virginia Woolf and her oeuvre. As much as Laura Brown, Cunningham fashions himself as Woolf's ideal reader: He has read *Mrs. Dalloway*, let "the dust of reading" settle and conceived of the novel in a new shape. Whereas Laura's thoughts and her subsequent reactions manifest her dialogic involvement with *Mrs. Dalloway*, *The Hours* is Cunningham's attempt at dialogue with Woolf and *Mrs. Dalloway*, the evidence of his ongoing debate and involvement with a book he first read as a teenager.[28] *The Hours* constitutes an act of *writer-response* that relies on Woolf's understanding of reading and her notions that "the most successful reading is when, as we finish the book, we feel that 'it leaves us with the impulse to *write* it all over again'" (Lee, *Woolf* 404;

---

[26] "The first process, to receive impressions with the utmost understanding, [...] must be completed, if we are to get the whole pleasure from a book, by another. We must pass judgement upon these multitudinous impressions; we must make of these fleeting shapes one that is hard and lasting [...] the book will return, but differently. It will float to the top of the mind as a whole. And the book as a whole is different from the book received currently in separate phrases. Details now fit themselves into their places. We see the shape from start to finish [...]" ("How Should One Read a Book?" 8).

[27] Hussey also regards Woolf as an "early reader-response critic" (xviii) "It seems that the state to which a reader should aspire is one in which he or she could *write* the book. [...] Throughout her oeuvre Woolf stresses the *experience* of reading and the necessity of reading creatively" (xvii). Compare also Lee "Essays" 95-96. The assumption that "readers make the literary event" is of course consistent with the novel's privileging of process over product and its pragmatic concept of art.

[28] "I've just had this thing with *Mrs. Dalloway* since I was very young, and it has always felt like a part of me [...] I don't exactly know why. I don't know if it was the greatest book ever written. I don't know if it's the greatest book Virginia Woolf ever wrote. But I read it when I was pretty young and it just stuck with me like nothing else has, to the point that it felt as much like something for me to write about as my childhood, my first

italics mine).[29] Writing *Mrs. Dalloway* all over again, by appropriating Woolf's biography and her general thematic concerns, is Cunningham's project in *The Hours*. Thus he does not only prove to be a successful writer, but also presents himself as Woolf's ideal reader. Additionally, Cunningham's attempt to integrate elements and motifs of Woolf's life into his novel can again be seen as a parallel to Woolf's own strategy in *Mrs. Dalloway*, a novel that according to Lee is highly informed by autobiographical elements.[30] Furthermore, by integrating Woolf's notions on reading into his book, Cunningham again uses the modernist icon's notions on art to justify his own artistic endeavors and literary strategies.[31]

Difference

However, a close analysis shows that *The Hours* is not as perfectly interwoven with Woolf's oeuvre as Cunningham would have us believe. Despite intricate similarities in the presentation and understanding of the content, production and consumption of art, there is a marked difference between Cunningham's and Woolf's "aesthetics" that runs against the general grain. As demonstrated above, one major difference between Woolf's and Cunningham's "artists in life" is an increased degree of self-awareness and the emphasis on the importance of their creative efforts in spite of an admitted triviality by Cunningham's characters. In this aspect, Cunningham's aesthetics are a development and a radicalization of Woolf's aesthetic notions. Still, the more striking differences are to be found on a formal rather than on a thematic level and these are more ambiguous.

Differences in style between *The Hours* and *Mrs. Dalloway* are obvious. Woolf uses her famous stream of consciousness and interior monologue techniques to focus on her characters' inner lives, to "record the atoms as they fall upon the mind in the order in which they fall, [...] trace the pattern, however disconnected and incoherent in appearance, which each sight or incident scores

---

love affair, or all the more traditional material we're supposed to draw on as novelists" (Cunningham in an interview with David Bahr, *Poets & Writers*, July-August 1999: 20).

[29] However, in the original essay, "A Character Sketch," Woolf discusses the merits of a good biography, and not of a good novel.

[30] According to Lee, *Mrs. Dalloway* is Woolf's "most dramatic mixing of autobiography and history" (Lee, *Woolf* 336). Cunningham draws on Woolf's, but also on his own biography in *The Hours*, for example in portraying a reader's involvement with *Mrs. Dalloway* and his mother's life in the "Mrs. Brown" strand of narrative.

[31] Cunningham therefore can be said to engender an intricate instance of popular culture's intake of figures of high culture in its "search for cultural legitimacy" (Freedman 211; also see Silver 175). Nevertheless, as has been shown above, Woolf's notions of art and her attitude toward the canon render her an adept ally in Cunningham's quest.

upon the consciousness" ("Modern Fiction" 107). In long sentences that are loosely connected by various conjunctions, Woolf portrays the meandering of thoughts and impressions that are not yet fully rationalized or organized in a logical order, allowing "[i]nterior monologue and exterior description [to] flow into one another" (Nicholls 265) and merges present with past by making them grammatically indistinguishable.[32] To convey life's and reality's "constant state of flux" (Whitworth 152) in Woolf's novels, language had to give up its linearity and become more fluid itself.

In contrast, Cunningham's language and sentence structure in *The Hours* rely largely on the traditional "grid" of language. Although Cunningham imitates Woolf's style to a certain extent, for example by supplementing a main clause by an observation or thought put in parenthesis, the overall structure of his characters' thoughts remains orderly and the "binding function of syntax" (Minow-Pinkney 57) is never loosened. The limits of grammar and sentence structure are never stretched. The reader receives insights into the characters' thoughts, but does not gain immediate access to their minds as the train of thoughts of Cunningham's characters are always already fully verbalized and ordered in a more or less logical way by some superordinate mind: past and present, self and other, can always be easily distinguished grammatically and in terms of sentence structure. Accordingly, despite the fact that Clarissa Vaughan is likened to her literary predecessor, Clarissa Dalloway, in her attitude towards the past and her city surroundings, past and present, outer reality and inner thoughts remain separate; her self's boundaries remain stable whereas Clarissa Dalloway's self is continually "contracting and dilating," dissolving in its surroundings and reverting upon itself. Whereas Clarissa Dalloway "lives" the city and merges with it, Clarissa Vaughan observes and cherishes the city—but she is always kept at a distance from her surroundings and her past. Rather than reflecting the fluidity of self and world in Woolf's writing, Cunningham's style conveys linearity and stability as it largely adheres to a more conventional usage of language.[33] Compared to Woolf, Cunningham's stance towards language, his attitude

---

[32] This is true for Woolf's characters in general, not just Clarissa Dalloway. The tendency to merge past and present, inner life and outer reality in sentence structures that stretch language to its utmost possibilities derives from the "general modernist inclination [...] to see life and reality as fluid, continuous, perpetually creative, but falsely apprehended by the divisive, dissecting apparatus of the intellect—clocks, calendars, concepts, categories or whatever" (Stevenson 178). Imposed systems of order were inimical to modernist conceptions of world and self, and their rejection was extended to literary aesthetics. Traditional usages of language were perceived as a "grid imposed on a vital 'tumult'" and had to be overcome to convey "the true fluidity of life and consciousness" (ibid.).

[33] This does not mean that his characters' relations to their surroundings are necessarily less problematic.

towards reality and the expression thereof, is thoroughly positivist. His style appears more simplistic, tending towards the superficial and shallow against Woolf's. Thus, while on a purely thematic level, differences between Cunningham and Woolf constitute an extension of Woolf's concerns towards a pragmatist aesthetics, the implications of Cunningham's style are twofold—and, to some extent, contradictory: Cunningham's style reflects a pragmatic attitude towards art on a formal level, while at the same time manifesting a lack of meaning conveyed by style in comparison to Woolf. Whereas Woolf's style added to and conveyed meaning in itself, the discrepancy between what Cunningham's characters allegedly feel, think, or experience and the verbal conveyance thereof raises questions as to the compatibility of pragmatism and art, or the appropriateness of a pragmatic attitude towards art.

A Visual Hypertext

Sharing many of *The Hours'* thematic concerns and using a visual leitmotif technique of recurring images reminiscent of both *The Hours* and *Mrs. Dalloway*, the film version of The Hours[34] can be regarded as a hypertext to Cunningham's novel, and as yet another "re-visitation" of Woolf and *Mrs. Dalloway*.[35] As a hypertext, the film does not just constitute a visual version of the novel, but is a reinterpretation of it. On the other hand, the novel provides a frame and filter for the film's approach to the historic Virginia Woolf and *Mrs. Dalloway* that considerably influences and prescribes their cinematic representation.

Thematically, the film singles out the life-death-madness theme and thus considerably narrows down both Woolf's and Cunningham's thematic concerns. Even though the film treats these themes with intensity and empathy, the consequences of its limited focus for the main female characters are disturbing: while their ruptured relationships towards life and their mental instability are emphasized, their artist-identity is marginalized, becoming less apparent and less important. In the film, Clarissa's preparations for the party do not reach the same level of artistic preoccupation with detail that is so vital for both *The Hours* and *Mrs. Dalloway* in terms of presenting the women as artists in life. Instead of minutely arranging and re-arranging flowers or pillows, Clarissa is engaged in

[34] *The Hours*. Dir. Stephen Daldry. Miramax-Scott Rudin, 2002. The film was released in the United States on December 27, 2002.

[35] The leitmotifs used to grant the unity of the film's three strands of narrative include ringing clocks, flowers, mirrors, the "plunge" of cold water in the morning, kisses, parties, and literature. As in the novel, these images connect *The Hours* with *Mrs. Dalloway* and Woolf's life.

basic preparations such as cleaning the kitchen and/or bathroom or removing staples of manuscripts from the furniture rather than giving her apartment artistic finish. Similarly, Laura's first cake and Kitty's reaction to it suggest that Laura is just an incapable housewife rather than an artistic perfectionist in life. "I don't know why you find it so difficult," Kitty says as the spectator's view is directed to the spoiled cake. Laura helplessly agrees. The women's high demands on themselves and the artistic aspect of their creations are trivialized, and their identification with their tasks lacks immediacy. Cunningham's pragmatism has been reduced to a level where it has lost its reference to art.

In the case of the fictional Virginia Woolf, the over-emphasis on life, death, madness and the marginalization of creativity are even more provocative. Woolf is almost always presented with eyes unfocused and with a slight squint—especially when she is working. The element that the film focuses on is her deviancy from what is considered normal: it is her squint rather than her insight, her attraction to death, the ridicule of her nephews and Leonard's exasperation that become much more prominent than her genius. This depiction is a throwback for Woolf scholars and uses a cliché of the author that is more concerned with her possible illness than with her creative mastery of her art. Other inaccuracies further make it difficult to accept the film's representation of Woolf. Woolf's house and garden are out of scope and so is the depiction of the Bells—whose clothes suggest London high society rather than Bloomsbury avant-garde life.[36] Even more importantly, Vanessa does not seem at ease with her sister and Virginia's kiss comes across as yet another signal of her psychological instability rather than her close relationship to her sister. The judgmental depiction of same sex female relationships is not limited to the Woolf strand of narrative. While Woolf's kiss does not seem quite natural, Laura's kiss also lacks sensuality and seems out of place—disturbing if not actually disturbed—and Clarissa's relationship to Sally is devoid of sexual attraction while her fixation on Richard is emphasized and naturalized. Whereas Cunningham suggested bisexual attraction as the norm rather than an aberration, the film uses the women's attraction to their own sex to emphasize their critical mental states. While Cunningham's female characters are artists whose special sensitivity is a source of both their creativity and their sense of failure, this creative aspect has largely given way to the more problematic aspects of the women's lives in the film. For Laura Brown, Clarissa Vaughan, and the fictional Virginia Woolf, their filmic exploitation entails a loss of essential parts of their identities and motivations through trivial-

---

[36] Both facts are also criticized by Lee with regard to both novel and film ("Dying").

ization. The visual hypertext misrepresents the female characters' ambitions, sexuality, and creativity and presents a misogynistic reading of female identity.[37]

Closing Gaps

Following Leslie Fiedler's demand to "cross the border—close the gap," a great amount of contemporary literature attempts "to pull art back into the maelstrom of daily life" (MacGowan 585). While the literature of high modernism has created a highly intellectual, elitist aesthetic sphere, postmodern writers question hierarchical, self-contained closed systems and close the gaps "between high and low art forms" (Hutcheon 44) and thereby between art and life. Cunningham participates in this endeavor and combines it with an intertextual practice of revisiting canonical works of literature to reinterpret or modernize them. He uses the modernist icon Virginia Woolf to bridge the gap between his own work and a canonical modernist literary tradition. However, Woolf gives leeway to Cunningham's practice. In "rethinking the assumptions and practices

[37] Critical response to the film version of *The Hours* has been as ambivalent as responses to the novel. Jane Marcus criticizes Cunningham's novel as "a tiny insignificant spinoff from a great book" and points out that neither novel nor film "capture the multilevel quality of *Mrs. Dalloway*" (cp. Cohen). In the film, "the great brilliance of Virginia Woolf" has been "turned into this absolutely maimed fool with a really ugly nose" (ibid). Silver also criticizes Woolf's misrepresentation as a "neurotic, suicidal, bad-to-the servants kind of woman" in the film and was much annoyed by the "faux Virginia Woolf" in the novel (ibid.). In contrast, Neverow objects to the film's representation of Woolf "as helpless emotional vampire" but generally considers both film and novel as "worthy creative efforts" and DeSalvo actually admired *The Hours* as "one of the great books of the 20th century" (ibid.). Lee considers Cunningham's novel "a bold invention" but acknowledges reservations (Lee, "Dying"). She criticizes Cunningham's depiction of Woolf's thoughts and concerns, and finds idiosyncracies even more apparent in the film. Furthermore, she objects to the misrepresentation of social detail in both renderings, as well as to the prettification of the death scene in the film, and its "sentimental expressiveness." Nevertheless, she maintains that in their focus on suicide, novel and film "come together in an impressive tribute to Woolf" (Lee, "Dying"). Rubenstein's critique of the film version concurs with essential points of my own reading, pointing out that "Daldry's film [...] domesticates, even trivializes, his subject." While Kidman's portrayal emphasizes Woolf's struggle with depression, Rubenstein argues that it minimizes the writer's "utterly original imagination, her uncompromising intelligence, her scalpel-sharp wit" and fails to convey her struggle with "language to express her unique vision." Woolf is diminished to "a slightly fey, rather dowdy-looking woman, who, even as she ponders the details of 'Mrs. Dalloway,' her novel in progress, seems somehow far less than the sum of her groundbreaking fiction." Doris Lessing also finds fault with the film's depiction of Woolf as "a sensitive suffering lady novelist [...] whose permanent frown shows how many deep and difficult thoughts she is having" (ix). Lessing does not seem to find much else that distinguishes Woolf as an artist character in the film. Furthermore, the film smoothes out Woolf's edges, disregards her joy in life when she wasn't ill, and victimizes her (ibid).

of a modernist literary tradition, Woolf raised many questions now informing our discussions of postmodernism" (Caughie xii), for example, questions concerning "the assumption that the artist is a *special* and *self-sufficient* individual, that the artwork is *original* and *autonomous*, and that art is a means of providing order and revealing *truth*" (ibid. 29). Her appreciation of the reader in the literary process, as well as her prediction of the development of new genres and above all more unconventional contents of literature, anticipate attacks on the canon that have dominated literary criticism for the past thirty years and provide links for Cunningham's book. Choosing Woolf's life and work as hypotexts for a novel that attempts to establish a pragmatic concept of art has two functions: while Cunningham clearly relates back to Woolf and her oeuvre and engages the reader in a quest for intertextual relationships and "original" meaning, the "implied" Woolf is constructed to point forward to *The Hours*' aesthetic concept.[38] "Postmodern" traits of her work and her aesthetic theory are foregrounded to let *The Hours* appear as a logical development of Woolfian intent. The "implied" Woolf legitimizes *The Hours*' concept of art, and more indirectly, Cunningham's acts of appropriation in terms of a writing strategy that encompasses closing gaps and crossing borders on various levels: the deconstruction of formal distinctions between fact and fiction, modernism and postmodernism, high art and popular art, originality and imitation, and ultimately, between art and life.

Interrelations with Woolf and her oeuvre are used to generate different aspects of this process. For example, Woolf is present in *The Hours* in a "literary" way not only through the novel alluded to by the title, but also by providing the structural principles for Cunningham's novel and by anticipating his thematic concerns. Extensive intertextual relations to Woolf and her oeuvre foreground the novel's ambivalent status between originality and imitation while questioning formal distinctions between both categories.[39] Secondly, Virginia Woolf's presence is conjured up in the form of a fictional character in the novel.

---

[38] I use the term "implied Woolf" as an entity that can be inferred by readers from Cunningham's novel, i.e. an image, or version, of Woolf that is suggested by the text's construction of Woolf and her aesthetic concerns. As such, it differs from the historical person (just as the implied author differs from the real author) as well as from the fictional character Virginia Woolf in Cunningham's novel. The "implied Woolf" encompasses, but at the same time transgresses the fictional character as each of the three strands of narrative contribute to the idea of Woolf that can be inferred from the fictional text.

[39] Notably, Woolf's own working process raises similar questions. According to Genette, diaries, letters, and first drafts can function as hypotexts of fictional works and thus pose questions as to the intertextual status of supposedly "original" work. Compare Genette, 313, 376ff, 527.

However, the fictional character is no mere "fiction."[40] Interweaving "fact" and "fiction," Cunningham blurs and questions traditional categories of genre, a contemporary trait that in itself again establishes links to Woolf who was averse to "fixed generic categories and final conclusions" (Nünning 300-301) and prophesied the development of new genres.[41] Thirdly, and most importantly, *The Hours* evokes Woolf's aesthetic concerns. Both Cunningham and Woolf depict "the common" as a worthy content of fiction and try to close the gap between art and "ordinary" experiences. In contrast to Woolf's Clarissa Dalloway who reflects on her artistic endeavors—although not as being a kind of art—but does not seem to analyze them critically, Clarissa Vaughan and Laura Brown realize the triviality of their creative efforts, but assert their pragmatic value in spite of banality. Thus, the dominant concept of art in *The Hours* extends the line of argument that underlies *Mrs. Dalloway* and *To the Lighthouse* in several ways: the forthright assertion of the pragmatic value of art and creativity, the universal application of this principle within the novel, its legitimization by paralleling the artistic endeavors of the three female characters with that of the historical Virginia Woolf, and finally the explicit reflections on their art that the characters—and foremost the fictional Virginia Woolf—display.

The attempt to overcome formal distinctions between life and art in *The Hours* is illustrated by the main female characters and their relation to literature, namely to *Mrs. Dalloway*. Cunningham's fictional Virginia Woolf creates literature and writes *Mrs. Dalloway*; Clarissa Vaughan lives a life that is basically a modernized version of Woolf's character Clarissa Dalloway; Laura Brown is captivated by the novel she reads, which is, again, *Mrs. Dalloway*. *The Hours* describes and celebrates a community constituted by (a work of) literature beyond the bounds of time and place. However, despite the fact that Woolf's concept of reading favors the notion of a community established by literature and values the reader's immersion and involvement with a work of fiction, her texts, due to the intricacy of Woolf's literary aesthetics, were hardly accessible for a

---

[40] Neither is the person that Woolf's biographers resurrect from the past mere "fact." The difficulties of differentiating between "fact" and "fiction" is extraordinary in the case of Woolf. Different opinions about Woolf and about the nature and causes of her mental problems demonstrate that most biographies straddle a similar line between "fact" and "fiction" as Cunningham does in *The Hours*. Even Woolf's biographers have no claim to an "absolute truth." Cunningham's method would seem different only in degree from that of most biographers. Furthermore, Woolf preceded Cunningham's attempt to inform a novel with historical elements by mixing autobiographical elements with her own fiction.

[41] In "The Narrow Bridge of Art" Woolf predicts that new generic categories will be needed in the future.

[42] As "Mrs. Brown" is Woolf's synonym for an "ordinary" woman, she can certainly be taken to figure as an "ordinary," or "common" reader, too.

"common" reader or a broad reading public.[42] *The Hours* closes this gap between literature and an "ordinary" reader and between high art and popular culture in so far as it does not require special literary knowledge or highly developed reading skills. Instead, like many postmodernist novels, it can be read and enjoyed on various levels, "is both academic and popular, elitist and accessible" (Hutcheon 44). However, a knowledge of *Mrs. Dalloway*—although not essential for *The Hours*—certainly adds to the reading experience. Cunningham's "invitation" of the reader to the intellectual game of finding out which elements of his bricolage are "original" and which are intertextual allusions and of tracing these allusions to their origins is certainly lost on an uninitiated reader.

Thus, *The Hours* relies on the paradox of attempting to close the gap between art and life, "literature" and the "common" reader on one level, while opening it on another. The alleged "predicament" of *Mrs. Dalloway*, namely the problem of accessibility for a "common" reader, is only transferred to a different level. Furthermore, the fact that *The Hours* contains such an intricate web of references to Woolf and her oeuvre as well as being an intellectual challenge for the informed reader raises the question whether its characters' insights as to the pragmatic value of art can by and large be extended to Cunningham's understanding of his own artistic creation. The appropriation of the epitome of high modernism for his own novelistic endeavors seems to indicate the contrary. Nevertheless, despite extensive parallels and acts of appropriation, the fact that Cunningham also deliberately distances his novel from his literary predecessor and closes the gap between art and audience that Woolf allegedly left open on a formal level is an acknowledgement that mirrors his characters' pragmatic attitude. Read in this way, an impression of shallowness and superficiality evoked by Cunningham's style as compared to Woolf's is a writing strategy, a vehicle for Cunningham's comment on present day life and art that links to the novel's overall concept of art. The "yes-no relationship," the playing with high claims and banality, with obvious and hidden meanings, emphasizes how firmly *The Hours* is situated in contemporary literary debate and the modernism-postmodernism paradigm. Thus, despite intending to be his "artistic book" and being deeply concerned with concepts and functions of art, *The Hours* embraces banality while at the same time reasserting its pragmatic value as a work of art, questioning the distinctions between high art and popular culture that have previously excluded the Judith Shakespeares from the literary canon.

Works Cited

Abel, Elizabeth. "Narrative Structure(s) and Female Development: The Case of *Mrs. Dalloway.*" *The Voyage In: Fictions of Female Development.* Ed. Elizabeth Abel et. al. Hanover, NH: UP of New England, 1983. 161-185.

Bahr, David. "The Difference a Day Makes: After *Hours* with Michael Cunningham." *Poets and Writers* July-August 1999: 18-23.

Barth, John. "The Literature of Exhaustion." *The Friday Book. Essays and Other Nonfiction.* New York: Putnam's, 1984. 62-67.

Boone, Joseph Allen. *Libidinal Currents: Sexuality and the Shaping of Modernism.* Chicago, London: U of Chicago P, 1998.

Borges, Jorge Luis. "El otro tigre." *Borges und Ich.* 1960. Trans. Gisbert Haefs and Fritz Arnold. Frankfurt-Main: Fischer, 1993. 82-85.

Bowlby, Rachel. *Virginia Woolf: Feminist Destinations.* Oxford: Blackwell, 1988.

Caughie, Patricia L. *Virginia Woolf and Postmodernism: Literature in Quest and Question of Itself.* Urbana and Chicago: U of Illinois P, 1991.

Cohen, Patricia. "The Nose Was the Final Straw." *The New York Times* February 15, 2003. B9+11.

Cunningham, Michael. *The Hours.* 1998. London: Fourth Estate, 1999.

Dewey, John. *Art as Experience.* New York: Minton, Balch & Company, 1934.

Eder, Richard. Rev. of *The Hours*, by Michael Cunningham. *The Los Angeles Times Sunday Book Review* Nov. 15, 1998.

Fiedler, Leslie. "Cross the border—close the gap." 1960. *The Collected Essays of Leslie Fiedler.* Vol. II. New York: Stein and Day, 1971. 461-485.

Freedman, Jonathan. "Autocanonization: Tropes of Self-Legitimization in 'Popular Culture.'" *Yale Journal of Criticism* 1 (Fall 1987): 203-217.

Freund, Wieland. "Erfolgreich Schwarzfahren." Rev. of *The Hours*, by Michael Cunningham. *Die Literarische Welt* Feb. 26, 2000.

Friedan, Betty. *The Feminine Mystique.* 1963. New York, 1984.

Genette, Gerard. *Palimpseste: Die Literatur auf zweiter Stufe.* 1982. Transl. Wolfram Bayer and Dieter Hornig. Frankfurt-Main: Suhrkamp, 1993.

Gilbert, Sandra M. and Susan Gubar. *No Man's Land: The Place of the Woman Writer in the Twentieth Century. Vol. III: Letters from the Front.* New Haven: Yale UP, 1994.

Gillespie, Diane F. *The Sisters' Arts: The Writing and Painting of Virginia Woolf and Vanessa Bell.* Syracuse, NY: Syracuse UP, 1988.

Hasler, Jörg. "Virginia Woolf and the Chimes of Big Ben." *English Studies* 63 (1982): 145-148.

Holmesland, Oddvar. *Form as Compensation for Life: Fictive Patterns in*

Virginia Woolf's Novels. Columbia: Camden House, 1998.
Howard, Maureen. "Introduction." Virginia Woolf. *Mrs. Dalloway*. 1925. San Diego: Harcourt, 1981. vii-xiv.
Hussey, Mark. *The Singing of the Real World: The Philosophy of Virginia Woolf's Fiction*. Columbus: Ohio State UP, 1986.
Hutcheon, Linda. *A Poetics of Postmodernism: History, Theory, Fiction*. London: Routledge, 1988.
Ingram, Penelope. "'One Drifts Apart': *To the Lighthouse* as Art of Response." *Philosophy and Literature* 23.1 (1999): 78-95.
Lee, Hermione. *Virginia Woolf*. 1996. New York: Vintage, 1999.
———. "Virginia Woolf's Essays." *The Cambridge Companion to Virginia Woolf*. Ed. Sue Roe and Susan Sellers. Cambridge: Cambridge UP, 2000. 91-108.
———. "Ways of Dying." *The Observer* February 8, 2003.
Lessing, Doris. "Foreword." Virginia Woolf. *Carlyle's House and Other Sketches*. Ed. David Bradshaw. London: Hesperus Press, 2003. vii-xii.
Littleton, Jacob. "Mrs.. Dalloway: Portrait of the Artist as a Middle-Aged Woman." *Twentieth Century Literature* 41.1 (Spring 1995): 36-53.
McGowan, John. "Postmodernism." *The Johns Hopkins Guide to Literary Theory & Criticism*. Ed. Michael Groden and Martin Kreiswirth. Baltimore, London: Johns Hopkins UP, 1994. 585-587.
Marcus, Laura. "Woolf's feminism and feminism's Woolf." *The Cambridge Companion to Virginia Woolf*. Ed. Sue Roe and Susan Sellers. Cambridge: Cambridge UP, 2000. 209-244.
Marsh, Nicholas. *Virginia Woolf: The Novels*. London: Macmillan, 1998.
Minow-Pinkney, Makiko. *Virginia Woolf and the Problem of the Subject: Feminine Writing in the Major Novels*. Brighton: Harvester, 1987.
Morgan, Genevieve Sanchis. "Performance Art and Tableau Vivant—The Case of Clarissa Dalloway and Mrs. Ramsay." *Virginia Woolf: Texts and Contexts. Selected Papers from the Fifth Annual Conference on Virginia Woolf*. Ed. Beth Rigel Daugherty and Eileen Barrett. New York: Pace UP, 1996. 268-273.
Morris, Jill. *Time and Timelessness in Virginia Woolf*. Hicksville: Exposition, 1977.
Nicholls, Peter. *Modernisms: A Literary Guide*. London: Macmillan, 1995.
Nünning, Ansgar. "Mapping the Field of New Hybrid Genres in the Contemporary Novel: A Critique of Lars Ole Sauerberg, *Fact into Fiction* and a Survey of Other Recent Approaches to the Relationship between 'Fact' and 'Fiction.'" *Orbis Litteratum* 48 (1993): 281-305.
Rabinowitz, Peter J. "Reader-Response Theory and Criticism." *The Johns

Hopkins Guide to Literary Theory & Criticism. Ed. Michael Groden and Martin Kreiswirth. Baltimore: Johns Hopkins UP, 1994. 606-609.
Randall, Alice. *The Wind Done Gone.* New York: Houghton Mifflin, 2001.
Rose, Phyllis. *Woman of Letters: Virginia Woolf.* New York: Oxford UP, 1978.
Rosenman, Ellen Bayuk. *The Invisible Presence: Virginia Woolf and the Mother Daughter Relationship.* Baton Rouge, London: Louisiana State UP, 1986.
———. *A Room of One's Own: Women Writers and the Politics of Creativity.* New York: Macmillan, 1994.
Rubenstein, Roberta. "To the Litehouse." *The Washington Post* January 26, 2003: B03.
Showalter, Elaine. Introduction. *Mrs. Dalloway.* By Virginia Woolf. 1925. Ed. Stella McNichol. London: Penguin, 1992. xi-xlviii.
Shusterman, Richard. *Pragmatist Aesthetics: Living Beauty, Rethinking Art.* Oxford: Blackwell, 1972.
Silver, Brenda R. *Virginia Woolf Icon.* Chicago: U of Chicago P, 1999.
Stevenson, Randall. *Modernist Fiction: An Introduction.* Hemel Hempstead: Harvester Wheatsheaf, 1992.
Tambling, Jeremy. "Repression in Mrs. Dalloway's London." *Essays in Criticism: A Quarterly Journal of Literary Criticism* 39.2 (April 1989): 137-155.
Tomalin, Claire. "Introduction." Virginia Woolf. *Mrs. Dalloway.* 1925. Ed. Claire Tomalin. Oxford: Oxford UP, 1992. xii-xxxxii.
Urquhart, James. Rev. of *The Hours*, by Michael Cunningham. *Financial Times* Jan. 23 1999.
Weber, Robert W. "Die Glocken von Big Ben: Zur Strukturierungsfunktion der Uhrzeit in 'Mrs. Dalloway.'" *DVJS* 39 (1965): 246-258.
Whitworth, Michael. "Virginia Woolf and Modernism." *The Cambridge Companion to Virginia Woolf.* Ed. Sue Roe and Susan Sellers. Cambridge: Cambridge UP, 2000. 146-163.
Wood, Michael. "Parallel Lives." Rev. of *The Hours*, by Michael Cunningham. *The New York Times Book Review* Nov. 22 1998.
Woolf, Leonard. *Downhill all the Way: An Autobiography of the Years 1919 to 1939.* 1967. San Diego: Harcourt, 1975.
Woolf, Virginia. *The Diary of Virginia Woolf.* Vol. I2: 1920-1924. Ed. Anne Olivier Bell. San Diego: Harcourt, 1980.
———. *The Diary of Virginia Woolf.* Vol. 3: 1925-1930. Ed. Anne Olivier Bell. San Diego: Harcourt, 1980.
———. "How Should One Read a Book?" *Collected Essays.* Vol. 2. Ed. Leonard Woolf. London: The Hogarth Press, 1966. 1-11.

———. *The Letters of Virginia Woolf.* Vol. 5: 1932-1935. Ed. Nigel Nicolson and Joanne Trautmann. San Diego: Harcourt, 1982.
———. "Modern Fiction." *Collected Essays.* Vol. 2. Ed. Leonard Woolf. London: The Hogarth Press, 1966. 103-110.
———. "Mr. Bennett and Mrs. Brown." *A Woman's Essays: Selected Essays.* Vol. 1. Ed. Rachel Bowlby. London: Penguin, 1992. 69-87.
———. *Mrs.. Dalloway.* 1925. Ed. Stella McNichol. Intro. Elaine Showalter. London: Penguin, 1992.
———. "The Narrow Bridge of Art." *Collected Essays.* Vol. 2. Ed. Leonard Woolf. London: The Hogarth Press, 1966. 218-229.
———. "Professions for Women." *Collected Essays.* Vol. 2. Ed. Leonard Woolf. London: The Hogarth Press, 1966. 284-289.
———. *A Room of One's Own.* 1929. London: Penguin, 1945.
———. *To the Lighthouse.* 1927. Ed. Stella McNichol. London: Penguin, 1992.
———. "Women and Fiction." *Collected Essays.* Vol. 2. Ed. Leonard Woolf. London: The Hogarth Press, 1966. 141-148.

I would like to thank the members of the American Studies Colloquium at Goethe University, Frankfurt am Main, for their stimulating comments in a discussion of an early version of this article. My special thanks go to Susanne Opfermann and Neil Cormier for their help and support.

Woolf's Ethnographic Modernism: Self-Nativizing in *The Voyage Out* and Beyond

Carey Snyder

> From the start of my own field-work, it has been my deepest and strongest conviction that we must finish by studying ourselves through the same methods and with the same mental attitude with which we approach exotic tribes.
> —Bronislaw Malinowski, *First Year's Work*

At the heart of Virginia Woolf's first novel, *The Voyage Out* (1915), is an expedition to a remote Amazonian village undertaken by a group of English tourists. The veteran traveler among them, Mr. Flushing, adopts the role of impromptu ethnographer, bidding the party to "remark the signs of human habitation"—signs he confidently assumes that he can interpret, his imperious approach reflecting the assumption that they are the spectators while the natives are the spectacle, and that "native life" is transparent, readily legible to an outside observer (284). Such assumptions are almost immediately belied, however, when the observers find that they themselves are observed. A sleight of perspective turns the English into strangers, as the point of view shifts from the tourists to the native women who are the subject of the first sentence below:

> The women took no notice of the strangers, except that their hands paused for a moment and their long narrow eyes slid round and fixed upon them with the motionless inexpressive gaze of those removed from each other far, far beyond the plunge of speech. Their hands moved again, but the stare continued. It followed them as they walked, as they peered into the huts where they could distinguish guns leaning in the corner, and bowls upon the floor, and stacks of rushes; in the dusk the solemn eyes of babies regarded them, and old women stared out too. (284)

Reversing the conventional dynamic of a colonial encounter, the native women's insistent, wandering eyes pursue the English until the English look away, ashamed. The encounter is imbued with a sense of bewilderment by pronoun referents that shift in an unpredictable way—"their," "they," and "them" signify interchangeably the tourists and the natives—such that the reader is made as disoriented as the characters come to be. Despite intense scrutiny on both sides, these would-be ethnographers seem to arrive at an impasse: separated by a vast linguistic gulf ("far, far beyond the plunge of speech"), neither group can forge a meaningful understanding of the other.

By staging a cross-cultural encounter in *The Voyage Out*, Woolf was tapping into the primary discourse that grappled with making sense of imperial England's newly recognized cultural diversity: modern anthropology. Inasmuch as this scene insists upon the opacity of other cultures, it might seem to undermine the premise of a discipline that seeks to elucidate realms of difference. Yet by defamiliarizing English culture and turning English characters into "natives," the novel participates in a reflexive mode wholly characteristic of ethnographic and anthropological writings in this period.[1] Clifford Geertz calls this mode "self-nativizing," or turning an ethnographic eye back on the home culture and using "extravagant otherness" as a means of "self-critique."[2] In the introduction to *Argonauts of the Western Pacific* (1922), which has been regarded as a disciplinary manifesto, Bronislaw Malinowski suggests that the principal justification for anthropological fieldwork is that by studying other cultures, "we shall have some light shed on our own" (25). This statement inverts the apparent aims of fieldwork by placing the emphasis on the ethnographer's "own culture" (an ambiguous category in this instance),[3] suggesting, perhaps dubiously, that cultural "others" should be of personal "use." The self-nativizing move cannot be regarded as simply "self"-serving, however, since it enables cultural critique and often destabilizes identities.

In *The Voyage Out*, Woolf bends modern anthropology's self-nativizing perspective to a novelist's purpose to simultaneously scrutinize English culture and reformulate fictional character, reflecting the profound dislocations and de-centerings of modernity. Ordinary customs, institutions, and artifacts of Englishness become strange to the novel's main characters as they travel to a fictitious South American town and into the Amazon, encountering cultures that they perceive to be radically different from their own. Voyaging out thrusts the novel's protagonist Rachel Vinrace into a morass of existential uncertainties that launch a career for Woolf of aesthetic experimentation with and philosophical interrogation of character. The elaboration of a new model of character—the nebulous, incoher-

---

[1] In *Anthropology as Cultural Critique: An Experimental Moment in the Human Sciences*, George Marcus and Michael Fischer argue that although anthropological writings often engage in a critique of the writers' own culture, this propensity is heightened during experimental phases in the discipline, such as that in the 1920s and '30s, as illustrated by the writings of Ruth Benedict, Margaret Mead, and Bronislaw Malinowski.

[2] *Works and Lives: The Anthropologist as Author*, 107, 113. Geertz coins this phrase to describe Ruth Benedict's *Patterns of Culture* (a work discussed below), which he argues should be read as a satire of American culture rather than as a source of knowledge about the cultures with which it is overtly concerned: the Dobu, Kwakiutl, and Zuñi.

[3] James Clifford has connected Malinowski's complex positioning to that of Joseph Conrad, also prone to using phrases like "one of us," in that both are of Polish descent and upbringing, and join British professions and communities of writing (see *Predicament of Culture*).

ent, fragmented "modernist self"—is intertwined with a critical examination of English culture in this novel: Rachel is struck both by the way that "the whole system" in which the English live appears "quite unfamiliar and inexplicable" (36) and by what she calls "the unspeakable queerness" of her own being (125), vivified in a foreign context. For the novelist, then, "nativizing the self" entails not only looking at English culture in a new light but also revolutionizing character—a central component of the modernist project.

Using what may be considered ethnographic tools, Woolf makes her first foray into experimental subjectivity in *The Voyage Out*; at the same time, while the novel deflates imperial identities and represents the disintegration of its central character, it begins to trace the contours of a scaled-back version of Englishness, one that is anchored in everyday customs and artifacts. In presenting the English as one culture among others, and presenting character as more porous and fluid than it had previously been conceived, Woolf does more than register the dislocations of modernity in her first novel: with the anthropologists and ethnographers of her day, she moves toward a new understanding of English culture and character, one that she will continue to explore in later writings.

In this essay, I situate Woolf's work in an early twentieth-century anthropological milieu that includes the writings of the British classicist and anthropologist Jane Ellen Harrison, who published her influential *Ancient Art and Ritual* in the same year that Woolf completed *The Voyage Out* (1913), also turning an ethnographic eye back on English culture. The essay goes on to trace connections between *The Voyage Out* and the U. S. anthropologist Ruth Benedict's *Patterns of Culture* (1934)—the paradigmatic example of "self nativizing" for Geertz, and a key text in popularizing the idea of cultural relativism. The final section shows how Woolf continues to employ and interrogate ethnographic methods and premises in her later writings, as illustrated by "Street Haunting: A London Adventure," a text that brings participant observation geographically home.

More ambitiously, I hope that by elaborating some connections between Woolf's major innovations in the representation of character and the ethnographic methods and motifs emerging in this period, I may begin to argue for the usefulness of a category of writing I call "ethnographic modernism," which I believe has wide applicability that can only be alluded to here. I mean "ethnographic" in the broad sense defined by James Clifford in *Predicament of Culture* to refer to "a characteristic attitude of participant observation among the artifacts of a defamiliarized cultural reality" (121). Defined in this way, much of Woolf's oeuvre may be considered ethnographic, for though she does not take up the theme of cross-cultural encounter so overtly again (except perhaps in the gypsy episode in *Orlando*), she persistently estranges the familiar and interrogates the premise that it is possible to know others.[4]

Modern Anthropology: Ourselves Exposed[5]

Before considering the constellation of anthropological and literary texts mentioned above, it will be useful to clarify what I mean by "self-nativizing." Following Geertz, I intend "self-nativize" to signify the move to regard one's own culture through the estranging lens of ethnography, such that familiar customs, artifacts, and beliefs are rendered strangely visible—an anthropological version of the modernist dictum, "make it new." This "home-coming" of anthropology as Malinowski dubs it, whereby we study "ourselves through the same methods and with the same mental attitude with which we approach exotic tribes,"[6] may be considered an instance of the fundamental reflexivity of modernity, "a major engine" of which, according to Michael North, "is the oscillation between local and global points-of-view."[7]

Such self-reflexivity is also characteristic of what James Buzard has recently termed "metropolitan auto-ethnography," a "utopian" genre whereby "Western societies self-consciously represent themselves" as a defensive act of self-definition in the context of increasing global "entanglements" perceived to threaten cultural integrity.[8] Buzard refutes Stuart Hall's imputation that in Victorian England forces of globalization blithely engulfed ethnic differences,

---

[4] A large subset of modernist fiction can be considered ethnographic, considering the pervasive figuring of encounters with cultures represented as "exotic" or alien. A short list would include virtually all of Joseph Conrad's work (except perhaps *The Secret Agent*), much of E. M. Forster's work, Jean Rhys's *Voyage in the Dark*, D. H. Lawrence's *A Plumed Serpent* and *St. Mawr*, and Aldous Huxley's *Brave New World*.

[5] My subtitle is meant to connect Malinowski's idea that anthropology should serve to illuminate "ourselves" with the end of Woolf's novel *Between the Acts*, where the actors in a country pageant turn makeshift mirrors on the audience, who respond in bewilderment and embarrassment: "What's the notion? Anything that's bright enough to reflect, presumably, ourselves?/ Ourselves! Ourselves!/ Out they leapt, jerked, skipped. Flashing, dazzling, dancing, jumping. Now old Bart... he was caught. Now Manresa. Here a nose... There a skirt... Then trousers only... Now perhaps a face... Ourselves? But that's cruel. To snap us as we are, before we've had time to assume...And only, too, in parts... That's what's so distorting and upsetting and utterly unfair./ Mopping, mowing, whisking, frisking, the looking-glasses darted, flashed, exposed" (183-184).

[6] See Malinowski's concluding essay in *First Year's Work 1937-38 by Mass-Observation* (103). Mass-Observation was a popular movement in England from 1937 to 1949, concerned with letting ordinary, untrained observers conduct an "anthropology of ourselves." See Buzard's essay on this topic as well.

[7] *Reading 1922*, 15. North builds on Anthony Giddens' assertion in *The Consequences of Modernity* that modernity is "fundamentally reflexive."

[8] "Ethnography as Interruption," 450. Buzard has adopted the term "auto-ethnography" from Mary Louise Pratt's *Imperial Eyes*, where it applies to the colonized representing

"translat[ing] everything in the world into a kind of replica of itself," by arguing that the nineteenth-century novel (exemplified, in Buzard's brilliant analysis, by *Bleak House*) performs a kind of ethnographic salvage of *English* culture, deliberately "turning away from that seemingly boundariless world in which the nation's destiny, identity, and 'culture' (its way of life) are embroiled" ("Anywhere" 11).

While auto-ethnography is a useful concept, I want to move in a somewhat different direction here. To begin with, unlike the metropolitan auto-ethnographies that Buzard discusses, *The Voyage Out* maps a touristic trajectory *into* that "seemingly boundariless world" and *away from* stable, familiar realms of Englishness (as the title suggests); far from being utopian, it shows the perils of acute self-consciousness. Moreover, by making the cross-cultural encounter central to the narrative, *The Voyage Out* foregrounds the epistemological uncertainty that surrounds ethnographic fieldwork, even as it facilitates the project of turning English culture into an ethnographic object.

"Self-nativize" also suits my purposes in that it draws attention to the cornerstone of the new ethnographic fieldwork methodology that was taking shape while Woolf was writing her first novel: the move to inhabit "the native's point of view."[9] Detailed in a 1912 field manual, the emerging aim of fieldworkers was "to enter into their [informants'] feelings, to think as they did, and to become for the time being one of themselves."[10] The notion of presuming to inhabit the perspective of "the native"—the second meaning I have in mind for "self-nativize"—has of course been subsequently critiqued as politically and

---

themselves through a negotiation with the terms of the colonizers. Buzard intends to liberate "the ethnographic perspective" from its exclusive association with "the aggressive force of a colonizing gaze" ("Anywhere's Nowhere," 10).

[9] In a recent essay on globalization, Melba Cuddy-Keane dubs this move to critically examine one's own culture by imaginatively adopting another culture's perspective "critical globalization." Since my focus is more overtly on the confluence of anthropological and literary modes of unsettling identity than on globalization per se, and since Cuddy-Keane's term reflects only one facet of what I'm calling "self-nativizing," I have not adopted her terminology. Nonetheless, my essay may be construed as an affirmative response to her provocative question: "did increasing encounters with cultural others help to produce the multipersonal novel?" (540).

[10] Stocking, *Observer Observed*, 85. The field manual is the "General Account of the Method," in the 1912 edition of the Royal Anthropological Institute's *Notes and Queries on Anthropology*, and its principle author was W. H. Rivers, the most prominent practitioner of the new methods prior to Malinowski. Rivers participated in what Stocking identifies as an important precursor to the modern fieldwork method, the Torres Straits Expedition of 1898-99, organized out of Cambridge University. It is likely that the Cambridge-educated Bloomsbury group would have been familiar with the work of Rivers, since their social circle overlapped substantially with his.

methodologically dubious.[11] Woolf partially anticipates these critiques, even as she experiments with the fictional possibilities inherent in a model of subjectivity that unsettles fixed identities.

Harrison's writing exhibits both senses of "self-nativize" outlined thus far. Part of the Cambridge Ritualist school who believed that art and myth shared common roots in ritual, Harrison studied Greek art and archaeology at the British Museum, traveled extensively to archaeological sites, and taught courses at Newnham College for women at Cambridge after they made her a fellow in 1898—a fact Woolf playfully alludes to in pretending to glimpse her at "Fernham" (Newnham) in *A Room of One's Own*, paying homage to Harrison's stature as an important female intellectual: "could it be the famous scholar, could it be J— H— herself?" (17). Given that Harrison's earlier works such as *Prolegomena to the Study of Greek Religion* (1903) concern themselves with the matriarchal origins of Greek myth, Woolf scholars have tended to focus on Woolf's use of Harrison's texts as a reservoir of feminist myths, a counterpoint to James Frazer's androcentric emphasis on dying-and-reviving gods in *The Golden Bough*.[12] What I do here instead is to explore the self-nativizing device in Harrison's work, especially *Ancient Art and Ritual*, and its connection to the kind of fluid subjectivity we see in Woolf's modernism.[13]

Though she could not have read Harrison's book before completing *The Voyage Out* (in 1913, the year *Ancient Art and Ritual* was published),[14] Woolf

---

[11] See for instance Geertz, "From the Native's Point of View," and Trinh's chapter from *Woman Native Other*, "The Language of Nativism," in which she speaks of the patronizing and dehumanizing effects of nativizing discourse.

[12] The feminist scholar Jane Marcus has called Harrison Woolf's "great role model and mentor" (139), and has analyzed Harrison's influence on texts including *A Room of One's Own, The Years,* and *The Pargiters*. In a book-length study of Harrison's influence on modernist writers, Martha Carpentier traces the connections between Harrison's *Themis* and Woolf's *To the Lighthouse*, arguing that both writers affirm the "transcendence of the female principle" (173). Finally, Madeline Moore asserts that, perhaps unconsciously, Woolf drew on Harrison's discussion of the "Earth Mother" in *Prolegomena* to construct the character of Helen Ambrose in *The Voyage Out*.

[13] Anticipating a generation of anthropologists that would include Benedict and Malinowski, Harrison conforms to Geertz's definition of self-nativizing in her insistence that the main justification for studying other cultures is to better understand her own. To this end, Harrison juxtaposes rituals of the Huichol Indians with those of European folk and of antiquity not to illuminate the rituals themselves, but to illustrate her point that art has roots in "primitive" ritual, and finally, to highlight the deficiencies of modern art. Harrison's professed aesthetic bent may help to explain her popularity among modernist writers, including T. S. Eliot and D. H. Lawrence, as well as Woolf. (See K. J. Phillips for a discussion of Harrison's centrality to modernism.)

[14] *The Voyage Out* has a complicated textual history, but the bulk of the manuscript material that exists was composed between 1908-1913.

had read Harrison's earlier work, and it is possible that she would have been familiar with the ideas of Harrison's work-in-progress through her friendship with Roger Fry.[15] A study of the ritual roots of classical theater, *Ancient Art and Ritual* culminates in a critique of the social stagnation of Harrison's own age, and, in particular, the impotence of modern art. Whereas for "us," ritual has become "a dull and formal thing," a meaningless repetition, for primitive cultures, Harrison argues, ritual is alive, motivated by intense desire, and infused with meaning and purpose (27). "The earnest, zealous *act*" of the savage is contrasted with the "folly and futility" of modern rituals enacted in spiritual desiccation, by so many "hollow men." Echoing a refrain of literary modernism, Harrison laments that modern ritual has been reduced to hollow mimicry: "We mimic not only others but ourselves mechanically, even after all emotion proper to the act is dead" (27). She proposes that anthropologists' study of "primitive ritual" can school modern artists in the proper function of their work. For Harrison, art "rises by way of ritual out of emotion, out of life keenly and vividly lived" (235), and in turn, revivified by its encounter with the primitive, art can regenerate society; in its ideal form, Harrison writes, art "invigorates, enhances, promotes actual, spiritual, and through it physical life" (209).

Just as Harrison's critique of modern art as impotent and incommensurate with modern experience is familiar to modernist scholars, so is her solution: a collaboration between anthropology and art that T.S. Eliot would also call for in lauding Joyce's use of "the mythical method" in place of traditional narrative structure.[16] As if taking a cue from Eliot, a generation of scholars traced the mythic content of modernist literary texts to their anthropological or archetypal

---

[15] Fry first heard Harrison lecture in the 1890s (Peacock 61), and may have attended her lecture at Cambridge in 1909; moreover, in 1912 one of Fry's sisters was privy to a private reading of portions of Harrison's manuscript of *Ancient Art and Ritual*, with which she was favorably impressed (Ackerman 153). During this period, Fry enthusiastically referred to Harrison's book on the "topology of Athens" (probably indicating *Primitive Athens as Described by Thucydides* [1906]) and praised her interesting conversation and her great intellect, describing her to his sister with this perhaps backhanded compliment: "She has a very masculine mind and is quite apostolic" (August 15, 1895; *Letters*, 163). Critics have noted a nod to Fry's fascination with local Turkish art in *The Voyage Out* in Woolf's characterization of Mr. Flushing, whose pursuit of native artifacts provides the justification for the tourists' journey to "see the natives in their camps" (*TVO* 244); yet given Fry's interest in primitive anthropology as well as tribal artifacts, his mark on *The Voyage Out* almost certainly exceeds the representation of a minor character.

[16] Harrison concludes that the study of primitive ritual potentially revitalizes modern art: "Science, then, helps to make art possible" (223). In "*Ulysses*, Order, and Myth," Eliot seems to echo and revise Harrison's statement, making a somewhat grander claim: "Psychology, [...] ethnology, and *The Golden Bough* have concurred to make possible what was impossible even a few years ago. Instead of narrative method, we may now use

roots in Frazer, Jung, or Harrison.[17] But the "method" that I am interested in here is not the use of myth (or, in Harrison's terms, ritual) to impose new order or coherence on the "chaos" of modern life; rather it is the methods of the new anthropology and ethnology that potentially unsettle and reformulate identities. By "using" other cultures to spotlight the deficiencies of her own and thus anticipating what would become the dominant mode of anthropology between the wars, Harrison subtly destabilizes a hegemonic view of English culture: insofar as the new anthropology turns the home culture into a defamiliarized object of critique, it potentially de-centers national identities.[18] This auto-critique is achieved partly through the assumption of the native's perspective, which enables the ethnographer to speak with authority from an imaginary position outside her own culture.

Harrison went to unusual lengths for an armchair anthropologist to "grasp the native's point of view"; her theatrical lecturing style at Cambridge included not only lantern slides and special effects, but also dramatic role playing: in a presentation on the ritual origins of the *Bacchae*, for instance, Harrison assumed the part of the inspired maenad (Peacock 62). Her teaching involved a kind of transportation to an alien realm of experience, moving one student to assert that she "stood for all true magic and mystery of the unknown" (Prins 68). In a review of Erwin Rohde's *Psyche*, Harrison again puts herself in the ancient worshippers' shoes, mediating between the perspective of the Dionysian revelers and that of the "rational," "modern" scholar: "To dance till we are dizzy, to toss our heads in ecstasy, may not seem to us the best means of promoting spirituality, but to anyone who has watched either the dancing or the howling dervishes at work the whole faith becomes historically intelligible" (165). Reminiscent of Woolf's slippery pronouns in the opening passage, the referents are unstable here. The sentence enacts a metamorphosis: the Greek maenads, the referent of the collective pronoun of the opening clause ("we" dance; "toss *our* heads"), are transformed into the anthropologist-guided readers dubious about this unfamiliar ritual, the "us" of the main clause. Using the plural form, Harrison takes the reader with her as syntactically she bodies forth a flexible, mobile form of identity, moving seamlessly from the ancient "savage" to the "modern" point of view.

---

the mythical method. It is, I seriously believe, a step toward making the modern world possible for art" (178).

[17] See John Vickery, "Literary Criticism and Myth, Anglo-American Critics" (1980), for a discussion of myth criticism, which had its heyday from WWII through the 1960s.

[18] Christopher Herbert has suggested that anthropology's propensity to de-center the subject is rooted in the comparative method of the late Victorian period, such that Sir James Frazer "shared the revolutionary dislocations of Einstein himself" (4).

In this way, thinking "like a native," whatever its political dubieties, stretches the boundaries of the self. Harrison's anthropological practice (writing and lecturing) may have contributed to her understanding of the self as elastic and fluid, in contrast to what she envisioned as an earlier, more clearly bounded model of identity, reflecting "a time when man was very sure of his own selfhood and separateness, when lines were sharply drawn and selves were envisaged as solid bodies in space mutually exclusive, not as forces interacting" (*Alpha and Omega*, 44). One of the major authors of this innovative model of selfhood was of course Woolf, whose novels Harrison read with interest.

Indeed, Harrison sounds like a Woolfian character—a Rachel Vinrace or a Mrs. Dalloway—when she describes how after reading the psychologist William James, suddenly she "seemed to go to pieces, to lapse into a stream of consciousness, an ill-defined compound, or tendency, partly [herself], partly other people" (*Alpha and Omega*, 38). In attributing her altered view of her self to new ideas from psychology (a discipline itself intertwined with anthropology in this period), Harrison overlooks both the propensity within her own discipline for unsettling identities and the example of modern fiction, with its fragmented, dislocated characters. I turn now to the colliding cultures and de-centered identities elaborated in *The Voyage Out*, which answers Harrison's call to use anthropology to revitalize art, while at the same time, performing a reciprocal critique of that discipline.

Modern Fiction: Self-Nativizing in *The Voyage Out*

In nativizing the English, Woolf spotlights not only the fracturing of modern British society and lack of vitality in modern rituals, but also the complacency of pre-1914 England, based on an inflated image of the empire as vast and omnipotent—a complacency surprisingly resilient after such imperial trials as the Boer War.[19] At the same time, working against the grain of the novel of personal development,[20] *The Voyage Out* depicts a character that dissolves further and further into "unspeakable queerness," signifying a potent critique of the stability of personal as well as national identities, and giving rise to a genre that perhaps

---

[19] In *Social Imperialism*, Bernard Semmel argues that although the intense jingoism of the 1880s and '90s was significantly checked by the infamy of the Boer War, it is still possible to consider the years up to World War I an era of "social imperialism"—a period when patriotism and pride in empire continued to prevail. Discussing *The Voyage Out*, Dorothy Brewster characterizes "pre-1914 England" in terms suggestive of an attitude of "complacency," as a time of "distinct classes, a politics of progress, awareness of the Empire, a leisurely atmosphere" (87).

[20] Elizabeth Abel speaks of *The Voyage Out* as a failed *Bildungsroman*, since, following the literary conventions of nineteenth century fiction, Woolf kills her heroine off rather than letting her develop against the grain of social conventions.

should be dubbed "the novel of personal dissolution."[21] If "the fashioned wholes of a self and of a culture" can function as "mutually reinforcing allegories of identity" as James Clifford argues in *Predicament of Culture* (104), the converse seems to apply in this case: *The Voyage Out* simultaneously unsettles a cultural narrative of national supremacy and the fiction of a unified self. But rather than leaving self and society dismantled, Woolf's text points the way for constructing a new, more fluid, and relativistic model of identity.

The imperial mindset that the novel undermines is encapsulated by the then-minor character Clarissa Dalloway's effusion on the glory of Englishness, uttered aboard the *Euphrosyne* as the group of English tourists approach South America:

> Being on this ship seems to make it so much more vivid—what it means to be English. One thinks of all we've done, and our navies, and the people in India and Africa, and how we've gone on century after century, sending out boys from little country villages—and of men like you Dick, and it makes one feel as if one couldn't bear *not* to be English! (50-51)

The expansiveness of Clarissa's remark, encompassing whole continents as well as centuries of British rule, is significantly deflated by other descriptions of England and of the English characters in the text. While the novel treats Clarissa's jingoism with irony, the implication of her remark that the contours of national identity become "much more vivid" when thrown into relief against an unfamiliar backdrop is germane to the concerns of the whole book. As anthropologist Roy Wagner puts it in *The Invention of Culture*: "the culture in which one grows up is never really 'visible'—it is taken for granted, and its assumptions are felt to be self-evident" (4). What it means to be English—the ceremonies, institutions, and artifacts of these characters' everyday lives—becomes "vivid" (because strange) as the characters journey farther away from English "civilization," and encounter cultures that they perceive to be radically different from their own. While the English characters sporadically seek out these cross-cultural encounters—yearning for new experiences and insight into different lives—ultimately, the text reiterates the anthropological conceit that to contemplate another culture is to scrutinize oneself, as the tourists are converted into objects of ethnographic study.

The self-nativizing tendency of the novel begins when the tourists glimpse their capital with new eyes, from the vantage point of a departing ship: "It seemed dreadful that the town should blaze for ever in the same spot; dreadful at least to people going away to adventure upon the sea, and beholding it as a circumscribed mound, eternally burnt, eternally scarred. From the deck of the ship

---

[21] Joseph McLaughlin suggested this phrase to me when he read a draft of this article.

the great city appeared a crouched and cowardly figure, a sedentary miser" (17-18). The *fin de siècle* slogan for the British empire, "the land where the sun never sets," is given an ironic recasting as the idea that "no darkness would ever settle" in London becomes a thing of horror; the abiding light conventionally symbolizing the vastness and supremacy of the empire is instead "dreadful," conjuring hellish pictures of being "eternally burnt." Rather than the vast expanse that Clarissa Dalloway associates with being English, the capital city is figured by this shift of perspective as a "circumscribed mound," at once evocative of a burial mound (bringing to mind Conrad's *sepulchral* city) and of an archaeological site, subject to future excavations and anthropological study.[22]

The impression of the smallness or strangeness of the nation is reinforced by a series of images that figure England or London as increasingly diminutive. The narrator remarks, "Not only did it [England] appear to them to be an island, and a very small island, but it was a shrinking island in which people were imprisoned" (32), echoing an observation Woolf made in her journal when she visited Greece in 1906: "Out here [...] The Times loses its stately proportions: it is the private sheet of a small colony of islanders, whose noise is effectually shut up in their prison" (*PA* 345). Elsewhere, the capital is figured ingloriously as a stranded ship—"They had left London sitting on its mud" (27). The deflating of a grandiose image of an imperial nation is one of the major manifestations of cultural critique in *The Voyage Out*, often enacted through dramatic shifts of perspective such as these. Just as England appears distorted and greatly diminished from the vantage point of the South American shore, the English appear, in turn, unrecognizable: it is unclear "whether they were really live creatures or only lumps of rigging" (87). The pompous classicist Mr. Pepper (who has been meditating on their destination, Santa Marina, as a lost colonial opportunity) comes in for particular ridicule as he is "mistaken for a cormorant, and then, as unjustly, transformed into a cow" (87), his "mutability," according to Elizabeth Lambert, undercutting "both his authority as a man of facts and the glory of civilization's artifacts" (11). By showing the strangeness of Englishness when viewed from another vantage, the novel acknowledges that the appearance and value of other cultures is a function in part of perspective—the multitude of cultures within the empire providing a multitude of vantage points from which to observe and be observed. Foreshadowing a major motif for Woolf and for modernism in general, the sometimes jarring shifts of perspective here can be linked to the emerging concept of cultural relativism, given the novel's conspicuous

---

[22] The figure brings to mind the passage in *Mrs. Dalloway* where Clarissa has a vision of some curious person sifting through the ruins of London in the distant future, tapping into the idea that today's civilization will yield tomorrow's archaeological digs.

move to de-center its English characters, juxtaposing them with South American others.

As ordinary customs and appearances are defamiliarized, Rachel is increasingly bewildered by the conventions of her own society: "She could not explain to herself why suddenly, as her aunt spoke, the whole system in which they lived had appeared before her eyes as something quite unfamiliar and inexplicable, and themselves as chairs or umbrellas dropped about here and there without any reason" (36). Pried out of its ordinary context like an object in a museum, or like the deliberately incongruous juxtapositions in a surrealist painting, Rachel's culture loses its semblance of coherence.[23] The English class structure appears through this estranging lens to be equally exotic in an image that makes you feel Rachel has fallen down the rabbit hole: "Out here it seemed as though the people of England must be shaped in the body like the kings and queens and knights and pawns of the chessboard, so strange were their differences, so marked and so implicitly believed in" (99). Repeatedly, the protagonist is astonished by the peculiarity of everyday customs of the upper class, such as the appearance of her aunt with a message: "The utter absurdity of a woman coming into a room with a piece of paper in her hand amazed Rachel" (124).

For the critic Andrea Lewis, following Gayatri Spivak's lead from "Three Women's Texts and a Critique of Imperialism," *The Voyage Out* serves "to empower a definition of bourgeois feminine individualism occurring at the margins of empire" (115); Lewis reads Rachel's identity as consolidated "by the erasure of colonized culture [... and] by the ability to set oneself apart from that silenced culture" (118). This reading ignores the significantly different imperial dynamic displayed in Woolf's text than in, for example, *Jane Eyre*, where, Spivak argues, the heroine's identity is fortified through the immolation of a colonial other. Instead of being "empowered" by her voyage out, Rachel is stranded in a kind of liminal, no-person's zone. Rather than serving to shore up the protagonist's identity, the quasi-colonial encounter erodes an already nebulous sense of self. Helen regrets that there is "nothing to take hold of in girls—nothing hard, permanent, satisfying" (20), and Rachel's displacement further attenuates this seemingly diffuse character. She is increasingly unable to get

---

[23] The move Woolf makes to portray her own culture as strange is illuminated by James Clifford's concept of *ethnographic surrealism*, which he explains in this way: "I am referring to a [...] general cultural predisposition that cuts through modern anthropology and that this science shares with twentieth-century art and writing. The ethnographic label suggests a characteristic attitude of participant observation among the artifacts of a defamiliarized cultural reality. The surrealists were intensely interested in exotic worlds, among which they included a certain Paris. Their attitude, while comparable to that of the fieldworker who strives to render the unfamiliar comprehensible, tended to work in the reverse sense, making the familiar strange" (121).

her bearings, until sitting in the villa in Santa Marina, she is "overcome by the unspeakable queerness of the fact that she should be sitting in an arm-chair, in the morning, in the middle of the world [...]. Her dissolution became so complete she could not raise her finger any more, and sat perfectly still" (125). This odd figuring (in an English novel) of a South American port town as "the middle of the world" contributes to the de-centering of the imperial self. A brief vision "of her own personality, of herself as a real everlasting thing...unmergeable" may seem to stabilize, center, and concretize the self, but the text emphasizes instead how that vision "flashes" through Rachel's mind, its very transience serving to highlight her general state of dislocation and diffusion (84). Rachel's insubstantial character can be read partly as an indictment of a patriarchal society that has failed to provide the heroine with an adequate education, partly as a means of raising ontological issues that reflect simultaneous transformations in society and the individual,[24] and partly as an aesthetic end in itself, reflecting Woolf's first endeavor to redefine "character" in modern fiction. Crucially, the text achieves all of these narrative and political objectives by bringing anthropology "home" as it were, by applying techniques designed for the far-flung subjects of Empire to English culture and character.

With characters as well as English culture voyaging beyond conventional parameters in this novel, Woolf embarks on the project of reformulating fictional character, later elaborated in her famous quarrel with Arnold Bennett.[25] Harvena Richter was among the first to counter the impression that *The Voyage Out* is traditional in its form, arguing for the novel's innovative "emphasis on the subject's experience of the object," and specifically, the distorting effects of the subject's "angle of vision" on perception (viii).[26] If Richter's meaning is broadened to include other human beings as well as inanimate entities as "objects," this statement becomes eloquent of the self-nativizing move in the novel that I have

---

[24] For a reading that examines the heroine's limited education, see Ruotolo, 31. On the general topic of the "modernist self" as reflecting various dislocations of society, see Levenson.

[25] In "Modern Fiction," Woolf asks whether Bennett's characters fail due to "some limitation imposed by the *method* as well as the mind" (italics mine). Though the iconoclastic tone seems to eschew method altogether, in fact Woolf incites English writers to creative revolution by advocating a wider range of *methods* in a bold new era of experimentation that draws on other disciplines (most obviously psychology, but also seemingly physics, as writers are urged to "record the atoms as they fall upon the mind"), in order to revitalize English fiction. I am suggesting that anthropology and ethnography lent imaginative writers another set of adaptable methods with which to forge a new aesthetic.

[26] More recently, Pamela Caughie has noted the "postmodern" features of Woolf's first novel, including the perpetually shifting perspectives and scenes that point to the indeterminacy of language, "undermining identification and representation" (204).

been discussing. For it is not only, or even primarily, physical objects that take on a changed appearance when viewed from different angles in this novel, it is English culture itself which becomes an object of scrutiny, as well as the ethnographic others whose perspective the novel temporarily adopts (as discussed below). Indeed, many of the attributes of the Woolfian subject developed more fully in her later writings—fluidity of perspective, a sense of dislocation, the perceived dissolution of the boundaries of the self, the multiplicity and discontinuity of different "selves"—can be linked here to the novel's ethnographic perspective.

The potential within ethnography for unsettling fixed identities is suggested in an extreme form by Bronislaw Malinowski's fieldwork diary from the Trobriand Islands, written 1914-1918 (and published posthumously in 1967). In its moody pages (which may be read as a tool for catharsis in the field[27]) Malinowski writes of the impossibility of maintaining a "unified personality" (296), which anthropologist Anthony Forge suggests is the "dilemma of every anthropologist in the field—that of retaining his/her identity while being as much as possible involved in the affairs of the local society" (xxvi).[28] The diary registers a radical sense of alienation and self-questioning, with Malinowski even wondering whether or not he has succumbed to "tropical madness" (69). The English tourists' sense of being "cut off" from the familiar is obviously less acute than Malinowski's, but their experience in "the field" nonetheless destabilizes unified identities in the novel, threatening the protagonist with psychic disintegration.

The defamiliarization of English identities and corresponding critique of English culture in *The Voyage Out* culminate in the main characters' expedition to the remote Amazonian village. The trip "up the river [to] see the natives in their camp" (235) is proposed as an antidote to the banal routines of the English tourists abroad—like Rachel and Helen's exploration of the streets of Santa Marina, a means of potentially revitalizing a lifeless and trivial society. Yet as I've already indicated, the impact of the scene relies upon frustrating these expectations.

---

[27] The diary expresses a range of emotions elicited by the pressures of fieldwork, including frustration, boredom, loneliness, and depression; the image of the empathic fieldworker who participates in the daily life of a people (which Malinowski was largely responsible for founding) was seriously shaken by publication of the diary, given the contempt that Malinowski at times expresses for his native informants, whom he refers to at one point as "neolithic savages" (54).

[28] James Clifford considers the diary a "polyphonic" text, one that reveals a "mercurial" fieldworker-writer who seems to try on "different voices, personae" (297). Raymond Firth, in his 1988 Introduction to the diary, refers to Malinowski's character as "protean" (xxi).

> Stepping cautiously, they observed the women, who were squatting on the ground in triangular shapes, moving their hands, either plaiting straw or kneading something in bowls. But when they had looked for a moment undiscovered, they were seen, and Mr. Flushing, advancing into the centre of the clearing, was engaged in talk with a lean majestic man, whose bones and hollows at once made the shapes of the Englishman's body appear ugly and unnatural. (284)

The English control the terms of the encounter for little more than a sentence: *they observe*, wielding what is meant to be an unobtrusive gaze, voyeurs in the jungle, until they are discovered in a reversal that sets the tone for the whole encounter. In contrast to their South American foils, the English are represented as "ugly and unnatural," and as "treading cumbrously like tight-coated soldiers among these soft instinctive people" (285)—descriptions that resonate with the cultural critique Harrison performs. This is not the romantic primitivism of Jane Harrison or D. H. Lawrence, however, and the scene's principle function is not to idealize these ultimately inscrutable strangers, but rather to underscore the ambivalence of an encounter where the observers acknowledge their vulnerability to observation.

For their part the villagers are depicted as impervious to the interruption of their daily lives by the English interlopers:

> But soon the life of the village took no notice of them; they had become absorbed into it. The women's hands became busy again with the straw; their eyes dropped. If they moved, it was to fetch something from the hut, or to catch a straying child, or to cross the space with a jar balanced on their heads; if they spoke, it was to cry some harsh unintelligible cry.

The otherwise omniscient narrator pauses on the threshold of this different culture, observing surfaces, but refusing to speculate about meanings, dwelling instead on the "unintelligibility" of the language to the English auditors and on actions whose very simplicity seems to deny the need for interpretation. Suggesting a critique of anthropology's presumptiveness, *The Voyage Out* retreats from the possibility of knowing another culture, and focuses on the move to nativize the English.

Woolf obliquely invokes "the native's point of view" in *The Voyage Out* by depicting the English as objects of the native's gaze,[29] only to retreat from the possibility of attaining any meaningful insight into this other culture. From the

---

[29] To an extent, the new method was put into practice by Leonard Woolf, who returned from Ceylon in 1911, where, anticipating one of the conventions of modern anthropology, he stressed that he was a lone interloper in an alien culture: the district was "pure Sinhalese, no planters, no Europeans at all" (*Diaries in Ceylon*, lxxvii). During his extended stay, Leonard learned the language and studied the customs of the Sinhalese and Tamils of Ceylon, and out of this experience shaped his first novel, *The Village in the*

perspective enforced by the passage quoted at the beginning of this essay, it is the English who are incomprehensible, viewed by the unfamiliar tribe with "the gaze of those removed from each other far, far beyond the plunge of speech" (284)—a formulation that emphasizes the vast distance between cultures, a distance unbridgeable by language. The "incomprehensibility" of the English makes them intriguing objects of ethnographic study, but what the passage goes on to underscore is the unease of being subjected to an inquisitive gaze:

> As they sauntered about, the stare followed them, passing over their legs, their bodies, their heads, curiously, not without hostility, like the crawl of a winter fly. As she [one of the native women] drew apart her shawl and uncovered her breast to the lips of her baby, the eyes of a woman never left their faces, although they moved uneasily under her stare, and finally turned away, rather than stand there looking at her any longer. (284-5)

The English experience the gaze viscerally, as a fly *crawling* over their flesh, which in turn is anatomized (as the fly traverses legs, bodies, heads)—the parasitical gaze traversing their bodies as though they were corpses. The passage conveys the sense of dehumanization that potentially goes along with being nativized, an impression evoked powerfully by Trinh T. Minh-ha through the metaphor of the anthropologist-as-naturalist who presumes to have "captured, solidified, and pinned ['his natives'] to a butterfly board" (*Woman Native Other* 48), yet here the observers are the ones caught and pinned. Juxtaposed with the somewhat hostile gaze is the image of the native woman breast-feeding, an image at once potentially sacred (evocative of an exotic Madonna) and semi-pornographic, one that conventionally would invite voyeuristic consumption in ethnographic writings.[30] The syntax subtly realigns the power dynamic of this encounter, however: the gaze that the native woman wields forms the subject of the main clause, such that she is identified as the actor, while the would-be voyeurs are the objects her gaze acts upon. In this way, the sentence structure further dislocates the English tourists, making them uncomfortably aware of competing wills, desires, points of view.

Describing the phenomenon of *culture shock*, Roy Wagner suggests that "the local 'culture' first manifests itself to the anthropologist through his own *inadequacy*; against the backdrop of his new surroundings it is he who has become 'visible'" (7). Feeling inadequate perfectly characterizes the English response in

---

Jungle (1913), in which he adopts the vantage point of the indigenous people of the region—an unusual move for a colonial novel of the day. While revising her first novel, Virginia read drafts of Leonard's novel; each would dedicate his/her novel to the other.

[30] See Hansen et al., "Pornography, Ethnography, and the Discourses of Power" and Torgovnic's *Gone Primitive*, where she discusses the pornographic dimensions of Malinowski's *The Sexual Life of Savages*. See also Mark Wollaeger, who has persuasive-

this instance, as reflected by Terence's remark: "it makes one feel insignificant, doesn't it?" (285). The characters feel vulnerable because although *they* sought out this experience, they have not controlled the terms of the exchange; they are sized up and seem to come up short. In this way their subject positions as English travelers no longer appear stable or unassailable. Rachel repeats her abiding question in this text about the permanence of identity: "Are we on the deck of a steamer on a river in South America? Am I Rachel, are you Terence?" (289).

On the whole, the encounter leaves the English tourists unsettled: "Peaceful, and even beautiful at first, the sight of the woman who had given up looking at them made them feel very cold and melancholy" (285). St. John is depicted walking "slowly down to the river, absorbed in his own thoughts, which were bitter and unhappy, for he felt himself alone" (285). Shaken by the seemingly tame, uneventful encounter, Helen blames the Flushings for having compelled them to have "ventured too far and exposed themselves" (286)—self-exposure signaling the price of seeing oneself as a native. Her thoughts wander from the vulnerability of the "flesh of men and women, which breaks so easily" to envisioning a boat in London capsized at mid-day: "It was morbid, she knew, to imagine such things; nevertheless she sought out the figures of the others between the trees, and whenever she saw them she kept her eyes fixed on them, so that she might be able to protect them from disaster" (286). England has been depicted as a stretch of mud, a tiny island in which people are "imprisoned," and in this figure it shrinks even farther, as the nation allegorically becomes a precarious craft that tips over, imperiling all of its passengers.

As the novel charts the progressive fragmentation and eventual dissolution of its heroine through an encounter with cultural others, it exposes the fragility of not only personal but also national identities, identities that perhaps cohere primarily through anxious reiteration.[31] Within the frame of the novel, the central ethnographic encounter is represented as disturbing, even fatal, since it is immediately after the expedition that Rachel contracts a tropical disease and dies,

---

ly illustrated that this scene owes something to the simulacrum of recreated "native villages" on display in imperial exhibitions in European and American cities at this time, and to the vogue of circulating semi-pornographic, "exotic" colonial postcards.

[31] I am suggesting that, as Butler argues for gender identities in *Gender Trouble*, national identities might endure largely through the mechanism of repeated performance. Adapting Victor Turner's terms, Butler interprets gender as a "ritual social drama," wherein mundane acts are codified and legitimated through repetition (140). Analogously, what Benedict Anderson refers to as "the imagined communities" of nations may be conceived as maintaining themselves through a process of constant reinvention. In *The Voyage Out*, Woolf potentially dramatizes this idea by showing the process of cultural invention faltering, as English routines are taken out of context, interrupted, and metaphorically put under a microscope.

such that the novel functions as a kind of anti-advertisement for ethnographic tourism. In this sense, *The Voyage Out* may be read at once as debunking Harrison's romantic idea that the "primitive" can revitalize English culture, as well as participating in potentially racist thinking that links cultural others with the idea of contamination. Stepping outside the frame of the novel, Woolf may be thought of as "using" the ethnographic encounter to help refashion character. Woolf describes hers as an age in which "character is dissipated into shreds,"[32] and her fiction self-consciously represents that dissipation, as, throughout her career, she foregrounds the raveling and unraveling of character. In *The Voyage Out*, the tool for reshaping character in this way is the ethnographic perspective that turns an estranging eye on English customs and subjects English characters to the shock of the unfamiliar.

Along with *nativizing* character, the novel's ethnographic perspective reveals customs to be arbitrary and local, rather than universal. Yet though the novel deflates an imperial model of nationality, it also works to recuperate the value of local cultures—in the new, plural, modern sense. When they have returned from their expedition into the Amazon and the tourists' provisional routines resume, Rachel experiences a brief interlude of clarity before receding into a new existential fog, this time induced by tropical fever: "She felt herself amazingly secure as she sat in her arm-chair, and able to review not only the night of the dance, but the entire past [...] as if she had been turning in a fog for a long time, and could now see exactly where she had turned" (314). With this new clarity, Rachel reflects that after all "things formed themselves into a pattern [...] and in that pattern lay satisfaction and meaning. When she looked back she could see that a meaning of some kind was apparent in the lives of her aunts, and in the brief visit of the Dalloways...and in the life of her father" (314).

In the last pages of the novel, what has been depicted as an incoherent and strange culture while decontextualized resolves itself into a familiar pattern for St. John Hirst as well. He is comforted in his grief over Rachel's death by noticing that "the movements and the voices [of the English circle] seemed to draw together from different parts of the room, and to combine themselves into a pattern before his eyes"—a pattern which Hirst is "content to sit silently watching [...] build itself up" (374). The novel closes with a description of the activities of the displaced English tourists which resonates with the description of the natives in the Amazon; as St. John falls asleep, "across his eyes passed a procession of objects, black and indistinct, the figures of people picking up their books, their

---

[32] She wrote this in her diary after completing *Jacob's Room* (*D2* 248). The problem of character is of course brought to the fore in "Mr. Bennett and Mrs. Brown" as well as in "Modern Fiction," and explored in such novels as *Jacob's Room* (1922) and *Orlando* (1928), which revel in the uncertainty of identity.

cards, their balls of wool, their work-baskets, and passing him one after another on their way to bed" (375). It is in this procession of familiar artifacts, and in the pattern of local, customary activities, that the novel anchors meaning in a text which has been concerned with defamiliarizing national and personal identities.

Patterns of Englishness

Interestingly, "pattern"—the word both Rachel and Hirst use to describe the shape of their culture coming into focus—is the same word the US anthropologist most famous for popularizing the idea of cultural relativism, Ruth Benedict, will use in her 1934 *Patterns of Culture* to describe the variable forms that different, but, she will insist, "equally valid," cultures take (278). Benedict read *The Waves* while writing *Patterns of Culture*,[33] and one is tempted to imagine that Woolf's innovative way of imagining the interrelations between characters in that novel (which Woolf described in her diary as a "mosaic" of voices [*D*3 298]) influenced Benedict's way of visualizing the integration of cultures into specific configurations.[34] In seizing on "pattern" to describe the emerging meaning of the everyday lives, artifacts, and customs of her English characters, Woolf anticipates (and perhaps helps to generate) the anthropological sense of the term that Benedict will turn into "a household word."[35]

Patterns of Culture is a study of three contrasting cultures that illustrate Benedict's famous statement that culture is "personality writ large"—the "Apollonian" Zuñi of New Mexico, the "treacherous" Dobu of Melanesia, and the "megalomaniacal" Kwakiutl of the Pacific Northwest—along with, the reader can infer, a fourth: "our own," its foibles reflected in what Geertz describes as

---

[33] It is equally provocative to me that Woolf in turn read *Patterns of Culture* while she was writing *Between the Acts*, though her diary entry about it is enigmatic: "I'm reading Ruth Benedict with pressure of suggestions—about Culture patterns—which suggests rather too much" (*D*5 306).

[34] Judith Modell argues that the typological approach of Benedict's work resembles the "six sharp examples" that Woolf uses in *The Waves* "to convey complex social and personal interactions" (28). In a 1932 letter, Benedict inquires of Margaret Mead, "Did you like *The Waves*? And did you keep thinking how you'd set down everybody you knew in a similar fashion? I did. I suppose I'm disappointed that she didn't include any violent temperaments, and I want my group more varied. [...] Mrs. Woolf's types are circumscribed; she never does anything that isn't essentially mild"; nevertheless, Benedict concludes, "This way of setting people down seemed very exciting to me..." (*An Anthropologist at Work*, 318).

[35] This is Modell's phrase (27). Rachel's description of chaos resolving into coherent meaning echoes Woolf's description of the process of composing *The Voyage Out*, as described in a letter to Lytton Strachey in 1916: "What I wanted to do was to give the feeling of a vast tumult of life, as various and disorderly as possible, which should be cut short for a moment by the death, and go on again—*and the whole was to have a sort of pattern and be somehow controlled*. The difficulty was to keep any sort of coherence" (*L*2 82).

the fun house mirrors of the other three (115). Principally setting out to undermine ethnocentricity and foster an appreciation of cultural diversity, Benedict also aims to "nativize" the West, an objective that, she states, "can most economically be arrived at by [the] detour" of studying others (56). Critics have justifiably found the goals of promoting tolerance and illustrating diversity at odds with Benedict's reductive typological approach and her apparent willingness to distort or caricature other cultures in order to critique her own (a contradiction that also marks Woolf's text, which exposes the foibles of the English in part by caricaturing South Americans as "soft instinctive people").[36] What I want to explore is the congruence between Woolf's and Benedict's elaboration of the shifting concept of culture.

The idea of cultures, plural—as complex, integrated wholes that are geographically bounded[37]—was under construction in this period. While the humanistic, Arnoldian model of capital "C" Culture and the increasingly relativist Boasian-Malinowskian model of small "c" *cultures* seem almost diametrically opposed, recent studies have suggested that the literary and anthropological senses of the concept emerged in tandem, and were interconnected in significant and complex ways.[38] In *Culture, 1922: The Emergence of a Concept*, Marc Manganaro identifies Benedict as a major early twentieth-century "architect" of the culture concept, and I want to suggest that her way of conceptualizing culture may illuminate Woolf's way of conceiving of Englishness in *The Voyage Out*.

Benedict describes the process of ascertaining the dominant shape of a culture as a gradual one punctuated by sudden moments of clarity, where "hundreds of details fall into over-all patterns" (*The Chrysanthemum and the Sword*, 12)—a formulation evoking the way that quotidian details of English life suddenly appear to have a discernable shape for both Rachel and Hirst in Woolf's novel. Woolf's characters become ethnographers of themselves, glimpsing the shapes of their lives from afar, as previously unexamined details of English life (eating, dancing, mating rituals) coalesce into a pattern, much as in Benedict's moment of anthropological inspiration.[39] *The Voyage Out* enacts Benedict's colleague

[36] *TVO*, 296. See Geertz, ibid., and cf. Hegeman, 96-103.
[37] In *After Tylor*, Stocking points out that E. B. Tylor's founding definition of "culture" bears resemblance to the modern usage of "small c" culture: "that complex whole which includes knowledge, belief, art, morals, law, custom, and any other capabilities and habits acquired by man as a member of society" (*Primitive Culture* [1871]). However, as Stocking observes, Tylor was constrained by his belief in evolutionism and the superiority of the English, so that his definition does not acknowledge a plurality of cultures.
[38] See Hegeman and Manganaro.
[39] Judith Modell argues that Benedict drew on the aesthetic ideas of Bloomsbury in conceptualizing the idea of cultural "patterns." Noting that Benedict read the journals in

Edward Sapir's idea that "culture is not something given but something to be gradually and gropingly discovered,"[40] as the characters and the novel itself grope toward a new understanding of Englishness—as a culture among *cultures*, or, in Benedict's terms, one of many possible cultural configurations.[41] Indeed, *The Voyage Out* may be read as an imaginative ethnography of English culture, a tour through English customs (tea-taking, English dances, drawing-room concerts), rites of passage (coming of age and courtship), institutions (marriage, empire), and so on. To describe the novel in these terms is to invoke a lineage that might include the novels of Austen or the anglophilic Henry James,[42] but Woolf's representation of English customs and manners departs significantly from the tradition of the novel of manners in its heightened ethnographic self-consciousness: Woolf's first novel is filled with scenes that throw into relief not only English culture but also the self-nativizing device that renders it visible.

If Woolf's first novel registers the emergent idea of cultural pluralism, as I have been suggesting, it does not do so in a utopian mode. *Patterns of Culture* provides a possible explanation. Benedict observes that until recently, cushioned by imperial successes, the West has been deluded into regarding its own customs and mores as universal and absolute (6), and the erosion of this belief has sent shock waves through society:

> [t]he sophisticated modern temper has made of social relativity, even in the small area it has recognized, a doctrine of despair. It has pointed out its incongruity with the orthodox dreams of permanence and ideality and with the individual's illusions of autonomy. It has argued that if human existence must give up these, the nutshell of existence is empty. [...] It rouses pessimism because it throws old formulas into confusion, not because it contains anything intrinsically difficult. As soon as the new opinion is embraced as customary belief, it will be another trusted bulwark of the good life. We shall arrive then at a more realistic social faith, accepting as grounds of hope and as new bases

---

which Roger Fry published (*The Dial, Athenaeum, The Nation*), Modell detects a resonance between Fry's model of a work of art, characterized by "form, harmony, and structured arrangement," and Benedict's model of culture.

[40] David G. Mandelbaum, *Selected Writings of Edward Sapir* (Berkeley: U of Cal P, 1968), 592.

[41] Or "a tribe among tribes," as Melba Cuddy-Keane suggested upon hearing an earlier version of this paper at the 1999 MLA, on a panel called "Woolf and Englishness" that Cuddy-Keane organized. See also Sonita Sarker on the topic of Woolf and Englishness. In a discussion of *The London Scene*, Sarker argues that Woolf tends to elide race and nation, taking Anglo-Saxon as the unmarked norm of English identity.

[42] In *Ethnography of Manners*, Nancy Bentley suggests that Henry James' novels of manners and Bronislaw Malinowski's ethnographies engage in the parallel enterprise of "refashioning an earlier, more provincial genre of manners, [...] a new way of seeing and writing about social life" (1).

for tolerance the coexisting and equally valid patterns of life which mankind has created for itself from the raw materials for existence. (278)

In *The Voyage Out*, the trope of the diminished nation, the impression of mechanistic behavior surrounding especially courtship and religion, and finally, the collective English response to the encounter with a different culture—the sense of self-exposure, "insignificance," and vulnerability—all partake of the pessimism Benedict describes. The novel represents a world in which "old formulas" have been thrown "into confusion."

In place of the grandiose image of empire that prevailed in the popular press, *The Voyage Out* presents a much-scaled-back image of the English as just another culture "hovering off the edge of Europe, with their own language, their own peculiar customs, their rituals, their myths,"[43] reflecting the new cultural relativism that Benedict would help to popularize after the war. The "old stable ego"[44] might be viewed as a kind of casualty of the new relativistic outlook in this book, given that the main character, deprived of an elusive (and perhaps illusive) solid ground of culture, metaphysically deteriorates and then dies. But in the last pages, the narrative that has been verging toward bleakness shifts to a more hopeful tenor. Moreover, in Woolf's subsequent writings, similar experimentation with character is not shadowed by the same sense of loss, perhaps because elastic, fluid modern subjectivities come to be regarded not as part of what Benedict calls "the doctrine of despair" surrounding cultural relativity, but instead as a realm of new possibilities. I will close by briefly exploring one example of this shift in attitude.

Not Tethered to a Single Mind

A text that revels in the artistically generative potential inherent in the ethnographic practice of adopting the native's point of view is Woolf's 1930 essay "Street Haunting: A London Adventure," in which the narrating writer-observer celebrates the liberation from restrictive identity afforded by the anonymity of London streets, where "one can put on briefly [...] the bodies and minds of oth-

---

[43] This is Stuart Hall's characterization of what he calls "new style globalization," in contrast to that of the Victorian era, when, he argues, the English mistook their own limited perspective for "sight itself" (21-22). While this division of globalization into "old" and "new" styles may be overly schematic (Buzard makes a good case for Victorian novels exhibiting the kind of cultural self-consciousness Hall associates with the twentieth century), it is a helpful way of thinking about a general shift in attitude that Woolf and Benedict record. Woolf shows the "old style" ethnocentrism persevering in the character of Richard Dalloway, and the emergence of "new style" globalization in the "pattern" of ordinary customs that Rachel and St. John Hirst each self-consciously observe in the last pages of *The Voyage Out*.

[44] D. H. Lawrence uses this phrase in the following remark about *The Rainbow*: "You mustn't look in my novel for the old stable *ego*—of character" (qtd Langbaum 72).

ers"—of a street singer, a dwarf, or a society woman—"penetrating" each "far enough to give oneself the illusion that one is not tethered to a single mind" (165). Far from recoiling from encounters that destabilize identities as in *The Voyage Out*, in this essay such encounters are courted, yet the exuberant identity hopping that ensues emerges as a more likely methodology for novelists than for social scientists since the practice is predicated, in the wording of the previous sentence, on "illusion."[45] "Street Haunting" is an illuminating companion piece to *The Voyage Out* because it likewise employs and interrogates the self-nativizing device, and at the same time suggests a powerful connection between the ethnographer's and the fiction writer's respective "fieldwork" methods.

Even as the essay hints at the fictiveness of vicariously inhabiting other identities, it replicates the structure of the "participant observation" approach to modern fieldwork, which in James Clifford's description, entails a "continuous tacking between the 'inside' and 'outside' of events" or, in "hermeneutic terms," "a dialectic of experience and interpretation" (34). The street haunter is subsumed by the power of observation, transfigured into an "enormous eye," suggestive at once of a fantasy of undetected voyeurism (the body is left behind; only spectral vision remains) and a comment on the potential monstrosity of an ethnographic gaze. The eye alternates between "gliding" and "delving," between skimming and imaginatively plunging into another's experience, presuming to penetrate an alternate reality. The representatives of alterity in this essay, rather than "primitives" in an Amazonian jungle, include indigent and disabled Londoners and a wealthy woman of Mayfair, delineating a model of national culture riven along lines of class and physical ability. Unlike Woolf's first novel, this essay is less interested in the contours of English culture per se than in the internal divisions that divide this geographical space. The fanciful inhabitation of different selves and perspectives suggests an intra-cultural relativism figured as exhilarating (as opposed to the mainly disorienting relativism of *The Voyage Out*), but not one that escapes the problematic power dynamics of ethnographic observation.

Cued by the question, "What, then, is it like to be a dwarf?" (157), the narrator of "Street Haunting" seamlessly passes into this person's consciousness, relating her thoughts and emotions, a technique perfected in Woolf's fiction of the 1920s. The writer-observer then pulls back from this close-identification with

---

[45] The critique of ethnographic methodology that Woolf's essay provocatively suggests has subsequently been made from within the discipline. Refuting Malinowski's near mystical model of "anthropological understanding," Clifford Geertz asserts, "The ethnographer does not, and [...] largely cannot, perceive what his informants perceive" ("From the Native's Point of View" 27). Instead of presuming to "think like a native," Geertz favors the hermeneutic approach of interpreting a culture's symbolic forms.

an urban other, assuming a distanced vantage point from which the young woman and a band of disabled and indigent pedestrians appear as "human spectacle," grotesques whose lives become unfathomable (159). This move is reminiscent of the central ethnographic encounter of *The Voyage Out*, where the narrator adopts and then rescinds the native's point of view, ultimately insisting on the opacity of the foreign culture. In both cases, Woolf's tacking back achieves a different sort of distance than that of the participant-observer who extricates him or herself from native life to produce an authoritative, theoretically informed ethnographic monograph. The distancing move in "Street Haunting," as in *The Voyage Out*, renders the scene from what emerges as another limited vantage point—one that is somewhat cringe-inducing because it is clearly prejudicial (the "dwarf" becomes a grotesque, and the Amazonian natives, stereotypically "instinctive" people), yet one that stakes no claim of objectivity.

Woolf scholars have debated the significance of the oscillating perspective in "Street Haunting." The essay concludes with a seemingly cozy return to old identities: "it is comforting to feel the old possessions, the old prejudices fold us round; and the self, which has been blown about at many street corners [...] sheltered and enclosed" (166). (This narrative trajectory resembles that of *The Voyage Out*, though I have argued that rather than returning to old identities, the novel revises personal and national identities.) Susan Squier argues that "Street Haunting" ultimately enacts a politically conservative "retreat" into a safe-house of economic and physical privilege, away from "the multiple selves it explores and temporarily affirms," and that this retreat cuts short the potential for social criticism that an "outsider's" perspective may have offered (50).[46] But I have to agree with Pamela Caughie's response to Squier that the resumption of stable identities is not finally the point here; rather than positing a choice between fixed subject positions (in the Squier-Caughie debate, between hegemonic and marginal, or feminist and aesthete), the essay "explores the relations between [these positions]" (123). The conclusion doesn't undo the destabilizing effects of the rest of the essay, which emphasizes the departure from "the straight lines of personality" and shows the limitations of fixed perspectives.

In "Street Haunting," the mutable consciousness returns home with resources for writing, much as the ethnographer returns to transmute the messy stuff of fieldwork into a professional monograph. The oscillations of the self-

---

[46] Squier uses the terms "insider" and "outsider" in their colloquial sense to mean, respectively, hegemonic versus marginal (the latter use typified by the phrase "outsider art"). The ethnographic sense of these terms is effectively reversed since the "outside" perspective is aligned with the self-authorizing voice of the ethnographer. For Squier, then, the dwarf is an "outsider"; in my discussion, the dwarf is an "insider".

nativizing consciousness that assumes and relinquishes different points of view help to generate a fluid model of identity characteristic of Woolf's novels, as prefigured in *The Voyage Out*. To recall Harrison's words, selves are no longer "envisaged as solid bodies in space mutually exclusive"—they are relative and provisional, a premise integral both to new fieldwork methods and to Woolf's technique. Adopting the other's point of view is disconcerting to the English tourists in *The Voyage Out* and celebrated in "Street Haunting," but in both texts, it functions as a fertile creative strategy. Using ethnographic tools, Woolf carves out new aesthetic terrain in these texts, participating in the shift to more relativist models of personal and cultural identity, and installing herself as a "major architect" of an innovative model of character.

Works Cited

Abel, Elizabeth, Marianne Hisch, and Elizabeth Langland, *The Voyage In: Fictions of Female Development*. Hanover: UP of New England, 1983.
Ackerman, Robert. *The Myth and Ritual School: J. G. Frazer and the Cambridge Ritualists*. London: Garland Publishing Inc, 1991.
Benedict, Ruth. *An Anthropologist at Work: Writings of Ruth Benedict*. Edited Margaret Mead. Boston: Houghton Mifflin, 1959.
——. *The Chrysanthemum and the Sword: Patterns of Japanese Culture* (1946). Vermont and Tokyo: Charles E. Tuttle Company, 1954.
——. *Patterns of Culture* (1934). Boston: Houghton Mifflin Company, 1959.
Brewster, Dorothy. *Virginia Woolf*. NY: NYU Press, 1962.
Buzard, James. "'Anywhere's Nowhere': *Bleak House* as Autoethnography." *The Yale Journal of Criticism* 12.1 (1999) 7-39.
——. "Ethnography as Interruption: *News from Nowhere*, Narrative, and the Modern Romance of Authority." *Victorian Studies* 40.3 (Spring 1997): 445-74.
——. "Mass Observation, Modernism, and Auto-ethnography." *Modernism/modernity* 4.3 (1997) 93-122.
Carpentier, Martha C. *Ritual, Myth, and the Modernist Text: The Influence of Jane Ellen Harrison on Joyce, Eliot, and Woolf*. NY: Routledge, 1998.
Caughie, Pamela. *Virginia Woolf & Postmodernism, Literature in Quest & Question of Itself*. Urbana and Chicago: U Illinois P, 1991.
Clifford, James. *The Predicament of Culture: Twentieth-Century Ethnography, Literature, and Art*. Cambridge, MA: Harvard UP, 1988.
Cuddy-Keane, Melba. "Modernism, Geopolitics, Globalization."

Modernism/modernity 10.3 (Sept. 2003): 539-58.
Eliot, T. S. *Selected Prose of T. S. Eliot*, ed. Frank Kermode. NY: HBJ, 1975.
Fry, Roger. *Letters of Roger Fry*, Volume I. Ed. Denys Sutton. New York: Random House, 1972.
———. "The Art of the Bushmen" (*Burlington Magazine*, 1910) and "Negro Sculpture" (*Athenaeum*, 1920), in *Vision and Design* (1924). New York: Chatto and Windus, 1947.
Geertz, Clifford. "'From the Native's Point of View': On the Nature of Anthropological Understanding." *Local Knowledge: Further Essays in Interpretive Anthropology*. NY: Basic Books, 1983: 55-70.
———. *Works and Lives: The Anthropologist as Author*. Stanford: Stanford UP, 1988.
Hansen, Christian, Catherine Needham and Bill Nichols, "Pornography, Ethnography, and the Discourses of Power," in *Representing Reality: Issues and Concepts in Documentary*. Bloomington and Indianapolis: Indiana UP, 1991.
Harrison, Jane Ellen. *Alpha and Omega*. London: Sidgwick & Jackson Ltd., 1915.
———. Ancient Art and Ritual. London: Williams and Norgate, 1913.
———. "Rohde's *Psyche*, Part II." *The Classical Review* (April 1894): 165-66.
Hegeman, Susan. *Patterns for America: Modernism and the Concept of Culture*. Princeton: Princeton U P, 1999.
Lambert, Elizabeth. "'and Darwin says they are nearer the cow': Evolutionary Discourse in *Melymbrosia and The Voyage Out*." *Twentieth Century Literature* 37.1 (Spring 1991): 1-21.
Lee, Hermione. *Virginia Woolf*. London: Chatto & Windus, 1996.
Levenson, Michael. *Modernism and the Fate of the Individual*. NY: Cambridge UP, 1991.
Lewis, Andrea. "The Visual Politics of Empire and Gender in Virginia Woolf's *The Voyage Out*." *Woolf Studies Annual* 1 (1995): 106-120.
Malinowski, Bronislaw. Argonauts of the Western Pacific (1922). Prospect Heights, ILL: Waveland Press, Inc., 1984.
———. "A Nationwide Intelligence Service," in *First Year's Work (1937-1938) by Mass Observation*, ed. Charles Madge and Tom Harrison. London: Lindsay Drummond, 1938.
Manganaro, Marc. *Culture, 1922: The Emergence of a Concept*. Princeton: Princeton UP, 2002.
Marcus, George, and Michael Fisher. *Anthropology as Cultural Critique*. Chicago: U of Chicago P, 1986.
Marcus, Jane, *Virginia Woolf and the Languages of Patriarchy*. Bloomington and

Indianapolis: Indiana UP, 1987.
Modell, Judith. "'It is besides a pleasant English word'—Ruth Benedict's Concept of Patterns." *Anthropological Quarterly* 62.1 (1989), 27-40.
Moore, Madeline. "Some Female Versions of Pastoral: *The Voyage Out* and Matriarchal Mythologies" in Jane Marcus, ed., *New Feminist Essays on Virginia Woolf*. Lincoln: U of Nebraska P, 1981: 82-104.
North, Michael. *Reading 1922: A Return to the Scene of the Modern*. NY: Oxford UP, 1999. *Notes and Queries on Anthropology* (fourth edition). London: The Royal Anthropological Institute, 1912.
Peacock, Sandra J. *Jane Ellen Harrison: The Mask and the Self*. New Haven: Yale UP, 1988.
Phillips, K. J. "Jane Ellen Harrison and Modernism." *Journal of Modern Literature* 17.4 (Spring 1991): 465-487.
Pratt, Mary Louise. *Imperial Eyes: Travel Writing and Transculturation* NY: Routledge, 1992.
Prins, Yopie. "Greek Maenads, Victorian Spinsters." In Richard Dellamora, ed. *Victorian Sexual Dissidence*. Chicago: U of Chicago P, 1999: 43-81.
Richter, Harvena. *Virginia Woolf: The Inward Voyage*. Princeton: Princeton U P, 1970.
Ruotolo, Lucio P. *The Interrupted Moment*. Stanford: Stanford UP, 1986.
Sarker, Sonita. "Locating a Native Englishness in Virginia Woolf's *The London Scene*." *NWSA Journal* 13.2 (Summer 2001): 1-30.
Spivak, Gayatri Chakravorty. "Three Women's Texts and a Critique of Imperialism." Henry Louis Gates, ed. *"Race," Writing, and Difference*. Chicago: U of Chicago P, 1986: 262-80.
Squier, Susan. *Virginia Woolf and London: The Sexual Politics of the City*. Chapel Hill and London: U of North Carolina P, 1985.
Stocking, Jr., George W. *After Tylor: British Social Anthropology, 1888-1951*. Madison: U of Wisconsin P, 1995.
———. "The Ethnographer's Magic: Fieldwork in British Anthropology from Tylor to Malinowski," in *Observers Observed: Essays on Ethnographic Fieldwork*. Madison: U of Wisconsin P, 1983.
Trinh T. Minh-ha. *Woman Native Other*. Bloomington and Indianapolis: Indiana UP, 1989.
Wagner, Roy, *The Invention of Culture: Revised and Expanded Edition*. Chicago: U of Chicago P, 1975.
Wollaeger, Mark. "Woolf, Postcards, and the Elision of Race: Colonizing Women in The Voyage Out," in *Modernism/modernity*. 8.1 (January 2001): 43-75.
Woolf, Leonard. *Diaries in Ceylon: Records of a Colonial Administrator (1908-*

1911). London: Hogarth Press, 1963.

———. Growing: *An Autobiography of the Years 1904-1911*. NY: Harcourt, Brace & World, Inc., 1961.

Woolf, Virginia. *Between the Acts* (1941). NY: Harcourt Brace Jovanovich, 1969.

———. *Collected Essays*. London: Hogarth P, 1967.

———. *The Diary of Virginia Woolf*. (Volume 3: 1923-1928) NY: Harcourt Brace Jovanovich, 1977.

———. *The Diary of Virginia Woolf*. (Volume 5: 1932-1935) NY: Harcourt Brace Jovanovich, 1979.

———. *Melymbrosia: An Early Version of* The Voyage Out, ed. Louise A DeSalvo. NY: New York Public Library, 1982.

———. *A Passionate Apprentice: The Early Journals of Virginia Woolf*, ed. Mitchell A. Leaska. London: Hogarth P, 1990.

———. *A Room of One's Own* (1929). NY: Harcourt Brace Jovanovich, 1957.

———. *Three Guineas* (1938). NY: Harcourt Brace Jovanovich, 1966.

———. *The Voyage Out* (1915). NY: Harcourt Brace Jovanovich, 1948.

I am grateful to the following individuals for giving me feedback at various stages of the development of this project: John Marx, Joseph McLaughlin, Adrienne Munich, Eric Haralson, Helen Cooper, Renato Rosaldo, Melba Cuddy-Keane, Heidi Johnsen, Jessica Yood, Paul Jones and the rest of my colleagues in the junior faculty writing group at OU, and my anonymous reviewers at WSA. *A previous incarnation of this essay, entitled "Woolf's Ethnographic Fiction: Othering Englishness in* The Voyage Out,*" was presented at the 1999 MLA Convention in Chicago.*

Virginia Woolf and the Curious Case of Berta Ruck
Diane F. Gillespie[1]

In *A Story-Teller Tells the Truth* (1935), journalist and popular romance novelist Berta Ruck (1878-1978) (*figure 1*) recalls how much she has enjoyed getting "pen-and-ink bouquets from unknown readers" (188).[2] Perhaps because Ruck considered a "fan-letter from a colleague" an especially "rare and helpful variant" of the genre (194), she occasionally sent one to another writer. In 1928, for instance, she wrote to Virginia Woolf about *Orlando*.[3] The letter alludes to the fact that, to Woolf, Ruck is no "unknown reader." The two women had been known to each other since the publication of *Jacob's Room* in 1922. In chapter 11 of the novel, Woolf describes Mrs. Flanders and Mrs. Jarvis strolling through the churchyard and reading "the legends on the tombstones [...], brief voices saying, 'I am Bert*h*a Ruck,' 'I am Tom Gage'" (133; italics mine). On that occasion, Woolf received the opposite of a fan letter. Berta Ruck, along with her family and friends, strongly objected to Woolf's having given her a premature burial and threatened legal action (Bell 2: 91; Spater and Parsons 147). In a short paragraph entitled "Buried Alive—By Virginia Woolf" in *A Story-Teller Tells the Truth*, however, Ruck does not mention litigation. She does say she notified her "'grave-digger'" that when she dies, she "meant never to own a grave, but to be cleanly burnt and scattered upon the air" (260).

---

[1] I wish to thank Manuscripts, Archives and Special Collections at Washington State University (Pullman, Washington), the owners of the unpublished letter from Virginia Woolf to Berta Ruck, as well as the Society of Authors which, on behalf of the Estate of Virginia Woolf, has allowed me to quote it. I would also like to thank the University of Sussex Special Collections, owners of Berta Ruck's unpublished letter to Virginia Woolf. The reproductions of the dustjackets for Woolf's *Orlando*, Ruck's *The Disturbing Charm*, and Ruck's *Love on Second Thoughts* are courtesy of Manuscripts, Archives and Special Collections at Washington State University. I am grateful to those who have assisted in my efforts to locate and contact all holders of copyrights still in effect and would welcome any information as to errors or omissions. Finally, I wish to thank the two anonymous readers of this essay for *Woolf Studies Annual* whose helpful comments stimulated some final revisions.

[2] Leavis thinks that, in part through fan letters, a popular writer, however "identical with his public in background of taste and intellectual environment," continues to take the pulse of actual and potential readers (42).

[3] Ruck also wrote to Katherine Mansfield in 1922 about *At the Bay*. Mansfield replied (24 March 1922), rather ungraciously, "You scarcely say anything about the black holes in my book (like the servant's afternoon out)" (Alpers 346).

Figure 1. Portrait of Berta Ruck in Winter. Levonde is identified as photographer. From A Storyteller Tells The Truth: Reminiscences & Notes *(London: Hutchinson & Co. 1935).*

Biographers after Quentin Bell, with the exception of George Spater and Ian Parsons, show little, if any, interest in this curious incident. Given Ruck's popularity, Bell says, "Virginia must have seen that odd name and unconsciously distorted it a little, adding an *h*." Ruck herself eventually accepted Woolf's theory that "it had been a freak of subconscious memory" (*A Story-Teller* 260). Oliver Onions, Ruck's writer husband, however, had more trouble believing Woolf's claim never to have "heard of Berta Ruck," even though her "name and fame were emblazoned even on the tops of London omnibuses" (Bell 2:91). Onions apparently suspected Woolf of a highbrow joke on a popular writer. Indeed, Lytton Strachey and Carrington teased Woolf about just such a motive when they sent her a letter purportedly from "Thomas Gage" (the name on the other tombstone). "Gage" objects to Woolf's attempt to "injure the literary reputation" of his "honoured friend" Berta Ruck, just because she is a "literary rival, the circulation of whose books in England, the British Dominions, and the United States, you may hope in vain to equal." "Gage" reveals, confirming Woolf's suspicions of a hoax, that his health has been so compromised by the incident that he has "been forced to resign [...his] position as superintendent of the Lavatory at Oxford Circus" (Spater and Parsons 147-8; *L2* 602). Onions' angry reaction and the Bloomsberries' love of teasing aside, it seems unlikely that Woolf could have been so jealous of Ruck's kind of popularity that she would have mocked her publicly.[4]

Private mockery, in this case a complex blend of amused appreciation and disdain, was another matter. In the six years between the publications of *Jacob's Room* and *Orlando*, Woolf recorded, and often caricatured, in personal letters and in her diaries, several encounters with Ruck. Also, some years after the *Orlando* fan letter, Ruck included several brief references to Woolf, similarly contradictory or ambiguous in tone, in *A Story-Teller Tells the Truth*. Although the personalities and aesthetic interests of these two readers and writers fundamentally diverged, they seem to have found their differences stimulating. There may even be, in Woolf's writing, a few submerged echoes of her experiences with Ruck. More important for this essay, what was it about Woolf's *Orlando* that so excited a woman dubbed by her *DNB* biographer "one of the leading popular romantic novelists of her day" (Alderson 740)?[5] Any consideration of this

---

[4] At the same time, in something of this one-upping spirit, Leonard Woolf advertised *Orlando* with a positive comment from an essentially dismissive review by Arnold Bennett (Stape xxi).

[5] Ruck's *His Official Fiancee* (1913) was the first of her many novels. Although not mentioned in *Fiction and the Reading Public* (1932), Ruck was, "in 1930, among those best-selling authors approached by Mrs Q. D. Leavis" while doing research for her book

question begins with each woman's view of the diverse and volatile cultural dynamics of early twentieth-century Britain.

I

Both Woolf and Ruck were aware of the literary divide between so-called "highbrow" and "lowbrow." In *Hunting the Highbrow* (1927), as Melba Cuddy-Keane observes, Leonard Woolf attacks as mere "'pseudo-highbrow[ism],'" clichés that associated highbrows with elitist "sneers at popularity," with snobbery and "affectation," and with their own brand of ephemeral trendiness (60).[6] In the fall of 1932, responding in part to a public debate about literary value conducted in BBC talks and in the pages of the *New Statesman and Nation*, Virginia Woolf wrote but did not send a letter to the editor on the subject. In the letter, she reexamines the terms commonly used in the debate. Embracing the dismissive label, she defines a "highbrow" as "the man or woman of thoroughbred intelligence who rides his mind at a gallop [...] in pursuit of an idea," whereas a "lowbrow," whose practical skills are equally deserving of respect, has "thoroughbred vitality" and "rides his body in pursuit of a living" ("Middlebrow" 176, 178). Highbrows, who "cannot do things" as lowbrows can, and lowbrows, who do not have the ability to reveal what "lives look like," as highbrows do, are mutually dependent. They should unite, Woolf says, against the "middlebrow," who pursues both art and life, "mixed indistinguishably, and rather nastily, with money, fame, power, or prestige" (179-80). Although highbrows also may write for money, Woolf admits, once they have it, they enjoy living. Middlebrows, in

---

(Alderson 740). Leavis notes that she sent out questionnaires to sixty of "the most popular living novelists" and got twenty-five responses (33). Most recently, Ruck appears among popular fiction writers of 1900 to 1918 in Bloom's *Bestsellers*. Along with Ethel M. Dell and E. M. (Edith Maude) Hull, Ruck was so admired by Barbara Cartland (Bloom 86) that the current "Queen of Romance" has condensed some of Ruck's books ("Ruck," 184, 930).

[6] In 1925, Leonard Woolf pondered what makes a book popular. He distinguishes between "the ordinary popular novel," which "has something mechanical about it" and is written out of "no intense conviction, no passion, no real belief in what the typewriter is tapping out," and the truly popular novel, like Marie Corelli's *La Princesse Lointaine*, which has a "quality of passionate conviction. Instead of an ancient plot dipped into a thin mixture of sentimentality and bathos, you have a fierce orgy of both. And that goes straight to the heart of the great public" ("The World" 777).

Virginia Woolf, in her obituary of Lady Ritchie, defines popularity by what it is not. Lady Ritchie "wrote neither for the busy man who wants to be diverted, nor for the earnest who wishes to be instructed; she offered neither sensation nor impropriety, and her beauty and distinction of manner were as unfailing as they were natural. Such characteristics are not those that appeal to a large public" ("Lady Ritchie" 279).

contrast, conservatively accumulate "Georgian style" houses in South Kensington, "sham antiques," and works by dead painters and writers (185-6).

Q. D. Leavis, who discusses all three brow levels in *Fiction and the Reading Public* (1932), classifies "absolute bestsellers" as "lowbrow" and Woolf's *To the Lighthouse* as an example of "highbrow" fiction (45, 20). It is "not a popular novel," she adds, "(though it has already taken its place as an important one), and it is necessary to enquire why the conditions of the age have made it inaccessible to a public whose ancestors have been competent readers of Sterne and Nashe" (223).[7] Leavis gloomily concludes that "the reading capacity of the general public" is lower than it ever has been (231), that "Dr. Johnson's common reader" is completely out of touch with "the living interests of modern literature," and that modern literature is now in the hands of a "critical minority" that is cut off from "the general public and threatened with extinction" (35). Although Woolf does not refer to *Fiction and the Reading Public* in her letters or diaries of this period, it seems likely that she at least would have read reviews. One wonders why did she not send her letter on brow levels to a periodical editor and publicly join the debate. It was Leonard Woolf who finally published her letter as "Middlebrow" in the posthumous collection *The Death of the Moth and Other Essays* (1942). Was Virginia Woolf reluctant to air snide remarks about middlebrows that may have been more therapeutic to write than wise to publish? Or was she reluctant to join an argument about literary value carried on in what she later called Mrs. Leavis's "high and dry" academic manner (*L5* 425)? The title of Woolf's *Common Reader* collections of essays, the second volume of which appeared in the same year as Leavis' book (1932), certainly suggests a challenge, if not to Leavis, then at least to the academic orientation and concerns she represented. As in "Hours in a Library" (1916), Woolf identifies, not with a sedentary specialist reading "on a system" in search of "some particular grain of truth," but with a nonprofessional lover of reading whose motivation is "intense curiosity" (*E2* 55-57). Even redefined and realigned in "Middlebrow," the brow levels, like many attempts by Woolf's characters to label and classify people, also may have proved too confining.[8] A case in point is the application of "lowbrow" or "middlebrow" to a writer like Berta Ruck.

Ruck, in *A Story-Teller Tells the Truth*, is equally aware of the highbrow/lowbrow cultural divide. Using "highbrow" in the clichéd, derogatory sense, she writes, "If I minded stuffy highbrow reviews about '*sprightly style*'

---

[7] Leavis is here relatively positive about Woolf's work, at least compared to her later reaction to *Three Guineas* in the September 1938 issue of *Scrutiny*.

[8] An early example is St. John Hirst's reduction of people to types versus Terence Hewet's insistence that "No two people are in the least the same" (*TVO* 107).

and '*popular appeal*' and '*the usual Ruck*,' I'd be dead by now" (279). Says one such condescending reviewer in a periodical classified by Q. D. Leavis as middlebrow (20), "If her sprightliness keeps her for the most part among the shallows, they are at any rate sparkling in the sun" (Anon. *TLS*, 518). "The style of the story would undoubtedly be called 'sprightly,'" says another. "It is always cheerful and amused at itself" (Anon. *Literary Review*, 551). And, says one more, "While the work cannot boast of any great depth, it is ingenious in a rattle-brained sort of way" (Anon. *New York Times*, 18). Certainly there also was a lot of "the usual Ruck." As Leonard Woolf says, writers of popular novels characteristically are prolific (*Hunting* 25). Berta Ruck, who lived to be 100, wrote some eighty romance novels, often publishing two per year. Her "modest niche," as she describes it, is "as a writer for—and about—young girls" (*A Story-Teller* 146, 189). In her books, typically, young women confront a variety of obstacles, but eventually gain loving, successful husbands. Readers liked the books, says Ruck's *DNB* biographer, because she found seemingly endless, ingenious ways of delaying her couples' unions, meanwhile entertaining her readers with a wealth of "contemporary detail," narrator commentary (Alderson 740), and practical advice.

Ruck thought of Woolf as an intellectual, but not according to the positive definition of "highbrow" in "Middlebrow." Instead, Ruck adds to the highbrow/lowbrow discourse of her time a conventional gender distinction that associates brain with masculinity, and body, heart, or emotion with femininity. She recalls a comment about educated women made by an elderly male professor of zoology and anatomy— "'I am afraid [...] that the more aptitude they showed for what I had to impart to them, the less conscious they remained of their biological reason for being.'" Then Ruck sighs, in parentheses, "(Shades of Virginia Woolf!)" (*A Story-Teller* 310). As a writer, Ruck allies herself with a feminine stereotype. She describes how her husband Oliver Onions tried to "teach [her] form, as he conceived it," and how she fought the efforts of his "alien, masculine mind" to organize the "'gay and shallow chaos'" of her "slender talent" (*A Story-Teller* 197-8). In spite of the fan letter she wrote to Woolf about *Orlando*, the women writers Ruck says she most admires are Colette, Vita Sackville-West for her poetry, and especially Rebecca West who "writes better than any woman now holding a pen" because, beneath her penchant for "unsparing criticism," she appeals to the heart rather than to the brain (*A Story-Teller* 238, 228, 251).[9]

---

[9] That Ruck may have communicated similar criteria to Q. D. Leavis is indicated by her quotation from a "bestseller" in response to her questionnaire: "'Even if many of them [bestsellers] are not works of art, they are on the whole (except the very bad ones) closer

Some of Ruck's earlier books about heterosexual love manifest her concern about the apparent gender role reversals of her time. During World War I, for example, she published a book of short stories called *Khaki and Kisses* (1915). As Jane Potter points out, the stories transform "flippant coquette[s]" or aggressive suffragettes into "serious lad[ies]" with maternal characteristics, and potentially degenerate aesthetes become manly men in uniform (87-8, 90). In 1915 too, Ruck published *The Lad with Wings*. This patriotic novel pits highbrow intellectuals and aesthetes who treat the Russian Ballet, not as a "*pastime*," but as "*a matter of Life and Death*," against practical people who "*made Life and Death matters their pastime*" (207), who designed, built, and flew airplanes in defense of their country. In *The Lad with Wings*, a young pilot and his new wife (who has worked in an airplane factory to help the war effort, then, to be with her husband, has disguised herself as his co-pilot) are shot down over the English channel in what Ruck presents as the glorious consummation of their deferred honeymoon.

Virginia Woolf, a pacifist who would have been out of sympathy with Berta Ruck's priorities and with her patriotic effusions during the Great War, exchanged letters with her after the fracas over *Jacob's Room*. The two women even met, and, Woolf reports, became "great friends" (*L2* 602). Less ironically and more accurately, Ruck became for Woolf a fascinating, sometimes off-putting study of a life-affirming, middle-aged woman who was both sensual and maternal. Her experience of Ruck could well have borne fruit in characters like the older, more conservative Sally Seton with her "five enormous boys" in *Mrs. Dalloway* (171) or especially like that "wild child of nature" Mrs. Manresa in *Between the Acts* (41). Although she has William Dodge in tow, Mrs. Manresa is attracted by the conventional masculinity of Giles Oliver whose contempt for Dodge's homosexuality is apparent. She sees the blood on Oliver's snake-stomping boots as proof of his "valour for her admiration" (107).

In a 1924 letter to Marjorie Joad, Woolf wrote a breathless parody, not of Ruck's writing, but of her way of speaking. Woolf imagines Joad buried in manuscripts, sacrificing all pleasures for "the profit and glory of the Hogarth Press. Do you know what has set me off writing in this incoherent way?" Woolf continues,

---

to the fundamentals of life and of romance than much of the cleverer stuff that springs mainly from the brain and so fails to reach the *heart*'" (68). In chapter thirty of *A Story-Teller Tells the Truth*, Ruck describes her bewildered and resentful reaction to a questionnaire about the novel sent to her by a fellow of Girton College who has the "academic urge to classify" (270). It was very likely Leavis's questionnaire.

> Mrs Berta Ruck. I fell into her arms—which are wide and brawny—at Maynard's party the other night; and a whole room full stood agaze to see the lady novelists embrace. She said Oh if I were Virginia Woolf! I said Oh Berta, if I were you! And for Gods sake, I said, tell me how you do it, and what you get for it, whereupon Berta, rolling her fine eyes about, replied, 'Would you believe me Mrs Woolf I abominate my own books more than I can say, and they only bring me in £400 a piece, and I have to write two every year so long as I and my husband and our boys do live, and its almost impossible to find another plot [...] for there are only ten plots in the world; and Ethel Dell is my only rival;[10] [...] but what can you do, Mrs Woolf, when you've two darling boys and I want them to have the best of everything—Eton, sports; you should see them Mrs Woolf; for you have written in Jacobs room such a description of the beauty of young manhood'...(here we embraced once more) and with tears in my eyes I swore to come down to a rosy bower on the river, where they live 'like anybody else' she said; but I doubt it" (*L*3 119-20).

Ruck, denigrating her own work and linking her love for her sons with Woolf's understanding of "young manhood" in *Jacob's Room*, clearly seeks common ground. Ruck also encourages Woolf to see her, if not as an intellectual, at least as "a cultivated woman. I read the classics, I know French; and if only I could write a paragraph [...] like Mr. Lytton Strachey, I'd retire tomorrow" (*L*3 120). Woolf, revealing in this letter her flirtatious awareness of Ruck's physical presence (her "wide and brawny" arms and "fine eyes"), also reveals her professional writer's and publisher's curiosity about books that make money.

Ruck remained realistic about her abilities. Introducing her own complexities into the highbrow/lowbrow controversy in *A Story-Teller Tells the Truth*, she writes, "I am not clever enough to make good Art out of a bad show. Always I would rather be 'good Bad' than 'bad Good'" (405).[11] This comment seems to make Ruck one of Woolf's "middlebrows," who produce neither "well written; nor [...] badly written" mixtures "of geniality and sentiment" ("Middlebrow" 181-2). Yet, in 1924, Woolf offered Roger Fry a qualified defense of Ruck. Woolf writes that the Hogarth Press has invested heavily in Freud's works, "which will sell they say because he has cancer; but I doubt any book selling that isnt by

---

[10] Q. D. Leavis includes Ethel M. Dell (1881-1929) among the "great names of popular fiction" (62). Bloom says of the tremendously successful and wealthy Dell, "Her easy style and clear eroticism made her an illicit favourite with middle-class adolescents and working-class servants and gained her the title of 'the housemaid's choice' for her success in writing what Rebecca West called 'tosh'" (134). Ruck's books were more conventionally wholesome.

[11] Although Woolf would never have defined herself as a writer of "bad good" or "good bad" books, she nervously used the word "bad" about *Orlando* at least four times in letters (*L*3 437, 475, 506, 512).

Berta Ruck." As a woman writer, though, Woolf identifies with Ruck. "You are rather hard on 'lady novelists'," she tells Fry, "or perhaps my corns are tender [....] The best sellers are gentlemen, like Hugh Walpole, and Compton Mackenzie, of a peculiarly poisonous breed."[12] Alluding to her recent encounter with Ruck, she adds, "The Rucks do it to send their sons to Eton, which, though not my ambition in life, is comparatively harmless" (*L3* 133). In other words, if you are honest about the quality of what you write, and if you do it to earn a living for your family, then you may be more a practical, life-loving lowbrow than an opportunistic middlebrow.

In Ruck's novel *The Disturbing Charm* (1919), a character named Mrs. Cartwright is a popular journalist and novelist much like her creator. Ruck thus shows herself capable of both self-mockery and self-defense. Mrs. Cartwright first produces articles (signed "Domestica") like "What to do with the Cold Mutton" (47). These "articles had put plenty of nourishing beef gravy into little Keith;" we are told, "and when Reggie had nearly gone out with bronchitis she had settled the doctor's bills with her brightly-written instructions as to always keeping a smiling face [...] for when Hubby got back from a hard day's work" (47-8).[13]

> Business-like columns on Emigration and Fruit Farming for Women paid for her boy's first reefer-coats. Their school-kits came out of the long serials to which she had at last attained, and which became a never-failing joke with those of her acquaintances who had cultured literary tastes [....]
>
> After all, these literary tastes of her acquaintances were no more "superior" than the thickness of the new woollies that she was then going on to buy for her son's wear.
>
> Moreover, the woollies were of more use (48).

---

[12] There is some evidence that, in this context, Woolf and Ruck would have allied themselves against Arnold Bennett's proclamations too. Ruck recalls overhearing Bennett say, "'there isn't anything you can tell me that I don't know about any w-w-women. I know them inside and out and backwards and forwards. I know what any one of them is going to say or do next. I know them like I know my p-p-pocket.' 'Fancy,' I thought, and went on reading Colette'" (*A Story-Teller* 238).

[13] In a similar vein, in *The Lad with Wings* (1915), Ruck makes of her character Leslie Long a kind of advisor to younger, more innocent girls on dating and mating. Several chapters detail her advice: "The girl who pleases is the girl who is hard to please" (97), "*half the 'nice' girls we know don't wash enough. That's* why they don't get half the attention they'd like. Men like what they call a 'healthy-looking' girl" (102). "Attractive shoes, even with an unfashionable skirt, will pull you through" (104). "Be awfully careful about your collar, the ends of your sleeves and the hem of your skirt" (105). "For the stimulation of an admirer's interest, jealousy. Jealousy and competition" (158).

Woolf did not have the practical motive of keeping sons in woollies; that had been her sister Vanessa's job. Her niece, Angelica, however, was still young enough to benefit from *Orlando*'s success. Remembering their own deprivations as girls, Virginia wrote to Vanessa, "I think she ought to have a little money to throw away on clothes etc." (*L4* 264).[14] That Woolf should have used some of the proceeds from a novel that sold well to provide discretionary money for her niece is consistent both with her recognition of a woman's need for money of her own and with her defense of Berta Ruck to Roger Fry.

It is no coincidence that Woolf's meeting with the exuberant Berta Ruck, as described to Marjorie Joad, was at Maynard Keynes's. Lydia Lopokova was a mutual friend. Woolf reports ambiguously that "(poor Berta was overcome)" by a transvestite ballet designed by Duncan Grant and staged at the Keynes' party (*L3* 120). A diary account in 1925, upon her return from a Greek play she had attended with Berta and Lydia, serves as a partial gloss (*L3* 182).[15] Woolf recorded, "I'm jangled & jaded, having sat next the sea horse Sally Onions [Ruck's married name], who oozes lust at the sight of young men dancing" (*D3* 18). Ruck's *The Disturbing Charm* provides a further gloss. She appropriately describes her semi-autobiographical character Mrs. Cartwright as reaching a point in her career when she earns enough not only to take care of her sons, but also to supply herself with silk underwear and suede shoes, and to discover herself still sexually attractive (49). Literature, Mrs. Cartwright complains, has given us stories of exceptional women like Cleopatra who take up with younger men, "But the stories of matrons of to-day who had married their sons' contemporaries hadn't drifted across the writer's experience," only "pathetic" and

---

[14] "As I grew older and she grew richer," Angelica Garnett recalls, "Virginia made herself responsible for my dress allowance, which was £15 a quarter, quite enough for clothes and minor pleasures" (*Deceived* 111).

[15] The play, according to Anne Olivier Bell, was a Cambridge Amateur Dramatic Company performance of Euripides' *Helen* and *Cyclops* "in versions by J. T. Sheppard." Bell says that Ruck "misremembers the performance as being of *The Frogs*" (*D3* 17 n. 9). Ruck recalls that Woolf took her "to the Greek Plays at the Queen's Theatre, Hammersmith." She calls herself "virgin soil to Greek humour," describes her "purest delight in drinking from the very spring of comic drama," and compares modern comedy to that of Aristophanes (*A Story-Teller* 260).

Much later (1971), in a letter to Quentin Bell, Ruck remembers another aspect of the Greek play experience—Lydia's desire to get up and leave in the middle *The Frogs* because, as she said "in her enchantingly original English," the play was "'so doll.'" Berta and Virginia tried to dissuade her, Ruck writes, because the three of them were "much to [sic] noticeable [....] Your famous Aunt wore a very large black sombrero hat, I was as tall as she, and had fat black plaits done over my ears, Lydia between us was small, but always outstandingly striking in movement and manner" (Bell 2: 92).

"ugly" stories of desperation and failure (156).[16] Whether out of unacknowledged jealousy over Ruck's attraction to "young men dancing" (in drag or not) rather than to women like herself, or just out of simple disgust at its blatancy, Woolf's inability to share Ruck's visceral responses confirms her fictional Mrs. Cartwright's perception of the standard reaction.[17]

Recording, in the same diary entry as her account of the Greek play, "a meagre meal with the Sangers whose mediocrity of comfort & taste saddens me," Woolf adds, "'oh for a little beauty in life,' as Berta Ruck might say." Her next comment, however—"A lewd woman that, deposited in a lewd South Kensington House [...] & her front teeth with a red ridge on them where her lips had touched them" (*D*3 18)—underscores Woolf's fascination/revulsion reactions where Berta Ruck was concerned. If not her enthusiasm for young men, at least the South Kensington house she now owned, apparently moved her into Woolf's middlebrow category. Yet Quentin Bell also mentions a Bloomsbury party at which the ebullient "Berta Ruck gave a most spirited rendering of 'Never allow a Sailor an inch above your knee'—a performance which," he says, "filled Virginia with amazement and delight" (Bell 2: 92).

II

A few years later, against this background, Ruck typed her fan letter to Woolf about *Orlando* (now in the University of Sussex Special Collections).[18] Although Quentin Bell concludes that the women quickly forgot their differences over the *Jacob's Room* tombstone (2: 92), Ruck immediately recalls the incident in her letter. She apologizes for not having written sooner about the book and asks, rhetorically, "Will you allow one whom you once buried (deeper than Caesar) now to praise it?" "To praise is an impertinence," she continues, "but

---

[16] Ruck records her preference for female and young male characters and her inability to draw middle-aged males because so many of them are overweight and, in other ways, aesthetically unappealing (*A Story-Teller* 279-80).

[17] However overt Ruck's sexuality may have been in real life, she and Woolf might have agreed, as writers, on what Ruck calls her "verbal prudery complex....Let me be left to my old-world habit of leaving some things unmentioned" (*A Story-Teller* 298). Woolf discusses her own reticence when writing about the body in "Professions for Women."

[18] *Orlando* was published on 11 October 1928. Ruck's letter is dated "22nd December, 1928." She thinks "it may be just as well" that she did not write sooner because by now "there has abated what has no doubt been a spate of letters about your last book." The letter is typed, except for the last line (from "will accept it" to "ever sincerely") and the signature, both hand-written in ink. With her pen, she also underlined several words for emphasis, added one set of parentheses, and capitalized "Great Frost" and "Great Damp."

Lord, how I did enjoy it."[19] As evidence she offers the fact that, after having read a library copy, she went to the "extreme length" of buying one for herself.

> I also read it aloud to my husband. This was on the evening of the day when I had dragged him up for the first time into an aeroplane; with the result that the two things are inseparably connected in his mind. As he saw for the first time the country side looking so different, so he also felt that it was from an aeroplane that he received this vivid, brilliant glimpse down onto English history. The Great Frost was marvellous but beaten, if I may say so, by the Great Damp a couple of centuries later. I hope you will not think all this is gratuitous, but will accept it as a small acknowledgement of great pleasure given to yours ever sincerely,
>
> Berta Ruck

Manuscripts, Archives and Special Collections at Washington State University has Woolf's unpublished, typed reply. Parodying Ruck's jocular tone, Woolf matches burial for burial, aeroplane for aeroplane, and husband for husband:

> I am more pleased than I can say that you survived my burial. Never will I attempt such a thing again. To think that you should have bought my book! As you say, it makes my hair stand on end. And then that you should have liked it—I am tremendou[s]ly pleased, and read your letter aloud to my husband as a tribute that I insisted upon his hearing. His sympathies are all with your husband. Poor man, he said, to be taken up in an aeroplane and then to read Orlando. But it was something of that very effect I tried to give. How very charming of you to write and tell me!
> A thousand thanks--
> Yours very sincerely
>
> Virginia Woolf [signed]

---

[19] In *A Story-Teller*, Ruck describes her reaction to *Orlando* as "unmixed," just like her "purest delight" in Aristophanes (260).

When Woolf writes that Ruck's purchase of her book, "makes my hair stand on end," she quotes one of the clichéd expressions that characterizes Ruck's speech (as she had quoted "oh for a little beauty in life" in her diary account of dinner with the Sangers). Connoting anything from extreme pleasure to horror, the expression suggests Woolf's combined surprise and dismay. It also is worth noting that Woolf, although she read Ruck's letter to Leonard, did not reciprocate by even mentioning a Ruck novel.

So we return to our initial question: Why did *Orlando* appeal to Berta Ruck? The letter itself provides some reasons: in addition to the Great Frost and the Great Damp that are highlights in Woolf's romp through English history,[20] Ruck's fascination with airplanes. "Grand," she exclaims, "to have lived at an epoch when the thrill of Flight was new!" (*A Story-Teller* 365). Woolf never flew, but she remained fascinated with the negative and positive possibilities of flying (Beer 135). Ruck, on the other hand, took every opportunity to fly, followed the development of planes and the fortunes of particular flyers (*A Story-Teller* 375), and introduced a succession of flyers into her fiction.[21] She therefore would have enjoyed the ending of *Orlando* where, as Gillian Beer notes, the airplane is "an emblem of modern life" with "individualistic, erotic and heroic" connotations (147-8). Shelmerdine, the ship's captain, re-emerges in the 1920s in a bird-like plane that has burst out of the clouds, and is guided to Orlando by the pearls on her bared breast, burning "like a phosphorescent flare in the darkness" (329). Orlando is, in fact, very like the "Mooring Mast for air-ships" invented by the hero of Ruck's *The Subconscious Courtship* (published in the same year as *Jacob's Room*), an invention "as necessary" to England's "sky-liners," Ruck writes, "as were her light-houses to her ships that ploughed her seas!" (32). One result of Ruck's articulation of the parallel between Woolf's overview of British history in *Orlando* and the view of the landscape from a plane may well have been Bart Oliver's plane's-eye-view of the history of the landscape in *Between the Acts*: "From an aeroplane, he said, you could still see, plainly marked, the scars made by the Britons; by the Romans; by the Elizabethan manor house; and by the plough, when they ploughed the hill to grow wheat in the Napoleonic wars" (*BTA* 4).

---

[20] The anonymous review in the *Times Literary Supplement* of two months earlier picks these two passages to quote (414), and Leon Edel singles out these same two examples of Woolf's "most brilliant writing" (447).

[21] If, in Woolf's *Mrs. Dalloway*, a sky-writing plane is a commercial novelty (Beer 143), in Ruck's *To-Day's Daughter* (two years earlier), the plane advertises romance as the pilot hero, searching for the woman he loves, "writes her name in the sky" (*A Story-Teller* 371). In *Love on Second Thoughts* (1936), Ruck's hero arrives in Austria in an airplane that crashes into a tall tree, from which, as a kind of *deus ex machina*, he climbs down to claim the woman he loves.

In her letter, Berta Ruck does not mention that the appearances in *Orlando* of people she knew gave special meaning to the book, as they must have done. Woolf uses Lydia Lopokova's "beauty of movement" as a metaphor for Orlando's changing her clothes (*O* 315). More importantly, Ruck was related on her maternal grandfather's side to the Sackvilles, and Ruck's mother corresponded regularly with Lady Sackville, Vita's mother. Berta Ruck, therefore, must have observed the dedication of the book to Vita, recognized the photographs of her, and enjoyed Woolf's rendition of the history of the family and, simultaneously, of Vita's life. Ruck remembers Vita as a "handsome, serious, dark-eyed, long-haired little girl," coming with her mother to visit them in Wales (*A Story-Teller* 228). Vita's hand-me-down, kid-leather boots, in fact, were on Ruck's feet when she was confirmed in Bangor Cathedral; her mother and sister urged her to read Vita's books as they appeared; and Vita's poems were once a Christmas present to Ruck from her mother (*A Story-Teller* 228-9). In 1913, her mother and younger sister attended the wedding of Vita Sackville-West and Harold Nicolson at Knole. Ruck quotes her sister's descriptions of the gifts, the chapel, the flowers, and Vita's "poise and self-possession" (*A Story-Teller* 228). Woolf's description of the marriage of Orlando and Shelmerdine is very different, with its "movement and confusion" and the obliteration of the word "Obey" by a "clap of thunder." (*O* 262). Still, Ruck must have been fascinated by this high-spirited (even "sprightly"?) treatment of an event known to her, and also by Woolf's sympathy for the needs of a woman writer.

Orlando is, as Quentin Bell puts it, "Virginia's most idealised creation; he/she is modelled near to the heart's desire[...]—near, in fact, to the glamorous creations of the novelette" (2: 118). Although it has so much more, *Orlando* also has a number of the characteristics of popular romance fiction, as some early reviewers noted (e.g. Anonymous 413, MacCarthy 225). It is worth asking, however, if Woolf parodies those characteristics to the degree that she does elements of biographical and historical writing. The answer is yes, especially if one accepts, as a description of such a parody, Leslie Hankins' treatment of *Orlando* as an "enveloping heterosexual text" that "protects the lesbian note and allows it to be transmitted under the nose of the censor" (187). A more difficult question is whether or not Ruck was attracted by Woolf's lesbian subtext, by the ways in which "heterosexuality is interrupted, side-lined, and undercut throughout the novel" (Hankins 188). Ruck was not naive. She had gone to art schools (the Slade in London and Colarossi's in Paris) and was familiar with bohemian studio life, fancy-dress dances, as well as art, medical, and theatrical students' antics before she encountered any Bloomsbury variants.[22] Ruck may have been

---

[22] Ruck left the Slade school right around the time that Vanessa Bell began her short sojourn there.

as "selfishly pleasure-seeking" as her cohorts (*A Story-Teller* 81), but, whatever self-censorship she may have imposed on her memoir, I detect no hints that, so far as sexual pleasures went, her own included women. Because, in the early decades of the twentieth-century, "the term [lesbian] was not yet accepted" (Jeffreys 100), and because *Orlando* did not come "out of the closet as a lesbian text" until the 1970s (Hankins 181), Ruck, like most of Woolf's other contemporaries, probably would not have recognized the precise nature of Woolf's parody.[23]

Ruck's enjoyment of *Orlando* more likely stemmed, in part, from what she saw as Woolf's playful use of familiar romance novel characteristics than from her thorough subversion of them.[24] In spite of her enjoyment of Woolf's book, Ruck advocated a more straightforward tone: "Story-tellers who write with the tongue in the cheek do not succeed in pleasing any Public for over twenty years," she notes (*A Story-Teller* 105). Critical in her early career of a breakdown between masculine and feminine roles, however, Ruck must have recognized Orlando's gender ambiguities and their relation to clothing, as well as Orlando's "many lives and many lovers" and the chance to be male, not just feel male (Gilbert 205). If Ruck still saw gender slippages as dangerous, she does not say so. She simply may have noticed that, however much Woolf plays with stereotypical "him[s] and her[s]" (*E3* 10) caught in plots with the happy endings that best define romance novels (Radway 66-67; Leavis 27), she still provides Orlando with what she desires. Although Orlando's marriage is partly one of convenience, it nevertheless gives her the much-coveted freedom to write as well as considerable friendly comradery. Woolf still characterizes Shelmerdine, his own gender ambiguities aside, as courageous and devoted, and she treats childbirth and parenthood for Orlando as painless and burden-free (Moore 470). Woolf also gives Orlando literary success: a publisher and praise for her long poem, "The Oak Tree." More than anything, though, Woolf unabashedly grants Vita Knole, the family estate entailed away from her in real life. Ruck, with her knowledge of Vita's family, especially must have appreciated Woolf's fictional fulfilment of this desire.

---

[23] In spite of her link with Vita Sackville-West's family, Ruck also would have missed, like most early readers, the private jokes, tensions, and nuances of Woolf's own relationship with Vita that Suzanne Raitt and others have more recently described.

[24] Even if Woolf had not read popular romance novels of her day, like Ruck's, there are a number of ways she would have known the characteristics of traditional romance fiction, as the books in her library reveal. Remaining in the Woolf library at Washington State University are, for instance, two volumes of the 1795 edition of Ann Radcliffe's *The Mysteries of Udolpho*, all twenty-five volumes of Scott's *Waverley Novels*, and George Sand's *Elle et Lui* which Woolf inscribed and bound.

Ruck defended the happy endings of popular romance. Although, she says, she cannot possibly "include *all* things I believe to be true," she insists that she "never wrote what I believed to be untrue." Some people, like herself, are better able to see "the romantic and rosy side of life" than others. Although she acknowledges a world of war, "disease, poverty, crime," cruelty, and death, she insists that these evils "cannot destroy a happier knowledge" (*A Story-Teller* 105, 407). Ruck further defines happy endings as necessary to her essentially Platonic definition of reality. Considering what she calls "'compensating dream fiction,' not as opiate, but as tonic," she no doubt would have been pleased to see Orlando get what she wants—husband, child, literary success, and family estate—even with Woolf's tongue-in-cheek modifications. Wish fulfilment, Ruck writes, is not a "flight from reality." Instead, it is "the entrance into the original, or real, world" that "has been all messed up by one accident after another." If she could be "a beneficent witch, and change it back," Ruck says, she would wave her wand and "conjure up all that they ought to have for all my friends."

> Every man-Jack should have perfect fitness, ideals, and ambitions all but within his grasp, a stimulating, beautiful and amusing Love, congenial surroundings, and a job interesting, settled, progressive and adequately paid; every girl I knew should have the same, until she chose to add to them home, husband and children, all of the most satisfactory. I can't do this. I can only wave my pen (*A Story-Teller* 409, 406).

Perhaps because of enough similar pen-waving, however parodic, *Orlando* made Woolf, in some sense, popular.[25] In five years, 38,000 copies of the first English and American editions had to be printed (Langham 231).

When Leonard Woolf calls *Orlando* "the turning-point in Virginia's career as a successful novelist" (*Downhill* 143-5), though, he means that she "had to write a bad book [*The Years*] and two not very serious books [*Orlando* and *Flush*] before her best serious novels were widely understood and appreciated" (*Downhill* 147). Was it because Orlando elicited fan letters from popular writers like Berta Ruck and Hugh Walpole[26] that Leonard had to label it "not very serious"? Virginia herself called it "not, I think 'important' among my works" (*D3*

---

[25] "I am writing *Orlando* half in a mock style very clear & plain, so that people will understand every word," she wrote in her diary (*D3* 162). There is an implied distinction here between a style that general readers could recognize and comprehend and layers of meaning that only certain readers, like Vita Sackville-West, would detect.

[26] Hugh Walpole, a best-selling novelist whom Woolf had called "poisonous" in contrast to Ruck in her letter to Roger Fry (*L3* 133), wrote to praise *Orlando* (*L3* 547) and reviewed it positively. Woolf's reply is exaggeratedly gracious, as it is to Ruck's fan letter, but in both cases she seems to struggle for common ground. She writes to Walpole, "How so rapid and various, and generally gifted and busy and successful a man can yet

Figure 2. Courtesy of Manuscripts, Archives and Special Collections. Washington State University, Pullman, WA.

184).[27] Neither Woolf lived to see how new feminist, lesbian, and cultural studies approaches have challenged such evaluations.

III

The packaging of *Orlando* and of a small sample of Berta Ruck's novels for their respective marketplaces reveals further nuances in the highbrow/lowbrow cultural divide, especially where the two women's treatments of gender are concerned. The Hogarth Press, which printed writing that "would have little or no chance of being published by ordinary publishers" (L. Woolf, *Beginning* 236), also made no attempt to make their books look like those of more commercial houses. Still, the cover of the first edition of *Orlando* (*figure 2*) could not be decried, "reproachfully," as "post-impressionist," like those of other Woolf novels with jackets by Vanessa Bell (L. Woolf, *Downhill* 76). Instead we have what seems to be a more conservative, illustrative cover, a reproduction of a sixteenth-century painting supposedly of Vita Sackville-West's ancestor, Thomas Sackville.[28] The armed and active figure reinforces swash-buckling masculine stereotypes. The beginning of the book, however—"He—for there could be no doubt of his sex, though the fashion of the time did something to disguise it" (13)—directs our attention away from the weapon and shield and towards the figure's elegant costume. The design may be illustrative, but it is not, in the context of *Orlando*, conservative. It announces the fluidity of dress in relation to a historical succession of socially constructed categories and hierarchies that Woolf vigorously deconstructs in the book.

---

be so generous on such a large scale, I cant conceive. Seriously, I am more than grateful, and very proud into the bargain. Don't you, after all, share my passion for Waverley?—and lots of other things" (*L3* 552).

[27] Although the early reviews were generally positive, Woolf did get a couple of condescending ones. J. C. Squire dismissed the book, as he might have done one by Berta Ruck, as "a pleasant trifle" (*L3* 547 n.1) and Arnold Bennett called it the current topic of obligatory dinner-party chatter in a review that relegates the book, in Bowlby's opinion, "to superficiality, ephemerality and snobbery, all three at once" (151).

[28] Stape indicates that this "allegorical portrait c. 1570" was inscribed on the frame in the nineteenth century, "THOs. SACKVILLE created Baron BUCKHURST 8th of June 1567. Afterwards Earl DORSET. Died 19th of April 1608." Sent to London from the Worthing Museum for cleaning, the painting was destroyed during the blitz. Stape notes that although the identity of the man in the painting has been questioned, clearly Vita Sackville-West and the Hogarth Press considered it a portrait of Thomas Sackville (Stape 191-2, note for p. xxxii).

Figure 3. Courtesy of Manuscripts, Archives and Special Collections. Washington State University, Pullman, WA.

Figure 4. Courtesy of Manuscripts, Archives and Special Collections. Washington State University, Pullman, WA.

The illustrations on a small sampling of Ruck's dustjackets suggest a different market. Her British publisher frequently was Hodder and Stoughton,[29] a firm known, since its founding by religious Dissenters in 1868, for its publication of theological books and journals. In the 1880s, in spite of the "abhorrence of fiction characteristic of Dissent" (Collin 145), the firm began to publish conservative novels for women readers.[30] Its fiction list eventually included "all the popular genres" but never "any improper or immoral work" (Collin 147). Hodder and Stoughton's dustjackets for Ruck's novels frequently call attention to her stories' emphases on traditional love and marriage. On the unsigned pastel jacket chosen for *The Disturbing Charm* (1919) (*figure 3*), for instance, is the delicate drawing of a heart, within which two pudgy cupids hold blue ribbons attached to a small envelope. It is a saccharine, but straightforward visual reference to an alleged love charm that the heroine, to test its potency, gets lonely individuals to wear, in little packets, on their persons.[31] Yet this novel also is the one containing Mrs. Cartwright, the defensive, semi-autobiographical writer character who pushes the boundaries of heterosexual love to include relationships between older women and younger men. Ruck's subversions of tradition seem mild, compared to Woolf's, but they are there.

The jacket for a later Ruck novel, *Love on Second Thoughts* (1936) (*figure 4*), offers more ambiguities. In the center, between the two women on the dustjacket, is a rectangular clock. It is tempting to see a visual allusion to the clock in Vanessa Bell's jacket design for Woolf's *A Room of One's Own* (1929)—its hands (on 11 and 1) forming the "V" that suggests Virginia, Vanessa, and Vita (Hankins 197-8). We know, from a reference in *A Story-Teller Tells the Truth*, that Ruck had read Woolf's book (172, cf 175), but we know nothing about the identity of the *Love on Second Thoughts* jacket designer, beyond the hand-printed name "Greenup." Nor do we know if Ruck had any control over the cover. Its

---

[29] Ruck did publish with other British presses, including Hutchinson and Co., Cassell and Co., and (in later years) Hurst and Blackett and Mills and Boon. Her American publisher was pretty consistently Dodd, Mead, although occasionally *Harper's Bazaar* printed one of her works. A number of her books were translated into Spanish, French, and Portuguese.

[30] The first were serialized romantic novels by Annie S. Swan. The firm continued publishing novels in the style of Swan, who defined her own work as "serious and innocuous fiction for the delectation of babes" (qtd. Blain, et. al., 1050). In 1917, the press introduced its popular two-shilling yellow-jacket novels. Some writers, including Rose Macaulay, left Hodder and Stoughton during the twenties "to escape the stigma of popularity in a yellow jacket" (Collin 147).

[31] Potter publishes the design for Ruck's early *Khaki and Kisses* (1915) with her article. Again, a large heart is prominent. Within it are a handsome, dark-haired man in uniform and a laughing blonde woman who partially embraces him but demurely leans back in his arms.

clock, with hands positioned at two o'clock, probably is a visual reference to the *two* female characters whose contrasting qualities cause Ruck's hero, Dick Herrys, to have *second* thoughts about his approaching marriage to one of them. More generally, it may suggest other time constraints upon him. Upper-class Dick Herrys scrambles to fulfill the conditions of his eccentric grandfather's will that require him, every week for a year, to earn money secretly "by some [different] piece of manual labour" (27).

Instead of symbols of love—hearts and cupids or images of a man and a woman—the design emphasizes the heads and shoulders of the two women in Dick Herrys' life. Its representational quality makes it the kind of jacket to which Leonard Woolf contrasts Vanessa Bell's design for *Jacob's Room*, which is devoid of "a desirable female or even Jacob or his room" (*Downhill* 76). The colored drawing on Ruck's *Love on Second Thoughts* dustjacket includes, on our left, a brunette wearing a brown hat with a brim over brown hair apparently pulled straight back. She also wears a brown tailored suit with a red scarf. She looks, to our right, at a curly-haired, round-faced blonde with a pale-blue ruffled collar and pearls. The blonde looks, not at the brunette, but out of the picture space at, perhaps, the third main character, a man not pictured but introduced on the alliterative jacket blurb:

> His first thoughts: Dorothea, daughter of a wealthy ship-building magnate; she was spoilt, jealous and dictatorial, but irresistibly attractive. His second thoughts: Rosemary, the hard-working daughter of a country doctor; she had no time for the cheap frills of life. Dick Herrys alternated between Daimlers with Dorothea and rough riding with Rosemary until a moonlight picnic helped him to make his decision.

In spite of the direction of the gazes on the cover, the novel does not describe a love triangle in which Rose Mary is attracted to Dorothea who is attracted to Dick Herrys.

Sensitized to the kinds of parodies and subtexts now evident in *Orlando*, some twenty-first century readers of Virginia Woolf might want to read a lesbian subtext into the dustjacket picture of the two contrasting women, and into Ruck's post-*Orlando* novel.[32] Parallel to the possibility that Ruck appreciated the lesbian subtext in Woolf's parodic use of romance novel characteristics in *Orlando* is the possibility that the heterosexual unions she celebrates in her own novels

---

[32] Such suspicions indeed were voiced when I presented a short, early version of this essay at the Twelfth Annual Conference on Virginia Woolf at Sonoma State University, June, 2001. Although one may read anything one pleases into the dustjacket with the two contrasting women, it is dangerous to assume that the same readings apply to the novel or, further, to Ruck's life.

were the results of publisher and audience expectations and fear of censorship rather than of personal conviction. Yet again, it would be difficult to prove that, in *Love on Second Thoughts*, Ruck is encoding gay or lesbian sexual preferences. True, Ruck is sensitive to clothes and their ability to define people. There also is cross-dressing in the novel, but it is class-related, not primarily sex or gender-related as in *Orlando*. To fulfill the terms of his grandfather's will, Dick Herrys has a closet full of costumes in which he impersonates working men in what his manservant calls "'Tom-fool Duke-in-disguise acts'" (21). Herrys dons his costumes, not to pick up working-class male lovers, but, as his grandfather had hoped and predicted, to lose some of his aristocratic affectations and to learn social responsibility. Ruck, in fact, gets in a clothes-related dig at Bloomsbury when Herrys criticizes a Chinese jacket of Dorothea's as "'Bloomsbury-studio-party [...] So's that hand-painted cocktail suit" (83). In Dick's eyes, these clothes, along with her "unsuitably Jean Harlow frock" (199), are evidence of Dorothea's affected and immature tastes. More likely than a lesbian subtext in *Love on Second Thoughts* is a mildly unconventional supratext, i.e., an acknowledgment of obvious changes in social behavior that still are contained, even overwhelmed by the novel's traditional values.

For instance, both the jacket design and the novel itself ring variations on the long cultural tradition of opposing kinds of women—blonde and brunette, puritanical and passionate. To her characterization of Rose Mary, the brunette, Ruck has added, somewhat belatedly in the history of such characters, elements of the "New Woman"[33] juxtaposed to one more old fashioned in dress and manner. Dick Herrys admiringly describes Rose Mary as the "best type of the modern Rosalind....'A little bit independent,' he thought." Her "neat tweeds" are not masculine dress but, he notes, the garb "of any hardworking young business or professional woman" (12).[34] Although Rose Mary earns her living as a skilled medical massage therapist—her patients ranging from injured children to the elderly, from rheumatic violinists to pampered rich women (one of whom is Dorothea's mother)—she remains conventional enough to want to retain "introductions and formalities and surnames" unlike, Dick Herrys notes, "half the young women who earn their own living" (23). She comes from a loving family, and dancing with Dick "like the unified halves of a sea-shell" (98) does not lead to pre-marital sex. Heterosexual marriages remain major components of the happy ending in *Love on Second Thoughts*. Ruck's moderate innovation is that

---

[33] The "new woman" has been much discussed. See, for example, Ardis, Gardner, and Nelson. Ardis, who follows appearances of the new woman from the Victorian into the early modern period, does not include any by Ruck on her list of relevant novels.

[34] Rose Mary wears a version of the "tailor-made costume" favored by the New Woman since the 1890s (Adburgham, 227).

the more independent brunette—not the pampered, blonde child/woman—gets Dick Herrys, himself chastened and improved by his movements up and down the socio-economic scale.

Even when Ruck's brawny arm of coincidence causes Rose Mary and Dorothea to go on a trip to the continent together to escape their disappointments with, unbeknownst to each other, Dick Herrys, there is no erotic attraction between them. Although the narrator and a number of the other characters, young and old and of both sexes, use child and especially domestic animal imagery to describe Dorothea (whose nickname is "Duckie"), far from being a coded "language of lesbian desire" as in some of Woolf's writings (Lilienfeld 41), the tone of these animal descriptions ranges from indulgent to critical.[35] In a metageneric moment, for example, Ruck has Dick Herrys' formidable aunt describe the engaged Dorothea as looking like "the pet who, being now well fed on Romance has now given up canary-stalking" (44). As for Rose Mary, she consistently describes herself as reluctant to take on the duties of the child-like Dorothea's nanny, governess, even mother, but she has done so because it is part of her "modern, feminine creed" not to "leave another girl stranded" (182-3). However angry she is at his apparent deceptions, Rose Mary loves Dick Herrys. Dorothea, although she becomes less selfish, has eyes only for the men competing for her attention until her conventional femininity is drawn by the old-fashioned masculinity of an Austrian Baron. A look at Ruck's *Love on Second Thoughts* in connection with *Orlando*, then, only serves to emphasize the degree to which Ruck, despite her introduction of a toned-down version of the new woman, stays well within the conventional bounds of the romance genre, and does so transparently, without suggestions of parody or submerged meanings.

There is no evidence in published letters or diary entries that Woolf read this or any other novel by Berta Ruck. Since actually purchasing one no doubt would have made her hair stand on end, none remain among the books in the Woolfs' library. The Woolfs owned Oliver Onions' *The New Moon: A Romance of Reconstruction* (1918), however,[36] and one wonders if Woolf at least might have been curious enough to borrow the Ruck novel published in the same year as the flap over the tombstone in *Jacob's Room*? In *The Subconscious Courtship* (1922), along with the "Mooring Mast for air-ships" already mentioned in connection with Orlando guiding Shelmerdine's plane, Ruck, like Woolf, shows her interest in "Silence, or the Things People Don't Say" (Woolf, *TVO* 220). Ruck can't find a way, however, past graceless sentences like "Thinking one thing, she

---

[35] It would be a misreading to take this animal imagery out of the context of the novel as a whole.

[36] Hodder and Stoughton, who was Ruck's publisher, also brought out Onions' novel.

uttered another thing" (*Subconscious* 148).[37] More interestingly, a concerned observer in Ruck's novel notes, "Every pair of lovers invent a special 'little language' of their own" (*Subconscious* 134-5). In *Orlando*, Shelmerdine and Orlando speak and send telegrams in a coded language comprehensible only to them, and, in the last section of *The Waves*, Bernard feels the same need for "a little language such as lovers use" (295).[38] Still, the evidence is slender.

IV

The curious relationship between Virginia Woolf and Berta Ruck, their respective fictional genres, and their positions on the highbrow/lowbrow cultural continuum, then, stand up to scrutiny in a number of amusing and illuminating ways. Clearly, different kinds of publishers marketed their novels for different kinds of audiences. Woolf, with her own *avant-garde* press, was free to experiment with new fictional forms and to parody traditional ones, still retaining the interest of increasingly large numbers of curious, intelligent, but not exclusively academic readers. Ruck, with her conservative publisher, could be only mildly subversive, but it would be difficult to prove, by using her own comments or by searching for subtexts in her novels, that she wanted to be anything else. Looking back on her career in *A Story-Teller Tells the Truth*, Ruck has a clear idea of her place in the literary pantheon of her time. She defines herself as an unpretentious, "good Bad" writer who writes primarily to support her family. She prefers to do a good job with a popular genre than to fail at *avant garde* writing. At the same time, she defends the popular romance with its heterosexual marriages, financial successes, and happy endings; its appeals to the hearts of a wide range of primarily young female readers; and its ability to recreate a "real" world in which desires are fulfilled.

In spite of what seem like unbridgeable chasms between presses, writers, and audiences in early twentieth-century London, that world remained a relatively small one. Woolf could not help but see Ruck's popular name, possibly in advertisements or reviews, and she inadvertently echoed it in the *Jacob's Room* cemetery scene. Also, it is not surprising that two professional women like Woolf

---

[37] Both writers also take cues from painting, and both provide impressionistic descriptions capturing the fleeting effects of light on quotidian activities. Here is Ruck on the Henley Regatta in one of her early novels: "Timbers jarred timbers as the punts drove closer together, making one heaving, swinging, floating floor....All around was a speckle of faces; sun-browned, rosy, radiant,[...]" (*Subconscious* 292).

[38] As Ruck puts "little language" in quotation marks, perhaps there was a common source.

and Ruck, both married to writers, both with interests in visual and other art forms, would have mutual friends, meet socially, and share the experience of important cultural events.[39] In their different ways, too, Woolf and Ruck both knew Vita Sackville-West's family, not only because of its prominence in society, but because of more personal contacts. No wonder Ruck's enthusiastic fan letter about *Orlando* and Woolf's amusing response eventually travelled up and down the highbrow/lowbrow continuum.

Both Virginia Woolf and Berta Ruck, as we have seen, were intensely aware of these classifications of readers and writers, including themselves, as "highbrow," "middlebrow," and "lowbrow." Although Woolf redefined and embraced the "highbrow" label, she chose not to join the public debate, unlike Leonard Woolf and Q. D. Leavis, perhaps in part because such labels were difficult to apply to real people, as Virginia's own fluctuating comments on Berta Ruck confirm. Ruck defensively used "highbrow" to dismiss the reviewers who damned with faint praise her "sprightly" writing and her prolific output. According to her gendered view of the distinction, Ruck associated Woolf with highbrow intellectuals and thus with appeals to the brain rather than to the heart. Nevertheless, Ruck read at least *Jacob's Room*, *A Room of One's Own*, and *Orlando* and, in *A Story-Teller Tells the Truth*, seems proud of her encounters with their celebrated author (259-60, 236-7). Woolf, whether or not she actually read any of Ruck's fiction, clearly made a study of her various enthusiasms, was curious about her financial success, and initially granted her some respect for being an honest woman with a worthy, practical motive for her prolific output. If Ruck caricatured Woolf as intellectual in a pejorative sense, however, Woolf caricatured Ruck as distastefully sensual, even lewd.

Ruck's attraction to *Orlando* was multilayered. Shelmerdine's arrival from the sky at the end of the novel must have appealed to Ruck's love of airplanes. People Ruck knew appear in Woolf's book—Lydia Lopokova and especially, Vita Sackville-West, to whom Ruck was distantly related. She also would have enjoyed Woolf's playful use of romance novel conventions, quite apart from the lesbian subtext that we now see as a thorough subversion of the genre. Since happy endings fit Ruck's definition of reality, she especially could have identified with Woolf's decision to grant Orlando so much of what she desires. But in addition to the wish fulfillment, Ruck may have responded to the virtuosity and sheer poetic beauty of the writing which, as "Thomas Gage" wrote to Virginia Woolf about Ruck's fame, she "may hope in vain to equal" (Spater and Parsons 147). Ruck, using words like "brilliant" and "vivid" in her fan letter, specifical-

---

[39] Ruck also spotted Woolf at the "first night of the Russian Ballet" (*A Story-Teller* 236-7).

ly complimented Woolf on her renditions of the "marvellous" Great Frost and, surpassing even that, the Great Damp. One can imagine her delighted response to Shelmerdine's return at the end of the novel:

> "Marmaduke Bonthrop Shelmerdine!" she [Orlando] cried, standing by the oak tree.
> The beautiful, glittering name fell out of the sky like a steel blue feather. She watched it fall, turning and twisting like a slow falling arrow that cleaves the deep air beautifully. He was coming, as he always came, in moments of dead calm; when the wave rippled and the spotted leaves fell slowly over her foot in the autumn woods; when the leopard was still; the moon was on the waters, and nothing moved between sky and sea. It was then that he came [....]
> "Here! Shel, here!" she cried, baring her breast to the moon (which now showed bright) so that her pearls glowed like the eggs of some vast moon-spider. The aeroplane rushed out of the clouds and stood over her head. It hovered above her. Her pearls burnt like a phosphorescent flare in the darkness. (*Orlando* 327-8, 328-9)

Whether, as writers, they were "highbrow" or "good Bad," Woolf and Ruck would have shared an appreciation of words and all they could evoke. "'Oh for a little beauty in life,'" Woolf wrote, "as Berta Ruck might say" (*D3* 18).

Works Cited

Adburgham, Alison. *Shops and Shopping 1800-1914: Where, and in What Manner the Well-dressed Englishwoman Bought her Clothes*. London: George Allen and Unwin, 1964.
Alderson, Brian. "Ruck, Amy Roberta (Berta)." *Dictionary of National Biography 1971-80*. Blake, Lord and C. S. Nicholls, eds. Oxford: Oxford UP, 1986. 740-1.
Alpers, Antony. *The Life of Katherine Mansfield*. New York: Viking, 1980.
Anonymous review of *Orlando*. *Times Literary Supplement* (11 October 1928), 729. Reprinted in *Virginia Woolf: Critical Assessments*. Ed. Eleanor McNees. Vol. 2. Mountfield, East Sussex: Helm Information Ltd., 1994. 413-15.
Anonymous review of *Disturbing Charm*. *Times Literary Supplement* (25 September 1919), 518.
Anonymous review of *Wrong Mr. Right*. *Literary Review* (1 April 1922). 551.
Anonymous review of *Wrong Mr. Right*. *New York Times* (23 April 1922). 18.
Ardis, Ann. *New Women New Novels: Feminism and Early Modernism*. New Brunswick: Rutgers UP, 1990.

Beer, Gillian. "The Island and the Aeroplane: The Case of Virginia Woolf."
Virginia Woolf. Ed. Rachel Bowlby. London: Longman. 1992. 132-61.

Bell, Quentin. *Virginia Woolf: A Biography*. 2 vols. London: Hogarth, 1972.

Bennett, Arnold. "Virginia Woolf's *Orlando*." *Evening Standard* (8 November 1928), 5. Reprinted in *Virginia Woolf: Critical Assessments*. Ed. Eleanor McNees. Vol. 2. Mountfield, East Sussex: Helm Information Ltd., 1994. 422-3.

Blain, Virginia, Patricia Clements, and Isobel Grundy, eds. *The Feminist Companion to Literature in English: Women Writers from the Middle Ages to the Present*. New Haven: Yale UP, 1990.

Bloom, Clive. *Bestsellers: Popular Fiction Since 1900*. New York: Palgrave Macmillan, 2002.

Bowlby, Rachel. "*Orlando*: An Introduction." *Feminist Destinations and Further Essays on Virginia Woolf*. Edinburgh: Edinburgh UP, 1997. 149-72.

Cuddy-Keane, Melba. "Brow-Beating, Wool-Gathering, and the Brain of the Common Reader." *Virginia Woolf Out of Bounds: Selected Papers from the Tenth Annual Conference on Virginia Woolf*. Ed. Jessica Berman and Jane Goldman. New York: Pace UP, 2001. 58-66.

Edel, Leon. "Time." *Literary Biography: The Alexander Lectures, 1955-6*. London: Rupert Hart-Davis, 1957. 81-104, 109. Reprinted in *Virginia Woolf: Critical Assessments*. Ed. Eleanor McNees. Vol. 2. Mountfield, East Sussex: Helm Information Ltd., 1994. 440-56.

Gardner, Vivien. "Introduction." *The New Woman and Her Sisters: Feminism and Theatre 1850-1914*. Ed. Vivien Gardner and Susan Rutherford. Ann Arbor: U of Michigan P, 1992. 1-14.

Garnett, Angelica. *Deceived with Kindness: A Bloomsbury Childhood*. London: Chatto & Windus/The Hogarth Press, 1984.

Gilbert, Sandra M. "*Orlando*: Introduction." *Virginia Woolf: Introductions to the Major Works*. Ed. Julia Briggs. London: Virago, 1994. 187-217.

Hankins, Leslie Kathleen. "*Orlando*: 'A Precipice Marked V' Between 'A Miracle of Discretion' and 'Lovemaking Unbelievable: Indiscretions Incredible.'" *Virginia Woolf: Lesbian Readings*. Ed. Eileen Barrett and Patricia Cramer. New York: New York UP, 1997. 180-202.

Jeffreys, Sheila. *The Spinster and Her Enemies: Feminism and Sexuality 1880-1930*. London: Pandora, 1985.

Langham, Linda J. "Virginia's Pages: Collecting Woolf's First Editions & Letters." *Virginia Woolf: Emerging Perspectives: Selected Papers from the Third Annual Conference on Virginia Woolf*. Ed. Mark Hussey and Vara Neverow. New York: Pace UP, 1994. 230-38.

Leavis, Q. D. *Fiction and the Reading Public* (1932). New York: Russell & Russell, 1965.

Lilienfeld, Jane. "'The Gift of a China Inkpot': Violet Dickinson, Virginia Woolf, Elizabeth Gaskell, Charlotte Brontë, and the Love of Women in Writing." *Virginia Woolf: Lesbian Readings*. Ed. Eileen Barrett and Patricia Cramer. New York: New York UP, 1997. 37-56.

MacCarthy, Desmond. "Orlando." *Sunday Times* (14 October 1928), 10. Reprinted in *Virginia Woolf: The Critical Heritage*. Ed. Robin Majumdar and Allen McLaurin. London: Routledge & Kegan Paul, 1975. 222-26.

Moore, Madeline. "*Orlando*: An Imaginative Answer." *The Short Season Between Two Silences: The Mystical and the Political in the Novels of Virginia Woolf*. London: George Allen & Unwin, 1984. 93-115. Reprinted in *Virginia Woolf: Critical Assessments*. Ed. Eleanor McNees. Vol. 2. Mountfield, East Sussex: Helm Information Ltd., 1994. 457-73.

Nelson, Carolyn Christensen, ed. *A New Woman Reader: Fiction, Articles, Drama of The 1890s*. Peterborough, Ontario: Broadview Press, 2001.

Onions, Oliver. *The New Moon: A Romance of Reconstruction*. London: Hodder & Stoughton, 1918.

Potter, Jane. "'A great purifier'; The Great War in Women's Romances and Memoirs 1914-1918." *Women's Fiction and the Great War*. Ed. Suzanne Raitt and Trudy Tate. Oxford: Clarendon, 1997. 85-106.

Radway, Janice A. *Reading the Romance: Women, Patriarchy, and Popular Literature*. Chapel Hill: U of North Carolina P. 1991.

Raitt, Suzanne. *Vita and Virginia: The Work and Friendship of V. Sackville-West and Virginia Woolf*. Oxford: Clarendon, 1993.

"Ruck, 'Berta', Amy Roberta." *The Feminist Companion to Literature in English: Women Writers from the Middle Ages to the Present*. Virginia Blain, Patricia Clements, and Isobel Grundy, eds. New Haven: Yale UP, 1990. 930.

Ruck, Berta. *The Disturbing Charm*. London: Hodder and Stoughton, 1919.

———. *The Lad with Wings*. London: Hutchinson, 1915.

———. *Love on Second Thoughts*. London: Hodder & Stoughton, 1936.

———. *A Story-Teller Tells the Truth: Reminiscences and Notes*. London: Hutchinson & Co. 1935.

———. *The Subconscious Courtship: A Novel*. New York: Dodd, Mean and Company, 1922.

Stape, J. H., ed. *Orlando: A Biography*. Oxford: Shakespeare Head Press/Blackwell Publishers, 1998.

Woolf, Leonard. *Beginning Again: An Autobiography of the Years 1911-1918*. New York: Harcourt Brace Jovanovich, 1964.

———. *Downhill All the Way: An Autobiography of the Years 1919 to 1939*. New York: Harcourt Brace Jovanovich, 1967.

———. *Hunting the Highbrow*. London: Hogarth, 1927.

———. "The World of Books: The Bestseller." *Nation and Athenaeum 36* (March 7, 1925). 777.

Woolf, Virginia. *Between the Acts* (1941). New York: Harcourt Brace Jovanovich, 1969.

———. *The Essays of Virginia Woolf*. Vol. 3. Ed. Andrew McNeillie. San Diego: Harcourt Brace Jovanovich, 1988.

———. *Jacob's Room* (1922). San Diego: Harcourt Brace Jovanovich, 1978.

———. "Lady Ritchie." *Times Literary Supplement* (6 March 1919). Reprinted as Appendix A in Winifred Gerin. *Anne Thackeray Ritchie: A Biography*. Oxford: Oxford UP, 1981. 280-84.

———. "Middlebrow." *The Death of the Moth and Other Essays*. New York: Harcourt, Brace and Company, 1942. 176-86.

———. *Orlando: A Biography* (1928). New York: Harcourt Brace Jovanovich, 1956.

———. *The Voyage Out* (1915). New York: Harcourt Brace Jovanovich, 1948.

———. *The Waves* (1931). Harcourt Brace Jovanovich, 1959.

Virginia Woolf and Literary History
Part II

Edited by Jane Lilienfeld, Jeffrey Oxford
and Lisa Low

Virginia Woolf and Literary History Part I (*Woolf Studies Annual* 9 [2003])

Jane Lilienfeld	Introduction: Virginia Woolf and Literary History
Merry Pawlowski	Exposing Masculine Spectacle: Virginia Woolf's Newspaper Clippings for *Three Guineas* as Contemporary Cultural History
Jeanette McVicker	"Six Essays on London Life": A History of Dispersal. Part One
Evelyn Haller	Alexandria as Envisioned by Virginia Woolf and E. M. Forster: An Essay in Gendered History
Miriam Wallace	Thinking Back Through our Others: Rereading Sterne and Resisting Joyce in *The Waves*
Lisa Low	Feminist Elegy/Feminist Prophecy: *Lycidas*, *The Waves*, Kristeva, Cixous

Virginia Woolf and Literary History Part II

Jeanette McVicker	"Six Essays on London Life": A History of Dispersal. Part Two.
Patricia Cramer	Vita Nuova: Courtly Love and Lesbian Romance in *The Years*
Vara Neverow	The Return of the Great Goddess: Immortal Virginity, Sexual Autonomy and Lesbian Possibility in *Jacob's Room*
Meena Alexander	"The Shock of Sensation": On Reading *The Waves* as a Girl in India, and as a Woman in America
Mónica G. Ayuso	The Unlike[ly]Other: Borges and Woolf
Jane Lilienfeld	Shirking the Imperial Shadow: Virginia Woolf and Alice Munro
Beth Rigel Daugherty	Teaching Woolf/Woolf Teaching

"Six Essays on London Life": A History of Dispersal Part II

Jeanette McVicker

In the first part of this essay (*WSA* 9 [2003]: 143-65), I suggested that as Virginia Woolf was making the transition between finishing *The Waves* and beginning *The Pargiters* in the early 1930s, she became increasingly attuned to the multiple conditions affecting women's entrance to the professions, their role in the public sphere, and their ability to finally tell "the truth" about their bodies. My reading of the *London Scene* essays sketches out their small, but I believe significant contribution to this overall development in Woolf's thinking, especially if one reads these pieces together with the Speech to the London Society for Women's Service that preceded their composition by only weeks. Highlighting the significance of the enigmatic "Portrait of a Londoner" as the concluding piece of the group of "Six Essays on London Life" written for British *Good Housekeeping* (*GH*) in April 1931, I suggest that Woolf already intuited the double-edge for women (as well as men) implicit in the transformation of an imperial to a liberal democratic consumer capitalist formation, though it would take her nearly the rest of the decade to articulate the full impact of such a transformation in her thinking. More specifically, I read the London essays as one of Woolf's preliminary meditations on the way space—public and private, institutional and discursive, "official" and common—participates in the construction and maintenance of knowledge, truth, and power, and what happens when these are reconstituted into new social, economic, political, cultural and (inter)national formations.[1]

The permission of the Society of Authors as the Literary Representative of the Estate of Virginia Woolf to quote from *The London Scene* is gratefully acknowledged.

[1] Responding to the increasing momentum in modernity towards globalization, Susan Stanford Friedman stresses that the space of geopolitics must be added to feminist critiques of identity and culture. By "space in this context," she writes, "I mean...not a static or empty essence, but rather the spatial organization of human societies, the cultural meanings and institutions that are historically produced in and through specifically spatial locations. Thinking geopolitically means asking how a spatial entity—local, regional, transnational—inflects all individual, collective, and cultural identities" (*Mappings*, 109-10). While my essay does not specifically deal with identity issues as such, her argument, with which I emphatically agree, contributes an important component to the reading of Woolf's *Good Housekeeping* essays I've undertaken through the lens of Foucault's genealogy of the "regime of truth," specifically of his analysis of the way this regime constructs knowledge for the formation of a disciplinary society. The one blindness I find in

Perhaps it is too obvious to point out that the *Good Housekeeping* essays are constructed as a kind of walking tour of particular and often prominent places (generally in the City of London) and function as a series of keen, witty observations about temporality, historicity, tradition, and geography for a specific gender and class audience between December 1931 and December 1932, a time of tremendous upheaval in British life domestically and throughout the empire. Woolf's "tour" locates its readers at the "heart" of London from multiple temporal and historical directions and offers both observation and critique of how space is constructed, inhabited, and utilized for particular ends by the dominant culture. "London," for Woolf, is a geopolitical space as well as an idea, ceaselessly in transition and yet always "the same"; it carries its history, tradition, and past glories into the present, where they are monumentalized and inscribed for both present and future; its famous and anonymous dead commingle with the living at nearly every step; its past as well as present power reverberates beyond the island to the whole world. Every essay in the series offers us a palimpsestic view of London functioning in a multitude of ways, depending on one's angle of vision—one alternately inflected by ontology, language, race, ethnicity, class, gender, nationality, and purpose. Together with the Women's Service speech, one might say that they allow Woolf to connect the various ways in which temporality, history, space and language are shifting to accommodate as well as normalize and discipline women's greater public participation, a theme that will become more prominent as she struggles with the novel-essay that will eventually become *Three Guineas* and *The Years*.

Each of the six essays focuses on a particular kind of institutional and discursive space—"The Docks of London" and "Oxford Street Tide" deal with economics and culture, over time, through history, across class and national boundaries; "Great Men's Houses" offers a contrast in how culture-producers—in this case writers—become commodities themselves under the aegis of "tradition"; "Abbeys and Cathedrals" points out the ways in which the dead and the spaces which house them contrast with the living; "'This is the House of

---

Friedman's important contribution is her omission of the way in which the ontological site engages the geopolitical in constructing being. By invoking antitraditionalist social scientists such as James Clifford without fully acknowledging the contribution that poststructuralist philosophers have made to the question of knowledge production, especially their disclosure that the "objective truth" of modernity is the fictional consequence of an ontology that precisely *spatializes*—and colonizes—time, her otherwise insightful and illuminating extension of the feminist focus on identity to include the geopolitical site remains limited. Her admonition to feminist critics to "always spatialize!" (130) thus needs more nuance, I'd suggest, given that it is precisely the spatialization of temporality and the differences time makes possible that has enabled the technologization of the planet and the domination of the beings that inhabit it by the dominant culture.

Commons'" juxtaposes the distinctive men of past politics with their contemporaries and the ways they are "stamped" into history; "Portrait of a Londoner" offers us the drawing room of a Victorian hostess and the "nest" she has constructed, not only for herself, but for those who "wish to know London not merely as a gorgeous spectacle, a mart, a court, a hive of industry, but as a place where people meet and talk, laugh, marry, and die, paint, write and act, rule and legislate" (*GH* 132). All of them reveal the multiple ways by which "London" extends its space into the arena of the global, an extension in the process of tremendous transformation as political, economic, social and cultural affiliations are being reformulated. Through imperialism, parliamentary democracy, commodity capitalism, the English tradition of literature, language, culture, social manners and customs, London by turns dominates/influences/impacts the nations of the world. The world, in turn, including the subjected nations of empire, naturally reciprocates such influence, however minutely or invisibly. Thus "London" is always London, yet it is never the same at any particular moment.

Woolf seems clearly responsive to this phenomenon, noting its positive implications, particularly for women, but she registers its negative complications as well. This thematic element of continuous flux within/under a façade of permanence (for example, the "timelessness of the British Empire," which is actually under continuous renegotiation across the spectrum mentioned above, both domestically and throughout the world), which could be said to have had its conception in *The Waves*, will dominate her work throughout the decade. Each essay explores the relay of spatial, historical, temporal, discursive and ontological shifts taking place in this iconographic city, and as a whole they suggest that, while some aspects of London's greatness are passing, the changes taking place enable white, middle class women to enter the professions, take more visible roles in the public sphere, and wield both the language and the position needed for speaking the truth about their bodies. At the same time, however, the newly emergent social formations vying for prominence as imperialism wanes—democratic consumer capitalism as well as fascism—are already attempting to appropriate women's desires for greater visibility through surveillance, normalization, commodification, "hero-worship" and technological progress, including the new entertainment industries and magazines written for mass distribution such as *Good Housekeeping*.

III The Center "Elsewhere" and the Politics of Desire

The *Good Housekeeping* essays begin by marking the arrival of raw materials from throughout the world as they come into the London docks and then are weighed, measured and valued, according to the laws of efficiency and commerce, to be transformed into the finished products that will be bought and sold in Oxford Street (the subject of the second essay in the series). The entire process is undertaken for "our" benefit, Woolf writes, in the first essay "The Docks of London," including herself among the readers of the magazine:

> The only thing, one comes to feel, that can change the routine of the docks is a change in ourselves...It is we—our tastes, our fashions, our needs—that make the cranes dip and swing, that call the ships from the sea. Our body is their master. We demand shoes, furs, bags, stoves, oil, rice puddings, candles; and they are brought us. Trade watches us anxiously to see what new desires are beginning to grow in us, what new dislikes. One feels an important, a complex, a necessary animal...(*LS* 14).

The second essay, "Oxford Street Tide,"[2] provides an immediate translation of how "trade" has not only gauged our desires but how it *produces* desire. Oxford Street (unlike Bond Street) is glitzy, cheap and tawdry. Everything about Oxford Street depends on its ability to continuously transform itself by manufacturing ever "new" consumer tastes, a vicious cycle of creating demand and then satisfying it. On the one hand, it seems clear that Woolf is fascinated by the creation and invention that produces this commodity-driven consumer capitalism, which is not only replacing the old sovereign/imperial logic, but also produces and then attends to the needs and desires of precisely the emergent professional women

---

[2] In Part I, I gave an incomplete list of critics who have written on the *London Scene* essays, which I hope to correct here. Pamela Caughie's extended discussion of the first two essays in "Purpose and Play in Woolf's *London Scene* Essays," *Women's Studies* 5. 16, 1989—revised slightly for *Virginia Woolf & Postmodernism*—is still the benchmark in reading "The Docks of London" and "Oxford Street Tide." Her counterarguments to Susan Squier's reading in *Virginia Woolf and London: The Sexual Politics of the City* are especially insightful. While Caughie's focus on language contributes a salient perspective most critics ignore, it tends to minimize what I find to be the deep historical focus of these essays.

Sonita Sarker's essay, "Locating a Native Englishness in Virginia Woolf's *The London Scene*" appears in the *National Women's Studies Association Journal* 13.2 (2001): 1-30. Leslie Kathleen Hankins reconstellates "Oxford Street Tide" along with several other Woolf essays, with Benjamin in "Virginia Woolf and Walter Benjamin Selling Out(Siders)" in *Virginia Woolf in the Age of Mechanical Reproduction*, ed. Pamela L. Caughie (New York: Garland, 2000, pp. 3-35). Michael Whitworth makes a brief reference to "Oxford Street Tide" as well, in "Virginia Woolf and Modernism," *The Cambridge Companion to Virginia Woolf*, ed. Sue Roe and Susan Sellers. Melba Cuddy-Keane's *Virginia Woolf, the Intellectual, and the Public Sphere* (Cambridge UP, 2003) includes a discussion of two *London Scene* essays: "Abbeys and Cathedrals" and "'This is the House of Commons.'" I am very grateful to her for sharing page proofs from this section of the book while I was making final revisions to this essay. Again my apologies if I have left out other work on the London essays.

who have finally won the vote and are earning their own incomes. They are indeed "necessary animals" to this new economy of desire. On the other hand, it seems equally clear that Woolf feels uneasy about the way women's consumer-driven desires are being catered to and manipulated by commodity capitalism, and how this new importance of women to the economy inevitably supports the horrendous conditions of the laboring men who work the docks of London—unloading ships, running cranes—and who live in the sordid tenements lining the docks; the workers who are there to satisfy the needs of consumers—almost exclusively figured as female—and, ultimately, the greed of the (male) owners/producers. This essay, as well as the others, reveals Woolf's ambiguous attraction to *and* distaste for the new "transparent" London, a reaction that has its roots in her "however uneasy" identification with a certain sort of "Englishness" which I will explore below. This identification with an aspect of "Englishness" suggests the degree to which Woolf herself is caught within the transformation of the imperial center into an invisible regime of truth, even as she intuits the changes, both positive and negative, taking place.

Reading the Women's Service speech together with the London essays in light of Foucault's analysis of the disciplinary panoptic gaze and its extension, the repressive hypothesis, helps contemporary readers think through the implications of the new economy of desire produced by the transformation of the imperial center, to which Woolf points. The center/panoptic gaze she invokes remains as a mechanism that controls the relations of power, but it is now a "center elsewhere,"[3] i.e. *invisible*. It necessitates the inscription of a value system based on the accommodation of desire to the unitary structures of commodity capitalism at home and on "development" abroad (e.g., granting certain former colonies Dominion status, providing them with just enough independence to make them want to continue their "special" economic connection to Britain). This "center elsewhere" promises economic freedom and autonomy as well as democratic rights and privileges, but as the Oxford Street scene clearly reveals, it has simply reinscribed desire into a machinery of commodity production and "fulfillment." Working class men are still reduced to backbreaking labor and squalid working conditions; working class women who are not domestics or factory workers find a place in the "underground" world of prostitution and crime. The middle-class woman becomes not only a "necessary" animal to the captains

---

[3] While Foucault and Derrida have quite different projects, they both invoke the privileged metaphorics of (super)vision as part of a philosophy of presence, a fundamental component in the way modern disciplinary power works. For Derrida's discussion, see especially "Structure, Sign and Play in the Discourse of the Human Sciences," *Writing and Difference*. For Foucault's discussion of panopticism, see *Discipline and Punish*, trans. Alan Sheridan (New York: Vintage, 1995).

of trade but a metaphorical one who, consumed by greed and envy, "pounces." The merchant seeks only the maintenance of the illusions of grandeur at the least possible cost ("It taxes all my wits to think how I can display my goods with the minimum of waste and the maximum of effectiveness." *LS* 21). All these people have become bodies assigned by a disciplinary regime of truth to their "proper" places in the capillated whole, where they can be most useful at the least possible cost to its power. This reinscription of desire will figure prominently in *The Pargiters* and, by the end of the decade, emerge full-blown in *The Years*.

The "gaudy, bustling, vulgar" Oxford Street provides Woolf a glimpse of the "center elsewhere." It reveals how daily life has shifted to accommodate the masses of people who depend on commerce for their survival: "A thousand such voices are always crying aloud in Oxford Street. All are tense, all are real, all are urged out of their speakers by the pressure of making a living, finding a bed, somehow keeping afloat on the bounding, careless, remorseless tide of the street" (*LS* 21). Even those who consider themselves members of a higher class (such as the "moralist" who observes the streetlife with derision, whom Woolf mocks[4]) recognize that this street and its inhabitants are caught up in the same battle for human survival: "that life is a struggle; that all building is perishable; that all display is vanity" (*LS* 22). This post-Victorian Oxford Street and the docks that support it are symptomatic of the shift from an imperial center, which *visibly* assigned bodies and products to their proper places in the home and the factories as well as in the civil service and the administration of the empire, to a "center elsewhere," which renders bodies docile and useful ("necessary animals") for commodity capitalism by producing and accommodating desire. Thus, Woolf suggests, as the center elsewhere becomes increasingly invisible—moves "beyond the reach of free play" or critical engagement in Derrida's terms—the struggle over what human dignity might mean in the modern era of increasing technology and dehumanization is never articulated.

---

[4] Woolf posits a type of foil commentator in "Oxford Street Tide," whom she simply refers to as a "moralist," and against whose stuffy arrogance she elaborates on the street scene. For example, in the second paragraph: "Oxford Street, it goes without saying, is not London's most distinguished thoroughfare. Moralists have been known to point the finger of scorn at those who buy there, and they have the support of the dandies" (*LS* 16). Several paragraphs later: "And again the moralists point the finger of scorn. For such thinness, such papery stone and powdery brick reflect, they say, the levity, the ostentation, the haste and irresponsibility of our age" (*LS* 19). While it is clear that she is mocking this "moralist"—one presumes him to be the typical, stuffy Victorian male—which enables her critique of Victorian morality, it is also clear that in some ways this "moralist" reveals an English attitude with which Woolf—despite her critique—identifies in some degree. I hope to make this aspect of the series more clear as I proceed with my analysis. Squier reads this "moralist" very differently than I do; see *Virginia Woolf and London*, pp. 57-61, as does Caughie (see Note 2).

The three essays that follow "Oxford Street Tide"—"Great Men's Houses," "Abbeys and Cathedrals" and "'This is the House of Commons'"—together reveal the cultural, social, and political discourses which made possible the transformation of the visible center into an invisible one in the everyday lives of the British public. In discussing them together in the next section I hope to demonstrate the degree to which Woolf is attentive to the ingenious way these multiple discourses of power establish norms by means of which average citizens are accommodated to the regime of truth.

IV The Monumental Past in the Age of the Masses

1

The "London life" depicted in these essays is a life constructed by layers of history, tradition and culture, which the city itself has metaphorically and literally monumentalized. In direct contrast to the cheap and ephemeral glitter of Oxford Street, which is "built to pass," stands virtually the rest of the city, which is not only "built to last" but functions as a vast network of tombs and memorials in and around which the masses struggle to eke out their living. Yet even what was "built to last" is the result of continuous demolition and reconstruction, as the churches mentioned in "Abbeys and Cathedrals" overtly reveal. If masterpieces of architecture and "great men" were fundamental to the production of the definition of "Englishness" that held the imperial center in place, what will define "Englishness" in the time of the masses?[5] Through a series of repetitions and contrasts, Woolf calls attention to the ways in which the imperial center marshalled the cultural and socio-political institutions that reached most directly into people's daily lives. While Woolf makes clear her critique of patriarchal imperialism, particularly through the use of ironic juxtaposition, her discussion of

---

[5] Defining "Englishness" has become an important focal point of much recent Woolf scholarship. The International Virginia Woolf Society sponsored a panel, organized by Melba Cuddy-Keane, at the 1999 Modern Language Association on "Woolf and Englishness"; panelists included Carey Snyder (SUNY Stony Brook) discussing "Woolf's Ethnographic Fiction: Othering Englishness in *The Voyage Out*"; Ayako Yoshino-Miyaura (U of Sussex) on "Redefining Englishness: *Between the Acts* and the History of the Modern Pageant"; and Sonita Sarker (Macalester C) on "Siting Englishness in Woolf's *London Scene*." Recent issues of the *Selected Papers from the Annual Conference on Virginia Woolf* and *Woolf Studies Annual* (Pace UP) provide some additional sources for recent Woolf scholarship on this topic. Jane Garrity's *Step-Daughters of England: British Women Modernists and the National Imaginary* (Manchester and NY: Manchester UP, 2003) provides a cogent discussion of Woolf's nostalgia for Englishness and has a very useful bibliography. Her book was published too late for its insights to be included here, but see my review in this volume (392-95).

Britain's cultural and political traditions reveals a wariness about this post-imperial, anonymous age of the mass public. Even as she celebrates the changes that provide women with economic and political freedom and the means by which they might "speak the truth about women's bodies," she is uncertain about the way in which those changes are taking place and the consequences that might ensue. This ambiguity or tension comes through in each of the next three pieces in the *Good Housekeeping* series.

In "Great Men's Houses," the third essay in the series, Woolf takes her reader-tourists through the houses of Thomas Carlyle and John Keats. She begins by invoking the commodification of tradition represented by the National Trust, which purchased Carlyle's house in 1895—"London, happily, is becoming full of great men's houses, bought for the nation and preserved entire with the chairs they sat on and the cups they drank from, their umbrellas and their chests of drawers" (*LS* 23)—presumably for use in the post-imperial era. In a time, moreover, of the emergence of the masses, especially the "intrusion" of women into the professions, the "stamp" of great men must be made visible as a resonant sign of a great "manly" English tradition that should be maintained.

Woolf subverts that intention of the dominant culture in her guided tour of Carlyle's house by focusing on the material existence of that eminent household: they had "no water laid on." Woolf insistently uses the metaphors of war in describing life in the household of the great "Victorian sage," who wrote as a reformer of his own time while maintaining the gender codes that kept an intelligent woman such as his wife, Jane Welsh, locked in a battle with dirt, cold and bugs. This is no accident: his reform work and writings left completely intact the power relations controlled by the patriarchal, imperial center. Woolf would, throughout her career, position him as both a remarkable user of the English language *and* as a significant upholder of the Victorian moral system she so despised (though, as Michael Whitworth notes, Victorians such as Carlyle and Ruskin provided her with "the possibility of an 'impassioned prose' which would address the feelings and imagination without taking on the 'overdressed' appearance of the prose poem"[6]). Woolf may or may not have known Carlyle's profoundly racist and anti-democratic tendencies, particularly those expressed toward the end of his life. In spite of his genuine efforts to bring about needed reforms in the mid-Victorian age, his writings, Woolf implies, contributed to the

---

[6] In "Virginia Woolf and Modernism," Whitworth suggests that "Woolf was particularly indebted to the Victorian non-fictional prose writers"—especially Pater, Carlyle and Ruskin—(152) while at the same time, "[I]n rejecting Victorian 'materialism,' Woolf is rejecting the Victorian idea of reality itself" (151). I will come back to this latter point of Whitworth's in my discussion of the sixth essay, "Portrait of a Londoner."

concealment of the center of power by its emphasis on a particular kind of morality that operated as a type of normalization.[7] The struggle to maintain "civilization" that produced great men and through them the canonical English tradition was waged to a large degree, Woolf implies, by those who lived "underground"—women and servants—as Susan Squier first compellingly pointed out (Squier 61-63). In other words, the imperial center held in check the relations of power across the spectrum: maintenance of the patriarchal Victorian household required the cultural, political, and economic institutions of British life, which sustained British hegemony to the furthest outposts of empire. Woolf's discussion of Carlyle in this series seems to imply his quite visible role in that process, hence her mocking tone toward this great Victorian man and the monumentalizing of his house by the English culture industry.

---

[7] Woolf reviewed the volumes of letters written by Carlyle and his wife, Jane Welsh Carlyle (published posthumously) and wrote an essay on the Carlyle household and marriage, in addition to the essay in the *Good Housekeeping* series. See especially "Geraldine and Jane" in *The Common Reader, Second Series* (New York: Harcourt, Brace and Co., 1932); a review of "The Letters of Jane Welsh Carlyle"in *E*1 54-58; and a review of "More Carlyle Letters" *E*1: 257-61. Woolf frequently invoked Carlyle as an important 19th century thinker and writer, and praised his literary style throughout her life. For example, she includes Carlyle among "the greatest [prose] writers of our time" with Dostoevsky and Tolstoy ("Mr. Symon's Essays," *E*2, 70).

Given Leslie Stephen's influences on Woolf's thinking, it seems likely but not certain that she knew, for example, Carlyle's "Occasional Discourse on the Nigger Question" (1853). Critic Deirdre David characterizes the piece as "written with the wild energy and linguistic abandon" so typical of Carlyle's prose, and summarizes it thus: "the 'Nigger Question' argues that black West Indians are destined 'to be servants to those that are born wiser than you, that are born lords of you; servants to the Whites, if they *are* (as what mortal can doubt they are) born *wiser* than you.' Sharing none of his contemporaries' belief in mid-Victorian moral superiority to late-eighteenth-century moral laxity, Carlyle finds mid-Victorian Britain sunk 'in deep froth-oceans' of rubbish about benevolence, fraternity, emancipation, and philanthropy, its citizens deaf to what is, for him, their 'everlasting duty': to work." See David's *Rule Britannia: Women, Empire, and Victorian Writing*, 97-100. *The Norton Anthology of English Literature* (v.1, ed. M. H. Abrams et. al. [New York: W.W. Norton & Co., 1986]), perhaps not surprisingly, doesn't include the "Occasional Discourse on the Nigger Question" in its section on Carlyle.

In terms of the Victorian legacy Woolf inherited, it is interesting to contrast Carlyle's views on race and imperialism with her father's. Stephen was ardent in his support of the North in the American Civil War, for example, and "an enthusiastic champion of slavery emancipation," according to the online *Dictionary of National Biography* (of which he was, of course, the first editor). Stephen traveled to the U.S. in 1863 to view the war firsthand and subsequently published "*The Times* on the American War, by L. S."(1865), "in which he sought to refute the English arguments in favour of the South."

Significantly, I think, the discussion of "great men's houses" ends not with Carlyle the patriarch (though Squier's otherwise brilliant analysis does). Woolf takes her readers from Cheyne Row in fashionable Chelsea to the "little white house behind wooden palings" of John Keats, in Hampstead. Born the same year as Carlyle (1795) but dying 60 years before him of tuberculosis, Keats left his "stamp" upon the house "not of fever, but of that clarity and dignity which come from order and self-control" (*LS* 27). His "heroic equanimity" contrasts positively with Carlyle's authoritarian "hero worship," Woolf implies, which qualifies him as a different kind of "great man." It is the distinction she makes in the meaning of what constitutes a "great man" that is the basis of the contrast in this essay, and will continue in the next two.

Keats's house near Hampstead Heath, a space of 700 acres just four miles north of the city center, was not on any tour of Monumental London. Woolf praised Keats often in her writing, but very differently from the way she praises Carlyle: he had a "fine and natural bearing...profound insight and sanity."[8] There is also something very different, having to do with Hampstead's place in the city, in the way Woolf represents Keats's house as a symbol of his kind of "greatness": "By some miracle, too, Hampstead has always remained not a suburb or a piece of antiquity engulfed in the modern world, but a place with a character peculiar to itself. *It is not a place where one makes money, or goes when one has money to spend.* The signs of discreet retirement are stamped on it...It has style and intention as if designed for people of modest income and some leisure who seek rest and recreation" (*LS* 26; my emphasis).

What Woolf seems to imply in contrasting the homes of these two writers is a difference in the way they inhabit space, which has implications for the ways in which they became "great men" in the service of maintaining "tradition." One space, supporting a visible network of power relations, lends itself to monumentalization (for example, by the National Trust). The other is "peculiar to itself" and unassuming: it resists appropriation and commodification by the culture industry. The essay implies another distinction, this one less overt (at least in the section on Keats): it has to do with Carlyle's and Keats's inscription within patriarchy, which has implications for how such writers, and their memorialization by the tradition, contribute to "the truth about women's bodies." Carlyle's relationship with Jane Welsh, Woolf implies, is more like that of a tyrant than a partner; the essay suggests that the monumentalization of this great man is in fact a celebration of a tyrannical tradition. There is no suggestion of this in the section on

---

[8] "How It Strikes a Contemporary," *The Common Reader*, 1st series, ed. Andrew McNeillie, p. 234.

Keats, even though he was, despite his deep love for Fanny Brawne, also susceptible to the patriarchal conventions of his day.[9]

In the conclusion of the essay, Woolf's focus shifts to the view of London from the top of Parliament Hill (on Hampstead Heath), providing the reader with a panoptic prospect that collapses the historical past into the present and complicates the positive implications of the above contrast:

> One sees London as a *whole*—London crowded and ribbed and compact, with its dominant domes, its guardian cathedrals; its chimneys and spires; its cranes and gasometers; and the perpetual smoke which no spring or autumn ever blows away. London has lain there time out of mind scarring that stretch of earth deeper and deeper, making it more uneasy, lumped and tumultuous, branding it for ever with an indelible scar. There it lies in layers, in strata, bristling and billowing with rolls of smoke always caught on its pinnacles (*LS* 28-29; my emphasis).

From this elevated perspective, which enables the perception of historical layering, the reader can view London in its modern ugliness, a chaotic London that scars and pollutes the earth. This could be London as Carlyle might have characterized it: the monuments and the factories, the masses and the smoke all coalescing into a whole that calls for its transformation through an emphasis on moral reform, work, and a political system, grounded in patriarchal values, that celebrated a heroic tradition of strong leaders. This tradition, which has as its purpose the triumph of order over disruption, has manifested itself as chaos. The panoptic perspective reverses this and manifests itself in Carlyle's remedy for such an industrial nightmare; despite its positive implications for improvements in workers' conditions, it represents one precursor to the fascism emerging across Europe as Woolf penned these essays. Contemporary readers might, with the hindsight provided by our 21st century location, also see Carlyle's remedies as part of an emergent disciplinary formation, as I believe Woolf in her own way intuited: a formation that would bring about an era of ever-increasing normalizing techniques that would mask itself as an era of liberal democracy and consumer capitalism. However, Woolf offers us a second, qualified glance at London from this panoptic perspective:

---

[9] Woolf chastised Keats for complaining that his beloved Fanny Brawne "danced too much" in Hampstead: "The divine poet was a little sultanic in his behaviour; after the manly fashion of his time apt to treat his adored both as angel and cockatoo. A jury of maidens would bring in a verdict in Fanny's favour." One can note here both the fleeting "oriental" reference as well as, ironically, the reference to an angel—a variation on the one I have been discussing. See "Indiscretions," *E3* 460.

And yet from Parliament Hill one can see, too, the country beyond. There are hills on the further side in whose woods birds are singing, and some stoat or rabbit pauses, in dead silence, with paw lifted to listen intently to rustlings among the leaves. To look over London from this hill Keats came and Coleridge and Shakespeare, perhaps. And here at this very moment the usual young man sits on an iron bench clasping to his arms the usual young woman (*LS* 29).

The last lines offer the reader a different view of London, a culturally historical one rooted in the pastoral tradition that celebrated love, nature and poetry. This is Keats's London, where the din and rush of life were stilled into timeless beauty. Yet there seems something wrong with this picture, too: what should be the lyric beauty of multifaceted nature seems reduced to a formulaic, sentimental and banal scene of "birds singing in the woods" and an anonymous couple clasping each other "as usual" on iron benches. Woolf seems to suggest that for all their intimations of the dehumanizing logic of the Enlightenment tradition, the English Romantics' answer was a withdrawal from the public into the subjective reality of the poet awed by beauty, a withdrawal that left the regulating center of power intact.

In other words, while Keats perhaps offers a more positive model of a "great man" than Carlyle, the changes being wrought on the London of *Good Housekeeping* would have made it impossible in 1931 to write the kind of poetry Keats (or Shakespeare for that matter) wrote. In order to accommodate the growing masses, among them the increased number of women entering public life and the middle class, Woolf implies, the transformation of the center of power is accompanied by a calculated efficiency that renders daily life anonymous. This ambiguity is even more pronounced in the next two essays.

2

The theme of monumentalizing the past is articulated more overtly in "Abbeys and Cathedrals" and "'This is the House of Commons,'" as Woolf undertakes a concrete "tour" of several London churches together with a visit to the gallery of the Commons to contrast the distinctive personality of the past with the increasingly lackluster politicians of the present. It is significant, I believe, that all these geographical places are located in Whitehall, the seat of political power, or in the old city center, the legal and financial district. Even more significantly, "Abbeys and Cathedrals" is not, as readers might suspect, thematically about the religious tradition or the role of religion in English daily life as such, but rather about the way the dead share space with the living. The essay focuses on architecture and public space, the ways in which human beings inhabit and have their lives reflected through such spaces over time and through history, and the ways in which ideologies and politics come to saturate and "carve" such spaces and legacies. By invoking only churches designed or renovated by Sir Christopher Wren, Woolf perhaps makes a subtle reference to seemingly timeless institutional monuments such as St. Paul's and Westminster Abbey, which were, upon closer scrutiny, demolished and rebuilt over and over again.[10] London itself can thus be seen as a dynamic, not static, city in perpetual transformation.

The reader can now begin to appreciate the connections Woolf invites us to make as we leave the "great men's houses" and move to these "abbeys and cathedrals" (next, to the House of Commons), all of which participate in the forging of an apparently seamless iconic representation of the English tradition—but one that is in fact a series of much more discreet fragments and personalities that have become welded into something timeless and continuous for the sake of maintaining an *idea* of Englishness, a tradition that can be imposed as ideology on the citizen or packaged and sold to the consumer. From the culture industry that literally enshrines great writers and poets to the religious and state monuments that permeate London, this walking tour reveals how multiple institutional and discursive spaces are overcoded with meaning. Woolf's essays, however, disperse those meanings for her audience of readers, primarily women entering the middle classes who are attempting to become "insiders" for the first time.

Woolf begins the fourth essay noting that St. Paul's "dominates" London: "It swells like a great grey bubble from a distance; it looms over us, huge and menacing, as we approach" (*LS* 30). Woolf uses historical contrast to comment on the way daily life under this ominous bubble has become depersonalized in the present:

> ...The fields are gone and the fish ponds and the cloisters; even men and women seem to have shrunk and become multitudinous and minute instead of single and substantial. Where Shakespeare and Jonson once fronted each other and had their talk out, a million Mr. Smiths and Miss Browns scuttle and hurry, swing off omnibuses, dive into tubes. They seem too many, too minute, too like each other to have each a name, a character, a separate life of their own (*LS* 30).

---

[10] All the churches mentioned by name were designed or renovated by Sir Christopher Wren (1632-1723), Great Britain's foremost architect, though he was first a brilliant mathematician and astronomer. Wren constructed a plan to rebuild the city of London following the Great Fire of 1666, and though his plan was not fully adopted, he did execute construction of 52 London churches, among them St. Paul's Cathedral (in which he is buried), St. Clement Dane's in the Strand, and St. Mary-le-Bow; with Nicholas Hawksmoor, he built the western towers of Westminster Abbey, all of which are referenced in Woolf's essay. Wren's use of simple baroque style (an architectural complement, perhaps, to Keats's "heroic equanimity"?) provides yet another kind of "stamp" of a great man—in this case, Wren's imprint which permeates London.

Even the inglorious dead seem to have more substance, character and identity than the "usual" "Mr. Smiths and Miss Browns" of the present, and are afforded greater space than the living.

Woolf makes use of two levels of contrasts in this essay: the first juxtaposes a temporal and spatial dimension of the past as a time of expansive reflection and space with the hectic and constraining present, where "keeping alive" reduces Londoners to a life devoid of the open physical or mental space necessary for contemplating their humanity. While St. Paul's will increasingly function in Woolf's work as a symbol of a sedimented tradition of patriarchal power,[11] in this essay it still offers, despite its threatening aura, "that pause and expansion and release from hurry and effort which it is in the power of St. Paul's, more than any other building in the world, to bestow" (*LS* 31). Nevertheless, the meaning of Woolf's reference to St. Paul's monumental dead is unmistakable. Even Lord Nelson and "the contorted and agonized figure" of John Donne find repose here. It is the *way* that St. Paul's monumentalizes its dead, similar to the National Trust's preservation of "great men's houses," which Woolf ironizes. These monumentalized dead are represented as upholders of the imperial center in whose behalf their erratic life has been reduced to a ceremonial national virtue: "But death and the corruption of death are forbidden to enter. Here civic virtue and civic greatness are ensconced securely" (*LS* 32). With the exception of Donne and Nelson, these "great dead men" are anonymous in Woolf's essay, but that is precisely the point: their anonymity is given iconic memory as selfless agents of the great British imperial tradition. To refer to Donne—the metaphysical poet and dean of St. Paul's—and Lord Nelson—the naval hero who restored the power of the British navy during the Napoleonic Wars—is enough to demonstrate how their individuality is reduced and accommodated to the great aristocratic tradition.

This national memorializing of the great is juxtaposed in the essay on a second level of contrast with the great who are buried in Westminster Abbey.[12] "Far from being spacious and serene, the Abbey is narrow and pointed, worn, restless and animated," Woolf writes. "One feels as if one had stepped from the demo-

[11] In her diary on Feb. 16, 1932, Woolf wrote that she had amassed so much factual information about patriarchal abuses from biographies and newspapers that she had "enough powder to blow up St Pauls" (*D4* 77), all of which would be utilized extensively, first in *The Pargiters* and then in *Three Guineas*.

[12] To further gloss what I understand as a theme of the whole series of essays and particularly of these middle ones—i.e., that "London" is both geographically and geopolitically a space and an idea in continuous flux and transformation yet represented as the center of a timeless, unchanging English tradition—I find it interesting that St. Paul's began as a Saxon cathedral in 1087, and was replaced with a Norman structure in the 13th century. After burning partially in 1561, it burned beyond repair in the great

cratic helter skelter, the hubbub and hum-drum of the street, into a brilliant assembly, a select society of men and women of the highest distinction" (*LS* 32-33). These "great dead" include those with inordinate force of personality, such as Gladstone and Disraeli (who will dominate the next essay): the abbey is filled with kings and queens and poets (Spenser, Chaucer, Dryden, Gay)—the dead who "have lived to the full" (*LS* 33). The implication of this contrast seems to be that these monumentalized dead convey something beyond civic, military and cultural greatness in the service of an imperial hegemony right through to the period of Enlightenment, even while they unquestionably signify and maintain "Englishness." Woolf condemns a predatory imperial tradition which reduces human existence—"effort, agony, ecstasy"—to the solemnity of national monuments, yet she is unwilling to condemn an English past that sparkled with the individual personality of a Chaucer or a Dryden, a Gladstone or a Disraeli. Even the lives of the obscure are worth noting, as the tombs in St. Mary-le-Bow remind us. Woolf thus seems to criticize two contemporary trends: on the one hand, the rise of a technological mass society that promises freedom, convenience and comfort but reduces individuals to anonymity, and human life generally to a banal efficiency; and on the other, the identification of "Englishness" solely with the imperial tradition for the edification of those new masses. As such, these *Good Housekeeping* essays effect a transition from the cultural project of *A Room of One's Own*, in which Woolf positively attempts to resurrect the "lives of the obscure" in order to establish a tradition for women artists, to the more overtly political project of the 1930s to encourage women, such as the members of the National Society for Women's Service, to seek education and entrance to the professions. At the same time, Woolf expresses a wariness about the potential for the leveling of personality and the erosion of all aspects of "Englishness," concerns that will come to dominate *The Pargiters* and the texts it eventually produces.

Pointing out that, while "London, after all, is a city of tombs," it is also "a city in the full tide and race of human life" (*LS* 35), "Abbeys and Cathedrals"

1666 fire, at which time Wren was allowed to completely demolish and rebuild the cathedral, which was completed in 1710. Westminster Abbey, similarly, began as part of a Benedictine monastery and was rebuilt over a former Norman church; it was continuously reconstructed between the 13th-16th centuries; Wren and Hawksmoor added the western towers between 1722-40. Almost every English monarch since William I has been crowned in the abbey; of course, several major English poets—more "potent" royalty—are also buried there in Poets' Corner, as Woolf notes. The fact that two of the most iconic architectural structures of the English tradition experienced nearly perpetual reconstruction and ideological imprinting plays out Woolf's focus, in my view, on the differences temporality ceaselessly proliferates against the monistic pressures of monumentalization. My historical source is *The Concise Columbia Encyclopedia*.

ends with two more stops, in which the dead and the living commingle more casually, but it is what the living are doing that bears comment. A wedding is taking place at St. Clement Dane's in the Strand (the church where Arnold Bennett's funeral took place while Woolf was writing this series[13]); even the celebration of a wedding must take place amid the "roar of omnibuses" (*LS* 35). Searching for a place of peace and quiet in the city center, some unnamed place that cannot be construed as a London monument, Woolf notes that only in "old graveyards which have become gardens and playgrounds" can one find the daily routine of present individual lives merging with the space of the dead: "Flowers light up the turf, and there are benches under the trees for mothers and nursemaids to sit on, while the children bowl hoops and play hopscotch in safety. Here one might sit and read *Pamela* from cover to cover" (*LS* 35). Here are women—presumably women who might read *Good Housekeeping* on the weekend, after working all week?—fulfilling the prescribed roles that the center has always demanded of them, with this difference: they are also acting according to a norm that is being evoked through appeal to a national tradition. Life goes on, but this too is part of "Englishness." The evocation of a pastoral tradition in which women peacefully watch children play in an overgrown cemetery while reading *Pamela*, a novel that prescribed "conduct" for women in the 18th century,[14] would suggest that Woolf is lamenting the loss of some aspect of that tradition when it is ideologically reduced to a monumentalized one in order to provide the masses with a benign sense of "Englishness." I find this to have relevance for an understanding of the complexity of Woolf's project in this particular historical moment; it suggests her awareness of the uses of patriarchy as they are reconfigured from an imperial hegemony to a neo-imperial one, while also revealing an aspect of her own cultural blindness. Women's entrance into social and professional life, Woolf suggests, has profound implications for the imperialist mechanisms of

---

[13] See the *Diary* for 28 March 1931: "Arnold Bennett died last night; which leaves me sadder than I should have supposed...." The editor's note gives additional details on the funeral (*D4* 15-16).

[14] There is an interesting irony here in Woolf's casual reference to Richardson's *Pamela*, which, as critics note, reinforced gender norms. According to Amy B. Wieber, "Novels such as *Pamela* reinforced and augmented the same ideology preferred in conduct books that situated women as domestic beings, docile bodies that could be molded to function specifically as agents that not only fit into the emerging economics of the middle class, but also the socio-political distinctions of the public and private realms." See Lynne Agress, *The Feminine Irony: Women on Women in Early Nineteenth Century Literature* (Cranbury, NJ: Associated University Press, 1978) and Nancy Armstrong, *Desire and Domestic Fiction: A Political History of the Novel* (Oxford UP, 1989).

power. For the readers of *Good Housekeeping*, this newfound economic freedom is accompanied by efforts to manipulate their desire: it would turn them into a mass of anonymous consumers while transforming the imperial tradition into a monumentalized past that will seek to maintain the old value structures under a mask of bourgeois liberalism. Woolf seems to suggest that there *are* aspects of the English past worth preserving, but not by celebrating a tradition of "great men" of virtue and glory interred under marble in St. Paul's or Whitehall. Woolf foregrounds this contrast above all in the fifth essay in the series, "'This is the House of Commons.'"

3

Like the other essays that precede it, "'This is the House of Commons'" develops according to a series of historical, temporal and spatial contrasts. Woolf's tourist-readers enter the Houses of Parliament greeted by the monumentalized past of the imperial tradition, as they were in St. Paul's, though this time that past is represented by statues rather than tombs. Woolf's description is acutely sarcastic:

> Outside the House of Commons stand the statues of great statesmen, black and sleek and shiny as sea lions that have just risen from the water. And inside the Houses of Parliament...here, too, are statues—Gladstone, Granville, Lord John Russell—white statues, gazing from white eyes at the old scenes of stir and bustle in which, not so very long ago, they played their part. (*LS* 37)

William Gladstone (1809-98) was the most important Liberal prime minister during Queen Victoria's reign; the 2nd Earl Granville (1815-91) served as Foreign Secretary in Gladstone's government; Lord John Russell (1792-1878), active in several governments, is best known for his efforts to reform Parliament and education policy. All three are linked with the great Victorian age of reform, which, while having profoundly positive effects on the conditions of the working classes, also consolidated the economic and political transformation to commodity capitalism, a neo-imperialism that would maintain the dominance of "whiteness" within the empire as well as domestically. Within the text, Woolf's emphasis on the interior statues' whiteness contrasts not only with the statues outside Parliament that look like "shiny black sea lions" but also, and more overtly, with the (black) "granite plinths" that will mark the mass monumentalizing of contemporary politicians. I would not suggest that Woolf is overtly aware of the implications of "whiteness" here, except that as a matter of course all the great men celebrated by statues would have been white; however, her present-day readers will be aware of such implications. In spite of the statues, and "vague though *our* history may be," Woolf continues, "we somehow feel that we common people won this right [to self-representation] centuries ago, and have held it for centuries past, and the mace is our mace and the Speaker is our speaker and we have no need of trumpeters and gold and scarlet to usher our representatives into our own House of Commons" (*LS* 38; my emphasis).[15] The untidiness of the Commons, its apparent informality, help to establish a connection between "we" common people and these representatives, members of the House of Commons. These common statesmen "remind one of a flock of birds settling on a stretch of ploughed land" (*LS* 38).[16] Woolf's repetition of "our" and "common" in the essay stands out sharply and, I suggest, implicates "*us*"—women entering into public political life having obtained the vote, just as the use of *we* in the first essay implicated *us* in driving the economic machine—in the business of empire even as it is fading, and with the neo-imperialism that is rapidly taking imperialism's place.

One gets lulled into a sense that these male politicians, "well fed and given a good education doubtless," are still quite like the rest of us; one must consciously (read: sarcastically) say to oneself "severely, 'But this is the House of Commons. Here the destinies of the world are altered. Here Gladstone fought, and Palmerston and Disraeli. It is by these men that we are governed. We obey their orders every day of the year. Our purses are at their mercy. They decide how fast we shall drive our cars in Hyde Park; also whether we shall have war or peace'" (*LS* 39). Yet as the heaviness of history and tradition begin to weigh upon "our" consciousness, in spite of the "commonness" we felt earlier—and even in spite of the subtle sarcasm with which Woolf began—eventually the reader begins to attend to the effect that Woolf has been subtly pointing out, experiencing a growing sense of difference and alienation from these men and this place:

---

[15] Woolf will savagely critique such ceremonial costumes and symbols of patriarchal authority by means of photographs and description in *Three Guineas*, but one must consult the Oxford UP edition (ed. Morag Shiach, 1992), rather than the Harvest/HBJ edition, to find these telling photographs.

[16] The reference to the "ploughed land" is an interesting one in this context if one recalls the etymology of "agriculture" and considers the gender dynamics of "improving the land" and "planting the seed" that have their basis in Roman imperialism: "culture," "cultivate," "colony," "colonization" all derive from the same Latinization (*colon* or *agricola*—farmer) of the Greek *agrios*, which originally meant "wild, monstrous" and which the Romans "seem to have substituted for the more original and originative Greek words for these: *georgia* (*gea+ourgos*: earth working) and *georgos* (earth-worker)": see William V. Spanos's discussion of this etymology in the history of imperialist thinking in *America's Shadow: An Anatomy of Empire*, page 97 but throughout the chapter "Culture and Colonization." See also Anne McClintock's *Imperial Leather* (Routledge, 1995) for a specifically gendered reading of colonization and land.

> ...[The Commons] has somehow a code of its own. People who disregard this code will be unmercifully chastened; those who are in accord with it will be easily condoned. But what it condemns and what it condones, only those who are in the secret of the House can say. All we can be sure of is that a secret there is" (*LS* 39).

Once she has established "our" complicity, Woolf focuses on those elements that keep "us" separate, outsiders; these have to do with tradition *and* with the disciplinary formation that is rapidly subsuming it. The women entering the professions and exercising their newly won right to vote do not want to be outsiders anymore, do they? For the second time in the essay—now in the context of recognizing a secret code of the House of Commons—"we" become aware of surveillance, of being monitored. Earlier, in the context of the statues inside the Commons, a policeman handed out "green cards" of admittance; now "Perched up high as we are, under the rule of an official who follows the prevailing informality by crossing his legs and scribbling notes on his knee, we feel sure that nothing could be easier than to say the wrong thing, either with the wrong levity or the wrong seriousness, and that no assurance of virtue, genius, valour is here sure of success if something else—some indefinable quality—is omitted" (*LS* 39-40). This is precisely the way the panoptic gaze functions, as Foucault reminds us: it describes a situation in which discipline has become internalized.

Woolf makes in this essay a profoundly important point that, I suggest, will achieve its full force in *Three Guineas*, in which she will indict "the daughters of educated men" (including herself) by claiming that "we cannot dissociate ourselves from that figure [of the dictator] but are ourselves that figure. It suggests that we are not passive spectators doomed to unresisting obedience but by our thoughts and actions can ourselves change that figure."[17] The initial connection of a shared purpose and common ground with statesmen is indicative of a sense of "Englishness," and even young women with their recently-won vote (1928, for women 21 and over) are encouraged to feel part of the democratic tradition which, foregoing the trappings of aristocracy, is on display in the Commons. Yet this democracy, like the imperial tradition it is replacing, is not without its own codes and secrets; neither is it unmonitored. The Angel in the House is replaced by the gradual internalization of the disciplinary gaze; the policeman is "there to remind us." The "center elsewhere" continues its silent work of surveillance and of stamping itself onto these most ordinary-seeming men, Woolf's humorous

---

[17] *Three Guineas*, p. 142. Of course, the essay portions of *The Pargiters*, which Woolf began while writing this series, eventually became *Three Guineas*, the companion to *The Years*, and in which Woolf expressed her most insightful and scathing anti-fascist, anti-patriarchal views.

sarcasm notwithstanding: even Mr. Baldwin, who has "all the look of a country gentleman poking pigs," will eventually undergo the inevitable transformation, which Woolf describes in an extraordinary passage beginning with the Secretary for Foreign Affairs' discussion of "some difficulty with Germany":

> And as he spoke so directly, so firmly, a block of rough stone seemed to erect itself there on the Government benches...Matters of great moment, which affect the happiness of people, the destinies of nations, are here at work chiselling and carving these very ordinary human beings. Down on this stuff of common humanity comes the stamp of a huge machine. And the machine itself and the man upon whom the stamp of the machine descends are both plain, featureless, impersonal. (*LS* 41-42)

The sculptured monuments of the aristocratic, imperial tradition become the machine-fabricated slabs of the age of the masses and of the commodity. This begins a long section in which Woolf returns to the strategy of the preceding essays, which thematizes the contrast between the "great man" of the English tradition and the anonymous man of the present. In this essay, however, the contrast is sharper and most explicit, more clearly suggesting the transformation of the visible imperial center into an invisible "center elsewhere" with all its power nevertheless intact. Imperialism valorized the great individual political man—Carlyle, Gladstone, Disraeli, Pitt, Palmerston—as well as the individual of the cultural tradition, so that even Keats can be celebrated, however differently. In an era circumscribed by the invisible "center elsewhere" of liberal democratic commodity capitalism, the need to uphold and maintain the glorious English tradition is greater than ever, but the force of the charismatic individual personality can no longer sustain it:

> Pitt thundered; Burke was sublime. Individuality was allowed to unfold itself. Now no single human being can withstand the pressure of human affairs. They sweep over him and obliterate him; they leave him featureless, anonymous, their instrument merely. The conduct of affairs has passed from the hands of individuals to the hands of committees. Even committees can only guide them and hasten them and sweep them on to other committees. The intricacies and elegancies of personality are trappings that get in the way of business. The supreme need is despatch. A thousand ships come to anchor in the docks every week; how many thousand causes do not come daily to be decided in the House of Commons? Thus if statues are to be raised, they will become more and more monolithic, plain and featureless. They will cease to record Gladstone's collars, Dizzy's curls and Palmerston's wisp of straw. They will be like granite plinths set on the tops of moors to mark battles. The days of single men and personal power are over. Mr. MacDonald is addressing not the small separate ears of his audience in the House of Commons, but men and women in factories, in shops, in farms on the veldt, in Indian villages. He is speaking to all men everywhere, not to us sitting here. (*LS* 42-43)

The "center elsewhere" attends to the individual human being *as a body only*, for purposes of deindividualization. In this context, one feels *as if* one is a free individual, but in fact the individual body is being inscribed by discipline, on the one hand, and documented as part of the "population" on the other—control via *normalization* of the masses.[18] The production of monolithic granite plinths, not statues of individual men, are its way of honoring the great tradition. But this new center must be perceived, unconsciously, as continuous with that prior tradition of great men in order to justify its control over the masses of people who now think of themselves as free citizens, whether they are working class women in the Co-operative Guild or women entering colleges and attending meetings of the Society for Women's Service or residents of the Dominions. Woolf seems acutely aware that the positive possibilities of the post-imperial age are many. She has supported the effort of women and the working classes to gain education and greater economic and political power. She and others have envisioned a social collectivity of genuine equality and economic cooperation. The articulation of that dream will occupy her work for the next several years and find its greatest expression in *Three Guineas*. But in 1931-32, that future is by no means assured. It is threatened outrightly by the relentlessness of commodity capitalism, which, as her previous essays on "The Docks of London" and "Oxford Street Tide" have suggested, seems already entrenched. On yet another level, it is jeopardized by the appearance, even in Britain, of fascism. The stamp of anonymity and the constant grinding of technological progress that turns the lives of people into dehumanized machines without beauty or a moment for solitude and reflection is a theme of all these essays. Woolf implies that mass disillusionment is one of the conditions that leads to the longing for a "great man" in the form of a charismatic leader, such as was being felt in Germany, Italy and Spain—that is, the longing for a *visible center of power*.

[18] Foucault describes this dual process of inscription in "Truth and Power": "In the seventeenth and eighteenth centuries a form of power comes into being that begins to exercise itself through social production and social service. It becomes a matter of obtaining productive service from individuals in their concrete lives. And, in consequence, a real and effective "incorporation" of power was necessary, in the sense that power had to be able to gain access to the bodies of individuals, to their acts, attitudes, and modes of everyday behavior. ...But, at the same time, these new techniques of power needed to grapple with the phenomena of population, in short, to undertake the administration, control, and direction of the accumulation of men (the economic system that promotes the accumulation of capital and the system of power that ordains the accumulation of men are, from the seventeenth century on, correlated and inseparable phenomena): hence there arise the problems of demography, public health, hygiene, housing conditions, longevity, and fertility. And I believe that the political significance of the problem of sex is due to the fact that sex is located at the point of intersection of the discipline of the body and the control of the population" (66-67).

Woolf also calls the "age of granite plinths" the "age of architecture" at the end of this essay. As the narrator leaves the House of Commons, she thinks: "Let us rebuild the world then as a splendid hall; let us give up making statues and inscribing them with impossible virtues...Let us see whether democracy which makes halls cannot surpass the aristocracy which carved statues" (*LS* 43). But she is shaken out of her reverie by the reality that there are "still innumerable policemen. A blue giant stands at every door to see that we do not hurry on with our democracy too fast. 'Admission is on Saturdays only between the hours of ten and twelve.' That is the kind of notice that checks our dreaming progress" (*LS* 43). This "center elsewhere" of liberal capitalist democracy promises freedom but utilizes constant surveillance, so that for a moment Woolf's daydreaming becomes a bit heretical, indeed, somewhat treasonous under the policeman's gaze: "Must we not admit a distinct tendency in our corrupt mind soaked with habit to stop and think: 'Here stood King Charles when they sentenced him to death; here the Earl of Essex; and Guy Fawkes; and Sir Thomas More'" (*LS* 43-44). In different ways, each of these figures challenged the disciplinary relations of power in their day (even Charles could be said to have challenged the Puritan version of discipline, though of course he embodied above all the imperial center and thus doesn't fit the mold of the other three). In this era of the "center elsewhere," one must monitor one's own thoughts. The policeman is there to remind us.[19] Woolf ends the essay—one should bear in mind that in *The London Scene* reprint this is the end of the book—with this wish: "So let us hope that democracy will come, but only a hundred years hence, when we are beneath the grass; *or that by some stupendous stroke of genius both will be combined, the vast hall and the small, the particular, the individual human being*" (*LS* 44; my emphasis). The choice of the future tense must have stood out to the 1932 reader, who no doubt believed that democracy already *had* come to England. Woolf's recognition that the imperial center was still operating as a "center elsewhere" seems apparent in such a rhetorical move. Yet even with that understanding she can hope for a different outcome. But it is the last part of that sentence, which I have italicized, that seems to be the key to this essay—indeed, to all three essays under discussion in this section. Woolf's acute sense of the depersonalization taking place across the social ranks implies that it is just as damaging, and as deadening, as the monumentalizing of the individual within the old heroic

---

[19] Many thanks to Mark Hussey for reminding me of the remarkable connection between this early policeman and Mr. Budge's speech as a traffic policeman during the pageant in *Between the Acts* (160-63).

nationalist tradition that sustained the imperial center. Both disfigure or erase the real living person, an important observation as women begin increasingly to enter the public sphere, aspiring even to Parliament. That last wish, "*that by some stupendous stroke of genius both will be combined, the vast hall and the small, the particular, the individual human being,*" is significant for the writing Woolf was soon to undertake in *The Pargiters*. It articulates her insight that the invisible center of power is already threatening to co-opt what was an opportunity, particularly given the greater visibility of women in public spaces, for a change in the way "the truth about women's bodies" could be told, and thus, for a genuine transformation in human relations.

For the original readers of *Good Housekeeping*, this essay on the House of Commons was not the final installment. "Portrait of a Londoner" would conclude the series in December 1932. The geopolitical implications of Angelica Garnett and Quentin Bell's decision to exclude it from the 1975 Frank Hallman edition of *The London Scene: Five Essays by Virginia Woolf*—complete with dust jacket by Angelica in the style of her mother Vanessa, depicting the dome of St. Paul's dominating the London skyline on the front cover, and an aproned woman with bucket ascending a set of stairs on the back cover (Jane Welsh Carlyle or her maid?)—might be more clear if one attends to the inner jacket blurb, which announces the subject matter this way:

> These five sparkling essays on those aspects of London that have changed little since Virginia Woolf wrote of them in the 1930s show Woolf at the top of her form, blending together in her own unique fashion solid information and imaginative flights of fancy, fact and poetry. 'London,' she wrote, 'is a city in the full tide and race of human life.' It still is. The Docks, Oxford Street, the great men's houses within its confines—Keats', Carlyle's—its abbeys and cathedrals, the House of Commons, today reflect those same enduring qualities that Virginia Woolf observed so perceptively (*LS* inner front cover).[20]

By omitting the final essay on Mrs. Crowe—who clearly lacks "enduring qualities"—and her tea-table gossip, the historical London undergoing tremendous turmoil in the 1930s is reduced to "the London Scene" of 1975, stable, staid, connected to a great English tradition even though it has witnessed the emergence of a youth counterculture, the welfare state and postcolonialism, and relinquished

---

[20] I am referring to the 1982 Random House edition of *The London Scene*, which lists Quentin Bell and Angelica Garnett as copyright holders (1975) and credits Angelica Garnett with the jacket illustration. The Random House edition reproduces the limited-edition Hallman publication of 1975 and is the American reprint of the Hogarth Press edition published in 1982 in London.

its position as "leader of the free world" to the neo-imperialist USA. The editorial (and commercial, one assumes) erasure of the final essay from *The London Scene* testifies to the fulfillment of the imperative of the "center elsewhere" in 1975 that had begun its transformation in Woolf's day.

V Full Circle: Mrs. Crowe's Drawing Room

The London essays begin at the metaphorical, ideological and literal space at which Britain meets the world—the docks. As goods and people come in, power and influence go out, mediated through commerce, politics, language, desire. The world passes into London through the refinement of goods displayed in Oxford Street as well as the imperial travelers returning to Mrs. Crowe's teatable (in the modern age, it also enters via the wireless, the cinema, and mass produced cultural forms such as popular magazines). Woolf concluded the series with the essay "Portrait of a Londoner," which opens not with someone dreaming of "genuine democracy" but with these lines: "Nobody can be said to know London who does not know one true Cockney—who cannot turn down a side street, away from the shops and the theatres, and knock at a private door in a street of private houses" (*GH* 28). The reader-tourist is brought to a flat presumably in the East End, into a dark hall, up a narrow staircase, into the front of a double drawing-room, gradually to be introduced to Mrs. Crowe, "in her black dress and her veil and her cap," who for sixty years could be found "there by the fire in winter, by the window in summer" (*GH* 28). The entire rhetorical and thematic strategy of the series seems displaced; we are no longer in the realm of the public world but of the private house. We seem to have been transported to another age: one in which the public world entered the consciousness of middle class women almost exclusively through mediation by the private house. And indeed, it *is* another age compared to that depicted at the end of the previous essay, which evokes in the reader a sense that the imperial center might give way to the multiple possibilities of a truly democratic social-collectivist future. Yet, here, we find ourselves in a dark, Victorian drawing-room filled with 18th-century furniture and peopled for the past 60 years (i.e., since about 1870) by the faithful servant Maria, Mr. Graham (an ever-present "elderly man in the corner by the cabinet who seemed, indeed, as much a part of that admirable piece of eighteenth-century furniture as its own brass claws") and, of course, the Angel in the House, who makes certain that the talk is "not too deep" and "not too clever" (*GH* 29). At Mrs. Crowe's tea-table, everything "new" is accommodated to her knowledge of the present, her sense of the past, her vision of the future. "Change" is sought but only as it can be accommodated to what already *is*; difference, temporality, genuine conversation are all reduced to sameness, to "idle talk" meant merely to entertain, not to illuminate, provoke or educate. Mrs. Crowe and the world that produced her rely on the façade of the perceived continuity of a tradition that annulled change. "But even London itself could not keep Mrs. Crowe alive" (*GH* 132): modernity's force of change is too great; the old center of visible power yields to the new, and yet that center *does not disappear*, it merely moves out of visible sight, and inscribes itself in different, *invisible*, relations of power. The death of this Angel in the House, who functioned at one level as a kind of monitor for "the truths of women's bodies" and at another level as the preserver of a domestic order that provided a foundation for imperialism, will have tremendous implications for the next generation of women, and for London itself—and hence for the world. And yet that transformation is itself taking place with multileveled and ambiguous consequences for women.

My reading of the complete set of six essays suggests that without the final piece, readers of the 1975 Hallman/Random House edition are denied Woolf's extraordinary vision of how such a transformation in relations of power, and particularly their implications for the roles of women in public and private life, were taking place at the beginning of the 1930s, as she herself was, I believe, attempting to understand them. Deleting "Portrait of a Londoner" provides us with only witty journalism and Woolf's trademark style, as the inner sleeve of that edition makes clear. Keeping the set of six essays intact, in contrast, allows us to glimpse Woolf's effort to work out several thematic, aesthetic, political and cultural problems that were specific to that historical occasion. The project of searching for a new aesthetic form in order to render the transformations taking place, particularly for the emerging middle class of professional women, became *The Pargiters*. Woolf could only finally resolve the issue of socio-politics and aesthetics, however, by writing two books, not a new "hybrid" form of novel-essay. Perhaps the shift in tone and style readers experience when coming to "Portrait of a Londoner" is an early indicator that Woolf would be unable to merge granite and rainbow in the way she had hoped.

Two thematic/literary devices Woolf had utilized with exquisite results in *The Waves*, which she had just completed, come into relief when one adds "Portrait of a Londoner" to the other five essays in the series, both of which comment on the passing of an imperial order into one dictated by the market. One is Woolf's constant notation of changing light—artificial and natural—in our sensory experiences of atmosphere and affect as one strolls along this tour of London; the second is the concept of "talk," whether this takes the form of gossip, speechifying, street utterance or tabloid journalism. To illustrate this point, let me provide two examples that bring "Oxford Street Tide" directly into connection with "Portrait of a Londoner." The first: "The buying and selling [on

Oxford Street] is too blatant and raucous. But as one saunters towards the sunset—and what with artificial light and mounds of silk and gleaming omnibuses, a perpetual sunset seems to brood over the Marble Arch[21]—the garishness and gaudiness of the great rolling ribbon of Oxford Street has its fascination" (*LS* 16). This artificially induced perpetual sunset seems a mocking reference to the famous dictum that the "sun never set on the British Empire" and thus the blatant, raucous transparency of Oxford Street signals one kind of demise of the imperial order. The death of Mrs. Crowe, perpetually in her dark drawing-room, winter and summer, signals another, perhaps equally important marker of empire's passing. Mrs. Crowe's geographical (and geopolitical) space is claustrophobically atmospheric in that old Victorian sense. As Michael Whitworth notes generally,

> In rejecting Victorian 'materialism,' Woolf is rejecting the Victorian idea of reality itself. This marks her experimental work from the outset. In 'The Mark on the Wall' (1917), the narrator identifies a whole range of Victoriana, such as 'mahogany sideboards and ... Landseer prints,' as having once been 'the standard thing, the real thing' (*CSF* 86). ...Throughout her fiction and criticism, Woolf expresses a preference for a reality which is semi-transparent, combining the solidity of granite and the evanescence of rainbow (Whitworth 151).

[21] The Arch was erected as part of Buckingham Palace renovations in 1827-29 by John Nash to commemorate British victories at Trafalgar and Waterloo. According to the Talking Cities tourism website:

> Originally located in front of Buckingham Palace, John Nash's Marble Arch was intended to be the building's main entrance (and solely for royal use). However, as enlargement to the Palace in 1851 effectively made it a redundant 'White Elephant,' the arch was moved to Hyde Park where today, it continues to serve as a gateway between Bayswater and Marylebone. Although Marble Arch now stands rather unceremoniously on a traffic island in one of the busiest (and most polluted) parts of town, convention still dictates that only senior members of the royal family, the Royal Horse Artillery and King's Troop are allowed to pass underneath the arch. With three archways of Corinthian columns, it still makes for an impressive sight, although the meaning behind the arch's sculpted reliefs, which represent England, Scotland and Ireland, are somewhat lost amidst the chaos and traffic fumes.
> More intriguing however, is the history of the area that surrounds the triumphal arch. For it was here that London's old Tyburn Gallows stood. With a history dating back to the 12th century, Tyburn was the hanging gallery of choice for the city's notorious criminals, petty thieves and political prisoners. The name, which is derived from a local brook which flowed into the Thames, became synonymous with large-scale public executions right up until 1783.

Woolf's use of the location is even more fascinating with this history in mind, in my view.

The transformation of natural light into artificially produced light not only satirizes the metaphor relating to empire but overtly frames the way the new commodity culture is replacing—by deception, manipulation and marketing—the imperial formation, which saw itself as "natural." The new culture, too, will attempt to pass itself off as "natural." Woolf's contrast underscores the constructedness of each order, even while each utilizes a different apparatus of power to control people's lives.

If one contrasts as well the role of "talk" or gossip in both these essays, we have yet another connection between the passing of the imperial order and the rise of the democratic commodity capitalism that is quickly replacing it. Again in "Oxford Street Tide":

> Taking all this into account—the auctions, the barrows, the cheapness, the glitter—it cannot be said that the character of Oxford Street is refined. It is a breeding ground, a forcing house of sensation. The pavement seems to sprout horrid tragedies; the divorces of actresses, the suicides of millionaires occur here with a frequency that is unknown in the more austere pavements of the residential districts. News changes quicker than in any other part of London. The press of people passing seems to lick the ink off the placards and to consume more of them and to demand fresh supplies of later editions faster than elsewhere... (*LS* 17).[22]

It is precisely gossip that Mrs. Crowe requires as admittance to her "club." What can we make of this contrast between the tabloid gossip of a teeming, modern Oxford Street and the "talk" of Mrs. Crowe's drawing room, a talk that is neither intimate nor brilliant, not too deep and not too clever, but general, "a glorified version of village gossip" (*GH* 29)? Mrs. Crowe controls the gossip brought to her tea-table and arranges it into blank sameness; it is "idle talk" that merely

---

[22] Hermione Lee notes, in her essay for *The Cambridge Companion to Virginia Woolf*, Woolf's conflictedness toward reviewing for the popular press and writing "journalism" even as these works helped her develop a stronger novelistic technique:

> Her development into the kind of novelist she wanted to be, in the 1910s and 1920s, was worked out in large part through the essays of that period—reviews of individual writers, and more discursive, synthesising considerations of 'modern' writing...
> But her feelings about the market-place, and about the side of the mind she used for non-fiction, were very mixed. ...[But] she had a horror of identifying herself with 'Grub Street' or with professional journalism. She was caught between 'writing as a job and writing as art'. Her antipathy to the 'intellectual harlotry' of reviewing (a phrase from *Three Guineas*), and to the censorship, corruption and hierarchies of the professional literary world, hardened up in her later years and became ever more involved with her critique of a capitalist male-dominated society (Lee 92-93).

entertains rather than actually communicating new ideas and world events, to invoke Heidegger's important concept.[23] She is part of an imperial order that draws everything around a visible center of power in order to domesticate and control it. The teeming "forcing house of sensation" of Oxford Street, on the other hand, seems out of control, wild and chaotic. In that flux and excitement of talk there is at least the possibility for something new, something different and potentially important. Yet the market will do everything it can, particularly through the tabloid press that Woolf so loathed, to rein that potentiality for difference and change back into an inscribed context—but it will do so according to the logic of a center that has become invisible, a center elsewhere. Thus the people working and shopping on Oxford Street will have a sense of possibility and freedom, of liveliness and newness, even as they are all quietly being inscribed into the disciplinary society that Foucault described so meticulously in "Truth and Power."

By reading this sixth and final installment back into the context of the series as a whole, we readers come "full circle": Woolf returns us to the beginning, back to the imperial context, after having taken her readers on an offbeat tour of London's landmarks, noting how they have all in some way contributed to the creation and maintenance of Mrs. Crowe, and by extension, the imperial center. How suffocating that old corbie and her parlor seem to us now! We feel relief that Mrs. Crowe dies at the end of the essay—that the imperial center is fading away. Imperialism was already in the process of being transformed into a network of power relations with no visible center; the magazine *Good Housekeeping* itself plays a major role in this shift to a disciplinary framework of power.[24] Such changes must have seemed palpably refreshing to the generation of women Woolf was addressing, as they took on new responsibilities and experienced greater freedoms. Woolf, too, must have felt a great sense of liberation given her relentless critique of Victorian values and ideology throughout her life and writing. As Whitworth notes, Woolf "directs her most forceful satire at

---

[23] In Part I of this essay I alluded to Martin Heidegger's concept of the "idle talk of *Das Man*" as one way of reading the emptiness of the "talk" assembled at Mrs. Crowe's tea table. I refer readers to pages 160-161 of McVicker, and especially note 24, p. 160. See Heidegger's *Being and Time*, trans. John Macquarrie and Edward Robinson (New York: Harper and Row, 1962), pp. 211-224 for a full discussion of the concept.

[24] Readers familiar with the first part of this essay will recall my observation that magazines such as *Good Housekeeping* served as cultural bridges between an imperial order and a democratic capitalist one for the emerging middle class woman reader. Not only did the magazine regularly deliver sensationalized features on the most exotic outposts of the British Empire to her living room; increasingly, it also brought the disciplinary gaze of scientific management theory and consumerism into the home. See McVicker 158-9.

imposed systems of order, whether the 'real and standard things' of Victorian life, the social hierarchies contained in Whitaker's Table of Precedency, or Mr Ramsay's idea of thought progressing from A to Z. These systems of order are all based either on ideas of linearity, or of hierarchy, the Victorian 'pyramidal accumulation'. ...Woolf extends her rejection of these systems to literary aesthetics, criticising 'Bennett, Galsworthy and so on' for adhering to a formal railway line of sentence. ..." (Whitworth 154). Yet what I hope to have offered in a symptomatic analysis of these essays is a way of thinking about that transformation as Woolf might have glimpsed it but was not fully able to name, a transformation that would effect her everyday life and preoccupy her mind for the decade of the 1930s as she struggled to find a new form that would be adequate to the task of representing this new kind of power. It was a transformation that promised social liberation, genuine political citizenship, and economic freedom, yet it was already one that was reinscribing power relations in ways that would increasingly discipline both the individual and the collective body.

Woolf experimented with form throughout her career, but in my opinion, the experiments that attempted subversions from "inside" the literary tradition begin to shift with *The Waves*. From 1930 on, Woolf's experiments with new forms I suggest should be read as an effort to reimagine the possibilities of an altered historical past together with opportunities to enact—not simply reflect—a more radical present and future.[25] What might a novel-essay accomplish if it undertook an exploration of the past from the point of view of women caught between the monumental imperial tradition and the age of the consumer masses? Could such innovations in form begin the process of providing space for a different, more authentic—or de-centered—way of constructing what passes for "truth," particularly as it concerns the sexual lives of women, their social bodies, and human relations more generally? The last projects Woolf worked on, "Anon" and "The Reader," seem to indicate that she had not yet exhausted such a search for

---

[25] Michael Whitworth's observation that while rejecting Victorian "order" and aesthetics Virginia Woolf was also heavily influenced by certain Victorians' attempts to find a "rhythm in prose" is an important one for my argument about her search for new aesthetic forms in this period:

> There may also be a concealed intellectual debt to the Victorian sages, and, beyond them, to the Romantics, in Woolf's recurrent distinction between mechanical and rhythmic modes of thought....Woolf's fluid syntax indicates the ease with which borders could be crossed. Such conversational acquaintance with ideas [as was apparent in Bloomsbury] creates fragmentary, unsystematic knowledge, but, for these very reasons, is all the more valuable to the literary artist. The systematic treatise can stifle rather than stimulate (Whitworth 148; 152).

an aesthetic—and literary historical—form that would continuously engage readers caught up in such transformative times.

For the women reading the last of the "Six Essays on London Life" in *Good Housekeeping*, December 1932, the Labour Government of Ramsay MacDonald had collapsed only months before and Hitler would be named Chancellor in January. The economic and political peril of this time is strikingly evident, while the desire of the masses is already being manipulated by a variety of forces vying for authority by means of the "center elsewhere." Woolf, on the other hand, was already at work on *The Pargiters*, exposing that center in ways that continue to inspire us, her readers in another century.[26]

---

[26] I am indebted to Jane Lilienfeld for inviting me to write this essay, one which I've had scattered in my head for quite a long time, and for her work as a careful, enabling editor during its long period of writing and revision. She and Jeffrey Oxford kept the idea of a volume on Woolf and Literary History alive despite unbelievable setbacks; deep gratitude must go to them as well as to Mark Hussey, for (finally) giving the volume a home. My additional thanks to Mark for allowing this essay to remain intact by breaking it into two issues of *WSA*. Melba Cuddy-Keane not only provided cogent suggestions for revision at an early stage, but graciously shared her work on *The London Scene* essays prior to publication of her forthcoming book. My co-panelists at the 10th Annual Conference on Virginia Woolf, Sonita Sarker and Janet Winston, gave valuable feedback to that draft. The earliest thinking I did on the London essays was presented initially at the 5th Annual Conference (and published in its *Selected Papers*, ed. Beth Rigel Daugherty and Eileen Barrett [New York: Pace UP, 1996]). Finally, I am thoroughly indebted to William V. Spanos, whose enthusiasm for this project was sustaining and whose insights throughout its multiple revision stages strengthened the paper in innumerable ways. He has been for me *the* model of what it means to be a scholar, however much I continue to fall short of his example.

Works Cited

Caughie, Pamela. "Purpose and Play in Woolf's *London Scene* Essays," *Women's Studies* v. 16, 1989, 389-408.

——. *Virginia Woolf & Postmodernism*. Champagne-Urbana, IL: U of Illinois P, 1991.

——, ed. *Virginia Woolf in the Age of Mechanical Reproduction*. New York: Garland, 2000.

The Concise Columbia Encyclopedia, ed. Judith Levey and Agnes Greenhall. New York: Columbia UP, 1983. (Entries on Christopher Wren, 931; St. Paul's Cathedral, 743; Westminster Abbey, 916.)

David, Deirdre. *Rule Brittania: Women, Empire, and Victorian Writing*. Ithaca, NY: Cornell UP, 1995.

Derrida, Jacques. "Structure, Sign and Play in the Discourse of the Human Sciences," *Writing and Difference*, trans. Alan Bass. Chicago: U of Chicago P, 1978. 278-293.

Foucault, Michel. "Truth and Power," trans. Alessandro Fontana and Pasquale Pasquino, rpt. in *The Foucault Reader*, ed. Paul Rabinow. New York: Pantheon, 1984. 50-75.

Friedman, Susan Stanford. *Mappings: Feminism and the Cultural Geographies of Encounter*. Princeton UP, 1998.

Lee, Hermione. "Virginia Woolf's Essays," in *The Cambridge Companion to Virginia Woolf*, ed. Sue Roe and Susan Sellers. Cambridge UP, 2000. 91-108.

McVicker, Jeanette. "'Six Essays on London Life': A History of Dispersal," Part I. *Woolf Studies Annual* 9 (2002): 143-65.

Oxford Dictionary of National Biography Online. 1999-2003. Oxford UP. 22 September 2003. <http://www.oup.com/oxforddnb.info/> (Entry on Leslie Stephen.)

Spanos, William V. *America's Shadow: An Anatomy of Empire*. Minneapolis, MN: U of Minnesota P, 2000.

Squier, Susan Merrill. *Virginia Woolf and London: The Sexual Politics of the City*. U of North Carolina P, 1985.

Talking Cities Online. July-August 2003. <http://www.talkingcities.co.uk/london_pages> (Entry on Marble Arch.)

Whitworth, Michael. "Virginia Woolf and Modernism," in *The Cambridge Companion to Virginia Woolf*, ed. Sue Roe and Susan Sellers. Cambridge UP, 2000. 146-163.

Wieber, Amy B. "Reweaving Pandora: Mary Shelley, Romantic Hellenism and

Re-Vision," unpublished dissertation. Department of Comparative Literature, SUNY Binghamton, Binghamton, NY. 1999.

Woolf, Virginia. *Between the Acts*. 1941. New York: Harvest/HBJ, 1969.

———. *The Common Reader*, ed. Andrew McNeillie. 1925. New York: Harvest/HBJ, 1984.

———. *The Diary of Virginia Woolf*, 5 vols., ed. Anne Olivier Bell, asst. by Andrew McNeillie. New York: Harvest/HBJ, 1978.

———. *The Essays of Virginia Woolf*, 3 vols., ed. Andrew McNeillie. New York: Harvest/HBJ, 1986.

———. *The London Scene: Five Essays by Virginia Woolf*. New York: Random House, 1975. Rpt. Of *The London Scene*, first published by Frank Hallman, New York, 1975.

———. "Six Essays on London Life,"*Good Housekeeping* magazine. London: The National Magazine Company, Ltd. 1931-1932.

———. *Three Guineas*. 1938. New York: Harvest/HBJ, 1966.

Vita Nuova: Courtly Love and Lesbian Romance in *The Years*

Patricia Cramer

> I hope to compose concerning her what has never been written in rhyme of any woman.
> Dante Alighieri.
> *The Vita Nuova* (99)

> ...I see a porpoise in a shop window at Christmas and pearls and a pink coat—a jersey was it?—anyhow you wore gaiters, and it was the sight of the gaiters ... that inspired Orlando—the gaiters and what lies beyond.
> Virginia Woolf (*L5* 157)

Between 1931 and 1937, as she composed her novel *The Years*, Virginia Woolf was reluctantly accepting the demise of her love affair with Vita Sackville-West. In 1935, Woolf writes, "I could here analyze my state of mind these past 4 months, & account for the human emptiness by the defection of Vita; Roger's death; & no-one springing up to take their place" (*D4* 287). Vita's "defection" was partly due to her preoccupation with Gwen St. Aubyn, but also due to Vita's increasing preference for solitude and gardening. During the thirties, Vita became more withdrawn from social life preferring to spend her time restoring Sissinghurst Castle, working on her gardens, and writing in her tower (Glendinning 265; 285).[1] In fact, Woolf's favorite jokes about Vita during the 1930s as she adjusted to the loss of their intimacy, depict Vita alone, writing in her tower, surrounded by pigeons. In 1933, Woolf writes about Vita, "do let her

---

[1] Gwen's Catholicism and its influence on Vita's writing and thinking may have inspired Woolf's challenge to Christianity in *The Years* (Glendinning 265). And, as Vara Neverow pointed out to me, the play on Vita's name in Dante's title could not have escaped Woolf. For an excellent review of Woolf's views on and revision of the sacred in the companion piece to *The Years*, *Three Guineas*, see Froula. Lipking offers an excellent discussion of Woolf's characters' tendencies to make gods of others in this novel. References to Christianity, uncharacteristic of Woolf, appear throughout the novel. Members of the Pargiter and Rigby families turn to the language of hell and damnation when they want to express rage at patriarchal institutions such as war and the nuclear family (284; 330; 417); recall the devil (245; 285) as well as the Christian father and son (229); visit St. Paul's (226) and read prayer books (244). Eleanor reads Renan's *Life of Jesus* (150), quotes Dante's Canto 14 from *The Divine Comedy* (212), and wonders about the original meaning of the phrase "God is Love" (154). The significant visionary characters in the novel—Kitty, Eleanor, and Sara—are subject, like Dante's poet/lover in the *Vita Nuova*, to disorienting swoons and faints which prefigure shifts in imaginative vision and ecstatic experiences (267; 381; 384; 365).

come down from her rose-red tower where she sits with thousands of pigeons cooing over her head" (*L5* 266).

Although Vita had had other love affairs—for example, with Mary Campbell and Hilda Matheson—Vita's relationship with Gwen inaugurated a breach between Vita and Virginia that the other affairs had not.[2] In 1936, Woolf writes about Vita to Dame Ethel Smyth: "I don't think she will ever come back, wholly: I think G. [Gwen St Aubyn] answers to something deeper in her than I ever did" (*L6* 4). This time there was a finality to the withdrawal of Vita's romantic interest in Virginia that Woolf, reluctantly, learned to accept. In a diary entry in 1935 Woolf writes, "[m]y friendship with Vita is over. Not with a quarrel, not with a bang, but as ripe fruit falls" (*D4* 287). Vita had been lover, confidante, and muse for Woolf for about ten years: according to Woolf's sister, Vanessa Bell, Vita was "the person Virginia loved most…outside her family" (474). In her letters and diaries, Woolf repeatedly attests to the sensuous joy she found only with Vita. In 1926, she describes to Vita "*a sensation I get only from you…physically stimulating, restful at the same time I feel supple and anointed*" (*L3* 540; emphasis added). As late as January 1933, Woolf complains that when Vita is gone, "a whole patch of my internal globe [becomes] extinct" (*L5* 148).

Despite her characteristic irony when speaking of Vita and Gwen, Woolf's hurt and grief were considerable. In 1937, she describes herself as "hardened and battered" by love (*L6* 194); and after pointedly describing to Vita "[t]wo Comma butterflies…copulating on the cabbages," Woolf complains, "[a]ll the romance of my life is to me centred…in a Red underwing sipping sugar on a beech tree" (*L5* 226). But as Woolf reluctantly began to accept her loss of intimacy with Vita as unavoidable, her letters, as well as Vita's, began to focus on fond remembrances of their former passion. In 1935, Virginia asks to see Vita, adding, "[m]ere affection—to the memory of the porpoise in the pink window" (*L5* 370). Woolf's 1937 letter to Vita confirms her determination not to let even infidelity overshadow the happy memories of their former love: "Why, 'once' Virginia?…Just because you choose to sit in the mud in Kent and I on the flags of London, thats no reason why love should fade is it? Why the pearls and the porpoise should

---

[2] Vita's earlier affair with Mary Campbell may have inspired *Orlando*: In 1927, Woolf writes to Vita, "If you've given yourself to Campbell, I'll have no more to do with you, and so it shall be written, plainly, for all the world to read in *Orlando*" (*L3* 431). However, in contrast with *The Years*, Woolf's novelistic response in *Orlando* is playful and seductive, suggesting a confidence in 1927 that her jealousy and seduction would matter to Vita. See Hankins for an excellent reading of *Orlando* as lesbian seduction. Four letters from Virginia to Vita recently discovered hidden in a drawer in Vita's writing table suggest that Virginia's sexual expectations in regard to Vita survived into the thirties. A letter dated August 8, 1938 complains "it was nice having you …even in its less pronounced form" (Woolf, "Four Letters" 2).

vanish" (*L6* 186)? In 1940, Virginia wrote to Vita, "You have given me such happiness" (*L6* 424); and Vita to Virginia, "Darling, thank you for my many happy hours with you. You mean more to me than you will ever know" (Sackville-West 437).

This end to the most important romance of her life prompted Woolf to write *The Years* as a memoir of her love life: a retrospective elegy to her beloved, Vita, and a reassessment of the impact of lesbian desire on her self-development and her vocation as an artist.[3] Virginia Woolf initially intended *The Years* to be "about the sexual life of women" (*D4* 6) and the drafts as well as published version reflect her preoccupation with sex and romance during its composition. The opening "1880" chapter of *The Years* introduces this theme by depicting a range of "in love" experiences typical for people of Woolf's generation and class: Delia and Milly's shameful and competitive interest in their neighbor's son; the Colonel's hidden affair with Mira; Eleanor's unacknowledged attraction to Miss Levy's daughter; Kitty's secret romantic attachment for Miss Craddock; and the self-denying homoerotic triad: Edward, Ashley, and Gibbs. Presiding over all these underground sexual feelings is the "approved" romantic liaison—the marriage of the heroic male (the Colonel) and his "beloved," his dying wife, Rose.

Again and again in the novel, the Pargiters and Rigbys question the meaning of sexual love in their own and each other's lives. Eleanor wonders "why do men think love affairs so important?" (155); later comparing the flirtation between Sarah and the homosexual Nicholas with the "old ways of love," she decides: "they are aware of each other; they live in each other; what else is love?" (370). Kathleen Phillips suggests that when Rose buys flowers and Sarah takes them (*TY* 174), Woolf revises a heterosexual dating ritual (30). Sarah begs her mother, Eugenie, to tell her the "true [love] story" of her youth (143), and in the final chapter, Peggy asks Martin what being "in love" (356) meant to his generation. "We were all in love" he brags, and then Woolf has her private joke when Martin, trying to impress Peggy on the abilities of his generation to "fall in love" with the opposite sex gives the homosexual Edward ("he was very much in love" [357])[4] as the exemplar of what being "in love" meant to his generation. In the last lines of the novel, Patrick recalls "buying roses for a certain lady" and Delia and Eleanor silently recall old romances (433).

Woolf's exploration of the meaning of sexual love in *The Years* necessarily confronts the lack of adequate literary models for her lesbian love story. Woolf's

---

[3] See also Cramer, "Pearls" on *The Years* as lesbian memoir.
[4] According to Jeri Johnson, in the ho lograph Edward as well as Nicholas is homosexual (318). Consider also Edward's fondness for undergraduates. The holograph is similarly more overt about Rose's lesbianism than the published version: Maggie speaking to Eleanor says, "Besides if Rose loved anybody...it wasn't a man....Look at her

alienation from available heterosexual romance traditions in "real life" and in the arts was so thorough-going that she has often been misread as indifferent to or frightened of sex entirely. The following comment is typical of Woolf: "What I meant was that *sexual* relations bore me.... oh but how dull, how monotonous, and reducing its young men and women to what abysses of mediocrity!" (*L*3 136; emphasis in original). Similarly, in response to Ralph Partridge's confidences about his love affair with Dora Carrington she writes, "[h]is stupidity, blindness, callousness, struck me more powerfully than the magic virtues of passion"; & how, having made those convenient railway lines of convention, the lusts speed along them, unquestioning" (*D*2 177; 78). Woolf was particularly turned off by sexual behavior which split the mind off from the body, once raving to Roger Fry: "and how anyone can be such a fool as to think the mind dull compared with the body, Lord knows. Im sure I live more gallons to the minute walking once round the square than all the stockbrokers in London caught in the act of copulation" (*L*3 386). Heterosexual romantic passions in the arts left her similarly cold: "I went to Tristan the other night; but the love making bored me" (*L*3 56).

However, all this boredom and contempt typical of Woolf's attitude toward heterosexuality entirely disappear in her reactions to lesbian lust and romance. In Woolf's responses to Vita Sackville-West, for example, we find all the fascination ("These Sapphists *love* women; friendship is never untinged with amorosity" [*D*3 51; emphasis in original]), romance ("I have a perfectly romantic and no doubt untrue vision of you in my mind—stamping out the hops in a great vat in Kent—stark naked, brown as a satyr, and very beautiful" [*L*3 198]); and lust ("If you could have uncored me—you would have seen every nerve running fire—intense but calm" [*L*3 306-07])—missing in her autobiographical and fictional representations of heterosexual lust and love.

Additionally, Woolf's alienation from heterosexual romance was more profound than a simple lack of interest in men as potential lovers, for, politically motivated as she was, Woolf seems to have decided to alter the aims and emotional bases of sexual desire itself. A 1935 diary entry suggests that she was thinking about how to undo the conjunction of sexuality and violence central to war and romance traditions during the composition of *The Years*. Shortly after

---

clothes," she said. And her hands" (*H*4: 69). In this essay the published section of Woolf's draft is cited as *The Pargiters*; all references to the unpublished drafts are to the Berg holograph, [Virginia Woolf. *The Years*: the Pargiters:] a novel-essay based upon a paper read to the London, National Society for Women's Service. Holograph. M42. The Berg Collection of English and American Literature at The New York Public Library. References to the unpublished draft are cited as *H*, followed by volume and page number. For further discussion on Woolf's parody of British sexual hypocrisies, see Nelson-McDermott.

an argument with her nephew, Julian, about why men need war, she asks, "whether one can give people a substitute for war...*Lust & danger*. Cant cut them out at once. Must divert them on to some harmless object. But what. Some fantasy must be provided...I made up some of my Professions book" (*D4* 307; emphasis added).

In *The Years*—an outgrowth of the "professions book" she alludes to in response to Julian's rationales for war—Woolf rejects the merging of sex, violence, and heroism Julian falls for, and self-consciously constructs sexual fantasies attached to more life-affirming and liberating impulses. Toward this aim, Woolf parodies heterosexual romance conventions throughout her book and she engages critically with the "giants" of heterosexual romance traditions: most apparently Jane Austen, Richard Wagner, and Dante.[5] For example, Joanna Lipking has pointed out that Woolf may be revising a scene from Austen's *Emma* when she replaces the heterosexual coupling celebrated there with the "romance" between Sarah and the homosexual Nicholas: when Sarah rises to dance with Nicholas her words "I will dance with you" (371) nearly repeat Emma's words to Mr. Knightley on a similar occasion (Lipking 142). As Jane Marcus notes, in *The Years* Woolf "takes the structure and technique" of Wagner's *Ring of the Nibelung* in order to illustrate how "Wagnerian ideas, with their own superman hero and anti-Semitism...heralded the doom of the nineteenth and twentieth centuries" ("Greek Drama" 295). In Kitty's confused sexual responses to Wagner's *Siegfried* Woolf shows how "great art" contributes to the eroticization of violent men. The dwarf's "hammer, hammer, hammer" intermingled with the music which "exalted her" (183) accompanies the entrance of the lover/warrior, Siegfried. The seductive music eroticizes the heroic Siegfried; the background noise of the hammering of Siegfried's sword reminds us of the violence implicit in that romantic ideal.[6]

---

[5] In *The Years* Woolf engages with another major figure in romantic love literature, Marcel Proust. However, in contrast to her revisionary stance in regard to Austen, Wagner, and Dante, Woolf seems to turn to Proust as ally and "fellow insider" to the travails of unrequited homosexual romantic love. See Cramer, "Pearls."

[6] Leaska points out that originally Alf Carter was George Carter and Woolf may have altered the name to downplay the too obvious reference to George and sexual molestation ("A Reading" 183). The erotic confusion Woolf alludes to in Kitty's sexual memories becomes more complicated when we recall that Vita had a similar adolescent encounter with a farmer's son, Jackie, who nearly raped her (Glendinning 22). In adulthood, Kitty's memory confuses genders and introduces a woman—Margaret Marrable—into this scene of sexual initiation (271). Also, during the thirties Vita wrote and sent to Virginia a poem entitled "The Bull" and Woolf consequently associated Vita herself with this animal: (for example, see *L5* 153). Woolf may be exploring here how lesbian desire becomes interconnected with available sexual norms based on the eroticization of dominance and

The most prominent figure in Woolf's engagement with the founders of romance conventions in the arts is Dante.[7] Woolf greatly admired Dante's craft: in a 1930 diary entry on reading Dante she writes, "this makes all writing unnecessary. This surpasses 'writing' as I say about Shre [Shakespeare]" (*D3* 313). Woolf could recognize in Dante imaginative and verbal gifts equal to her own; but as an atheist, lesbian, socialist, and feminist, she could hardly share Dante's views, especially his predilection for passive women, chastity, Christianity, and empire. Nevertheless, given her focus in *The Years* on romantic love and memoir, Dante's *Vita Nuova*—"the classic...of idealized lyric love" (Briffault 184-85)—is an appropriate model for Woolf's revisionary project. Like the troubadours and Dante, Woolf is most concerned in *The Years* with exploring and redesigning the nature and meaning of romantic love. As Robert Pogue Harrison notes, the "core" [of the *Vita Nuova*,] is pervaded by a simple, yet obsessive question: "What is love?" (38); *The Years* is preoccupied with this same question. By rewriting Dante and the courtly love tradition he perpetuates, Woolf revises one of the most influential ideals of western culture. As Meg Bogin points out, "[t]his medieval poetry...continues to determine a good portion of the Western world of feeling. Through Dante's Beatrice, love was proclaimed the supreme experience of life, and the quest for love, with the lady as its guiding spirit, became the major theme of Western literature" (10). As Susan Noakes notes, Dante aims in the *Vita Nuova* to elaborate "a new poetic model" based on the "poetic and...theoretical integration of divine and human love" ("Hermeneutics" 41). In *The Years*, Woolf parodies Dante and the romantic love tradition he perpetuated and she elaborates "a new theory of love" that is secular and lesbian-based.

In the following discussion I juxtapose Woolf's version of romantic love with Dante's partly in order to trace the considerable influence of the *Vita Nuova* on the novel. However, even when these juxtapositions rely on comparisons that

---

submission. For excellent discussions of sexuality in *The Years*, see Gottlieb, Phillips, Squire and, especially, Sears.

[7] Although Woolf seems to have read Dante periodically throughout her writing career, as early as 1917 (*D1* 84), the majority of references to reading Dante occur between 1931 and 1937 during the composition of this novel (for example, *D4* 264; 291; 320); she was reading Renan's *Life of Jesus* and the *New Testament* at the same time (*L5* 362). The Library of Virginia and Leonard Woolf held in Manuscripts, Archives and Special Collections at Washington State University Library contains a copy of the *Vita Nuova*, translated by Charles Eliot Norton and published in 1867. See Comstock; Leaska, "A Reading"; Lipking; Marcus, "Greek Drama, Domestic Novel." Louise A. DeSalvo notes that Woolf's comment in a reading notebook indicating her intentions to write a story about Dante and "what happens to the mind" was probably written in 1930 and refers to *The Years* (139).

are not indisputably incidences of direct influence or imitation on Woolf's part, I carry through with the comparison in order to more fully articulate the significance of the differences between them. As Sara Sturm-Maddox notes, in the *Vita Nuova*, Dante sustains a close relationship with the tradition which preceded him, courtly love, in order to highlight the novelty of his own love experience and poetic model of romantic love. Following Woolf's lead, I place her romantic ideals beside Dante's for similar reasons: in order to highlight the inadequacies of romance conventions to express lesbian love passion, and to accentuate what is new in her experiences and fictional representations of lesbian romance.

Woolf herself invites this extended comparison of the *Vita Nuova* and *The Years* by sustaining a close dialogue with Dante and Christianity throughout the novel. For example, Woolf's draft indicates that she initially intended that the structure for this novel would more overtly imitate the *Vita Nuova* than the final version. *The Pargiters*, the published version of her first draft, alternates essay commentaries with narrative passages (Leaska, "Introduction"). This original plan may have been borrowed from Dante's *Vita Nuova*, which was written as a series of poems accompanied by essay commentaries. At times, Woolf borrows incidents and lines directly from the *Vita Nuova*. For example, in the holograph, Woolf blames Elvira's (renamed Sara in the published version) damaged shoulder on the "god of love"—a clear reference to this figure, who appears to Dante's poet/lover in the *Vita Nuova* as the representative of courtly love. Thus, in the holograph we find: "the god of love forced me out of his arms," says Elvira, "down the kitchen stairs—...naturally she dropped me." Maggie explains that a nurse had dropped the infant Elvira to race down the stairs to greet her lover, "the bootmaker" (*H* 3: 134).

In the published version, Woolf takes one of Dante's lines for Beatrice's grandiose walks and rephrases it. In the *Vita Nuova* we read: "when she walked down the street people ran to see her;...Crowned and *clothed with humility*, she would go her way, displaying no pride at what she saw and heard. Often people said, when she had passed: 'This is not woman; this is one of the fairest angels of Heaven.' And others said, 'She is a miracle; blessed be the Lord who can create such marvels!'" (75-6; emphasis added). In Woolf's version—Dante's "clothed with humility" becomes Kitty's "clothed in starlight" (187): when Kitty enters the suffrage meeting "[e]verybody looked up" (176); as Sara recalls it, "[t]here were pigeons cooing...And then a *wing darkened the air*, and in came Kitty *clothed in starlight*; and sat on a chair" (187; emphasis added). Woolf's "wing darken[ing] the air" echoes Dante's references to the portents of Beatrice's death when he saw "the sun grow dark and stars turn to such a colour that I thought they were weeping" (65). Woolf's deflated version of Dante's scenario—she "sat on a chair"—is typical of her ironic repetitions of heterosexual love norms: she both embraces and steps back from the grandiosity claimed for sexual love by her predecessors. In the holograph, Woolf seems to be actually recalling the lines from the *Vita Nuova* from memory. Sara tries to find the words to describe Kitty's entrance to the suffrage meeting: "[a]nd she came in like *starlight hid with jewels*"; and later "and she came in like *starlight clothed with*...I can't remember how it goes..." (*H* 4: 65; 67 emphasis added).

In *The Years*, Woolf's most pervasive engagement with Dante's love ideal occurs through her parody of Dante's beloved, Beatrice.[8] In *The Years*, Woolf links Beatrice with the dreaded "Angel in the House"; she mocks Dante's "pallid...lady lying dead and cold" (69), and elevates her own "arrogan[t]" (*D3* 380), "passionate" (*L3* 303), and "divinely lovely" (*L3* 86) beloved, Vita, in her place. Toward this end, Woolf has filled *The Years* with caricatures of the virginal beloved, modeled on the silent lady of the troubadours and the enervated Beatrice. There is the "placid, smiling portrait of their mother [Rose Pargiter]" which reappears throughout the novel (150); the Princess of Wales (96); Queen Alexander ("[s]he had a face like a flower petal" [160]); Edward's Antigone ("in the white and blue dress" [51]); Queen Anne (227); and the "cadaverous statue" of a "woman in nurse's uniform holding out her hands" (336). When Sara refuses to play the lady "waving a white handkerchief for a knight in armour" (287), and when Renny and North mock Queen Alexandra as "the face that launched a thousand ships" (389), Woolf applauds their rejection of the muse tradition per-

---

[8] By engaging with Dante, Woolf participates in a widespread modernist dialogue with Dante and his work. As Stuart Y. McDougal notes, Dante is a common presence in the literature of modernist writers, appearing in citations, allusions, imitation, and parody in the work of such contemporaries of Woolf as T. S. Eliot and Ezra Pound. In addition to Pound and Eliot, McDougal mentions Arthur Rimbaud, Paul Claudel, Giuseppe Ungaretti, Osip Mandelstam, Eugenio Montale, Yeats, Beckett, Wallace Stevens, and Auden (but not Woolf) in his list of modernist writers engaged with Dante (*Dante Among the Moderns*). See also Mary T. Reynolds, *Joyce and Dante*. According to Kathleen Verduin, writers of Woolf's generation were especially preoccupied with the figure of Beatrice who became for many—for example, E. M. Forster and D. H. Lawrence—a symbol of the bifurcation of body and soul this generation had mostly rejected (226-27). See also Ann Loades on "Dorothy L. Sayers and Dante's Beatrice." Woolf's revision of the troubadour tradition is also in keeping with her modernist peers' preoccupation with revitalizing and revising this tradition (most notably T. S. Eliot, William Butler Yeats, and Ezra Pound). McDougal points out that this generation of writers responded to an outburst of European scholarship on the troubadours published in the late nineteenth and early twentieth centuries. This scholarship regarded Provençal poetry as the first European literature in the vernacular and as the origin of modern European poetry (*Ezra Pound and the Troubadour Tradition* 4-5). Thus in rewriting courtly love conventions, Woolf revises the foundations of western literature. See also Saarriluoma on Woolf's narrative innovations in *The Years*.

petuated by Dante and the synthesis of sexual love and war romanticized in courtly love conventions.

The funniest satire on Dante's Beatrice is Woolf's comic representation of Edward Pargiter's Dante-like beatification of his cousin, Kitty Rigby (51). In the essay section Woolf omitted from the published version, she explains that Edward "forms[s] an ideal of womanhood" to repress his sexual feelings because he is more attracted to his classmate, Jevons, than to Kitty. Here, Woolf recognizes the repressed homoeroticism some critics have identified in Dante's eroticization of a dead woman and preoccupation with male figures—mortal and divine.[9] Edward's idealized fantasy of Kitty allows him "not to desire [women] but to produce something which their spirit...the spirit of all that was holy & pure and lovely...would reward" (*Pargiters* 67-68).

Like Woolf's *The Years*, the autobiographical inspiration for Dante's *Vita Nuova* is the loss of the beloved. Most scholars agree that Dante composed his love memoir between 1292-94, shortly after the death of Beatrice, the woman he met and fell in love with when he was just nine years old (Barolini 24). Framed as a retrospective memoir of his love for Beatrice, the *Vita Nuova* traces Dante's gradual realization of Beatrice's meaning for his poetic and spiritual life. Looking back on the emotional excesses of his youth, Dante recognizes how much his early experiences and lyric expressions of romantic love were influenced by courtly love, a tradition he later rejected. Although courtly love originated and flourished as a literary convention in twelfth century France, it was extremely popular in Dante's region, Tuscany, during his lifetime (Collins 20).[10] Like the troubadour poets he imitates, Dante celebrates the transformative and ennobling powers of romantic love by singing the praises of his beloved. The courtly love conventions—the need for secrecy; the submission of the loyal lover to his unattainable beloved; the love anguish; and the obsessive enumeration of their scarce love contacts—are all present in Dante's love lyrics. However, as Sara Sturm-Maddox notes, the *Vita Nuova* is less an imitation of courtly love than a "systematic testing of the sentiments and solutions" (130) of the courtly

---

[9] On the homoeroticism in Dante's love triangle, Beatrice-Dante-God, see Holsinger and Camille. On Bruno Latini and Dante's views on sodomy see also Della Terza and Noakes, "Other Sodomites."

[10] See Barolini for an excellent summary of Dante's relationship to the courtly love movement of his time. It is a commonplace among Dante scholars that love as desire (or to borrow Marc Cogan's terminology "appetition") informs both the *Vita Nuova* and *Divine Comedy*. As Cogan notes, "it is desire in the guise of a journey that gives shape to the overall narrative of the *Commedia*" (286). In *The Years*, Woolf puts love as desire at the center of her social critique as well. For further discussions of Dante's views on sexual love see also Boyde, and Lewis.

lover role. Sturm-Maddox further notes that the *Vita Nuova* is "a coherent story of the poet's attempt to coordinate his affective experience and his poetic vocation, and for that vocation the tradition itself is the essential context" ("Transformations" 131).

As Bogin notes, the influence of medieval romantic love on the "Western world of feeling" is pervasive: "[r]omantic love—love as perpetual torment, as ennobling force, as obstacle course (making its way around barriers of distance, class, and marriage)...is so much a part of our culture that it almost seems biologically determined" (18). Woolf mistrusted sexual emotions—even her own: "loves the devil" she writes to Dame Ethel Smyth in reference to her feelings of jealousy and longing for Vita during the thirties (*L5* 379). Yet despite her profound alienation from romantic love norms, when she was "in love," Woolf found herself experiencing all the torments, longing, and vitalizing emotions ennobled by the very tradition she mistrusted. Thus, Woolf's attempts to coordinate her lesbian love experiences with her political and aesthetic values also necessarily occur within the context of the romance traditions she inherited. Therefore, by juxtaposing the *Vita Nuova*, Woolf's autobiographical love writings, and *The Years*, I am not consistently insisting on a simple pattern of influence with Dante at the head. Instead, I suggest that Woolf participates in and engages with romance traditions in her private life as well as fiction—just as Dante repeats and revises the courtly love conventions he inherited in the *Vita Nuova*.

The lesbian autobiography in *The Years* becomes readily apparent when sections of Woolf's letters and diaries addressed to Vita are juxtaposed with comparable sections of the novel. These autobiographical sketches reflect her complex sense of herself as a lover—both of and outside her culture's constructions of sexual emotion—as well as a thorough familiarity with literary romance traditions. As the letters to and about Vita suggest, Woolf was making up her lesbian love story as she lived it, often conjuring up images of ancient romances—like "coloured windows, red towers, moats, and swans" (*L5* 153)—when speaking to her lady love. Through self-parody and, at times, unabashed sentimentality, Woolf's autobiographical writings as well as fiction explore the ways in which desire, culture, and narrative are interconnected. Through ironic repetitions of her culture's romantic love norms, Woolf assimilates and transforms those norms to create a romantic love ideal and lesbian love classic of her own.

For example, Woolf seems to have assumed the role of the male courtly lover in relation to Vita, playfully (but with serious intent) exploring the erotic possibilities and limitations of that role in her personal life and in her fiction. In the courtly love tradition, much is made of the superiority of the beloved and inferiority of the knightly lover in relation to her. She is usually—like Vita—a married woman from a social class higher than the lover-knight. The courtly lover's commitment to keeping the identity of his beloved secret may also have appealed to Woolf's delight in coding references to her beloved muse, Vita, into her fiction.[11] The language of courtly love sustains the feudal master/slave dynamic of class inequality. In the *Vita Nuova*, Dante translates the superiority of the beloved from courtly love into spiritual rather than class terms, and he transposes the class servility of courtly love to Christian humility; but the sado-masochistic posturing of courtly love remains, for Dante, intact. For example, on the superiority of his beloved, Beatrice, Dante writes "and I saw that in all her ways she was so praiseworthy and noble that indeed the words of the poet Homer might have been said of her: '[s]he did not seem the daughter of a mortal man, but of a god'" (30).

Woolf's delight in Vita's class superiority was integral to their erotic play. She liked to call Vita "my aristocrat" (*L*3 155), and Vita's class arrogance—unlike Beatrice's humility—was part of what made Vita so attractive to her. For example, in 1923, when Woolf describes the first time she met Vita, we can see how Vita's aristocratic arrogance and her Sapphic allure were intertwined in Woolf's erotic imagination: "[s]nob as I am, I trace her passions 500 years back, & they become romantic to me, like old yellow wine" (*D*2 235-36); and in 1924, Woolf writes, "…I like her being an honourable, & she is it; a perfect lady, with all the dash & courage of the aristocracy" (*D*2 313). In *The Years*, Kitty and Eleanor act out the rituals of Virginia and Vita's courtship and love affair. Kitty embodies the "authoritative manner" (421) Woolf admired in Vita; and other parallels between Kitty and Vita are numerous and easy to find: both drive huge motor cars; both garden; appear frequently accompanied by dogs; and Kitty, like Vita, loses an estate because, as a woman, she cannot inherit the land she loved. Like Vita, Kitty increasingly withdraws in mid-life to her country home, and she chooses a marriage that in her mother's words "could give her what she wants—scope" (83). In the novel, Eleanor (that "queer old bird" [328]) and Kitty ("one of those well-set-up rather masculine old ladies" [393]) play out all the recognizable pathos and comedy of two lesbians in love but closeted to each other and themselves. Kitty pursues Eleanor and Eleanor is drawn to her—but neither seems aware of the sexual possibilities of their mutual attraction.

At the same time, this courtship of the closet reenacts Woolf's fondest memories of her courtship and romance with her lover, Vita. So, in Eleanor's awe at Kitty's magnificence, Woolf playfully recalls her own love-struck—though real-

---

[11] For fuller discussions of Woolf's coding methods see Cramer, *Lesbian Readings*, esp. Cramer, "Introduction" and "Pearls"; Krystyna Colburn; Leslie Hankins; Annette Oxindine; Ruth Vanita; Janet Winston.

ly humble—admiration of Vita's aristocratic charms. Looking admiringly at Kitty, Eleanor muses, "[t]hat's the manner I like...authoritative, natural...[t]he great ladies' manner" (177). And in the letters, we find nearly the identical words: "[t]hen there was Vita, very striking...but rather awkward, forced indeed to take her stocking down and rub her legs with ointment at dinner...I like this in the aristocracy: I like the legs; I like the bites; I like the complete arrogance and unreality of their minds...." (*L3* 380). However, for Dante, this sense of inferiority on the part of the lover is much more serious, and the courtly-lover's self-abasement is key to the erotic charge of the love-relation. For example, when Dante writes of love, the master and slave dynamic is invariably present: for example, "[s]o long have I been subject to Love's sway / And grown accustomed to his mastery..." and "[t]hus by her merest glance I am *unmanned*, / And pride so *humbled*, none could understand" (78; emphasis added).

In contrast, Woolf liked to exaggerate the class differences between her and Vita, flirtatiously but in ways that are not seriously self-abasing. In 1926, for example, Woolf's pretense for not coming to dinner at Knole uses the same excuse Eleanor gives to Kitty in the novel. In a letter to Vita we find, "so I don't see how I can come to Knole, all in holes, without a pin to my hair or a stocking to my foot. You'd be ashamed" (*L3* 311). But in a follow-up letter, Woolf makes it clear that her expressed inferiority is merely a joke: "I was partly teasing. I don't mind being dowdy, dirty, shabby red nosed middle classed and all the rest—its only a question when and how—I do want to see you, I do—I do" (*L3* 313). And in the novel, we find that Eleanor "felt shabby and dowdy compared with Kitty who stood there in full evening dress...flustered and dowdy, as if she were a schoolgirl suddenly" (179). When Kitty asks Martin why Eleanor had not come to her party, he answers "[s]he hasn't the right kind of hairpin" (262).

In courtly love, the beloved appears hopelessly unattainable to the anguished lover and the lady's rejection or inaccessibility is a necessary test to the troubadour's love service which is given without hope of reward. Dante expresses this inaccessibility in terms of Beatrice's unapproachable perfection: "Love says of her: 'How can a mortal thing / Have purity and beauty such as hers?' /...She is the sum of nature's universe. / To her perfection all of beauty tends" (56). Likewise, in Woolf's erotic imagination, Vita's inaccessibility is sometimes a stimulant to Woolf's sexual desire. In 1927, during the early days of their love affair, Woolf writes: "[t]his year you seem to me, imaginatively, more unattainable, more pearled, powdered, [and] white legged...than ever" (*L3* 342). However, during the thirties, as Woolf was writing *The Years*, when Vita became actually less available to Virginia due to her involvement with Gwen, Vita's inaccessibility was no longer so romantic. Nevertheless, though heartbroken, Woolf took this estrangement as an opportunity to manufacture a new romantic fantasy—this time of Vita as the inaccessible lady locked away in her impregnable tower. In 1933, she writes about Vita, "[b]ut do let her come down from her rose-red tower where she sits with thousands of pigeons cooing over her head" (*L5* 266); and in 1934, she complains to Dame Ethel Smyth, "Vita never rings me up; but then she's sitting among the pigeons at the top of the pink tower watching the moon rise between the hop poles" (*L5* 312). Pigeons are a lesbian signature in *The Years*: pigeons herald Kitty's characteristically grand entrance to the suffrage meeting (176) and pigeons circle about Kitty just after her visit to Miss Craddock awakens her lesbian desire and sets her to dreaming about Eleanor (75).

Rejection by the beloved and the subsequent anguish felt by the lover are key to the courtly love experience. Shortly after Beatrice ignores him when he passes her on the street, Dante writes to Beatrice: "[w]ith your companions you make fun of me, / Not thinking, Lady, what the reason is / I a figure in your eyes / When, raising mine, your loveliness I see" (49). Nevertheless, convention dictates that rejection merely stimulate the poet-lover's desire to see her more: "as soon as I imagine her wonderful beauty the desire is so powerful that it utterly destroys anything in my memory that might rise up against it; that is why my past sufferings do not restrain me from trying to see her" (50).

This determined pursuit of the beloved, despite rejection, is humorously dramatized in Kitty's stubborn and book-length attempt to get Eleanor into her car. Here, Woolf indulges in another romantic fantasy as she imagines a role reversal from what was actually happening in her life: perhaps living through Eleanor those now bygone days when she was pursued as well as pursuer—when Vita familiarly picked her up in her "large blue motor car" (*L3* 210). In the following juxtaposition of lines from the letters and novels, we can see how closely this autobiographical memoir, *The Years*, mirrors the ritual rejection and pursuit familiar to loyal lovers and to Woolf during the 1930s.

> For example, in 1931, Woolf complains to Ethel Smyth:
> "Yes, yes; I am still unfortunately attached to the woman I never see; the vision in the fishmongers shop" (*L4* 365).

> In the novel, Kitty complains to Martin when she realizes that Eleanor is not coming to her party:
> "Then why wouldn't she come tonight?" said Kitty (262).

> In 1930, Woolf is reduced to pleading with Vita:
> "But how am I ever to see you...Is an afternoon alone never possible?" (*L4* 240).

> Just as Kitty begs Eleanor, unsuccessfully, to see her again:
> "But must you get out? Do come and see me—do let us meet again soon, Nell." (180)

Like Kitty, Woolf did not easily give up:
"Please come snuffing up my stairs soon...in your red jersey. Please wear your pearls" (*L5* 170).

While in the novel
"[Kitty] wished she saw more of Eleanor...but she never could get her to come and dine. It was always 'Papa's expecting me' or some other excuse, she thought rather bitterly..." (180).

Repeated rejection from Vita does not stop Woolf from asking Vita to bed:
"So to bed. And whats bed without—? And when—? And what—? (*L* 4 356).

And at the very end of the novel, Kitty importunes Eleanor yet again:
"Can't I give you a lift back, Nell?...I've a car waiting...I've a car...(433).

This interchange illustrates how Woolf slips lesbian autobiography into her "realist" narrative so that the lesbian story takes on a narrative life of its own: Woolf's lesbian autobiography, when abstracted from the manifest narrative, tells the story of Woolf's lesbian love history. In a 1926 article entitled "Life and the Novelist," Woolf writes, "the writer's task is to take one thing and let it stand for twenty: a task of danger and difficulty" (45). The lesbian allusions in *The Years* are part of the network of meanings carried by Woolf's allusive metaphors. Thus, at the manifest level of the text, Eleanor and Kitty are simply two cousins fond of each other; at the same time, when the pattern of Kitty's pursuit of Eleanor is lifted out of the "realist" text, the allusion to Woolf's lesbian romance with Vita becomes apparent.

Another example of the narrative autonomy of Woolf's lesbian autobiography in this novel is Eleanor's anxious pacing outside Delia's window in the 1891 section. In the "realist" narrative Eleanor is waiting for Delia to come home to discuss Parnell's death with her. At the same time, Eleanor's pacing beneath the window recalls Woolf's frequent references to Vita locked in her tower and herself as the forsaken lover beseeching Vita "to come down from her rose-red tower" (*L5* 266). Also recalled are romance conventions depicting courtly lovers and their descendants pacing beneath the windows of their beloveds. In this passage, I doubt that the lesbian allusions are intended to depict Eleanor as sexually attracted to her sister, Delia; rather, they carry the plot of the lesbian memoir within the novel without interrupting the manifest narrative.[12]

[12] See also my discussion in "Pearls" (234-36) on the allusions to Proust's *Remembrance of Things Past* in this scene. Leaska also recognizes in *The Years* "the complex scaffolding of the novel's visible structure as fiction, as well as...its barely discernible sub-structure as autobiography" ("A Reading" 186).

Woolf's expression of love anguish is less melodramatic than Dante's, but not less sincere. In the *Vita Nuova*, Dante's poet-lover names himself "[t]he keep and key / [o]f all torments sorrow can combine" (35), and laments "O vos omnes qui transitis per viam, attendite et videte si est dolor sicut meus. [All ye that pass by, behold and see if there be any sorrow like unto my sorrow]" (*Jeremiah* 1:12 qtd in *Vita Nuova* 36). Woolf writes more simply to Ethel Smyth: "I've never a word from V. which rather hurts me, save that I know what is to be has to be. And whats the good of complaining" (*L*5 435). Kitty mirrors Woolf's pain in her reaction to Eleanor's rejection: "[s]he felt hurt. She could not help it" (262).

Dante's "book of...memory" (29) relies on a recall of a few key memories of Beatrice which appear as "sightings: of the nine year old Beatrice in her crimson and white dress; on the day she first greeted him; in church; on the day she denied him her greeting; at the marriage feast; and walking behind Giovanna down the street" (Hollander 1-2). In *The Years*, Woolf similarly recalls romantic rendezvous with her beloved and muse, Vita. Woolf has "filled [*The Years*] with dreams of romantic meetings" with Vita (*L*5 370): for example, Vita's habit of sitting on the floor, leaning on Virginia's knee (384; Sackville-West 119); their trip to Paris (396; *L*3 531); Vita's present of a miniature alpine garden (65; *L*3 210); their journey to see an eclipse in northern England (270-78; "The Sun and the Fish"); and Vita's custom during the heydays of their love affair of picking Virginia up in her "sweeping black car" (433; *L*6 232).

But for the courtly lover, the first meeting is by far the most important and most reverently recalled. As Robert S. Briffault notes, in the works of poet-lovers, "the occasions of their first beholding their ladies are described in minute detail" and typically, the lover dwells repeatedly on a few key details of dress or appearance" (186). As Mark Musa also notes, precious erotic memories such as these appear in the love lyrics of troubadours like "a single crystallized moment...forever repeated" (142). Dante's memory of his famous first meeting with Beatrice has this numinous quality to it: "[she was] dressed in...a decorous and delicate crimson...," he recalls, [t]he moment I saw her I say in all truth that the vital spirit, which dwells in the inmost depths of the heart, began to tremble so violently that I felt the vibration alarmingly in all my pulses, even the weakest of them" (29). For Dante, the crimson garment remains a key erotic stimulant which recurs to him in sexual fantasies associated with Beatrice's death: before she dies—"sleeping, wrapped lightly in a crimson cloth" (31)—and after she dies: "in glory, clothed in the crimson garments in which she first appeared" (94).

Similarly, Woolf dwells repeatedly in her letters and diaries on a "single crystallized moment" in December 1925, when she came upon Vita standing in a fishmonger's shop in Sevenoaks during the first days of their love affair. Reminiscing with Vita about these early days of their love, she writes in 1927,

"Aint it odd how the vision at the Sevenoaks fishmongers has worked itself into my idea of you?" (*L*3 326). And again in 1933, "What fun to see you at the bottom of the stairs, like a fishmongers shop again. Wasn't it about this time of year we saw the porpoise? You wore a pink shirt and pearls. Lord how I remember it!" (*L*5 260) In the novel, the fishmonger's shop memory appears associated with Kitty when she appears at the end of the novel as that "well-dressed lady...like a ball on the top of a fishmonger's fountain." Significantly, Eleanor, looking at Kitty "vibrating in the door" thought "it had all happened before" (369). As Maurice Valency notes, courtly love relied on a "a heightening of sensuality...the concentration of enormous libidinous energy upon such casual contacts as ordinarily have no special erotic significance...[A] glance, a touch of the hand, a word of greeting could be transformed into an event of crucial character" (28). For Woolf, beloved objects associated with Vita which recur in *The Years* are Vita's pearls, which reappear to Eleanor's admiring eye on Mrs. Levy's daughter (30) and on the Princess of Wales (96); and the porpoise which appears in passages suggesting life-renewing forces (47).

To the courtly lover, his lady is first among women—her unique magnificence augmented whenever she walks among "lesser" human beings. She stands out: luminous, transformative, miraculous. In the *Vita Nuova*, Dante's poet/lover enjoys dwelling on Beatrice's effects on crowds:

> ...she ennobles all she looks upon.
> Where e'er she walks, the gaze of everyone
> She draws; in him she greets, such tremors rise,
> All pale, he turns his face away, and sighs,
> Reflecting on his failings, one by one.
> Fleeing before her, wrath and pride are gone....
>   All gentleness and all humility...
> So rare and strange a miracle is she. (60-61)

In the letters Woolf creates similar fantasies of Vita—striding in grandeur— "emerg[ing] like a lighthouse, fitful, sudden, remote" (*L*3 215). In fact, picturing Vita as "a lamp or torch in all this petty bourgeoisdom" (*L*3 204) is one of Woolf's favorite romantic fantasies of Vita. In 1927, Woolf imagines "Vita stalking in her Turkish dress, attended by small boys, down the gallery, wafting them on like some tall sailing ship" (*D*3 125); and similarly, in 1929, "What I think of is arriving and seeing Vita black and scarlet under a lamp with a dog on a string. ...strid[ing] through a crowd of dumpling shaped greasy grey women to meet us" (*L*4 2).

Dante is perhaps most praised by admiring critics for the breadth of his metaphors: the extent to which he is able to make Beatrice—a "mere woman"— mean so many things. Maurice Valency, for example, praises Dante for "devis[ing] a compliment to a woman's eyes in which was involved all the history of the world and the hope of *man*kind" (255; emphasis added). Robin Kirkpatrick commends Dante's ability in the *Vita Nuova* and its sequel, the *Divine Comedy* "to investigate nothing less than the whole of the physical and spiritual universe through the experience of romantic love" (1). Noakes identifies Dante's achievement in the following way: "Dante links together, powerfully, what is disparate: eros, beauty, morality, judgment, religion, philosophy"; and notes how Dante's "integration of disparate forms of social activity" aims "to persuade a broadening readership to affiliate itself with such integration" ("Hermeneutics" 54-55).

Dante achieves this extension of the meaning of Beatrice through a carefully constructed network of parallels between Beatrice and Christ. Fundamental to this comparison are the similarities he creates between the feelings of romantic love and the emotions inspired by the soul's desire for God. Through word play and Biblical allusions, Dante sustains this emotional congruence between romantic and religious ecstasy so that by the end of the *Vita Nuova*, "where simile gives way to metaphor" (Barolini 21), Beatrice seems so "like" Christ that she is almost indistinguishable from him. For example, the "bliss" (31) the poet-lover experiences when first greeted by Beatrice is easily recognized as a boyish response to first love—but is also "like"—according to Dante's verbal directions—the ecstasy of the devout Christian soul in relation to Christ; and Dante's choice of the word "beatitudine" for bliss makes Beatrice a source of divine blessings (Levy 54; Noakes, "Hermeneutics" 51; Singleton 6). By praising Beatrice as "this gracious being," Dante simultaneously suggests feminine and divine grace; when he calls her "la donna de la salute"—"the lady of the greeting," the word "salute" means greeting but is also a word customarily reserved for Christ (Singleton 22). Beatrice appears in Dante's nightmare draped over the arms of the god of love, a posture reminiscent of Christ in the Pieta, because a lover's grief at the thought of the death of the beloved is like the anguish of Christ's mother faced with her son's death (Nolan 42-43). This "underground" resemblance between Beatrice and Christ is, as Singleton notes, "the controlling metaphor of the whole construction" (23) of the *Vita Nuova*. Singleton expresses what is a consensus view among Dante scholars that "[t]he unique achievement of the *Vita Nuova* as a theory of love is the seeing how love of woman may be kept all the way up to God" (114).

Perhaps the fact that Dante's "true love" is male and immortal, and Woolf's is female and alive, accounts for the key differences in their metaphoric expressions of sexual desire: that Dante contrives similitudes that link sexual desire with death, and Woolf just as consciously constructs a language of desire which attaches sexual feelings to life-affirming impulses. For example, long before

Beatrice actually dies, the poet/lover foresees her death and longs for his own. Imagining his "lady lying dead," he is "filled with such serenity at the sight of her," that he can no longer differentiate the yearnings of love from the desire for death: "Sweet Death," he writes, "Come now to me, for I greatly desire you; see, I already wear your colour!" (65-66) Because in Dante's view, a man's love for a mortal woman interferes with his prior allegiance to God, Beatrice's death is a precondition and "final cause" (Barolini 96) of Dante's love quest. Therefore, Dante's erotic imagination evinces a morbidity absent from Woolf's language of love. This is evident when the types of images called up for each by sexual emotions are compared. Dante's erotic preoccupation with Beatrice's death produces nightmare images to his erotic imagination: "women all ...shedding tears," "fiery arrows," and "[b]irds flying in the air...dead" (68).

In contrast, Woolf's metaphoric responses to Vita in her letters produce a plethora of images of natural fertility: "grapes, pink with pearls" (*L3* 224); "beech trees, waterfalls" (*L3* 227); "June nights...roses flowering" (*L3* 275); and "bumble bees and suet pudding" (*L3* 205) are typical. In the following diary entry, we can more closely follow the pattern of Woolf's struggle to find the words to express Vita's "miraculous effect" (*VN* 40) on her:

> Two nights ago, Vita was here; & when she went, I began to feel the quality of the evening—how it was spring coming...I had a tremendous sense of *life beginning*; mixed with that emotion, which is the *essence of my feeling*, but escapes description...& all the doors opening; & this is I believe the moth shaking its wings in me. I then begin to make up my story whatever it is; ideas rush in me. (*D3* 287; emphasis added)

In "The Sun and the Fish," Woolf's discussion of the metaphoric nature of memory can help elucidate her metaphoric strategies in *The Years*. In this essay, she explains the "unexpected logic of memory" as governed by emotional similitudes: "a sight will only survive in the queer pool in which we deposit our memories, if it has the good luck to ally itself with some other emotion by which it is preserved. Sights marry, incongruously, morganatically...and so keep each other alive" (211). Thus, like Dante's, Woolf's metaphors for love are based on similarities in feeling: the ecstasy she feels in Vita's presence is like the joy one feels with "spring coming," and similar to the expansive optimism suggested by "doors opening" and "life beginning." Likewise, Woolf's search for the emotional equivalents for her love passion leads to her "revelation" that for her, sexual feeling is closely aligned with her creative and visionary faculties—that "essence of her feeling"—that inspires fresh ideas and story making.

Perhaps this power of the "in love" experience to generate deep resources of energy, optimism, and fertility which Dante and Woolf say they discovered when they fell in love explains why male poets have spent so much time writing love lyrics in their own self-interest, and why Woolf works so assiduously to redirect women's sexual aims toward more woman-centered and liberating goals. Dante titles his love memoir *Vita Nuova*—a life made new in love—to emphasize the regenerating power of love. However, as Maurice Valency notes, Dante's "New Life...centers on death" (266)—of the woman, not himself. Beatrice's death is the precondition for the *Vita Nuova* and his erotic fantasies dwell longingly on her death even before she has, in fact, died. This assimilation of the life-giving energies of sexual love to death wishes is where Woolf most differentiates herself from Dante and the tradition he perpetuates.

While the violence attached to male sexual impulses was—ideally at least— projected outward against the so-called enemy in courtly love, Dante projects masculine erotic violence more overtly against the woman because Beatrice's death is a precondition for his salvation in relation to a patriarchal god as well as the success of his poetic career. As Singleton notes, "[t]he effects of love on the lover and the praise of the lady belong to the [courtly love] tradition. The death of Beatrice does not" (101). Therefore, in *The Years*, Woolf represents heterosexual passion as dangerous to women because female sexuality driven unquestioningly along the "railway lines of convention" (*D2* 178) usually leads women to share in Beatrice's fate, literally dead like the Pargiters' mother, Rose, or "soul-dead" like Milly and Delia whose degrading marriages illustrate the "rewards" of becoming the beloved chosen by a heroic male.

Woolf perceived that women's desires for sexual love and their yearnings for intellectual freedom were incompatible impulses within a culture in which a dominant man "in love" with a submissive woman is the romantic ideal. As noted earlier, in the letters and diaries, Woolf links lesbian desire with creative and visionary powers through metaphors suggestive of the fertility of nature. In *The Years*, she further extends the power of lesbian desire by adding feminist rage and rebellion to her metaphoric entailments. Alienated by sexual models available to her, Woolf writes her way back into her body by creating a lesbian sexual fantasy which eroticizes rebellion against tyranny, intellectual and creative endeavors, and keeps women focused—through sex and romantic love—on themselves and each other rather than on men. As James Wheelock notes, in the *Vita Nuova*, Dante set himself "the task of reconciling two traditions [courtly and religious love] that were in their purest, unaccommodated states, structurally incompatible" (277). In *The Years*, Woolf reconciles seemingly incompatible traditions as well by reuniting romantic love with feminist aims.

In the *Vita Nuova*, Dante adopts the position of the mature narrator looking back on the exaggerated love feelings of his youth to discover patterns in his relationship to Beatrice not apparent to him at the time. Likewise, in *The Years*,

Woolf adapts Dante's narrative strategy to express the point of view of the experienced lesbian reassessing the meaning of her sexual love for women within the context of her life patterns. In retrospect, Dante redefines Beatrice as a liberating force on his life, the impetus for a new poetic style and his salvation. When Dante's God of Love appears in a dream vision announcing "Ego dominus tuus," he recalls the story of Moses and the liberation of the Jews from Egypt, thus identifying Beatrice as a "figure of deliverance" and romantic love as a "way out of enslavement" (Noakes, "Hermeneutics" 51; see also Scott 19). Similarly in *The Years*, Woolf depicts lesbian desire as a liberating influence, even for closeted lesbians who are not fully conscious of the aims and consequences of their erotic feelings.

For example, Kitty's heart, aglow with lesbian passion, opens up to unacted potentialities in her self and in life following a visit from Miss Fripp: feeling "the glow on her cheek" from Miss Fripp's kiss, Kitty "stand[s] at the open window," dreaming of escape to America. Inspired by the lingering "pleasure" from a woman's kiss, Kitty decides "she didn't want to be a don's wife and live in Oxford forever. No, No, No!" Kitty's rebellious decision is followed by the fertilizing rain, Woolf's metaphor for the regenerating feelings released by lesbian desire attached to feminist aims (60-62). In Kitty's love for her history teacher, Miss Craddock, Woolf reconsiders the influence of her adolescent crush on her Latin teacher, Janet Case, on her erotic and creative imagination. Like Dante, Woolf "links together…disparate forms of social activity"—here, learning and romantic love (55). Just as Dante's poet-lover has difficulty distinguishing between yearnings for love and for death, Woolf's would-be lesbian lover, Kitty, gets her love for learning and for Miss Craddock mixed up. In the *Pargiters* draft, Kitty thinks "that learning was a wonderful thing: or was it that Miss Craddock was a wonderful woman; or was it both together" (102).

The consequences of Kitty's metaphoric imagination are acted out in the published version of this novel. After coming home from her visit to Miss Craddock's, "everything was romantic" to Kitty's adoring eyes. The quickening of lesbian desire Kitty experiences in Miss Craddock's presence once again awakens feminist rage at her entrapment at Oxford, and unconscious lesbian yearnings for her cousin, Eleanor. Kitty thinks, "[b]ut for a moment all [of Oxford] seemed to her obsolete, frivolous, inane. The usual undergraduate in cap and gown with books under his arm looked silly." Just as the fertilizing rain follows Kitty's rebellious thoughts after Miss Fripp's kiss, nature appears once again, this time in the form of the key lesbian signature in this novel—the pigeons—which appear cooing nearby. Kitty's unarticulated lesbian feelings cause her to think, of course, of her beloved, Eleanor: "'I want…What would Nell think of this, she thought'" (74-75).

In a chapter excluded from *The Years*, Eleanor finds herself unexpectedly aroused by a visit to Kitty (see Radin). As Eleanor prepares to leave Kitty's home, Kitty gives Eleanor a flower. In linking flowers with lesbian romance, Woolf participates in a lesbian metaphoric convention which has adapted the longstanding link between flowers and romantic love for lesbian sexual aims. In her lesbian classic, *The Highest Apple*, Judy Grahn identifies the rose as a recurrent image for lesbian eroticism, symbolizing "the vulva with its birthing sexual creative and menstrual/intuitive powers" (93). Woolf frequently compares Vita to flowers, as in 1926 when she writes to Vita: "[t]he flowers have come, and are adorable, dusky, tortured, passionate like you—" (*L3* 303; see also *L3* 275; *D2* 306).[13] In the holograph Kitty also kisses Eleanor, and Eleanor responds with, "[b]ut thats wicked" (*H* 6: 7). Woolf traces the pathway of Eleanor's unconscious lesbian desire—the "tingling, the tension"—that impels her, like Kitty's adolescent emotions, toward forbidden desires and rebellious decisions. Startled by the beauty of Kitty's daughter-in-law she passes on her way out, Eleanor "felt the need to walk off some little quickening of feelings—caused by what? The big room; the staircase; the footman, *the lady in black*" (emphasis added). Sexual feelings send Dante's poet-lover's erotic imagination leaping from images of wailing women to fiery arrows to dead birds and a prostrate Beatrice, and they intensify his loyalty to the Christian male deity and the devaluation of women and the body Dante's version of god demands. In contrast, the trajectory of Eleanor's lesbian desire releases feminist rage at heterosexual norms and male sexual violence against women. Sexual arousal heightens Eleanor's perceptions so that she discovers similitudes between disparate events not previously apparent to her: she disapprovingly connects her parents' "brass bed" with her father's secret affair with Mira and the heterosexual arrogance which would put her homosexual friend, Nicholas, in prison. Once again, similitude gives way to revelation: Eleanor suddenly understands why she cannot walk alone at night (see Radin, *Evolution*, Appendix: 161-79 [Galley F 19-30]).

In these and other passages linking lesbian desire with rebellious feelings, Woolf solicits the power of romantic love to inspire heroic ambitions, what Carl Goldberg has identified as the potential of "passionate yearnings...to vitalize our personality and influence our willingness to pursue the conditions of self-worth in social and political missions" (14). In the *Pargiters* draft, we can see Woolf exploring the interconnections between sexuality, creativity, and heroism. She

---

[13] For further discussion of flowers as lesbian codes see Priscilla Pratt and Paula Bennett. On flowers as lesbian metaphors in Woolf's fiction, see Cramer, "Lesbian Ritual," and Colburn.

complains that men's resistance to women writers talking about their "bodies...their passions" (xxxix) prevents women from fully developing their imaginative potential, while at the same time speaking of women in the professions in heroic terms; she praises them as "explorers" who "discover new lands and...found civilizations" (7), and commends Dame Ethel Smyth as "one of the ice breakers, the gun runners, the window smashers" of her time (xxviii). In the published version of this novel, Woolf more subtly exploits the links between romantic love and heroism central to Dante's notion of the ideal Christian lover and courtly love's poet-knight. Like his troubadour predecessors, Dante writes out of a tradition in which "[l]ove and the noble heart are one thing" (*VN* 59). By synthesizing poet, statesman, warrior, and saint within an ideology of sexual love, Dante and courtly love channel the life energies of sexual feeling into a concept of nobility which keep men focused on each other and masculine aims. In *The Years*, Woolf redefines heroic as well as romantic ideals. In the context of the social forces waged against them, Woolf posits Kitty's refusal to marry an Oxford don and Eleanor's secret ravings as heroic as any deed inspired by a male poet/lover's lady love.

Dante has been described "as a poet concerned with 'directing the will'"—his own and Beatrice's—into absolute obedience to the will of the Father God, what Rachel Jacoff aptly calls "a progress toward the congruence of legitimacy and desire, toward an Edenic situation defined precisely by the identity of the desirable and the permissible" (129). Dante's redirecting of sexual desire culminates in the final lines of Dante's sequel to the *Vita Nuova*, the *Divine Comedy*. Here, Beatrice, seated at the "Eternal Rose," smiles at the poet/lover, turns her eyes back to the "Eternal Fountain," and then disappears for good. Dante prays to Beatrice,

> Preserve in me your great munificence
> so that my soul which you have healed may be
> pleasing to you when it slips from the flesh
> ...And she, so far away,
> or so it seemed, looked down at me and smiled;
> then to Eternal Light she turned once more. (*Paradiso* 368)

Turning toward the "Eternal Light," Beatrice redirects the poet-lover's desire away from her and toward God; subsumed by a masculine metaphor and patriarchal aims, Beatrice's "gaze," as Joy Hambeuchen Potter notes, "remains eternally fixed upon God as its end" (79).

At the very end of *The Years*, in the "Present Day" chapter, Woolf's secular version of Dante's *Paradiso*, Eleanor answers Kitty's lesbian overture—her invitation to give her a ride in the car—with a gesture borrowed from Beatrice's directing of Dante's desire and will toward God. Eleanor does not answer Kitty directly, but points in a direction away from male ideals, represented by the God and the king praised on the nearby gramophone record. In a gesture much like Beatrice's directions to the Dante figure in the *Divine Comedy*, Eleanor answers Kitty's unspoken lesbian desire by directing Kitty's attention toward lesbian aims: "'Listen'...said Eleanor, raising her hand. Upstairs they were playing God save the King on the gramophone; but it was the pigeons she meant; they were crooning" (433). Here, Woolf replaces Dante's god with the pigeons she associated with Vita and the transformative power of lesbian love. As Marianne Shapiro notes, for Dante, "the love of God disembodied from all other loves becomes the unique goal and object" ("Woman Earthly" 152); as Dante "moves through images recorded in memory" (Nolan 53), his metaphoric entailments progressively narrow and sublimate sexual aims to a single male god. In contrast, Woolf's metaphoric associations culminate in Eleanor's open-ended gesture toward a lesbian future, presented by images borrowed from nature—a group of pigeons in flight. Dante severs but Woolf retains erotic ties with the body and nature when she acculturates the mind, rebellious and communal impulses, and the will to create into her lesbian erotic ideal.

By concluding her novel with Eleanor's reversal of Beatrice's final gesture toward Dante's god, Woolf finalizes her break with the erotic and political aims of Dante's love classic, as well as the subsequent romance traditions he helped to found. At the most obvious level, she redefines what makes a woman desirable and worthy of love by rejecting a long-standing male romance tradition which eroticizes passive virgins and punishes independent, sexually active women with death or social exile. Unlike Dante, Woolf is attracted to independence, authority, and vitality in a woman—qualities epitomized for her by Vita's "gay, gallant and adventurous" ways (*L3* 342). Woolf eroticizes female power, but divorces this erotic tie from power as domination and love as pleasurable humiliation. As Jacoff suggests, for Dante all female desire and perhaps any desire attached to "'specific corporealities'" is transgressive; in contrast, Woolf celebrates her "seductive" (*L5* 425) Vita's "specific corporealities"—especially her legs (*L3* 412). Potter suggests that Dante's disembodying techniques in his treatment of Beatrice are designed to rid himself of a troubling desire for a woman he cannot get (70); Woolf at least works through her disappointment and rage at sexual rejection from her beloved so that she can celebrate Vita as a living presence in her fiction and in "real life." Also, for Dante, and the troubadours, sexual love always refers to something more than itself: the longings and heroic ambitions awakened by the love passion seek visionary experiences that reach far beyond the female beloved. Thus in rewriting Dante and the muse tradition, Woolf not only redefines what makes a woman sexually desirable, but also the springs of creative and visionary desire.[14] If we recall that the *Vita Nuova* is also "a myth about the origin and goal of writing," then in juxtaposition with Dante's love story, Woolf's love memoir can be more easily recognized as her counter-testament: a "praise-song to her beloved" and eulogy to lesbian passion as the origin and aim of her creative achievements. She claims a place for herself and other women writers as living creators of their own desires and of art, and she attaches female desire to more life-affirming and self-sustaining aims than the sadomasochistic eroticism sanctified by Dante and conventional romance.

In juxtaposing Woolf's version of romantic love with Dante's, I have accentuated the differences between them. But of course neither Dante nor Woolf's sexual feelings can be fully accounted for by the opposition I establish by placing her erotic ideals on the side of life and his on death. When Dante "explain[s] what happens to [him] when [he is] near [Beatrice]" (50), we sometimes find that liberating exuberance—that life-enhancing discovery of unsuspected potentialities in the self and the beloved—typical of the best moments of being "in love." Dante's poet-lover experiences "unendurable bliss...excess of sweetness," and "joy, which often exceeded and overflowed"; he explains: "I felt I had not an enemy in the world" and "glowed with a flame of charity which moved me to forgive all who had ever injured me" (41). At times like these, Dante's language of love is almost indistinguishable from Woolf's—as, for example, when she writes shortly after meeting Vita: "But life, life! I long to take you in my arms & crush you out!" (*D2* 238); or when, Peggy, inspired by Eleanor's lesbian dreams, recalls "real laughter, real happiness...and this fractured world was whole, vast, and free" (390). Similarly, Woolf's feelings about Vita could not always be truthfully compared to "sunny patch[es] on a hot bank" (*L3* 440) and "bees[ ] mingling in the asparagus beds" (*L3* 275). For example, Woolf's jealousy over Vita's other love affairs could give rise to fantasies of violence more overt than any found in Dante, as when Woolf warns Vita to be "careful...in [her] gambolling, or [she'll] find Virginia's soft crevices lined with hooks" (*L3* 395); Woolf's 1940 nightmare in which Vita appears with a blackened nose blown up like a pig contains as much "horror and guilt" (*L6* 396) as the dead birds and wailing women in Dante's morbid dream about Beatrice.

Nevertheless, I argue that both Dante and Woolf tend toward this one-sidedness in their fictionalized autobiographies because they are visionaries as well as

---

[14] On women writers revising muse and courtly love traditions see Mary DeShazer and Meg Bogin. See especially Mary J. Carruthers on lesbian writers and the muse. I suggest that Woolf's lesbian romance classic, *The Years*, is a forerunner of and co-visionary within the lesbian feminist literary tradition Carruthers so brilliantly defines in this essay. On Woolf's revision of the courtly love paradigm in *The Waves*, see Marcus, "Britannia Rules *The Waves*."

historians of romantic love: explorers and creators, not simply recorders of their own and their culture's sexual fantasies. As self-conscious myth-makers, Dante and Woolf deliberately construct romantic ideals and metaphoric alliances consistent with their disparate political and aesthetic aims. Thus in Dante's Christ-like Beatrice and Woolf's pigeons, porpoises, and pearls, we find two visionary artists exploiting the power of metaphor to alter as well as describe experiences by "highlight[ing] certain features while suppressing others" when combining "domains of experience" (Lakoff and Johnson 141; 117) normally kept separate. As Terry Hawkes further notes, by "juxtapos[ing] elements whose interaction brings about a new dimension for them...metaphor can reasonably be said to create new reality and to secure that reality within the language where it is accessible to the people who speak it" (43). The troubadour-knights combined "domains of experience"—warfare and heterosexuality—previously kept separate; similarly, Dante subsumes male heterosexual desire within the confines of divine love. Despite these superficial differences, both the courtly love poets and Dante idealize "what love...is" (59) within a social and political context in which male domination is the norm. Dante's superb lyric skills, particularly his exceptional use of the futuristic possibilities of metaphor,[15] have made the *Vita Nuova* a classic within a romance tradition which has seduced many of his own and subsequent generations to misconstrue submission as pleasurable and domination as love.

The Years, like the *Vita Nuova*, is a lyric expression of the "dreamworld of ecstatic love" (Reynolds 11), and an intervention into that "twilight zone between fantasy and reality" (Moller 162) where long-standing cultural patterns are eroticized and acted out. In her sexual metaphors, Woolf commingles female sexual desire with fantasies of freedom and fertility, and creates a language of love more seductive than his. By blurring the boundaries between "facts" and "vision" (*D4* 151-52) in her fictionalized autobiography of her lesbian love life, Woolf has left behind in *The Years* a record of what lesbian love felt like to her, and she creates, through metaphor and fantasy, a lesbian romance classic potentially as influential as the "revolutionary ideology" (Noakes, "Hermeneutics" 55) and "new cult of emotion" (Jaeger 268) inaugurated, respectively, by Dante and courtly love.

---

[15] For an excellent discussion of Dante's use of metaphor to enact fundamental changes in emotions and perception see Marianne Shapiro, "Figurality."

Works Cited

Barolini, Teodolinda. "Dante and the Lyric Past." *The Cambridge Companion to Dante*. Ed. Rachel Jacoff. Cambridge: Cambridge UP, 1993. 14-33.

Barrett, Eileen and Patricia Cramer, eds. *Virginia Woolf: Lesbian Readings*. NY: NYUP, 1997.

Bell, Vanessa. *Selected Letters of Vanessa Bell*. Ed. Regina Marler. New York: Pantheon Books, 1993.

Bennett, Paula. *Emily Dickinson: Woman Poet*. London: Harvester, 1990.

Bogin, Meg. *The Women Troubadours*. New York: Paddington Press Ltd., 1976.

Boyde, Patrick. *Perception and Passion in Dante's Comedy*. Cambridge: Cambridge UP, 1993.

Briffault, Robert S. *The Troubadours*. Bloomington: Indiana UP, 1965.

Brownlee, Kevin. "Dante and the Classical Poets." *The Cambridge Companion to Dante*. Ed. Rachel Jacoff. Cambridge: Cambridge UP, 1993. 100-19.

Camille, Michael. "The Pose of the Queer: Dante's Gaze, Brunetto Latini's Body." *Queering the Middle Ages*. Eds. Glen Burger and Steven F. Kruger. Minneapolis: Minnesota UP, 2001.

Cogan, Marc. *The Design in the Wax: The Structure of the Divine Comedy and Its Meaning*. Notre Dame: Notre Dame UP, 1999.

Carruthers, Mary. "The Re-Vision of the Muse: Adrienne Rich, Audre Lorde, Judy Grahn, Olga Broumas." *The Hudson Review* (Summer 1983): 293-322.

Colburn, Krystyna. "Flowers Between Them: Virginia and Vanessa." *Sixth Annual Conference on Virginia Woolf*. June 13, 1996. Clemson University, Clemson, South Carolina.

Collins, James. *Pilgrim in Love: An Introduction to Dante and His Spirituality*. Chicago: UP, 1984.

Comstock, Margaret. "The Loudspeaker and the Human Voice: Politics and the Form of *The Years*." *Bulletin of the New York Public Library* 80.2 (1977): 252-75.

Cramer, Patricia. "Notes from Underground: Lesbian Ritual in the Writings of Virginia Woolf." *Virginia Woolf Miscellanies: Proceedings of the First Annual Conference on Virginia Woolf*. Eds. Mark Hussey and Vara Neverow-Turk. New York: Pace UP, 1991. 177-88.

——. "'Pearls and the Porpoise': *The Years*—A Lesbian Memoir." In Barrett and Cramer: 222-40.

Dante Alighieri. *La Vita Nuova*. Trans. Barbara Reynolds. New York: Penguin Books, 1969.
——. *The Divine Comedy*. Vol 3. *Paradise*. Trans. Mark Musa. NY: Penguin Books, 1986.
DeSalvo, Louise. "A Note on the Beginning of *The Years*." *Bulletin of the New York Public Library* 80.2 (1977): 139.
DeShazer, Mary K. *Inspiring Women: Reimagining the Muse*. New York: Pergamon Press, 1986.
DiBaetani, John Louis. *Richard Wagner and the Modern British Novel*. London: Associated University Presses, 1978.
Froula, Christine. "St. Virginia's Epistle to an English Gentleman; or, Sex, Violence, and the Public Sphere in Woolf's *Three Guineas*." *Tulsa Studies in Women's Literature* 13.1 (1994): 27-56.
Glendinning, Victoria. *A Biography of Vita Sackville-West*. New York: Alfred A. Knopf, 1983.
Goldberg, Carl. "The Role of Passion in the Transformation of Anti-Heroes." *Journal of Evolutionary Psychology* 9.1-2 (1989): 2-16.
Gottlieb, Laura. "*The Years*: A Feminist Novel." *Virginia Woolf: Centennial Essays*. Ed. Elaine K. Ginsberg and Laura Moss Gottlieb. Troy, New York: Whitson, 1983. 215-29.
Grahn, Judy. *The Highest Apple*. San Francisco: Spinsters Ink, 1985.
Hankins, Leslie. "*Orlando*: 'A Precipice Marked V': Between 'A Miracle of Discretion' and 'Lovemaking Unbelievable: Indiscretions Incredible.' In Barrett and Cramer: 180-202.
Hawkes, Terry. *Metaphor*. London: Methuen and Co, Ltd., 1972.
Harrison, Robert Pogue. "Approaching the *Vita Nuova*." *The Cambridge Companion to Dante*. Ed. Rachel Jacoff. Cambridge: Cambridge UP, 1995. 34-44.
Hollander, Robert. "*Vita Nuova*: Dante's Perception of Beatrice." *Dante Studies* 92 (1974): 1-18.
Holsinger, Bruce W. "Sodomy and Resurrection: The Homoerotic Subject of the *Divine Comedy*." *Premodern Sexualities*. Eds. Louise Fradenburg and Carla Freccero. New York: Routledge, 1995.
Jacoff, Rachel. "Transgression and Transcendence: Figures of Female Desire in Dante's *Commedia*." *Romantic Review* 79.1 (1989): 129-42.
Jaeger, C. Stephen. *The Origins of Courtliness: Civilizing Trends and the Formation of Courtly Ideals—939-1210*. Philadelphia: Pennsylvania UP, 1985.
Kirkpatrick, Robin. *Dante: The Divine Comedy*. Cambridge: Cambridge UP, 1987.

Lakoff, George and Mark Johnson. *Metaphors We Live By*. Chicago: Chicago UP, 1980.
Leaska, Mitchell. "Introduction." *The Pargiters: The Novel-Essay Portion of The Years*. Ed. Mitchell Leaska. New York: Harcourt Brace Jovanovich, 1977.
———. "Virginia Woolf, the Pargeter: A Reading of *The Years*." *Bulletin of the New York Public Library* 80.2 (1977): 172-210.
Levy, Bernard. "Beatrice's Greeting and Dante's 'Sigh' in the *Vita Nuova*." *Dante Studies* 92 (1974): 53-62.
Lewis, R. W. B. "Dante's Beatrice and the New Life of Poetry." *New England Review* 22.2 (2001): 69-80.
Lipking, Joanna. "Looking at the Monuments: Woolf's Satiric Eye." *Bulletin of the New York Public Library* 80.2 (1977): 141-45.
Loades, Ann. "Dorothy L. Sayers and Dante's Beatrice." *Seven: An Anglo-American Literary Review* 10 (1993): 97-106.
Marcus, "Britannia Rules *The Waves*." *Decolonizing Tradition: New Views of the Twentieth Century 'British' Literary Canon*. Ed. Karen R. Lawrence. Urbana: Illinois UP, 1992. 136-62.
———. "*The Years* as Greek Drama, Domestic Novel, and Götterdämmerung." *Bulletin of the New York Public Library* 80.2 (1977): 276-301.
McDougal, Stuart Y. *Dante Among the Moderns*. Chapel Hill: North Carolina UP, 1985.
———. *Ezra Pound and the Troubadour Tradition*. Princeton: Princeton UP, 1972.
Moller, Herbert. "The Social Causation of the Courtly Love Complex." *Comparative Studies in Society and History* 1 (1958-59): 137-63.
Musa, Mark. *Dante's Vita Nuova: A Translation and an Essay*. Bloomington: Indiana UP, 1973.
Nelson-McDermott, Catherine. "Disorderly Conduct: Parody and Coded Humor in *Jacob's Room* and *The Years*." *Woolf Studies Annual* 5 (1999): 79-95.
Noakes, Susan. "Hermeneutics, Politics, and Civic Ideology in the *Vita Nuova*: Thoughts Preliminary to an Interpretation." *Texas Studies in Literature and Language* 32 (1990): 40-59.
———. "From Other Sodomites to Fraud." *Lectura Dantis*. Eds. Allen Mandelbaum et al. Berkeley: California UP, 1998. 213-25.
Nolan, Barbara. "The *Vita Nuova*: Dante's Book of Revelation." *Dante Studies* 88 (1970): 51-76.
Nolan, Barbara. "The Vita Nuova and Richard of St. Victor's Phenomenology of Vision." *Dante Studies* 92 (1974): 35-52.

Oxindine, Annette. "Rhoda Submerged: Lesbian Suicide in *The Waves*." In Barrett and Cramer: 203-221.
Phillips, Kathleen. *Virginia Woolf Against Empire*. Knoxville: Tennessee UP, 1994.
Potter, Joy Hambeuchen. "Beatrice, Dead or Alive: Love in the *Vita Nuova*." *Texas Studies in Literature and Language* 32 (1990): 60-84.
Pratt, Priscilla. *"Then Sunrise Kissed My Chrysalis": Figurations of the Erotic in the Poetry of Emily Dickinson*. Dissertation. February 1991. University of Minnesota.
Radin, Grace. *Virginia Woolf's* The Years: *The Evolution of a Novel*. Knoxville: Tennessee UP, 1981.
———. "'Two enormous chunks': Episodes Excluded during the Final Revisions of *The Years*." *Bulletin of the New York Public Library* 80.2 (1977): 221-51.
Renan, Ernest. *The Life of Jesus*. London: A. L. Humphreys, 1906.
Reynolds, Mary T. *Joyce and Dante: The Shaping Imagination*. Princeton: Princeton UP, 1981.
Saariluoma, Liisa, "Virginia Woolf's *The Years*: Identity and Time in an Anti-Family Novel." *Orbis Litterarum: International Review of Literary Studies*. 54.4 (1999): 276-300.
Sackville-West, Vita. *The Letters of Vita Sackville-West to Virginia Woolf*. Ed. Louise DeSalvo and Mitchell A. Leaska. New York: William Morrow, 1985.
Scott, J. A. "Notes on Religion and the *Vita Nuova*." *Italian Studies* 20 (1965): 17-24.
Sears, Sally. "Notes on Sexuality: *The Years* and *Three Guineas*." *Bulletin of the New York Public Library* 80.2 (1977): 211-20.
Shapiro, Marianne. "Figurality in the *Vita Nuova*: Dante's New Rhetoric." *Dante Studies* 97 (1979): 107-127.
Shapiro, Marianne. *Woman Earthly and Divine in the Comedy of Dante*. Lexington: Kentucky UP, 1975.
Singleton, Charles S. *An Essay on the* Vita Nuova. Cambridge: Harvard UP, 1958.
Squire, Susan. "The Politics of City Space in *The Years*: Street Love, Pillar Boxes and Bridges." *New Feminist Essays on Virginia Woolf*. Ed. Jane Marcus. Lincoln: Nebraska UP, 1981. 216-37.
Sturm-Maddox, Sara. "Transformation of Courtly Love Poetry: *Vita Nuova* and *Canzoniere*." *The Expansion and Transformation of Courtly Literature*. Eds. Nathaniel B. Smith and Joseph T. Snow. Athens: Georgia UP, 1980.
Terza Della, Dante. "The Canto of Brunetto Latini." *Lectura Dantis*. Ed. Allen

Mandelbaum et al. Berkeley: California UP, 1998. 197-213.
Valency, Maurice. *In Praise of Love: An Introduction to the Love-Poetry of the Renaissance*. New York: Octagon Books, 1975.
Vanita, Ruth. "Bringing Buried Things to Light: Homoerotic Alliances in *To the Lighthouse*." In Barrett and Cramer: 165-179.
Verduin, Kathleen. "Sayers, Sex, and Dante." *Dante Studies*. 111 (1993): 223-32.
Wheelock, James. "A Function of the Amore Figure in the *Vita Nuova*." *Romantic Review* 68 (1977): 276-86.
Winston, Janet. "Reading Influences: Homoeroticism and Mentoring in Katherine Mansfield's 'Carnation' and Virginia Woolf's 'Moments of Being: "Slater's Pins Have No Points."'" In Barrett and Cramer: 57-77.
Woolf, Virginia. *The Diary of Virginia Woolf*. 5 vols. Ed. Anne Oliver Bell. New York: Harcourt Brace Jovanovich, 1984.
———. Four Letters to Vita Sackville-West. *Virginia Woolf Miscellany* 43 (Special Summer Issue 1994): 1-3.
———. *The Letters of Virginia Woolf*. Ed. Nigel Nicolson and Joanne Trautmann. 6 vols. New York: Harcourt Brace Jovanovich, 1975-80.
———. "Life and the Novelist." *Granite and Rainbow*. New York: Harcourt Brace Jovanovich, 1958. 41-47.
———. *The Pargiters: The Novel-Essay Portion of* The Years. Ed. Mitchell A. Leaska. NY: Harcourt Brace Jovanovich, 1977.
———. "The Sun and the Fish." *The Captain's Death Bed and Other Essays*. New York: Harcourt Brace Jovanovich, 1950. 211-18.
———. *TheYears: the Pargiters*: a novel-essay based upon a paper read to the London, National Society for Women's Service. Holograph. M42. The Berg Collection of English and American Literature at the New York Public Library. [Holograph, unsigned, dated 11 Oct. 1932-15 Nov. 1934. 8 vols.] Mark Hussey, ed. *Major Authors on CD-ROM: Virginia Woolf*. Woodbridge, CT: Primary Source Media, 1997.
———. *The Years*. New York: Harcourt Brace Jovanovich, 1937.

The Return of the Great Goddess: Immortal Virginity, Sexual Autonomy and Lesbian Possibility in *Jacob's Room*

Vara S. Neverow

In *Jacob's Room*, Woolf invokes the traditions of pre-Hellenic Goddess culture and by this gesture inverts patriarchy in the novel, pre-empting the history of male dominance and reclaiming both a mythic and a historical matrifocal past in which women enjoyed social and sexual autonomy. In so doing, she establishes the possibility of "lesbian narrative space" (Farwell) in the novel. Even Woolf's revisions of the manuscript reveal that she consciously chose to emphasize female lineage and matriarchal tradition. Edward Bishop aptly notes in "The Subject in *Jacob's Room*" that, in the manuscript, "Woolf begins not with Betty Flanders but with Jacob on the beach" (149). In the published version, Woolf brackets the entire narrative of Jacob's brief life with the prior and subsequent presence of Betty Flanders, Jacob's mother, the woman who not only gives birth to him and survives him, but who has a very distinct narrative existence separate from him. This bracketing emphasizes the ancient and eternal primacy of the female in contrast to the ephemeral, vulnerable and secondary male, the dying and rising god and son-lover of the goddess. When the novel is read from this perspective, even the title of the work shifts in significance. Jacob's first room is his mother's womb; his final room is the earth itself—the womb of the great Goddess whose presence subtly pervades the book.

"[T]he accent falls differently now" in *Jacob's Room* ("Women and Fiction" 49; "Modern Fiction," *CE2* 106), emphasizing the female rather than the male. This difference in accent focuses on what Woolf would later term "those unrecorded gestures, those unsaid or half-said words, which form themselves, no more palpably than the shadows of moths on the ceiling, when women are alone" (*AROO* 88). Indeed, in *Jacob's Room*, some of these gestures and half-said words are recorded for, as the narrator notes, "how interesting [Mrs. Flanders'] letters were, about Mrs. Jarvis, could one read them year in, year out—the unpublished works of women, written by the fireside in pale profusion, dried by the flame" (91). *Jacob's Room* thus documents a little of what occurs when women are alone together—and some of what occurs is at very least suggestive of lesbian possibility, of an emotional intimacy verging on the erotic particularly with regard to the relationship of Clara Durrant and Elsbeth Siddons and that of Mrs. Flanders and her close friend Mrs. Jarvis.

In her reversal of patriarchal history and her invocation of a mythic matriarchal pre-history, Woolf is clearly relying on her own familiarity with Greek mythology and literature as evidenced, for example, in her essay "On Not Knowing Greek," which is primarily a meditation on the intensity of Greek tragedy, poetry and philosophy including the *Bacchae* and the *Agamemnon*, the poetry of Sappho and the works of Plato. Woolf also taught Greek mythology at Morley College and traveled to Greece in 1906 with her sister Vanessa, her intimate friend Violet Dickinson and her brothers, Thoby and Adrian (*PA* 317-347).[1]

Woolf's personal knowledge of ancient Greek culture is almost certainly supplemented by Jane Ellen Harrison's studies of ancient Greek religious practices and beliefs. In *Jacob's Room*, Woolf relies particularly heavily on Harrison's *Prolegomena to the Study of Greek Religion* (1903). In the *Prolegomena*, Harrison argues that patriarchal culture and religion displaced Goddess-centered civilizations when the Olympian pantheon supplanted the "primitive goddesses [who] reflect...a relationship traced through the mother, the state of society known by the awkward term matriarchal" (*Prolegomena* 261). By drawing on Jane Harrison's work, Woolf is also able to accent the lesbian possibilities of what Harrison terms the "early, matriarchal, husbandless goddesses," especially "the duo of mother and maiden or the trio of three women" discussed in the section of the *Prolegomena* entitled "The Maiden Trinities" (see Cramer; Harrison, *Prolegomena* 286-92; Maika; Marcus, "*The Years*" 37, and 194 n5).[2] Like Woolf, Harrison regards the patriarchal family structure as inherently oppressive and misogynist and she defends the female deities who have been so rudely displaced: "so stately and yet so pitiful are the ancient goddesses that our hearts are sore for the outrage on their order" (*Prolegomena* 320). The focus on the Goddess in *Jacob's Room* enables Woolf to invert the patriarchal hierarchy and reposition Jacob in a secondary role as Dionysus, the subordinate and sacrificial son-lover of the Goddess.

Woolf's depiction of the Goddess in *Jacob's Room* is especially indebted to the chapter "The Making of a Goddess" in which Harrison details the characteristics of the deity. In Harrison's view, the dyadic relationship of Demeter and Persephone, the mother and the maid, is flanked by the triadic "Maiden goddesses," the Great Goddess in her manifestations as Aphrodite, Hera and Athena. Artemis—the quintessential maiden Goddess—is not discussed at length in this section of Harrison's work but is central to Woolf's invocation of the Goddess in the novel. As Harrison argues, when the Goddess is manifested in a mother and

---

[1] It was this fateful journey that culminated tragically with Thoby's death from typhoid fever in November of that year. The novel has been identified by some critics as an elegy for Thoby (e.g. Mepham, Spilka, Schaefer).

[2] Woolf was also familiar with the *Epilegomena to the Study of Greek Religion* for she notes in her diary that James Strachey "leapt on to my bed, directly I left it, & lay reading Jane's pamphlet" [*D2* 136, Monday 12 September 1921]).

daughter dyad like that of Demeter and Persephone, this dyad is "two persons through one god," "not Mother and Daughter, but Mother and Maiden[.]...They are...merely the older and younger form of the same person" (Harrison, *Prolegomena* 273-274). Marija Gimbutas indicates that even in the archeological record the Goddess is consistently represented by patterns of doubleness and tripleness: "The number two and doubleness...meant a blessed multiplication" (Gimbutas 317) while tripling "is linked with the triple Goddess, an astonishingly long-lived image[.]...continuous throughout the whole of pre-history and history" (Gimbutas 97).

In *Jacob's Room*, lesbian possibility is powerfully situated in the doubling and tripling of the Goddess, a pattern of twinning, mirroring and fusing which, as Bonnie Zimmerman notes, is a metaphor frequently used to describe lesbian relationships (87-89). While there are no explicitly lesbian passages in *Jacob's Room*, many of the Goddess motifs mark the space of what Marilyn Farwell would term a lesbian subtext. Farwell, in her article "Heterosexual Plots and Lesbian Subtexts: Toward a Theory of Lesbian Narrative Space," argues that heterosexist narrative dualism can be destabilized by "a disruptive space of sameness as opposed to [the] difference which has structured most Western narratives" (93). The sameness which is a defining element of lesbian narrative is also an essential attribute of the Goddess herself.

Like Farwell, Terry Castle traces the erasure of lesbians in literature. In The *Apparitional Lesbian*, she identifies a curiously elegiac phenomenon which she refers to as "'seeing ghosts.'" In "[t]he literary history of lesbianism" lesbians vanish due to the "[p]anic [which] seems to underwrite...obsessional spectralizing gestures: a panic over love, female pleasure, and the possibility of women breaking free—together—from their male sexual overseers" (Castle 36). Yet, Castle points out that the very strategy for spectralizing the lesbian in literature can be appropriated by the lesbian author with remarkably subversive repercussions:

> the supernatural metaphor itself, obviously, suggests a different and perhaps more subtle way of thinking about the matter. A ghost...is a spirit believed to appear in a "bodily likeness." To haunt, we find, is "to visit often," "to recur constantly and spontaneously," "to stay around and persist," or "to reappear continually." The ghost, in other words, is a paradox. Though nonexistent, it nonetheless appears. Indeed, so vividly does it appear—if only in the "mind's eye"—one feels unable to get away from it. (Castle 46)

Castle argues that this phenomenon constitutes a "rhapsodical embodiment," "a ritual calling up" in which "the dead are indeed brought back to life; the absent loved one returns" (47). In *Jacob's Room*, "the absent loved one returns" when Woolf invokes the Great Goddess. The haunting supernatural element which constitutes spectral lesbian presence in *Jacob's Room* is not a ghost but the Goddess herself, a powerful female pagan deity suppressed by centuries of patriarchal religion.

Thus, as I will argue, Woolf's use of the Goddess motifs in *Jacob's Room* not only destabilizes the patriarchal tradition but also alludes to lesbian possibilities. Although *Jacob's Room* probably should not be called a lesbian novel, it unquestionably can be read as a work alluding to women's emotional and erotic same-sex passions. This reading is justified by Woolf's repeated references to the Maiden goddesses. As Harrison notes, "Virginity was to these ancients in their wisdom a grace not lost but perpetually renewed, hence the immortal maidenhood of Aphrodite" (*Prolegomena* 312). These goddesses are virgin not in the conventional patriarchal sense of "maiden inviolate" but in the radical sense of "maiden alone, in-herself"; the root meaning of the word "virgin" is "belonging-to-no-man," "one-in-herself" (Hall 11) and is associated with female freedom. Gimbutas observes that, in keeping with this gradual subordination of women in patriarchal culture, the Goddess tradition was eventually "assimilated into [androcentric] Indo-European ideology" and in the process, the Goddess herself was "militarized," acquiring armor and weapons while "[p]arthenogenetic goddesses creating from themselves without the help of male insemination gradually changed into brides, wives, and daughters and were eroticized, linked with the principles of sexual love, as a response to a patriarchal and patrilineal system" (318).

As Nor Hall observes, "the prostitute and the virgin are both archetypes or archaic images of the free woman, as opposed to domesticated woman, the wife and helpmeet, whose life goal is union with the male" (Hall 11-12). In *Jacob's Room*, Florinda, the "little prostitute" (94), is linked to Aphrodite, one of the Maiden Goddesses who, like Athena and Hera, is annually restored to virginity in a sacred bath regardless of her numerous sexual liaisons (Harrison 312; Puhvel 131). Florinda is fascinated with her own virginity. Her name, according to the narrator, "had been bestowed upon her by a painter who had wished it to signify that the flower of her maidenhood was still unplucked" and "she talked more about virginity than women mostly do; and had lost it only the night before, or cherished it beyond the heart in her breast, according to the man she talked to" (77). Further, Florinda is given to frequent bathing (she loves "hot baths") and when she returns to her flat after her initial sexual encounter with Jacob, "she first washed her head." The narrator also observes that "Florinda and her sort have solved the question by turning it into a trifle of washing the hands nightly before going to bed, the only difficulty being whether you prefer your water hot or cold" (79).

Woolf specifically endows so many of the "minor" female characters in *Jacob's Room* with attributes of the Great Goddess that they become, incrementally, composite aspects of the main character—the Goddess herself. One might even argue that the Goddess is the very medium in which the narrator and all of the characters live and move and have their being (see Miller). The names of all the female characters in the novel refer in some way to the Goddess (see Grundy for a discussion of Woolf's use of names).[3] As the inventory of characters documents, several even share the same name, an indication that Woolf consciously and deliberately chose to emphasize the doubling and tripling of the Goddess: There are, for instance, two Julias (both of whom are spinsters) and three characters who share names that are variants on Elizabeth. The origin of the name "Julia" illustrates exactly how important the names of the minor characters are in this novel for "Julia" is a direct reference to one of the Maiden goddesses: "The ancient Roman clan of the Julii claimed direct descent from...Aphrodite... through her son Aeneas" (Cresswell 140), who fled the ruins of Troy to found Rome. This obliquely embedded reference to the Trojan War is part of a larger pattern in which Woolf situates the Trojan War, the consummate instance of patriarchal military violence, as the archetypal parallel to World War I, even to the extent of naming Clara Durrant's dog Troy and comparing Jacob explicitly to both Ulysses and Achilles.

The female characters who bear the names of the Goddess also possess one or more of the Goddess's attributes such as her perpetual virginity or her doubled manifestation as the mother/daughter dyad. Affiliations with the Goddess in the novel not only include references to her traditional activities but to her symbols, her sacred creatures, and her companions. Julia Eliot's photographic tripod invokes Athena. Elizabeth Durrant, in her association with Demeter, is depicted expressing concern about the proper cultivation of potatoes and driving her own carriage drawn by ponies, an image that echoes both Artemis "being drawn by two harts or four stags with golden antlers" and Demeter in her chariot with her sheaf of wheat (Jobes 132). Mrs. Durrant is constantly attended by her daughter, Clara, who is closely associated with both Persephone and Artemis as well as with the mythic sacrificial victims Iphigeneia and Andromeda. Woolf also alludes on occasion to the representation of the Goddess in artwork and to the legends of her deeds. Thus, a friend watching Clara Durrant walking her little

---

[3] The surnames of most of the characters are derived from the names of habitations or topographical sources. For example, Fanny Elmer's last name derives from *Allmor* which in Welsh means "a valley or a dale" (Hanks and Hodges) while Elizabeth Siddons' surname, also from Welsh, means "a farm" (Arthur). These references to the earth itself and to agriculture may be interpreted as allusions to the Great Mother Goddess worshipped in ancient cultures.

Aberdeen terrier thinks she "look[s] like a huntress...some pale virgin with a slip of the moon in her hair" (166). In many sculptures of the Classical era, Artemis "is shown as a young huntress, austere, beautiful, stately, in a short tunic with bow and arrow followed by her dogs" (Jobes 132) and "crescent moonlike horns rest upon her head." Lady Rocksbier, too, rides to the hounds and her name, like Clara's, means light. Madame Lucien Gravé, whose body type echoes the voluptuous curves of the Venus of Willendorf, also bears a name (Lucien) that means light.

When Woolf's narrator introduces Lady Rocksbier, she makes quite clear that Lady Rocksbier is an exceptionally privileged woman who enjoys a truly remarkable degree of liberty:

> The Countess of Rocksbier sat at the head of the table alone with Jacob....[F]ed upon champagne and spices for at least two centuries (four if you count the female line)[,] the Countess Lucy looked well fed. A discriminating nose she had for scents, prolonged, as if in quest of them; her underlip protruded a narrow red shelf; her eyes were small, with sandy tufts for eyebrows, and her jowl was heavy...whatever the deficiencies of her profile, [she] had been a great rider to hounds. She used her knife with authority, tore her chicken bones, asking Jacob's pardon, with her own hands. (100)

Lady Rocksbier, one of the few women of her era whose aristocratic title obscures her marital status, is a commanding presence. Unlike most women, she has somehow managed to have access to power, sensual pleasures and costly luxuries usually restricted to male enjoyment. Appropriately, she is seen seated at the head of the table, taking second place to no man for she has, after all, been treated much like a Goddess and "fed upon champagne and spices for at least two centuries." Rather than being neglected or systematically deprived of gratification, the Countess Lucy has been pampered, even cherished—quite an achievement in a patriarchal culture that regards the desires even of upper class women as either trivial or scandalous. The Countess Lucy's lineage, startlingly, is traced through the female line—a remarkable departure from patriarchal tradition which also hints at the immortality of the Goddess (four centuries, after all, is longer than even Woolf's Orlando lives) and this anomaly is reinforced by the root meaning of "Rocksbier."

"Rocksbier" obviously suggests that the Countess is somewhat obdurate and impervious (like stone), but more importantly, the prefix, *rock*, is also a "metonymic occupational name for a spinner of wool or a maker of distaffs (from ME *rok* distaff)" (Hanks and Hodges, *Surnames*).[4] The emphasis on the distaff

---

[4] The suffix *bier* is similarly occupationally linked—it means "brewer of beer"; beer is a grain product that is associated with Demeter and with Isis, who "in Egypt is addressed as not only Our Lady of Bread but also Our Lady of Beer" [Harrison, *Prolegomena* 422].

side of the Countess's genealogy is a punning invocation of the Great Goddess for, like the Fates, "[s]pinning and weaving are occupations proper to the...Great Mother and it is probably not accidental that two parts of spinning-wheel machinery are called 'the maiden' and 'mother of all'" (Wilkins 97 quoted in Baring and Cashford 559). Countess Lucy's given name links her to Artemis for Lucy means light (derived from the Latin *lux*; Hanks and Hodges, *First Names* 212) and is a reference to St. Lucy or Lucia of Syracuse, a virgin-martyr. Accounts of her martyrdom included such details as her being "denounced as a Christian by a rejected suitor, and miraculously saved from exposure in a brothel" (Attwater 216). Thus, St. Lucy is a powerful illustration of a marriage resister.

Lady Rocksbier is described as a rider to the hounds and, by implication, an accomplished hunter (Jacob, too, who is "somehow connected to the Rocksbiers," "rode to the hounds—in a fashion" [153]). She not only possesses a skill which distinguishes her from the majority of women whether aristocratic or otherwise; her sporting expertise links her to Artemis both in her manifestation as the virgin huntress, the Lady of Wild Things, and as the fearsome Hecate with her dogs. As Baring and Cashford document, "[t]he hounds that dismember Actaeon are also Artemis's sacred animals, and her priestesses wore the masks of hunting dogs" (332). Nor Hall indicates that Hecate rides a horse in one of her manifestations (204).

In open defiance of the cultural norms dictating that women must be demure and eat with great delicacy if they eat at all, Lady Rocksbier devours her food with gusto, wields "her knife with authority" and is described as "well-fed." Such a lust for life in a woman radically counters the self-effacing demeanor required by patriarchy and enforced by the Angel in the House (Woolf, "Professions for Women"). Instead of nibbling unobtrusively on the bony wing of the chicken as the Angel would have done, Lady Rocksbier devours the entire bird, ripping it apart with her bare hands. In Woolf's work, "well fed" usually refers to male privilege at the expense of women and can be extended to refer to intellectual deprivation as well. In *A Room of One's Own*, the novelist Mr. A possesses a "well-nourished, well-educated, free mind" (103) while in *Three Guineas*, Arthur's Education Fund translates for the daughters of educated men into "petticoats with holes in them [and] cold legs of mutton"(5).[5] By contrast with the cramped and narrow lives these women lead, Lady Rocksbier's unconcealed pleasure in her food creates an image of a powerful, totally self-possessed,

---

Beer is also an interestingly earthy contrast to the grape-based champagne which Lady Rocksbier has enjoyed for two centuries. However, *bier* is also a reference to burial rituals and thus is suggestive of the cyclical pattern of the dying and rising god.

[5] See Delphy for a discussion of the politics of women and consumption.

unabashedly sensual woman who has no qualms whatsoever about gratifying her bodily desires.

Given that well-fed women are extremely rare in Woolf's works,[6] the figure of Madame Lucien Gravé becomes another important reference to the Goddess, for she is an ample woman, a woman oblivious to patriarchal standards of female pulchritude. Jacob's disapproval of the zaftig Madame Lucien Gravé ("'Damn these women!...How they spoil things'" [151]) is clearly founded as much on her physique as her effrontery when he first discerns her

> perched on a block of marble with her kodak pointed at his head. Of course, she jumped down, in spite of her age, her figure, and her tight boots—having, now that her daughter was married, lapsed with a luxurious abandonment, grand enough in its way, into the fleshy grotesque; she jumped down, but not before Jacob had seen her. (151)

The description of Madame Lucien Gravé seems to be derived from Woolf's own observations during her trip to Greece in 1906:

> No place seems more lusty & alive than this platform of ancient dead stone. The fat Maidens who bear the weight of the Erechtheum on their heads, stand smiling tranquil ease, for their burden is just meet for their strength. They glory in it; one foot just advanced...& spring in to the air...still virile & young. (*PA* 323)

If one is to see Madame Lucien Gravé as a manifestation of the Great Goddess, her Kodak camera becomes an amusingly modernized version of Artemis's bow and arrow. The narrator indicates that Madame Gravé, like Lady Rocksbier, actively revels in her own physical female being and—unlike most women in Woolf's novels—has given herself over deliciously to "the fleshy grotesque." Her name—Lucien—means, of course, light (derived from the Latin *lux*, it also is a punning link to her "luxurious abandonment"). Her last name, Gravé, can mean either "pitted" or "carved" (as in "*pierre gravé*," a "carved stone" [Cassell's]); when deprived of its accent, "grave" means both a place of burial (an evocative reference to the dying and rising god motif strongly reinforced by the pattern of references to graves throughout the novel) and "heavy," thus giving emphasis to "the fleshly grotesque" that strongly evokes the vast amplitude typical of the Great Goddess. In fact, "her age, her figure, and her tight boots" suggest that Madame Lucien Gravé actually resembles the ancient figurine of the Venus of Willendorf with its enormous breasts, belly and buttocks and its tiny attenuated feet. Since there is specific mention that her daughter has married (thus suggesting the relationship between Demeter and the abducted

---

[6] As Roger Poole has indicated, Woolf herself may have had an eating disorder which developed after her marriage; see 126-136.

Persephone), it is probable that Madame Lucien Gravé manifests the Great Goddess as the Corn Mother, the female fertility deity who is most closely associated with the delights of the harvest.

While the Goddess returns in *Jacob's Room* in her many forms as Aphrodite, Athena and Hera, as Demeter and Persephone as well as Hecate, her most frequent manifestation is as Artemis, the virgin Goddess of the moon. Artemis is a Goddess worshipped by women and chaste men (Morford and Lenardon 140; 142-143) and was especially revered by the Amazons (Salmonsa 20; Grahn 172; Hall 109-132). The characteristics of Artemis indicate strongly that she exists outside the patriarchal definition of womanhood. In her guide to mythology, Edith Hamilton notes that Artemis is known as "the Lady of Wild Things, Huntsman-in-chief to the gods" and comments wryly that this position seems "an odd office for a woman" (31).

Artemis is often recognized as an archetypal lesbian figure (Baring and Cashford; Hall; Grahn). The emphatically counter-patriarchal (and distinctly butch) qualities that Artemis embodies are vividly expressed in Robert Graves's account of the young Goddess's prayer to Zeus when he asks her what she desires most:

> Pray give me eternal virginity; as many names as my brother Apollo; a bow and arrow like his; the office of bringing light; a saffron hunting tunic with a red hem...; sixty young ocean nymphs...as my maids of honor; twenty river nymphs to...feed my hounds when I am not out shooting; all the mountains in the world; and lastly, any city you care to choose for me, but one will be enough, because I intend to live on mountains most of the time. (*The Greek Myths* vol. 1: 83, quoted in Hall 116)

As Merlin Stone observes, Artemis was associated with rituals intended to "keep young women 'safe from marriage'" (Stone 383) and Judy Grahn links Artemis to the berdache figure of tribal culture (158-159; see also Carpenter, cited in Hall 132). As Hall points out, Artemis is indeed a gender-bending Goddess for she "encourages women to express their masculine natures. At the Korythalia, a festival in her honor, women would dance with exaggerated phalli attached to their male costumes. In their imitation of men, women would enact male sexual gestures" (129). Baring and Cashford, affirming Hall's research, note that "nine-year-old girls in their 'tomboy' phase were her favoured companions" (326).

Artemis, always surrounded by her maids of honor, may have been the lover of Kallisto, one of her companion-nymphs, whom Artemis turned into a bear because Kallisto had been impregnated by "Zeus or perhaps Apollo who had taken the guise of a woman to seduce her" while she "thought she had been making love to Artemis" (Hall 120; see also Morford and Lenardon 135-139 for a variant in which Kallisto is raped by Zeus and turned into a bear by Hera). The companions and priestesses of Artemis all "take vows of celibacy" (Jobes 131).

To protect her virginity from male assault, Artemis "always carried her own quiver," "hanging it by the door to her dwelling" so that " it would seem to all who pass that there was a man in there with her. [Artemis] herself was called a mannish woman" (Hall 127). She was prepared to kill any man who so much as glimpsed her nudity (and such was the fate of Actaeon—see Baring and Cashford 331-332) and any man who harassed one of her nymphs (thus died Orion for harassing Eos, the Dawn [Murray 111]—or perhaps for attempting to rape Artemis herself [Morford and Lenardon 140]).

Jacob is situated in the novel as the dying and rising god, the son-lover of the Goddess who manifests not only as Dionysus but as other gods as well. Dionysus is equated by Plutarch with Osiris (Baring and Cashford 268), a link that Harrison discusses in her *Prolegomena* (567). He is associated as well with Adonis, the beloved of Aphrodite. In the Zagreus-Dionysus myth, the twice-born dying and rising god comes to a violent end, "killed, dismembered, and devoured by the Titans" (Eliade 360; see also Hamilton 61,146, 401-403, 416, 439; Baring and Cashford 268, 373-374), an elegiac foreshadowing of Jacob's death in the Great War. Jacob, of course, will never be resurrected; nonetheless, a ritual of renewal and rebirth is tragically echoed in the novel. In keeping with this ancient lineage, the narrator observes that Jacob is "descended on his mother's side from a family of the greatest antiquity and deepest obscurity" (71). Associated with the Goddess, he is tragically subject to the bitter fate of the dying and rising vegetation god. It is at Olympia in Greece that Jacob meets Sandra Wentworth Williams, an older married woman inclined to engage in sexual escapades with younger men. Her relationship with Jacob is a further indication of his role as the consort of the Goddess. Like so many of the other female characters in the novel, Sandra's given name is directly linked to the Goddess. "Sandra" is derived from "Alexander," meaning "defender of men," one of the epithets of Hera (Hanks and Hodges, *First Names*). Significantly, Harrison maintains that Hera "has been forcibly married, but she is never really wife" and certainly never practiced submission to her husband (*Prolegomena* 316). Sandra, by cuckolding her husband, Evan, reverses the sexual prowess of Zeus, notorious for his liaisons. "Beautiful but dangerous," she says aloud when she sees Jacob enter the dining room. She is ostensibly referring to the pink melons served for dessert, but both she and her husband know that the phrase is a double entendre, for while she simultaneously thinks to herself regarding Jacob, "Ah, an English boy on tour" (143) the narrator comments: "Evan knew all that too. Yes, he knew all that; and he admired her. Very pleasant, he thought, to have affairs" (143). Evan tolerates her proclivities without many objections though he occasionally succumbs to jealousy (143, 145).

Woolf is quite explicit in connecting Jacob to Dionysus. Allusions to Dionysus include Jacob's tendency to appear and disappear without warning and his reiterated association with grapes. Additional connections include his power to arouse female sexuality and his frequent association with theatrical productions (as Harrison observes, "from the religion of Dionysus sprang the drama" [567]) and other festive occasions. Jacob's given name, which is Semitic in origin and means "usurper" or "supplanter," links him directly to the patriarchal culture of Hebrew monotheism which displaced the worship of the Goddess. Indeed, Jacob's namesake was one of the founding patriarchs of the religion—he is also known as Israel (Jobes 859). The Biblical Jacob is particularly noted for his clever techniques for breeding sheep[7]—a form of animal husbandry that rather obviously parallels the domestication and control of female sexuality under patriarchy. Like the Goddess, the dying and rising god is manifested more than once in the novel. Thus, Jacob's death is duplicated in that of a young man named Jimmy who "refused to marry a woman called (if memory serves) Helen Aitken" and now "feeds crows in Flanders" (96, 97). While Jacob's doom is foreshadowed in his very surname—Flanders, a site of military slaughter in the Great War—the reiteration of his first name becomes a motif of the dying and rising god for the name "Jimmy," a diminutive of James, is derived from the same origin as Jacob (Hanks and Hodges, *First Names* 171). Two other characters share the same name: the young grandson of Lady Rocksbier is called Jackie—the "informal pet name of James" (Hanks and Hodges, *First Names* 169) and Sandra Wentworth Williams's son (almost certainly fathered by Jacob) is called Jimmy. "'Jacob would be shocked,'" Sandra thinks as she watches "[t]he perambulator...going through the little gate in the railing. She kissed her hand; directed by the nurse, Jimmy waved his" (169).

In keeping with his connection to Dionysus, Jacob is given to disappearing and reappearing suddenly. When the novel opens, Jacob is missing. He has wandered away on the beach and is lost. His brother Archer seeks him, calling his name. When the novel ends, Jacob is missing again, lost in the war. His friend

---

[7] Given his association with his Hebrew namesake, it is perhaps not coincidental that Jacob Flanders, in the first scene of the novel, discovers a sheep's skull on the beach and possesses himself of its jawbone. Reinforcing Jacob's connection to the Goddess culture, it is especially interesting that Gimbutas establishes that "the ram is...the sacred animal of the [Neolithic] Bird Goddess" (317). Not only does Jacob find a sheep's skull, he also lives in a flat that has "over the doorway a rose, or a ram's skull...carved in the wood" (70; 176).

Richard Bonamy calls Jacob's name aloud as Jacob's mother stands in his vacant rooms, holding a pair of her son's old shoes (176). As Mircea Eliade observes, "[b]y his epiphanies and his occultations, Dionysus reveals the mystery, and the sacrality, of the conjunction of life and death" (Eliade 359).

Jacob's association with grapes is first introduced while he is visiting the Durrants. Just before Jacob is to leave for London, Clara Durrant gathers hothouse grapes for Jacob in an abortive courtship scene: "One bunch of white, and two of purple," she said, and she placed two great leaves over them where they lay curled warm in the basket" (62). If this were the only reference to the grape motif, one might not view this segment as an allusion to Dionysus, the god of wine. However, there is another, even more explicit passage describing Guy Fawkes festivities:[8]

> "We think," said two of the dancers, breaking off from the rest, and bowing profoundly before [Jacob], "that you are the most beautiful man we have ever seen."
> So they wreathed his head with paper flowers. Then somebody brought out a white and gilt chair and made him sit on it. As they passed, people hung glass grapes on his shoulders, until he looked like the figure-head of a wrecked ship. (75).

This passage seems to allude to the Homeric Hymn to Dionysus (Morford and Lenardon 210-212).

Dionysus is irresistible to women (and, indeed, numerous women are attracted to Jacob). For example, the young artist's model Fanny[9] Elmer is depicted as a maenad when she is instantaneously smitten with Jacob within moments of meeting him for the first time: "she started angrily. For never was there a more irrational passion. And Jacob was afraid of her for a moment—so violent, so dangerous it is when young women stand rigid; grasp the barrier; fall in love" (118). In a variant of the Dionysus myth, his mother is Persephone, impregnated by her own father Zeus in his disguise as a serpent (Baring and Cashford 367) and he is equated by Plutarch with Osiris, another dying and rising god (Baring and Cashford 268), a link Harrison discusses in her *Prolegomena* (Baring and Cashford 373-374), thus bringing him into conjunction with the goddesses Demeter and Persephone and therefore Artemis. Harrison, in fact, argued that "the maenads used the bull, the phallus and the thyrsus or ivied rod in their worship of Dionysus...to partake of male power and to deny the division between male and female" (Marcus, "Taking" 139). Hall

---

[8] The burning of Guy Fawkes in effigy evokes the use of effigies in the rites of Adonis (Baring and Cashford 363).

[9] "Fanny" is, according to Eric Partridge, a nickname for the female genitalia.

acknowledges that Dionysus is, in some sense, "the god of women" (Reis 179), for Dionysus "pulls women out of their contexts and evokes their eager potential for maenadism, their lust for the wilds, their desire for unrepressed female sexuality, and fusion with nature" (Reis 184). Even more significantly, "for women, Dionysus represents a return to the Great Goddess.... a divine epidemic" in which women leave the "bounds of regulating social arrangements" as "individuality breaks down and collective female energy is aroused" (Reis 185). Dionysus is particularly powerful because of his "ability to dissolve sexual boundaries" (Reis 187).[10]

Clara Durrant, seen by most critics as a young woman cheated of matrimonial bliss by Jacob's death in the war, actually seems to have a rather pronounced aversion to marriage, an aversion which associates her with Artemis, the eternal virgin and ultimate marriage resister. The reader first encounters Clara the evening Jacob—her best matrimonial prospect in the heterosexual marketplace—arrives at her home at the end of his boating adventure with her brother Timothy. In this initial encounter, the reader sees Clara through Jacob's eyes. He "named the shape clad in yellow gauze Timothy's sister, Clara" (57). Clara, whose name also means "light" (Hodges and Hanks 64), is dressed in misty yellow—a color that is suggestive of hazy moonlight and is the same hue as the tunic Artemis demands from Zeus (see quotation from Robert Graves above). Interestingly, Clara's surname, Durrant (or Durant), means "enduring" (it is the "pres. part. of *durer* to endure, last L. *durare*, from *durus*, hard, firm" [Hanks and Hodges, *Surnames*]). The name Durrant not only meant "Steadfast" but was also used as a nickname meaning "obstinate" (Hanks and Hodges)—a hint that Clara, despite her apparent delicacy and compliance is capable of resisting the patriarchal agenda. Not only does she seem, after all, to "ha[ve] a spark of her mother's spirit in her—[be] somehow heroic" (154)—her last name suggests a likeness to two other very determined female figures, Lady Rocksbier and Madame Lucien Gravé, discussed earlier.

If Clara longs to wed Jacob, it is surely ironic that she actively dreads the possibility of a proposal from him. Clara's consternation regarding marriage is illustrated in the curious courtship scene during which she gathers the grapes for Jacob: "'You're too good—too good,' she thought, thinking of Jacob, thinking that he must not say that he loved her. No, no, no." (63). Although it is possible that Clara longs for Jacob's declaration of love so intensely that she is in denial

---

[10] As Eliade indicates, "Dionysiac ecstasy means, above all, surpassing the human condition, the discovery of total deliverance, obtaining a freedom and spontaneity inaccessible to human beings,...[and] deliverance from prohibitions, rules, and conventions of an ethical and social order...which explains, in part, the mass adherence of women" to his cult (365-366).

for fear it will not occur (and, in fact, it does not), her close association with Artemis suggests that she genuinely dreads any marriage proposal.

A subsequent encounter between Jacob and Clara affirms the profound ambivalence both share with regard to their social obligation to marry. At a party, Jacob moves abruptly toward Clara out of apparent boredom: "Jacob shifted perhaps five inches to the left, and then as many to the right. Then Jacob grunted, and suddenly crossed the room. 'Will you come and have something to eat?' he said to Clara Durrant" (87). Clara accepts his invitation and then, as soon as a competing social obligation occurs, she assumes the new responsibility and thereby avoids spending any time with Jacob. In the traditional marriage plot, this incident would serve to increase narrative tension by thwarting the lovers' longing to be together and intensifying the reader's desire for their union. In *Jacob's Room*, the event seems to serve as a deflection of anxiety.

The only times the reader actually sees Clara in a state of euphoria is when she is with her friend Elsbeth Siddons. On the evening when Clara first meets Jacob, everyone at the Durrants' goes out for a stroll after dinner. Rather than choosing Jacob as her walking companion, Clara, like Artemis with her nymphs, keeps company with another woman, her house guest Elsbeth. The next time we see Elsbeth, she is singing at an evening entertainment in London: "Then to Silvia let us sing,/That Silvia is excelling;/She excels each mortal thing/Upon the dull earth dwelling./To her let us garlands bring." As Clara watches Elsbeth, she sighs repeatedly: "'Ah!' Clara exclaimed out loud [at the end of the performance], and clapped her gloved hands" (88). "Elsbeth" (a variant of "Elspeth") is derived from "Elizabeth" (Hodges and Hanks, *First Names* 100), a name shared not only with Jacob's mother, Mrs. Betty Flanders, but with Clara's own mother, Elizabeth Durrant. The name is directly associated with Artemis through Edmund Spenser's *The Faerie Queen* in which he celebrates his monarch, Elizabeth I, as the virgin Goddess of the moon—a volume Jacob has in his own library (39).

This scenario closely parallels the lesbian moment in *Mrs. Dalloway* when Sally Seton kisses Clarissa whose name derives from the same root as Clara (see Cramer). Clara returns from this stroll with Elsbeth disoriented, bemused and distracted: "'Oh, mother! I didn't recognize you!' exclaimed Clara Durrant, coming from the opposite direction with Elsbeth. 'How delicious,' she breathed, crushing a verbena leaf" (59). Perhaps the phrase "the opposite direction" is merely a descriptive detail, but it can be seen as Woolf's reference to an alternative sexuality—an opposition that challenges heterosexuality. After all, in the language of flowers, verbena means "you enchant me" (Jobes 1645). Verbena has an herbal significance as a powerful magical and healing substance. Also known as vervain, the herb is "sacred in…many cultures. In Egypt, vervain was believed to have originated from the tears of Isis" (one of the manifestations of the Great Goddess), while in Greek culture, being "sacred to Venus, vervain was used in love potions" (Bremness 146; see also Stuart 279; *Magic and Medicine* 323).

Throughout the novel, Clara continues to evade romantic liaisons with men, for when another young man who is courting her celebrates Clara's domestic virtues in bad poetry, ending his verses "And read their doom in Chloe's eyes," he "cause[s] Clara to blush at the first reading, and to laugh at the second, saying it was just like him to call her Chloe when her name was Clara" (84). Chloe,[11] a variant of the Greek name Khloe, "was originally used in the classical period as an epithet of the fertility goddess Demeter" (Hanks and Hodges, *Surnames* 62) and means "a young green shoot" (Withycombe 64), one of the terms associated with the Goddess Kore/Persephone. Clara may be blushing from affronted modesty because the comparison to Demeter, the Corn Mother, might suggest the reproductive fertility of heterosexual intimacy. Alternatively, she may blush because as a true marriage resister, a dedicatee of Artemis, any proposal of marriage suggests to her the loathsome and forcible wedding of Persephone who was abducted and raped by Hades with the consent and collusion of her own father, Zeus. When the young man actually proposes marriage to Clara, "la[ying] his life at her feet[,] she ran out of the room and hid herself in the bedroom," "sobbing" (85), a response that indicates a significant degree of terror or revulsion. (Of course, it is possible to interpret the passage in a more conventional fashion, arguing that Clara weeps from sheer disappointment and frustration because Jacob, with whom she might be profoundly in love, has failed to propose to her.)

It is immediately after the traumatic incident of the marriage proposal that Clara finds solace in her friendship with Richard Bonamy, a man "who couldn't love a woman and never read a foolish book" (140)[12] and who is himself in love with Jacob (85). After all, Artemis—among her other titles—is known as "sister to all men" (Hall 109). Clara's mother, Mrs. Durrant, thinks this new connection is a potential match but Clara resists this idea, defying her mother's injunction to marry despite her mother's peremptory rejection of her protest:

---

[11] It may or may not be relevant that it is Chloe who likes Olivia in *A Room of One's Own* (86) and that both are associated with the maiden Goddesses—Chloe with Persephone and Olivia with Athena, whose sacred plant is the olive tree.

[12] Clara's choice of a male homosexual as a dear friend and a dance partner—but not as a spouse—is reminiscent of Virginia Woolf's mercifully brief and abruptly terminated engagement to Lytton Strachey in 1909.

"But I could never marry a man with a nose like that," said Clara
"Nonsense," said Mrs. Durrant....
Clara, losing all vivacity, tore up her dance programme and threw it in the fender. (85)

The chorus of "character mongers" believe—reinforcing Mrs. Durrant's view—that Richard Bonamy and Clara are well-suited to each other. Their comments suggest that the match might be a success because Richard and Clara are both attracted to their own sex: "'sometimes it is precisely a woman like Clara that men of that temperament need...' Miss Julia Eliot would hint" (154). Bonamy's perceptions of Clara emphasize her profound affinity with the ever-virgin Artemis for he marvels in "amazement at an existence squeezed and emasculated within a white satin shoe...until the virginity of Clara's soul appeared to him candid; the depths unknown" (152). The use of the word "emasculated" is oddly provocative in its juxtaposition with the word "virginity," perhaps as a further reference to Artemis and her androgynous fusion of such male-identified activities as hunting with her essentially female, everlasting virginity. The word *candid* is particularly rich in meanings. Its figurative meanings include "splendid, illustrious; fortunate" while its archaic meanings highlight the intense significance of Clara's relation to whiteness (the white satin shoe, the moon itself) and the Goddess-like attributes of purity, clarity; stainlessness and innocence ("candid" *OED* 1; 2a; 2b).

In the reader's final glimpse of Clara, she is apparently thinking of Jacob while she stands in front of a statue of Achilles as a riderless horse gallops past (167). In this passage, she is linked to Iphigeneia, the daughter Agamemnon sacrificed to Artemis. Agamemnon, to deceive his wife Clytemnestra into sending the girl to him, claimed to have arranged a marriage to Achilles (Jameson 240-241). In one version, Artemis intervenes in the sacrifice, substituting a fawn for the girl and makes Iphigeneia a priestess of her cult in Taurus, an Amazon stronghold (now Crimea). There, Iphigeneia becomes "the battle princess of the cruel goddess," sacrificing all shipwrecked sailors to Artemis (Salmonsa 124-125). In Taurus, Iphigeneia is actually one of the names of the Goddess Artemis. The reference to Achilles, which, of course, foreshadows Jacob's death, suggests yet again that Clara, like Iphigeneia, belongs to the Goddess. Clara is positioned repeatedly as a victim of patriarchy (Jacob sees her as Andromeda, "a virgin chained to a rock [somewhere off Lowndes Square] eternally pouring out tea for old men in white waistcoats" [123]). Reinforcing this image, the narrator notes that "Clara only wondered why...Jacob had never come. . . . And Clara would hand the pretty china teacups, and smile[.]..."Jacob! Jacob!" thought Clara" [166]). However, the allusions to Iphigeneia and the abducted Persephone again suggest that Clara genuinely dreads wedlock. After all, in her diary she notes that

"'I like Jacob Flanders....though he's frightening because...'" but breaks off without completing the thought (71). As a modern Persephone, the stifled daughter of a domineering Demeter, Clara is constantly threatened with the violation and imprisonment that constitutes Persephone's forcible marriage to Hades: "Devoted to her mother, Clara sometimes felt her a little, well, her mother was so sure of herself that she could not understand other people" (166). The word "devoted" of course carries religious significance and Clara, even in her unhappiness, thinks like a dutiful daughter: "Ought she not to be grateful? Ought she not to be happy? Especially since her mother looked so well [...]" (166).

In each of the episodes that Clara encounters the prospect of marriage—whether it be to Jacob or to another man—she evinces tremendous anxiety and even anguish. Her resistance to marriage and her fleeting attempts to forge an alternative connection with another woman place her in what Farwell would call lesbian narrative space. Clara's few ecstatic moments with Elspeth are interrupted and never consummated in the novel. Only the musings of Miss Julia Eliot suggest that Clara may someday defy the social sanction against same-sex passion and discover her own possibilities of pleasure as do, perhaps, the dowagers Betty Flanders and Mrs. Jarvis.

Appropriately, in a novel that is only partially about Jacob, Betty Flanders, Jacob's mother, is literally the alpha and omega of the work—she has the first and last word. In a patriarchal plot, Mrs. Flanders, as Jacob's mother, would be classified as a significant but ultimately minor figure in Jacob's tragic drama, his dithyramb (Eliade 373 n27). Instead, Woolf offers an alternative matriarchal plot which locates Betty Flanders as an aspect of the Great Goddess and positions Jacob symbolically in the subordinate role of her son-lover. This mythic sexual connection between the mother and the son is expressed most vividly when Betty Flanders' letter to Jacob becomes a witness to his tryst with Florinda:

> [Betty Flanders'] letter lay upon the hall table; Florinda coming in that night took it up with her, put it on the table as she kissed Jacob, and Jacob seeing the hand, left it there under the lamp, between the biscuit-tin and the tobacco-box. They shut the bedroom door behind them.
> The sitting-room neither knew nor cared. The door was shut; and to suppose that wood, when it creaks, transmits anything save that rats are busy and wood dry is childish...But if the pale blue envelope lying by the biscuit-box had the feelings of a mother, the heart was torn by the little creak, the sudden stir. Behind the door was the obscene thing, the alarming presence, and terror would come over her as at death, or the birth of a child. Better, perhaps, burst in and face it than sit in the antechamber listening to the little creak, the sudden stir, for her heart was swollen, and pain threaded it. My son, my son—such would be her cry, uttered to hide her vision of him stretched with Florinda, inexcusable, irrational, in a woman with three children living at Scarborough. (91)

Woolf depicts Betty Flanders as a woman with her own life, her own passions, and her own desires. The counter-patriarchal relationship between Betty Flanders and her friend Mrs. Jarvis constitutes a precise example of how Woolf ensures that the accent falls differently for, through almost imperceptible incremental references, she creates an emotionally intimate, flirtatious relationship between these two ordinary middle-aged women, a widow and a clergyman's wife. The relationship shows how the dyadic aspect of the Great Goddess can serve as a metaphor of erotic tension between women.

Mrs. Elizabeth Flanders, Jacob's mother, is already two years into widowhood at the very beginning of the novel. Like Clara Durrant, Mrs. Flanders' given name immediately associates her with Artemis. Mrs. Flanders has three young sons—Jacob, Archer and John—and maintains a rather curious relationship with one Captain Barfoot, with whom she corresponds.[13] Since Captain Barfoot is married to an invalid, the townspeople suggest a degree of impropriety in his relationship with Mrs. Flanders: "[s]he's very attractive still"—"Odd she don't marry again!"—"There's Captain Barfoot to be sure—calls every Wednesday, as regular as clockwork, and never brings his wife" (15).

Clearly, "Elizabeth Flanders, of whom this and much more than this had been said and would be said" is a juicy topic of gossip as "a widow in her prime ...half-way between forty and fifty" (15). But for Betty Flanders herself, Captain Barfoot is a safe companion: not only is he married, he walks with the aid of a "rubber-shod stick" for "[h]e was lame and wanted two fingers on the left hand, having served his country" (25). These castration images suggest he lacks sexual drive and that Mrs. Flanders is thus able to benefit from the social connection with a male who in no way poses a sexual threat to her (see also Bishop 160).

And does Mrs. Flanders wish to remarry? Not in the least, apparently. She is what might be termed a "remarriage resister" and rejects her one suitor, Mr. Floyd, with little hesitation. She responds initially to the offer with some excitement—excitement that is quickly quenched by a seemingly incongruous encounter with her youngest son. Even as she reads the letter, recalling her deceased husband nostalgically, she looks up to see "three geese, half-running,

---

[13] David Bradshaw, in his rollicking and provocative paper "*Jacob's Room* and 'The Complexity of Things,'" presented at the 13th Annual Conference on Virginia Woolf: Woolf in the Real World (June 2003), also engaged with the tacit aspects of the novel, suggesting that Betty Flanders's youngest son, John, might have been fathered by Captain Barfoot and this indiscretion might have been the unstated reason that, as she writes in her letter to him, she had to leave. For a detailed account of this interpretation, see *Winking, Buzzing, Carpet-Beating: Reading* Jacob's Room, the published version of Bradshaw's 2003 Birthday Lecture for the Virginia Woolf Society of Great Britain, pp. 3-12.

half-flying, scuttl[ing] across the lawn with Johnny behind them, brandishing a stick" (20-21). The sight of the male child chasing the almost certainly female geese with his stick absolutely infuriates Mrs. Flanders. She flushes with anger and chastises her son, "snatch[ing] his stick away from him." The child offers an excuse ("'they'd *escaped*!'") But Mrs. Flanders does not relent: "'I won't *have* you chasing the geese!' she said,...crumpling Mr. Floyd's letter in her hand." Suddenly she sees the connection for herself: "'How could I think of marriage!' she said to herself bitterly...She had always disliked red hair in men, she thought ...for she saw Johnny chasing the geese, and knew it was impossible for her to marry any one" (21; emphasis in text). This castrating gesture is reiterated in a notorious passage just one page later. Here, her thought process reveals that she associates Topaz (the male kitten Mr. Floyd had given to Johnny as a parting gift) with Mr. Floyd himself: "'Poor old Topaz,' said Mrs. Flanders...and she smiled, thinking how she had had him gelded and how she did not like red hair in men. Smiling, she went into the kitchen" (22-23).

Betty Flanders' response to this attack on her fowls is evocative of the Goddess's jealous guardianship over her sacred creatures, for "even at fifty, [Betty Flanders is] impulsive at heart, sketching on the cloudy future flocks of Leghorns, Cochin Chinas, Orpingtons" (91), but she has a thoroughly antagonistic relationship with her rooster: "The rooster had been known to fly on her shoulder and peck her neck, so that now she carried a stick or took one of the children with her when she went to feed the fowls" (16).

Early on in the novel, the reader is given a glimpse of the way that Mrs. Jarvis views Mrs. Flanders in a fashion suggestive of the grieving Demeter, for "widows stray solitary in the open fields, picking up stones, gleaning a few golden straws, lonely, unprotected, poor creatures" (8). This passage also alludes to the devotion of the biblical Ruth who, once widowed, devotes her life entirely to Naomi, her mother-in-law (Ruth apparently marries Boaz solely to provide for her mother-in-law). Mrs. Jarvis's seemingly innocent observations suggest an unusually tender and protective impulse toward Mrs. Flanders and also provide an intriguing but subtle foreshadowing of a possible erotic relationship between the two women. The reader first encounters "Mrs. Jarvis, the rector's wife" at church, observing Mrs. Flanders "while the hymn tune played." But, despite (or because of) her immediate relationship to these patriarchal religious practices, Mrs. Jarvis is neither a docile wife nor a happy one:

> Had she again been pacing her lawn late at night? Had she again tapped on the study window and cried: "Look at the moon, look at the moon, Herbert!"
> And Herbert looked at the moon. (27)

Although this passage is in some respects humorous, it is also both pathetic and prophetic. When Mrs. Jarvis demands that her husband see the same moon she sees as she paces on the lawn, her urgency evidences her desperate attempt to connect with him in a meaningful way. At another level, the passage functions as an invocation of Artemis, associating Mrs. Jarvis (like the Countess Lucy, Madame Lucien Gravé, Clara Durrant and Elizabeth Flanders) with the moon goddess herself. Herbert, the obtuse clergyman, insulated by his Christian faith, cannot hope to respond to his wife's eager prompting. Safely ensconced in his cozy study, he can cooperate with his wife's peculiar request only by dutifully but perfunctorily glancing at the moon. To him, it is merely the moon, ordinary and dull—not a manifestation of the Goddess or an index of his wife's secret longings. Since Mrs. Jarvis's husband cannot understand her needs, the moon arouses in her discontentment and an illicit desire—perhaps for a woman's love:

> Mrs. Jarvis walked on the moor when she was unhappy, going as far as a certain saucer-shaped hollow...and there she sat down[.]...She was not very unhappy, and, seeing that she was forty-five, never perhaps would be very unhappy, desperately unhappy that is, and leave her husband, and ruin a good man's career as she sometimes threatened. (27)

Like Mrs. Jarvis, Mrs. Flanders wanders on the moors and finds her way to the "raised circle of the Roman camp" (19), a place to which the two women will return together. It is quite possible that Woolf knew that the circle, the mound and the ring are all sacred to the Goddess (Jobes), also representing—as her contemporary Olive Schreiner observes in *Women and Labor* (1911)—the circle of the cervix "through which the head of the human infant passes at birth" (quoted in Hall 45). As Hall points out, those women who do leave "marriages that kept them [like Persephone] too much in the dark" (125) can still retreat "to the protective circle of the virgin" (Hall 131).

Although Mrs. Jarvis is not yet prepared to break the bonds of marriage, she remains a malcontent. As Hall phrases it:

> the spirit of Artemis...calls [girls] into her service at an early age. They may leave her for marriage,...[b]ut for those who do leave, the imperative to reconnect with the lost experience may come up later in life in the desire to make friendships with women more central....[and] it may 'come out' in a woman's recognition of her desire to form love relationships with women. (Hall 130).

Mrs. Jarvis must wrestle with her inchoate longings, longings which, as the narrator reiterates, jeopardize her marriage, "there is no need to say what risks a clergyman's wife runs when she walks on the moor. Short, dark, with kindling eyes...Mrs. Jarvis was just the sort of woman to lose her faith upon the moors—to confound her God with the universal that is" (27). The narrator's reference to the "universal" invokes the Goddess, the founding female principle that creates, undergirds and nurtures the world. When Mrs. Jarvis does find what she seeks with Mrs. Flanders, the narrator reminds the reader of this prior passage, noting that "Mrs. Jarvis found it difficult to think of herself to-night....Neither did Mrs. Jarvis think of God" (132).

As the novel progresses, it becomes evident that Mrs. Jarvis and Betty Flanders have developed a very close and erotically charged relationship, for "Mrs. Flanders liked Mrs. Jarvis,[14] always said of her that she was too good for such a quiet place, and, though she never listened to her discontent[,]...Mrs. Flanders knew precisely how Mrs. Jarvis felt" (91). As the relationship between Mrs. Jarvis and Mrs. Flanders evolves, the narrator devotes an unusually long passage to describing their interaction. The passage in question establishes the affinity between Mrs. Flanders and Mrs. Jarvis and displays many of the thematic elements Woolf routinely uses to indicate women's passional relationships and romantic friendships.

However, the possibility of a sexual connection between the two women is only metaphorically suggested and the relations between Betty Flanders and Mrs. Jarvis are eloquently allusive without being at all explicit. The two women are alone together at Mrs. Flanders' house. They are apparently engaged in a desultory conversation about Jacob while Mrs. Flanders sews: "Mrs. Jarvis thought of Paris. At her back the window was open, for it was a mild night; a calm night; when the moon seemed muffled and the apple trees stood perfectly still" (130). The setting is very sensual, the reference to Paris suggests same-sex erotic attraction between women (see Neverow-Turk), and the mention of the moon invokes the presence of Artemis.

The reference to Paris also seems to be a link to Hope Mirrlees' *Paris: A Poem* which definitely manifests the Sapphic content surrounding goddess imagery. Woolf was fully aware that Mirrlees was Jane Harrison's "'ghostly daughter' and companion" (editor's note *D1* 75 n10). In a letter to Clive Bell about her *Times Literary Supplement* review of Hope Mirrlees' *Madeleine, One of Love's Jansenists* (9 October 1919), Woolf comments: "I have to review Hope Mirrlees[.] ...It's all sapphism so far as I've got—Jane [Harrison] and herself" (1093: 24 September 1919 *L2* 391). The Hogarth Press published Mirrlees' *Paris: A Poem* in 1920. Woolf commented in a letter to Margaret Llewelyn Davies on 17 August 1919: "Last weekend,...we had a young lady [Hope Mirrlees] . . . [who] is Jane Harrison's favourite pupil, and has written a very obscure, indecent, and brilliant poem [*Paris*], which we are going to print" (1075: 17 August 1919 *L2* 385). The poem alludes to the erotic lesbian aspect of

---

[14] Again, one is reminded of Woolf's phrasing in *A Room of One's Own*: "Chloe liked Olivia."

the Great Goddess as well as to the lesbian community in Paris where Harrison and Mirrlees "shared a flat" (editor's note *L2* 385 n1).

In the poem, several lines are strongly suggestive of the lesbian sexuality Woolf consistently associates with Artemis. Calling attention to itself, one section of the poem is typeset in a challenging and suggestive fashion with a single line set vertically (Woolf herself typeset the publication):

<pre>
          The first of May
               T
               h
               e
               r
               e

               i
               s

               n
               o

               l
               i
               l
               y

               o
               f

               t
               h
               e

               v
               a
               l
               l
               e
               y
</pre>

There was a ritual fight for her sweet body

> Between the two virgins—Mary and the moon
> The wicked April moon (13-14)

This segment of the poem makes direct reference to the tension between "the two virgins" Mary and Artemis. Not coincidentally, it was in Ephesus, the site of the most elaborate temple to Artemis, that "Mary, mother of Jesus, was declared to be Theotokos, 'Mother of God'" (Baring and Cashford 330). The two manifestations of the Goddess—the holy virgin mother and the pagan and possibly lesbian goddess of the moon are here engaged in a "ritual fight" for a "'sweet body'" represented by the lily. The ritual suggests the rites of the mystery religions that Harrison studied while the sweet body itself suggests the different manifestations of female sexuality as the sacred/ maternal/heterosexual Goddess co-opted and subordinated to patriarchal religion in conflict with the powerful pagan/erotic/lesbian Goddess of ancient matriarchal worship.[15]

When Mrs. Jarvis comments to Mrs. Flanders "'I never pity the dead'" as she moves suggestively, "shifting the cushion at her back, and clasping her hands behind her head," one must consider the significance of this distinctly sensual pose, a pose that certainly might indicate her sexual availability. By referring to the dead, Mrs. Jarvis perhaps situates Mrs. Flanders as Persephone, Queen of the Underworld, suggesting that she leave Hades, end her exile and return to Demeter. Mrs. Jarvis's next conversational ploy is openly seductive, an echo of Clara and Elsbeth strolling on the terrace:

> "You never walk at this time of night?" she asked Mrs. Flanders.
> "It is certainly wonderfully mild," said Mrs. Flanders....
> "It is perfectly dry," said Mrs. Jarvis, as they shut the orchard door and stepped on to the turf. (131)

Earlier in the novel, Mrs. Flanders had herded her frightened geese back into the orchard through that same garden gate as she decided to reject Mr. Floyd's offer of marriage[16]—but now, she steps beyond that domestic barrier on to the turf. The usually impulsive Mrs. Flanders is cautious and somewhat hesitant:

> "I shan't go far," said Betty Flanders...."Now, my dear, I am going no further"
> ...They had climbed the dark hill and reached the Roman camp.

---

[15] The poem is also striking in that it refers explicitly to the lesbian bar-scene on the Left Bank: "*I dont like the girls of the night-club—they love/women*" (21).

[16] It is perhaps only a coincidence that Eric Partridge notes that *goose girl* means: "A Lesbian: since ca. 1918. Ex the synon. Fr. s. *gousse*." However, the association with French slang seems particularly suggestive and apt in this context.

> The rampart rose at their feet—the smooth circle surrounding the camp or grave. How many needles Betty Flanders had lost there! and her garnet brooch....Mrs. Flanders rubbed the turf with her toe, thinking of her garnet brooch. (132)

The reference to the lost garnet brooch is a further allusion to Persephone. The name of the semi-precious stone comes from *granum*, the Latin word for seed, and, as Jobes observes, "is so called because its color resembles that of the seed of the pomegranate" (Jobes)—six of which Persephone ate in the underworld and thus doomed herself to spend part of the year in Hades as a prisoner-spouse.

As the novel progresses, the ancient pagan sites become more identified with female sexuality. Both women independently visit the Roman ruins which obviously predate patriarchal Christianity and coincide historically with both the practice of the Goddess religions in Britain and the worship of Diana in the Roman Empire. It is here, in the smooth circle, that Betty Flanders has lost darning needles (a possible reference to the Goddess as needleworker, weaver and spinner) as well as the garnet brooch. It is here that Mrs. Flanders herself makes the oblique but possibly sexual gesture, "rubb[ing] the turf with her toe, thinking of her garnet brooch" (see Bennett, McKenna).

Unlike the sexually charged but equally oblique encounter between Jacob and his lover, Sandra Wentworth Williams, that occurs a few pages later, this moment of communion between the two women is exquisitely peaceful: "It was so calm. There was no wind; nothing racing, flying, escaping. Black shadows stood still over the silver moors" (132). However, for Jacob and Sandra, "the night was dark...obscuring the moon and altogether darkening the Acropolis, the clouds passed from east to west. The clouds solidified; the vapours thickened; the trailing veils stayed and accumulated....Violent was the wind." For Mrs. Flanders and Mrs. Jarvis, the Roman fort is a smooth circle while for Jacob and Sandra "[t]he Acropolis was a jagged mound." Mrs. Flanders and Mrs. Jarvis walk casually out through the garden gate but Jacob and Sandra must risk breaking and entering: "'I suppose they leave the gates open?' he asked. 'We could climb them!' she answered wildly" (159-160).[17] Mrs. Flanders and Mrs. Jarvis have arrived at a place where "[t]he moonlight destroyed nothing" and "[t]he moor accepted everything" (134). By contrast, "[a]s for reaching the Acropolis who shall say that we ever do it, or that when Jacob woke next morning he found anything hard and durable to keep for ever?" (161).

Ordinarily unhappy and discontented, Mrs. Jarvis is no longer agitated or distraught—not needing to evade heterosexual tyranny (like the fleeing geese

---

[17] This section seems to allude to Andrew Marvell's "To His Coy Mistress," especially to the lines "Let us...tear our pleasures with rough strife / Through the iron gates of life" (ll. 43-44).

half-flying away from the boy with the stick who tries to prevent their escape). In fact, nothing at all is "racing, flying, escaping." The Sapphic moon and not the patriarchal God (who would surely disapprove of these rites) blesses this moment of female communion. At the moment when Mrs. Flanders picks up a pebble (see Bennett)—not the garnet brooch she believes she is seeking—Mrs. Jarvis (who has been longing for someone to give herself to) realizes suddenly that "sometimes people do find things." However, Mrs. Flanders and Mrs. Jarvis do *not* find the garnet brooch which echoes the fateful pomegranate seeds that force Persephone to reside in Hades in a coerced marriage away from her beloved mother six months out of the year.

The loss of the garnet brooch may be of particular significance in Woolf's system of symbols. In *To the Lighthouse*, another proto-lesbian character, Minta Doyle, loses an heirloom brooch given to her by her grandmother while on an excursion with Paul Rayley, the man she will soon wed—a marriage that later devolves into tolerant adultery (see Neverow-Turk). Mrs. Flanders has lost her brooch, given to her by her son (a possible reiteration of his son-lover relationship to her), while she is accompanied by a man—a man whom, as it turns out, neither she nor Mrs. Jarvis like:

> A garnet brooch has dropped in the grass. A fox pads stealthily. A leaf turns on its edge. Mrs. Jarvis, who is fifty years of age, reposes in the camp in the hazy moonlight.
> "...and," said Mrs. Flanders, straightening her back, "I never cared for Mr. Parker."
> "Neither did I," said Mrs. Jarvis. They began to walk home. (133-134)

Woolf's reiterated references to the age of Mrs. Jarvis and Mrs. Flanders is intriguing—both are women over the age of forty (like Woolf herself) and have fulfilled their patriarchal obligations to marry (and, in the case of Mrs. Flanders, to bear children). Now, seemingly, they are free to move beyond these obligations: "Betty Flanders's darning needles are safe too and her garnet brooch.... [A]t midnight .... it would be foolish to vex the moor with questions—what? and why?" But patriarchal time ultimately intrudes on the women: "The church clock, however, strikes twelve" (131-134). Mrs. Jarvis and Mrs. Flanders have been together out on the moors since before ten o'clock, an extraordinarily long time, perhaps even a scandalously long time. While the moor, the moon, the night, the female-identified natural world, and the Goddess herself "accepts everything," the patriarchal clock in the phallic church steeple (a reminder of Mrs. Jarvis's husband, the rector) sounds harsh, striking twelve judgmentally as the women depart.

Is this interlude between Betty Flanders and Mrs. Jarvis actually an occluded instance of lesbian desire, a physically consummated erotic lesbian relationship, a lesbian merging of Demeter and Persephone? Such a claim cannot be verified. Certainly, it is a subtly nuanced and obliquely articulated episode of female-centered eroticism. Similarly, Clara Durrant, explicitly associated as she is with Artemis, could be regarded as a character struggling with lesbian panic in the patriarchal web of compulsory heterosexuality.[18] The Goddess motifs in the novel reclaim the eternal virginity of these women whether wife, widow or maiden. The traditional linear plot of *Jacob's Room* culminates in the tragic but ironic justice of Jacob's death—offstage—in the Great European War of 1914-1918, a slaughter in which he chose to participate (e.g., Handley; see also Schaefer; Ingram). The counterplot—invoking the mythic pattern of the Goddess religion—undermines not only the chronological and historical plot structure but redefines the limits of female sexuality, freeing women to reclaim their divine Virginity and enter lesbian narrative space.

[18] See Smith for a discussion of lesbian panic.

Works Cited

Arthur, William. *An Etymological Dictionary of Family and Christian Names with an Essay on Their Derivation*. New York: Sheldon, Blakeman, 1857. Detroit: Gale Research, 1969.

Baring, Anne and Jules Cashford. *The Myth of the Great Goddess: Evolution of an Image*. New York: Viking, 1991.

Bennett, Paula. "Critical Clitoridectomy." *Signs*. 18: 2 (Winter 1993): 235-259.

———. "The pea that duty locks: Lesbian and Feminist-Heterosexual Readings of Emily Dickinson's Poetry." *Lesbian Texts and Contexts: Radical Revisions*. Eds. Karla Jay and Joanne Glasgow. New York: New York UP, 1990. 104-125.

Bishop, Edward L. "The Subject in *Jacob's Room*." *Modern Fiction Studies* 38:1 (Spring 1992): 147-175..

Bradshaw, David. "*Jacob's Room* and 'The Complexity of Things,'" 13th Annual Conference on Virginia Woolf: Woolf in the Real World, Smith College, June 2003.

———. *Winking, Buzzing, Carpet-Beating: Reading* Jacob's Room. Southport, UK: Virginia Woolf Society of Great Britain, 2003.

Bremness, Lesley. *The Complete Book of Herbs*. New York: Viking, 1988.
Castle, Terry. *The Apparitional Lesbian*. New York: Columbia UP, 1993.
Cramer, Patricia. "Notes from Underground: Lesbian Myth and Ritual in the Writings of Virginia Woolf." *Virginia Woolf Miscellanies: Proceedings of the First Annual Conference on Virginia Woolf*. Eds. Mark Hussey and Vara Neverow-Turk. New York: Pace UP, 1992. 177-188.
Delphy, Christine. "Sharing the Same Table: Consumption and the Family." *Close to Home: A Materialist Analysis of Women's Oppression*. Trans. and ed. Diana Leonard. Amherst: U of Massachusetts P, 1984. 40-56.
Eliade, Mircea. *From the Stone Age to the Eleusinian Mysteries*. Chicago: Chicago UP, 1978. Vol. 1 of *A History of Religious Ideas*. Trans. Willard R. Trask. 3 vols. 1978.
Gimbutas, Marija. *The Language of the Goddess*. London: Thames and Hudson, 1989.
Grahn, Judy. *Another Mother Tongue*. Boston: Beacon, 1990.
Grundy, Isobel. "'Words without meaning—wonderful words': Virginia Woolf's Choice of Names." *Virginia Woolf: New Critical Essays*. Eds. Patricia Clements and Isobel Grundy. Totowa: Barnes and Noble, 1983. 200-220.
Farwell, Marilyn. "Heterosexual Plots and Lesbian Subtexts: Toward a Theory of Lesbian Narrative Space." *Lesbian Texts and Contexts: Radical Revisions*. Eds. Karla Jay and Joanne Glasgow. New York: New York UP, 1990. 91-103.
Hall, Nor. *The Moon and the Virgin: Reflections on the Archetypal Feminine*. New York: Harper, 1980.
Haller, Evelyn. "Isis Unveiled: Virginia Woolf's Use of Egyptian Myth." *Virginia Woolf: A Feminist Slant*. Ed. Jane Marcus. Lincoln: U of Nebraska P, 1984. 109-131.
Hamilton, Edith. *Mythology: Timeless Tales of Gods and Goddesses*. New York: The New American Library, 1942.
Handley, William. "War and the Politics of Narration in *Jacob's Room*." *Virginia Woolf and War: Fiction, Reality, and Myth*. Ed. Mark Hussey. Syracuse: Syracuse University Press, 1991: 110-33.
Harrison, Jane. *Epilegomena to the Study of Greek Religions* (1927) and *Themis, a Study of the Social Origins of Greek Religion* (1921-1927). New Hyde Park, NY: University Books, 1962.
———. *Mythology*. New York: Cooper Square Publishers, 1963.
———. *Prolegomena to the Study of Greek Religion*. 1903. New York: Meridian, 1960.
Hanks, Patrick and Flavia Hodges. *Dictionary of First Names*. New York:

Oxford UP, 1990.

———. *Dictionary of Surnames*. New York: Oxford UP, 1989.

Ingram, Angela. "'The sacred edifices': Virginia Woolf and Some of the Sons of Culture." *Virginia Woolf and Bloomsbury: A Centenary Celebration*. Ed. Jane Marcus. Bloomington: Indiana UP, 1987. 125-145.

Jameson, Michael H. "Mythology of Ancient Greece." *Mythologies of the Ancient World*. Ed. Samuel Noah Kramer. New York: Doubleday, 1961. 219-276.

Jobes, Gertrude. *Dictionary of Mythology, Folklore and Symbols*. 2 vols. Part I and II. New York: Scarecrow Press, 1962.

Little, Judy. "*Jacob's Room* as Comedy: Woolf's Parodic Bildungsroman." *New Feminist Essays on Virginia Woolf*. Ed. Jane Marcus. Lincoln: U of Nebraska P, 1981.

Maika, Patricia. *Virginia Woolf's* Between the Acts *and Jane Harrison's* Con/spiracy. Ann Arbor: UMI Research P, 1987.

Magic and Medicine of Plants. Pleasantville: Readers Digest Associates, 1986.

Marcus, Jane. "*The Years* as Götterdämmerung, Greek Play, and Domestic Novel." *Virginia Woolf and the Languages of Patriarchy*. Bloomington: Indiana UP, 1987. 36-56.

———. "Taking the Bull by the Udders: Sexual Difference in Virginia Woolf—A Conspiracy Theory." In *Languages*: 136-62.

McKenna, Kathleen. "The Language of Orgasm." *Re: Reading, Re: Writing, Re: Teaching Virginia Woolf: Selected Papers from the Fourth Annual Conference on Virginia Woolf*. Eds. Eileen Barrett and Patricia Cramer. New York: Pace UP, 1995. 29-38.

Mepham, John. "Mourning and Modernism." *Virginia Woolf: New Critical Essays*. Eds. Patricia Clements and Isobel Grundy. Totowa: Barnes and Noble. 137-156.

Mercatante, Anthony S. *Facts on File Encyclopedia of World Mythology and Legend*. New York: Facts on File, 1988.

Miller, J. Hillis. "Virginia Woolf's All Souls' Day: The Omniscient Narrator in *Mrs. Dalloway*." *The Shaken Realist: Essays in Modern Literature in Honor of Frederick J. Hoffman*. Eds. Melvin J. Friedman, John B. Vickery, and Philip R. Yannella. Baton Rouge: Louisiana State UP, 1970. 100-27.

Mirrlees, Hope. *Paris: A Poem*. Richmond: Hogarth Press, 1919.

Morford, Mark P. O. and Robert J. Lenardon. *Classical Mythology*. 2nd ed. New York: Longman, 1977.

Murray, Alexander S. *Who's Who in Mythology: Class Guide to the Ancient World*. New York: Crescent, 1988.

Neverow-Turk, Vara. "'Mrs. Rayley is out, Sir': Re-reading that Hole in Minta's

Stocking." *Virginia Woolf Miscellany* 39 (Fall 1992): 9.
Partridge, Eric. *A Dictionary of Slang and Unconventional English*. 8th ed. New York: Macmillan, 1984.
Reis, Patricia. *Through the Goddess: A Woman's Way of Healing*. New York: Continuum, 1995.
Risolo, Donna. "Outing Mrs. Ramsay: Reading the Lesbian Subtext in Virginia Woolf's *To the Lighthouse*." *Virginia Woolf: Themes and Variations: Selected Papers from the Second Annual Conference on Virginia Woolf*. Eds. Vara Neverow-Turk and Mark Hussey. New York: Pace UP, 1993. 158-171.
Schaefer, Josephine O'Brien. "The Great War and 'This Late Age of World's Experience' in Cather and Woolf" in *Virginia Woolf and War: Fiction, Reality, and Myth*. Ed. Mark Hussey. Syracuse: Syracuse UP, 1991. 134-50.
Smith, Patricia Juliana. "'Things people don't say': Lesbian Panic in the *Voyage Out*." *Lesbian Readings of Virginia Woolf*. Eds. Eileen Barrett and Patricia Cramer. New York: New York UP, 1996. 128-45.
Spilka, Mark. *Virginia Woolf's Quarrel with Grieving*. Lincoln: U of Nebraska P, 1980.
Stone, Merlin. *Ancient Mirrors of the Goddess: A Treasury of Goddess and Heroine Lore from Around the World*. Boston: Beacon, 1979.
Withycombe, E[lizabeth] G[idley]. *The Oxford Dictionary of English Christian Names*. New York: Clarendon, 1977
Woolf, Virginia. *The Diary of Virginia Woolf*. Ed. Anne Olivier Bell assisted by Andrew McNeillie. Vols. 1 and 2. New York: Harcourt Brace Jovanovich, 1978. 5 vols. 1977-1984.
———. *Jacob's Room*. 1922. New York: Harcourt Brace Jovanovich, 1950.
———. *A Room of One's Own*. 1929. New York: Harcourt Brace Jovanovich, 1963.
———. *The Letters of Virginia Woolf*. Ed. Nigel Nicolson and Joanne Trautmann. vols. 1 and 2. New York: Harcourt Brace Jovanovich, 1976. 6 vols. 1975-1980.
———. "Professions for Women." *Women and Writing*. Ed. Michèle Barrett. New York: Harcourt Brace Jovanovich, 1979. 57-63.
———. *To the Lighthouse*. 1927. New York: Harcourt Brace Jovanovich, 1964.

"The Shock of Sensation": On Reading *The Waves* as a Girl in India, and as a Woman in America

Meena Alexander

> We have no ceremonies,
> only private dirges and no conclusions,
> only violent sensations, each separate.[1]
> —Virginia Woolf, *The Waves*

I was twelve or thirteen when I first read *The Waves*. I was in my grandmother Mariamma's bedroom in Kozencheri, a small town in Kerala, South India. The walls were whitewashed, with a bluish tinge to their color. There were photographs of family all over the upper edge of the wall—broad foreheads, dark eyes peering down—and, in the single bookshelf to the right of grandmother's bed, beneath the wooden cross, a motley array of English books, which did not belong to her, for my grandmother Mariamma never read English books. Perhaps they had belonged to my other grandmother, who loved English literature and had died before I was born or perhaps one or two of the books had come from my father's collection. There they were, stacked upright: The Bible, a volume of Shakespeare, Tagore, H. G. Wells, Conan Doyle, Dickens, Emily Brontë, and a copy of Virginia Woolf's *The Waves*. I recall how I sat at the edge of the bed and pulled *The Waves* off the shelf.

Before I opened the book, I glanced out of the window. There were no humans visible, but I could see the brown cow tugging at its rope, nuzzling into sweet hay; a goat tipsy with heat; white doves scrambling awkwardly towards the seeds in the dovecote, hardly bothering to flap their wings. Life seemed suspended in a heat haze. And grandmother herself, perhaps saying her prayers in the next room, or supervising the cook as she made sambar or coconut chutney, was nowhere to be seen. I thumbed through the book, knocked dust off the bottom edge, then opened the cool pages. As I buried my nose in the shining letters, I felt I was falling into water.

The editors gratefully acknowledge permission to reprint "'The Shock of Sensation': On Reading The Waves *as a Girl in India, and as a Woman in America." We thank Meena Alexander for her kind permission to reprint the essay, as well as Myriam J. A. Chancy, editor of the journal* Meridians, *where the essay first appeared in Volume 1, Number 1 (Autumn 2000), pages 179-86.*

[1] Virginia Woolf, *The Waves* (New York: Harcourt Brace, 1959), 157. All subsequent page references are to this edition.

I had never before encountered prose that danced quite in that way, drawing me over the surface of shining particles, then tugging deep, deep to the gulf that underlies sense.

It was between the dark covers of that copy of *The Waves* that I first encountered the sense that truth could be verified by what was felt on the skin and in the bloodstream, that the body, as Woolf put it "goes before me like a lantern down a dark lane, bringing one thing after another out of darkness into a ring of light" (129). This sense was critical to me, coming as it did as part of Woolf's notion of scattered bits and pieces, sensorial beckonings, of a "shattered mind which is pieced together by some sudden perception" (39). Reading *The Waves* I recognized in a deep, if unspoken awareness, a kindred spirit, one who took for granted the walls of old houses, ancestral gardens, the migrancy that time enforces.

By then I had spent so many years of my childhood traveling between India and North Africa. My father had been "seconded" to the Sudan by the Indian government and, starting from the age of five, I had to learn to pack and unpack myself, accept that "reality," far from being solid, was singularly insubstantial, its loveliness could turn breathless in seconds. Solid walls could vanish, ancestral gardens could melt away. The sedimentation of the soul that I was starting to learn, my childhood and teenage years cut by border crossings, India and the Sudan, the hundreds of miles of ocean or blue sky that layered them, drawing me into a difficult sense-making, one I did not have a ready pattern for. What kind of creature was I, if what I had known and loved was always to be cut away, the passage of space casting veils over what the body had touched?

There was no simple narrative I could draw between the parts of my worlds. How could I speak of what I knew if the self could scarcely be taken for granted? And what might memory mean?

And holding a fresh copy of *The Waves* in my hand, for that old dark book in my grandmother's bedroom has vanished, I sit in my room in Manhattan, the green trees of summer outside my window. I try to recall what sense I made of two figures, each no more than an outline, yet unfolding between them the whole tapestry of the book. One is a woman, the other a child. The woman maintains order by the sheer fact of her maturity, her stillness at the centre of a bustling garden. She is "the lady" who "sits between two long windows writing" (17). She is as necessary to the growth of the garden as the men with their long brooms, sweeping. She calms the chaos, stills the fearful children. She does not look up from her writing. In my mind, she is linked to the poet in Wallace Stevens's poem "Mozart, 1935" with the haunting, troubling invocation: "Poet, be seated at the piano." Even if stones are thrown in the streets, or there are gunshots, riots outside the garden walls, the lady must maintain her seat, be wrapped in meditation, keep writing. It is she who keeps "reality," the word that Woolf puts to such fierce use at the end of *A Room of One's Own*.[2]

The other figure is that of the child, the girlchild cast out. Forced outside the loop of time, she starts to write. I will never forget the nervous thrill of reading the lines that follow, the origin of the imaginary, but, at the end, the writer herself, by her own hand, it would seem, forced out. What stringent necessity lay in this, what tragic foreshadowing of Virginia Woolf's end?

But we need to think beyond this, and ponder how these seeming fixities might be unlinked, how we might write beyond this ending:

> "I begin to draw a figure and the world is looped in it, and I myself am outside the loop; which I now join—so—and seal up, and make entire. The world is entire and I am outside of it, crying, 'Oh, save me, from being blown forever outside the loop of time!'" (22)

Why should the writing child be flung outside the loop of time? Why should her hand tremble with fear as she writes? And how did she so painfully, so carefully acquire the discipline that turned her into the woman in the garden, writing?

The child is mother to the woman. I am only learning this now. What the child draws into the quick of her flesh is what the writing woman must etch into the lineaments of her landscape, her characters of knowledge, her tall green trees. But what kind of world does this woman inhabit? Must she forever be unhoused? I ponder Woolf's line: "my body passes vagrant as a bird's shadow" (66).

Her hold on the body was tenuous and puts me in mind of Wordsworth, who in his Fenwick note to the Immortality Ode speaks of how, as a child on his way to school, overcome by the sense of the unreality of all that was around, put out his foot and touched a wall, a stone, a tree to recall himself "from the abyss of idealism to reality." So too Woolf's speaker in *The Waves* feels herself slip "into nothingness" and must bang her "hand against some hard door to call herself back to the body" (44).

But perhaps it was this very dissolution of the bodily hold on things that allowed for the textured layering of spaces, sharp and disjunctive sensations that, wrapping themselves one over the other, could free the woman writer from an imprisoning social world. And if the simple self is set at risk, then that too forces a recognition of its impossible nature. There is nowhere one can simply be:

> This is the first day of a new life, another spoke of the rising wheel. But my body passes vagrant as a bird's shadow...I coerce my brain to form in my forehead; I force myself to state, if only in one line of unwritten poetry, this moment; to mark this inch in the long, long history that began in Egypt, in the

---

[2] Virginia Woolf, *A Room of One's Own* (New York: Harcourt Brace,1957), 113-4.

time of the Pharoahs when women carried red pitchers to the Nile. I seem already to have lived many thousand years. But...I sit in a third-class railway carriage full of boys going home for the holidays...(66)

Reading these lines again, at the tail end of the century, at a time of mass migrations, transnational crossings, gendered postcolonial reflections, I realize how my reading of *The Waves* quickened my girl's mind, a mind in search of form. The sharp disjunctions of space, the shock of motion, the edginess of sensation, even a violence to it so that the self can scarcely discover an underlying continuity in the flow of consciousness, all this sparked a quick recognition in me.

And where did that recognition lead me? I sense now how close to me, how buried under my own skin was my own reading of Virginia Woolf's "flaw" in creation, a crack in the world (25). How her fear of even stepping over a puddle, or of what the looking glass might reveal, reverberates in me. And always on the other side is the civilized world, others who are "immaculate," watching, staring.

The sense of a fault in things, of a broken-up, fissured earth courses through my poetry and prose. A few years ago I published a memoir called *Fault Lines*. In it, I try to reflect on the ways in which my being here, in America, is underwritten by multiple border crossings, languages, voices. I try to brood on the palimpsest of memory, intrinsic to making up the present. In this way, each moment of reflection becomes a threshold.[3] Though Virginia Woolf in no way entered consciously into my mind as I wrote *Fault Lines* it seems to me now, in hindsight, that Woolf's influence on me, rich and subterranean, was all the more intense for being hidden. So that while I had read and even taught *Mrs Dalloway* and *To the Lighthouse* to my students at Hunter College and had alluded to Woolf's essays in my work *Women in Romanticism*, never ever had I alluded to the one book that had marked me so deep, so early.[4] Something kept me away from *The Waves*, a dark shadow, a hand.

But *The Waves* was the work I drank so deeply of in the whitewashed room in my paternal grandmother's house, a house with lime trees outside the window, the footmarks of a baby elephant, its round grey body and sinuous trunk puffing dirt and bits of broken leaf all night in the lower garden, in an attempt to cool

---

[3] For an elaboration of memory as a threshold "that deepens what it is that migration or dislocation does," see the interview in which I speak of this: "Gold Horizon: The Unquiet Borders of Memory," in Eileen Tabios, *Black Lightning: Poetry in Progress* (New York: Asian American Writers Workshop, 1998), 195-226.

[4] Meena Alexander, *Women in Romanticism: Mary Wollstonecraft, Dorothy Wordsworth and Mary Shelley* (London: Macmillan, 1989). See the chapter entitled "Natural Enclosures."

itself. As the lines of *The Waves* turned in my head, the snorting sounds of the baby elephant drifted up to me, and, when I looked through my parents' window, I could see its dark shadow, grey, humped in between the mango trees and the rubber trees.

But what happened to me when I could no longer see the baby elephant? When the "I" that saw the elephant no longer existed? Forced dislocations made a simple narrative—and then and then and then—hard, even untenable for me.

These days, I am engaged in my usual practice: in between poems, scribbling prose, the chaos of identity just about balanced by the edginess of aesthetic form. The one and the other always entwined for me as the questions continue to haunt: Who am I? Where am I? When am I? Again and again I feel as if I were forced to start from scratch, each time and all over again making up self and world.

And I need to ask, how did Virginia Woolf, in the early years of this century, have such a vivid sense of dislocation, living, as she seems to have done, so close to home? Could it be, that over and above the physical facts of migrancy, there is an essential condition that etches itself into visibility through the wound of traumatic loss? No quick answer is possible. I have my work cut out for me. It seems that I need to reflect on this question slowly, carefully in the years to come.

But perhaps this was why *The Waves* spoke to me, in the many voices of an English woman who had never traveled very far from home, a great and difficult writer, her soul marked by inner motion, speed unsettling a psyche that deliberately maintained the most tenuous hold on its bodily station, all the better to underwrite a language of fraught, splintered, bejeweled sensation.

And there it lies, right at the heart of the modernist enterprise, I tell myself—Woolf's writing, a glistening palimpsest of bodily knowledge, a body of work immensely useful to a postcolonial imagination in search of dissolving structures.

But something else has to be spelt, as crucial as right hand is to left, given the integrity of the body, or left foot to right, for one who would seek out her own mobility in the realm of letters. My early awareness of Woolf's power and my love of her writing was cut by another emotion in me, a distinct refusal, a rage at the white, colonial world in which she lived, moved and had her being.

How could I doubt that I would forever be part of that "Oriental problem" she alluded to in *The Waves*, the dark, poor world Percival was riding into, the world of those who are pitiful and do not speak good English. And didn't she write of how the "violent language" that Percival uses to solve the problem, sets things right (136)? If I sensed the irony in Woolf's tone, it cut no ice with me, for I was clear on which side she stood, the side of those Gandhi had struggled against, those to whom India would forever be a series of flat pictures, dark natives, painted dancers, mud, heat, dust—all the "fragility and decay" of a lesser ontology, an elsewhere that could never compete with the English present, an India that seemed illusory, never more than "temporarily run-up buildings in some Oriental exhibition" (136). And while she had the flow of English, and bathed in the river of the language, I was forever cast to the rocky shores, my feet against the sharp stones, the jagged syllables I was forced to repeat over and over again by my British tutor: "cut," "cut," "mutt," "mutt," the violence of a colonial pedagogy, its sense of utter rightness—of one world, one Empire, hurting my child's mind, making me recoil from the very language I needed to live and breathe and move in as a writer.

Then too the storybooks my tutor gave me—this British woman my parents found to teach me when we traveled to North Africa—had pages filled with little white children who wore pinafores and had pink cheeks and drank milk and ate muffins. I had no doubt that had they caught sight of me, or of my grandmother Mariamma, they would have run a mile, perhaps hidden out in their bungalows. Or cried out to their soldiers to come and push me back into the jungle where I belonged. And as a girl I had no doubt, that Virginia Woolf, for all her anguish, all her resistance, came from that very British world. The avowal, indeed the complicated truth, that each and every one of us is part of a historical moment and must bear its burdens, could not in any way have eased what I felt.

And so the affiliation with a foremother was cut by the sense of disenfranchisement, the awareness of a racialized world which would force my own body into the shadows, into the bushes, away from the "immaculate others." And this in spite of, perhaps even intensified by, the fact that Woolf herself understood what it meant to be robbed of identity.

So the layered, sedimented worlds, the opposite histories from which we came, the density of the whiteness that clung to her, invaded me. And later, in the years that I was studying the writings of Mary Wollstonecraft, I felt that by casting aside her own rage, exiling it in works like *Three Guineas* and *A Room of One's Own*, Virginia Woolf was whitewashing her fiction, paying too heavy a price for the exquisite fabric of sensation. And there were years when I did not read her work, could not read her work.

In the past few months, I feel I have reached a watershed in my own writing life, a period when after intense labor I can stop, turn back, reflect on what has entered into the texture of writing, what has gone into the making of my visible world. I realize now my deep indebtedness to Woolf, to the ways in which she etches in the strangeness that lies just under the surface of our skin, the shadows pinned under doves that circle slowly to the dovecote, in an ancient garden I no longer return to.

And in my room in New York City, thousands of miles from that garden, ever so slowly I murmur her lines again: "The structure is visible. We have made a dwelling" (164).

And the dwelling is one made of words, words of a colonial language I have stripped and polished down, then torn with my own hands so that the homeless voices of my generation can enter in. My novel *Manhattan Music* focuses on the life of an Indian woman haunted by her memories of the past. Sandhya, an immigrant, tries to adjust to life in the new world. During the Gulf War she goes to an antiwar protest and, listening to descriptions of ongoing bombardment, senses her own mind at the brink of disintegration. Voices pour through her. The body is pitched against its own need to simply have and hold and can barely shelter these homeless voices. It's only at the very end of the novel that Sandhya is able to walk freely into the city, filled with a sense that she can survive the present.

I do not doubt that in my need to braid in these voices, I have taken what I could from Virginia Woolf. And if she were to hear them and, clapping her hands over her ears, turn away—sensing nothing but the dark crudity of a face that peers in over the shoulder, invading the gilt-framed mirror—then let that too, be part of our story, part of our lives in a postcolonial theatre, a world cut from ancient ceremonies, filled with what Woolf once called "the shock of sensation" (130):

> ...Voices stirred...drawing her down to a rough basement—a dark, muddy place where syllables stirred their moist roots.
> She heard her sister Nunu cry out in the Sanskrit her tutor forced on her: "*Aham patashala getchami*!" the singsong of recitation. She heard Arabic from the lyrics Rashid learnt from his mother, a burial song, a woman with a swan-like neck, exiled in life, returned to her native soil in death. She heard voices from the streets of Bosnia, Rwanda, Sri Lanka, strange countries bruised as plums might be in a gunny sack. Voices too, from mats and torn mattresses stained with virginal blood, moans and sharp cries of pleasure, exhalations of delight, gasps as smoke is inhaled from burning cities where tanks rumble.
> These sounds played within her in a ceaseless cacophony, struggling to become speech: the homeless voices of Sandhya Maria Rosenblum.[5]

---

[5] Meena Alexander, *Manhattan Music* (San Francisco: Mercury House, 1997), p.193. For related questions of self-identity and border crossings, see Meena Alexander, "Rites of Passage," *Interventions: An International Journal of Postcolonial Studies* (Inaugural Issue: Vol. 1, No. 1, 1998-99): 14-17.

The Unlike[ly] Other: Borges And Woolf
Mónica G. Ayuso

In a story of doubling called "The Other," published in *The Book of Sand* (1975), a young Jorge L. Borges—not quite twenty as the real Borges would have been in 1918—meets his alter ego, a man of seventy-some-odd years as he would have been in 1969, the fictional time of the story. After the initial shock of the face-to-face encounter, the young Borges refers to the most prized possessions of his older counterpart in an attempt to offer foolproof evidence of his legitimate authority. He is Borges. He is not lying. He says,

> In the wardrobe closet in your room, there are two rows of books: the three volumes of Lane's translations of the *Thousand and One Nights*—which Lane called *The Arabian Nights Entertainment* [...] Quicherat's Latin Dictionary, Tacitus' *Germania* in Latin and in Gordon's English version, a *Quixote* in the Garnier edition, a copy of Rivera Indarte's *Tablas de Sangre* signed by the author, Carlyle's *Sartor Resartus*, a biography of Amiel, and [...] a paperbound volume detailing the sexual customs of the Balkans. (*Collected Fictions* 412)

Except for the last heterodox item in the series, the list is exemplary of what made both the real and the fictional Borges a bibliophile throughout his life: the shelf with books, at home, in the library, opening up to the universe of reading, the world of books. But if this list is exemplary for its bookish nature, it is no less exemplary for its polyglotism.

The real Jorge L. Borges became a member of the first editorial board of *Sur*, published in Argentina under the leadership of Victoria Ocampo between 1931 and 1970. He made more than 170 contributions to the literary magazine that helped fulfill one of its missions: making foreign culture accessible to a wide Spanish-American readership. As José Bianco has indicated, Borges' notable contributions alone justified publication of the journal (*Borges en Sur*, editor's note, 7). Though never explicitly stated in editorials, the mission of bridging intellectual culture was evidenced by its publishing practice. As a result, Borges served not only as creative writer and literary critic for Spanish readers but also as translator of works in French and in English, the language he loved most. Virginia Woolf was among many contemporary prose writers whose work Borges was asked to translate.[1] She was a personal acquaintance Ocampo had befriended through Aldous Huxley in 1934 at the London opening of the Man Ray photography exhibition and with whom she stayed in touch until 1941, the

---

[1] He translated a number of German lyrics, Faulkner, Whitman, Melville, Carlyle, Swedenborg, and others.

year of Woolf's suicide. Borges' translation of *A Room of One's Own*, issued from December 1935 to March 1936, was followed by that of *Orlando: A Biography* in 1937; both were undertaken by *Sur* and were later published by the prestigious Sudamericana Press. They also became, as did most of what Sur published, the standard texts from which a Spanish-American readership got acquainted with new ideas and works of fiction. These were the standard translations in Spanish of Virginia Woolf's work through the mid-twentieth-century.

In this essay, I will focus on Borges' *Un Cuarto Propio* as I draw also on my readings of his *Orlando: Una Biografía*. To my knowledge, incredibly, no full-length translation studies have been published on either of the two renditions of Woolf's work by Borges, renditions that raise any number of interesting questions. Having read the translations closely, I will answer three sets of related questions. Knowing that Borges was handling the tricky standardization of Spanish, that the readers of *Sur* were eclectic, and that the Spanish vernacular they were familiar with differed as much from country to country as it differed from each Spanish-American-speaking country and Spain, I will first determine the elements essential to Woolf's aesthetics that Borges rejected and those he accepted. Second, I will define the most important features of Borges' translations, the compromises he arrived at, the tough decisions he made, and his management of the original to produce a readable Spanish version that kept faithful to the original while it captured the Englishness of Woolf's. Finally, I will examine the gender issues involved in the decisions he made as male translator of a woman's work.[2] I will determine the way he positioned himself as a man *vis-à-vis* two foreign texts by the same female author and will answer the question of whether his decisions are consistent throughout both translations or—if not—note the places where he seems to position himself differently in each. In short, I will address his handling of Woolf's experiments with gender.

In at least two ways, Borges seems an "unlikely other" to read and recreate, as he thought successful translators invariably did, the work of Virginia Woolf. As Andrew Hurley has maintained, "Borges seemed, sometimes, to come from a place more distant than Argentina, another literary planet" (517). He also seems to have been on at least two occasions openly critical of Woolf's narrative style. In the preface to Adolfo Bioy Casares' *The Invention of Morel*, he lambasted, in

---

[2] In her observations on the process of translating *A Room of One's Own* into French, Clara Malraux argued that it was easier for her to translate a woman's work than a man's. She argued that "Virginia Woolf's long and sinuous sentences, her way of picking up and dropping a metaphor without ever abandoning it, fitted in with my capacities." She, like Woolf, had discovered that "we write with our bodies, their motor impulses and breathing rhythms, their proportions and disproportions" (198).

characteristically censorious style, all novelists who preferred the "psychological" novel, Woolf's specialty. Such a novel, he said, "would have us forget that it is verbal artifice" (5-7). At the opposite end of the spectrum is detective fiction, he maintained forcibly, the sub-genre of plot-driven stories that appealed to him most. This genre, mastered in his opinion by Edgar A. Poe, afforded the writer "the classic virtues of a beginning, a middle and an end—of something planned and executed" (Borges 5-6). Then, in an interview with Fernando Sorrentino, he argued directly against Woolf's excessive disruption of chronological time which was for him "the natural order of the narrative" (61). Second, Borges' renowned postmodern denial of individual agency opposed the relational, socially-developed self so prevalent in the work of the British writer.

In some other ways, however, Borges as translator was an excellent fit. He admired her work. An account in the weekly "El Hogar" (a capsule biography appearing on October 30, 1936, in between the publication of Borges' translations of Woolf in *Sur*) leaves no doubt of his admiration of her style. He calls Woolf's imagination and mind among the most sensitive of the English experimentalists and *Orlando* an extremely original novel; he describes its prose as musical not only on account of its language but of the novel's structure which isolates certain motifs that combine and recur. Borges equally applies the adjective "musical" to the prose of *A Room of One's Own* ("El Hogar" 38-39). Furthermore, he shared a fundamental concern with Woolf, at least as the writer of *Orlando: A Biography*. Both were envisioning innovation of a similar nature: to make the translator and the biographer respectively much more central to the creative activity than each had been in its respective tradition. They were both trying to liberate, the biographer from the facts of life, the translator from the original.

Borges had always regarded translations and exercises related to them— even those not completely successful—as literary practices worth pursuing in their own right.[3] Some critics have argued that the acknowledged English flair of Borges' own Spanish prose is precisely the quality that makes his own work in translation exquisitely readable in English.[4] So his coming in and out of lan-

---

[3] For example, he attempted a translation of *Macbeth* but abandoned it because he deemed Shakespeare's rendering of Germanic and Latinate words impossible in Spanish (*Conversaciones de Jorge L. Borges con Antonio Carrizo*, 180). However, in his youth, he had composed some poems in Shakespeare's idiom that he never found sufficiently embarrassing to disown. Rather, he included them in his *Obras Completas*, published by Emecé at the end of his life.

[4] Ilan Stavans made this observation most recently in his review of Borges' *Collected Fictions* translated by Andrew Hurley. Also, Norman Thomas di Giovanni, who worked with Borges from 1968 to 1972, has argued that "Borges' sentence structure is often molded on English sentence structure" (Sorrentino 174).

guages seems to have been regarded by him and his critics as a process that, if anything, enhanced rather than hampered his literary style. Throughout his literary career, he worked tirelessly on translations of both prose and poetry. He thought highly of a genre that he knew was an indispensable means of making foreign texts available to readers who could not access the language of the original. As a member of the editorial board of *Sur*, he expatiated repeatedly on what he was convinced was a shamefully underrated craft when he collaborated with other translators on an issue entitled *"Problemas de la Traducción"* (1976). As a result, he fought for specific material concerns related to the profession of translator, like the proper remuneration of the translator's work, unquestionably considered lower than that of the creative writer. In part he owed the global fame he attained as a fiction writer in the early sixties (his first short story in English was published in the U.S. in 1962) to the multiple translations of his work into multiple languages. He had such respect for the skill of some translations of his own work, especially of his poetry, that he acknowledged them as improvements on the originals.[5] His ample knowledge of foreign language and culture had taught him both the intellectual as well as the practical challenge posed by the translator's job of the creative writer. Finally, he made the translator a protagonist of legendary tales of ambition (Pierre Menard), obsession (Funes, the Memorious), defeat (Averroes), and erudition but always placed his task at the center of the narrative.

With *Orlando*, on the other hand, Woolf was breaking with Victorian biographical modes and releasing the biographer from as similar a position of servitude to the subject matter as Borges was trying to release the translator from the creative writer. In the early stages of Woolf's thinking about biographical form, she had indicated her allegiance to more contemporary styles of manipulating facts and departing from strict observation of reality. In the essay entitled "Literary Geography" (1905), Woolf evaluates positively the creative impetus of writers like Thackeray and Dickens who not only picture but "interpret" geographical facts (33). In this review essay, Woolf praises the transformation of the city of London in their fiction to the point that it becomes a territory within a writer's own brain, a fictional landscape unmatched by "tangible brick and mortar" (35). Years later, reviewing the work of Vita Sackville-West's husband,

---

[5] Borges made this comment in "El arte de traducir," an essay published in an issue of *Sur* exclusively devoted to the subject of translation and published in Buenos Aires in 1976. A few of the essays on translation compiled in this issue had been published in English as part of the proceedings of the Conference on Literary Translation held in New York City in May 1970 under the auspices of PEN American Center (120). Norman Thomas di Giovanni has also maintained that Borges allowed himself to intervene backwards as it were: from translation back to original (Sorrentino 171-172).

Harold Nicolson, in *Some People*, Woolf published an essay, "The New Biography" (1927), in which she applauds Nicolson's blend of reality and imagination. Biography has served two aims, Woolf suggests, the search for both truth and personality, which she translates into "granite" and "rainbow." The twentieth century, Woolf argued, had been characterized by a change in biography wherein the biographer is no longer relegated to a position of subservience to his subject but is an artist in his or her own right. In Woolf's opinion, Nicolson comes close to accomplishing the marrying of granite and rainbow. "For it would seem that the life," Woolf wrote, "which is increasingly real to us is the fictitious life; it dwells in the personality rather than in the act. Each of us is more Hamlet, Prince of Denmark, than he is John Smith of the Corn Exchange" (155).

Borges left scattered testimony that allows us to envision his stance on translation. For example, he discussed the negative criticism his own rendition of Faulkner's circuitous sentences elicited as if he, as translator, were responsible for their length. He studied carefully the different versions of *The Thousand and One Nights* and described the characteristics of each (92-109). However, he left no record of the specific challenges he faced with Woolf's work except bizarre statements of vagueness surrounding the authorship of *Un Cuarto Propio*. It is common knowledge that this translation is attributed to Borges but that his mother, Leonor Acevedo, had some important—albeit vague—role in its production. In one instance at least Borges referred to collaboration; he admitted to having signed the translation and to his mother having polished it (Christ 407). In the case of these two translations, a reader is left with little more than the translations themselves, some specific comments on the function of translation, and a general sense of Borges' stance on prose. For example, Borges' authorial presence is deceptively self-effacing in his fiction; he has a great capacity for ventriloquism. Juxtaposing his work as writer-translator with his short- and non-fiction allows one to share in his conviction that some translations can surpass the original in quality, a concept he adopted as critical truism and a belief he upheld repeatedly when evaluating the capable translations of his own work. Consider, for example, "Las versiones Homéricas" (1932 in Spanish; trans. 1976). In this essay, Borges conceives of the reader-translator. He argues that any translation involves interpretation (110-112) and that each is not the definitive translation of Homer in this case (or of any other author for that matter) but a "version" that adds itself to an infinite possible number of versions. The sum of all approximates the metaphorical palimpsest of an Ezra Pound or a Hilda Doolittle. Or consider the dazzling parable of "Pierre Menard: Author of the Quixote" (published in 1941, a bit later than his translations of Woolf) as one of the early fictional texts in the evolution of Borges' thinking about translation. This text casts serious doubt on the superiority of original over translation. According to the narrator, Menard's undertaking to recreate the *Quixote* was not an exercise in futility. Even though the version he creates from Nîmes in the thirties may look identical to that of the famed sixteenth-century Cervantes, Menard proves no servant to Cervantes, and his version is no parasite living off the original either. Menard's is richer and more startling because he accesses Cervantes' experience "through the experiences of Pierre Menard" (Hurley 91). That was the challenge.

And that, one presumes, was Borges' challenge when faced with Woolf's texts. Undoubtedly, he was more than well-equipped to face the task. He was a stylist with mastery of Spanish and thorough familiarity with British English. His daunting job was to provide a "version" of her works so as to integrate them into the Spanish-American conception of life. But for someone so intent on championing the genre and liberating the translator from the pressure of producing a definitive text of the original in the new context, Borges translates quite literally. About Nicholas Greene, Woolf writes:

> That he did not know a geranium from a carnation, an oak from a birch tree, a mastiff from a greyhound, a teg from a ewe, wheat from barley, plough land from fallow; was ignorant of the rotation of the crops; thought oranges grew under ground and turnips on trees; preferred any townscape to any landscape;— all this and much more amazed Orlando who had never met anybody of this kind before. (Woolf, *Orlando* 92)

Borges translates almost word by word:

> Que no distinguiera un geranio de un clavel, una encina de un chopo, un mastín de un sabueso, un borrego de una oveja, el trigo de la cebada, la tierra arada de la tierra en reposo; que ignorara la rotación de las siembras; que pensara que las naranjas crecen bajo tierra y los nabos en los árboles; que prefiriera cualquier rincón de Londres al mejor paisaje del campo—todo esto y mucho más azoraba a Orlando, que no había conocido nunca una persona así. (Borges, *Orlando* 62)

This literalness results in accurate and concise translation. Except for some radical license at paragraphing in both *Un Cuarto Propio* and *Orlando*, the changes he makes to the original are far from substantial. Some seem to be guided by a desire to make allusion of a foreign nature accessible. A reference easily understood by the audience of the original may not be so in the new cultural context. Thus, Borges eliminates references to place setting that Woolf prefers somewhat vague. In the passage quoted above, she leaves Anglophone readers to elicit the beauty of any town; Borges denies the Hispanophone reader that possibility by attributing that beauty specifically to London (62). When Orlando travels back from Constantinople as a woman, she recalls the benefits of being a man and "sit[ing] among my peers" (158), which Borges translates as "sentarme en el

Parlamento" (104). In *Un Cuarto Propio*, the morning paper announces "a big score in South Africa" (33). In Spanish the big score is in cricket (34). With similar logic, when the narrator envisions gender role changes likely to take place in a hundred years, like "the shop-woman will drive an engine" (40), Borges chooses to specify what kind of engine, a locomotive (41), as one of the most gender-defiant roles a woman can undertake. Conversely, a reference may be obscure in Spanish. Borges drops the specific reference to Guy Fawkes (158) for a very general "mamarracho" (104), an embarrassing fool.

Other interventions are much more interesting and deserve some commentary. They seem recreations of certain detail. When Marlowe predicts that Shakespeare will be a celebrated poet but does not live to see the prediction come true—for "he was killed two nights later in a drunken brawl" (90)—Borges describes the manner of Marlowe's death more explicitly than does Woolf. He is killed, "apuñalado" (60), he writes; that is, he dies of wounds inflicted with a fist, or knife, or some similar violent means. Here Borges appears to slip briefly into the glorification of manliness and toughness such as the one he exalted in his own bloody descriptions of knife fighters, throat-slitters, evil and casually violent men and women.[6]

Possibly more interesting still are the passages in *Orlando* and *Un Cuarto Propio* that highlight gender concerns. They reveal a translator, who in theory approves of entanglements with the translation, at work with a narrator-biographer, who in turn approves of entanglements with his/her subject matter. In the masque of chapter 3, Borges takes a number of liberties. These liberties neutralize gender content in radical ways. Borges changes paragraphing. The climactic "[…] we have no choice left but confess—he was a woman" (137) is rendered a one-sentence paragraph in Spanish: "Debemos confesarlo: era una mujer" (90), followed by another one-sentence paragraph: "The sound of the trumpets died away and Orlando stood stark naked" (138). In Spanish Borges writes, "La voz de las trompetas se apagó y Orlando quedó desnudo" (90). It may be safe to assume that in this instance the effect of the change is added emphasis. But when, for the sake of transition, Orlando's biographer carries both masculine and feminine structures together, he blends them in the plural form and refers to them together:

> The change in sex, though it altered their future, did nothing whatever to alter their identity. Their identities remained, as the portraits prove, practically the same. (138)

The translator is hard-pressed to find the strategy that will successfully do so—without confusion—for the Spanish reader. Unwilling to go for the plural in

Spanish, Borges-translator nails the masculine much faster by ascribing a singular noun and by compressing the narrative:

> El cambio de sexo modificaba su porvenir, no su identidad. Su cara, como lo pueden demostrar sus retratos, era la misma (90).

Similarly, in chapter 4, the biographer intervenes repeatedly to draw attention to the way in which Orlando is gradually taking to the attributes of femininity after her metamorphosis. References to "the biographer or the historian"/ "the poets and the novelists" (192), with the capacity to convey the gender-ambiguity crucial to *Orlando* in English, are rendered masculine in Spanish (125) as are references to a universal reader in this passage (199) and throughout. The Spanish language may be thought to leave no such possibility of gender ambiguity because of the scarcity of neuters; most adjectives, articles, and nouns are designated either masculine or feminine (*lector* or *lectora*). However, the possibility exists to translate certain Spanish words both in the feminine and the masculine. In poetic contexts one can choose the feminine rendition of "the ship" ("la barca") over the more common "el barco" to represent its elegance, its smooth sailing, or its majestic nature. Not every Spanish noun offers that potential, though. But one should not forget that Borges was a poet, and an *ultraista* poet at that, with recourse to the neuter-bound potential of language by countless other means. But as translator he chose to tamper with the material in other ways. In a parenthetical intervention, the biographer says:

> (It must be remembered that she was like a child, entering into the possession of a pleasaunce or a toycupboard; her arguments would not commend themselves to mature women who have had the run of it all their lives) (*O* 156)

Borges translates:

> (Debemos recordar que era como un niño, que toma posesión de un jardín o de un armario de juguetes: sus razonamientos no podían ser los de una mujer ya madura que ha disfrutado de esas cosas toda su vida) (103)

Borges changes feminine into masculine and singular into plural. So the female child becomes a boy, and the plural "women" is singularized. Then, he renders "to have the run of it"—in the sense of having the opportunity or the freedom to do—with the Spanish verb "disfrutar," which means literally "to enjoy." The question of choice is sidestepped, and there may be in this rendition a move towards erasing "women" and favoring an iconic representation of "woman."

A few scholars have recently documented Borges' interventions over material that may prove controversial or inflammatory. Daniel Balderston noted the suppression of homoerotic material in his critical essays and his prejudiced stance on homosexuality in general (29-45). More to the point of Borges' work as translator, Eduardo Gonzalez has observed the erasure of explicitly homosexual content from Borges' rendition of Walt Whitman's *Leaves of Grass* (50-51).

The changes noted in *Orlando* are all consistent with those he allows in *Un Cuarto Propio* where he consistently favors the masculine subject throughout. A well-known passage in chapter three reads,

> When [...] one reads of a witch being ducked, of a woman possessed by devils, of a wise woman selling herbs, or even of a remarkable man who had a mother, then I think we are on the track of a lost novelist, a suppressed poet, of some mute and inglorious Jane Austen [...] (50-51)

I will call attention to "one reads," "uno lee," and "novelist," "un novelista" (49-50). These decisions in which the universal reader is subsumed as masculine, a matter of style in Spanish, are worthy of commentary for two reasons. First, they are easily avoided even by the novice translator by substituting the first-person plural "leemos" or the indefinite "one reads" or simply by the use of a passive construction that would make the translation literal, "se lee." Second, these decisions seem almost over-determined by the rhetorical situation. The audience Woolf was addressing at Newnham and Girton on the subject of women and fiction was female, and the items on the list that follow the tricky gender of pronouns, namely Jane Austen and Emily Brontë, were also female.

Borges' 1937 translation of *Orlando: A Biography* was subsequently published by Sudamericana Press in 1943, 1945, 1951, and 1968. His rendition of Woolf's work added itself to the numerous texts instrumental in forming a community of readers in Spanish America. When Borges translates literally and accurately, his voice is that of a purveyor of high culture responsible for transmitting, as transparently as he can, the ideas he received and so greatly admired. In this instance he positioned himself vis-à-vis Woolf's text almost as an absence. His presence is more clearly felt in the rendering of gender, undoubtedly the most overreaching thematic concern of *A Room of One's Own* and the most challenging function of *Orlando* as text. In his handling of gender he adopts a critical masculine presence which sabotages the texts.

---

[6] Fernando Alegría makes a similar point when he evaluates Borges' translation of Walt Whitman's "Song of Myself" (Greenspan 208-219).

Works Cited

Alegria, Fernando. "Borges's 'Song of Myself." *The Cambridge Companion to Walt Whitman*. Ed. Ezra Greenspan. Cambridge: Cambridge UP, 1995. 208-219.

Balderston, Daniel. "The 'Fecal Dialectic.'" *Entiendes? Queer Readings, Hispanic Writings*. Eds. Emilie Bergmann and Paul J. Smith. Durham: Duke UP, 1995. 29-45.

Borges, Jorge Luis. *Collected Fictions*. Trans. Andrew Hurley. New York: Penguin, 1999.

———. "El arte de traducir." *Sur*, Enero-Diciembre, 1976. 117-120.

———. Interview with Antonio Carrizo. *Borges el Memorioso*. Mexico: Fondo de Cultura Económica, 1982.

———. "Translators of the Thousand and One Nights." *Selected Non-Fictions*. (Ed.) Eliot Weinberger. New York: Penguin, 1999. 92-109.

———. *Orlando*. Trans. Jorge L. Borges. Mexico: Hermes/Sudamericana: 1968.

———. Prologue. *The Invention of Morel and Other Stories*. By Adolfo Bioy Casares. Trans. Ruth L.S. Simms. Austin: U of Texas P, 1986. 5-6.

———. *Textos Cautivos: Ensayos y reseñas en "El Hogar"*. Eds. Enrique Sacerio-Gari and Emil Rodriguez Monegal. Barcelona: Tusquets Editors, 1986. 38-39.

———. *Un cuarto propio*. *Sur*. 5.15 (1935), 7-29; 6.16 (1936), 26-58; 6.17 (1936), 41-61; 6.18 (1936), 46-81.

Christ, Ronald. "Borges at New York." Newman Charles and Mary Kinzie. *Prose for Borges*. Evanston: Northwestern U, 1974. 396-411.

Del Carril, Sara L. and Mercedes Rubio de Socchi. Nota del Editor. *Borges en Sur: 1931-1980*. By Borges. Buenos Aires: Emecé, 1999. 7-8.

Di Giovanni, Norman, Daniel Halpern and Frank MacShane (eds.) *Borges on Writing*. New Jersey: The Ecco Press, 1972.

Gonzalez, Eduardo. *The Monstered Self: Narratives of Death and Performance in Latin American Fiction*. Durham: Duke UP, 1992. 50-51.

Fuentes, Ana, Carol Maier, and Lynda Privitera. "The Construction of 'Further, Alternative Signs': Notes from a Workshop in Translating Women Writers." *Letras Femeninas*. Número Extraordinario Conmemorativo: 1974-1994. 167-175.

Hurley, Andrew. "A Note on the Translation." Jorge Luis Borges, *Collected Fictions*. New York: Penguin, 1999. 517-521.

Malraux, Clara. "Translation and Complicity." *The World of Translation: Papers Delivered at the Conference on Literary Translation*. New York City, 1970. New York: PEN American Center, 1971. 195-201.

Stavans, Ilan. *Times Literary Supplement*, January 29, 1999. 24-25.
Sorrentino, Fernando. *Seven Conversations with Jorge L. Borges*. Zlotchew, Clark, trans. Troy: The Whitston Publishing Co., 1982.
Woolf, Virginia. *A Room of One's Own*. 1929. New York: Harcourt Brace Jovanovich, 1957.
——. "Literary Biography." *The Essays of Virginia Woolf. Volume I: 1904-1912*. Andrew McNeillie, ed. New York: Harcourt Brace Jovanovich, 1986.
——. *Orlando: A Biography*. 1928. New York: Harcourt Brace Jovanovich, 1956.
——. "The New Biography." *Granite and Rainbow: Essays*. New York: Harcourt Brace Jovanovich, 1958. 149-155.

Shirking the Imperial Shadow: Virginia Woolf and Alice Munro*

Jane Lilienfeld

Can one hypothesize, as some Canadian critics do, that female is to male as periphery is to Empire[1] (Fraser xviii-xix; Irvine 50-51)? Materialist feminists working in Postcolonial studies have long argued that women occupy relative positions of privilege within systems of gender, race, and colonial domination (Ashcroft, et al. 249; Donaldson 34). Posthumously, the icon of Virginia Woolf (Silver), anti-imperialist, may have cast a not disempowering shadow over the dominion/ated writer, Alice Munro.[2]

When in the early 1950s Alice Munro first encountered Virginia Woolf, numerous Canadians whose forebears came from the United Kingdom experi-

*I wish to express my gratitude for a Canadian Studies Research Grant that enabled me to spend the summer term of 2001 working in the Alice Munro *Fonds*, housed in the Special Collections of the Mackimmie Library of the University of Calgary, Calgary, Alberta, Canada. I thank Apollonia Steele, Special Collections Librarian, and her staff for their generous assistance as I worked with selected materials in the Alice Munro Fonds. The Canadian Studies Research Grant sustained not only my work on primary reference materials, but also my extensive reading of critical literature about Alice Munro in the Mackimmie Library general collection. For generous help with additional reference materials, I wish to thank Marcia Deihl, Staff Assistant at Tozzer Library, Harvard University, Gregory A. Finnegan, Ph.D., Associate Librarian for Public Service and Head of Reference, Tozzer Library, Harvard University, and Michael Cook, Executive Staff Assistant to the Director of the Library, University of Missouri, Columbia. This paper is dedicated to Michael Beard, with my deepest thanks.

[1] As a white woman aware of living in a government devolving from colonial power, Woolf was herself oppressed while also situated in relative privilege vis à vis indigenous peoples. JoAnn McCaig holds a similar view of Munro's positionality in contextualizing Munro's struggle for publication and recognition. McCaig reads Munro at the start of her career as excluded from serious consideration as a writer by gender and by "provincial" nationality in the Canadian backwater of the Commonwealth (32-6, 121). Herb Wylie questions in what ways might Canadian literature be interrogated as Postcolonial, arguing that in "settler-invader" cultures such as Canada, Australia, and New Zealand, "English Canadian" writers had to distinguish themselves from the British [male] establishment, but were a part of that "invader" culture that absorbed the lands of those indigenous peoples they displaced (139-40). As analyzed by Wylie, then, Munro may be seen as excluded by gender from equality with the English Canadian and British literary elite males, while nevertheless having national and white skin privilege in relation to indigenous Canadians and immigrants. See note 8 for a further discussion of this point.

[2] In articulating similarities, of course, I am not arguing that Virginia Woolf was the only foremother whose works illuminated a pathway that Alice Munro may have fol-

enced themselves as very much a part of the British Empire. Growing up as a Polish immigrant in Canada, for example, Alice Hoffman noted that the coronation of Queen Elizabeth II on June 2, 1953 was an event even more celebrated in some parts of the dominion of Canada than in London (101-102). At the time that Alice Munro became acquainted with her work, Virginia Woolf was disparaged by segments of the British intelligentsia. So soon after World War II, Woolf's socialist, feminist, pacifist views were seen by some as suspect, and her suicide was interpreted as cowardice in wartime by others (Reid 455). The Leavises' view of her, certainly, excoriated Woolf's elite class status, underpinned, they insisted, by her co-ownership of the Hogarth Press and, to them, her uncomplicated access to the opinion-shaping power wielded by the male homosocial elite of the Bloomsbury Group (Marcus, *Languages* 76, "Wrapped" 18-20).

Newly married to a young man from a well-off family, Alice Munro was living at this time what she herself termed a double life. Like Woolf, Munro had begun writing as a young girl, telling interviewers later that

> I always did value myself terribly, but I had to pretend I didn't for the purpose of disguise [...]. And then when I got married quite young and started having kids and lived in the [Vancouver] suburbs, I went on [...] living two completely different lives [...] I worked out a way of living by pretending to be what people wanted me to be [...] (Munro, qtd. in Ross 17-19).

---

lowed. Although similarity by no means proves causality, a comparison of narrative techniques used by both writers highlights significant parallels, which this essay will explore. Like all successful writers, Munro assimilated and absorbed numerous disparate influences. For example, Munro herself cites the importance to her craft of American Southern women writers such as Eudora Welty, Flannery O'Connor, Carson McCullers (Munro, qtd. in Struthers 8). (Significantly, Eudora Welty has acknowledged the influence on her work of Virginia Woolf.) Nora Robson calls these "the authors of the Faulknerian school [...]" in her excellent study of the influence of such writers on Munro's style and content (84). Additionally, Robert Thacker has argued for Willa Cather's influence on Alice Munro ("Cather"). Further, Scots-Irish literature is seen as an important influence on attitudes and plots in Munro's works (Waterson 248-56; Redekop, "Scottish").

Beverly Rasporich questioned Alice Munro about the possible literary influence of Virginia Woolf on her work, as I will discuss below. Asked as a part of an interview in 1975 by Barbara Martineau about the similarity to her own of Woolf's views on women writers' anger at male oppression, Munro downplayed the comparison (*MsC* 37.20.20.f28-9). Unfortunately not explored further in her superb book on Alice Munro is the tantalizing paragraph that Coral Ann Howells wrote in 1990, comparing the two writers' narrative strategies: "In these late stories Munro comes close to Virginia Woolf's abnegation of authorial omniscience in *Jacob's Room* (1922), a novel whose very title suggests comparison with Munro's 'enclosed spaces,' or Woolf's decentering strategies of *Between the Acts* (1941). In both these women's fictions there is always excess and incompleteness, where determination of meaning is no longer possible" ("Indeterminacy" 151).

When first encountering Virginia Woolf and works about her, Munro appears to have had a complicated response to this symbol of the prominence of British writing (Rasporich 9-11), under the shadow of which was written what readers and writers of it alike later came to call "Can Lit," Canadian literature (Atwood, 11, 29).[3]

What would Munro have been likely to read? By 1953 all of Woolf's novels, many of her stories, *A Room of One's Own*, *Three Guineas*, four books of essays and criticism, and familiar essays published in popular magazines were available, and Leonard Woolf's edition of his wife's *A Writer's Diary* was published in 1954. Munro notes that for her, writing is a natural outgrowth of reading (Ross 42-44) and that at this period she read omnivorously, acknowledging—among others—the influence of American Southern women's stories (qtd. in Struthers 8). Munro had access to literature through her jobs in a university and then a public library,[4] but it seems that it was within a subversive female friendship, augmenting what Munro had found in the library, that Alice Munro discovered Virginia Woolf. Munro and a woman friend—on the surface, ordinary housewives and mothers living in suburban Western Vancouver—

> would 'spend every Tuesday afternoon [. . .] drinking coffee and smoking until we were dizzy [...] We read all the books by and about D. H. Lawrence, Katherine Mansfield, the Bloomsbury Group, and then we would get together and we'd talk with incredible excitement' [...] (Munro, qtd. in Rasporich 9).

Following Lawrence and Mansfield, Virginia Woolf is not named, but subsumed into the Bloomsbury Group, appearing to signify that which Munro could never be: established, upper-class, British. Did Munro feel more aligned with Lawrence, from a working class family, and Mansfield, New Zealand rebel against wealth and bourgeois respectability?

---

[3] The journal *Canadian Literature* was first published in Summer, 1959, and Klinck's authoritative three-volume edition of *The Literary History of Canada* first appeared in 1965.

[4] Alice Munro had a part-time job in the University of Western Ontario library from 1949 through 1951, working as well in the public library in London, Ontario (Ross 10, 46-47). After her marriage, Munro worked in the public library in Vancouver, British Columbia from 1952 through 1955 (Ross 52). Discussing her wide reading in these years, Munro told Struthers that "I learned nothing at university about new books, though I did stumble on some books. [...] So the most important work I did [at university] was reading in the library. Then that just went on. After I was married and was having children, I was led from one title to another. [...]" (7-8; see also Ross 47, 52).

Feminist scholars brilliantly debate the vexed personal and literary relations between Mansfield and Woolf (*D2* 225-227; Dunbar; Kaplan; A. Smith; Winston). Evelyn Haller succinctly argues the main points of critical debate: Virginia Woolf resented, envied, and adapted certain of Katherine Mansfield's techniques, felt class antagonism, and experienced complex sexual attraction and disparagement of her literary rival. One could certainly speculate that Katherine Mansfield's work had an equally profound effect on Alice Munro as it did on Woolf, for, as Munro told John Metcalf in 1972, "I was very influenced by Katherine Mansfield at one time" (57). While both Mansfield and Woolf textualize the female body, a central preoccupation of Munro's fiction, below I will suggest that Munro learned from Woolf how to disguise and disperse narratorial voice through a multilayered discourse that filters female experience through plots representing random circumstance.[5]

Alice Munro, in an interview given to Beverly Rasporich in the 1980s, suggests that Woolf's colonial and class privilege shaped Munro's conceptualization of Virginia Woolf. Referring to the now heavily-contested site of Woolf's *Diary* entries excoriating James Joyce for his vulgarity (*D2* 14, 199, 203-4), Munro seems to read the entry at face value, championing Joyce for his refusal to lie about the human body (qtd. in Rasporich 21). Ascribing to Woolf the supposed prissiness of her social class, Munro dismisses Woolf's aversion to the body. Is it likely that in 2003 after a career spent as a feminist writer,[6] Munro would view either Woolf or Joyce as she did at the time of the interview? It is possible that the newer work by diverse writers such as Patricia Moran, Patricia Cramer, Pam Olano or Patricia Juliana Smith would convince Munro to reconsider how Virginia Woolf textualizes the lesbian body. It is equally possible that the feminist revision of the then-esteemed body of Molly Bloom (Henke) would give Munro pause, thereby troubling her privileging of Joyce's representations. On the other hand, it is also possible that Munro would still maintain such views about Woolf, for Munro ascribes these views to Woolf based on an analysis of the social class differences dividing the two writers. Throughout her discussion about this with Rasporich, Munro insistently contrasts Woolf's elite British/Empire status with Joyce's colonized/Irish poverty.

[5] Dunbar's analysis of the narrative voice deployed in Mansfield's works attempts to demonstrate the existence of multiple narrative sites in some of the stories. More convincing are Dunbar's strong readings of the aboriginal "other" in Mansfield's earlier works.
[6] Alice Munro has repeatedly stated that she espouses many of the goals of the women's movement. See for example, her interview with Kem Murch during which she told Murch that "I'm intellectually a great supporter of the women's movement" (43). See also her comments about the effects on her of being a female writer in Hancock 102, Gibson 249-50, 254, Metcalf 59-60.

Indeed, viewed as subjects of the British Empire, Virginia Woolf grew up in the Metropolis, whereas Alice Munro grew up in the Huron River Valley in Ottawa, Canada on a failed fox farm. Nestled in "the Victorian Intelligentsia," (Annan 5-6), the Stephen family into which Virginia Woolf was born in 1882 was economically secure, owned property, and, like many Victorian families of their social milieu, employed numerous servants. When Alice Munro was born in 1931, the economic depression of those years impacted her parents' already-insecure financial circumstances.

Alice Munro's paternal forebears were impoverished Scots farmers who emigrated in 1818 to the British territories in Canada (Ross 27-28). In 1850, they obtained "crown lands" in the Huron Valley bush (Ross 27-28); that is, lands obtained from indigenous tribes by the subterfuges of colonial practices, were ceded to them in return for a token sum. Even after two generations, however, their descendants lived a disadvantaged rural existence. As Munro could have discovered in reading about Woolf, Leslie Stephen's forebears, too, had begun as industrious Scots colonists; but Stephen's grandfather had emigrated to the West Indies, and with his return and subsequent attachment to the abolitionist Wilberforce elite, his fortunes had risen (Annan 6-7). Woolf's paternal and maternal forebears had profited in money and status from a colonial system in which Munro's ancestors, with much less success, had found themselves inscribed.[7]

Certainly the metropole/periphery and social class differences separate the two writers, although, in fact, they were both descended from colonizing families. Further, their family structures had some similarities. Whether in London, England or in Wingham, Ontario, both their fathers believed that women were second class citizens in the home—where their duty was to take care of men—and in the state. Much less well off than Leslie Stephen, who had objected to his

---

[7] As did Virginia Woolf in *The Voyage Out* (Abel), *To the Lighthouse* (Phillips), and *The Waves* (Abravanel), in her fiction Munro investigates the ambiguous situation of white women within colonial Empire. For example, Munro's story "Eskimo" uses the colonized consciousness of its adulterous narrator, whose lover/boss is racially prejudiced, to explore this white woman's response to her conflicting feelings about a woman whose ambiguous identity seems to the narrator to mark the woman as abused, masochistic, "Eskimo." A more frequently discussed example in the critical literature is Munro's story "Meneseteung," which creates a narrator who seeks to understand the fictional figure of a nineteenth century forgotten female poet and through her, to interrogate "colonial constructions of middle-class femininity [within the poet's] family's pioneer history" (Howells 106). Significantly, "[t]he story's title is the ancient Indian name for the Maitland River, at the mouth of which Goderich [the town where the action is set] is situated" (Howells 107).

daughter Virginia's attending university,[8] Robert Laidlaw, Alice Munro's father, strictly enforced the separate spheres inhabited by his son and daughters.[9] Munro was expected to perform the rigorous housework required on the family's fox farm while her brother did farm chores and roamed the outdoors (Rasporich 8). Munro's education was further curtailed by the family's financial difficulties, and only hard work in the rural Wingham public schools had enabled her to earn a minimal two-year scholarship to the University of Western Ontario. Not having the money to continue her education when the scholarship expired, Munro had left college and married (Ross 49-50). Like Virginia Woolf, personal experience and political observation had made Alice Munro a feminist writer.

Not only their fathers' upholding rigid sex role differentiation separating sons and daughters connects Woolf and Munro. The lives of both writers' mothers were complicated by the Victorian ideology of upper- and middle-class white women's roles. Julia Stephen understood that there was a life beyond sacrifice of self to others: "I had all along felt that if it had been possible for me to be myself, it would have been better for me individually; and that I could have gotten more real life out of the wreck if I had broken down more" (qtd. in Stephen 40). Yet her strong sense of duty convinced her that such a choice was not possible for her: "But there was Baby to be thought of and everyone around me urging me to keep up, and I could never be alone which sometimes was such torture" (qtd. in Stephen 40)). Because of her severe depression and her inability to break free of the sacrificial self, Julia Stephen was emotionally inaccessible to her children (DeSalvo 118), a severely wounding experience to Virginia Woolf. Woolf deeply resented her mother's insistence on serving her own mother first, then others outside the home, and, only then, her children. That others would raise one's children was normative; it was expected that Victorian children of Woolf's social class would be primarily raised by nannies. Such children were expected to see their parents only for a certain small time period each day. During that time period, Virginia Woolf felt that her mother was rushed and distracted: "Can I remember being alone with her for more than a few moments? Someone was always interrupting" (*MOB* 83). Woolf was angry at her mother's clear favoritism of her sons, particularly of Woolf's younger brother Adrian: "Him she cherished separately; she called him 'My Joy'" (*MOB* 83).[10] Julia Stephen's complicated accession to the Victorian ideology of womanhood led her to sign

---

[8] In spite of the fact that his niece Katherine Stephen was Vice-Principal of Newnham College, Cambridge.

[9] Alice Munro's brother Bill is five years younger, and her sister Sheila is six years younger than herself. Alice Munro's eldest daughter has written a memoir that provides some information about Munro's younger siblings.

[10] Louise DeSalvo considers this favoritism to have been pathological (49-56).

an anti-suffrage document (Gillespie and Steele 15), for she strongly opposed women's right to vote, as did her husband. It is perhaps no accident that after her parents' deaths, Virginia Woolf advocated women's rights and was friends with many whose lives were devoted to the cause of suffrage.[11]

Julia Stephen embodied an emotionally inaccessible ideal of beauty, while Alice Munro's mother Anne Chamney Laidlaw was a flamboyant, creative woman whose artistic talents and business acumen garnered ridicule by townspeople and family members instead of approbation. Munro's shame at her mother's difference bears some similarity to Woolf's resentment of her mother's remote perfections. Munro has attested more than once to the constricting conventionality which was part of the ethos of her town and of her family, particularly the paternal side: "with many people of this sort of Scotch-Irish background in that part of the country. One doesn't try because one may fail...[sic]" (Munro, qtd. in Gibson 247). Showiness and aggression, even in men, were frowned upon, and Munro speculates that her father's chances to gain more than a rudimentary education were shattered because he was not able to contravene the insistence on not rising above oneself ("Working" 9-11). It is not by accident that Munro's story collection was entitled in Canada, *Who Do You Think You Are?* (when published in the United States it was entitled *The Beggar Maid*) with its direct echo of words that Munro perhaps heard more than once in her extended family. Anne Chamney Laidlaw's insistence on using correct grammar and a reader's extensive vocabulary, her using good dishes and antiques representing her artistic tastes (even her laying out of the kitchen linoleum showed flare and individuality [Hancock 100]) abashed her family and bemused her neighbors in Wingham, Ontario (Ross 33). To help her husband sell his fox furs in 1941, Anne C. Laidlaw boldly became an entrepreneur, going alone to the wealthy "American" hotel to market fox scarves and capes to individual buyers (Munro, "Working" 20, 24-7). While feminists today might applaud such courage and resourcefulness, at the time, such behavior was considered so unconventional and unfeminine that it stigmatized rather than gained approval. Both daughters suffered from the cultural assessments of their mothers; Munro shared her paternal grandmother's, great aunt's, and father's embarrassment at her mother (Ross 41-2), while Woolf resented the fact that her mother embodied the Victorian female ideal. In fact, in rejecting the traditional social class and female role prescribed for her, Munro lived out something of Woolf's example and her feminist precepts.

---

[11] Repudiating her mother's views, Woolf worked for women's suffrage. After her marriage, the Woolfs were friends with many politically active feminist women. Chapman and Manson examine the complex interconnections of this important "milieu," emphasizing its complex, consistent effects on Woolf's adult life.

The writers' complicated relationships with their mothers were further distorted by the sickness of each mother. Scholars increasingly focus upon the severity and long-lasting nature of Julia Stephen's depression, tracing its inception from the death of her first husband, when she was twenty-four (Caramagno 115-24; Love 63). Her overextension of herself into the hard work of constant service to others wore Julia Stephen out, and her health broke down when she was a comparatively young woman. When Julie Stephen died, exhausted, at 47, pictures of her taken shortly before her death give the impression that she could have been a woman of 75 (DeSalvo 232 ff). Virginia Woolf was thirteen when her mother died, a vulnerable time.

Alice Munro was twelve when her mother became sick. Anne Chamney Laidlaw's illness was not correctly diagnosed for some years, and the family at first thought her symptoms were more shaming than that these were indications of serious illness: "We were *all* embarrassed by my mother *before* she got sick. When she got sick, that put the cap on it" (Munro, qtd. in Ross 36; italics in original). Living in a small town, Alice Munro was fully aware that familial appearances influenced one's place in the town's social hierarchy, a position made precarious by the family's financial challenges and their living not in Wingham proper, but in Lower Town, "a rural slum" the area on which their fox farm was located (Ross 23). Prior to her illness, Anne C. Laidlaw had been a source of embarrassment, but also an example that a woman could rebel against the narrow and rigid roles assigned to them, an example that Munro herself increasingly followed in her thirties and after (Ross 36). But when Alice Munro was twelve, the "bizarre," (Ross 39) not-yet diagnosed symptoms of her mother's illness made Anne C. Laidlaw someone from whom the daughter sought some distance.

Munro read omnivorously and first began to make up stories in her head around the age of 8. She began writing at age 11, coincident with the onset of her mother's Parkinson's Disease (Ross 43-4). Woolf, too, wrote stories from an early age. Munro was able to posit an alternative existence in the literature she conceptualized and then wrote. However, Munro outwardly conformed to the traditional female role, as this was instilled by the teachings and example of her paternal relatives and the mores of the Wingham bourgeoisie. In this impersonation of a conventional woman with a hidden, artistic life of the mind were intertwined both the roots of her writing career and her terrified rejection of her mother's strangeness.

More than one Woolf scholar has interrogated the complex intersection of illness and gender-roles in Woolf's background. Leslie Stephen's ailments and his emotional instability elicited his wife's constant attention, that is, unless she were serving her mother. Maria Jackson, Julia's mother, had been wracked by rheumatism since 1856, and Julia had taken over the nursing care of her mother by her sixteenth year. Even during her marriage to Sir Leslie, Julia put her mother's needs before those of her husband. When Julia was not helping her mother or husband in times of illness, she was nursing members of her extended family (Gillespie and Steele xx-xxii). So insistent was Julia on helping the ill, that she volunteered as a nurse in St. Ives, Cornwall, where the family summered, and was remembered there via a scholarship (Gillespie and Steele 21; Lilienfeld, *Reading* 179-84). Julia's treatise on nursing, much praised in its time, led Jane Marcus to remark: "the world of the sick is a little empire, and the nurse is queen" ("Violin" 183). The message is clear: to merit Julia's love and attention, one had to be either male or an invalid: "there were two modes of life for a Victorian girl of [Woolf's] class, to nurse or to be nursed, to care for invalids or to be an invalid" (Marcus, "Violin" 183). In different ways, their mother's relationship to illness profoundly impacted both Woolf and Munro.[12]

On first reading Woolf in the 1950s, Munro may not have known of the several similarities between herself and Woolf; nevertheless, I think it unlikely that Munro would have fully assented to "the Leavisite view" of Woolf.[13] Refusing to reduce literature to ideology, Munro might have gathered strength from study-

---

[12] "Munro reworks the sick mother story again and again" (Howells 23), while Virginia Woolf believed that she had escaped her mother's haunting her imagination by writing *To the Lighthouse*. "Until I was in the forties [...] the presence of my mother obsessed me. I could hear her voice, see her, imagine what she would do or say as I went about my day's doings [...] [In writing *To the Lighthouse*] I suppose I did for myself what psycho-analysts do for their patients. I expressed some very long felt and deeply felt emotion. And in expressing it, I explained it and then laid it to rest [...]" (*MOB* 80-1; For further discussion of Woolf's fictional use of the mother figure, see my essay "Mother Love").

The desire to purge the internalized figure of the mother takes fictional form in the multilayered interior monologue of the narrator of what Howells describes as the "most unabashedly autobiographical" of Munro's fiction (24), "The Ottawa Valley": "The problem, the only problem, is my mother. And she is the one of course that I am trying to get [...] To mark her off, to describe, to illumine, to celebrate, to get *rid*, of her; and it did not work, for she looms too close, just as she always did. [...] I could go on, and on, applying what skills I have, using what tricks I know, and it would always be the same" (Munro, "Ottawa" 246.) Emphasis and punctuation in original.). Indeed, Munro has redrawn, reshaped, revised the never-disappearing mother for much of her career in such stories as "The Peace of Utrecht," "The Progress of Love," "Friend of My Youth" among others. Madeline Redekop's book *Mothers and Other Clowns* provides an excellent analysis of mothers and mothering in Munro's fiction (See also Ross 38-42; Howells 19-25, 90-2, 102-5; Smythe). In light of feminist readings of Munro's use of the mother figure in fiction, Robert Thacker's interrogation of the blurred generic lines in Munro's seemingly autobiographical works is an excellent critical intervention, "'So Shocking a Verdict in Real Life': Autobiography in Alice Munro's Stories."

[13] Brenda Silver interrogates "the Leavisite view" of Woolf in *Icon*; see especially 108-16.

ing Woolf's "Modern Fiction." There Virginia Woolf promulgates what might be called her manifesto of narratological revolution. Her essay suggests a reconsideration of what constitutes plot, a focus on consciousness, and on the so-called trivial. Woolf stated that in modern fiction, the plots of the Edwardians must be jettisoned in favor of what had heretofore been called the inconsequential: "At once, therefore, the accent falls a little differently; the emphasis is upon something hitherto ignored [...] the emphasis is laid upon such unexpected places that at first it seems as if there is no emphasis at all [...]" (Woolf, "Modern" 156-7). Significantly, Woolf's "Modern Fiction" concludes with mention of Chekov, a writer to whom Munro is often compared (Ozick, qtd. in McCulloch and Simpson 229; Giles 66). Indeed, as if seemingly following the suggestions laid out in "Modern Fiction," Munro's earliest fiction reconsiders what constitutes plot, uses consciousness, not only as the focus of the story but as its central narrative strategy, and focuses on what some readers might still view as quotidian and trivial.

In addition to "Modern Fiction," in Woolf's stories and novels Munro would have learned Woolf's methodologies, so suitable to her own needs and tastes. Through complex and freighted skeins of allusion rather than political pronouncements, Woolf's narratives represent a feminist, anti-imperial worldview, one skewering patriarchal institutions' on-going class and racial domination (Marcus, *Languages* 38, 42, 132-133). Both Woolf and Munro satirize traditional marriage plots, focusing on the seemingly random happenstance of daily life, on human relationships and consciousness rather than on external events (DuPlessis 48, 56-60). Both deploy a multi-situated, polyphonic narration to represent fictions of women who, while seemingly entrapped in patriarchal settings, circumvent circumstance. Although Woolf is best known for novels and Munro for stories, in fact, both writers trouble generic boundaries. Munro's recent works are novellas (Howells 11), and Woolf's experiments in form emerged from her short stories (*D2* 13-14).

Published in 1974 in the volume entitled *Something I've Been Meaning to Tell You*, Munro's short story "How I Met My Husband" is a feminist critique of the romantic view of marriage, presented through a combination of retrospective first person narration and disguised narratorial commentary couched in free indirect discourse.

The setting in Ontario, Canada, is a large house on land that used to be a rural farm but is fast becoming suburbanized. The suppressed native claims to this tract of land shimmer almost visibly in the background,[14] creating a palimpsest through which are visible subtle variations on colonization.

---

[14] These native claims may be glimpsed in the reader's mind from the anti-hero's airplane in which Edie never flies. For a demonstration of the airplane as a trope of colonial

Munro's story builds plot out of the squalid realities of a working class Canadian life constricted by gender. The protagonist Edie's growing awareness of her own sexuality is mapped onto her service as hired help in a middle-class professional household immediately after World War II. Raised in dire rural poverty, Edie had received only a 37 out of 100 on her first-year high school exams and subsequently had left school, facing limited opportunities. The improbable—but entirely believable—appearance of a bush pilot named Chris, who lands his small plane near her employers' rural property, leads to a plot which juxtaposes Edie to three older women, separated from her by minute variations in social class, yet united by facing gender inequities. The recognition scene forces Edie to acknowledge that she is a younger version of Alice Kelling, Chris's rejected fiancée. Munro contravenes a reader's expectations of romance, freeing Edie not by seduction, but first by Chris's lost erection (Munro, "How" 60) and then by Edie's recognition of female solidarity and agency.

Waiting by the mailbox for the promised summons from Chris, Edie smiles at the mailman daily for many months in happy anticipation of the letter that never comes. Ironically, the mailman thinks she is attracted to him. Shaping unanticipated events to meet her needs, Edie refuses to be victimized. Having acknowledged her sisterhood to Alice Kelling—both are conned and rejected by Chris—Edie can accept the mailman's offer of marriage, understanding that her "prince charming" came, not in an airplane, but in the mail truck (Munro, "How" 64-65). He is not a sexually attractive man, but he is a member of a family with a good reputation in those parts, a steady worker, with a government job, and a pension plan. Working in a job to which her social class and gender had consigned her, through luck and intelligence Edie was able to circumvent the cultural conscription into Romance and live comfortably ever after.[15]

I see Virginia Woolf more than Katherine Mansfield as a foremother of this story. Seduction, female jealousy, and traditional romance are mocked; economic consideration as partial cause of female sexual choices is subtly suggested. Events occur in retrospect, making narrative voice more central than dramatic confrontation. Consciousness is primary, and its revelation is methodologically reminiscent of Woolf's strategies. The story's multilayered narrative voices demonstrate Munro's mastery of one of Woolf's greatest legacies, the depiction of a multisituated polyphonic narrative voice, weaving together personal and cul-

---

domination, see Beer. A significant feature of Munro's narrative representations of temporal discontinuities can be seen in her mapping of overlaid spatial domains: see Ross 22, 70 and Howells 68.

[15] For a very different reading, see Robert Hampson, who regards this short story as a piece of fluff, Munro's attempt to write for glossy women's magazines (70-2).

tural memories with the narrative present, past times, and varied settings. Like Virginia Woolf,

> Munro does not simply tell a story from a particular perspective in time but includes the experiences of the intervening years implicitly in the tones and attitudes of the narrating voice; and sometimes briefly intrudes as if from another reality, creating dimensional resonance like the echoes of memory within the reader's mind. (Moss, qtd. in Rasporich 160)

Like Woolf (*D*3 106-107; Lilienfeld, *Reading* 185-8), Munro's crafting a polyvocal narrative voice is the result of conscious artistic intervention. In a 1985 interview Munro acknowledged that:

> [...] it's so difficult to write a story within the voice of a woman who is not very articulate [...] It's when you have to get the narrator to do something analytical that you have to be so careful, because the story will need that insight, and [...] it will have to be given in a very oblique way [...] (qtd. in Bonetti).

As Munro notes here, inherent in the manipulation of free indirect discourse is the author's ability to wield judgment and commentary without overt intervention. In the expertly shaped narratives of Woolf and Munro, authorial control exists but remains unobtrusive, enabling the reader to participate in the making of meaning, for the reading process itself requires interpretive attention. Hence, in the multilayered narrativity of both Woolf and Munro "time shifts and shifts in narrative perspectives unsettl[e the fiction] [...] so that multiple and often contradictory meanings have room to circulate in structures of narrative indeterminacy" (Howells 11). For both Woolf and Munro, such narrative method has political implications: "Narratives that allow the equal participation of many voices signal a new form of relating—one in which authority and dominance are irrelevant, replaced by the communal recomposition of experience" (Mayberry, "Strategies" 57). Strikingly, although Katherine Mayberry was here referring only to Alice Munro, Rachel Blau DuPlessis uses the terms "communal" and "choral" about Virginia Woolf's multiple narrative foci as protagonists and narrative consciousnesses, a strategy that she too sees as political (48, 162-3).

One of Munro's greatest strengths as a writer is her ability to depict the random chaos of life in such a way that the chaos is given full reign, while the story is shaped into a work of art. Her plots recreate a sense of chaos in tightly organized arrangements of incidents, mimicking chaos without replicating it structurally (Hoy 16; Canitz and Seamon 69-70). Event dominates character (often painfully); consciousness grows out of the impingement of circumstance, but cannot always make sense of events (Mayberry, "Strategies" 63-4, "Limits" 535-6). Because of this, Munro's work impresses the reader with a representation of what lived life may feel like to those who are not always in positions to dominate events and resources. Was the Munro-plot not something like that which Woolf had in mind when she stated: "the moment of importance came not here but there; so that if a writer were a free man [sic] and not a slave, if he could write what he chose, not what he must, if he could base his work upon his own feeling and not upon convention, there would be no plot, no comedy, no tragedy, no love interest, or catastrophe in the accepted sense [...]" (Woolf, "Modern" 154)?

If Munro's "How I Met My Husband" demonstrates Munro's development of the legacy of Woolf's mastery of the polyvocal mediations of consciousness, then Munro's "Accident" reveals the authorial manipulation of incident to foreground the randomness, rather than the human control of events, that shapes human lives. In fact, "[w]hat I want now in a story is the admission of chaos," Munro told Janet Watts (qtd. in Ross 88). With her emphasis on the unplanned and the contingent, Munro is an heir to Woolf's subversive fictions, which interrogate the trajectory of women's lives by emphasizing the unexpected incident, not the predictable perfection of foregone plot conclusions (DuPlessis 50-4).

Originally published in 1977, "Accident" appeared in the collection entitled *The Moons of Jupiter* in 1982. Frances Wright, a high school music teacher living during World War II in Hanratty,[16] a small town in Ontario, Canada, is having an adulterous affair with Ted Makkavala, the high school chemistry teacher. Frances is convinced no one knows of their sexual assignations, conducted in the woods, in the supply closet of Ted's second-floor classroom, and in proximity to that area of the United Church where the choir performs, a delusion resulting from her "lack of small town instincts [...]." (Munro, "Accident" 80) Frances is not conventionally beautiful, as she is intermittently aware (Munro, "Accident" 78-9) nor is the middle-aged, "slightly stooping" (Munro, "Accident" 83) Ted, with his bombast, impatience, and intolerance of religion, the stuff of romantic dreams. The affair has been going on for at least a year, and "Frances caught more than glimpses [of Greta, Ted's wife]. She caught the Makkavala's family's colds. She began to feel that she was living with them in a bizarre and dreamlike intimacy" (Munro, "Accident" 99). That adultery should result in the common cold is yet another deft deflation of myths of romance.

A reader versed in escape fiction might predict that the affair would end unhappily, perhaps culminating in Ted's decision to become faithful once again to his wife, or Frances's termination of the situation, perhaps because her mother's eventual death might have enabled her to move to a larger, more cosmopolitan city. Instead, Munro insists upon the solidity of the affair. Frances comes alive sexually, astonished that what she had read about but never before

---

[16] Hanratty is a fictional version of Wingham, Ontario, the site of Munro's birth. Wingham is also named Jubilee and Dalgleish in Munro's fiction.

experienced had been true: "But no, it wasn't a fraud, it was all true, it surpassed everything [...]" (Munro, "Accident" 83). More than sex gives the relationship its power, for Ted treats Frances as a rational friend with whom he can discuss political realities and philosophical questions. "When something amused or outraged him—a number of things did both, and at the same time—he thought of telling Frances" (Munro, "Accident" 87).

Frances and Ted are in the midst of making love in the science room supply cabinet when the school secretary interrupts them by knocking on the door. "Like everybody else in town, she had known about them for some time" (Munro, "Accident" 86). When no one answers the door immediately, the secretary calls out, "Mr. Makkavala! I'm sorry! Your son's been killed!" (Munro, "Accident" 87). Munro occludes Ted's leaving the closet. Frances hangs back, waiting until later to vacate the premises, a pointless reluctance, for her car remained parked at the school in plain view. Deflating romance in the interruption of sexual intercourse by death is at once a brilliant and poignant plot maneuver. That the announcement comes from the school secretary, who knows exactly where to find the couple who think they are invisible, is even more effective. The grand European narratives of adultery here become tawdry, yet suggest a tenderness toward actual, ordinary people who have nowhere to go but the school's chemistry supply closet, and even so, are spied out by the inhabitants of the small town.

As Ted waits with Greta at the hospital, the townspeople in Hanratty discuss how twelve-year-old Bobby Makkavala and his friend, the young O'Hare boy, had tied their sled during the snow storm to the trunk of Fred Beecher's car. Fred, not knowing they were coasting along behind him, drove up a hill by the school en route to Post Office Square. Suddenly another car skidded on the hill, slammed into Fred's car, and this accident pushed the boys' sled under Fred's car. The O'Hare boy died instantly, but Bobby, extricated from the wreck, was taken 70 miles away by ambulance (due to the bad weather this took four hours) to London, Ontario, where he died some time later.

Ted and Frances both realize that Bobby's death could and perhaps "should" have resulted in the termination of the affair. Disgusted with himself for being irrational, Ted nevertheless is tempted for a moment: "Give up Frances, give her up for good, and Bobby would not die" (Munro, "Accident" 88). A confirmed agnostic and rationalist, Ted watches his mind in horror present this idea to him as a means of controlling his son's destiny. Frances, too, understands that this very choice would present itself to Ted:

> He would come back to Hanratty but he would not come back to her. Because he was with her when it happened he would hate her; at least, he would hate the thought of her, because it always made him think of the accident. And suppose

somehow the child survived, crippled. That would be no better, not for Frances […] (Munro, "Accident" 97).

Both Ted and Frances were wrong.

After Bobby dies, Ted does not give up Frances; he leaves Greta and marries Frances. This conclusion arises naturally out of Ted's character. Those whom the narrator refers to as "Various Hanratty busybodies" (Munro, "Accident" 102) inform Greta's sister, Kartrud, that Ted is having an affair with Frances. Outraged, Kartrud demands action from the high school principal and the United Church minister, both of whom had known of the affair and both of whom had been reluctant to interfere. The high school principal is thus forced to confront Ted who, far from being apologetic, flies into a rage, quits, and announces that he had planned to marry Frances all along (Munro, "Accident" 104).

Ted then goes to Frances and tells her what had happened, making his proposal of marriage as rather an afterthought. Frances doubts that, in fact, Ted had planned to marry her from the start of the affair, as he claimed. When, a few days earlier, Ted had told Frances the story of Bobby's time in the hospital and about the conflict over the funeral ceremony, she had understood that he had been engaged in a power struggle with his sister-in-law over Greta, and over his right to conduct a non-religious ceremony at his son's funeral. Frances "could not help seeing this and she did not like it. She could not help seeing how much she did not like it" (Munro, "Accident" 103). In this moment Frances sees Ted as an intransigent agnostic whose obsessional beliefs matter more to him than his wife's feelings or his son's spiritual needs. What she describes as his selfishness does not end her love, but it ends her illusions: "she had not stopped loving him. But there was a change" (Munro, "Accident" 103).

Ted had not left Greta due to romantic love. He had not proposed out of his love and need for Frances, although he did love and need her. He proposed because in that way he could punish Kartrud, get revenge for losing control of Greta, and leave a marriage which his son's death might have poisoned irrevocably. Ted left Greta and married Frances (with whom he relocated to Ottawa) due entirely to accident.

> There was a long chain of things, many of them hidden from her, that brought him here to propose to her in the most proper place, her mother's living room. She had been made necessary. And it was quite useless to think, would anyone else have done as well, would it have happened if the chain had not been linked exactly as it was? (Munro, "Accident" 106-7).

Nor does Frances forget that what becomes her happy marriage occurred as a result of mere chance. Returning to Hanratty years later for her sister-in-law Adelaide's funeral, Frances sees Fred Beecher once again.

If he had not gone out in the snow that day to take a baby carriage across town, Frances would not live in Ottawa now, she would not have her two children, she would not have her life, not the same life. That is true. She is sure of it, but it is too ugly to think about. The angle from which she has to see that can never be admitted to; it would seem monstrous (Munro, "Accident" 109).

Frances recognizes that random events and ordinary tragedy shaped her life, making her "incidental" to Ted's choices. "Thus, there is no necessity to a major portion of [Frances'] life; it does not flow from her character, as it would in the classical formulation in which character is fate and fate is character; her life would have been very different, and therefore, so would she" (Canitz and Seamon 70). The narrative thus insists on displaying its own devices, foregrounding the artful construction of a plot that captures the unplanned moment: "[T]he acknowledgment of contingency occurs in a story whose title [...] clearly signals the importance of contingency" (Canitz and Seamon 70). Such barring of the mechanism is a hallmark of metafiction, and its increasing use by Munro[17] aligns her with Woolf, whose fictions repeatedly call attention to their own narrative mechanisms.[18]

"Accident," like "How I Met My Husband," cleverly punctures the tropes of magazine fiction romance. Munro's representation of female consciousness and her mastery of plots based on the contingent add to the power of these stories. Conflating tragedy and comedy, moving with ease through the various voices focalized in the stories, Munro deftly continues and develops several aspects of the pathways in fiction that Woolf's stories and novels helped pioneer. Consciousness, the random event, and the ironic rewriting of "the marriage plot"

---

[17] Linda Hutcheon (46-7, 109, 133) and Kit Stead, for example, make this point. Beverly Rasporich vigorously disputes such a view, insisting that to see Munro as a Postmodern deliberately obscures Munro's depiction of women's lives as shaped by forces beyond individual control (162-5). Such debate over categorization and its political implications is a part of Woolf studies as well. Caughie analyzes Woolf as a Postmodernist. In her two volume text, Bonnie Kime Scott categorizes Woolf as Modernist and Postmodernist.

[18] For example, in *Jacob's Room* the theme of epistemology is manifested in numerous ways. The narrative voice repeatedly announces that character cannot be known and describes its hunt for knowledge of Jacob as fascinating and hopeless, remarking, "[b]ut something is always impelling one to hum vibrating, like the hawk moth, at the mouth of the cavern of mystery, endowing Jacob Flanders with all sorts of qualities he had not at all [...] what remains is mostly a matter of guess work" (73). Similarly, in *To the Lighthouse*, the painter Lily Briscoe wants to create a painting in which would be realized her vision of "the colour burning on a framework of steel; the light of a butterfly's wing lying upon the arches of a cathedral" (75), a metaphor for the novel's construction. Isa in *Between the Acts* reads about physical violence against women (20) while also herself experiencing emotional battering (48, 219).

are three elements of each of the stories that show Munro practicing the suggestions Woolf laid out for "Modern Fiction."

Now recognized as one of the greatest of Canadian writers, often called the equal of Chekov, Alice Munro has been forced to emerge from her youthful disguise (Ross 91). Munro has repeatedly told the truths of the female heterosexual body, insisting on her right to voice that which Woolf urged women to fictionalize (Munro, qtd. in Rasporich 21-22; Woolf, "Speech" xxxvi-xxxix). As indigenous and postcolonial voices gain increasing prominence in Canadian fiction,[19] Munro's oeuvre—with its development of tasks Woolf left for others to realize—will serve, perhaps, as Woolf's may have served for Munro, as a compelling force to be resented and emulated, for that is one way in which a writer may inadvertently serve as an inspiring embodiment of "the Mother Country."

[19] After *The Life of Pi* won the Mann Booker Prize, the *New York Times* noted in an article headlined "For Canada's Top Novelists, Being Born Abroad Helps," that "a good many if not a majority of the leading lights in Canadian letters today are immigrants, making Canadian literature a multicultural amalgam of exotic flavors and imagery" (Krauss). (The subsequent scandal over Yann Martel's possible plagiarism of the main idea for his novel was also duly noted and was widely discussed ["Booker"]). The prestigious Oxford University Press canonized the contemporary literary contributions of Canada's indigenous peoples by publishing in 1985 the first edition of *An Anthology of Canadian Native Literature in English*. Moses and Goldie, the anthology editors, reprint a discussion, one of many they had in the process of selecting and editing the work to be included, about the problems of appropriation and canonization (xix-xxi). During the course of their debates, Terry Goldie stated, "I think there is a global problem with the 'fourth world.' That is George Manuel's term, the fourth world being indigenous peoples' cultures which are controlled by the non-indigenous, like Canada or New Zealand or Australia [...]. The fourth world is not allowed to develop [...]" (xxiii).

Works Cited

Abel, Elizabeth. "Matrilineage and the Racial 'Other': Woolf and Her Literary Daughters of the Second Wave." The Third Annual Conference on Virginia Woolf. Jefferson City, MO. 13 June 1993.

Abravanel, Genevieve. "Woolf in Blackface: Identification Across *The Waves*." *Virginia Woolf Out of Bounds: Selected Papers From the Tenth Annual Conference on Virginia Woolf*. Ed. Jessica Berman and Jane Goldman. New York: Pace UP, 2001. 113-19.

Annan, Noel. *Leslie Stephen: The Godless Victorian.* 2nd ed. New York: Random House, 1984.
Ashcroft, Bill, Gareth Griffiths, and Helen Tiffin, eds., *The Post-Colonial Studies Reader.* London and New York: Routledge, 1999.
Atwood, Margaret. *Survival: A Thematic Guide to Canadian Literature.* Toronto: Anansi, 1972.
Beer, Gillian. "The Island and the Aeroplane: The Case of Virginia Woolf." *Nation and Narration.* Ed. Homi K. Bhabha. London and New York: Routledge, 1990. 265-90.
Bonetti, Kay. *Interview with Alice Munro in Clinton, Ontario.* Videocassette. APR, 1987.
"Booker Winner in War of Words." *BBC News World Online.* 8 Nov. 2002. 28 May 2003. <http://www.news.bbc.co.uk/2/hi/entertainment/2416613.stm>
Canitz, A. E. Christa and Roger Seamon. "The Rhetoric of Fictional Realism in the Stories of Alice Munro." *Canadian Literature* 150 (1996): 67-80.
Caramagno, Thomas C. *The Flight of the Mind: Virginia Woolf's Art and Manic-Depressive Illness.* Berkeley: U of California P, 1992.
Caughie, Pamela. *Virginia Woolf and Postmodernism: Literature in Quest and Question of Itself.* Urbana and Chicago: U of Illinois P, 1991.
Chapman, Wayne and Janet M. Manson. *Women in the Milieu of Leonard and Virginia Woolf: Peace, Politics, and Education.* New York: Pace UP, 1998.
Cramer, Patricia. "'Pearls and the Porpoise': *The Years*—A Lesbian Memoir." *Virginia Woolf: Lesbian Readings.* Ed. Eileen Barrett and Patricia Cramer. New York: NYUP, 1997. 222-40.
DeSalvo, Louise. *Virginia Woolf: The Impact of Childhood Sexual Abuse on Her Life and Work.* Boston: Beacon UP, 1989.
Donaldson, Laura E. *Decolonizing Feminisms: Race, Gender, & Empire-Building.* Chapel Hill: U of North Carolina P, 1992.
Dunbar, Pamela. *Double Discourse in Katherine Mansfield's Short Stories.* New York: St. Martin's, 1997.
DuPlessis, Rachel Blau. *Writing Beyond the Ending: Narrative Strategies of Twentieth-Century Women Writers.* Bloomington: Indiana UP, 1985.
Fraser, Wayne. *The Dominion of Women: The Personal and the Political in Canadian Women's Literature.* New York: Greenwood, 1991.
Gibson, Graeme. *Eleven Canadian Novelists Interviewed by Graeme Gibson.* Toronto: Anansi, 1973. 241-64.
Giles, Jeff. "The Heart of Her Matter: Munro's Lonely Terrain." *Newsweek.* 12 Nov 2001: 66.

Gillespie, Diane and Elizabeth Steele, eds. *Julia Duckworth Stephen: Stories for Children, Essays for Adults*. New York: Syracuse UP, 1987.
Haller, Evelyn. "Virginia Woolf and Katherine Mansfield: or The Case of the Declassé Wild Child." *Virginia Woolf Miscellanies: Proceedings of the First Annual Conference on Virginia Woolf*. Ed. Mark Hussey and Vara Neverow-Turk. New York: Pace UP, 1992. 96-104.
Hampson, Robert. "Johnny Panic and the Pleasures of Disruption." *Re-Reading the Short Story*. Ed. Clare Hanson. New York: St. Martin's, 1989. 69-85.
Hancock, Geoff. "An Interview with Alice Munro." *The Canadian Fiction Magazine* 45 (1982): 71-114.
Henke, Suzette. "Stephen Dedalus and Women—A Portrait of the Artist as a Young Misogynist." *James Joyce and the Politics of Desire*. New York: RKP, 1990. 82-107.
Hoffman, Eva. *Lost in Translation: A Life in a New Language*. New York: Penguin, 1989.
Howells, Coral Ann. *Alice Munro*. Manchester: Manchester UP, 1998.
——. "Alice Munro's Art of Indeterminacy: The Progress of Love." *Modes of Narrative: Approaches to American, Canadian, and British Fiction*. Ed. R. M. Nischik and B. Korte. Wurzburg: Konighousen & Neumann, 1990. 140-52.
Hoy, Helen. "Alice Munro: 'Unforgettable, Indigestible Messages.'" *Journal of Canadian Studies* 26.1 (1991): 5-21.
Hutcheon, Linda. *The Canadian Postmodern: A Study of Contemporary English-Canadian Fiction*. Toronto: Oxford UP, 1988.
Irvine, Lorna. "Questioning Authority: Alice Munro's Fiction." *CEA Critic* 50.1 (1987): 57-66.
Kaplan, Sydney Janet. *Katherine Mansfield and the Origins of Modern Fiction*. Ithaca: Cornell UP, 1991.
Krauss, Clifford. "For Canada's Top Novelists, Being Born Abroad Helps." *New York Times*. 5 Nov. 2002, late ed.: E1.
Leavis, Q. D. "Caterpillars of the Commonwealth, Unite!" *Scrutiny* 7.2 (1938): 203-214.
Lilienfeld, Jane. "'The Deceptiveness of Beauty': Mother Love and Mother Hate in *To the Lighthouse*." *Twentieth Century Literature* 29.3 (1977): 345-376.
——. *Reading Alcoholisms: Theorizing Character and Narrative in Selected Novels of Thomas Hardy, James Joyce, and Virginia Woolf*. New York: St. Martin's, 1999.
Love, Jean. *Virginia Woolf: Sources of Madness and Art*. Berkeley: U of California P, 1977.
Marcus, Jane. "Virginia Woolf and Her Violin." *Mothering the Mind: Twelve*

Studies of Writers and Their Silent Partners. Ed. Ruth Perry and Martine W. Brownley. New York: Holmes & Meir, 1984. 181-201.

———. *Virginia Woolf and the Languages of Patriarchy.* Bloomington: Indiana UP, 1987.

———. "Wrapped in the Stars and Stripes: Virginia Woolf in the U.S.A." *South Carolina Review* 29.1 (Fall 1996): 17-23.

Martel, Yann. *The Life of Pi.* New York: Harcourt, 2001.

Martineau, Barbara. "Transcript of Interview with Alice Munro, February 16, 1975 in London, Ontario." Alice Munro *Fonds.* The Alice Munro Papers. First Accession. Special Collections, University of Calgary Library. Edited and Compiled by Jean M. Moore, Jean F. Tenner, Apollonia Steele. *MsC* 37.20.20.f1-31.

Mayberry, Katherine J. "'Every Last Thing...Everlasting': Alice Munro and the Limits of Narrative." *Studies in Short Fiction* 29.4 (1992): 531-41.

———. "Narrative Strategies of Liberation in Alice Munro." *Studies in Canadian Literature* 19.2 (1994): 57-66.

McCaig, JoAnn. *Reading in Alice Munro's Archives.* Waterloo, Ontario: Wilfred Laurier UP, 2002.

McCulloch, Jean and Mona Simpson. "The Art of Fiction, Interview with Alice Munro." *Paris Review* 131 (1994): 227-64.

Metcalf, John. "A Conversation with Alice Munro." *Journal of Canadian Fiction* 1.4 (1972): 54-62.

Moran, Patricia. *Word of Mouth: Body Language in Katherine Mansfield and Virginia Woolf.* Charlottesville: U of Virginia P, 1996.

Moses, Daniel David and Terry Goldie, eds., *An Anthology of Canadian Native Literature in English.* 2nd ed. Toronto: Oxford UP Canada, 1998.

———. "Preface to the First Edition: Two Voices." Moses and Goldie xviii-xxix.

Munro, Alice. "Accident." *The Moons of Jupiter.* New York: Vintage, 1991. 77-109.

———. "Eskimo." *The Progress of Love.* New York: Penguin, 1995. 248-73.

———. "Friend of My Youth." *Friend of My Youth: Stories by Alice Munro.* New York: Knopf, 1990. 5-26.

———. "How I Met My Husband." *Something I've Been Meaning to Tell You, Thirteen Stories.* New York: Penguin/Plume, 1974. 45-66.

———. "Meneseteung." *Friend.* 50-73.

———. "The Ottawa Valley." *Something.* 227-46.

———. "The Peace of Utrecht." *Dance of the Happy Shades and Other Stories.* New York: Penguin, 1983. 190-210.

———. "Working for a Living." *Grand Street* 1.1 (1981). 9-37.

Munro, Sheila. *Lives of Mothers and Daughters: Growing Up with Alice Munro.*

Toronto: McClleland & Stewart, 2002.
Murch, Kem. "Name: Alice Munro, Occupation: Writer." *Chatelaine* 48.8 (1975): 43+.
Olano, Pamela J. "'Women alone stir my imagination': Reading Virginia Woolf as a Lesbian." *Virginia Woolf, Themes and Variations: Selected Papers from the Second Annual Conference on Virginia Woolf*. Ed. Vara Neverow-Turk and Mark Hussey. New York: Pace UP, 1993. 158-71.
Phillips, Kathy. *Virginia Woolf Against Empire*. Knoxville: U of Tennessee P, 1994.
Rasporich, Beverly J. *Dance of the Sexes: Art and Gender in the Fiction of Alice Munro*. Edmonton, Alberta: U of Alberta P, 1990.
Redekop, Magdalene. "Alice Munro and the Scottish Nostalgic Grotesque." *The Rest of the Story: Critical Essays on Alice Munro*. Ed. Robert Thacker. Toronto: ECW Press, 1999. 21-43.
———. *Mothers and Other Clowns: The Stories of Alice Munro*. London and New York: Routledge, 1992.
Reid, Panthea. *Art and Affection: A Life of Virginia Woolf*. New York: Oxford UP, 1996.
Robson, Nora. "Alice Munro and the White American South." *The Art of Alice Munro: Saying the Unsayable*. Ed. Judith Miller. Waterloo, Ontario: U of Waterloo P, 1984. 73-84.
Ross, Catherine Sheldrick. *Alice Munro: A Double Life*. Toronto: ECW Press, 1992.
Scott, Bonnie Kime. *Refiguring Modernism*. 2 Vols. Bloomington: Indiana UP, 1996.
Silver, Brenda. *Virginia Woolf Icon*. Chicago: U of Chicago Press, 1999.
Smith, Angela. *Katherine Mansfield and Virginia Woolf: A Public of Two*. New York: Oxford UP, 1999.
Smith, Patricia Juliana. *Lesbian Panic: Homoeroticism in Modern British Fiction*. New York: Columbia UP, 1997.
Smythe, Karen. "Sad Stories: The Ethics of Epiphany in Munrovian Elegy." *University of Toronto Quarterly* 60.4 (1991): 493-506.
Stead, Kit. "The Twinkling of an 'I,' Alice Munro's *Friend of My Youth*." *The Guises of Canadian Diversity*. Ed. Serge Jaumain and Marc Maufort. Amsterdam and Atlanta: Rodopi, 1995. 151-64.
Stephen, Leslie. *Sir Leslie Stephen's Mausoleum Book*. Ed. Alan Bell. Oxford: Oxford UP, 1977.
Struthers, J. R. [Tim]. "The Real Material: An Interview with Alice Munro." *Probable Fictions: Alice Munro's Narrative Acts*. Ed. Louis K. Mackendrick. Toronto: ECW Press, 1983. 5-36.

Thacker, Robert. "Alice Munro's Willa Cather." *Canadian Literature* 134 (1992): 42-57.

——. "'So Shocking a Verdict in Real Life': Autobiography in Alice Munro's Stories." *Reflections: Autobiography and Canadian Literature*. Ed. K. P. Stich. Ottawa: U of Ottawa P, 1988. 153-61.

Waterson, Elizabeth. *Rapt in Plaid: Canadian Literature and Scottish Tradition*. Toronto: U of Toronto P, 2001.

Winston, Janet. "Reading Influences: Homoeroticism and Mentoring in Katherine Mansfield's 'Carnation' and Virginia Woolf's 'Moments of Being: "Slater's Pins Have No Points."'" *Virginia Woolf: Lesbian Readings*. Ed. Eileen Barrett and Patricia Cramer. NY: NY UP, 1997. 57-77.

Woolf, Virginia. *A Room of One's Own*. New York: Harcourt, Brace & World, Inc. 1928.

——. *Between the Acts*. New York: Harcourt, Brace & World, Inc., 1941.

——. *The Diary of Virginia Woolf, Volume 2: 1920-1924*. Ed. Anne Olivier Bell, Assisted by Andrew McNellie. New York: Harcourt Brace Jovanovich, 1980.

——. *The Diary of Virginia Woolf, Volume 3: 1920-1924*. Ed. Anne Olivier Bell, Assisted by Andrew McNellie. New York: Harcourt Brace Jovanovich, 1980.

——. *Jacob's Room & The Waves*. New York: Harcourt, Brace & World, Inc., 1959.

——. "Modern Fiction." *The Common Reader, First Series*. New York: Harcourt, Brace & World, Inc., 1953. 150-58.

——. *Moments of Being: Unpublished Autobiographical Writings of Virginia Woolf*. Ed. Jeanne Schulkind. Sussex: U of Sussex P, 1976.

——. "Speech before the London/National Society for Women's Service, January 21, 1931." *The Pargiters by Virginia Woolf: The Novel-Essay Portion of* The Years. Ed. Mitchell A. Leaska. New York: NY Public Library: 1977. xxvii-xxxxiii.

——. *To the Lighthouse*. New York: Harcourt, Brace & World, Inc., 1955.

Wylie, Herb. "Regionalism, Postcolonialism, and Canadian Writing: A Comparative Analysis for Postnational Times." *Essays on Canadian Writing* 63 (1998): 139-61.

Teaching Woolf/Woolf Teaching[1]
Beth Rigel Daugherty

I begin here: despite the historical and cultural gulfs that lie between us—era, nationality, class, context, career, education, audience, and so on—Virginia Woolf, in the teaching she did at Morley College and performs in her essays, has something to teach me about teaching literature. Why do I feel this connection? Because Woolf is intensely aware of the obstacles to learning and intimately acquainted with the paradox of being simultaneously an outsider and an insider, a paradox I myself live in. So while preparing and teaching a seminar on Virginia Woolf, I think about our different situations, about her teaching at Morley, and about what I can learn from her attempts to cross barriers rather than erect them in her essays. I "read" her for her pedagogical lessons.

Before Virginia Woolf was a feminist, novelist, essayist, short story writer, diarist, letter writer, autobiographer, and biographer, Virginia Stephen was a teacher. In a very different time and context from mine, it is true, but a teacher nonetheless.

I walk into Roush Hall 331 on March 30, 1999, to begin teaching my first-ever seminar on Virginia Woolf. I'm almost 49, a professor of English at Otterbein College, where I have taught for fifteen years. The room has carpet, good lighting, and beautiful cherry tables we can move into a square for discussion. Otterbein is a four-year liberal arts comprehensive institution; it combines certain features of a traditional liberal arts college—ten liberal arts courses required of everyone and various liberal arts majors, for example—with strong pre-professional programs in business, education, and nursing. Our mission as a private, church-related institution has always been to balance education for its

Permission from the Society of Authors as the Literary Representative of the Estate of Virginia Woolf to quote from Virginia Woolf: Report on Teaching at Morley College (MHP A.22) is gratefully acknowledged.

[1] This essay grew out of a presentation at the Tenth Annual Conference on Virginia Woolf, "Virginia Woolf Out of Bounds," at the University of Maryland Baltimore County, June 10, 2000. I would like to thank Jane Lilienfeld for encouraging me to expand the discussion in that presentation and for her many good questions and suggestions over the course of its revision. I have used small portions of earlier publications, "Taking a Leaf from Virginia Woolf's Book: Empowering the Student," "Morley College, Virginia Woolf, and Us: How Should One Read Class?," and "Virginia Woolf Teaching/Virginia Woolf Learning: Morley College and the Common Reader," in this essay and want to acknowledge Pace UP and Contemporary Research Press for those previously published materials.

own sake, the liberal arts, with a belief in vocation, preparation for meaningful work. Located in Westerville, Ohio, a well-off "village" overtaken by Columbus' suburban sprawl, Otterbein enjoys both a small-town atmosphere and proximity to a major urban center.

Virginia Stephen walks into Morley College on January 18, 1905, to begin teaching her first course ever, in what subject, she's not sure: she refuses to teach grammar, composition is listed on the books (Martin 22), and according to her, Miss Sheepshanks has said to "combine amusement and instruction—a little gossip and sympathy, and then 'talks' about books and pictures" (*L1* 172). Only later does she discover that she has "been doing entirely the wrong thing at Morley—Sheepshanks showed wolf's fangs" (*L1* 194). During her nearly three years at Morley, she also teaches a history course, a composition course, and an English literature course (Rosenbaum 165). She's almost 23, a volunteer with no professional title and no formal schooling; she has educated herself in her father's library.[2] Her class is in a "great dreary room with tables & chairs & flaring gas jets" (*PA* 224), and Morley College, located on Waterloo Road in Lambeth, quite near Southwark on London's south side, is an urban institution offering an education "of a more advanced character" to working class adults (Richards 96).[3] In the debates of the time, Morley came down on the side of offering a liberal education, not just the three Rs, to its working class students (Sadler 138; Richards 91, 96); in 1901, when Morley lists 55 classes in 32 subjects, for example, it

---

[2] See "Learning Virginia Woolf: Of Leslie, Libraries, and Letters," 13-16, where I discuss the context, curriculum, pedagogy, and community represented by Leslie Stephen's library; "Morley College, Virginia Woolf, and Us: How Should One Read Class?" 126-28, where I summarize the advantages and disadvantages of Virginia Stephen's education; and "Virginia Woolf's Educational Inheritance: The Stephen Household and 19th Century Debates about Education for Girls," where I point out how nineteenth-century debates about women's education affected Virginia Stephen's education and Virginia Woolf's attitudes about education.

[3] As Denis Richards notes, Morley College was established at a time when "there was as yet scarcely any link" between a "comparatively newly organized system of elementary education and the older unsystematized institutions dispensing higher education" (87). Evening classes for the working classes were available in four basic formats: village schools for younger adults in the 3 Rs; Mechanics' Institutes focused on "scientific principles and their practical application" (90); socio-politically motivated institutions offering liberal, humanistic studies, such as the Working Men's College in London; and the university extension lectures (89-91). Morley College aimed "to promote by means of classes, lectures and otherwise, the advanced study by men and women belonging to the working classes, of subjects of knowledge not directly connected with or applied to any handicraft, trade or business; as subordinate or ancillary thereto, to assist in acquiring the requisite elementary instruction those whose age prevents them from making use of the ordinary elementary instruction; and to promote social intercourse among those following the above-mentioned pursuits" (91-92). It is difficult to know what "advanced study"

offers courses in science, literature, history, classical and modern languages, music, botany, and many other liberal arts subjects (Kelly 194). However, Morley, like the Mechanics' Institutes and some other adult education institutions, also has to offer basic courses to help its students catch up (Altick 193; Richards 93). Lambeth has an almost entirely working class population, with half of that population under the poverty line in 1890 (Richards 18-24; 95). In fact, Thomas Kelly, in his study of adult education in Great Britain, calls the Lambeth/Southwark area a slum (193-94), and Richards notes that some of Southwark's worst quarters appeared in the novels of Charles Dickens (18). Basing his information on Charles Booth's *Life and Labour of the People in London*, Denis Richards notes that the working class people above the poverty line in Lambeth have regular employment and are foremen and artisans. The half of the Lambeth population below the poverty line fall into four groups: the lowest (no family life, no work, alcoholism, crime); the very poor, with small and irregular earnings; the poor with well-paid but irregular work; and the poor with low regular wages (22-23).

My Woolf seminar has eight students, senior English majors, in their final quarter before graduation, plus one auditor.[4] There's a diversity of sorts, though at first glance they seem homogeneous, representative of a large portion of Otterbein's population: white, small-town or suburban, middle-class, midwestern. One young man is Mexican-American, for example, and I know if I explored cultural and ethnic backgrounds with them, as I have in freshman writing courses focused on autobiography, further ethnic variety would emerge. One young man is gay, four students are adults (as opposed to the traditional student age), three of the adults are married (two with children and one with a baby on the way), and one is a single mother with a young son. At a school where the female/male ratio is approximately 60/40, these English majors reverse the demographics: five are men, and three are women (the auditor is a woman). Two are

---

meant in this context. It seems as though "college" meant an organized collegiate atmosphere, not an institution of higher education offering the bachelor's degree, as it does in the United States. Was Morley College a link between elementary and higher education and thus more secondary in character? Or would some of its classes have offered university-level lectures? My guess, and it *is* a guess, is that Morley offered a range of opportunities to its students, from elementary to higher but that most of its classes were at the secondary level.

[4] I want to take this opportunity to thank the students in English 400—Beth Caldwell, David Firth, Eric Gamble, Rick Godfrey, Mary Pat Knight, Jessica Liebert, Nikki Schuler, Mark Snyder, and Matt Winter—for their open minds, lively talk, and caring hearts. They created a memorable class. They have also generously given me permission to quote from their written work in this essay.

planning to go to law school, one is going into secondary teaching, and one is headed for Actors Studio in NYC; none is headed for graduate school. Six have jobs, two of which are full-time. One, an engineer at Columbia Gas preparing the company for Y2K, has been getting a degree in English, one or two courses at a time.

Virginia Stephen's first students are "anaemic shop girls who say they would write more but they only get an hour for their dinner, and there doesn't seem to be much time for writing" (*L*1 210). In her July 1905 "Report on Teaching at Morley College," she describes the four female students in her summer term history class as possessing "more intelligence than I expected; though that intelligence was almost wholly uncultivated" (203).[5] One, Miss Williams, cranks out Grub Street reviews for a religious paper. In a composition class she teaches in autumn term 1906, she has both men and women, and mentions "an old Socialist," a "Dutchman who thinks—at the end of the class too—that I have been teaching him Arithmetic," and "my degenerate poet, who rants and blushes, and almost seizes my hand when we happen to like the same lines" in her letters (*L*1 210, 313); the latter is probably the Cyril Zeldwyn she writes to Nelly Cecil about, whom she describes as "a socialist, of a kind, and a poet; but also very clever and enthusiastic, and he can write short hand, and is a good man at accounts" (*L*1 321; Lee 219).[6] As Denis Richards points out, the founders of Morley wanted to provide the local working class population of Lambeth and Southwark with an education, but the College also attracted students from outside the manual laboring class, students who were clerks and shop-assistants, for example (94-95).[7] Thus, though not all Morley students would have been considered true working class, all Morley students worked for a living; its description of itself as a college "For Working Men and Women" was accurate (Richards 95).

---

[5] Virginia Stephen has canceled the following phrase in her draft of this report, "In spite of warning, I found them of a higher standard on the whole," suggesting that the assumption about her students' intelligence may not have been entirely her own. Monks House Papers, A. 22, in Special Collections, Library, University of Sussex.

[6] Woolf surely uses Zeldwyn as one of her models for Septimus Smith, who falls "in love with Miss Isabel Pole, lecturing in the Waterloo Road upon Shakespeare" and goes to France "to save an England which consisted almost entirely of Shakespeare's plays and Miss Isabel Pole in a green dress walking in a square" (*MD* 84-86). See "Taking a Leaf" 39n1 and "Morley College" 133.

[7] Many well-intentioned educational institutions for the working classes, using teaching methods that had been used in institutions for the middle and upper classes, attracted lower-middle-class students; as a result, the working classes for whom the institutions had been intended, often stayed away. See Altick 191-94, 209-11.

The students in English 400 live in an educational and economic culture that aspires to universal secondary education for all its people, begins to promote higher education as early as elementary school, and promotes that education as a key to upward mobility. Many of their schools have guidance counselors who help students think about their options, colleges have visitation days, brochures, and web pages to show students what they offer, and students with good and even not-so-good grades can get scholarships, need-based financial aid, and work-study jobs on campus. Although the tuition at Otterbein can be a barrier to some students, over 90% of the students who attend receive some form of aid, and if they cannot afford Otterbein, they do have other higher education options in Ohio, such as the eight state universities and numerous community colleges. Unfortunately, students who might benefit from higher education still fall through the cracks; race, class, gender, disability, and the preparation often tied to any or all of those factors can still erect high barriers to a college education. In addition, as we're currently observing, it remains all too easy for institutions to suddenly close doors that have only recently been opened. But relatively speaking and in comparison to the past, a college education is accessible in the United States, so much so that colleges often compete for students and the middle class seems to perceive a college education as a job requirement, not a luxury available to just a few. As Steven Marcus notes, in 1900, colleges and universities in the United States were educating 2% of the cohort of the young; in 2000, that statistic was close to 40%. (Interestingly enough, close to 40% of Otterbein's students are the first members of their families to attend college.)

Virginia Stephen's students in 1905, if they are similar to what Richards notes was true of the demographics in 1890,[8] are between 15 and 35 years old and thus born between 1870 and 1890. As a result of the 1870 Education Act, they probably (though not certainly) received an elementary education, which in England was the term used for the education provided to the working classes. This act made it possible for communities to form local non-denominational school boards and to establish schools to "supplement the existing places provided by the church schools." These schools could receive government funds, so with their establishment, the slow move toward a national system was begun; the eventual aim was an elementary education available to all (Copeland 379). However, the Education Act of 1870 did *not* make elementary education "mandatory or free" (McAleer 14). Not until the Education Act of 1880 was school attendance made mandatory from the ages of 5 to 10, and then compulsory attendance caused financial problems for working class families (they were "paying"

---

[8] In 1890, almost all the students at Morley College were under 31, with more than half over 20 (and almost half under 20) (Richards 100-01).

twice, through a fee to the school and through a loss of income) and thus, attendance problems for schools. School fees were finally abolished in 1891, but employers could make part-time arrangements for hiring children who were also attending school until 1918 (Hurt 188). Thus, it is possible that some of the students in Virginia Stephen's classroom did not have even the most basic of educations, and of those students who did, many would have left school at 12 or younger and worked part-time before they left (Burnett 168-70).[9] In addition, secondary education was not possible for other than the privileged classes until 1902 (Curtis 193-94; Arata 56), and access to higher education at the established universities was impossible for all except the most extraordinary working class student. Early in the 19th century, for example, when Oxford and Cambridge were the only institutions of higher learning in England, they shared about 1500 students between them (Heyck 195). The education they offered, in the classics or mathematics, was reserved for the upper classes, and its purpose was to prepare those young men for service to Church or State. Such severely limited access to education had created a strong desire for it, and Mechanics' Institutes, the Workers' Education Association, the founding of the University of London in 1828 as a secular institution and an alternative to Oxford and Cambridge, the university extension system, and institutions like Morley College, all part of a burgeoning adult education movement, were attempts to feed a people hungry for knowledge.

The students in my class have access to libraries and to library networks that makes getting books and information incredibly easy. Otterbein's location puts it in the Columbus Metropolitan Library system, one of the best in the country, and a student with a Westerville Public Library card can quickly get a book from any library branch in the system. Otterbein is also part of a group of libraries called the Ohio Private Academic Libraries (OPAL), which in turn is part of OhioLink. If Otterbein does not have a book, a student can search the OhioLink database containing almost all the academic library card catalogs in the state, order it online, and pick it up at the Otterbein circulation desk within days. In addition, although some students are intimidated by complicated search strategies or do not like libraries, faculty can at least assume that all of them have had access to some kind of library as children, even if it was only the Bookmobile, the small two-room public library, or the room in the elementary school.

---

[9] It is also possible, on the other hand, that her classrooms contained working class people who had educated themselves in the face of overwhelming odds. See J. F. C. Harrison (292-94), Paul Thomas Murphy, Altick (193, 211), and Jonathan Rose's *The Intellectual Life of the British Working Classes*.

Virginia Stephen's students have limited, if any, access to a library, since libraries in England were not truly free or public until 1919 (McAleer 48; Altick 213-39). Libraries existed, but almost all charged a fee. The London Library, for example, established by Thomas Carlyle and others in 1840 and opened in 1841, charged a £2 annual subscription (Inwood 673). The great Victorian commercial circulating libraries, such as Mudie's, charged readers a guinea a year to borrow books (Altick 295), and even libraries that functioned as "side lines to the barbering, confectionary, news-vending, stationery, and tobacco trades" in London charged a penny a volume rental fee (Altick 217). According to Stephen Inwood, public libraries could be funded by a penny in the pound tax on ratepayers beginning in 1855, "if two-thirds of ratepayers agreed. But ratepayers, who could afford to subscribe to commercial libraries, were not convinced that the poor should be 'civilized' at their expense [...]" (673-74). Richard Altick agrees, pointing out that "Opposition was particularly strong in London. In 1887, only two parishes in all of metropolitan London had rate-supported libraries, although the impetus of the Queen's Jubilee [...] subsequently added a number to the list" (227). In addition, since the purchase and maintenance of buildings often took most of the rate-provided funds, leaving little money for books, "the shelves were often laden with the dubious harvest of housecleaning time or the specialized collections left by local clergymen and amateur scholars" (Altick 228-29). Mechanics' Institute libraries depended upon the same kind of philanthropy for their holdings, could contain "only books that were proper for mechanics to read," which meant a ban on anything considered "controversial" by conservative middle class sponsors, often including poetry, drama, and novels (Altick 194-95), and charged a subscription fee, ranging from 5 to 20 shillings a year (Altick 194). Even after World War I, as Ida Rex, a teacher in Hackney notes, poor children had very little access to books: "children borrowed books to take home, although there was a very poor library at the school. I don't remember much about the public libraries—there wasn't one in Hackney Wick" (29) Finally, as Melba Cuddy-Keane points out, even when free libraries began to make books available to the working and lower middle classes at the beginning of the century, "methods of book borrowing were still nothing short of intimidating" (1).

Although all the students sitting in English 400 have had access to elementary and secondary education that went beyond rote learning of the three Rs, not all have had what they or their professors would call a good education. Funding for public schools in Ohio comes from property taxes, which means that some districts are much poorer than others; many buildings in both urban and rural districts are crumbling, sometimes even unsafe; and even when teachers are bright and creative, they are often hampered by lack of funds for books and equipment or restricted by an emphasis on testing. School libraries vary from wonderful to laughable. In addition, my students live in a hypocritical culture that says it cares about families while it ignores children, demands education but disdains it, and deplores entertainment values while selling them. To maintain a love of reading, they must go against the grain of their generation's and increasingly, their country's culture. Generally, English majors at Otterbein like to read, but some do not have the time (particularly if they are working) or the inclination to read anything outside of class assignments, some have few interpretive strategies at their disposal, even as seniors, and too many still do not trust the interpretive strategies they do have. Of the students and auditor in this class, three are avid readers and three others are perceptive readers with too little time to focus. One student, I suspect, has difficulty reading, though he likes it well enough. He's what I would call a literal reader, someone for whom metaphors do not live; for him, language often obscures rather than illuminates. The other two are good students who read assignments, write papers, and pass tests, but rarely seem engaged with what they read. Much of these students' reading experience in the English major has been introductory, theme-based, or survey-oriented, covering as many authors out of an anthology as possible in a ten-week quarter. They will most likely have taken only two of the three English literature surveys (and one of the two American literature ones), they probably have taken those surveys out of chronological order, and some will have taken the 20th century English literature survey and some not; as a result, their historical background for the Woolf seminar is likely sketchy or confused.

  Those of Virginia Stephen's students *with* an elementary education have been taught under the most narrow of curricula, the Revised Code of 1862. This code was first applied in the day schools run by the Church Societies and then, after 1870, in the local board schools; it was enforced by government inspectors and remained officially in place until 1897, though its indirect effects, such as teaching and learning by rote, lingered longer (Curtis 267; Wardle 69, 107). Under the Code, or what was called the Payment by Results system, the amount of a school's annual grant from the government (and thus teachers' pay) depended upon pupil attendance and examinations passed in each of six Standards. As a result, teachers instructed working class students *only* in reading, writing, and arithmetic, and the instruction was mechanical, geared toward the examinations (Curtis 258-67); students had to memorize answers in constant drills, and "[t]he exams themselves became artificial performances by students for the Inspectors, with anxious teachers standing by nervously" (Heyck 208). The level of literacy expected in each Standard was low by today's standards, revealing either the level at which many students started or the expectations of those devising the

Standards. For example, in the Standard VI exam, the highest standard, a child "was expected to 'read a short ordinary paragraph in a newspaper,' write a similar passage of prose from dictation, and calculate 'a sum in practice or bills of parcels'" (Hurt 8).[10] Although composing a short letter was added to Standard VI in 1871 and although the Code was later expanded to make it possible for a school to add other subjects and for students to take one in addition to the basics, only one in 40 students did so, and the emphasis remained on learning by rote and teaching to the exams (Hurt 183). The move toward compulsory education in 1880 had tripled the number of children in the schools, caused a huge increase in the numbers of children with no formal teaching in their backgrounds, no tradition of attendance, and no family members with any history of schooling, and resulted in poor teaching conditions and huge classes.[11] It's hardly surprising, then, that in 1882, when just over 3 ½-million children were at the annual inspection, "only 47 per cent entered and passed one of the first four Standards in reading and 43 per cent in writing." During the 1880s, according to David Vincent, "there were on average no more than four Standard VI passes a year in each inspected school" (90-91). In the Johanna Street Council School in Lambeth, where none of the fathers of students had a regular job, a third of the children required free meals; the boys could not last through a full-length game of football (soccer); and 92 per cent of those in Standard I were older than they should have been, as were 85 per cent in Standard II and 80 per cent in Standard III—only 8 per cent ever achieved Standard V (Hurt 130). Even as late as the period between the wars, the majority of working class children received training only in the three Rs (Sanderson 146-47; Rex 29). Thus, Morley College's liberal arts curriculum would have been a new experience for many of its students.

---

[10] In the United States, current concerns about the quality of public education are rarely accompanied by any comparative or historical analysis of the term "literacy," though NCTE publications certainly make such information available. Although not all students in grade 6 meet the standards expected of them today in the U.S., surely they are expected to do more than read a paragraph in a newspaper, copy a passage from dictation, and do sums? Beyond the early elementary grades, surely U.S. teachers use the term "writing" to mean composing sentences, paragraphs, and essays rather than being literally able to form letters on the page? Examining historical uses of the term makes it clear that what we mean by "literate" or by "reading, writing, and arithmetic" today has grown to include more knowledge, more complex abilities, and more higher order thinking skills.

[11] The pupil to teacher ratio in 1870 was 123:1; in 1891, 67:1; and in 1899, 62:1 (Copeland 379).

My students are part of an educational context that for most of the United States' history has tied education to democracy; education is considered necessary for an informed citizenry. Fighting for the vote for women and for African-Americans meant fighting for education, too. Although free and universal public education has not been a part of the United States since its very beginning, towns, even those on the furthest frontier, generally established schools (Gutek 55, 69). Too, colleges and universities were established much more readily here than in England, partly because of the land grant tradition that made the idea of an accessible education part of U.S. culture.[12] Education has also been tied to upward mobility in the United States, and now increasingly to job security; marginalized groups have traditionally seen education as their ticket to a better life. Finally, education has become tied to the economy and considered necessary for a globally competitive workplace.

In Virginia Stephen's time, the idea that the working classes deserved an education, let alone that the nation needed educated workers *as* citizens, was relatively new in England. Education had been for ruling an Empire, not for participating in a democracy. As Jane McDermid points out, "the Church of England was extremely wary of education for the poor, fearing a potential threat to the social order" (117). What education there was for the working classes was almost always subtly or not-so-subtly geared toward keeping them in their place, not toward their questioning those places or moving out of them; thus, for example, education for working class girls and women was geared toward improving their homemaking skills and education for working class boys and men was aimed at improving their technical skills (McDermid 116-20; Altick 163-65, 194). Education for the working classes was not supposed to contribute to personal enrichment, social or political betterment, or upward mobility (Altick 141-44). Indeed, the increased availability of education for the working classes was creating anxiety, as Stephen Arata points out (56). He quotes Robert Buchanan, who complained that because of the Reform Bills and the Education Act, "'the great waters of Democracy' were 'arising to swallow up and cover the last landmarks' of high Victorian culture." Buchanan believed that "After the School Board has come the Deluge" (qtd. in Arata 57).

The students in English 400 are at an institution that cares about them as human beings, wants them to succeed, and tries to prepare them well for work

---

[12] Land-grant colleges and universities resulted from the Morrill Act (1862), which gave states federal lands on which to establish colleges offering programs in agriculture, engineering, and home economics, as well as traditional academic subjects and military training. The program was expanded with funds for research by the Hatch Act (1887) (*The Concise Columbia Encyclopedia* 463)

and life. The institution demands that students have a background in the liberal arts and has recently added a Senior Year Experience geared to help students see their education as a whole, connect their major and their requirements, and synthesize their learning across disciplines. Although students do not always see the coherence of their education until later, the institution does try to insure that the coherence is there and makes an attempt to communicate that coherence to students as well.

It is difficult to tell from historical accounts what a course of study at Morley College in the early years of the twentieth century consisted of; in fact, Richards writes in his 1958 history that "Morley College is not concerned with Degrees, and never has been" (85). The overall program was certainly not clear to Virginia Stephen, either, who was told, when she wanted to teach a course in English history, that "history [...] was the least popular subject in the College" ("Report" 202). She was convinced that it would not be difficult to educate her students "to give them a new interest in life"; they want "substance," something they "could really grasp" (203), she writes, which may have been why they begged her "to lecture steadily at English History [...] 'from the beginning'" (*PA* 255). As a result, she was angry when she was told she must "stop at King John," turn to teaching English Composition, and tell her students, if they wanted to continue learning history, that they "can hear eight lectures on the French Revolution" ("Report" 203). Her comment, that these lectures will be "dropped" into her students' minds, "like meteors from another sphere," and that they will be experienced as "disconnected fragments" by "people who have absolutely no power of receiving them as part of a whole" ("Report" 204), is not a criticism of her students' intellectual capabilities; rather, it's a criticism of Morley's lack of coherence—the College is not doing enough to help the students "piece together what they heard; to seek reasons; to connect ideas" ("Report" 203); to experience their education as a cumulative process.

I walk into my college classroom as a trained member of a profession: I have earned a B.A. (which included a secondary teaching certificate), an M.A., and a Ph.D. in English, taught for two years in a rural high school, participated in Rice University's graduate seminars on teaching freshman composition and supervised a fledgling writing center there, and worked part-time at the Ohio State University's Writing Workshop for students not ready for regular freshman composition classes. I have been part of a school environment since the age of 6, and have had many years' experience going to classes, watching effective and ineffective teachers, seeing what works and what doesn't.

Virginia Stephen is a volunteer, one of many, at an institution that is one small square in a patchwork quilt of efforts to educate the working classes. She is untrained. She has experienced some good individualized instruction in Greek from Janet Case, and she and her father have had almost daily discussions about literature at times. She does know how it feels to have a lecture go over her head: she records in her 1897 diary that her father's "lecture [on Pascal] was very deep rather too deep for the audience; very logical & difficult for the ignorant (i.e. Miss Jan [Virginia herself]) to follow" (*PA* 79). She has also talked with Thoby about his classes at Clifton and Cambridge, enough to know that she has "to delve from books, painfully and all alone, what you get every evening sitting over your fire and smoking your pipe with Strachey etc. No wonder my knowledge is but scant. Theres nothing like talk as an educator I'm sure" (*L1* 77). But other than a class or two in Greek and Latin from Dr. George Warr at the King's College Ladies Department in Kensington, she has had no experience of sitting in a classroom with a group of students on a regular basis, or of taking first one course, then another, or of watching different teachers at work. Morley has not provided any training, either, other than a party at the College where she discusses a class with "nice enthusiastic working women who say they love books" (*PA* 218). In Virginia Stephen's world, teaching had only recently begun to be thought of as a profession, requiring professional training and standards. Elementary school teachers, partly because they were recruited from the working classes and partly because they were required in great numbers after the Education Act of 1870 (Holcombe 34; Heyck 209), were perceived as needing professional status, and the state established standards for their training. Certified teachers had a secondary education and training at one of the teacher-training colleges, some of which were affiliated with universities and university colleges by the end of the 19th century (Holcombe 37), and a large majority of them belonged to the National Union of Teachers. (At the same time, the huge need for teachers to handle the growth in the number of pupils from 1,873,000 in 1875 to 5,392,600 in 1914 [Holcombe 34] meant that the numbers of untrained teachers with certificates and uncertificated or pupil-teachers also increased, the latter by as much as 24 times between 1870 and 1895 [Tropp, cited in Heyck 209]). Secondary teachers, on the other hand, were not as quick to professionalize, partly because of the belief that the "main requirement of a public school teacher was simply to be a gentleman" (Heyck 202), but also because secondary education was available to only a small part of the population. As more public schools were created, particularly for girls, and as the move toward a national system of secondary education gained momentum, however, secondary school teachers, generally from the middle classes, also demanded professional status. For women, this effort was tied to the demand for higher education (Holcombe 47-50). The move to professionalize teaching at the university level began with the tutors at Cambridge and Oxford who wanted to sever the connection between holy orders and careers, to have their teaching and scholarship valued, and to have access to better positions and the "academic career ladder" (Heyck 196-97). Women teachers in the universities were relatively "few in number," and most worked in the women's colleges (Holcombe 65). The first generation of women principals at the women's colleges, though superbly qualified in many ways, had not been able to attend university themselves and thus had to fight for professional standing with male colleagues (Levine 134), and until more women could attend university, the competition between men and women for positions, even at women's colleges, favored the better educated men. Although at the new coeducational universities positions were supposed to be open equally to men and women, "a woman had to be exceptionally well qualified and much more distinguished than a man in order to gain an appointment" (Holcombe 66). However, by 1900, as Thomas William Heyck points out, the four women's colleges "employed more than 50 women tutors and lecturers, whose career aspirations copied those of their male counterparts in combining research scholarship and teaching" (199).

I live in a time and in a country with a strong immigrant culture and background. Though this tradition offers little to Native and African Americans other than frustration at being once more excluded, it *has* created a narrative that moves from the hope of entry through the horror of discriminatory barriers to the achievement of access. This underlying narrative of equal or at least eventual access still has great power in our culture, and periodically, its power forces us, as a nation, to try to match reality to narrative for immigrant and non-immigrant groups alike. Thus, in this time and place, I am offered a bewildering array of arguments, beliefs, and positions about difference. Many teachers of my generation are aware of the individual stories of those who have been excluded and the history of our country's failures to meet its obligations to all. Racism, sexism, and classism still rear their ugly heads, but knowledge about racism, sexism, and classism, both everyday and theoretical, has become part of many teachers' cultural fabric. I am part of a generation of teachers who has read African-American literature as a matter of course; has founded and funded Black Studies, Women's Studies, and now Asian Studies, Hispanic Studies, Native American Studies, and so forth, on university campuses; has studied Jewish/Christian relationships; and has identified and discussed patterns in cultural conflicts and accommodations. Indeed, I am sometimes overwhelmed by the sheer amount of ethnic and cultural information available to me and by my sense of obligation to pay attention. Nonetheless, I have been trained to use the information, to consider difference in my teaching, to understand various learning styles, to be sensitive to exclusionary tactics on my own and my students' parts, to confront prejudice in my classroom and discrimination in my institution. I rarely feel as though I am succeeding, but I expect myself to. In this educational culture, some, maybe many, are at least trying to make progress and help our students make progress toward a more genuinely plural and diverse nation.

Virginia Stephen's "education" has given her no framework for understanding the working classes she has been asked to teach. Her knowledge has been limited to workhouse visits with Stella (*PA* 42-43; 56) and to the servants living in the household. But neither charity extended to the extremely poor nor the employer/employee dynamic of the mistress/servant relationship modeled by Julia Stephen has encouraged much real understanding of working class life (Stephen 248-52). Perhaps most important, though, Virginia Stephen knows little, if anything, about the education her working class students have received. She is truly a novice, with little theoretical information at her disposal about difference and little experience with it. Her everyday knowledge of class difference is anchored in maintaining it, not erasing it; hierarchies are breathed in and out as a matter of course, and many attitudes about difference are not identified, acknowledged, discussed, or questioned. It is hardly surprising, given her experience, her knowledge, and her context, that her comments about her students sometimes seem detached or condescending. Through current scholarship we now know that London was home to a great variety of people: tens of thousands of people in London in 1901 had been born in Czechoslovakia, Italy, and Germany; the Irish Catholic population was around 435,000; and by 1900, the Jewish population had risen to around 135,000 because of pogroms in Europe (Schneer 7-8). Other kinds of difference were perceived, inaccurately, it turns out, as being located in the Empire, not in London (Whitaker 481). For example, Jonathan Schneer estimates that in 1901, approximately 1,000 Indians lived in London (814); says that by 1911, approximately 1300 Chinese lived in England and Wales (he notes that the *Westminster Gazette* mentioned Chinese laundries in 1900) (266); and points out that "a sprinkling" of African and West Indian immigrants "organized the world's first Pan-African Conference" in 1900 with W. E. B. DuBois as the opening speaker (8). Yet little conscious awareness of London's diversity seems to have existed at the time. Whitaker's *Almanack* for 1917, for example, lists separate demographic information for only the Jewish population (290) and Irish "foreigners" (486-87). Thus, Woolf had little knowledge of other peoples in London and certainly no awareness that she *should* have such knowledge. The concept, let alone any resulting obligation, was simply not on the cognitive map.

I begin here: Virginia Stephen and I differ greatly as we walk into our classrooms at the beginning and end of the twentieth century. Our education and training differ, our students differ, and our contexts—national, institutional, educational, professional—differ. We have different career goals, different backgrounds, and different commitments. Yet even with all these differences, I believe Virginia Stephen/Woolf has something to teach me about teaching my students literature, but only if I read the pedagogical lessons in her essays carefully and take her suggestions and strategies seriously as I plan my Woolf seminar. I know what my goals are—I want the students in English 400 to experience the pleasure of studying an author in depth when most of their English major experience has been devoted to developing breadth; to understand at least some of Woolf's work even if they continue to dislike it; to think about how Woolf's life and work have been constructed and defined; and to leave the class with a clearer, more realistic view of Woolf as a person and writer. I want them to read widely, dig deeply, and enter the critical dialogue about Virginia Woolf and her work. But how can I help students with little experience or appreciation of modern literature reach those goals? In twice-weekly meetings of two hours in a ten-week quarter?

How did Virginia Stephen negotiate the great difference between herself and her students? Mainly, through identifying with them. She goes across the Waterloo Bridge, a significant passage in London at the time, and "trie[s] to *share* the fruits of [her] very imperfect education" (*L6* 419; my emphasis). And, as her diary, letters, and class preparations show,[13] she works very hard. She tries to make her talks more vivid (*L1* 191), writing a "pot boiler," for example (*PA* 227); she picks up books at the library (*PA* 221), thinking they might work for her classes; she tries to adjust to her audience, getting more comfortable with

---

[13] S. P. Rosenbaum has transcribed two of what seem to be Virginia Stephen "lectures" for Morley College, one on Benvenuto Cellini (*PA* 237) and one on "The Dramatic in Life & Art," and I want to thank him for so generously sharing those transcriptions with me. These lectures are in the University of Sussex Manuscripts Collection, Monks House Papers A.26.b and c. Stephen mentions taking "copious notes" of Green and Freeman for her English History lectures (*PA* 272) and these notes can be read in *PA* 278-80. At the rear of a bound volume of "Presscuttings from 1903 to March 13, 1913" in the Leonard Woolf Papers in the University of Sussex Manuscript Collections (LWP II.D.17.a), is a list of authorities on English history (including Green and Freeman) and a lengthy outline of English history dates and events in Woolf's hand. The existing outline consists of 32 numbered pages, but several pages have been torn out, including the first one. The date B.C. 410 is legible on the left hand side of that page, and the outline goes up to 1815. It's at least possible that this notebook was originally Virginia Stephen's, that she took these notes for her Morley College work, and that Leonard Woolf later used the notebook for his early presscuttings. If so, these notes join the evidence of the draft lectures and the notes in her journal to indicate that Virginia Stephen took her work at Morley quite seriously.

notes rather than written out lectures (*PA* 249; "Report" 203); and she begins to generate discussion (*L1* 177). She prepares handouts ("Report" 203), takes students on field trips (*L1* 192; *PA* 246), lends books, and encourages her students to write autobiographical essays ("Report" 203). But most important, she glimpses a similarity between their struggles to learn and her own: she sees that Miss Williams is the "germ of a literary lady" and that Miss Burke could have been a writer under different circumstances ("Report" 202-03).

Thus, she forges a link with others trying to educate themselves; they, too, have been excluded from a good education; they, too, desire learning, but are often overwhelmed by it; and they, too, must struggle to "piece together" what they're learning, "to connect ideas" into some cohesive whole ("Report" 202-04). Virginia Stephen is not pretending when she identifies with her students or sees how different material circumstances might have made them more like her (or vice versa?). Real similarities did exist between her education and theirs: education begun at home, irregular, and narrow in some way; education dependent on one's own initiative, motivation, and discipline; education fragmented and often interrupted. She identifies with the outsiders in her classes, who like her, have little money for education (the Stephen money was spent on the sons' educations)[14] and must struggle to educate themselves ("my own education [alone among books] was a very bad one" [*L6* 420]). Near the end of her life, in a talk called "The Leaning Tower" given to the Workers' Education Association in Brighton, she aligns herself with the working class men in her audience rather than with the university-educated men of her milieu. Yet she is also an insider, with access to the world of letters through the structure, coherence, and contextual wealth of her father's library; her awareness of that advantage is apparent in her criticism of Morley College for not providing a similar wealth, a context that would show students how the "disconnected fragments" of lectures and classes are "part of a whole" ("Report" 204).

[14] Although Woolf notes the difference in spending for Thoby and Adrian as opposed to herself and Vanessa, some proof of an even earlier gender disparity in educational spending within the Stephen household exists in Folder 13 ([Agnostic Women]) of the Julia Stephen Papers, Manuscripts, Archives, and Special Collections, New Holland Library, Washington State University, Pullman, WA. This folder contains the manuscript draft of Julia Stephen's reply to Bertha Lathbury's "Agnosticism and Women," which had been published in April 1880. On the verso of the last page of her draft is a household budget in Julia's hand, probably for the year 1880, given the names used, the date of Lathbury's article, Diane Gillespie's belief that Julia responded to Lathbury immediately (199), and my speculation that Julia grabbed the piece of paper containing her sketched-out budget and turned it over in her haste to finish her [agnostic women] draft. In any case, along with items such as house and clothes and rates, there's a line for education. It reads: "education boys £280 Stella £55 Laura £50 385." The "boys" were Gerald and George, 12 and 11 respectively in 1880; Stella and Laura were 10.

While teaching at Morley College from 1905-07, while trying to negotiate class difference for the first time, Virginia Stephen also begins serving her apprenticeship in essay writing. This double education—concurrently writing for a real audience she faces weekly and an audience she can only imagine, preparing and teaching classes for working class adults at Morley at the same time she is learning and practicing her craft as a writer—reverberates throughout her career, because what Morley College teaches the young Virginia Stephen about reaching an audience permeates the essays written by Virginia Woolf. In fact, teaching at Morley teaches Woolf how to teach—in print.

Woolf uses many of the same teaching strategies in her essays that she used in the classroom: identify with readers and acknowledge their presence and value; use conversation rather than lecture; communicate with vivid detail and narrative; and provide context (Daugherty, "Woolf Teaching/Learning" 63-65). When Woolf borrows the concept of the common reader from Samuel Johnson and recreates it in her introductory essay to *The Common Reader*, a collection of her essays, she recycles her Morley strategy of forging a link with the outsider and incorporates Morley student traits within her definition: exclusion from education, desire for learning, and attempt to form wholes out of scattershot reading. The common reader is thus "worse educated," less generously "gifted," and [h]asty, inaccurate, and superficial"; the common reader loves to read "for his own pleasure"; and the common reader instinctively attempts to "create, [...] out of whatever odds and ends he can come by, some kind of whole" (*CR*1 1). Woolf writes that "Every writer has an audience in view" (*CR*2 33), and she creates her essays with common readers in mind, an audience tied to her Morley students. Her essays become classrooms, spaces permeated with the "understanding of a teacher"[15] whose main goal is to motivate her students to read, talk, and learn, spaces where the teacher/writer and student/reader can talk comfortably as partners.

Woolf's essays aim to teach, then, some more overtly than others. For example, the essays that begin as lectures to students, women, and the working classes—"Mr. Bennett and Mrs. Brown," "How Should One Read a Book?," "The Narrow Bridge of Art," *A Room of One's Own*, "Professions for Women," and "The Leaning Tower"—all have a clear pedagogical subtext. "How Should One Read a Book?" takes the question seriously and attempts to answer it, for instance, whereas both "The Leaning Tower" and *A Room of One's Own* provide extensive reading lists.[16] The two volumes of essays that she collected into *The Common Reader* and *The Common Reader: Second Series* provide a crash course

---

[15] This phrase is Jeanne Dubino's, made in conversation.
[16] See "Taking a Leaf" for a more detailed discussion of these essays' pedagogical subtext.

in English literary history; in fact, the tables of contents look suspiciously like course syllabi. Woolf uses chronology, historical essays written specifically for the volumes, and transitions and comparisons between and among essays to transform collections of potentially random pieces into coherent volumes that literally model *how* to build literary knowledge. Again, she provides lists, summaries, and definitions; in addition, she encourages access by frequently using biography, autobiography, diaries, and/or letters; and she uses literary allusions in ways that include rather than exclude the reader.[17] Other of her essays are really about how to approach the difficult moderns, herself included. Finally, her essays respect and encourage the reader; in 1940, she urges the "commoners and outsiders" with whom she identifies to "trespass" on the "common ground" of literature because teaching ourselves "how to read and to write" will not only transform literature, but transcend the gulf between classes ("Leaning Tower" 181). Sometimes accused of being an elitist writing for a coterie,[18] Woolf actually persisted in reaching out, writing essays to educate readers not only for modern literature, but for literature in general. Thus, she works to widen the readership for literature ("I did my best to make [some of my books] reach a far wider circle than a little private circle of exquisite and cultivated people" [*L6* 420]), to make it more inclusive, and she insists on the reader's important role in that process: "The standards we raise and the judgments we pass steal into the air and become part of the atmosphere which writers breathe as they work" (*CR2* 269).

Virginia Stephen received almost no help in meeting and teaching students separated from her by class and education, whereas I receive a great deal of help, not the least of which is hers. As a teacher, Virginia Stephen worked to reach her students, and I'm convinced that her teaching at Morley College influences Virginia Woolf's essay style, that her Morley College students underlie her concept of the common reader, and that she teaches through her essays the rest of her life. It's not just her conversational tone. It's not just that her few public lectures are addressed to students, women, or the working classes. It's also that she creates entry points through narrative or biography, gives people background, shares the web of living literature, breaks down genre barriers, includes writers and works not in the canon, and shares her knowledge rather than withholds it.[19] So might not Woolf's efforts to reach a wider audience through her essays help me

---

[17] See my "Woolf Teaching/Learning" for a much fuller discussion of Woolf's teaching strategies in the *Common Readers*.

[18] See Alex Zwerdling, and for a more recent example, Jonathan Rose in Chapter 12, "What Was Leonard Bast Really Like?" 393-438.

[19] See my "Readin', Writin,' and Revisin'" and "Virginia Woolf's 'How Should One Read a Book?'" for additional discussion of Woolf's inclusive strategies.

plan and teach a senior seminar on Virginia Woolf to students who have most likely decided on the basis of one novel that they don't like her? Or who know absolutely nothing about her except that she was "crazy" and committed suicide? Might not Woolf's teaching teach me something about how to teach her work?[20]

Well, yes. A brief discussion follows of some of the strategies she "suggested" I try. Woolf's conversational tone and her emphasis on dialogue and multiplicity led me to call the course "Virginia Woolf: Multiple Voices, Multiple Writers"; I wanted students to break out of their one-dimensional view of Woolf and hear Woolf's many voices. I also wanted them to examine the relationship between voice and genre, so we read every genre she wrote in except drama, and they heard about *Freshwater*. Students kept a dialogic journal, which put them in dialogue not only with Woolf but with each other (each student commented on the reading for the week, and then group members exchanged journals, and commented on each other's responses). To make sure they heard their own voices and got their preconceptions on the table immediately, I asked them to come to class the first day ready to discuss what they already knew or thought they knew about Virginia Woolf, along with what they didn't know and wanted to learn. Each class session included lots of discussion, we met to discuss *To the Lighthouse* over dinner at my house, and half of the final exam was oral—each student had to discuss a favorite passage in Woolf and a favorite passage in the criticism.[21]

The close relationship between writing and reading in Woolf's essays suggests a close relationship between teaching and learning. To give students the experience of learning from teaching, to acknowledge and value their presence in the classroom more fully, and to give them more of a hand in creating the class, each student had to facilitate a half-hour discussion on the primary reading assignment for that week. This requirement not only encouraged discussion, the hearing of many voices, but it also put me in the position of learner, sitting and listening with wonder as a young man did a riff on *Mrs. Dalloway*, for example,

---

[20] This essay is another in a series of investigations into what Woolf might tell us as teachers: see "Empowering the Student," "Hungry to Talk" (with others), "Teaching *Mrs. Dalloway* and *Praisesong for the Widow* as a Pair," and the preface and introduction, with Mary Beth Pringle, to the MLA volume on teaching *To the Lighthouse*. These investigations are part of a longer study of Woolf and education that will include sections on Virginia Stephen's education, Virginia Stephen's work at Morley, Virginia Woolf's essays as education, and Woolf's pedagogical legacy.

[21] The written portion of the exam asked them to respond to two questions (out of five posed) with two essays. One question asked them to explore the relationship between voice and genre, one asked them to teach the teacher what to say (how would they answer typical student responses to Woolf? how would they help them read her?), another asked what they had learned about the relationship between life and literature from Woolf, one asked what she had taught them about the nature of reality, and the last asked what they had learned about being a writer from her.

or being reminded what it's like to be piecing together disconnected fragments, to not have the key concept that ties things together: "I never thought of writers writing in multiple genres. I figured that if they were poets, they only wrote poetry. If they wrote novels, they didn't write essays." Another student taught me a new metaphor for reading, especially for reading Woolf: "For me, reading Woolf was sort of like one of those magic eye puzzles, which is so full of detail it is distracting and you stare at it and don't see anything but ordered confusion. However, if you stare at it long enough it becomes a blur and it is from that that the 3-dimensional image of the puzzle jumps out." Perhaps this student's insight was really into the nature of learning.

Woolf's developmental model for learning how to read in "How Should One Read a Book?" continues to make me question how we teach literature in college. You'll recall that in the first stage, the reader reads widely and sympathetically, receiving impressions and attempting to become the author, not evaluate her, and reads lives, letters, and books on the rubbish heap: I call it the gluttony stage, and I've discovered that many Otterbein students have never experienced that pleasure. To give my students a taste of this stage, I sent them a letter near the end of winter quarter that encouraged them to read rapidly over spring break: for the first class, they were to read the diary and letter excerpts in Mitchell Leaska's *Virginia Woolf Reader*, a packet of supplemental selections from the diaries and the letters, and "Houses," the second chapter in Hermione Lee's Woolf biography.[22]

Second, the reader tries to see works as wholes and compare them to other wholes, which leads to the development of aesthetic criteria and values, to judgment. This stage occurred naturally as the students gained more knowledge and experience of Woolf's texts—their comparative comments and questions were much more frequent at the end of the quarter. Then, and only then, does the reader consult the critics and theorists, when she has questions to ask them and some perceptions of her own to test against theirs. But because the senior seminar has to include a research essay and because the students, with only ten weeks to work in, need to begin thinking about that essay early, I could not banish criticism until the end of the quarter, no matter how much I wanted to. However, I did schedule

---

[22] Although Lee's biography has flaws—blurring the fiction and the life (Hussey 197-98; Villeneuve 8), treating Virginia Stephen's abuse at the hands of her stepbrothers "as a side issue, a distraction" (Hussey 198), missing many opportunities to acknowledge 30 years of American scholarship (Hussey 199), and assuming knowledge of Woolf based on a problematic stance (Villeneuve 8-9), for example—her chapter on houses is useful for students with little knowledge of London or Cornwall. It packs a great deal of biographical context and an introduction to many of Woolf's works into a brief space.

the criticism about the primary text for the *second* class session of each week, and I restricted the criticism in two ways: for most weeks, I chose both a brief review of Woolf's work by a contemporary of hers and a critical essay that either undergraduates could read or I could use to model the critical essay's possibilities (Eleanor McNees' four-volume collection of criticism was excellent for this purpose).

Woolf's teaching experience and essays have taught me the most, however, about the importance of context. My students confirmed this lesson in their questions about what they wanted to find out about Woolf. "What was the cultural, social, and historical context of her time?" one asked. "What were her relationships to other people in her life like?" asked another. "How did she find time to write?" asked the aspiring playwright, and several wanted to know how her works were received at the time. They had purchased Mark Hussey's *Virginia Woolf A-Z*, a book they liked and consulted each week, and it was invaluable for such contextual work. I also identified a weekly "context building" topic on the syllabus and prepared a 10 to 15-minute presentation on it to frame discussion. For example, I talked about *The Common Reader* the week we read essays, about Thoby Stephen and Cambridge University the week we read *Jacob's Room*, about the *Dictionary of National Biography*, *Flush*, and *Roger Fry* the week we discussed *Orlando*, and about drama, history, and *Freshwater* the week we studied *Between the Acts*.

But the strategy that worked the best in terms of building context and in terms of helping students see Woolf and her work differently is one I learned from Pamela Caughie and Annis Pratt—that is, do not start with the novels. Pamela Caughie starts her Woolf seminars with *Three Guineas*, and Annis Pratt started hers with short stories. I started with the diaries and letters.

Reading a large selection of Woolf's diary entries and letters *first* had an enormous effect on the class.[23] For one thing, students heard two voices right away, generally reflective, hard-working, and focused on the work on the one hand ("The reader gets the feeling that she was just as nervous about her writing as any of [us] are") and generally outgoing, funny, and focused on the life on the other hand ("These letters portray Woolf as an individual with a sense of

---

[23] Mel Ankeny, an Ohio State University reference librarian and avid reader of and about Woolf, unknowingly corroborated the usefulness of this sequence when he shared with me that he tried to read Woolf several times as a young man with no success. What hooked him, he said, was reading the volumes of diaries and letters as they appeared in the 70s and 80s. After that introduction, he claimed, reading her work was easy.

humor"). For another, that early reading became a touchstone, something the students came back to time and time again—Woolf came alive for them there. It didn't matter that they did not "get" all the references—they experienced the web of people and events surrounding her, the complex life she was embedded in. They *felt* her context.

We then moved to Woolf, essayist and literary critic. The essays illustrated her clarity, her purpose, her embeddedness in the literary, and most of all, her desire to share that world with her readers. Next came Woolf, the feminist critic, whom they met by reading the first part of *A Room of One's Own* in the *Virginia Woolf Reader* (and portions of the last two chapters on reserve) and all of *Three Guineas*. Equal to the impact of the diaries and letters was the impact of *Three Guineas* on the class. It hit two of the young men especially hard; they had to grapple with its content emotionally, not just intellectually. For one, it was as though a veil had been ripped off the world; he was angry about how he had been socialized to love war. The other was wondering how he was going to withstand those social pressures to bring up the baby he and his wife were expecting in a different way: "Woolf has made me personally reconsider the way I view things."

We next read Woolf, the story writer. The stories gave students Woolf's fictional voice, experimentation, and style in manageable bites. It was week 5, then, midway in the quarter, before we turned to Woolf, the novelist. At that point, we read five of her novels in chronological order: *Jacob's Room, Mrs. Dalloway, To the Lighthouse, Orlando* (allowing me to include another genre and touch on Woolf, the biographer and historian), and *Between the Acts*. I cannot tell you how moving it was to read *Jacob's Room, Mrs. Dalloway,* and *Between the Acts* after *Three Guineas*. These students, who yes indeed had started the course thinking of Woolf as a flowery, out-of-it, "wasn't she crazy?" writer, needed absolutely no prompting to see the realism and political content of her novels. As one student wrote in the dialogic journal, "Woolf's apparent de-emphasis on character really isn't; it just appears that way because there is so much other information in her texts. It's because her texts are *alive*."

We ended with Woolf the autobiographer and "A Sketch of the Past," which gave a certain symmetry to the course. We had started with the diaries and letters, which revealed the life as it happened; we ended with the unfinished memoir, which revealed the life as shaped by the author. We had begun with a contemporary biographer's positioning of Woolf in "Houses"; we ended with Woolf's provisional positioning of herself. Using biography and autobiography as bookends gave students access to Woolf's life but encouraged them to move beyond using "true to life" as their only aesthetic yardstick; the life illuminated but did not overdetermine the art. Finally, the "Sketch" also allowed them to see

Woolf working, drafting, finding her way, in the midst of composing and revising, in the midst of having the last word.[24]

I begin here: Virginia Woolf can teach me a great deal about being a teacher. Her intense awareness of the obstacles to learning, her numerous attempts to cross barriers rather than to erect them in her essays, and her intimate acquaintance with the paradox of being both outsider and insider help me understand my own discomfort in my role as a teacher.

I often see my younger self when I look at my students. Like many of them, I too come from a small rural town with limited educational opportunities, provincial attitudes, and isolated people. My world was minuscule, and if it had not been for a grandfather who made a very small fortune twice (having lost the first one in the Depression), two grandmothers who earned college degrees and believed in the power of education, and two parents who loved reading, earned advanced degrees, and assumed their children would go to college, I might not have had the chance to enlarge it. Many of my forty-five high school classmates were not so privileged.

Virginia Stephen, though more divided from her students by class than I am from mine, also identified with her students. In a canceled passage of her draft "Report on Teaching at Morley College," she notes that she and the Grub Street reporter "found we had a good deal in common" (*MH* A.22). Understanding the frustration, desire, and struggle associated with being excluded from a good education ("Report" 202-03), she admires the "regular attendants," who come "with one serious desire in common" ("Report" 202).

---

[24] Mitchell Leaska's *Virginia Woolf Reader* is quite useful for seminars such as this one because it provides students with a sampling of Woolf's work in a relatively inexpensive format; no other book brings together so many different kinds of her writing. However, it should be noted that, as with any anthology, the selections made by the editor may not be exactly what the teacher wants. So I asked students to read Chapter 5 and the last part of Chapter 6 in *A Room of One's Own*, for example, to supplement what Leaska includes in his edition. I added "An Unwritten Novel," "A Society," "The Introduction," and "Moments of Being: 'Slater's Pins Have No Points'" to his selection of short stories and made sure they saw the tables of contents of the two *Common Readers* and got to read essays from each volume: "The Common Reader" and "The Duchess of Newcastle" in the first and "Dorothy Osborne's 'Letters'" in the second. I also asked them to read "Leslie Stephen," "The Art of Biography," and "The New Biography" to accompany their reading of *Orlando*. Teachers should also be aware that Leaska's edition, published in 1984, uses the 1st edition version of "A Sketch of the Past" (1976), not the longer 2nd edition version of 1985, and that the omissions from it, though always indicated by ellipses, are extensive.

No matter how much I empathize with my students' feeling as though they are on the outside looking in, trying to crack codes and tear down walls, however, I'm also on the inside, and they know it full well. Though I think I understand my students in some ways—I was there once—I'm also now separated from them by age, interests, and education. Sometimes I have the strangest bifurcated sense; one part of me is working on Woolf's manuscripts, reading Woolf scholarship, coming to conferences, and listening to and talking about topics such as postcolonialism and modernity, positionality and border crossings, cultural parataxis and new challenges to and within feminism, while another part of me is working to help students *read* Woolf, to become readers, period, and to consider ideas from first and second wave feminism. Woolf's wide reading and great learning still intimidate me, as do the convolutions of current theory; *my* reading and learning intimidate my students. I'm in that ambivalent, tense "place" Woolf so clearly identifies in *Three Guineas*: both outsider and insider, marginalized and privileged, periphery and center. No matter how much of an outsider I feel—Appalachian, rural, female—I *am* an insider: white, middle class, educated, employed, tenured, paid for mind work.

Woolf, too, was an insider, though as a formally uneducated woman, she perceived herself as an outsider and sometimes used the language of the outsider, a paradoxical position. Her awareness and openness about that paradoxical position has made her vulnerable to attackers who claim that her facts about women's exclusion from institutions are wrong, that she blindly participates in a pernicious class system, making her feminism suspect, and that she and her group enjoyed excessive (and corrupt) cultural power.[25] As Melba Cuddy-Keane points out, her "self-location on the common ground" with the working classes in "The Leaning Tower" was challenged even by friends such as Ben Nicolson (*L6* 413-14, 419-22), David Cecil (*D5* 352), and Desmond MacCarthy (*L6* 467-68) at the time. With almost no theoretical knowledge and no experience in confronting difference, her reaction to her own privilege is mixed. She both uses it, falls back on it, automatically calls on it, does not see *why* some workers might be conventional, for example (*L4* 228-29), and is highly aware of it, bothered by it, thoughtful in her attempts to interrogate it, frustrated by the upper middle class lens that hinders her understanding ("Life" xxviii). She lives in the place she so clearly and honestly articulates in *Three Guineas*, the outsider who is also the daughter of an educated gentleman. Those who see only the privileged insider

---

[25] See Q.D. Leavis; Tom Paulin; and Philip Hensher as described and quoted in Reed. Numerous Woolf scholars have documented how Woolf worked to cross various barriers, but those convinced that Woolf's class taints any cultural critique she might make are not persuaded by facts such as those gathered by Snaith, Tratner, and Pawlowski.

rarely give her credit for *seeing* the working classes,[26] attempting to widen her audience beyond the *Times Literary Supplement*,[27] or of inspiring women and men of widely varying backgrounds to join the literary conversation and *write*.[28] Christopher Reed's astute analysis of the English reviews of the 1999-2000 Bloomsbury exhibit could apply to such critics: he points out that the reviewers refuse to credit Bloomsbury's attempt to "spread [bourgeois values] to previously disenfranchised segments of the population" at the same time they refuse to see how they wrap their own comfortable existence in "the rhetoric and appearance, though certainly not the substance, of revolutionary Marxist analysis" (37-38).[29]

---

[26] Reginald Gibbons, in an interview in *The Writer's Chronicle*, notes that some classic middle-class suburban novels have been published in the United States in which hired people or people of the working classes simply were not there. It's certainly possible that "If no one in the book is *different*, [...] the characters themselves don't see the other people in their world. But all too often books are written this way because the *writer* doesn't see them, and that's not interesting to me" (Darrow 36). Woolf has been criticized, for example, for not giving a voice or agency to Mrs. McNab in *To the Lighthouse*, but at least, unlike in the novels Gibbons mentions, Mrs. McNab is *there*. The writer has seen her.

[27] In the draft of her letter to Ben Nicolson (*L6* 419-21), Woolf wishes she could have made "not merely thousands of people interested in literature; but millions" (420), but singles out the *Common Reader*, *A Room of One's Own*, and *Three Guineas* as attempts to reach a broader audience. As Michael Kaufmann notes, too, the *Times Literary Supplement* audience was not a coterie audience, since its subscribers numbered around 20,000, certainly not in comparison to *The Egoist*, whose subscribers ranged from 200-400. In addition, Woolf occasionally published articles in mass-market magazines like *The Forum* and *Vogue* (138). Kaufmann asserts that "Woolf spoke to a much wider audience, as a reader to other readers, thereby defining Modernism and literature in general as something available to all, not set apart for a select few" (137).

[28] To name just some current writers who acknowledge the influence of Woolf: bell hooks, Michelle Cliff, Jeanette Winterson, Tillie Olsen, Rosario Ferré, Nancy Mairs, and Michael Cunningham. In addition, as Melba Cuddy-Keane and Anna Snaith both make clear, Woolf often had great impact on ordinary readers' lives.

[29] See Reed's summary of Regina Marler's story in the *Los Angeles Times*, where she "noted the 'rich irony' of British journalists re-enacting their grandfathers' hostility to the first Post-Impressionist exhibition" (36). Reed also notes the spectacle of "British critics claiming the need to guide public taste today berat[ing] Bloomsbury's art-writers for guiding that taste eighty years ago" (38). What's more, they do so, not by assuming that the public has intelligence and wants to learn, as Woolf and other Bloomsbury figures did, but by emphasizing "their journalistic distance from other gallery-goers: 'the public has lousy taste'" complained one critic in *The Sunday Times* (36).

What do I do with my own privilege once I acknowledge it, I ask, just as I ask what Woolf was supposed to do with hers. Acknowledging privilege, seeing one's own complicity in power differences, even trying to challenge it within and without does not solve the problem of *having* it; nothing does. No matter what you do, being perceived as an insider can result in your efforts' being dismissed. Keen awareness of this complex dynamic does not prevent failure, either—Woolf could not always translate her knowledge of exclusion into more inclusive behavior, and with a great deal more theoretical knowledge and experience, neither can I. Such awareness can also paralyze: is any position on which I can stand untainted by power? is any voice with which I can speak uncorrupted by privilege? do I have the right to speak about any other voice than my own?[30] Woolf, it seems to me, has a great deal to teach me about living in that ambivalent, tense "place." Answering MacCarthy's criticism of her alignment with working men, she writes, "Compare my wretched little £150 education with yours, with Lytton's, with Leonard's. [...] Of course I'm not on the ground with the WEA but I'm about four thousand five hundred and fifty pounds nearer them than you

---

[30] As I struggled with the issues underlying this essay, a writing buddy noted, "you don't have the authority of a marginalized position," and Terry Eagleton notes a similar phenomenon when he writes that marginality, not centrality, "is the place to be" (8). Thus my discomfort with privilege simultaneous with a defensiveness about having no legitimate position from which to teach; thus, my support for protests from the margins simultaneous with a bewilderment about where to stand if the margins don't fit me. And doesn't my bewilderment sound suspiciously like the whining of a privileged kid who has had her toys taken away? The difficulties of our particular cultural moment as it relates to issues of teaching and authority are writ large in Nellie Y. McKay's "Naming the Problem That Led to the Question 'Who Shall Teach African American Literature?'; or, Are We Ready to Disband the Wheatley Court?" McKay, looking to the future without ignoring the sins of the past, argues that anyone who earns the knowledge and gains the training in African American literature should be able to teach it, just as anyone who earns the knowledge and gains the training in Renaissance literature should be able to teach it. Her courageous plea to pull down the walls of the "intellectual territories inside our common property" through training and learning (366-68) does not privilege race, class, gender, nationality, religion, political affiliation, or any other circumstance that might put one at the center or on the margins. It privileges learning, and in doing so, sounds a great deal like Woolf's plea at the end of "The Leaning Tower" (181). What McKay's essay does not comment on, however, is the dilemma confronting those who teach at small undergraduate institutions, and, I suspect, many others as well. Perhaps my specific situation will help clarify the nature of that dilemma: a specialist in 20th century English literature, I function most of the time as a generalist who must go outside my field in composition and literature courses designed for non-majors. How much knowledge and training in Renaissance or African American literature (or in medieval or Hispanic literature or in American or world literature) is enough in that situation?

are" (*L6* 467-68).[31] For her, then, the solution, no matter how problematic others find it, is to find some kind of common ground and build on that. Throughout her career, she finds that common ground with those who lack education, who receive a poor education, who must struggle to educate themselves. She asks the essential questions—what is a good education? is it right to tell the working classes to read Shakespeare? (*L6* 420, 421)—and by doing so, predicts my own struggles: what is the responsibility of the insider, the educated? if I teach part of the traditional canon (which now includes Woolf), do I replicate the imperialist underpinnings and power differences such a canon reflects? if I do not teach some of the traditional canon, do I shut marginalized groups out who want to either join or transform that tradition? if I learn and then teach other literatures with parts of the traditional canon, do *I* co-opt other teachers, other voices? how should *I* negotiate the insider/outsider, privileged/marginalized, center/periphery paradox? Woolf's answer seems to be that these questions are inherent, part and parcel of being educated, that teaching in and of itself *is* that tension, *is* that paradox. Her answer, reflected in the choices she makes in her essays, seems to be to open as many doors as possible; to share rather than withhold knowledge, information, and context; to learn all you can about how other people think, learn, work, and have fun; and to do all you can to ensure that your work empowers rather than imprisons.

What I hoped to achieve in the Woolf seminar was to make Woolf accessible to students who tend to fear her as difficult, strange, or snobbish. I think that happened, but if it did, it was because I took seriously the choices Woolf makes and the strategies she uses to make literature accessible in her essays. I cannot erase my privilege, but I can name my position and understand its inherent discomfort. I can continue to believe that it's better to be educated than uneducated, that it's meaningful to educate others, and that it's important to fight the forces that want to write students of one sort or another off. And when I fail to understand an individual student or a group, as I invariably do, I can learn from my misunderstanding, keep trying to cross the bridge, and encourage others to cross it, too.

When I get so tangled up in what to do with privilege that I wonder whether I should teach Woolf (isn't she racist, classist, anti-Semitic?), whether I should teach differently (shouldn't I interrogate, problematize, or call into question every position I or my students take?), and even whether I should teach at all (aren't I so blinded by my own context and insider status that I cannot bring anything to the classroom?), I take some comfort from the final exam written by the

---

[31] In her draft letter to Ben Nicolson, she writes "My father spent perhaps £100 on my education" (*L6* 419).

engineer, the techie, the oldest male in English 400. His response to a question about what Woolf's work had taught him about being a writer suggests that Anna Snaith's strategy—looking at actual readers' responses—and Anna Snaith's distinction—that Woolf can not (and did not want to) speak *for* working women (or students, or working men or people of color or colonized subjects or ...] but can speak *to* many people, across a great number of barriers (225)—have validity: "Being a writer, to Woolf, is being a hostess to the thoughts and feelings of life itself. She is, in some ways, a teacher or a guide to life. The reader is someone to be engaged in the business of intimacy, the business of connecting with a larger (or smaller!) community [...] As a writer, she appreciated the common reader. I am one of those to whom she speaks."

I end here: the gaps are often huge between the educated and the uneducated, between classes, between races, between cultures. But Woolf's impulse, throughout her life and work, to cross the gap and to invite people on the other side of the divide to cross it—"it's yours, too, so trespass! don't let them take literature from you," she implies—continues to inspire me, continues to urge me to keep at it.

And so I begin again ...

Works Cited

Altick, Richard D. *The English Common Reader: A Social History of the Mass Reading Public 1800-1900*. 1957. 2nd ed. Foreword by Jonathan Rose. Columbus: Ohio State UP, 1998.

Arata, Stephen. "1897." *A Companion to Victorian Literature and Culture*. Ed. Herbert F. Tucker. Oxford: Blackwell, 1999. 51-65.

Bell, Quentin. *Virginia Woolf: A Biography*. 2 vols. New York: Harcourt, 1972.

Burnett, John, ed. *Destiny Obscure: Autobiographies of Childhood, Education, and Family from the 1820s to the 1920s*. London: Allen Lane, 1982.

Copeland, Ian. "The Making of the Dull, Deficient, and Backward Pupil in British Elementary Education, 1870-1914." *British Journal of Educational Studies* 44 (1996): 377-94.

Cuddy-Keane, Melba. "Pedagogical Woolf: Between the Academic Devil and the Mass-Culture Sea." Paper presented at the session on Woolf as a Public Intellectual, MLA Convention, Toronto. 28 Dec. 1997.

Curtis, S. J. *History of Education in Great Britain*. 1948. London: University Tutorial P, 1967.

Darrow, Sharon. "An Interview with Reginald Gibbons." *The Writer's Chronicle* 32.2 (October/November 1999): 35-42.

Daugherty, Beth Rigel. "Learning Virginia Woolf: Of Leslie, Libraries, and Letters." *Virginia Woolf and Communities: Selected Papers from the Eighth Annual Conference on Virginia Woolf.* Ed. Jeanette McVicker and Laura Davis. New York: Pace UP, 1999. 10-17.

——. "Morley College, Virginia Woolf, and Us: How Should One Read Class?" *Virginia Woolf and Her Influences: Selected Papers from the Seventh Annual Conference on Virginia Woolf.* Ed. Laura Davis and Jeanette McVicker. New York: Pace UP, 1998. 125-39.

——. "Readin', Writin', and Revisin': Virginia Woolf's 'How Should One Read a Book?'" *Virginia Woolf and the Essay.* Ed. Beth Carole Rosenberg and Jeanne Dubino. New York: St. Martin's, 1997. 159-75.

——. "Taking a Leaf from Virginia Woolf's Book: Empowering the Student." *Virginia Woolf Miscellanies: Proceedings of the First Annual Conference on Virginia Woolf.* Ed. Mark Hussey and Vara Neverow-Turk. New York: Pace UP, 1992. 31-40.

——. "Teaching *Mrs. Dalloway* and *Praisesong for the Widow* as a Pair." *Virginia Woolf and the Arts: Selected Papers from the Sixth Annual Conference on Virginia Woolf.* Ed. Diane F. Gillespie and Leslie K. Hankins. New York: Pace UP, 1997. 175-82.

——. "Virginia Woolf Teaching/Virginia Woolf Learning: Morley College and the Common Reader." *New Essays on Virginia Woolf.* Ed. Helen Wussow. Dallas: Contemporary Research P, 1995. 61-77.

——. "Virginia Woolf's Educational Inheritance: The Stephen Household and 19th Century Debates about Education for Girls." Virginia Woolf: Turning the Centuries. The Ninth Annual Conference on Virginia Woolf. Newark, DE. 13 June 1999.

——. "Virginia Woolf's 'How Should One Read a Book?'" *Woolf Studies Annual* 4 (1998): 123-85.

——. With Mary Beth Pringle. "Preface" and "Introduction." *Approaches to Teaching Woolf's* To the Lighthouse. MLA Teaching World Literature Series. New York: MLA, 2001. xi-xiv; 3-22.

——. With Mary Beth Pringle, Marcia McClintock Folsom, Nancy Topping Bazin, Sally Jacobsen, Katherine Hill-Miller, and Susan Yunis. "Hungry to Talk: A Roundtable Discussion of Teaching *To the Lighthouse.*" *Virginia Woolf Miscellanies: Proceedings of the First Annual Conference on Virginia

Woolf. Ed. Mark Hussey and Vara Neverow-Turk. New York: Pace UP, 1992. 203-07.
Eagleton, Terry. "The centre cannot hold: outsiders are the literary mainstream now." *The Guardian.* 23 June 2001: 8.
Gillespie, Diane F. "Essays for Adults." *Julia Duckworth Stephen: Stories for Children, Essays for Adults.* Eds. Diane F. Gillespie and Elizabeth Steele. Syracuse: Syracuse UP, 1987. 195-213.
Gutek, Gerald L. *An Historical Introduction to American Education.* 2nd ed. Prospect Heights, IL: Waveland P, 1991.
Harrison, J. F. C. *The English Common People: A Social History from the Norman Conquest to the Present.* London: Croom Helm, 1984.
Heyck, Thomas William. "Educational." *A Companion to Victorian Literature and Culture.* Ed. Herbert F. Tucker. Oxford: Blackwell, 1999. 194-211.
Holcombe, Lee. "Women in the Classroom: The Teaching Profession." *Victorian Ladies at Work: Middle-Class Working Women in England and Wales, 1850-1914.* Hamden, CT: Archon, 1973. 34-67.
Hurt, J. S. *Elementary Schooling and the Working Classes 1860-1918.* London: Routledge & Kegan Paul, 1979.
Hussey, Mark. Rev. of Hermione Lee's *Virginia Woolf* and Regina Marler's *Bloomsbury Pie: The Making of the Bloomsbury Boom. Woolf Studies Annual* 4 (1998): 195-204.
———. *Virginia Woolf A to Z: A Comprehensive Reference for Students, Teachers and Common Readers to Her Life, Work and Critical Reception.* New York: Oxford UP, 1995.
Inwood, Stephen. *The History of London.* New York: Carroll & Graf, 1998.
Julia Stephen Papers. Manuscripts, Archives, and Special Collections, New Holland Library, Washington State University, Pullman, WA.
Kaufmann, Michael. "A Modernism of One's Own: Virginia Woolf's *TLS* Reviews and Eliotic Modernism." *Virginia Woolf and the Essay.* Eds. Beth Carole Rosenberg and Jeanne Dubino. New York: St. Martin's P, 1997. 137-55.
Kelly, Thomas. *A History of Adult Education in Great Britain from the Middle Ages to the Twentieth Century.* Liverpool: Liverpool UP, 1962.
Leavis, Q. D. "Caterpillars of the Commonwealth Unite!" *Scrutiny* 7 (September 1938): 203-14. Reprinted in McNees, Vol. II, 272-81.
Lee, Hermione. *Virginia Woolf.* New York: Knopf, 1997.
Levine, Philippa. *Feminist Lives in Victorian England: Private Roles and Public Commitment.* Oxford: Basil Blackwell, 1990.
Marcus, Steven. "The Humanities at the End of Centuries." Presentation at Otterbein College, Westerville, OH. 11 April 2000.

Martin, Lindsay. "Virginia Woolf at Morley College." *The Charleston Magazine* 4 (Winter/Spring 1991-92): 20-25.
McAleer, Joseph. *Popular Reading and Publishing in Britain 1914-1950.* Oxford: Clarendon, 1992.
McDermid, Jane. "Women and Education." *Women's History: Britain, 1850-1945.* Ed. June Purvis. London and New York: Routledge, 1995. 107-30.
McKay, Nellie Y. "Naming the Problem That Led to the Question 'Who Shall Teach African American Literature?'; or, Are We Ready to Disband the Wheatley Court?" Guest column. *PMLA* 113 (1998): 359-69.
McNees, Eleanor. *Virginia Woolf: Critical Assessments.* 4 vols. East Sussex: Helm Information, 1994.
Murphy, Paul Thomas. *Toward a Working-Class Canon: Literary Criticism in British Working-Class Periodicals, 1816-1858.* Columbus: Ohio State UP, 1994.
Paulin, Tom. *Virginia Woolf.* Dir. Jeff Morgan. *J'Accuse*. Channel Four Fulmar production. Videocassette. Media Matters, 1991.
Pawlowski, Merry M., ed. *Virginia Woolf and Fascism.* New York: Palgrave, 2001.
Reed, Christopher. "A Tale of Two Countries." *Charleston Magazine.* 22 (Autumn/Winter 2000): 35-39.
Rex, Ida. "Ida Rex, School teacher." *Working Lives: A People's Autobiography of Hackney.* Vol. 1, 1905-1945. London: Hackney WEA with Centerprise Publishing Project, 1976. 23-30.
Richards, Denis. *Offspring of the Vic: A History of Morley College.* Intro. by Harold Nicolson. London: Routledge and Kegan Paul, 1958.
Rose, Jonathan. *The Intellectual Life of the British Working Classes.* New Haven and London: Yale UP, 2001.
Rosenbaum, S. P. *Edwardian Bloomsbury: The Early Literary History of the Bloomsbury Group.* Vol. 2. New York: St. Martin's, 1994.
Sadler, M. E. *Continuation Schools in England & Elsewhere: Their Place in the Educational System of an Industrial and Commercial State.* Manchester: Manchester UP, 1908.
Sanderson, Kay. "'A Pension to Look Forward to . . .?' Women Civil Service Clerks in London, 1925-1939." *Our Work, Our Lives, Our Words.* Eds. Leonore Davidoff and Belinda Westover. Totowa, NJ: Barnes & Noble, 1986. 145-60.
Schneer, Jonathan. *London 1900: The Imperial Metropolis.* New Haven and London: Yale UP, 1999.
Snaith, Anna. "Virginia Woolf and Reading Communities: Respondents to *Three*

Guineas." *Virginia Woolf and Communities: Selected Papers from the Eighth Annual Conference on Virginia Woolf.* Ed. Jeanette McVicker and Laura Davis. New York: Pace UP, 1998: 219-26.

———. *Virginia Woolf: Public and Private Negotiations.* New York: St. Martin's, 2000.

Stephen, Julia Duckworth. "[The Servant Question]." *Julia Duckworth Stephen: Stories for Children, Essays for Adults.* Eds. Diane F. Gillespie and Elizabeth Steele. Syracuse: Syracuse UP, 1987. 248-52.

Stephen, Virginia. Early Writings c. 1902. Monks House Papers A.26.b&c. University of Sussex Manuscripts Collection SxMs18, University of Sussex Library, Falmer, UK.

———. Manuscript Report on teaching at Morley College dated July 1905. Monks House Papers A.22. University of Sussex Manuscripts Collection SxMs18, University of Sussex Library, Falmer, UK.

Tratner, Michael. *Modernism and Mass Politics: Joyce, Woolf, Eliot, Yeats.* Stanford: Stanford UP, 1995.

Villeneuve, Pierre-Eric. "Some Notes on Hermione Lee's Biography of Virginia Woolf." *Virginia Woolf Miscellany* 50 (Fall 1997): 8-9.

Vincent, David. *Literacy and Popular Culture: England 1750-1914.* Cambridge: Cambridge UP, 1989.

Wardle, David. *English Popular Education 1780-1970.* Cambridge: Cambridge UP, 1970.

Whitaker, Joseph. *An Almanack for the Year of Our Lord 1917.* London: Almanack Office, 1916.

Woolf, Virginia. *Between the Acts.* 1941. San Diego: HBJ, 1969.

———. *The Diary of Virginia Woolf.* Ed. Anne Olivier Bell. 5 vols. New York: HBJ, 1977-1984.

———. "Introductory Letter." *Life As We Have Known It, By Co-operative Working Women.* Ed. Margaret Llewelyn Davies. New York: Norton, 1931. xv-xxxix.

———. *Jacob's Room.* 1922. Dover, 1998.

———. *The Letters of Virginia Woolf.* Eds. Nigel Nicolson and Joanne Trautmann. 6 vols. New York: HBJ, 1975-1980.

———. *Mrs. Dalloway.* Foreword by Maureen Howard. 1925. San Diego: HBJ, 1989.

———. Notes of Virginia Woolf: Authorities, The English Kingdoms. Leonard Woolf Papers II.D.17.a. University of Sussex Manuscript Collections SxMs13, University of Sussex Library, Falmer, UK.

———. *Orlando, A Biography.* 1928. San Diego: HBJ, 1956.

———. *A Passionate Apprentice: The Early Journals, 1897-1909.* Ed. Mitchell A.

Leaska. San Diego: HBJ, 1990.

———. "Report on Teaching at Morley College." *Virginia Woolf: A Biography*. By Quentin Bell. Vol. 1. New York: Harcourt/Harvest. 202-04.

———. *Three Guineas*. 1938. San Diego: HBJ, 1966.

———. *To the Lighthouse*. Foreword by Eudora Welty. 1927. San Diego: HBJ, 1989.

———. *The Virginia Woolf Reader*. Ed. Mitchell A. Leaska. San Diego: HBJ, 1984.

Zwerdling, Alex. "The Common Reader, the Coterie and the Audience of One." *Virginia Woolf Miscellanies: Proceedings of the First Annual Conference on Virginia Woolf*. Eds. Mark Hussey and Vara Neverow-Turk. New York: Pace up, 1992. 8-9.

Guide to Library Special Collections

This guide updates the information in volume 9.

Name of Collection: The Beinecke Rare Book and Manuscript Library

Contact: Vincent Giroud, Curator of Modern Books and Manuscripts
Patricia Willis, Curator of American Literature

Address: Yale University Library
P.O. Box 208240
New Haven, CT 06520-8240

Hours: Mon.-Fri. 8:30AM-5PM

Access Requirements: Register at the circulation desk on each visit.

Holdings Relevant To Woolf: General Collection includes autograph manuscript of "Notes on Oliver Goldsmith." Comments on Edward Gibbon, William Beckford Collection. Letters from Virginia Woolf in the Bryher Papers, the Louise Morgan and Otto Theis Papers, and the Rebecca West Papers. Related material: 41 letters from Vita Sackville-West to Violet Trefusis; files relating to Robert Manson Myers's *From Beowulf to Virginia Woolf* in the Edmond Pauker Papers.

Yale Collection of American Literature includes typewritten manuscripts of "The Art of Walter Sickert," "Augustine Birrell," "Aurora Leigh," "How Should One Read a Book?" "Letter to a Young Poet," "The Novels of Turgenev," "Street Haunting." Dial/Scofield Thayer Papers: manuscripts of "The Lives of the Obscure," "Miss Ormerod," and "Mrs. Dalloway in Bond Street." Letters from Virginia Woolf in the William Rose Benet Papers, the Benet Family Correspondence, the Henry Seidel Canby Papers, the Seward Collins Papers, the Dial/Scofield Thayer Papers, and the *Yale Review* archive. Material relating to translations of Woolf in the Thornton Wilder papers. Related material: Clive Bell, "Virginia Woolf" (Dial/Scofield Thayer Papers); 43 letters from Leonard Woolf to Helen McAfee (*Yale Review*); 11 letters from Leonard Woolf to Gertrude Stein.

Name of Collection: The Henry W. and Albert A. Berg Collection of English and American Literature

Contact: Isaac Gewirtz, Curator

Address: New York Public Library, Room 320
Fifth Avenue & 42nd Street
New York, NY 10018

Telephone: 212-930-0802
Fax: 212-930-0079
E-mail: igewirtz@nypl.org

Hours: Tues./Wed. 11AM-6:00PM
Thurs.-Sat. 10AM-6:00PM
Closed Sun., Mon. and legal holidays

Access Requirements: Apply for an ACCESS card on the 3rd floor, and bring it with you when you apply for a card of admission at Office of Special Collections, Room 316. Traceable identification required. Undergraduates working on honors theses need letter from faculty advisor.

Restrictions: Virginia Woolf's MSS are now made available on microfilm. N.B. *All the Berg's Woolf MSS are on microfilm published by Research Publications and available at many research libraries.*

Holdings Relevant To Woolf: Manuscripts of *Between the Acts, Flush, Jacob's Room, Mrs. Dalloway* (notes and fragments), *Night and Day, To the Lighthouse, The Voyage Out, The Waves, The Years*; 12 notebooks of articles, essays, fiction and reviews, 1924-1940; 36 volumes of diaries; 26 volumes of reading notes; correspondence with Vanessa Bell, Ethel Smyth, Vita Sackville-West and others. Su Hua Ling Chen's Bloomsbury correspondence.

Name of Collection: The British Library Manuscript Collections

Contact: Manuscripts Enquiries

Address: 96 Euston Road
London NW1 2DB
England

Telephone: 0207-412-7513
Fax: 0207-412-7745
E-mail: mss@bl.uk

Hours: Hours: Mon 10:00-5:00PM
Tue-Sat: 9:30-5:00PM

Access Requirements: British Library Reader Pass (signed I.D. required and usually proof of post-graduate academic status, or other demonstrable need to use the collections—see www.bl.uk). In addition, access to most literary autograph material only available with letter of recommendation.

Restrictions: Paper Copies, Microfilms, and Photography of selected items available upon receipt of written authorization for photo duplication from the copyright holder.

Holdings Relevant To Woolf: Diaries 1930-1931 (microfilm); Mrs. Dalloway and other writings (1923-1925) three volumes; letter from Leonard Woolf to H. G. Wells (1941); two letters from Virginia Woolf and three letters from Leonard Woolf to John Lehmann (1941); letter written on behalf of Leonard Woolf to S. S. Koteliansky (1946); notebook of Virginia Stephen (1906-1909); A sketch of the past revised ts (1940); letters from Virginia Woolf in the correspondence files of Lytton and James Strachey; letter from Virginia Woolf to Mildred Massingberd; letter from Virginia Woolf to Harriet Shaw Weaver (1918); letters from Virginia Woolf to S. S. Koteliansky (1923-27); letter from Virginia Woolf to Frances Cornford (1929); letter from Virginia Woolf to Ernest Rhys (1930); correspondence of Virginia Woolf in the Society of Authors archive (1934-37); letter and postcard from Virginia Woolf to Bernard Shaw (1940); three letters (suicide notes) from Virginia Woolf (1941); two letters from Virginia Woolf and three from Leonard Woolf to John Lehmann (1941). "Hyde Park Gate News" 1891-92, 1895 (add. MSS 70725, 70726). Letters of Virginia and Leonard Woolf to Lady Aberconway, 1927-1941. Letter from Virginia Woolf to Frances Cornford.Collection of RPs ("reserved photo copies"–copies of manuscrips exported, some subject to restrictions).

Name of Collection: Harry Ransom Humanities Research Center

Contact: Research Librarian

Address: The University of Texas at Austin
P.O. Box 7219
Austin, TX 78713-7219

Telephone: 512-471-9119
Fax: 512-471-2899
E-mail: reference@hrc.utexas.edu
URL: www.hrc.utexas.edu/fa/woolf.virginia.html
Hours: Mon.-Fri. 9AM-5PM
Sat. 9AM-NOON

GUIDE TO SPECIAL COLLECTIONS 313

Closed holidays; intersession Saturdays; one week each in late May and late August.

Access Requirements: Completed manuscript reader's application; current photo identification.

Restrictions: Photocopies of selected items available upon receipt of written authorization for photoduplication from the copyright holder.

Holdings Relevant To Woolf: The manuscript collection includes the typed manuscript with autograph revisions of *Kew Gardens,* and the typed manuscript and autograph revisions of "Thoughts on Peace in an Air Raid." The Center holds 571 of Woolf's letters, including correspondence to Elizabeth Bowen, Lady Ottoline Morrell, Mary Hutchinson, William Plomer, Hugh Walpole and others. Further mss. relating to Virginia Woolf include letters to her from T. S. Eliot and reviews of her work. A substantial collection of the first British and American editions of Woolf's published works, as well as 130 volumes from Leonard and Virginia Woolf's library and a collection of books published by the Hogarth Press, is also housed. An art collection holds a landscape painting of Virginia's garden and a series of Cockney cartoons in a sketch book, signed "V.W." The center also has extensive holdings of materials related to Leonard Woolf, Ottoline Morrell, Mary Hutchinson, Lytton Strachey, Dora Carrington, E. M. Forster, Clive Bell, Roger Fry, Vanessa Bell, Bertrand Russell, Elizabeth Bowen, William Plomer, Stephen Spender and Hugh Walpole.

Name of Collection: King's College Archive Centre

Contact: Rosalind Moad, Archivist

Address: King's College
Cambridge CB2 1ST

Telephone: 01223-331444
Fax: 01223-331891
E-mail: archivist@kings.cam.ac.uk

Hours: Mon.-Fri. 9:30AM-12:30PM and 1:30PM-5:15PM. *Closed during public holidays and the College's annual periods of closure.*

Access Requirements: Proof of ID, letter of introduction, appointment in advance.

Holdings Relevant To Woolf: Woolf MSS and letters: Minute book, written up by Clive Bell, of the meetings of a play-reading society, with cast lists and comments on performances by CB. Dec. 1907-Jan. 1909, Oct. 1914-Feb. 1915. Players included variously Clive & Vanessa Bell, Roger & Margery Fry, Duncan Grant, Walter Lamb, Molly MacCarthy, Adrian & Virginia Stephen, Saxon Sydney-Turner. *Freshwater, A Comedy*—photocopy of editorial typescript prepared from the MSS at Sussex University and Monk's House; photcopy of covering letter from the publisher to "Robert Silvers," 1.29.1976. Papers relating to the Virginia Woolf Centenary Conference held at Fitzwilliam College, Cambridge, 9.20-22.1982. TS with corrections of "Nurse Lugton's Curtain." Typed transcript of R. Fry's memoir of his schooldays. Correspondence with Clive Bell, Julian Bell, Vanessa Bell, Richard Braithwaite, Rupert Brooke, Mrs. Brooke, Katharine Cox, Julian Fry, Roger Fry, John Davy Hayward, J. M. Keynes, Lydia Keynes, Rosamond Lehmann, Charles Mauron, Raymond Mortimer, G.

H. W. Rylands, J. T. Sheppard, W. J. H. Sprott, Thoby Stephen, Madge Vaughan. Woolf-related archival collections held: Charleston Papers; Rupert Brooke Papers; E. M. Forster Papers; Roger Fry Papers; J. M. Keynes Papers; J. T. Sheppard Papers; W. J. H. Sprott Papers. Various works of art by Vanessa Bell, Duncan Grant, and Roger Fry, held in various locations around King's College. Access via Domus Bursar's secretary. Roger Fry Papers: sketchbooks, 1880s-1920s. The papers of George Humphrey Wolferstan ('Dadie') Rylands (1902-99).

Name of Collection: The Lilly Library

Contact: Breon Mitchell, Director
Saundra Taylor, Curator of Manuscripts

Address: The Lilly Library, Indiana University
1200 East Seventh Street
Bloomington, IN 47405-5500

Telephone: 812-855-3143
Fax: 812-855-3143
E-mail: liblilly@indiana.edu, mitchell@indiana.edu
taylors@indiana.edu

Hours: M-F 9-6; Sat. 9-1; Closed Sundays and Major Holidays

Access Requirements: Valid photo-identification; brief registration procedure.

Restrictions: Closed stacks; material use confined to reading room; wheelchair accessible reading room and exhibitions (but no wheelchair-accessible restroom)

Holdings Relevant to Woolf: Corrected page proofs for the British edition of *Mrs Dalloway*; letters to Woolf from Desmond and Mary

(Molly) MacCarthy; 77 letters (published in *Letters*) from Woolf to correspondents including Donald Clifford Brace, Robert Gathorne-Hardy, Barbara (Strachey) Halpern, Richard Arthur Warren Hughes, Desmond MacCarthy and Molly MacCarthy; "Preliminary Scheme for the formation of a Partnership between Mr Leonard Sidney Woolf and Mr John Lehmann to take over The Hogarth Press" (includes contract signed by Lehmann, LW, and VW, and receipt for Lehmann's payment to VW to purchase VW's share in the Hogarth Press); photographs of VW, LW, Lytton Strachey, Strachey family, Roger Fry, and Vanessa Bell (Hannah Whitall Smith mss.); (Richard) Kennedy mss. (four hand-colored lithographs of VW: artist's proofs for RK's portfolio, VIRGINIA WOOLF: "AS I KNEW HER"; Sackville-West, V. mss. (10,529 items: includes the correspondence of Vita Sackville-West, and Harold Nicolson); MacCarthy mss. (ca. 10,000 items: papers of Desmond and Molly MacCarthy); correspondence between LW and Mary Gaither regarding publication of *A Checklist of the Hogarth Press* (1976, repr. 1986); Todd Avery, *Close and Affectionate Friends: Desmond and Molly MacCarthy and the Bloomsbury Group* (The Lilly Library / Indiana University Libraries, 1999).

Name of Collection: Archives and Manuscripts, University of Maryland, College Park, Libraries

Contact: Beth Alvarez, Curator of Literary Manuscripts

Address: University of Maryland Libraries
College Park, MD 20742

Telephone: 301-405-9298
Fax: 301-314-2709
E-mail: alvarez@umd.edu
Hours: Mon.-Fri. 10AM-5PM, Sat. Noon-5PM.

GUIDE TO SPECIAL COLLECTIONS 317

Access Requirements: Photo ID.

Holdings Relevant to
Woolf: Papers of Hope Mirrlees contain five autograph letters and postcards (1919-28) from Virginia Woolf to Mirrlees. Also in the collection are 113 letters from T. S. Eliot to Mirrlees, and three letters from Lady Ottoline Morrell to Mirrlees.

Name of Collection: Monks House Papers/Leonard Woolf Papers/Charleston Papers/Nicolson Papers

Contact: Dorothy Sheridan, Head of Special Collections

Address: University of Sussex Library
Brighton
Sussex BN1 9QL
England

Telephone: 01273-678157
Fax: 01273-678441
E-mail: Library.Specialcoll@sussex.ac.uk

Hours: By appointment

Access Requirements: Letter, to be received *before* visiting. Photocopying strictly controlled.

Holdings Relevant to
Woolf: The University of Sussex holds two large archives relating to Leonard and Virginia Woolf: The Monks House Papers, primarily correspondence and MSS of Virginia Woolf, including the three scrapbooks relating to *Three Guineas*; and The Leonard Woolf Papers, primarily correspondence and other papers of Leonard Woolf. (Monks House Papers are available on microfilm in many research libraries.) The Charleston Papers consist in the main of letters written to or by Clive and Vanessa Bell and Duncan

Grant which had accumulated in their home; the library houses Quentin Bell's photocopied set. Also included are c. 900 letters from Maria Jackson to Julia and Leslie Stephen (Charleston Papers Ad. 1); letters from Roger Fry, Maynard Keynes, Lytton Stachey, Virginia Woolf, Vita Sackville-West, E. M. Forster, T. S. Eliot, Frances Partridge and others. The Nicolson Papers complement these three Sussex archives relating to the Bloomsbury Group, and consist of Nigel Nicolson's correspondence relating to his editorial work as principal editor of the six-volume *Letters of Virginia Woolf*, published between 1975 and 1980.

The Bell Papers. A. O. Bell's correspondence relating to her editorial work on Virginia Woolf's Diaries. A parallel collection to Nicolson Papers.

Collection level descriptions may be accessed at www.archiveshub.ac.uk

Name of Collection: Archives & Manuscripts

Contact: Michael Bott, Keeper of Archives & Manuscripts

Address: The University of Reading, The Library, Whiteknights
P.O. Box 223
Reading RG6 6AE
England

Telephone: 0118-931-8776
Fax: 0118-931-6636
E-mail: g.m.c.bott@reading.ac.uk

Access Requirements: Appointment needed to consult material. Permission required to consult or copy material in the Hogarth Press and Chatto & Windus collections from Random House, 20 Vauxhall Bridge Road, London SW1V 2SA, UK.

GUIDE TO SPECIAL COLLECTIONS 319

Holdings Relevant to Woolf:	Hogarth Press (MS2750): editorial and production correspondence relating to publications of the Press including Woolf's own titles. Production ledgers 1920s-1950s. Correspondence between Leonard Woolf and Stanley Unwin about progress with his collected edition of the works of Freud. Chatto & Windus (MS2444): small number of letters 1915-25; 1929-31. George Bell & Sons (MS1640): 5 letters from Leonard Woolf 1930-66. Routledge (MS1489): Reader's report by Leonard Woolf on George Padmore's "Britannia rules the blacks" (1935); "How Britain rules Africa." Megroz (MS1979/68): 2 letters from LW, 1926. Allen & Unwin (MS3282): Correspondence with LW 1923-24; 1939-40; 1943; 1946; 1950-51, including letters concerning a reprint of *Empire and Commerce in Africa*, and concerning ill-founded rumors about the Hogarth press.
Name of Collection:	Frances Hooper Collection of Virginia Woolf Books and Manuscripts/Elizabeth Power Richardson Bloomsbury Iconography Collection.
Contact:	Karen V. Kukil, Associate Curator of Rare Books
Address:	Mortimer Rare Book Room William Allan Neilson Library Smith College Northampton, MA 01063
Telephone:	413-585-2906
Fax:	413-585-4486
E-mail:	kkukil@smith.edu
Hours:	Mon.-Fri. 9AM-5PM
Access Requirements:	Appointment to be made with the Curator.

Holdings Relevant to Woolf: The Hooper Collection emphasizes Woolf as an essayist but also includes many Hogarth Press first editions, limited editions of Woolf's works, and translations. The collection includes page proofs of *Orlando*, *To the Lighthouse*, and *The Common Reader*, corrected by Woolf for the first American editions, a proof copy of *The Waves* that Woolf inscribed to Hugh Walpole, and the proof copies of *The Years* and of *Flush*. The Collection also has one of the deluxe editions of *Orlando* that was printed on green paper. Other items include twenty-two pages of reading notes from 1926, three pages of notes on D. H. Lawrence's *Sons and Lovers*, thirty-three pages of notes for *Roger Fry*, a six-page ms. "As to criticism," a five-page ms. of "The Searchlight," and a fourteen-page ms. of "The Patron and The Crocus." The Hooper Collection also owns 140 letters between Woolf and Lytton Strachey as well as other correspondence, including a 13 February [1921] letter to Katherine Mansfield and ten letters to Mela and Robert Spira.

The Richardson Collection is a working collection of books and materials used by Richardson in preparing her *Bloomsbury Iconography*. It includes Leslie Stephen's photograph album, ninety-eight original exhibition catalogs dating back to 1929, clippings and photcopies of such items as reviews of early Woolf works, and Bloomsbury material from British *Vogue* of the 1920s. The Collection also has three preliminary pencil drawings by Vanessa Bell for *Flush*.

The Mortimer Rare Book Room also owns Woolf's 1916 Italian ms. notebook and her corrected typescripts of "Reviewing" and "The Searchlight." In addition, there is a 1923 photograph of Woolf at Garsington. Original cover designs for Hogarth Press publications include *The Common Reader, On*

Being Ill, and *Duncan Grant*. The Mortimer Rare Book Room also has a Sylvia Plath Collection that includes eight of Woolf's books from Plath's library, several of which are underlined and annotated, as well as Plath's notes from her undergraduate English 211 class at Smith (1951-2) in which she studied *To the Lighthouse*.

Recent Acquisitions: Virginia Woolf's 26 February 1939 letter to Vita Sackville-West, a 1931 bronze bust of Virginia Woolf by Stephen Tomlin, and a 1923 Hogarth Press edition of T.S. Eliot's *The Waste Land*.

Name of Collection: Woolf/Hogarth Press/Bloomsbury

Contact: Robert C. Brandeis

Address: Victoria University Library
71 Queens Park Crescent E.
Toronto M5S 1K7
Ontario
Canada

Hours: Mon.-Fri. 9AM-5PM
URL: http://library.vicu.utoronto.ca/special/bloomsbury.htm

Access Requirements: Prior notification; identification.

Restrictions: Limited photocopying.

Holdings Relevant to Woolf: This collection, the most comprehensive of its kind in Canada, contains all the work of Virginia and Leonard Woolf in various editions, issues, variants and translations; all the books hand printed by Leonard and Virginia Woolf at the Hogarth Press, including many variant issues and bindings, association copies and page proofs; a nearly comprehensive collection of Hogarth Press machine printed books to 1946 (the year Leonard Woolf and the Press joined Chatto & Windus) including presentation copies, signed limited editions, page proofs, variants as well as substantial amounts of ephemera. The collection is also very strong in Bloomsbury art, especially the decorative arts, and contains important examples of Omega Workshops publications and exhibition catalogues. Vanessa Bell correspondence/MSS; Leonard Woolf correspondence; Ritchie family materials and correspondence re: Anne Thackeray Ritchie/ Stephen family. Vanessa Bell dustwrapper designs for Woolf novels; Quentin Bell correspondence; S. P. Rosenbaum mss. Ephemera Collection. Bronze bust of Lytton Strachey by Stephen Tomlin (1901-37). A companion piece to Tomlin's bronze of Virginia Woolf. More than 150 additional items including Hogarth Press variant bindings and proof copies; translations of Virginia Woolf and Leonard Woolf; ephemera; including Hogarth Press: Complete Catalogue of Publications to 1939 with annotations by Leonard Woolf; materials relating to Bloomsbury Art and Artists including the catalogue of the second post impressionist exhibition, 1912, and catalogues relating to Vanessa Bell and Duncan Grant exhibitions.

Recent Acquisitions: 228 items, including Hogarth Press proof copies; Hogarth Press publication catalogues; bronze medal of Virginia Woolf by Marta Firlet; oil on canvas portrait of Amaryllis Garnett by Vanessa Bell (c.1958); Duncan Grant and Vanessa Bell designed Clarice Cliff dinner plates.

Name of Collection: Library of Leonard and Virginia Woolf (Washington S U)

Contact: Laila Miletic-Vejzovic, Head
Manuscripts, Archives and Special Collections

Address: Washington State University Libraries
Pullman, WA 99164-5610

GUIDE TO SPECIAL COLLECTIONS 323

URL:	www.wsulibs.wsu.edu/holland/masc/masc.htm
Hours:	Mon.-Fri. 8:30AM-5PM
Access Requirements:	Letter stating nature of research preferred; student or other identification.
Restrictions:	Materials must be used in the MASC area under supervision. Photocopying or photographing is permitted only when it will not harm the materials and is permitted by copyright.
Holdings Relevant to Woolf:	WSU has the Woolfs' basic working library including many works which belonged to Virginia's father, Sir Leslie Stephen, and other family members. Over 800 titles came from their Sussex home, Monks House, including some works bought at auction soon after Leonard Woolf died in 1969. Later additions include: 1,875 titles from his house in Victoria Square, London; 400 titles from his nephew Cecil Woolf; and over 60 titles from Quentin and Anne Olivier Bell. WSU has been actively collecting: all works in all editions by Virginia; all titles by Leonard; works published by the Woolfs at the Hogarth Press through 1946; books by their friends and associates, especcially those by Bloomsbury authors and about Bloomsbury artists; relevant correspondence and original works of art. Original artwork by Vanessa Bell; scattered letters by Vanessa Bell, E. M. Forster, Roger Fry, Leslie Stephen, Lytton Strachey, and Leonard Woolf. Original artwork by Richard Kennedy for illustrations in his book *A Boy at the Hogarth Press*; scattered letters by Roger Fry, Leslie Stephen, Ethel Smyth, and Leonard Woolf. Virginia Woolf's initialed copy of *Cornishiana*; Leonard Woolf's annotated copy of *An Anatomy of Poetry* by A. William-Ellis; Leslie Stephen's copy of *Lapsus Calami and Other Verses*, inscribed by James Kenneth Stephen. Several letters from Virginia

Woolf, including two written in 1939 to Ronald Heffer, and a letter to Edward McKnight Kauffer. New in the Hogarth Press Collection are a copy of E. M. Forster's *Anonymity, an Enquiry*, bound in cream paper boards, and what Woolmer calls the third label state of Forster's *The Story of the Siren*.

Name of Collection: Yale Center for British Art

Contact: Elisabeth Fairman, Associate Curator for Rare Books

Address: 1080 Chapel Street
P.O. Box 208280
New Haven, CT 06520-8280

E-mail: elisabeth.fairman@yale.edu

Hours: Tues.-Fri. 10AM-4:30PM

Access Requirements: Permission needed in order to reproduce.

Holdings Relevant to Woolf: Rare Books Department: 94 letters from Vanessa Bell and Duncan Grant to Sir Kenneth Clark. Prints & Drawings Department: 2 designs by Vanessa Bell and 2 studies by Duncan Grant. Paintings Department: 1 painting by Vanessa Bell, 2 by Duncan Grant (including a portrait of Vanessa Bell).

Reviews

Editing Virginia Woolf: Interpreting the Modernist Text
Eds. James M. Haule and J.H. Stape (London: Palgrave, 2002) xiv + 198 pp.

In the proliferation of Woolf studies, editing has remained a Cinderella, laying the fire and cleaning up the kitchen, so James M. Haule and J. H. Stape should, perhaps, be greeted as unlikely fairy godmothers, coming to her rescue. Can it really be the case that their collection of essays, *Editing Woolf: Interpreting the Modernist Text,* is the first book wholly devoted to this topic? If so, the high expectations occasioned by its title are rather rapidly deflated by the several disclaimers of the editors' introduction, where we are told that the "volume aims at no cutting-edge contribution to the field of editorial theory"(8), and, indeed, that "editing Woolf has just begun"(9). Or possibly, not yet begun? As a pioneer in the field, this volume offered an opportunity to air some of the larger problems of editing Woolf, many of which arise not from the absence, but the presence of a great deal of material evidence. Like so many of the modernists, Woolf left behind her a vast paper trail, much of it even now largely uninspected—from manuscripts, through uncorrected and corrected proofs to the various texts published in her lifetime. She was, as her husband Leonard explained, a compulsive reviser, and the reward of editing these texts at any level lies in how much they reveal of the artist at work.

If the title throws down a challenge, it is one that is never really taken up: this collection only engages with the big issues of Woolf editing tangentially, and insofar as they impinge on particular practice, and there is a shortage of active debate among its contributors. This may or may not be due to the fact that seven out of the ten are also editors of volumes in the Shakespeare Head Press reprint of Virginia Woolf, while two more sit on its Editorial Committee. The remaining contributor, Anne Olivier Bell, is the distinguished editor of Woolf's diaries, and while her account of that task makes delightful reading, it was first published elsewhere, in 1989. The main, if not the "only" begetter of the Shakespeare Head series was Andrew McNeillie, co-editor of the diaries with Bell, as well as editor of the four published volumes of Woolf's *Essays*, and curiously absent from this volume, given that his fellow members on the Editorial Committee have all contributed to it. When Woolf's work came out of copyright in Britain in 1992 (only temporarily, as it turned out), the Hogarth Press issued what they claimed as "the definitive edition," but only two volumes in the whole series (*The Voyage Out,* and *Mrs Dalloway*) had been edited, let alone definitively. At this point, McNeillie and others realized just how little work had been done on the history and transmission of the published texts (as opposed to the manuscripts), although significant differences between the American and British first editions were being identified. In response, the Shakespeare Head Press made a wholly admirable commitment to publishing carefully prepared and reliable texts, drawing on the skills of established American and Canadian scholars, even if that meant taking ten times as long—and charging ten times as much—as their main competitors in the field—the Penguin and Oxford World Classics paperbacks. The Shakespeare Head Press volumes were largely bought by libraries in single copies; they never went into paperback and some of the earlier ones are now out of print (188n1).

While this must have been frustrating for its editors, it is hardly a sufficient *raison d'être* for the various apologetics here on display. Of course, the best contributors fly happily past such temptations, and there are at least two excellent essays in the volume: Ted Bishop amusingly analyzes the different methods of transcription that have been adopted to represent Woolf's manuscripts in print. Diane Gillespie's essay, "The Texture of the Text," reflects on her edition of Woolf's *Roger Fry* for the Shakespeare Head Press—the high point of the whole series and a model of its kind. In this volume, she engages thoughtfully and constructively with Woolf's self-censorship in the process of revising her biography, as well as with "the architecture of annotation" as a general issue. With characteristic modesty, she claims no more than that her edition "inaugurates the dialogue," while not providing "the last word on the texture of this text" (109). Too many other contributors revisit their own editing achievements in order to celebrate their success.

Morris Beja commends the textual decisions and notes in his edition of *Mrs. Dalloway*, and in particular his discovery (subsequently disputed by David Bradshaw) that "Dalloway Day" was June 20, 1923 (137). Like several other contributors, he uses his essay as an opportunity to see off his rivals, sniping at Glenn Patton Wright's emendations in his edition of *Mrs. Dalloway* (for the Hogarth Press "definitive edition"); yet Wright makes one very important point: the Uniform edition includes a small number of textual variants, and is thus "not entirely a photo-offset reprint as Kirkpatrick claims," which opens up the further possibility that these variants may be authorial. Beja himself prefers the more convenient assumption that once Woolf "published her novels, she tended to leave them alone. So we do not have the problem of competing editions of *Mrs. Dalloway* within her lifetime" (131). The general policy of the Shakespeare Head reprints has been to ignore the Uniform edition, even though whatever changes occur there were made during Woolf's lifetime, and with her knowledge, or Leonard's. Moreover, in the case of *To the Lighthouse*, we know that Woolf herself re-read the text for publication in the Uniform edition because she tells us so, in a diary entry for Monday, November 25, 1929: "ought I not to be correcting *To the Lighthouse*," she asks, and the following Saturday notes that "Reading The Lighthouse does not make it easier to write" (*D3* 267, 268). *To the Lighthouse* appeared in the Uniform edition with a small number of alterations in February 1930.

The question of the Uniform edition and Kirkpatrick's descriptions, which Wright raises in the "Note on Editorial Method" in his edition of *Mrs. Dalloway*, is a significant one, although it is nowhere confronted in *Editing Virginia Woolf*. The Uniform edition has been consistently overlooked as a source of change—for example, when J. A. Lavin examined the *Lighthouse* variants in an article of 1972, he identified a particular group that occur in the 1938 Everyman/Dent edition, but most of these actually derive from the Uniform edition of 1930. As in the case of *Mrs. Dalloway*, this is another occasion where B. J. Kirkpatrick—bibliographer par excellence—is unintentionally misleading: her bibliography registers the Uniform edition of *To the Lighthouse* as the "First edition—fourth impression," and she adds, "This re-impression is incorrectly described as a 'New Edition' in the publication note on the verso of the title." But Leonard Woolf was far too conscientious to announce a volume as a "New Edition" without any justification. The problem here is what we understand by an "edition": Leonard knew that changes had been made in the text, and believed those changes justified its announcement as a new edition, whereas Kirkpatrick assumed, quite understandably, that since the typeface and page numbers had not changed, and the two books began and ended identically, this was only another impression of the first edition—both, in their different ways, were right. Since the Woolfs were practising printers, when they made changes to Virginia's published texts, they automatically made them in such a way as to keep alteration (and thus cost) to a minimum—only lines or part-lines would need to be replaced within plates. Even so, any alteration involved cutting into existing plates—charges to the Hogarth Press for these are listed in the ledgers of their printing firm, R. & R. Clark of Edinburgh.

Determining the authority of editions published during Woolf's lifetime, and in particular the status of the Uniform edition is a key issue in "Editing Virginia Woolf," and as such needs to be set in the context of related questions, such as the appropriate choice of base text, the procedures for analyzing textual transmission, the editorial responsibilities of emendation—and how technical information of this kind is to be presented in a "user-friendly" way. None of these issues is addressed in this collection, except incidentally, and there is something of an air of embarrassment, even anxiety, that debates of this kind will somehow be too difficult for the common reader (but could a book on editing ever be addressed to the common reader?). At times, particular points emerge from the shadows to light up inconsistencies in the Committee's thinking about what they wanted from their series. Discussing *The Waves*, James Haule acknowledges that "the first English edition is the more revised text"—this is, indeed, usually the case with Woolf's novels, and justifies the almost universal adoption of the first English edition as the text on which to base a critical edition. A few of the Shakespeare Head volumes, however, have taken Woolf's corrected American proofs as their base text, a procedure open to the objection made by Haule, above; moreover, a text thus based lacks the historical and social dimensions that textual critics such as Jerome McGann and the late D. F. Mackenzie have taught us to value. J. H. Stape's edition of *Orlando*, the subject of his essay, also adopts the American marked-up proofs as his base text, but tries to have it both ways by incorporating some of Woolf's later changes and emendations—a procedure that embraces the full eclecticism of traditional copy-text editing, making high demands on an editor's judgment and skill, yet, in the final analysis, the resulting edition is the work of no one but the editor. Elsewhere, James Haule warns that "scholars should be cautious about accepting the author's description of her text. As we shall see, the person least credible in such cases is often the artist herself" (173). Never trust the teller, trust the editor?

The least attractive aspect of *Editing Virginia Woolf* is its editors' eagerness to discredit their rivals: the Penguin and World's Classics editions of Woolf, we are told, feature "the same paratext" (4), a point contradicted in footnote 32 of Gillespie's article (113). More seriously, they assert that those editions "engaged in little editorial work at all." This is simply not true: for example, four volumes in the Penguin edition (for which I was general editor) had separate textual editors, in addition to the critic who provided the introduction and notes. Three of these (*Mrs. Dalloway*, *To the Lighthouse* and *Between the Acts*) were edited by Stella McNichol, the experienced and conscientious editor of *Mrs. Dalloway's Party*, who included the Uniform edition in her collation as a matter of course, thus providing editorial information not available in the Shakespeare Head Press editions. In 1993, Michèle Barrett's Penguin text of *A Room of One's Own* and *Three Guineas* not only lists a striking change made in the second impression of *A Room*, where "I like [women's] subtlety" has been altered to "I like their completeness," but also identifies the four places where Woolf extended the endnotes of *Three Guineas* for the American edition (*A Room* has not yet appeared in the Shakespeare Head series, and *Three Guineas* has only been available since 2001).

So if we cannot quite welcome Haule and Stape as the fairy godmothers they might have been, let us nevertheless take this volume as the first swallow, a token and a sign that we are finally turning our attention to the delightful task of editing Woolf. And this is a task that promises every sort of pleasure: the numerous drafts of essays and short stories provide a series of manageable exercises on which to practise editing skills. Woolf's incomplete autobiography still awaits a scholarly editor (Elizabeth Shih has made an interesting start). The surviving pages of manuscript and typescript of *Flush* and *Three Guineas* require patient analysis, and perhaps we could transcribe some more of the eight holograph notebooks of *The Years*. The web offers an ideal setting for the reproduction of holograph drafts and accompanying transcriptions. And let us also look forward to more innovative printed editions—can we not publish *Mrs. Dalloway* flanked by its opening and closing short stories? And why have we not restored those "enormous chunks" to their rightful place in *The Years*, thus reinstating its original twelve-part structure—we even have Woolf's own authority for doing so (*D5* 69). Above all, let us have new editions that unfold for us the wonderful history of their writing—a transformation that may at last carry Cinderella to the ball!

—Julia Briggs, *De Montfort University*

Virginia Woolf and the Visible World
Emily Dalgarno (Cambridge: Cambridge UP, 2001) xii + 215 pp.

Emily Dalgarno has produced a fascinating study in which the meanings of "visible" (and, inevitably, "invisible") mutate according to context and according to a loosely constructed history of Woolf's intellectual development. The congeries of ideas around the theme of visibility includes the visible as opposed to the invisible world of Greek tragedy—and "madness," in what Dalgarno sees as Woolf's ancient Greek-inflected understanding; the visible as a boundary-traversing category between Jacques Lacan's imaginary and symbolic registers; the visible as structured by historically specific codes of representation; and the visible as, on the contrary, opposed to the intelligible, which is also the ideological.

As this catalogue suggests, the ambition of this book is enormous. Dalgarno works with art history, the history of photography, visual theory, psychoanalytic theory, classical scholarship, political and social theory, feminist literary theory, various schools of phenomenology, philosophy of science, Woolf's manuscripts and notebooks, and a great deal of historical information. Her reach sometimes exceeds her grasp, in that individual readings can be partial (in both senses), and her influences and intertexts encourage her to read passages of Woolf's fiction monologically—a besetting sin of Woolf criticism that I will return to. But the scope of *Virginia Woolf and the Visible World* is impressive and a little dizzying. The visual clearly is involved in much of what is most important about Woolf's method and practice. Dalgarno's takes on several short stories, the great middle-period novels, "A Sketch of the Past" and *Three Guineas* are surprising, often satisfying, and even when off the mark, provocative. Anyone thinking seriously about Woolf and modernism will find Dalgarno's ideas stimulating.

The last two chapters are by far the strongest. Both are relatively narrow in focus and elegant in construction, and both seem to me persuasive. Chapter Five, on the famous mirror scene in "A Sketch of the Past," suggests that "Sketch" does not present Woolf as a complete subject, but rather, in its avowed focus on "the person to whom things happened," shows Woolf's identity in the process of being constituted. Autobiography, a liminal mode between public and private writing, enables a glimpse of the woman who in the process of being gendered was able to maintain a split between herself as speaker and herself as object.

Like many other readers of "Sketch," Dalgarno aligns the scene with the mirror in Woolf's memoir and Lacan's "mirror stage," or as she prefers, "mirror experience": a moment in the development of the very small child when a reflected image offers the first objectified notion of a consolidated self. But against virtually every other reader of this passage, Dalgarno argues that the young Virginia Stephen did not see herself in the mirror in the process of being molested by her half-brother Gerald Duckworth. Indeed, there is nothing in Woolf's description to indicate that the mirror was positioned directly opposite Virginia when Gerald was feeling under her clothes. Furthermore, as Dalgarno notes, the description itself is completely tactile. The mirror becomes important after the molestation scene, when Woolf describes having looked into it and seen the face of an animal. Dalgarno views this face not as a representative of Gerald, but as an objectification of Woolf herself as female, a Cassandra-like "sacrificed animal" with links to the "ancestresses" in the family who were photographed continually and famous for their beauty (145). Modifying Lacan, Dalgarno sees Woolf's "I" in "Sketch" as similarly split, "so that in memory the symbolic is admitted, but on terms that pair it insistently with the experience of the visible, and distance it from family relations" (148). Woolf's "I" in "Sketch" is the seer who has kept from coinciding with the seen. As a consequence, she can repair the effects of violence by restoring "what has been riven by violent action" to signification—which is to say, as Woolf herself wrote, she can make it real by putting it into words (147).

Chapter Six, on the photographs of "ruined houses and dead bodies" alluded to but not included in *Three Guineas*, is even more impressive. Here,

Dalgarno musters an array of historical evidence. She examines carefully Woolf's *Three Guineas* notebooks, paying particular attention to their chronology. She investigates the issues of the newspapers *L'Humanité* in France and the *Daily Worker* in England that printed the photographs to which Woolf refers. She goes into the history of censorship practices for mainstream newspapers like the London *Times*, as compared with their French equivalents, showing that different tactics of representation created different audiences for visual material and thus different reactions, especially to pictures of dead people. Carefully reading the ideology of these documentary photographs, which of course were published by supporters of the Republicans, Dalgarno points to the photographs' "appeal to the artist to create propaganda by representing the dead in terms of personal loss" and observes that they show a gendered divide "between brave soldiers and frightened women and children" (151, 161). Although she doesn't use the word, the appeal is sentimental in that it exploits gendered codes of innocence to create the division that propaganda seeks: they're guilty, we're innocent.

Reading a difficult comment in the *Three Guineas* notebooks in this context, Dalgarno establishes that Woolf actively resisted the emotional pull of such ideologically coded visual material. Woolf wrote, "'But you dont want tear[s]...You want / a suggestion how to prevent war'" (165). Neither sentimental emotion nor the appeal to English reactions of mastery—that is, of pitying those seen as powerless—are about putting an end to war: indeed, depictions of violated innocence are the most provocative kinds of war propaganda.

Most critics have taken Woolf at her word that in presenting such photographs as evidence, which she suggests both her male addressee and she will see in the same way, she accepts a naïve view of documentary photographs as unmediated, the truth about war in general available to any gaze. Dalgarno's careful, powerful argument maintains, however, that this initial position is satirical and that the effect is ultimately to show both female and male viewers as implicated in the ideology they at first failed to recognize: "Her sense of ideology would appear to be that which disquiets by its very invisibility" (178).

The other chapters are messier but interesting in many more local respects. For example, Dalgarno is particularly concerned that readers have overlooked Woolf's immersion in Greek language and culture, and has valuable insights into Greek aspects of imagery in *Mrs. Dalloway* (mostly Evans and those birds), *Jacob's Room*, *To the Lighthouse* (the ideal of beauty) and *The Years*. There are a couple of odd problems with the approach, however. For one thing, Dalgarno's emphasis in Chapter 2 is on how Woolf *did* know Greek well enough not to rely on translations ("On Not Knowing Greek" was a wittily disarming title for her *Common Reader* essay), and on how that knowledge enabled her, for instance, to represent how in the *Agamemnon* Menelaos' dream of Helen "troubles the sign, simultaneously stressing the capacity of language to translate the visible and stimulating its rhetorical power" (63). The observation is exciting—except that the analysis isn't grounded in Dalgarno's *own* reading of the Greek along with Woolf's translation and commentary, but in Woolf's translation and commentary along with the interpretation offered by classical scholar George Devereux. In other words, Dalgarno herself relies not only on others' translations (those contemporary with Woolf and more recent, such as the Lattimore versions of some of the tragedies) but on their interpretations, in order to make the point that Woolf gained enormous insight into Greek culture precisely because she didn't have to rely on others. It's an anomalous situation to be in. What strikes me as especially strange is that Dalgarno never openly refers to her own apparent "not knowing Greek," even though it seems she might have recuperated some of her points had she tried to theorize (and be wry about) her own position.

Another problem is that Dalgarno insists that Greek influences are dominant or even the only sources operating at many points in her readings of the middle-period novels For instance, "Septimus...represents the Greek idea that the mad see what the sane cannot" (30). I like the way this allows Dalgarno to take Septimus seriously, but surely the idea of privileged "mad" vision need not come only from Woolf's reading of Greek texts. For instance, much the same theme occurs in the novels of Dostoevsky, and Woolf was also translating Dostoevsky during the time she was writing *Mrs. Dalloway*. Then, too, the idea that great wits are to madness near allied came down through the English Romantics to Woolf's own doctors, who regarded her writing with dubiety for that reason. And of course there are Woolf's own reports on the experience of "madness," although Dalgarno believes "a biography that focused on her intellectual development would give priority to her study of the Greek language and literature," and not "the perspective of her family relationships, and...psychological damage..." (40). It's unclear to me why one source or kind of information need *supplant* others.

Another example is her take on the close of *The Waves*, where Bernard narrates himself riding a horse against Death. Dalgarno discerns the "homoerotic language" of "Plato's *Phaedrus*, and the contrast between the good horse who is noble and ruled by shame, and 'the lover's undisciplined horse...'" (128). This is a valuable reference, but surely one to layer with references to the Percival legend and *Parsifal*, poor King Canute's attempt to quell the British waves, and other quasi-heroic images of holy fools and futile attempts. Dalgarno accordingly sees the tone of the ending as "faintly ridiculous" and the scene as representing "the performative bent of Imperialism" (128). Again, fair enough, but can't this charged, overdetermined moment be *treated* as overdetermined? This culminating scene in the novel seems to me more than "faintly" ludicrous, but also heroic, also misconceived, also personally necessary (many scholars have pointed to Woolf's own embrace of the slogan "Fight! Fight!" in the face of death), also doomed, with the italicized description of the waves finally overwhelming the human—and of course overwhelming the storytelling voice. Twentieth-century literary language is usually double-voiced, as Bakhtin has taught us, and in practice that means multiple-voiced, with intonations that jostle each other, making conflicting claims for evaluating how a passage means. Of all the established modernists, Woolf seems to me to encompass the most nuanced voices, the most contrary intonations. Yet even her most intelligent critics too often approach her most multivalent texts by trying to substitute one meaning for another.

Dalgarno does a certain amount of this substituting: the birds singing in Greek "mean" nightingales (34); Clytemnestra in the *Agamemnon* is a figure "affirming the need for patriarchal values" (69) (what about that wonderful observation in "Character in Fiction": "Read the Agamemnon, and see whether, in process of time, your sympathies are not almost entirely with Clytemnestra"?); Rhoda's funeral urn refers entirely to Keats' Grecian urn (127) and not at all to Thomas Browne's "*Hydriotaphia*, or Urn Burial," which shows up in *Orlando*; Neville's "The lights of the world have gone out" alludes to Holman Hunt's painting *The Light of the World* (interesting), and therefore Neville's "the tree which I cannot pass" must be Christ's corpse (not as persuasive) (112, 114), and so on. Readings based on such univocal source-study are often useful but never definitive.

On the other hand, there are many gleaming nuggets of observation as Dalgarno juggles her theoretical modes to arrive at readings. One excellent analogy aligns Percival structurally with Kurtz in Conrad's *Heart of Darkness* and notes, "In both we see the desire for the inscrutable individual serves to organize the passionate attention of the characters" (117). Another important point, made in the introductory chapter, is that Woolf often allows the desiring subject to cross out of the domain of the visible, as when Septimus sees Evans (20). In this understanding, the visible is not the same as the real, an important point in *To the Lighthouse*, it seems, when Mrs. Ramsay simply appears for Lily—"There she sat" (202)—without any ontological cues about *how* she is present. Dalgarno, for reasons of her larger argument about this novel, wants this moment to represent Lily's operating "in the self-deceptive modes of the gaze and hallucination" (27), but I'm inclined to let her earlier judgment justify a more ambiguous reading of the reappearance scene. It also seems productive to think of Mrs. Ramsay's beauty functioning as a "master signifier" that closes off associations rather than making further creativity possible, and Lily's having to make her painting possible by redefining and ultimately failing to create beauty (88-95).

Given this scrupulous attention to *To the Lighthouse*, it is strange that Dalgarno reads the scene of arriving at the Lighthouse as only James's success at becoming a subject. Cam fails, it seems, because of the "tragedy of the Oedipal plot, in which a female fails to achieve subjectivity on any terms" (94). Perhaps here, Dalgarno is constrained by the limits of visibility as a topic. As Margaret Homans, especially, has argued, Cam is a very different sort of subject because she gains not the father's approval, but the mother's pre-Oedipal *voice*, narrating the incantatory words that first reconciled the green shawl with the skull: "It was a hanging garden; it was a valley, full of birds, and flowers, and antelopes..." (*TTL* 204). Dalgarno does not deal with this moment, surely worth treating in a psychoanalytic framework, perhaps because it doesn't fall under the lens of visibility. The slip makes me wonder if there might be a need for a parallel study of Virginia Woolf and the audible world.

—Molly Hite, *Cornell University*

Works Cited

Homans, Margaret. *Bearing the Word: Language and Female Experience in Nineteenth-Century Women's Writing*. Chicago: U of Chicago P, 1986.
Woolf, Virginia. *To the Lighthouse*. San Diego: HBJ, 1981.

Virginia Woolf and the Discourse of Science: The Aesthetics of Astronomy
Holly Henry (Cambridge: Cambridge UP, 2003) x iii+ 208 pp.

Scientific developments in the early twentieth century, especially new telescopes and the advances they made possible, created a "modernist human decentering and rescaling" that led to Virginia Woolf's "developing literary strategies that responded to this rescaling, and that offered possibilities for a radical rethinking of the social and political structures of the day." So argues Holly Henry in her study of links between "visualization technologies" and Woolf's aesthetics and politics.

Henry's study participates in the revision of the view of Bloomsbury as "effete and disconnected from the concerns of public audiences." She examines primarily popular versions of astronomic discourse, focusing on such diverse representations as works of the British mathematician and cosmologist James Jeans and Edwin Hubble's discoveries at Mount Wilson. Astronomy in this period became a subject of intense popular interest, helped along by Jeans's non-technical books such as *The Mysterious Universe* and *The Universe Around Us*. Simultaneously, scientists using new large telescopes such as the one at Mount Wilson were producing spectacular images of space. Hubble's calculation that the Andromeda galaxy, which he had photographed in October 1923, lay a million light-years beyond the Milky Way was news outside professional astronomic circles because until then, many scientists believed the edge of our galaxy was also the edge of the universe; Hubble's discovery meant that even non-scientists had to relocate themselves within a suddenly larger universe in which the earth had an even more insignificant place.

Combined with public interest in the solar eclipse of 1927, the first eclipse visible in England for 200 years, such discoveries fed an enormous popular engagement with astronomy. Woolf and her circle were as caught up in the frenzy as anyone; Woolf traveled to the Yorkshire Dales in order to secure a vantage point for the 24-second darkness, an experience she recorded in her diary (30 June 1927). Woolf was no johhny-come-lately to an interest in astronomy, however. The *Athenaeum*, later the *Nation and Athenaeum*, in which a number of her stories and essays were published, had throughout its history made a point of including articles on scientific discoveries and trends; with new editors in the 1920s, and with a number of compelling theories and discoveries to discuss, the paper increased its science coverage. Because both Woolfs wrote for the paper, they were brought into contact with some of the most prominent writers of popular science texts of the day, both personally and by having their texts on facing pages with the scientists'.

Discoveries such as the realization that the universe is made up of many galaxies and experiences like watching the sun's light extinguished during the eclipse encouraged many people to see human life as fragile and evanescent, and to see humanity's position in the universe as marginal and decentered. Woolf shared these attitudes, and they helped shape her aesthetic practices. Henry suggests that "photographs of intergalactic space printed in Jeans's popular science texts afforded Woolf fresh perspectives that informed her experiments in narrative form, as well as her radical pacifist stance on human aggression." But Woolf saw, she argues, that humanity's isolated and insignificant place in the universe could be a source of hope as well as a sobering reality check, because one could see humanity's evolution in the "nearly lifeless universe" as a sign of strength and tenacity.

Perhaps the most interesting segment of Henry's book is her discussion of the various ways one might look through telescopes, and what one might see there. Focusing on Woolf's story "The Searchlight," Henry discusses the evolution of the story from its origins as a tale told by a family friend, focusing on how telescopes might be seen as a trope for Woolf's narrative strategy. The telescope allows one to shift one's vision from near to far almost instantaneously; because the light of stars one sees through a telescope required measurable, and sometimes immense, amounts of time to travel to the viewer's eye, the telescope also allows one literally to see the past—events that are long over before they can be observed. Henry notes that E.M. Forster "also associated the telescope with looking back in time, and with memory" but that because Woolf "understood the telescope as a device that allows for a simultaneous co-existence of the past and present," she could engage in narrative experiments in which time and identity could become fluid. I found Henry's discussion of looking through a telescope or binoculars the wrong way to be particularly compelling. Woolf apparently engaged in this behavior, as well as writing about it, and Henry argues convincingly that the wrong-way telescope's ability to make the nearby seem distant is vitally connected to Woolf's narrative practices, in which both time and distance can become fluid and reversible.

Henry's chapter on maps and globes also presented a number of intriguing facts and ideas. Leslie Stephen had possessed a book, which Woolf might have seen, containing artists' renderings of the imagined look of the earth from the moon. First of all, these renderings, which are reproduced in Henry's book, are astonishingly accurate compared to the Apollo astronauts' photographs of the earth rising over the moon's horizon. But Henry gathers these images together with Woolf's musings in her diary about how she might appear to a visitor from the moon, going on to suggest that the images gave Woolf a "global aesthetic vision" that informs *The Waves*, as when the characters think of themselves in relation to universal time or Bernard uses images of a globe to represent his life.

The chief weaknesses of Henry's compact text are that it can sometimes seem repetitive—ideas are restated in nearly the same language only a page or two from their first appearance—and that her readings of Woolf's texts tend to be somewhat more distant than one might hope. While her argument seems persuasive while she is talking generally about Woolf, when she gets to specifics, one begins to lose faith because her examples can seem only tenuously connected to the point at hand. I would have loved a deeper and more prolonged engagement with Woolf's literary and critical texts than Henry provides here, because the facts Henry has dug up and the speculations they allow her suggest that her study is apposite.

Despite these reservations, though, Henry's book offers a useful new lens through which to view Woolf's narrative experiments. More than that, it is a fascinating compendium of details about early 20th century popular interest in

astronomy and how that interest changed how people—and modern writers—
saw themselves in relation to the universe.

—Jen Shelton, *Texas Tech University*

Einstein's Wake: Relativity, Metaphor, and Modernist Literature
Michael H. Whitworth (Oxford: Oxford UP, 2001) ix + 254 pp.

Michael Whitworth's *Einstein's Wake: Relativity, Metaphor, and Modernist Literature* is a thoroughly researched and compellingly argued analysis of the complex relationship between communities of writers and scientists in the modernist period of the early twentieth century, with a focus on the store of constitutive metaphors from which both communities drew. Whitworth closely examines the metaphors that helped to construct Einstein's theory as well as other scientific ideas related to it. He chooses to situate relativity "in its scientific rather than philosophical lineage, and so includes treatments of theories which were not Einstein's, in particular, the second law of thermodynamics, the school of epistemology known as descriptionism, and the new theories of matter from 1895 to 1913" (vii). For Whitworth, the metaphors emerging from these theories are of interest because they have shaped conceptions of literary form. Formal innovation was not only one of the hallmarks of literary modernism, but new physics chose to explain natural phenomena in formal rather than materialistic terms, with scientists "prefer[ring] to think in terms of 'description' rather than 'explanation,'" and with the second law of thermodynamics initiating that tendency (4). Whitworth explains that both in science and literature, it is necessary to discuss metaphors of form rather than form itself, because metaphors of form "are the only tangible material available for discussion" (5). Yet a long-lived dualism has refused to grant metaphor, deemed decorative, a constitutive function in science.

Underpinning Whitworth's analysis are poststructuralist tenets such as the Derridean idea that metaphor serves as the foundation for thinking and theorizing in all discourses and the Althusserian concept of interpellation or ideological "hailing" of the subject through the language of various institutions. Whitworth makes strategic use of such theoretical conclusions without bothering to be very self-reflexive about his use of them. He does not mention Derrida, and as he admits, "One need not accept every aspect of Lacanian theory to adopt a linguistic theory of the subject..." (15). He is resourceful, taking what he needs and distancing himself from the shortcomings of the positions of thinkers such as Stanley Fish and Richard Rorty. He also distinguishes his account of the function of metaphor from that of Lakoff and Johnson in their influential 1980 study *Metaphors We Live By*, by explaining that they do not, as does Althusser, factor the power of the hegemonic class into their analysis of rituals.

Whitworth carefully details the methodological problems common to the discipline of literature and science, and he avoids the anachronisms that result from the typical reliance on post-1945 accounts of science by using accounts and responses from the contemporary generalist periodicals. Central assumptions of his argument are that periodicals are as important as books and that the generalist publications are as important as the "little magazines," which have received more attention in literary scholarship. By analyzing generalist periodicals, he can convey something of the lively conversations between writers who were members of different publishing communities, for example Ezra Pound's exchanges with J.W.N. Sullivan, influential science popularizer and science writer for *The Athenaeum*. This method, with its focus on the local, gives us specific information about actual social networks rather than abstract and unhelpful notions of a general *zeitgeist*.

One of the main strengths of Whitworth's study is the rich context that he constructs in addressing the relationship between the popularization of science and modernism. He repeatedly argues that one cannot know this context and understand how these theories and metaphors circulated by looking at science books alone; we must examine reviews of these books in general periodicals. Whitworth considers the relationship in terms of rhetorical transactions and discursive construction of readers. He begins by pointing to the fact that graduates in the humanities dominated the universities and government in Britain in the 19th and early 20th centuries, requiring scientists to avoid using a technological framework and to translate their discipline into philosophical terms. Fortunately, the "cosmological frame on thermodynamics allowed them to do this" (29). The popular science article interpellated readers into ideologically determined subject positions: "...the reader is being told as much about himself as about dissipation, radiation, or the curvature of spacetime....[in] being told about his relation to the authority of 'science,' and his relation to the fragmented knowledge that characterizes modernity" (30). There is ample evidence that scientists as well as literary writers at the turn of the century read the popularizers. Explaining the inclusion of articles about science in *The Criterion*, T.S. Eliot argued that a narrow focus on literature would destroy "the life of literature" (44). But this cultivation of the well-rounded individual gave way in the 1930s to increasing emphasis on specialization and the separation of disciplines.

Whitworth takes up a series of themes that address the use of particular metaphors in modernist texts. The chapter on entropy and Conrad's *The Secret Agent* is superb, convincingly explaining the narrative description of London, the construction of the characters, and the complexity of the ironic tone. One of the few critics to have examined the anarchism in the novel in terms of the second law of thermodynamics is Alex Houen, who demonstrates the ways that the novel articulates a doomful vision of society which is threatened by the warring impulses of energies, fields, and masses. But Houen's analysis fails to connect this argument to the range of metaphorical versions of entropy that circulated in various contemporary communities. Whitworth traces metaphorical connections from entropy to earlier theories such as Max Nordau's notion of dissipation and degeneration. One of Whitworth's most significant claims is that the exchange of these ideas was not unidirectional; in the case of entropy, there was a multi-directional flow of exchange between the popularization of thermodynamics and social and moral criticism of the time. Numerous Victorian moral inflections were mapped on to the concept of dissipation—waste, distraction of energy, decadence, dissolution. Conrad was most concerned with the financial sense of dissipation; he connected such disintegration with the metropolis, and he feared the Communist annihilation of capital. Energy came to be equated with money and dissipation with expenditure. Another ascendant form of dissipation appeared in anxieties about the entropy of the nation/empire. In *The Secret Agent*, entropy is figured as disintegration, and Conrad paints a picture of ubiquitous fragmentation. Part of the novel's irony in Whitworth's reading is that not only would the sun set on the Empire, "but go out altogether" (80).

Whitworth also takes up the debate about reality, and in this discussion Woolf figures more prominently, beginning with her claim about reality's consisting of an "incessant shower of innumerable atoms." The discussion builds on the work of scholars such as Judith Ryan in its focus on various forms of descriptionism. The descriptionist school of science "rejected the idea that science *explained* the universe, preferring instead the more modest claim that it provided economic descriptions" (86). Whitworth examines the scientific debates about reality not to displace but to supplement well established theories such as Impressionism in art, Freudian theory of the unconscious, and the questions raised by William James, Ernst Mach, and Henri Bergson in their theories of perception. Like Ryan, he underscores the importance of Mach and the influence of Walter Pater's radical empiricism/individualism on both science writing and literary writing. Whitworth applies the concept of descriptionism to Woolf's experiments with perspective in the early stories such as "The Mark on the Wall" and "Solid Objects"; to the "alienated perspective" of the characters Peter, Clarissa, and Septimus in *Mrs. Dalloway*; to Mrs. Ramsay's abstract contemplation in *To the Lighthouse*; and to the tension between two kinds of perception and existence in *The Waves*—the world "without a self" and the world of Bernard's "phrase-making."

In examining the complexity of the response of literary modernism to science, Whitworth considers both the changes over time and the conflicted views held by some writers. Although there had been a long-lived Romantic antipathy (Wordsworth's "we murder to dissect") against science, which extended through Carlyle, Ruskin, and Arnold's opposition between mechanism and organicism, many intellectuals felt that culture should include science. During WWI, several influential memoranda were published that faulted the government and the civil service for scientific ignorance, against which a counter-argument arose that equated scientific training with specialization and finally with the kind of Prussian materialism against which Britain was fighting. Among the modernists, Conrad was the most clearly hostile to science. As Whitworth observes, in *The Secret Agent* Lombroso represents "not only bad science, but all science" (123). Whitworth disagrees with critics who read Lawrence as completely antipathetic to science; he sees Lawrence as markedly antipathetic but also as more enthusiastic about the new physics than Conrad. Lawrence's antipathy was "to science as mechanism," but he was fascinated by fields of force. Woolf, although also hostile to science, was curious about the concepts, images, and language of new physics. Insofar as Einstein was said to make a clean break with Victorian mechanistic perspectives, Woolf's comments about Arnold Bennett and other materialists could be read as "Einsteinian." The formal qualities of relativity theory gave it an aesthetic appeal. The popularizer A. S. Eddington described Einstein's theory as "beautiful." In addition, Einstein was depicted in the Romantic terms of intuitive genius, and Sullivan declared that he had the rare genius of perceiving things with a child's eyes. The figure of Einstein as well as the aesthetic appeal of his theory effected a rapprochement in the relationship between literature and science.

In the chapter "Invisible Men and Fractured Atoms," Whitworth discusses Wells and Woolf in terms of their use of elements from a pervasive set of antifoundational homologies connected to relativity that existed in science, philosophy, linguistics, and other fields. In terms of a theory of the self, "relativity" and the new ideas about matter meant that there was no essence, but rather that the self took shape in the social realm through relations with others. In this sense, the ambivalence about the solidity of matter acts as the organizing principle of self for each of the characters in *The Waves*. Whitworth argues that Woolf blended scientific concepts, such as those of Erwin Schrödinger, with ideas from Bergson's theory. In synthesizing, assimilating newer ideas with older ones, Woolf re-imagines both earlier theory and current theory—which reflects the process that scientists engage in as they continually replace, or rather re-place, old metaphors.

Numerous critics have analyzed simultaneity in modernist literature. Whitworth's analysis of simultaneity and the associated metaphors that Woolf employs in *Mrs. Dalloway*, *To the Lighthouse*, and *The Waves* is not altogether new, but still makes important points. For example, there is his wonderfully evocative claim about *To the Lighthouse*: "The novel cuts out sharply remembered moments from the flux of time, and sends them out into space" (183). Perhaps his most useful observation is that the simultaneity of *Mrs. Dalloway* is heterochronic while the simultaneity in *The Waves* is heterotopic.

Whitworth concludes his study by suggesting that some of these metaphors functioned in compensatory fashion: "If we place the metaphors of deep and flat selves at the centre of our account, then the other available metaphors for the self appear not as exchangeable equivalents, but as compensations. The possibility, for example of reaching out with rays of light and invisible filaments looks like a fantasy of control. The depths of spacetime compensate for the shallowness of the self" (236). Such compensatory moves would have gone unnoticed among the scientists and writers who made them, which highlights the importance of a study such as Whitworth's. Although it may be that his most valuable contribution is to the history of popular science writing, we can all benefit from his exhaustive archival work and his careful tracing of the shared use of a common set of metaphors that adds depth and breadth to the intellectual field of modernism.

—Molly Abel Travis, *Tulane University*

*Writing the Meal: Dinner in the Fiction of Early
Twentieth-Century Women Writers*
Diane McGee (Toronto: U of Toronto P, 2001) 221 pp.

This detailed, thoughtful study in seven chapters of the role of meals, principally dinners, in fiction by Edith Wharton, Katherine Mansfield, Virginia Woolf, Kate Chopin, and a few other early twentieth-century writers, assumes that meals have a particular resonance in women's writing. For women, after all, attending to some aspect of a household's meals is and historically has been a daily preoccupation. Without denying that men, from Plato to James Joyce, may also have written about meals, McGee addresses how, as women writers emerged from the kitchen or dining room at the beginning of the century, they found a voice in their domestic experience. While sometimes observing other meals, her study focuses on dinner as the most socialized and main daily meal, and the one most likely ritualized. Considering dinner "resonant, potent, full of meaning" (4), McGee moves beyond the physical aspects of serving and eating dinners to larger issues emanating from meals, at a time of significant social and cultural change, observing how in early twentieth-century women's writing, individual perspectives on dinner reflect an attitude towards society and its pressures that may range from alienation and rebellion to passivity and complacency.

McGee, who provides a wealth of background information throughout, lays the groundwork for reading the literary texts by drawing on thinkers from Claude Lévi-Strauss to Roland Barthes and Louis Marin (*Food for Thought*, 1989) to present the concept of the meal from an anthropological and sociological perspective as a communicative text and cultural locus. This she follows with an analysis of the turn-of-the-century social anxieties about formerly unquestioned areas of domestic life. The beginning of the twentieth century, that is, saw changes in gender roles and attitudes to the home, with the loss of past traditions replaced by a new world of consumerism and advertising as well as new forms of art. McGee, who is particularly effective at limning the cultural period, argues that even if fictions do not provide recipes and advice, "the meals that are central to these texts are also expressions of uneasy shifts in everyday life" (37).

Edith Wharton's 1920s *Age of Innocence*, which retrospectively explores conservative late nineteenth-century upper-class New York society, introduces McGee's detailed studies of literary texts. Her concern here is how the social ritual of fictional meals, so expressive of the defining manners and customs of a society, presents for the literary characters a means of understanding or of revising their social relations and for readers access to the author's perspective on her social world. Emphasis here falls on hostesses, but women may be guests at dinners too. McGee observes Wharton's *House of Mirth* and *The Custom of the*

Country as they focus on outsiders and marginal female guests who present a challenge to the accepted social world and show it to be on the verge of change. That change she finds in the writings of Katherine Mansfield, where the sometimes oppressive formal mealtime tradition has been replaced by a vacuum and empty freedom; the relaxation of nineteenth-century strictures now means loneliness and hunger of body and soul. In Wharton, society is defined largely by customs of dining and of sociability; in Mansfield's short stories, eating and attitudes to food are linked to modernist themes and predicaments, and meals reveal the contradictions attached to women's contemporaneously changing roles. (Highly selective in her choices of stories, McGee overlooks Mansfield's meal-oriented story "Sun and Moon," which focuses on a young boy's disillusionment as the aftermath of a dinner party, rather than on any women's issues.)

In discussing Mansfield's "Bliss" and some of her New Zealand stories and Virginia Woolf's *Mrs. Dalloway* and *To the Lighthouse*, McGee focuses on the traditional female roles that girls learn within the family and live some version of as women. Although domestic roles may be entrapping, in both authors McGee finds woman's traditional role as cook or organizer of dinner shown in a positive way, even sometimes honored, although with some authorial misgivings expressed as well. In both "Prelude" and *To the Lighthouse* she cleverly notes women given no first name "for whom 'Mrs.' is a sort of job title" (8)—Mrs. Fairfield and Mrs. Ramsay—who identify completely with their domestic role. But McGee is sometimes too intent on the issue of domestic roles. Thus, discussing Linda Burnell's repudiation of her domestic role in "Prelude"—"Linda sees maternity, like the entire domestic role, not as creative, but merely as burdensome" (McGee 174)— she overlooks the actual reason Mansfield provides for Linda's repudiation of her children. The burden is not domesticity; it is obligatory marital sex: "There were times when he was frightening—really frightening. When she just had not screamed at the top of her voice: 'You are killing me. [...] I have had three great lumps of children already'" (Mansfield 91). A similar problem occurs with *To the Lighthouse*. McGee properly contrasts Mr. Ramsay, as the highly abstract thinker and user of language, with Mrs. Ramsay, who is "grounded in the everyday, in the domestic objects which surround her" (135). But she is too quick to find domesticity in Mrs. Ramsay's every thought, for she sees her "merge with the domestic environment when Mrs. Ramsay '"often found herself sitting and looking [...] with her work in her hands until she became the thing she looked at—that light, for example' ([Woolf] 97)" (McGee 135). That nondomestic *light* is actually the beam of the lighthouse; Mrs. Ramsay is never limited to the quotidian in her sense of reality. The emphasis on domesticity also leads McGee to underestimate other of Woolf's imagery. To illustrate a contrast she overlooks, after Andrew Ramsay tells Lily Briscoe to think of a kitchen table when she is not there, in order to understand his father's work on subjective and objective perception of the nature of reality, what Lily sees is "a scrubbed kitchen table" (Woolf 38). That bare form provides an informative, clear contrast to Mrs. Ramsay's sociable and aesthetically gratifying dinner table which makes reality humanly bearable; Mr. Ramsay, who insists only on the unvarnished truth, has no use for such subjective distortions to improve upon life. The contrast in tables could have been useful to McGee. McGee's emphasis on Mrs. Ramsay as spiritual center of the novel in her domesticity also leads to some skewing of the book as a whole since McGee overlooks the validation of maleness in Part III, where Woolf reinforces her insistence on the need for androgyny by building up Mr. Ramsay and his way of being. But despite McGee's sometime tendentiousness with dinners and their ramifications, the overall intelligence of her discussion is not compromised, and she is led to fresh and perceptive observations by her focus on meals. For example, McGee credibly suggests that when the candles are lit at Mrs. Ramsay's dinner table, the effect is to create Mrs. Ramsay's own lighthouse and island refuge from the encircling flux. Likewise, in *Mrs. Dalloway*, McGee occasionally gets the details wrong, such as when she has Peter Walsh dining at a restaurant (128) although in fact he dines at his hotel, a kind of boarding house, before attending Clarissa Dalloway's party. But it is astute of McGee to call attention to the role of the ordinarily ignored preparty dinner to which only a select few guests are invited—not including Peter, whose current unimportance to Clarissa is thereby defined.

McGee believes that woman's role as purveyor of food can be celebrated because of its inherently creative quality; her final chapter thus explores the connection between the creativity of serving a meal and of producing a work of literature. The relationship of the writer to meals McGee posits as part of the larger issue for modernist women of whether to "think back through our mothers," as Woolf puts it, or reject their traditional roles. The possibilities for reinventing themselves would necessarily relate to the domestic center of their lives, reflected in explorations of creativity and depictions of artists' struggles, and in the structure of texts themselves. Modernist women's orientation to domesticity of course subjected them to the derogation of male modernism, with its contempt for everyday life. In the course of this discussion, McGee identifies modernist women writers who use dinners as a structural device, presenting a story or entire novel as if it were a meal offered the reader. Her detailed example is Kate Chopin's "The Awakening," constructed around a series of meals, which also depicts the conflict between being artist and traditional wife.

McGee finally argues that not only may the server of dinner become a model and an inspiration for the artist but also the meal itself may actually be transformed into a work of art through its literary presentation. For the writers she discusses, her introduction claims that dinner is not just the metaphorical center of their writing, but the meaning of change and defines them both as writers and as women. Whether or not one is willing to agree with her that meals in early modernist (and some later) fiction are all that she claims for them, certainly the significance of fictional meals is assured by the many perceptive readings in her book. If the metaphor is allowable, her book, which is tightly organized, specific and informative, clear and agreeably free of jargon and arguments with other critics, is also easy to digest.

—Harriet Blodgett, *California State University, Stanislaus*

Works Cited

Mansfield, Katherine. "Prelude." *Stories*. New York: Vintage, 1991. 51-96.
——. "Sun and Moon." *Stories*. New York: Vintage, 1991. 186-92.
Woolf, Virginia. *Mrs. Dalloway*. San Diego: Harvest/HBJ, 1990.
——. *To the Lighthouse*. New York: Harcourt, 1955.

The Life and Work of Jane Ellen Harrison
Annabel Robinson (Oxford: Oxford UP, 2002) xvi + 332 pp.

For many Virginia Woolf scholars, Jane Ellen Harrison's importance lies not so much in her contribution to the study of Greek religion, ritual, and art but in her role as Woolf's older mentor and friend to whom Woolf alludes in *A Room of One's Own*: "—could it be the famous scholar, could it be J—H—herself?" (17). As Annabel Robinson notes in the introduction to her biography, *The Life and Work of Jane Ellen Harrison*, Harrison served as the symbol of "what eluded Woolf, a university education and an academic career" (9). Indeed, as Woolf continues in the following sentence to compare "J—H—" to a "star or sword—the flash of some terrible reality leaping, as its way is, out of the heart of spring" (17), she conveys the powerful transformative effect of Harrison's exceptional genius, originality, humor, and vitality upon those who were privileged to be her friends or hear her unforgettable lectures. As a biographer, however, Robinson does not purport to explore here in any depth the relationship between Woolf and Harrison, nor does she attempt to employ feminist theory in her analysis of Harrison's scholarship, revolutionary views, or unconventional relationships with both women and men. To be fair, Robinson's introduction and later comments do underscore the ways in which Harrison "redefined the possibilities for academically gifted women" (10), yet Robinson has clearly chosen to employ her classicist background as the lens through which she focuses on Harrison's career as a lecturer at Cambridge University's Newnham College, her valuable contributions to the scholarship of her time, and her intense intellectual relationships with such other "Cambridge Ritualists" as Gilbert Murray, F. M. Cornford, and A. B. Cook.

Robinson has structured her biography chronologically, interweaving a detailed history of Harrison's life with an appraisal of her work. Beginning with Harrison's troubled childhood, Robinson sees as significant the death of Harrison's mother shortly after giving birth to her, providing her daughter with a lifelong sense of guilt (18). Her father eventually remarried, providing his daughter and her sisters with an unsympathetic stepmother. This unsatisfactory home life actually freed Harrison in many ways from the ties of family and permitted her to embark on a self-defined path, though her letters indicate that throughout her life she was subject to depression and profound loneliness as well as ill health. But at least she was among the few women of her time to receive an education, which encouraged her to take the London matriculation examination in 1870, newly opened to women, which she passed, and to eventually prepare for the Cambridge University Examination for Women. This, in turn, allowed her to win "the scholarship offered by Newnham College to the best candidate in this examination" (Robinson 33). Thus, in 1874, Jane Harrison was among the first handful of women to attend Cambridge University.

Her life at Newnham seems to have helped emancipate Harrison from the shackles of her Victorian society. Once there, she was usually at the center of her circle of friends, whom she apparently entertained nightly with her boundless humor and wit. As she became involved in Greek drama, she and several friends engaged in the unprecedented act of putting on a production of Euripides' *Electra*. As Robinson observes, "The very idea bears testimony for Harrison's gift of originality, perhaps also to her sense of the wholeness of things, that Greek tragedies were not texts but dramas, and would come to life only on the stage" (45). Harrison's lifelong interest in Greek ritual rather than mythology as the heart of Greek religion seems to have burgeoned at this time.

Where Robinson's authoritative biography most succeeds, however, is in the middle chapters that cover the period from 1879, when Harrison completed her studies at Newnham, through 1912, the years during which Harrison's theories about Greek art, archaeology, and religion were formulated. In these chapters Robinson chronicles Harrison's various travels to Greece and the new excavations at Troy, informs us of the various romances and attachments she experienced, cites the setbacks she encountered in her career because of her gender and her successful return to Newnham as a lecturer, and describes the gestation and completion of *Prolegomena to the Study of Greek Religion* (1903), among her most influential works. In *Prolegomena*, Harrison revolutionized her field by putting forth her belief that the mythology associated with the Olympian gods and depicted in Homer appeared much later than the Eleusinian, Dionysian, and Orphic Mysteries that were regularly enacted and that these Mysteries "were" Greek religion. These ideas were further refined and explicated in *Themis: A Study of the Social Origins of Greek Religion* (1912), which, though problematic, is still considered an important achievement. It was also during this period that Harrison established her lifelong friendships and collaborations with the other "Cambridge Ritualists," especially Gilbert Murray, with whom she regularly corresponded and exchanged ideas and to whom *Themis* was dedicated. Here Robinson seems most comfortable explicating Harrison's theories, the criticism she received, and the honest reevaluation of those theories to which Harrison subjected herself. Indeed, Robinson reveals that the Jane Harrison who dared to publish her innovative theories was also courageous and humble enough to recognize and admit when her thinking was flawed (87-91), and Robinson herself carefully explains why contemporary classicists have discredited aspects of *Themis*, especially those that rested on archaeological and anthropological arguments that have since been abandoned (227-233).

Nevertheless, one wishes at times that Robinson had paused to offer deeper analyses of her subject's later work and had seized opportunities for further reflection on Harrison's influence. For example, Chapter 2, "A Room of Her Own: Newnham College 1874-1879" (34), obviously alludes to Woolf's 1928 Newnham lecture and 1929 book, which is implicitly dedicated to Harrison (305), yet Robinson's observation that Harrison was able to make independent choices during this time because she received a modest annuity as an inheritance from her mother, allowing her the freedom to define herself and bring originality to her scholarship, is not examined in the context of Woolf's argument, while in a later chapter Robinson then claims somewhat gratuitously that Woolf's idea "that if a woman was to write she must have money and a room of her own [...] had first been articulated by Harrison, who called her room her 'cave' after her claim that the guardians in Plato's *Republic* were Orphic initiates in their cave" (187). Similarly, the title of Chapter 13, "*Via crucis, via lucis*: Cambridge, France, and London 1916-1928" (278), which cites the concluding line of

Harrison's last major work, *Epilegomena*, leaves one eager for more than the cursory discussion Robinson provides. Given Gilbert Murray's belief that, as he wrote Harrison in 1921, "[t]he last chapter [...] seems to me the best thing you have ever written about religion" (Stewart 182), Robinson gives short shrift to this culminating work, never bothering to explore Harrison's indebtedness "to the psychological work of Jung and Freud and to the less well known writings of the greatest of Russian philosophers Vladímir Soloviόv" (Harrison xv).

This study might also have profited from a final chapter summarizing Harrison's continuing influence on more recent work on Greek tragedy and the cults of Dionysos and Orpheus, especially that of French structuralists and poststructuralists Marcel Detienne, Jean-Pierre Vernant, Pierre Vidal-Nacquet, and René Girard. It would also benefit from editing such sentences as "The sad task fell to Curtius of burying his friend, mentor, and fellow-traveller at Colonus, the very place where Oedipus had been taken to heaven" (61), as if the "ascent" of Oedipus were a fact. Paragraphs often segue from one to the other with little in the way of transition: "Much of this material would find its way into [...] *Themis*, where she worked out a more satisfactory, if highly idiosyncratic, conclusion about the value of religion," for instance, is immediately followed with "Her heart still gave her problems" (210). Providing a more complete list of errata would have also been welcome. For example, John Stuart Mill's wife was Harriet, not "Helen" (36), and in Euripides' *Hippolytus*, Phaedra falls in love with her stepson, Hippolytus—not, as Robinson writes, "Phaedra is destroyed by her secret passion for her stepson, Theseus" (254).

Though in many ways this is a thorough biography, Robinson still notes with frustration the lack of background evidence concerning her subject's life. While "the biographer has a particular responsibility to [...] take as much care as possible that his or her own preconceived notions do not get in the way," writes Robinson, "[i]n the case of Jane Ellen Harrison, it is notoriously difficult to arrive at any undistorted account" (2). Because Harrison did not keep a diary and burned all her personal papers before she moved to Paris in 1921 with her former student, Hope Mirrlees, her companion for the last eight years of her life, her biographers have been forced to depend on letters she wrote to friends and colleagues, especially Gilbert Murray; subjective memories of friends and former students Stewart and Mirrlees; and Harrison's own short memoir, *Reminiscences of a Student's Life*, published by Hogarth Press in 1925. Yet the Harrison who studied comparative religion and mythology so assiduously was a mythmaker herself, and, complains Robinson, "Just to read *Reminiscences* in conjunction with the letters she wrote to Gilbert Murray is to be brought face to face with what deconstructionists might call *aporia*: a paradox of self-contradictions" (3). That Harrison had become a myth for many of her contemporaries complicates matters further. Perhaps because this is Robinson's first biography, she anticipated a more consistent image to emerge from Harrison's letters and memoir, but consistency in private and public personae is rarely found or perhaps actually desirable given the paradoxical nature of creative genius itself; what might make the biographer's task easier often contradicts the reasons why the subject of the biography is deemed worthy of examination in the first place.

Robinson's own resentment at being deprived of invaluable and irreplaceable primary sources surfaces when she unequivocally blames Hope Mirrlees for persuading Harrison to burn her personal papers before they left England, although no absolute evidence exists to verify Mirrlees's role. Consequently, her references to Mirrlees are often judgmental, just as her depiction of Harrison's final years describes an aging woman childishly fixated on her "stuffed bear" (238-242). Noting, for example, that "There had always been a silly side to Harrison, which was beginning to grow more pronounced as she grew older, perhaps as a way of disguising some of the physical and emotional pain she was suffering" (238), Robinson reveals her annoyance with Harrison's playful, imaginative, and affectionate side—the same qualities that probably allowed Harrison to remain youthful and open to new ideas throughout her life. She also appears to object to Harrison's choice of Mirrlees as a fitting companion, much as she disapproves of Harrison's departure from her earlier passion for ancient Greek religion and ritual that was increasingly replaced by a passion for Russian folklore, evidenced by her comments regarding Harrison's and Mirrlees's translations of Russian bear stories, *The Book of the Bear, Being Twenty-One Tales Newly Translated from the Russian* (1926): "The stories are Russian. They are also all inconsequential," writes Robinson (298).

In her effort to rupture the myths surrounding Harrison in order to present an "undistorted" portrait, Robinson at times vexes in her criticism of Harrison. As she herself admits, she decided to write a biography of Harrison because she "was looking for a research project at the moment" when she came across William M. Calder III's suggestion "that 'a woman might write the life or edit the letters of Jane Ellen Harrison,'" whose work "was a new departure for [her]" and whom she had never before read (Robinson vii). Had Robinson chosen to write about Harrison as a result of her own fascination with her subject, this well-researched biography, which is in many ways satisfying, might have even better reflected the unusual élan and genius of the great "J—H—."

—Helane Levine-Keating, *Pace University*

Works Cited

Harrison, Jane Ellen. *Epilegomena to the Study of Greek Religion and Themis: A Study of the Social Origins of Greek Religion.* New York: University Books, 1962 (1921; 1912).

Stewart, Jessie G. *Jane Ellen Harrison: A Portrait from Letters.* London: Merlin Press, 1959.

Woolf, Virginia. *A Room of One's Own.* San Diego: Harvest/ Harcourt Brace Jovanovich, 1989 (1929).

Invisible Work: Borges and Translation
Efraín Kristal (Nashville: Vanderbilt UP, 2002) xi + 213 pp.

Efraín Kristal's *Invisible Work* is a systematic demonstration of the crucial role that the underrated task of translation and exercises related to it played on the development of Jorge Luis Borges' literary world. The study amounts to a carefully researched compilation of scattered observations Borges left on the subject as well as deft readings and contextualizations of some major foreign texts the Argentine writer made available to a wide Spanish-speaking audience. In addition, Kristal demonstrates that Borges' translations fundamentally shape his prose fiction.

Kristal concentrates mostly on translations into Spanish of works published in English, but he also discusses a few translations of works originally published in other languages. Since *Invisible Work* is explicitly intended for an English-speaking audience, Kristal sets before the reader Borges' versions of foreign texts in English, not in Spanish. Sometimes Kristal resorts to translating the Spanish original into English himself and then includes Spanish versions in copious notes in the appendix. Kristal's purpose is to unveil Borges' engagements with the originals in order to expose the connections between his work as translator and as creative writer. Kristal, however, relegates Borges' translations of Virginia Woolf to a few passing comments. We shall see why below.

Through the discussion of Borges' pronouncements on translation, glossed over in chapter 1, Borges emerges as a bold, even unscrupulous, translator. He advances the view that all translation involves interpretation; that a literal translation would not necessarily be considered inadequate or unskillful if its judge could resist the privileging of the original over the translation; and—at his most radical—that certain translations can surpass the original in quality. This last tenet became a critical truism he upheld repeatedly when evaluating the capable translations of his own work. As a result of these beliefs, Borges emerges in chapter 2 as a translator free to take liberties with the original. For example, he excises or transforms whole passages and nuances or foregrounds secondary themes—all because he believes the function of translation surpasses the mere rendering of texts from one language into another.

Invisible Work does much more than illustrate Borges' mastery of his craft. Chapters 3 and 4 provide extensive arguments that link the role specific translations played in the development of themes fundamental to the gestation of famous poems and stories. For example, Kristal reconstructs the steady dialogue that Borges established with Walt Whitman's work between the announcement of the publication of his translation of *Leaves of Grass* in 1927 and the final appearance of the book in print in 1969 (48-49). In the evolution of his literary thinking, Kristal identifies 1930 as a watershed year, for Borges abandoned a belief in literature as transparently autobiographical, and he rejected nationalism. Armed with these two new aesthetic and political beliefs, Borges felt increasingly freer to develop a poetic persona less representative of Whitman's strict individualism (50). So Kristal juxtaposes two fragments, from 1929 and 1932 respectively, that show Borges' increasingly bold engagements with Whitman's poetry in ways more consistent with his new credo and that culminate in a translation Borges himself called "an interpretive recreation" (51). This evidence even prefigures Borges' fascination with the theme of cyclical time so frequently used in his own work.

Similar readings highlight the relationship of a host of his translations to his creative process. For instance, Kristal argues that at the time Borges was revising "Death and the Compass," he was also working on the translation of Poe's "The Purloined Letter" for inclusion of both in the 1946 anthology of detective fiction he was preparing with his life-long collaborator, Adolfo Bioy Casares. Kristal shows that the game of intellectual outwitting in "Death and the Compass" is prefigured in a secondary theme of Poe's and in the change of characterization of Minister D. from a "desperate" to an "unscrupulous and courageous man" (105). These changes of emphasis begin the metamorphosis of Poe's Dupin and Minister D. into Borges' Lönrot and Sharlach. Thus, Kristal illuminates the ways in which translation inspires Borges' creative mind, and the best of Borges' short fiction ("Emma Zunz," "The Lottery in Babylon," "The Garden of the Forking Paths" among many others) is related to the work of translation.

Kristal's compelling study does not claim to comprehend all of Borges' translations. For readers of Virginia Woolf one major disappointment will be the omission of Borges' translations of *A Room of One's Own*, published by Sur and issued from December 1935 to March 1936, and of *Orlando*, which followed in 1937. Both were published later by Sudamericana Press and became the standard translations of Woolf's work in Spanish-America during the mid-twentieth-century. Kristal relegates commentary on these to a passing reference. He rightly refers to *Orlando* as a literal translation (40) and then considers it a possible source of the theme of immortality in Borges' short story "The Immortal" (98). That is all. It is clear to close readers of either translation that Borges took very few substantial liberties beyond exercising some license over paraphrasing, changing an occasional reference of vague context in the original to a more familiar word in Spanish, and changing certain gender references. The scant scholarship on both translations shows that Borges' decision to resort almost invariably to literal—albeit accurate and concise—translation comes as a surprise, even a disappointment, considering the liberties he professed translators could take. More to the point, neither of Borges' translations of Woolf, important as they are in the circulation of culture, allows Kristal to advance his thesis. Borges simply does not come off as an adventurous, creative translator. There are no pyrotechnics. This fact does not invalidate Kristal's thesis, but it limits the thesis' application.

Still, with *Invisible Work* Efraín Kristal has opened up and signposted a brand new field for exploration. His book may be useful to a number of readers. It may ease literary critics into further interpretations of Borges' work; assist comparative literature experts in acquiring information that transcends national context; and help students of translation studies understand the tireless interventions of an important translation theorist. Finally, the general reader may gain an appreciation—without the difficulties of technical language—of the powerful literary mind of a writer who is by now a household name. The book concludes with an extended bibliography of sources intended to satisfy further reading interests.

—Mónica G. Ayuso, *California State University, Bakersfield*

The Great War and the Language of Modernism
Vincent Sherry (New York: Oxford UP, 2003) xiv + 395 pp.

In the last decade of the twentieth century, a student of Virginia Woolf and war, particularly World War One, would find a number of volumes specifically on the topic, including Mark Hussey's, *Virginia Woolf and War* (1991); Helen Wussow's *The Nightmare of History: The Fictions of Virginia Woolf and D.H. Lawrence* (1998); and my own *Virginia Woolf and the Great War* (1999). Moreover, there were a large number of books involving war in which Virginia Woolf figures prominently, including Lynne Hanley's *Writing War: Fiction, Gender, and Memory* (1991); Allyson Booth's *Postcards from the Trenches: Negotiating the Space Between Modernism and the First World War* (1996); and Suzanne Raitt and Trudi Tate's *Women's Fiction and the Great War* (1997). Books involving the Great War and history (cultural, military, or diplomatic), often without more than a passing reference to Woolf, are certainly more numerous, however, beginning with Paul Fussell's *The Great War and Modern Memory* (1975), the seminal study of the Great War and modern consciousness, which is the alpha (if not the omega) of almost every cultural study of the war since then. Others include (but are clearly not limited to) Samuel Hynes' *A War Imagined* (1991), and Jay Winter's *The Great War and the British People* (1986) and *Sites of Memory, Sites of Mourning: The Great War in European Cultural History* (1995). Since we entered the twenty-first century, as far as I know, there has been only one book relevant to the study both of the Great War and Virginia Woolf, Vincent Sherry's *The Great War and the Language of Modernism*; although a formidable study that makes use of most of the sources mentioned above, overlooking Wussow suggests a gap in the research, and in the book itself. What brings Wussow's much shorter book to mind (it is about half the length of Sherry's, includes no illustrations to the twenty-nine in Sherry's, but does have a bibliography, though the reader is deprived of even a list of works cited in *The Great War*...) is not only the use of history as the driving force (with nods to Foucault and Bakhtin) and its appreciation of the role of language at home during the war, but also the skill with which the book shows the influence of the Great War on important but markedly different writers. Sherry extends Wussow's coupling of strange bedfellows and focuses not only on writers separated by gender, temperament, and politics, but by genre and nationality. Moreover (*sans* explicit reference to Foucault and Bakhtin), his sense of historicity rests decidedly with the Great War (rather than a generalized idea of it as "conflict"), and, not limiting himself to one or two authors in his effort to trace the evolution of the "language of modernism," Sherry focuses on three: T.S. Eliot: American, poet/playwright; Ezra Pound, American, poet; and, Virginia Woolf, English, novelist.[1]

Quoting from Eliot's "Gerontion" (1919), "'History has many cunning passages, contrived corridors / And issues'" (3), Sherry begins what Marjorie Perloff (on the book's jacket) calls this "revisionist study." The word is itself problematic, Sherry himself asking whether his topic merits another full-length study (6). Certainly this is not a disingenuous question given the amount of work already done on the Great War and Modernism and each of the authors in this study.[2] By beginning with "Gerontion," Sherry points to a major conceit: "the validity of a noncombatant's imaginative part in the war" (7), which doesn't seem all that new to members of the Woolf community, and readers of the books referred to above. As Sherry points out, even Fussell admits, albeit parenthetically or in subordinate constructions, that writers who were moved "to recall in literary form the war they had *actually experienced*" were "*lesser talents*—always more traditional and technically prudent" (8).[3] But, Sherry's painstaking scrutiny of Eliot, Pound, and Woolf (and to a lesser degree, Gertrude Stein and Ford Maddox Ford, who are included in "interchapters") bears out his critique of Jay Winter, who, according to Sherry, asserts that accommodation rather than reorientation was the favored mode in postwar Britain; in fact, Sherry continues, "[F]ar from ushering in modernism, the Great War reinforced romantic values, particularly in poetry" and "encouraged" their promulgation in more diverse cultural representations. (8-9). When it comes to Woolf, whose subversive grammar and diction can resonate discordantly by design, and her unlikely fellow travelers, Sherry finds himself up to the task of demonstrating how their diction and syntax undercuts the language of political liberalism, that is, "public reason," in postwar England—and suggesting that "[t]he internal record of th[e] historical experience is revealed in the consistency of the shift these three writers exhibit" (14).

While equal attention is ostensibly given to Virginia Woolf as to Eliot and Pound in this revisionist historical study, Sherry places her in the shadow of the Liberal tradition to which she was born and presents a presumably new way of looking at her. Sherry doesn't totally eschew biography, but prefers to see in the language itself, the "vanguard awareness" of the writers: the "grammar and vocabulary through which the war was constructed in political Britain, in partic-

---

[1] See my review of Wussow's book in *Virginia Woolf Miscellany*. Sherry also overlooks William A. Evans, *Virginia Woolf: Strategist of Language* (1989), an early primer on the topic of Woolf's grammar and diction.

[2] Sherry is himself the author of *Ezra Pound, Wyndham Lewis, and Radical Modernism* (1993).

[3] Sherry adds the emphasis and cites pages 313-314 of *The Great War and Modern Memory*.

ular, represent an idiom whose coherence reaches deep into the major traditions of intellectual liberalism and, in its disturbance, opens into an equally profound range of resonance and implication" (19, 18). Thus, as the writers, "resident or relative aliens all" ("outsiders" by another name—see Wussow and Woolf herself) responded to the "discrepancy between the intellectual principles and practical actualities of British Liberalism," the crisis was thereby identified and assimilated into their imaginative literature—and it is the work of Sherry's study "to restore their poetry and fiction to a historical importance that is original, specific" (20-21). To do this, Sherry includes a prologue and epilogue, four parts (the last devoted to Woolf), and the three interchapters. The second and third parts, devoted to Pound and Eliot, respectively, each are divided into six, and each ends with an interchapter (the first interchapter follows part 1, "Liberal Measures," involving a "poetics of English Modernism"). The fourth part, "Woolf, Among the Modernists," is divided into five: "Voyaging Out"; "Shorts"; *Jacob's Room*; (interestingly) "*Mrs. Dalloway's* Insubordinate Clause," and "Unbracketed."

What makes Woolf special to Sherry "among the Modernists" is an "ambivalence [which] positions Woolf especially promisingly as a literary sensibility of the first postwar moment," both notwithstanding and because her social class and "genetic memory make hers one of the most indicative and expressive records of the loss on which her newfound power relies" (235) As Sherry reads Woolf, it is her intimate relation to the past, and particularly her allegiance with and recognition of the literary potential in the liberal tradition, that makes her future "power" so remarkable to Sherry—if not as unique and revisionary as the blurbs on the back cover would have us believe. William Handley, Rachel Blau DuPlessis, and James Haule, for example, fall along the way, under his critical ax, though not unkindly.[4] Sherry moves from *The Voyage Out* ("a [prewar] feminine *Bildungsroman*" that represents early on Woolf's critique of the Liberal culture [240]); to the short fiction and essays (evidence of the "coherent motive and style of pseudostatement" [261]); to *Jacob's Room* (where he disagrees with Handley's non-historicized treatment of Woolf and the war [272]), to *Mrs. Dalloway* (where he finds that while DuPlessis recognizes the "sentence broken," her emphasis is on the temporal and on gender conventions rather than the political and the Liberal idiom [291; 368n59]); to *To the Lighthouse* (where,

---

[4] Specifically, Handley, "War and the Politics of Narration in *Jacob's Room*"; DuPlessis, "Breaking the Sentence: Breaking the Sequence"; and, Haule, "*To the Lighthouse* and the Great War: The Evidence of Virginia Woolf's Revisions of 'Time Passes'" and "'Le Temps Passe' and the Original Typescript: An Early Version of the 'Time Passes' Section of *To the Lighthouse*."

again with full respect extended to James Haule, he takes issue with his "accept[ing] the premise of some universal language for art, a lexicon in which the parenthesis may assume a steady meaning and constant valence" [295]), thus asserting that Woolf's sensibility is grounded in the Great War, an "area of imaginative awareness [she shares] with the other major writers of English modernism" (297).

The Great War and the Language of Modernism is a demonstrably intelligent book written by a careful scholar. Does it add a new level to the discourse on war and modernism and Virginia Woolf? Yes, in some of the ways Helen Wussow did in linking D.H. Lawrence and Virginia Woolf in the context of the Great War, and in his meticulous attention to syntax and diction in the context of "Liberal England at war." Certainly it offers us a new way of seeing Eliot and Pound as well, be the three as strange bedfellows as Lawrence and Woolf—or stranger.

—Karen L. Levenback

Works Cited

Booth, Allyson. *Postcards from the Trenches: Negotiating the Space Between Modernism and the First World War.* NY: Oxford UP, 1996.

DuPlessis, Rachel Blau. "Breaking the Sentence: Breaking the Sequence." In *Writing Beyond the Ending: Narrative Strategies of Twentieth-Century Women Writers* (Bloomington: Indiana UP, 1985): 31-46.

Evans, William A. *Virginia Woolf: Strategist of Language.* Lanham, MD: UP of America, 1989.

Fussell, Paul. *The Great War and Modern Memory.* NY: Oxford UP, 1975.

Handley, William. "War and the Politics of Narration in *Jacob's Room.*" In Hussey: 110-33.

Hanley, Lynne. *Writing War: Fiction, Gender, and Memory.* Amherst: U of Massachusetts P, 1991.

Haule, James M. "'*Le Temps passe*' and the Original Typescript: An Early Version of the 'Time Passes' Section of *To the Lighthouse.*" *Twentieth-Century Literature* 29 (Fall 1983): 267-311.

——. "*To the Lighthouse* and the Great War: The Evidence of Virginia Woolf's Revisions of 'Time Passes'" in Hussey: 166-75

Hussey, Mark, ed. *Virginia Woolf and War: Fiction, Reality, and Myth.* Syracuse: Syracuse UP, 1991.

Hynes, Samuel. *A War Imagined: The First World War and English Culture.* NY: Atheneum. 1991.
Levenback, Karen L. *Virginia Woolf and the Great War.* Syracuse: Syracuse UP, 1999.
——. Review of *The Nightmare of History: The Fictions of Virginia Woolf and D.H. Lawrence* by Helen Wussow. *Virginia Woolf Miscellany* 58 (Fall 2001): 8.
Sherry, Vincent. *Ezra Pound, Wyndham Lewis, and Radical Modernism.* NY: Oxford UP, 1993.
Raitt, Suzanne and Trudi Tate, eds. *Women's Fiction and the Great War.* Oxford: Clarendon P, 1997.
Winter, Jay. *The Great War and the British People.* London: Macmillan, 1986.
——. *Sites of Memory, Sites of Mourning: The Great War in European Cultural History.* Cambridge, England: Cambridge UP, 1995.
Wussow, Helen. *The Nightmare of History: The Fictions of Virginia Woolf and D.H. Lawrence.* Bethlehem: Lehigh UP, 1998.

"Am I a Snob?" Modernism and the Novel
Sean Latham (Ithaca: Cornell UP, 2003) vii + 240 pp.

It is no doubt a challenge today to locate a fresh and original angle on Virginia Woolf (and modernism and the modern novel, for that matter), and Sean Latham should be highly commended for his new book which does just that. *"Am I a Snob?" Modernism and the Novel* explores the way various authors' concern with the question, "Am I a snob?" resulted in a new model of modernism, one which considered the privileges of elitism at the same time as it experienced anxiety about aesthetic autonomy, formalist innovation, and the fact that pleasures afforded by symbolic and economic capital were earned in a literary marketplace typically considered to be bourgeois and middlebrow. Readers of Latham's book will be immediately curious upon seeing its catchy (and effectively focused) title, and will be kept interested by the depth of his analysis and use of substantial evidence.

The book is extremely readable, and its subject matter is so that undergraduates as well as the most informed modernist scholars will find it offers original and helpful insights. Latham uses the question Virginia Woolf posed in the title of a paper she delivered privately to her Bloomsbury friends—"Am I a snob?"—

as an instigation for his analysis of the ways Thackeray, Wilde, Woolf, Joyce, and Dorothy L. Sayers tried to navigate their way through the literary marketplace as authors who participated in a modern literary project that inevitably found itself beset by the problems posed by aesthetic snobbery. Each chapter of Latham's book includes thorough, concrete evidence of these authors' experiences with their work and texts as products of a "culture" clearly preoccupied with the privileges and limitations of pretension and snobbery. The fascinating effect of Latham's method—intertwining the experiences of these authors, against the backdrop of Woolf's question, with the snobbery in which their texts intentionally or inadvertently engage—is that readers glean understanding not only of these authors' struggles with themselves and with their texts, but also of their place in a larger modern culture where art could not locate a realm of pure autonomy separate from the demands of fame and economic capital. Wonderfully, Latham's method also involves readers in the meaning-making process as we begin while reading his book to ask ourselves how snobbery functions for us in our own modern culture since we are the consumers and teachers of these texts.

In the first section of the first part, Latham uses a discussion of William Thackeray's publication from 1846 to 1847 of "The Snob Papers" to focus on what he considers to be one of two key moments in the history of snobbery. Until the first decades of the twentieth century, Latham explains, "[r]ather than describing the arrogance of an individual possessed of good taste and social refinement, snobbery initially described only those class climbers who vulgarly imitated the tastes and habits of the upper classes" (13). Latham argues that Thackeray's text rewrites this definition of the snob, transforming it instead into a set of behaviors that can be attained by anyone, regardless of class. Through intricate and convincing analysis of "The Snob Papers," Latham shows the way in which Thackeray redefines the snob as a celebrity who is able in a mass-mediated cultural marketplace to manipulate and counterfeit the signifiers of distinction in order to convey them as economic and social capital.

Latham examines the second of two key moments in the history of snobbery in his first part's second section. The first section on Thackeray defines what Latham refers to as "the logic of the pose," or "the process through which fashion evacuates an object and leaves behind only an empty sign of sophistication" (215). Latham discusses *The Picture of Dorian Gray* in this second section and argues that Oscar Wilde, like Thackeray, tries to escape from the logic of the pose by imagining for the arts an idealized space where aesthetic value could somehow exist untainted by the demands of the cultural marketplace. Both authors fail, Latham contends. Thackeray can only "construct the compensatory fantasy of arts and letters" (30) and Wilde "exploited his celebrity to reveal its aesthetic inadequacy" (56).

The two sections on Woolf in the second part of *"Am I a Snob?"* are particular highlights of Latham's book, demonstrating his extensive familiarity with Woolf studies. Latham is to be commended for achieving the difficult task of demonstrating through an impressive consideration of a good deal of Woolf criticism the way generations of critics from the 1920s to the present day have celebrated Woolf's achievements as a writer and/or criticized her apparent snobbery. In a discussion of David Denby, Alex Zwerdling, Jane Marcus, George Will, Nigel Nicolson, Frank Swinnerton, F.R. Leavis, and John Carey (to name just a few), Latham not only reveals the complicated nuances surrounding the historically evolving definition of the word "snob" but also carves out an appropriate niche within this critical context for his assertion that "[s]nobbery threads its way through Woolf's fiction, condensing the contradictions and discomforts that surrounded the mass-mediated institutions of cultural and social distinction in which she found herself ensnared" (63).

Latham interweaves discussion of excerpts from Woolf's diary with information about Woolf's experiences as she became increasingly famous, and he places this examination within the context of Woolf criticism and analysis of *Three Guineas*, *Jacob's Room*, *Orlando*, and *To the Lighthouse*. The result is that readers receive an informed and thorough sense through multiple angles of Woolf's life—her private writings, her public persona, her semi-public relationship with the Bloomsbury circle, her fiction, and others' reception of her—of the way

> the image of the snob as fashioned by Woolf is a highly successful performer whose public display of the seemingly counterfeit signs of sophistication effaces entirely what Woolf imagines to be a legitimate—if repressed—artistic culture. Having herself passed through the gauntlet of fame and sampled the pleasures of snobbery, Woolf sought escape in the narrowly conceived concept of the Outsider who could forge an autonomous art at the intersection of class privilege and social alienation. Wrapping herself in this shroud reserved primarily for the daughters of educated men, she may have appeared arrogant and even pretentious, but she believed that she had at last overcome the anxiety that underlay snobbery, free at last 'of vanity: of Virginia'
> (4:191) (117).

Latham's next chapter, which is on Joyce, is also a highlight of his book. In this chapter, Latham asserts that Joyce, like Woolf, found that the allure of fame and wealth acquired in a marketplace operating under the dictates of symbolic and economic capital threatened to compromise artists' potential. Latham contends that from the "Day of Rabblement" through *Stephen Hero* and the early stories of *Dubliners*, Joyce establishes a gap between the snobbish pretension of the artist and the challenging lives of those with whom he associates. Latham discusses "A Little Cloud" and sections of *Portrait* and *Ulysses* and concludes his chapter with the assertion that "[d]espite the great virtuosity of [*Ulysses*], despite its telling protest against the limitations of intellectual pretension, it still failed to exploit the critical potential of its own ambivalent snobbery and was appropriated by the very cultural hierarchies of value it sought to contest" (168).

Latham in this chapter again does an excellent job of establishing his own discourse and placing his argument within the context of current criticism and discussion so that readers gain a sense of the academic and popular concerns with snobbery that have surrounded the author and text. For example, through his consideration of Danis Rose's "readers' edition" of *Ulysses*, which we know added punctuation and simplified the formalistic complexity of *Ulysses*, Latham effectively conveys the way critics, scholars, as well as nonacademic audiences cannot help but become entangled in various aspects of snobbery, even while seeking to avoid such entanglement. Rose's is only one of numerous texts Latham explores as he creates a sense of presence within readers' minds of the complications that so completely surround issues of snobbery and modernism that it becomes difficult to talk about the modern novel without seriously considering the dilemmas that snobbery and pretension caused for these authors.

The remaining sections of this second part of Latham's book consist of a chapter on Dorothy L. Sayers and a concluding chapter entitled "The Problem of Snobbery." In another detailed discussion, Latham's Sayers chapter demonstrates the role her comic detective stories played in creating and propagating the concept of the modern snob. Latham asserts that "[f]or Sayers, snobbery appears as an apparently inescapable component of modernity itself, the by-product of a social system in which the easily counterfeited signs of cultural and social distinction can be made to yield institutional and individual profits" (213). Latham's concluding chapter returns to Woolf's question, "Am I a snob?" in order to outline the way others such as Roger Fry, F.R. Leavis, Arnold Bennett, and the New Critics have considered the problem of snobbery. Lastly, this concluding chapter offers a springboard for readers to consider that "only by insistently posing the question, 'Am I a snob?' can we demystify the operation of the cultural marketplace and begin to construct an aesthetic that does not evade the fact of its own commodification" (223).

"Am I a Snob?" Modernism and the Novel does an excellent job of placing the modern novel within its historical context in order to show that these texts, definitions we call forth when discussing these texts, and indeed our critical languages themselves contribute to our sense of history and at the same time exist as products of this same history. One of the greatest strengths of Latham's book is that it promotes active reading, whether one is an undergraduate or an experienced scholar. For example, it would be impossible, of course, for Latham to

offer a thorough discussion of the issues of snobbery and the literary marketplace in every text in which these issues are present. At the same time, it is impossible as one reads—because Latham's book is so engaging—not to consider how snobbery and the literary marketplace function for Dickens, for example, or for Charlotte Brontë, Mary Elizabeth Braddon, Lytton Strachey, Vita Sackville-West, Katherine Mansfield, or E.M. Forster. This is the most enjoyable kind of reading, reading which invites one to become an integral part of the meaning-making process at the same time it instructs, informs, and promotes collaboration between reader and author. Latham's book is therefore a valuable pedagogical tool and an important critical contribution to Woolf and modernist studies.

—Shannon Forbes, *University of St. Thomas*

From the Lighthouse to Monk's House: A Guide to Virginia Woolf's Literary Landscapes. Katherine C. Hill-Miller (London: Duckworth, 2001) 328 pp. *Virginia Woolf's Women.* Vanessa Curtis (Madison: U of Wisconsin P, 2002) 224 pp.; illustrated.

The title of Katherine Hill-Miller's *From the Lighthouse to Monk's House: A Guide to Virginia Woolf's Literary Landscapes* is entirely accurate. The book is a truly excellent guide to Woolf's sense of place, a solid introductory work for the uninitiated and a thoroughly useful reference work for the aficionado. "[A]imed at the audience Woolf cherished most—those whom Dr. Johnson described as 'common readers'—[the book] is an unabashedly hybrid work that combines literary biography, literary criticism and travel" (9). Delightfully, each chapter is prefaced with a beautiful decorative graphic by Stephen Barkway and, throughout the book, Hill-Miller includes especially lovely selections from Woolf novels, letters and diaries as well as passages from other sources such as the writings of Caroline Emelia Stephen, Leslie Stephen and Vita Sackville-West.

Tracing Woolf's experience of place from earliest childhood to death (thankfully, Hill-Miller does not pathologize Woolf in any way), the book is sensibly organized around a coherent and informative chronological summary of her life aligned with five of her major works and the places they evoke (the sections are sequenced based not on publication dates but on locations related to Woolf's lived experience)—*To the Lighthouse* (which includes St. Ives, Talland House,

22 Hyde Park Gate, Kensington Gardens, etc.), *Mrs. Dalloway* (mainly London), *Orlando* (primarily Knole, Long Barn and Sissinghurst), *A Room of One's Own* with a substantial sidebar discussion of *Three Guineas* (Cambridge), and *Between the Acts* (mostly Monk's House and Charleston). Each chapter begins with a brief but thorough overview of a particular life phase, followed by a lucid and accessible summary of a major work that illustrates key elements of place from that period. Each chapter concludes with meticulous directions and commentaries on noteworthy sites to visit (these sections list Woolf-related sites first and suggest other points of interest as additional possibilities for the energetic tourist including, of course, those of the armchair variety). The tours are very carefully thought out for those who wish to walk the paths and view the locations that inspired, influenced and grounded Woolf's life, imagination and work. Hill-Miller's travelogue provides the illusion of unmediated transparency free of any accounts of her personal experience. While in some ways this is a disappointment (for I am always curious about the author's own experiences), this strategy allows the reader's imagination to move effortlessly about the places described, accessing memories of previous visits, planning future adventures, or simply crafting the vivid fantasies of the traveler who embarks only on a journey of the imagination.

While the book is devised in such a way that each chapter and, indeed, each segment of a chapter, can be read independently (an organizational technique that necessarily relies on the repetition of certain material), one should not skim over the sections devoted to the walking tours as material relevant only to actual travelers. The historical material integrated into the walking tours is of particular interest to all readers since even very knowledgeable Woolfians may not know all the details. For instance, the origin of the Ready-Money fountain in Regent's Park (the fountain is unnamed in *Mrs. Dalloway*) where Lucrezia stands in despair (97) is not referenced even in Mark Hussey's *Virginia Woolf A to Z*. In fact, the *Mrs. Dalloway* section is particularly rich in the kind of trivia Woolfians thrive on and thus it is amusing to discover that Lady Bruton lives close to Bruton Street, Bruton Lane and Bruton Place. Similarly, Hill-Miller reminds the reader, when Peter Walsh appreciates the lingering twilight, he is enjoying the effects of British "summer time" (the equivalent of daylight savings time in the US) which was instituted while he was in India (83).

These glimpses of historical, cultural and geographical facts are so tantalizing that one longs for an even more detailed, more heavily annotated guide to Woolf's life and works. One hopes that there will be subsequent revised editions of *From the Lighthouse to Monk's House* if only because the essential travel information will, inevitably, change. To give just one example, in the interval since the book was published in 2001, 22 Hyde Park Gate has gone from a private home to a bed & breakfast managed by Jasmyne King-Leeder (you may contact her from the US at 011-44-20-7584-9404).

The very first sentence of the introduction notes that, although Woolf herself "worried about descending into sentiment when she visited the homes of famous writers, she enjoyed her literary tours immensely" (1)—and Hill-Miller's readers can enjoy the virtual literary tours she provides with equal zest. Pilgrimages to literary holy places are inspiring and intense experiences, the physical place uttering something that cannot be described in words or images. In this regard, Hill-Miller quotes from one of Woolf's earliest published essays, "Haworth Parsonage, November 1904," in which, referring to Charlotte Brontë's "muslin dress and small shoes," Woolf remarks: "'The natural fate of such things is to die before the body that wore them, and because these, trifling and transient though they are, have survived, Charlotte Brontë the woman comes to life'" (2). The introduction explores Woolf's sense of place, reminding us of our own affinities for, aversions to, and irrational but implacable associations with specific locations in the world, some intact and pristine, some inaccessible and forbidden, some now obscured, ruined or entirely obliterated, yet saturated with meaning nonetheless. As Hill-Miller observes:

> Near the end of her life, when Woolf sat down to write her autobiography and to consider her development as a writer, she returned to very specific places and invested them with the power to expand—or contract—the human spirit. In her essays about places, the idea of place acts as a fulcrum for the creative imagination. A place is the element that anchors memory. A place is continuous and solid, and therefore has the power to connect people to their pasts, and to the lives of people who have worked and died before them. Woolf discovers a sort of mortality in places, and it is in the idea of place that Woolf's fierce attachment to the natural world meets her urge toward transcendence,...inspir[ing]...a nearly mystical vision into the heart of reality. (3)

Hill-Miller offers engaging and lucid readings of Woolf's life and works that probably will not provoke any controversy among Woolf scholars, and she provides a thematic focus for each of her discussions of the major works. The first chapter deals primarily with *To the Lighthouse* because of the novel's indebtedness to Woolf's childhood memories of St. Ives and Talland House. Appropriately, the Godrevy Lighthouse is a constant point of reference, and, not surprisingly, Hill-Miller concludes her reading of the novel with the assertion that the line down the middle of Lily Briscoe's painting is, among other possible interpretations, the Godrevy Lighthouse itself. Hill-Miller also suggests that this line is Lily's (and by association Virginia Woolf's) psychological defense mechanism, a boundary separating her from the turbulent emotions related to the dead.

The section on *Mrs. Dalloway* is marked by the recurrent motifs of London's trees, windows, and buses (although Hill-Miller makes no reference to clocks striking). She links these elements to Woolf's lived experience in London and traces an intricate pattern of references to these images in the novel. In this same section, Hill-Miller asserts that Woolf has created a dichotomy between the inside and outside, designating the private house as a site of captivity and the public domain as a place of freedom and self-determination. When Septimus leaps out of the window into the open air of the street, he is defying the restrictive medical tyrannies of Dr. Holmes and Dr. Bradshaw. One of Hill-Miller's most emphatic readings is of Peter Walsh's inappropriateness as a mate for Clarissa. Hill-Miller provides a critique of his personality using the passage where, as he continues to finger his pocket knife, he stalks a young woman, fantasizing that she is sexually interested in him. With regard to Mrs. Dalloway's walk—and the walks of the other characters—Hill-Miller cites a variety of additional sources including David Daiches and Jean Moorcroft Wilson's work as well as Stuart N. Clarke's invaluable website. Those interested in following this thread might also want to read Andelys Wood's "Walking the Web in the Lost London of *Mrs. Dalloway*" in *Mosaic: A Journal for the Interdisciplinary Study of Literature* 36.2 (June 2003): 19-32.

In her chapter on *Orlando*, Hill-Miller deftly interweaves Woolf's and Vita Sackville-West's versions of Knole to craft an evocative and very beautiful impression of the vast, rambling building, its precious artifacts, and its lovely grounds. I felt, reading these intertwined narratives, a much greater affection and appreciation for a place which had to me seemed too huge and too austere to be truly beloved. This technique also fleshes out the setting of *Orlando* in ways that I had not previously imagined. And there are quirky details well worth noting. As Hill-Miller points out in this section, *To the Lighthouse* was published on the same day that Vita returned from Persia—and, as a homecoming gift, Woolf sent Vita a blank copy inscribed with the remark "In my opinion the best novel I have ever written." Hill-Miller also reminds us that Lady Sackville, Vita's mother, hated Virginia passionately. Not only did Lady Sackville buy up the entire Hogarth Press print run of Vita's poem *Sissinghurst* because it was dedicated to Virginia, she also "glued a newspaper photograph of Virginia inside the flyleaf of her own copy [of *Orlando*], and wrote beside it: 'The awful face of a mad woman whose successful mad desire is to separate people who care for each other. I loathe this woman for having changed my Vita and taken her away from me'" (176-177).

The chapter on *A Room of One's Own* (and *Three Guineas*) is particularly powerful and vivid. It brings into focus Woolf's lifelong ambivalence about universities and women's education, prizes and memberships. The chapter also revisits the historical contexts providing, for instance, information about the audience's reaction to Woolf's lecture, the accommodations at the women's colleges, and the luxuries of the men's colleges (including a seductive description of the paintings that Carrington did to decorate George "Dadie" Rylands's rooms, the place where a luncheon gathering which Woolf attended was transformed into her famous description of exquisite sole, delectable partridges and ever flowing wine). Hill-Miller also documents the mockery, contempt and even violent resistance that the advocates for women's access to the universities had to confront—behavior that Woolf integrates into *Three Guineas*, a work that Hill-Miller describes as "angry, resentful" (199)—but not without cause. When—in 1921—the University Senate finally voted that women at Cambridge could put "B.A." after their names:

> one elderly M.A. from Corpus Christi—the Reverend Pussy Hart, vicar of Ixworth—shouted to a mob of undergraduate men milling outside the Senate House, 'Now go and tell Newnham and Girton!' The mob surged, screaming, up Newnham Walk. When it reached the entrance to the college, someone found a coal cart, and the mob used it as a battering ram to smash down the Clough Memorial Gates. The principal of Newnham blocked the undergraduate men from entering the college and wreaking more havoc, but the damage had been done. (196)

Inevitably, the final chapter must focus on Woolf's struggle to maintain her equilibrium in a time of war. As Hill-Miller observes, *Between the Acts*, the novel which is the focal point of the chapter, "is the darkest and most violent of Virginia Woolf's novels. Yet, even *Between the Acts*...struggles toward and achieves an affirmative vision" (257). Because it is very much about Monk's House and Sussex, this chapter is also the affirming center of gravity for the reader for it focuses on the place where Woolf lived during one of the most productive periods of her life, the place where both Virginia and Leonard Woolf died and their ashes are buried, the place which (unlike Talland House, 22 Hyde Park Gate, 46 Gordon Square, or Asheham [now demolished]) is guaranteed to be an accessible and enduring remembrance of her life and work.

There are, of course, some tiny omissions and oddities. For example, although there is a walk to the new British Library near St. Pancras, there is no mention in that section that both Vanessa and Virginia were married at St. Pancras Registry. Ray Strachey is not referenced in a quotation from *A Room of One's Own* that is footnoted by Woolf as a passage from *The Cause*. Also, there is a slightly distracting paraphrasing technique, no doubt chosen to make reading smoother and less visually cluttered for common readers, in which Hill-Miller transcribes some passages virtually verbatim, footnoted but without quotation marks. These infinitesimal flaws are scarcely worth noting. Indeed, the book provides me with the rare and pleasant occasion to agree wholeheartedly with Nigel Nicolson who, on the book jacket, comments "I have read this book with enormous pleasure. It is accurate, original, tantalising, funny, useful and immensely enjoyable." For an ordinary reader unfamiliar with Woolf's life, work and environs, this book is truly a treasure trove of information—detailed and specific without being esoteric or overwhelming. For established Woolf scholars, it makes everything much, much easier. What could be more practical than a very sophisticated Baedeker guide dedicated to Virginia Woolf with carefully crafted directions that include not only the bus routes, tube stations, and train schedules and website addresses, but places to eat and estimated time of each phase of the expedition? To sum up, I suggest that you recommend the book to common readers who want to know more about Woolf, encourage your local library to acquire it, use it in your seminar course on Virginia Woolf, and keep a copy handy if you are planning to visit any (or all!) of the Woolf sites.

Vanessa Curtis's *Virginia Woolf's Women* (which includes a brief Foreword by Julia Briggs) provides biographical commentary regarding both Woolf and the women whose lives intersected with hers. The author, co-founder of the Virginia Woolf Society of Great Britain, has accessed some valuable archival materials including rare and interesting photographs as well as unpublished letters.

The project refracts Woolf's life from birth to death through the lens of the women who mattered most to her. These women range from immediate family to important female friends—Violet Dickinson, Ottoline Morrell, Katherine Mansfield, Dora Carrington, Vita Sackville-West and Ethel Smyth. Of the many biographical works on Woolf and her milieu, none take precisely this approach. Jane Dunn's *A Very Close Conspiracy*, Mary Ann Caws' *Women of Bloomsbury: Virginia, Vanessa, and Carrington*, Patricia Moran's *Word of Mouth: Body Language in Katherine Mansfield and Virginia Woolf* are narrower in scope while the much larger comprehensive biographies cannot be so selective in focus.

The introduction sketches out the themes that will be addressed. In the first few sentences of the book (a passage that is also quoted on the back of the dustjacket), Curtis observes that: "The women in [Woolf's] life gave her the stimulation, support, reassurance, and maternal care that Virginia, deprived of her mother at the age of thirteen, craved relentlessly. Women came to mean many different things to her, but even as writer of great eloquence, privileged enough to possess an army of words at her disposal, Woolf was unsure how to convey the importance of being a woman" (15).

In her concluding chapter, Curtis affirms that Woolf is often misinterpreted by "those who know little about Virginia Woolf other than from reading snippets of sensationalist reportage about her suicide and sexuality, or witnessing the tired portrayals in books and films of a 'mad' woman obsessed with suicide" (190-91). However, a glance at the index entries under "Woolf, Virginia" —listed in entirety below—suggests that Curtis, perhaps unintentionally, emphasizes Woolf's misfortunes, miseries, and failings: "Woolf, Virginia | & ageing, | attitudes to heterosexuality, | childlessness, | dealing with servants, | food refusal, | insecurity, | mental illness, | & music, | paintings of, | photographs of, | poor self-image, | sense of humour, | sexuality, | snobbery, | suicide attempts, | suicide" (224). Based on these recurrent themes, some readers may find Curtis's interpretation of Woolf's life too emphatically slanted toward pathology. For example, in her introduction, Curtis makes such claims as: "Very early on in life, Virginia came to realise that being ill was the only way of assuring Julia's, and later on, Leonard's, undivided attention." She also blames Woolf's eating disorders and aversion to food on Julia Stephen's influence: "As well as passing down a legacy that ensured that life would for many years still revolve around the ritualistic pull of the Victorian tea table, Julia and her claustrophobic household at 22 Hyde Park Gate imbued Virginia with lifelong eating distress" (17). Indeed, Curtis views 22 Hyde Park Gate as a site of trauma and reaffirms this viewpoint in her concluding chapter: "it is…astonishing that Virginia, formally uneducated, insecure and almost permanently in mourning during her teenage years, should have managed to fight back from such a difficult beginning; she not only survived life at Hyde Park Gate, but also was able to use it as an inspiration" (191).

The chapter on Vanessa offers Curtis's interpretative reading of several portraits of Virginia painted by her sister. Referring to Vanessa's 1912 painting of Virginia seated in a deckchair, Curtis comments that "The arms of the sitter are folded defensively, and if Vanessa had added features to Virginia's face, they would probably have been screwed-up with impatience and looking slightly confrontational" (74). In her concluding chapter, Curtis offers a similar analytic commentary on photographs of Virginia. For instance, referring to a photo taken just after the death of Woolf's half-sister Stella (the lower right image on the fourth page in the first section of photographs), Curtis comments:

> Skinny, hunched over and clad in black Victorian mourning dress, Virginia sits on a step at The Old Vicarage in Painswick, Gloucestershire. Two walking canes lie beneath her feet, suggesting that she was frail enough not to be able to walk unaided. Her eyes look up beseechingly towards the camera, imploring it not to take a photograph. Never did Virginia's later nickname of 'Sparroy' seem so terribly appropriate; in this mournfully sad photo, she resembles a fledgling that has fallen out of the nest away from its mother (indeed Virginia herself had been weaned too early from Julia)….Virginia, at age fifteen, was a sickly invalid. (194)

Even the caption to a delightful photograph of Virginia laughing as she watches her young nephew Julian Bell at play (facing 97) emphasizes the morbid: "this photograph was in fact taken during a period when she had suffered a less serious relapse of her 1904 breakdown." Yet, while she looks perhaps too often at the grimmer aspects of Woolf's life, Curtis definitely views Woolf as a survivor. As she states at the end of the book, Woolf "rose up into and maintained a position of great literary success, becoming more famous than any of her female friends and contemporaries. For this reason, whilst it is sometimes difficult to feel much warmth towards Virginia Woolf as a person (for, like most people, she could be cruel, dishonest and impatient), it is much more difficult not to respect her achievements" (191).

Scholars consulting this book should be aware that a peculiar indexing method effectively defeats any easy checking of sources (for example, Lucio Ruotolo's *The Interrupted Moment* is listed under his name but Eileen Barrett and Patricia Cramer's edited collection, *Virginia Woolf: Lesbian Readings* is referenced by the title, while Jane Lilienfeld—who contributed to this collection the article on Woolf and Violet Dickinson that Curtis references [94]—is not acknowledged). However, the book offers both common readers and Woolf scholars an innovative perspective on Woolf and the women in her life as well as access to some fresh and intriguing archival material.

—Vara Neverow, *Southern Connecticut State University*

Before Bloomsbury: The 1890's Diaries of Three Kensington Ladies: Margaret Lushington, Stella Duckworth and Mildred Massingberd
Ed. Anthony Curtis. (London: The Eighteen Nineties Society, 2003) 99 pp.

Anne Thackerary Ritchie gave us *Old Kensington* (1873), biographies of Leslie Stephen and Virginia Woolf, as well as Virginia's diaries and letters, give us some sense of the Kensington she grew up in, but here in short compass is the texture of that world as portrayed in the diaries of three young women. This is the Kensington in which the Stephen children were nurtured; these the elder sisters who might serve as their mentors or models, this the Kensington they left behind and repudiated.

Curtis' presentation makes life easy for the reader. He introduces us to the time and place of each diary item, sets forth the item itself, and supplies the necessary notes on persons, places, and things. He knows the Kensington world well, its dramatis personae and characteristic scenes, and writes of them in a style unpretentious and graceful. In addition he has supplied a set of photographs—portraits and family groups, including a Talland House scene of Virginia and Vanessa doing a theatrical with Walter Headlam and Jack Hills (hitherto unpublished).

Vernon and Julia Lushington had three daughters, Kitty, Margaret, and Susan, all educated at home or by a tutor (one being George Gissing), literate in French and the classics (in translation); they were all excellent musicians on a variety of instruments, music being the one vocation, as Curtis observes, then suitable for young ladies. They lived at 36 Kensington Square, the Massingberds at number 43, and the Stephens nearby at 22 Hyde Park Gate. Each family had a country house, the Lushingtons at Pyports in Surrey; the Massingberds, Gunby Hall in Lincolnshire, and the Stephens, farther off at Talland House, St Ives. The diaries tell of their goings and comings; how they were all constantly in and out of each others' houses (both town and country). Closest to the Stephen family were the Lushingtons, whose mother Jane had been a close friend of Julia Stephen, who nursed her in her final illness and took a lively interest in the daughters, especially Kitty. The daughters were of an age with George, Gerald, and Stella Duckworth; Gerald in fact was best man at Margaret's wedding to Stephen Massingberd, at which the young Ralph Vaughan Williams was organist. They went to Bayreuth together; at Georgie's urging they saw Ibsen's *A Doll's House* (Stella thought it "raving mad") and Elizabeth Robins in *The Master Builder* (Margaret thought it "too much," preferring the farce *Charlie's Aunt*); Verdi's *Otello* was "too ghastly for words, but very powerful." There were parties (Gerald's birthday), dinners with Julia Stephen, music concerts, family music (playing through *Lohengrin* at Talland House where there must have been a piano), plus hours of practice on the cello (Margaret), the violin (Sue), the piano, (Kitty). Some of the days were busy indeed; Mildred speaks of attending the National Gallery for an hour, changing her clothes, having tea before a lecture on Purcell, and scurrying off in the rain to dine at the Pioneer Club and hear Bernard Shaw lecture on music.

The diaries also throw light on events in the lives of the Duckworth and Stephen children. George is reported to be busy trying to find a job for Stephen on the eve of his wedding. Margaret's devotion to "dear Stella" and her mother, Julia, is a recurrent theme, and her diary provides us with new detail about Julia's death and its aftermath. Curtis prints two letters (hitherto unpublished), one from Leslie Stephen to Kitty after Julia's death, the other from Vanessa to Kitty after

Leslie's death. The latter is notable as it reveals Vanessa's affection and dependence on Kitty, and even more so, for what she says of her father is more positive than anything elsewhere recorded: "Even if one got irritated or cross it didn't matter and he gave a sort of balance and naturalness to it. I feel the greatness of his mind in ordinary life..."

This passage comes in Part II "After Years," when the Lushingtons gave up writing diaries; in this section, Curtis fills out the three lives in the years at the end of the 19th and in the early 20th century. Prominent is his attention to Kitty, whom he admires, her life and troubled connection with the Stephens. Drawing on her letters and diaries, Curtis gives us a detailed account of Virginia's ambivalent feelings about Kitty including remorse at snubbing her at a funeral in 1916. What seems to have happened is that when Kitty married Leo Maxse, she adopted his views on the tariff and imperialism and talked his politics, though, as Virginia noted, occasionally she slipped into being the attractive Kitty of past years. But the break was sharp: she disapproved of Bloomsbury and Bloomsbury of her. Even her supplying coals to the Woolf family during the Great War failed to soften their hearts. Yet Kitty haunted Virginia's imagination enough to become the source of Clarissa Dalloway's love of parties, nuances of Jinny in *The Waves*, and Kitty Lasswade's youth in *The Years*. Her diary response to the news of Kitty's death is poignant indeed.

As I have said above, this little book gives us the very texture of the lives of young women in the meritocracy at the turn of the century. There are links with the Darwins, games and walks and romance at Talland House, music and housing for soldiers in the Great War, bicycling (which liberated young women to go about on their own). Some of the stories are familiar, but are now told from the point of view of those who were there. Readers will not find any theory here, but a theorist may find grist for the mill, and certainly anyone interested in social history will find much to enjoy and note. Curtis supplies family trees, documentation, but no index. One's only real regret is that he did not give us more.

—John Bicknell

Modernist Women and Visual Cultures: Virginia Woolf, Vanessa Bell, Photography and Cinema. Maggie Humm (New Brunswick, New Jersey,: Rutgers UP, 2003) xii + 244 pp.

Why are literary critics attracted to certain topics, periods, and approaches and not to others? I pondered this question when I wrote *The Sisters' Arts: The Writing and Painting of Virginia Woolf and Vanessa Bell* (1988). Only in the dedication of the book to my own sister, a visual artist, did I reflect part of my motivation for examining the relationships between visual and verbal media, and between the collaboration and competition of sisters who practiced them. Women scholars are increasingly candid about their impulses to think through their personal and family histories. Diana C. Archibald, for example, accounts for her interest in *Domesticity, Imperialism, and Emigration in the Victorian Novel* (2002) in her Preface: "As the story goes, my great-great-grandmother was a mail-order bride" (ix). She is "the quintessential emigrant woman," whose short life suggested to her great-great-granddaughter a study of relationships between Victorian "heterosexist gender constructions" and the literature of emigration (x-xi). Similarly, Bonnie Kime Scott dedicates *Refiguring Modernism: The Women of 1928* (1995) in part to "Bhima." In her Introduction, Scott links this mysterious "lost grandmother" (whose watercolor paintings, photos, "flapper jewelry and scrapbooks" she has inherited) with the generation of women she studies (xli). Maggie Humm chooses the end of *Modernist Women and Visual Cultures* to reveal the connection between photo-induced memories of her mother, who "died aged forty-nine when I was thirteen, the same ages as Julia Stephen and Virginia Woolf at Julia's death," and her scholarship, "an obvious example of a need to acknowledge and move beyond the quintessential primary loss we all experience: the death or the disappearance of the mother" (223-4).

Do those of us who recognize a personal involvement in the material we study try especially hard to build strong cases for our conclusions, so as to avoid charges of subjective distortion? In spite of theoretical shifts from inviolable texts and artifacts to the varying perceptions of readers and viewers, I suspect we do. Humm marshals considerable evidence for "Woolf's obsession with the memory of her mother" (10), some from domestic photographs, gathered in album collections with pictures of Julia Stephen and of both parents mounted as "significant frontispieces" (19). In this gendered context, Humm also looks at Woolf's use of photographic techniques in a series of short, snapshot-like "Portraits," and at her photographic references and parallels both in *Three Guineas* and in her definitive essays on modernism. To outline her cultural studies and postmodern orientations to such varied materials, Humm makes abundant reference to psychoanalytic and feminist theories, to histories and definitions of both literary and visual modernisms (including useful detail about equipment and technologies), and to most of her relevant predecessors in literary critical studies and biographies (although there are a few surprising omissions, including Gevirtz's book on Dorothy Richardson and film). Primarily, though, Humm grounds her approach in the feminist, post-Lacanian, psychoanalytical theories of contemporary artist Bracha Lichtenberg Ettinger (4,7) who, with her "metaphor of the matrixial gaze"—defined in part as "self-reflexive gendered memories"—transforms "domestic photography into a palimpsest source of the maternal" and a revealing source of "feminine subjectivity" (8-9, 13). The advantage, or perhaps danger, of such an approach is that Woolf's maternal preoccupations need not be demonstrably conscious. Humm only need assume that the unconscious obsession is inadvertently, or inevitably, revealed in, for instance, the series of "'comfy chair' photographs" taken at Monk's House that, Humm says, evoke the primal photo of Woolf's parents sitting in the library at St. Ives (81). This assumption excludes other explanations for the chairs, like their mere convenience, or ubiquity. Even if the later photos do evoke the parental one, there are striking differences, like the visual interest in some of the photos (e.g. Humm's figure 13) of chair covers in Vanessa Bell's lively "Abstract" fabric, which creates a strong contrast with, even a rebellion against, the dark, plush, Victorian furniture of the parental photo.

Although four of Humm's seven chapter titles announce a focus on Virginia Woolf and photography, this book is not just about her or about that medium. The subtitle specifically adds Woolf's sister as well as cinema to the mix. Virginia Woolf and Vanessa Bell, Humm observes, were among "the first generation of women to be active photographers and cinema-goers from childhood" (18). Yet only one chapter, albeit a substantial one, is on Vanessa Bell. Two of the seven chapters—oddly bisecting those on photography—focus on cinema. Chapter 4 provides a brief overview of cinema and film theory in relation to modernism and then turns to specific film societies, journals (including the treatment of Black identities in *Borderline* and *Close Up*), and the "cinema masculinity" of prominent editors and directors. Chapter 5, however, reveals "how modernity's technologies did not necessarily force women into the mechanical, masculine critical rhetoric" that privileged avant-garde films and denigrated popular cinema and audiences of women and children (157). Here Humm introduces other female modernist figures, including Colette, Janet Flanner, Adrienne Monnier, H.D. (Hilda Doolittle), Bryher, Dorothy Richardson, Gertrude Stein and again, at the end, Virginia Woolf, all of whom wrote about the cinema from women's perspectives and tried to break down hierarchical barriers between types of films and audiences.

These imbalances in the book between Woolf and other modernist women, as well as between photography and cinema, seem, at least in part, products of Humm's attempt to pull together previous publications into a unified argument. Although many authors of book-length studies publish two or three portions first, five of Humm's seven chapters are substantially versions of articles published elsewhere. The result is less a coherent book than another valid type of publication for a senior scholar: a collection of related and provocative essays. Humm does have an overriding idea: "in their cinema writing and domestic photography, modernist women explore gender issues in a perhaps freer way than in their better-known work; and the book asks what such an exploration can tell us about gender and modernism" (4). The answer holds few surprises. Although repeatedly emphasizing her suspicion of overly neat gender binaries, Humm finds that Woolf and the other modernist women she discusses not only are more autobiographical and more focused on the everyday than their male counterparts, but also are more in touch with their emotions and more interested in common readers and viewers. The real value of the book lies in Humm's selection and scrutiny of artifacts and texts marginalized in many studies of modernism. Perhaps it is even appropriate for a study dealing in part with the fragmentary nature of snapshots arranged in albums, or of cinematic montage, to have some of that quality itself. Still, in part because of the large territory this book tries to encompass, and in spite of insightful comparisons that link some of the chapters, there is abundant room for more links and transitions, especially between the chapters on photography and those on cinema, but elsewhere as well. On the whole, though, I am stimulated less into a judgmental response than into what I hope is productive dialogue.

Humm's scattered references to color provide one example of missing links. Although other scholars she cites (including me), have established Woolf's fascination with both photography and painting, none of us (including Humm) deals with the relationship between the black-and-white nature of Woolf's photographic medium and, not just the ability of words to evoke colors, but the actual visual surface of her verbal medium, what she calls in "Pictures" (1925) a writer's starvation "diet of thin black print" (*E*4 245). Gisèle Freund photographed Woolf in color in the late 1930s (Humm 54), but for most of Woolf's life photography meant shades of black and white. It was painting, not photography, that she associated with color. "A still life painting of red-hot pokers," Woolf continues in "Pictures," in contrast to black print, is to writers "what a beefsteak is to an invalid—an orgy of blood and nourishment [...] We nestle into its colour, feed and fill ourselves with yellow and red and gold, till we drop off, nourished and content" (*E*4 245), as Woolf metaphor segues to color as mother's milk. In her introduction, Humm mentions Woolf's early descriptive piece "Blue and Green" (1921) in the context of G. E. Moore's recognition of the differences between variable subjective perceptions of color and what society defines as "blue" (3), but she does not deal with the piece as one of Woolf's early attempts to rival the painter's palette. However difficult to achieve, Woolf wrote later in Walter Sickert (1934), "all great writers are great colourists" (*CE2* 241). Yet Humm could have argued for a different kind of compatibility—as great as that between painting and writing—between black-and-white photography and writing, in that both require a more contemplative viewer or reader, one who must collaborate with photographer or writer to evoke color. Indeed, as Humm notes, Dorothy Richardson makes that point about the superiority of silent to sound films. Appropriately, therefore, Humm mentions color again in her treatment of women writers on the cinema (chapter 5). Women contributors to the film journal *Close Up*, she writes, "intially refused to be swayed [, not only by the addition of sound, but also] by the attractions of colour film, unlike [male] modernist photographers, who responded much more enthusiastically" (159). Here Humm associates color with masculinity. This is the only time, though, that she deals with possible gender implications of color, or lack thereof. The contrast between black-and-white and color media is usually conspicuous by its absence in, for instance, Humm's reference to Woolf's fascination with the 1927 eclipse (2), but not to her description of it, in "The Sun and the Fish" (1928), as a contrast between color and colorlessness. Another instance is Humm's discussion of Woolf's short verbal sketches known as "Portraits." Each slight "portrait" is like a (black-and-white?) photograph, Humm suggests, that defines a gendered gaze. Yet, not only do the sketches involve sounds and smells, as she admits, but the "visual surface" that she considers more important than appeals to the other senses also includes unacknowledged references to color—"grey-blue clouds," a "yellow and red" face, "yellowed" teeth, "rose red brick" (*CSF* 242-5). Can Woolf's black-and-white printed words evoke, for a collaborating reader, subjective experiences of colors? Do black-and-white photos of Woolf's parents or her mother evoke matrixial memories that, in her autobiographical sketches and fictional portraits, include color? Might the Woolfs even have used for their photo albums the French artists' sketch books with "Woolf's experimental coloured endpapers" (Humm 86) to encourage, by contrast to the black-and-white photos, such viewer participation?

Another example of provocative missing links is Humm's quotation, curiously without comment, in chapter 2, of Woolf's remarks to Vanessa (in 1928) about the photographs of Angelica for *Orlando*. "I'm showing them to Vita, who doesn't want to be accused of raping the under age. My God—I shall rape Angelica one of these days" (50). This kind of ribald joking between sisters, not unusual in their letters, raises issues of gender and sexual preference as well as of relationships between adults and children. When Woolf wrote this letter (*L3* 497), her niece was ten years old. As an adult, Angelica uses photographs to help her remember herself at age five: "In photographs of the time I am grave, round-eyed and healthy, held by a smiling Nellie or a Madonna-like Vanessa, whose long straight fingers are too apt to find their way into every crevice of my body" (*Deceived* 42). Humm might helpfully have connected such comments not only about, but also by, Angelica with the generally excellent chapter 3 discussion of "the tension [...] between eroticism and innocence" in Vanessa Bell's photographs, unusual for the time, of her naked children (115). Quentin Bell convincingly claims that these photos are natural and innocent, and that they often evoked to Vanessa "that time-honoured but still fascinating theme, the putto" which she used occasionally in her painting but more often in her decorative art (10). Most of the pictures, Humm agrees, show Vanessa's naked children, "comfortable in her world" (120) and unidealized, "even if the sheer saturation of their bodies moves in another direction" (123). Humm includes a few photos, however, that Quentin Bell and Angelica Garnett omitted from *Vanessa Bell's Family Album* (1981). To my knowledge, these photos have not been published before. One, in Humm's words, "taken from the rear, [is] of the naked Julian alone spread-eagled across the French windows at Asheham" (115), and one is of Judith Bagenal "lying [naked and] stretched out on her side on top of a short wall, her arm obscuring her face" (117). Although we also could view the latter as a version of the traditional odalisque, both children, as Humm convincingly argues, are artificially posed, distanced because of their hidden faces, and thus erotically objectified in ways that seem to me related to Woolf's joking comment in chapter 2 and thus to a tension between autonomous children's bodies and a proprietary adult attitude towards them.

Although she persuades us that some of the photographs of Vanessa's children are erotic objectifications, Humm maintains that "modernist women's private obsession with photography might represent an attempt to explore forms of representation outside the objectifications of masculine modernism" (5). This seeming contradiction raises questions about the degree of Vanessa Bell's feminine modernism or else about the motives of others in her household who might have been taking pictures. Humm does indicate that some of the photographs in Vanessa's collection are by the Woolfs, some by friends or acquaintances. Vanessa, for instance, is in a number of photographs she obviously could not have taken herself, as both Quentin Bell and Humm note. Yet, about one of Vanessa with a child on her lap, in the tradition of "madonna iconography of Renaissance painting," Humm asks, "Why did she need to represent herself as a madonna so frequently?" (108). If Vanessa were in charge even when she did not hold the camera, then perhaps the pose is an attempt to rival photos of her mother and to create matrixial memories for her own children. Given the fact that many of her friends were artistic men, however, isn't it also possible that one of them posed Vanessa and child as well as snapped their picture? Quentin Bell and Angelica Garnett indeed caption such a picture of Clive Bell and Vanessa holding the toddler Quentin at Asheham by saying "The pose suggests someone who knew and was in sympathy with the great Italians—Roger Fry very likely although it could have been Duncan Grant who already played a large part in the life of the Bells" (32). Yet, although Humm mentions him, without comment, as a recipient of some of Bell's photographs of her children, as a photographic subject, and a few times as an artist, she mostly excludes him, even from decorative projects like the Music Room at the Lefevre Galleries, the Queen Mary decorations, and the dinner set for Kenneth Clark (112)—all, in fact, Grant and Bell collaborations. I have argued in the past against the tendency automatically to *cherchez l'homme* in accounting for women's aesthetics, but this is more a case of accuracy than of influence. Roger Fry and his aesthetic theories get more attention. He may have dismissed photographs as art, but he edited with Woolf a volume of Julia Margaret Cameron's photographs, as Humm notes. She does not note that he also took snapshots. Caws and Wright, for instance, credit Fry with two (270, 309) and Lytton Strachey, another frequent guest of Vanessa's and Virginia's, with at least a half dozen (11, 32, 38, 41, 135, 203).

In chapter 2, in connection with Virginia Woolf's photo albums, Humm does a better job of dealing with male involvement. "Together with Leonard," she writes, Virginia "took, developed and preserved photographs in albums. Photography was a continuous part of the Woolfs' lives even if their photographic albums do not tell a coherent life story" (40). She even says, "it seems that the albums are a joint endeavour" between husband and wife. Still, two sentences later, it is "Woolf's [singular possessive] album-making" that "mirrors her aesthetics" (41). More than once "the Woolfs' albums" become "Woolf's albums" (e.g. 54). Humm contrasts the "documentary photographs" taken during Leonard's tenure as a colonial administrator in Ceylon (included in the first album) and the photographs of his family (loose in a box) with Virginia's selection and inclusion in the album of photographs from her "family past" (55). It might run against an all-too-common stereotype to treat Leonard as a man who shared some of the feminine attributes Humm ascribes to Virginia's photography and album keeping, not to mention being difficult in a book devoted to women modernists, but it would have been appropriate given the repeated demurrals in the book about oversimplified gender oppositions.

Do these "anti-chronological" (Humm 44) albums from Monk's House exist today just as Virginia, and later Leonard Woolf, left them? How secure are we in drawing conclusions, as Humm does, about Virginia Woolf and the albums based on the arrangements of photographs? These questions bothered me when I looked at the collection over a decade ago, and I wish this book addressed them. Humm writes that, in the Harvard Theatre Library, there are "seven albums, [...] together with four boxes containing over two hundred additional loose photographs" (40). George Spater and Ian Parsons, in their acknowledgments for *The Marriage of True Minds* (1977), indicate their good fortune "in being allowed to make full use of the photographs in the five Monks House albums now in the possession of Mrs Parsons" (x). When they pulled photographs for their book, and when Leonard Woolf chose photos for his autobiography, did they put them back in their exact places in the albums? Are some of them now among the loose photos in the boxes? How many other hands, I wonder, have tinkered with this uncatalogued collection in the more than sixty years since Virginia Woolf's death?

The layout of the book contributes to, or perhaps underscores, its somewhat fragmentary quality. The photo of the young Virginia Stephen on the cover has "ROUGH PROOF PLEASE RETURN" stamped diagonally beneath her chin. Until I read the cover credit on the back, I thought the stamp applied to some pre-publication, penultimate draft of the Rutgers paperback edition. Next, the text on each page is isolated by a linear black frame, and bulleted headings in bold black caps separate each chapter into a number of short sections. The page and figure numbers as well as picture titles appear in white print, enclosed within black boxes. These typographical and layout features, combined with the odd size (7 ½ x 9 3/4"), 45 illustrations, glossy paper, and wide margins, made me think I was looking more at a coffee-table book than at a scholarly study. The text, however, belied these first impressions, and Rutgers should be complimented at least on its willingness to include so many illustrations in a scholarly study.

Reading Humm's book may be something of a scramble, one that leaves plenty of room for raising questions and for positing further connections and qualifications. It is far easier, though, for me to wish for more than it was for Humm to gather together all that is already here. On the whole, she has written an ambitious and intellectually invigorating study, well worth reading.

—Diane F. Gillespie (Emeritus), *Washington State University*

Works Cited

Archibald, Diana C. *Domesticity, Imperialism, and Emigration in the Victorian Novel*. Columbia: U of Missouri P, 2002.

Bell, Quentin and Angelica Garnett. *Vanessa Bell's Family Album*. London: Jill Norman & Hobhouse Ltd., 1981.

Caws, Mary Ann and Sarah Bird Wright. *Bloomsbury and France: Art and Friends*. NY and Oxford: Oxford UP, 2000.

Garnett, Angelica. *Deceived with Kindness: A Bloomsbury Childhood*. London: Chatto & Windus/The Hogarth Press, 1984.

Gevirtz, Susan. *Narrative's Journey: The Fiction and Film Writing of Dorothy Richardson*. New York: Peter Lang, 1996.

Gillespie, Diane F. "'Her Kodak Pointed at His Head': Virginia Woolf and Photography." *The Multiple Muses of Virginia Woolf*. Ed. Diane F. Gillespie. Columbia: U of Missouri P, 1993. 113-147.

Gillespie, Diane Filby. *The Sisters' Arts: The Writing and Painting of Virginia Woolf and Vanessa Bell*. Syracuse: Syracuse UP, 1988.

Scott, Bonnie Kime. *Refiguring Modernism: The Women of 1928*. Vol. 1. Bloomington: Indiana UP, 1995.

Spater, George and Ian Parsons. *A Marriage of True Minds: An Intimate Portrait of Leonard and Virginia Woolf*. New York: Harcourt Brace Jovanovich, 1977.

Woolf, Leonard. *An Autobiography*. 5 vols. New York: Harcourt Brace Jovanovich, 1961-69.

A War of Individuals: Bloomsbury Attitudes to the Great War
Jonathan Atkin (Manchester: Manchester UP, 2002) iv + 250

The conception of this interesting but curiously constructed book seems out of sorts with its execution. It lays at the heart of a complicated matrix of largely forgotten World War I-era pacifist organizations the conscientious objection of numerous British individuals. That allows the author, in one chapter, to consider "Bloomsbury" too broadly defined and with odd blind spots and omissions. However, once one gets over the false advertising in the subtitle, one finds the book has something worth saying and does constitute a sense of comprehensiveness in spite of exceptions. The core premise of the book, like the warrant of a conscientious objector's argument, depends on *individuality*, "the notion of a person standing apart from the war and feeling an aesthetic or humanistic reaction against it" (4). The book has either few scholarly antecedents it chooses to acknowledge or limits itself to few sources not actually written by its many individual subjects. Atkin certainly read Martin Ceadel's *Pacifism in Britain 1914-1945: The Defining of a Faith* (Oxford, 1980) and Claire Tylee's *The Great War and Women's Consciousness* (London, 1990), which are frequently cited. The theme of individualism becomes a current that travels through several engaging chapters, although numbers 7 ("Obscurer individuals and their themes of response") and 8 ("Three [more] individuals") waste the momentum of the book proper, or the first six chapters. A bookseller and journalist in Manchester, the author constructs a credible sense of the milieu for anti-war reaction between August 1914 and November 1918 to "show for the first time that it existed through a far more widespread variety of individual experience than was generally assumed to be the case" (5).

"'Recognized' forms of opposition." This first short chapter sketches a context in the incidence of conscientious objection during those years—in four thousand young men of service age who were referred to the Pelham Committee by local tribunals, mostly for religious objections, although 240 of them gave no church affiliation with their personal reasons for refusing military and sometimes non-military service. We are introduced to the No Conscription Fellowship, an organization linked, in 1915, with religious anti-war factions such as the Fellowship of Reconciliation, the Young Men's Service Committee of the Society of Friends, the Stop the War Committee, and the National Council Against Conscription, which, after the Military Service Act of 1916, "threw their weight behind [individual] cases" (12). We make the acquaintance of leaders such as NCF chair Clifford Allen and Quaker John W. Graham, as well as COs such as Howard Marten, who put in prison-time and forced-labor in work camps for his beliefs.

"Bloomsbury"?—only generally speaking. This chapter is about how moral and aesthetic philosophy at Cambridge (with greater emphasis than usual on Goldsworthy Lowes Dickinson and Bertrand Russell, with G. E. Moore underplayed) influenced a handful of students who went on to significant fame, some of them as members of the so-called Bloomsbury Group or as associates of a sympathetic couple, Lady Ottoline Morrell and her husband Philip, at Garsington Manor in Oxfordshire. The connection between Dickinson, Roger Fry, and E. M. Forster (Dickinson's biographer) makes "Bloomsbury" the agitation Dickinson made for peace with the Bryce Group, the Society for a Durable Peace, and the League of Nations Society (later the League of Nations Union), though an easier way to do so would be through Leonard Woolf and the Webbs, the Rowntrees, and Quaker conferences. But Leonard is reserved for two paragraphs in the fourth chapter, as if a disciple of G. B. Shaw, which he was not. Even the connection between Margaret Llewelyn Davies, the Women's Co-operative Guild, and Bloomsbury is made through Virginia Woolf, rather than Leonard, in spite of his being the chief link and Virginia's being convalescent at the time. The explanation must be that Atkin does not know better. This book is no match, either, for Michael Holroyd's entertaining account of the recurrent episodes that Lytton and James Strachey had with the tribunals. But it does come through clearly that Bloomsbury was not unanimous on the war. Several of the men supported it at first (Clive Bell and Adrian Stephen, for example) until it began to go badly. Leonard Woolf was granted exemption from service for his nervous tremor, enabling him to care for his wife during her wartime mental breakdown. However, by far the most fascinating case in point is Maynard Keynes's fretful drafting of an application for CO status that he might not have sent, being exempted by the Treasury "above his head" (23). In resisting pressure from David Garnett and Lytton Strachey to resign his post in the government in protest of the war, Keynes has given his apologists to argue that he could give aid to his friends "from within" (24), a service Philip Morrell was able to perform as a character witness at the Hampstead Tribunal and then, with his wife, by turning his country estate into a "pilgrim's rest for individuals seeking escape from the war" (42).

"Academics at war—Bertrand Russell and Cambridge," the third chapter, seems somewhat displaced. Russell had a prominent early spot in the Bloomsbury chapter but, deemed "central to this book" (52), his actions in defiance of university and government authority were featured in a pivotal place. This exclusive focus may contradict the view that the stand taken by every individual in the anti-war movement was significant, since some individuals (e.g. Russell) will seem more significant than others. However, because of Russell's reputation as a major philosopher-mathematician and because of his zealous campaign to publicize his objections to the war effort, a chapter devoted to his case might sustain interest. And this one certainly does that. Important connections are missed between Russell, Norman Angell, and the Union of Democratic Control with Leonard Woolf, Dickinson, and others, as in the preceding and following chapter, yet the attention here to Russell's activities is simplified without being simplistic. Because Ottoline Morrell was his lover, of course, their correspondence is used to fill the narrative spaces between his speeches and writings between 1914 and his ostracism and dismissal by the Cambridge dons in 1916, scarcely to add his detention in 1918 and his resignation as an executive member of the No Conscription Fellowship. It is, above all, interesting that Russell was offered favorable treatment because of his useful knowledge of mathematics and, unlike Keynes, didn't take it.

"Writers at war" is not about war poets but about major writers whose misgivings about the war were sometimes pronounced in the form of public action. "Russell and the Bloomsbury circle" (77), Lowes Dickinson, Forster, and ruralist writer Edward Carpenter are cited by way of introducing contemporary writers' objection to the war's destruction of environment, both physical and psychological, as the Woolfs serve as example. The catalogue of major novelists includes Henry James, Arnold Bennett, Thomas Hardy, John Masefield, John Galsworthy, H. G. Wells, and D. H. Lawrence (obviously in reaction to Bloomsbury). But the chapter is devoted to George Bernard Shaw's anti-war projects in the name of Fabian Socialism somehow without the prolific involvement of Beatrice and Sidney Webb. (Here, at least, Patricia Pugh's *Educate, Agitate, Organize: 100 Years of Fabian Socialism* [London, 1984] might have helped.) Shaw's eight-page supplement of the *New Statesman*, "Common Sense About the War" (14 Nov. 1915), is presented as the antecedent to Leonard Woolf's book *International Government: Two Reports* (1916); and this is partly true, for Woolf wrote those reports, and co-authored a third (called "Articles Suggested for Adoption by an International Conference at the Termination of the Present War"), but in *collaboration* with Sidney Webb for the Fabian research department and for publication (true enough) as a *New Statesman* supplement. Shaw's office in the hierarchy of the Fabian Society and in the directorship of the journal made it convenient for him, in his enthusiasm, to send proofs to his publisher in New York, attaching an introduction of his own to Woolf's work without permission or pleasure from the author. Inadvertently, it seems, Atkin perpetuates Shaw's patronage (patronizing?) and may increase the irritation of historians, who will find no reference to the Webbs in the index or elsewhere in *A War of Individuals*.

"Writers in uniform" and "Women and the war" are complementary chapters that begin the drift and slide away from Bloomsbury altogether in subsequent pages. The tale is familiar: the young men who went to the war (Ivor Gurney, Siegfried Sassoon, Wilfred Owen, Richard Aldington, Isaac Rosenberg, Gerald Brenan, Edmund Blunden) find their subject but also that the war "blunts" or "blurs" their capacity to write about it. (You will find Rupert Brooke in the Bloomsbury and "Obscurer individuals" chapters, in company with Virginia Woolf and Lady Ottoline and the lamenting Monk Gibbon.) Robert Graves is the antipode for "smothering over his oscillating private reactions to the war" (118) by devotion to military regimen. A "pacifist in thought," he nevertheless counseled against "see[ing] too much" because, as he wrote Sassoon, "The only trouble is you're too sane[,] which is as great a crime as being dotty and much more difficult to deal with. That's the meaning of the anti-war complex" (119). Conversely, half of the leading women of the suffragist movement at home were opposed to war (131). Set brilliantly in the context of the London convention of the International Women's Suffrage Alliance, which began on the same day the war did, the women's perspective includes case histories of those whose activities were often affiliated with sister organizations with pacifist leanings such as the Women's Co-operative Guild or Quaker organizations such as the NCF (detailed in chapters 1 and 3). We brush up against Bloomsbury and Cambridge (and Dickinson and Russell) via Newnham College graduates Frances Partridge and Helen Wedgwood. After that, individual experiences surveyed are those of Sarah Macnaughton (*A Woman's Diary of the War*, 1914), Olive Dent (*A VAD in France*, 1917), Evadne Price (*Not So Quiet—Stepdaughters of War*, 1930), Mary Borden (*The Forbidden Zone*, 1929), Maude Onions (*A Woman at War*, 1929), Vera Brittain (*Chronicle of Youth—War Diary 1913-17*), Enid Bagnold (*Diary Without Dates*, 1918), and Mabel St. Clair Stobart (*A Flaming Sword in Serbia and Elsewhere,* 1916). Much as the men in uniform found to be true to their own unhappy experience, Atkin observes, quoting Stobart but going on to invoke a strategy promoted by Russell: "It was important that a woman both could and should...'go forth and see for herself the dangers that threaten life,' in order [to...] convey these dangers to others and [...] to channel destructive energies away from the battlefield towards more moral and social purposes" (160).

This book, unfortunately, does not stop, as it should, at such a good turn, leaving the "obscurer" folk (Stephen Graham, H. L. Currall, W. B. Kitching, Norman Cliff, J. E. Crombie, Charles Douie, Patrick MacGill, Wyn Griffith, William and A. V. Ratcliffe, C. G. Raven, George Kaufman, C. B. Purdom, E. G. Venning, Stephen Hewett, Stephen Winsten, Monk Gibbon, William Bell, Stephen McKenna, G. B. Manwaring, George Baker, R. H. Kiernan, Alan McDougall, H. S. Innes, E. H. Keeling, and D. H. Calcutt) dangling on a limb. This is a 45-page run up to Gilbert Cannan on the "herd instinct" in wartime, a reprise appearance of Shaw's *New Statesman* supplement of 1914, and an article in the *Nation* on "soldier minds" (221). This chapter of "Public commentary on [by now] familiar themes" is the end of a long figurative tail on an interesting animal, but the book is tired. A short chapter, called (unimaginatively) "Conclusion" calls attention to Bloomsbury for the first time, substantially, since chapter 4. Metaphors are mixed in what should be a moving final thought: "This book has attempted to put a mirror to the soul of the war as it triggered responses within men and women possessed of certain aesthetic, moral, or human sensibilities and thus capture something of the nature, cause and effect of the personal tragedies reflected therein" (231). Wars have souls? Souls have triggers? The Annie Oakley sharp-shooter analogy is too clever by half and misses the mark. This reviewer thinks that the individuals, "possessed" as Atkin says, constitute the mirror. He should say what he means.

—Wayne Chapman, *Clemson University*

The International Theory of Leonard Woolf: A Study in Twentieth-Century Idealism. Peter Wilson (London and New York: Palgrave Macmillan, 2003) xiv + 269.

Peter Wilson has taken on the daunting task of dealing with the enormous body of literature written by Leonard Woolf, who wrote at least two dozen books, numerous pamphlets, and hundreds of articles for various publications, including *The Nation, The Athenaeum, The Nation & Athenaeum, The New Statesman, War and Peace, The International Review, The Contemporary Review, The Political Quarterly*, and other periodicals and newspapers, not to mention the large number of reports and memos that he wrote for the Fabian Society's International and Colonial Bureaux, the Labour Party Advisory Committee on International Questions, and the Labour Party Advisory Committee on Imperial Questions. As the title of Wilson's book indicates, it focuses narrowly on Woolf's international theory and its place within twentieth-century idealist political literature. According to Wilson, not all modern political theorists of international relations can agree on a definition of "idealism"; nevertheless, the term has the following characteristics: a belief in progress, the use of reason to "overcome the problem of war" (12), the belief "that the scientific study of international relations has a large role to play in the prevention of war and the construction of a more peaceful world order" (13), and "that free trade will lead to peace" (14). Idealism in this sense and an examination of Woolf's political thought in light of the re-examination of E. H. Carr's *The Twenty Year's Crisis*, the seminal critique of post-World War I idealism, provide the rationale for *The International Theory of Leonard Woolf*. Carr and Woolf were contemporaries who disagreed on the viability of the League of Nations.

Although Wilson rightly acknowledges some of the achievements of Leonard Woolf—including the importance of *International Government* (1916) and *Empire and Commerce in Africa* (1920) in shaping political debate on a modern collective security organization (the League of Nations) and British colonial policies; Woolf's influence on British foreign policy by working with the Fabians and the Labour Party; his importance as a publicist for liberal policies through his many publications; and his success as a novelist, writer, editor, publisher, and businessman—*The International Theory of Leonard Woolf* is a flawed study. Leonard Woolf was not a political theorist, nor did he aspire to be one, so the body of his published work does not lend itself to examination as a collection of political theories on international government, colonial policies, or economic international and domestic policies.

Even though noting that Woolf wrote for a variety of literate audiences, Wilson does not take into account how this shapes the subject, tone, and terms of debate that Woolf uses in books such as *Quack, Quack!* (1937) and articles such as those published in *The Political Quarterly* (e.g., "From Sarajevo to Geneva," "The League and Abyssinia," etc.) that were written for a general audience. Some of Woolf's friends and colleagues were academics (most notably Goldsworthy Lowes Dickinson, John Maynard Keynes, Bertrand Russell, and Gilbert Murray), but Woolf did not write for an academic audience. Indeed, Virginia provides for us, in 1916, a description of Leonard's prodigious methods of writing: "Leonard is as usual writing away at about 6 books, and he has now trained himself to compose straight on to a typewriter, without a mistake in sense or spelling" (*L2* 83). An examination of his writings shows that he frequently used some of the same material, word for word, in various articles and books. This approach allowed him to publicize his views to a broader audience, a goal that Peter Wilson acknowledges.

Moreover, the noted scholar S. P. Rosenbaum has explained, in some detail, the importance of intellectual collaboration among members of the Bloomsbury Group, and this is especially true of Leonard Woolf and all of his political activities. By restricting this study primarily to Woolf's published writings, Wilson has overlooked the importance of the vast body of unpublished letters, committee reports, and memos that Woolf wrote that document the development of his political philosophy and the extent of his collaboration with friends and fellow political activists. For example, Woolf worked closely with fellow members of the Fabian Society and Labour Party committees while drafting reports and memos that he often revised two or three times at the suggestion of these fellow committee members. This process allowed him to work through a range of political positions that are then reflected in books and articles that he wrote for the broad literate audience that read periodicals such as *The Political Quarterly*. By comparing the different types of materials that Woolf wrote, we see him as the political pragmatist who drafted committee memos and reports (the writer who eluded Peter Wilson), and we can see Woolf as a publicist for liberal, political positions in the articles that he wrote for periodicals.

Thus, Wilson's study would have provided us with greater insight into Woolf's work if he had familiarized himself with a broader range of Leonard's work rather than relying on older, narrow studies, especially Duncan Wilson's *Leonard Woolf: A Political Biography* (1978). One assumes (though it is impossible to say) that Peter Wilson, who teaches at the London School of Economics, is familiar with its archival holdings on Woolf and Sidney Webb. To be sure, Wilson's examination of *International Government* and *Empire and Commerce in Africa*, which comprise four chapters of *The International Theory of Leonard Woolf*, would be more insightful if he had made use of Wayne K. Chapman's and Janet M. Manson's scholarship, especially "Carte and Tierce: Leonard, Virginia Woolf and War for Peace," in *Virginia Woolf and War: Fiction, Reality, and Myth* (1991) and "L.'s Dame Secretaire: Alix Strachey, the Hogarth Press and Bloomsbury Pacificism, 1917-1960," in *Women in the Milieu of Leonard and Virginia Woolf: Peace, Politics, and Education* (1998), which deal with the preliminary work that Leonard did, with Virginia's assistance, for *International Government* and *Empire and Commerce in Africa*. Had Wilson made use of "Carte and Tierce," besides Woolf's "Shall the Nations Enforce Peace?" in *War and Peace* (1917) and *The War for Peace* (1940), for example, he would have realized that Woolf was one of the early proponents of the use of force to maintain peace. (See *The International Theory of Leonard Woolf*, especially 70-1.) It is clear from Woolf's writings that World War II was his second war for peace, one that claimed his wife. (See especially *The War for Peace*, particularly 216-20 and *The Journey Not the Arrival Matters*, 1970.)

But, of course, Leonard Woolf's political writings is a big subject, and, to a large extent, Peter Wilson has focused his attention on Woolf's importance and significant achievements in shaping British foreign policy in the twentieth century. Indeed, Wilson puts his skill as a political scientist to good use by placing Woolf within the context of modern political theory, something that recent scholars have not done. Wilson's analysis of Woolf's and Carr's debate over the viability of the League is particularly insightful. Although Woolf was a liberal internationalist, Wilson concludes that he did not completely fit the idealist mold and certainly not the one that Carr fashioned.

—Janet M. Manson, *Clemson University*

The Reception of Virginia Woolf in Europe. Eds. Mary Ann Caws and Nicola Luckhurst (London and New York: Continuum, 2002) xxxviii + 450 pp.

This hefty volume is part of an ambitious project, published under the general editorship of Elinor Shaffer in the Athlone Critical Traditions Series, to study the reception not only of literary figures, but also philosophers, historians, scientists, and politicians; in fact, "writers in any field whose works have been recognized as making a contribution to the intellectual and cultural history of our society" (ix). As Mary Ann Caws remarks, Woolf is now "a larger-than-life, globally important figure" (xix) whose reception in every country has been primarily influenced by "the climate of receptiveness or refusal of feminism" (xx). Indeed, in nearly all the contributions to the book, the narrative of Woolf's reception from her own time until now is isomorphic with the fortunes of western feminism.

A fascinating timeline, with information on translations of Woolf's work and other significant moments in her critical reception in various countries, goes beyond Europe to include Argentina and Chile but not, surprisingly, Russia (Laura Marcus discusses Woolf's reception of Russian literature in her somewhat anomalous closing piece on "The European Dimensions of the Hogarth Press). There are also no accounts from Belgium or Holland. The "Europe" presented here is in some respects a rather idiosyncratic construction, heavily weighted in favor of the dominance of French and Spanish receptions, with the latter evoking that country's unresolved nationalist conflicts through essays on the Galician and Catalan Woolf, as well as its inevitable close ties to other Spanish-speaking cultures in South America.

As one might expect, translation issues dominate, and Nicola Luckhurst's superb introduction notes Woolf's own involvement in translating Russian works published by the Hogarth Press. Luckhurst suggests that "translation itself is the most significant encounter, the underlying constant in all these accounts of reception" (8). The *doubleness* of Woolf's reception history emerges as a significant theme in the introduction: Woolf as a modernist experimental writer is one identity; Woolf as a feminist (or *the* feminist) spokesperson another. These histories occasionally further divide within themselves: for example, the French publisher Stock rejected *Orlando*, *A Room* and *Three Guineas* after having published *The Voyage Out* and *To the Lighthouse*. In East Germany, Woolf's reception was interrupted by censorship hostile to modernism (9), but in the new market economy of 1990s Poland, Woolf's novels and *A Room* became bestsellers (similar to the situation in *perestroika*-era Russia, though that story is not told here).[1] Censorship itself emerges as an important aspect of reception history; Alberto Lázaro, reviewing Spanish Woolf scholarship, suggests almost an entirely new field of critical theory through his research in the postwar Spanish censors' files that record their readings of various works by Woolf.[2]

Although any volume of this type risks simply presenting lists of dates and translations, or summaries of critical works, there is enough variety among the contributors' approaches to ensure a reader's engagement with what will surely be quite new versions of Woolf for most Anglo-American scholars. Striking, too, are the number of instances in which a single individual has been the channel through which Woolf has entered a particular national culture. Victoria Ocampo in Argentina, for example, or Wolfgang Wicht in the German Democratic Republic, presented their own very influential versions of Woolf. It is possible in Denmark or Poland or Greece to be "the" Woolf specialist. Ocampo, similarly to Jacques Emile Blanche in France, was also responsible through her autobiographical accounts of meeting Woolf for what Luckhurst describes as "the double dissemination of Woolf as image and text" (6). Woolf's circulation as icon, clearly, began during her own lifetime and is noted by many contributors.

Luckhurst also cautions against reading Woolf's reception in specifically "national" terms, citing as the most telling example of why this can be misleading the widespread influence of Erich Auerbach's *Mimesis* in the academic reception of Woolf in several countries. This introduces yet another bifurcation, one which can be easily recognized in the American and British reception of

---

[1] It will be told in a forthcoming volume of papers from the "Virginia Woolf Across Cultures" symposium held at Russian State University for the Humanities, Moscow, in June 2003. Edited by Natalya Reinhold, this volume will include contributions from Korean, Japanese, Dutch, Portuguese, English, and U. S. as well as Russian Woolf scholars (Pace UP, 2004).

[2] *The Voyage Out*, for example, was praised by the censor as representing its characters "through a fine psychological and imaginative vision" (251), yet *The Waves* was redlined for references to God, the crucifix, the body, and the Spanish language.

Woolf, between the academic and the popular. Luckhurst mentions movie adaptations, documentaries, and films about figures associated with Woolf that have contributed to her international reputation, but, oddly perhaps, does not refer to Michael Cunningham's novel *The Hours*. In broad outline, she discerns a three-phase reception throughout Europe: as modernist and novelist; as essayist and author of foundational feminist texts; and as diarist, letter-writer and subject of numerous biographies.

Four essays discuss the reception of Woolf in France, beginning with Pierre-Eric Villeneuve's account of "the cultural impact Woolf had on the French intellectual scene, particularly on the thinking and works of writers of the generation that emerged following her death" (23). He exemplifies this impact through discussion of Simone DeBeauvoir, Natalie Sarraute and Maurice Blanchot. Not the kind of materialist history one is led to expect by Luckhurst's introduction, Villeneuve's literary critical essay has in every sentence the pressure of a book waiting to be written. It is a good example of the way that the establishment of Woolf as a global figure will foster a great deal of new and interesting work. Villeneuve points out the dialogue of DeBeauvoir's novel *L'Invitée* with novels such as *Jacob's Room* and *Mrs. Dalloway*, and comments on DeBeauvoir's use of Woolf in *Le Deuxième Sexe*. On the question of "influence" or even intertextuality, he shows how the selection of texts can be determinative: Sarraute and Woolf can be shown as antagonists, for example, if only "the lyrical side of Woolf's prose" is emphasized; Villeneuve finds the two writers' point of contact in *The Waves*. Blanchot's "notorious interpretation of *A Writer's Diary*" in 1959 saw Woolf as a poet of everyday life, treating her as a philosophical writer of the first rank, a reading that Villeneuve marks as "a milestone in the entire history of Woolf's reception" (34).

Focusing on the present state of French Woolf studies, Carole Rodier laments that Woolf has been appropriated by theoreticians who "overuse" critical tools. Her account of the highly formal structures of the French academy, with its centers and research teams, gives the impression that critical studies of Woolf are like lab reports, the tabulation of the results obtained by applying a grid to her texts. Narratology, psychoanalysis, and phenomenology are "the principle contexts in which Woolf's works are being most innovatively explored" (43), in contrast to the priority given by English critics to contextual elements of Woolf's work. The absence of women's or gender studies in the French academy explains for Rodier the lack of feminist approaches to Woolf. She also notes that the Société d'Études Woolfiennes is an exclusively academic society that holds its own, now international, symposium—quite a different milieu for discussion of Woolf than that represented by the British or American Woolf Societies.

Françoise Pellan and Mary Ann Caws contribute somewhat idiosyncratic pieces to the French section (Caws' quirky account of the 1974 Cerisy-la-Salle symposium and of Charles Mauron's translation of *Orlando* seems to me an exercise of editorial prerogative). Pellan notes Woolf's lack of interest in translations of her work, and reflects on her own experience of translating *To the Lighthouse* to exemplify the enormous challenges presented to a translator of Woolf by the essential differences between French and English. Although several contributors, including Luckhurst, refer to Mauron's translation of "Time Passes" published in *Commerce* in 1926, none refers to James Haule's commentaries on this piece, a surprising omission in so comprehensive a survey.[3]

The complex Spanish reception of Woolf is treated in several essays, beginning with an account by Laura Maria Lojo Rodríguez of the Argentine Victoria Ocampo's influence through the Sur group and the Sudamericana publishing house, following her meetings with Woolf in London in 1934.[4] The variety of approach in these contributions reflects the turbulent history of both Spain and Spanish-speaking countries in the first half of the twentieth century. These essays—as does, in fact, the volume as a whole—testify to the importance of publishing history in understanding the emergence of European modernism. For example, Lojo Rodríguez explains that "the publishing houses in Madrid focused primarily on the existing bond between Spain and the work of exiles, whereas Barcelona tended to publish European works which had played a seminal role in the process of cultural innovation. It is not surprising, therefore, that most of Woolf's works were—and still are nowadays—published in translation by editorial houses in Catalonia" (242).[5]

Jacqueline Hurtley notes that Woolf's writing "has occupied no mean place within the cultural production of Catalonia over the last seventy years" (296) and emphasizes that the reception of Woolf must be seen in the context of the struggle for women's rights from the late 1960s until the death of Franco in 1975. Both Hurtley and Alberto Lázaro comment on an exhibition held in Barcelona in

---

[3] James M. Haule, "'Le Temps Passe' and the Original Typescript: An Early Version of the 'Time Passes' Section of *To the Lighthouse*." *Twentieth Century Literature* 29.3 (Fall 1983): 267-311. James M. Haule, "*To the Lighthouse* and the Great War: The Evidence of Virginia Woolf's Revisions of 'Time Passes'." In Mark Hussey, ed. *Virginia Woolf and War: Fiction, Reality & Myth*. Syracuse: Syracuse UP, 1991: 164-79.

[4] See also Antonia García-Rodríguez, "Virginia Woolf from a Latin American Perspective." Mark Hussey and Vara Neverow-Turk, eds. *Virginia Woolf Miscellanies*. NY: Pace UP, 1992: 43-45.

[5] Publishers continue to shape reception history: it is hard to imagine what institutions or individuals will buy this book, which is priced at $160.

1986: "Lighthouses of the Twentieth Century" was "an audio-visual exhibition, composed of sections from Virginia Woolf's writings, reproduced on vertically hanging banners which formed a circle; a cone-like formation occupied the central space within this circle, made of a transparent fabric which enabled visitors to walk in and out of it at will. A video...showed a woman's body moving on the shore and through the sea" (311). This exhibition, which came about through the critic and translator Marta Pessarrodona's meeting Quentin and Anne Olivier Bell in 1983, attracted 20,000 visitors.

Of equal significance to the French and Spanish versions of Woolf is the German, where the Woolf "industry" is, according to Angsar and Vera Nünning, "second only to the Shakespeare industry" (98). A critical rethinking of Woolf's place in English literature, literary criticism, and feminism similar to that in the U. S. and in England is producing works that should be better known in English-speaking countries. The Nünnings' point made me wonder how well Europeans know each other's work: certainly, the work of (say) Japanese scholars does not have a presence on the U. S. critical scene, but is the same true of, for example, Italian writers' knowledge of German or French critics, or Spanish of Swedish? In other words, the insularity of scholars in English-speaking countries may not be all that different from any other country's literary scholars' tendency to read only what is translated into their own language. How many outside Germany, for example, know of the dozen articles on Woolf and "highly acclaimed monograph" of Willi Erzgräber? "It is not exaggeration," write the Nünnings, "to speak of an Erzgräber-school of German Woolf criticism" (79n15).

In the German Democratic Republic a single figure was responsible for bringing the "contraband" (121) of Woolf's work into the state. Wolfgang Wicht writes as an "insider," able to decode the "dominant ideological patterns" of the archive (105), and describes his own editing of Woolf as an "exemplary case of the general practise of publishing Western literature" (105). Again, Auerbach's impact is noted as challenging the socialist realism that held sway in the GDR. Looking back on the essays he wrote from within that ideological context, Wicht seems amused, affectionate toward, and occasionally irritated by his former self, embodying the constraints and challenges of a publishing history inflected by volatile politics and economic privations. Wicht writes that Woolf's novels "played a prominent role in widening the reader's horizon of literature and subverting the ruling ideological patterns of dogmatism" (126).

The essays in *The Reception of Virginia Woolf in Europe* will introduce many English-speaking readers to contexts of study previously unknown or even unknowable by monolinguists. Several contributors have found ways of conveying not only the raw data of reception history, in accounts of works translated or of academic meetings, but have also managed to give the texture of reader-response either through accounts of popular newspaper articles and reviews, or—as does Catherine Sandbach-Dahlström for the Swedish reception—of unpublished student papers. Sandbach-Dahlström uses her essay somewhat as a platform to criticize trends she disparages in Woolf criticism generally, but also aligns Sweden's democratic ideals of mass education with the Woolf of "The Leaning Tower." The "biographical," the poetic, and the political versions of Woolf seem to jostle one another in many other countries than just the United States or England. In Portugal, also, Woolf has played a "double role," being introduced as a modernist experimentalist and finding welcome as a writer who gives Portuguese women a language in which to express their own concerns. Graça Abranches takes the opportunity in her essay on the Portuguese reception to excoriate the well-distributed and cheap defective translations made in the 1990s. The quality not only of translations but also of the prefatory material accompanying them is of concern to several contributors.

Woolf's presence in the creative work of others is another significant aspect of the collective story of Woolf as a world writer articulated here. In *Tres mujeres* (Three Women), Ana Maria Navales (who has also written *Cuentos de Bloomsbury* [Bloomsbury Tales]) uses Woolf as a fictional character "through whom to construct an exploration of the female artist's relation to language and representation" (263). María José Gámez Fuentes notes "intertextual links between Woolf and modern Spanish women writers" such as Martin Gaite and Esther Tusquets. Manuela Palacios discusses the Galician Ramón Otero Pedrayo's creation of "Lady Woolf" as a British writer in his 1935 novel *Devalar* (Flowing), as well as references to Woolf in the work of Galician women writers in the 1980s and 1990s. Abranches describes a 2000 novel by the Portuguese writer Maria Velho da Costa, *Irene*, or the *Social Contract*, in which a character named Orlando is "handsome, politically aware and sensitive, multicultural, multilingual and multidimensional" (326); "the *mestizo* who 'will be a boy and a girl too,' stands, in superb homage to Virginia Woolf, as the metaphor for the future of Europe" (327). A metaphor, also, for the ideal reader of the internationalist Woolf that is shaped by these remarkable accounts of her European reception.

—Mark Hussey, *Pace University*

Step-Daughters of England: British Women Modernists and the National Imaginary. Jane Garrity (Manchester and New York: Manchester UP, 2003) x + 349pp.

Step-Daughters of England offers a meticulously researched, articulate and thoughtful intervention into the ongoing and often heated debate among "new modernism" and Woolf scholars regarding British women modernists' fraught positioning as female national subjects, their imbrication within discourses of imperialism and consumerism, and their use of aesthetic experimentation. While Virginia Woolf is only one of four primary writers studied in depth here, her presence and example permeate the book as a whole, and Garrity's handling of the myriad threads of this impressive study. Garrity addresses that "position of privilege" and traces it back to the interwar period (18) in ways that will perhaps surprise and in some cases, rile Woolf scholars. Garrity's provocative discussion of *The Waves* is reason enough to read the book, but it's the book in its entirety that underpins her nuanced understanding of the contradictions Woolf attempted to negotiate in that novel and that situate Woolf so carefully in relation to her peers. The book's major contribution to the field derives from Garrity's deft multidisciplinary, historical layering through which we engage with so many figures from the interwar era, from the four major writers—Woolf, Sylvia Townsend Warner, Mary Butts and Dorothy Richardson, who each have their own chapter—to Jane Ellen Harrison, Jean Rhys, Olive Moore, Marie Stopes, Winifred Holtby, Mina Loy, Cicely Hamilton, Mary Scharlieb, Radclyffe Hall, Ray Strachey, Eleanor Rathbone and many others. This complex web of historical layers, drawn from Garrity's incredibly wide range of both primary and secondary sources including diverse archival materials, affords contemporary readers a wealth of insight into the literary, political, aesthetic, social and sexual issues these women confronted, the affinities they shared, and the different approaches they undertook to resolve the dense knot of their own national and gendered subjectivity in relation to their professional and aesthetic work. The text builds on and engages in dialogue with the most recent scholarly work on Englishness and imperialism in relation to modernism, gender, and experimental form and breaks new ground in providing a way of critically exploring "a reliance on the *feminine* as an imaginative axis which organizes categories of race, sexuality, class and national identity in distinctive but mutually resonant ways" (6).

The book began as Garrity's 1994 dissertation at Berkeley, where she studied with Elizabeth Abel, Caren Kaplan, and Susan Schweik. Their critical influence echoes in the theoretical framework Garrity constructs for her exploration of these women and their texts, one that fuses Kristeva's work on the abject mother and the nation, Benedict Anderson's work on the national imaginary, and Simon Gikandi's work on Englishness in a fruitful, exemplary way.

Woolfians will already be familiar with this approach following Garrity's contributions on Woolf's writing in the 1920s in British *Vogue* to Pamela Caughie's edited collection *Virginia Woolf in the Age of Mechanical Reproduction* (Garland, 2000) and *Modernism/Modernity,* as well as a paper given at the 2002 MLA. She has also recently published on queer theory ("Mediating the Taboo: The Straight Lesbian Gaze," *Straight With a Twist: Queer Theory and the Subject of Heterosexuality*, ed. Calvin Thomas. [U of Illinois P, 2000]) and is at work on two edited collections (one with Laura Doan) that extend the theoretical constellating of gender, imperialism, nationalism and modernism, as well as a book project on Englishwomen travelers in the Middle East during the early decades of the 20th century. Her contribution here to the traces of racism and imperialism in Woolf's writing, particularly, will generate many important (and lively) (re)considerations.

Readers might wonder why Garrity chooses these four writers to put into primary dialogue with each other, given their disparate political and feminist affiliations. As she puts it at the beginning of her chapter contextualizing "nationality law, the social construction of femininity, and the discourse of maternalist imperialism" in relation to "British women's fantasies of cultural agency" (29):

> British women's perception of the global is informed by their awareness of the growing dimensions of the empire's reach, even when they question the effectiveness of that project. Symptomatically, while Richardson, Warner, Butts, and Woolf express varying responses to the principle of women's national responsibility, none puts her faith in parliamentary reforms. All of these writers register a gap between their subordinate status as female citizens and their desire to resist the State's repression of their cultural agency, reminding us of Jean Rhys's line: "everybody knows England isn't a woman's country". Putting Richardson, Warner, Butts, and Woolf into conversation with other British women writers and activists who similarly sought to remap the empire by championing femininity, this chapter explores how vexed the conceptual and the material realities of the female body were for British women, providing a historical basis for understanding why they imaginatively circumvent it (44).

For Garrity, each of these writers "highlights different key issues with respect to modernism and English national identity" and "portrays the female body as a site for recasting the nation as a whole" (5). Although these four writers "often balk at the supposition that the reproductive female body legitimizes women's participation in national life,"

> each nevertheless taps in to the correlative presumption that women are morally superior beings by trading on the idea of women's national responsibility and simultaneously alluding to the fact that Britain is already expressly gendered as a 'feminine' national body. British women modernists remain uneasily tied to

such dominant discourses of national belonging and imperial redemption, plagued by fierce emotions and irrational desires that inform their sacred loyalties to place and betray their varied unconscious attachments to England (2).

While I've personally never read Butts and have had only a limited engagement with Richardson and Warner, I found Garrity's constellation of these four writers in relation to so many additional writers and activists (female and male) of great historical and critical benefit, particularly coupled with a methodology that "foregrounds a range of cultural developments that coincided with the rise of modernism" as she discusses each of them. These cultural developments include "emerging visual technologies, the revival of British neo-medievalism, ethnographic work on primitive mysticism, and nostalgia for English ruralism" (4-5).

All of these threads come together in Garrity's breakthrough reading (in my view) of *The Waves*, one that has the same kind of "shock effect" that Jane Marcus's ("Britannia Rules *The Waves*") did about a decade ago. This 50-plus page chapter, "Mapping 'the body of our mother': national desire, imperial nostalgia and language in Virginia Woolf" is the climax of the book, toward which all the other chapters point, at least thematically. Invoking most of Woolf's primary texts in the course of her discussion, *The Waves*, Garrity says,

> suggests that the world is negotiated spatially, that female authorship (through the depiction of Elvedon) is located at the sacred core of national culture, and that the maternal (embodied improbably by Percival) is *the* principle of order, central to the national-imperial enterprise. Ultimately, Woolf delineates two distinct forms of nationalism that are fused in Percival: one, a militaristic nationalism that is associated with fascism and the symbolic order (and which the novel explicitly repudiates); the other, a more authentic ancestral Englishness that is tied to the semiotic, the recuperation of the mother/land, and primitive ritual (which Woolf celebrates) (243).

As she works through the chapter, building her argument section by section, Garrity provides a fascinating historical lens for the discourses of neo-medievalism (Harrison and Jessie Weston figure prominently in the discussion); "the interwar interest in the spiritual culture of landscape; the British feminist view that racial motherhood constituted the highest form of national responsibility; and the modernist engagement with matriarchal prehistory and *primitive* practices" (243). Her theoretical framework, anchored primarily but by no means exclusively by Kristeva, Anderson, and Gikandi, opens the novel to a multilayered engagement, enabling a sophisticated understanding of Percival's maternal and linguistic role in relation to the six male and female characters while it also articulates Woolf's ambitions as well as blindspots at the beginning of the 1930s. Garrity aims "to demonstrate how *The Waves*, although critical of it, simultaneously acknowledges imperialism as a precondition for locating oneself in the national imaginary....what *The Waves* ultimately calls for is the recovery of a repressed language," she asserts, "one drawn from the discourses of conquest and English prehistory, that would help to shape a feminizing of national space" (247). I was riveted by the discussion of the novel itself, and by Garrity's staging of Woolf's conflicted negotiations of Englishness, class privilege, and literary production, particularly by women.

Garrity takes Woolf to task in the introduction for not being more involved in helping her female peers gain access to a public. "If Woolf's competitiveness and disparagement of (in particular) best-selling female authors are inseparable from her anxiety surrounding her own popularity and the economic basis of her literary production, it is also true that, while she reviewed books by women throughout her career, she never used her considerable influence to further the careers of struggling British women novelists" (19). Garrity raises the issue in order to help explain the "relative obscurity of the other authors of this study" (19) and brings this subject back into dialogue with Woolf's discussion in *A Room of One's Own* of what it would take to establish a literary tradition for women, points that I found refreshing. While this review continues to privilege Woolf over the other writers in Garrity's study, my understanding of Woolf's project in *AROO* as well as the 1930s gained considerable depth, which will fuel my further reading of the other writers in this study. I'm sure I won't be alone in that effort.

Reading the book is a bit like participating in an engaging session at the annual Woolf conference where multiple reading strategies and critical approaches have contributed to new considerations of modernist texts and a lively question and answer period has spilled out into a coffee break or reception. This dialogic sensation stems partly from Garrity's fluid writing style and partly from her expansive reading of contemporary material on Englishness, imperialism, postcolonial theory, gender and sexuality studies and aesthetic reevaluations in relation to the primary interwar texts by British women modernists. These not only include citations from literary, historical and critical sources but letters and articles in such publications as *Time and Tide* and *The Woman's Leader*, based on her archival work. The footnotes and bibliography (the latter is 28 pages long) are particularly valuable as research tools on British women modernists in the interwar period as well as the multidisciplinary critical frameworks I've cited above. By engaging in its own dialogue with recent critical interventions put forward by "new modernist" scholars, the book allows readers to feel immersed, without feeling overwhelmed, within a fascinating conversation.

—Jeanette McVicker, *SUNY Fredonia*

Notes on Contributors

Meena Alexander is an award winning poet and Distinguished Professor of English and Women's Studies at Hunter College and the CUNY Graduate Center. Her works include the volumes of poetry *House of a Thousand Doors*, *River and Bridge*, and *Illiterate Heart*; a volume of essays and poems, *The Shock of Arrival: Reflections on Postcolonial Experience*; the memoir *Fault Lines*; the novels *Nampally Road*, and *Manhattan Music*. She is the author of two critical studies: *The Poetic Self: Towards a Phenomenology of Romanticism* and *Women in Romanticism: Mary Wollstonecraft, Dorothy Wordsworth and Mary Shelley*. She is currently at work editing the anthology *Indian Love Poems*.

Mónica G. Ayuso, born and raised in Argentina, is currently Associate Professor in the English Department at California State University, Bakersfield. Since she completed her Doctorate with a dissertation entitled "Thinking Back through Our Mothers: Virginia Woolf in the Spanish American Imagination," she has continued to work on comparative approaches to ethnic, racial, and gender issues.

Pat Cramer is Associate Professor of English and Women's Studies at the University of Connecticut at Stamford. She has published articles on feminist teaching, Chaucer, Blake, and Woolf and is co-editor of *Virginia Woolf: Lesbian Readings*. Her most recent article, "The Absent Lover in *The Waves*: Jane Harrison and Lesbian Plots" is forthcoming in *Studies in the Novel*. She is currently working on a book entitled *Virginia Woolf: The Lesbian Years*, which is the first full length study of the impact of Woolf's lesbianism on her writing.

Beth Rigel Daugherty teaches English, Integrative Studies, and Senior Year Experience courses at Otterbein College in Westerville, Ohio, site of the Fifth Annual Conference on Virginia Woolf. She co-edited, with Mary Beth Pringle, *Approaches to Teaching Woolf's* To the Lighthouse, and with Eileen Barrett, *Virginia Woolf: Texts and Contexts, Selected Papers from the Fifth Annual Conference*. She has published articles on *To the Lighthouse*, "Mr. Bennett and Mrs. Brown," "How Should One Read a Book?" and the *Common Readers*. Her work in progress is a book tentatively titled "The Education of a Woman Writer: Virginia Woolf's Apprenticeship," and she is also working on Woolf as an educator essayist and on Woolf's reception in the United States before 1975.

NOTES ON CONTRIBUTORS

Hans Walter Gabler is Professor of English Literature at the University of Munich, Germany, where, from 1996 to 2002, he directed an interdisciplinary graduate program on "Textual Criticism as Foundation and Method of the Historical Disciplines." He is editor-in-chief of the critical editions of James Joyce's *Ulysses, A Portrait of the Artist as a Young Man,* and *Dubliners.*

Diane F. Gillespie, Professor of English, Emeritus, at Washington State University, is author of *The Sisters' Arts: The Writing and Painting of Virginia Woolf and Vanessa Bell*, editor of Woolf's biography of Roger Fry for the Shakespeare Head edition of her works, editor of *The Multiple Muses of Virginia Woolf*, co-editor of a volume of Julia Stephen's writings, and co-editor of the selected papers from the sixth annual conference on Virginia Woolf. Her latest book is a co-edited edition of Cicely Hamilton's 1908 play, *Diana of Dobson's.* Having edited sections on May Sinclair and Dorothy Richardson for Bonnie Kime Scott's *The Gender of Modernism*, she is currently editing the section on modernist women painters for the forthcoming *The Gender Complex of Modernism.* She has also published numerous articles on Virginia Woolf, May Sinclair, Dorothy Richardson, Bloomsbury, and modern drama.

Jane Lilienfeld is a Professor of English at Lincoln University, an historically Black college in Jefferson City, MO. She has published essays on Willa Cather, Colette, Margaret Atwood, James Joyce, and feminist theory in addition to her work on Virginia Woolf. Her book *Reading Alcoholisms: Theorizing Character and Narrative in Selected Novels of Thomas Hardy, James Joyce, and Virginia Woolf* won a *Choice* Award as an outstanding academic book of 2000. With Jeffrey Oxford, she co-edited an anthology entitled *The Languages of Addiction.* Awarded a Canadian Studies Grant from the Canadian Government, Lilienfeld studied the manuscripts of Alice Munro at the University of Calgary in the summer of 2001. Her work on Alice Munro is part of her current project, tentatively entitled "Circumventing Circumstance: World Wide Women Tell Stories."

Lisa Low is an independent scholar who has published a number of essays on Virginia Woolf. She is also co-editor with Anthony John Harding of *Milton, The Metaphysicals, and Romanticism.*

Jeanette McVicker is Professor of English at SUNY Fredonia. Her scholarly interests include modernism, poststructuralist theory, globalization and the profession, and postmodern American literature and culture. She directed the Women's Studies Program 1996-2000 and currently directs the Journalism Program. Her work has appeared in *Women's Studies On Its Own*; *boundary 2*; *Crossings*; *Woolf Studies Annual* and, with Laura Davis, she co-edited the *Selected Papers* from the 7th and 8th Annual Conferences on Virginia Woolf

Vara Neverow is Professor of English and Chair of Department at Southern Connecticut State University She co-edited with Mark Hussey the first three volumes of the *Selected Papers* of the Annual Conference on Virginia Woolf; co-edited with Merry Pawlowski the Electronic Facsimile of the *Three Guineas* Reading Notebooks (online at CSU-Bakersfield), and has published many articles on Woolf. She is current President of the International Virginia Woolf Society; Managing Editor of the *Virginia Woolf Miscellany*. She is at work on a book-length study on Woolf, patriarchy and feminist utopias.

Jeffrey Oxford received his PhD from Texas Tech University and is Associate Professor of Foreign Languages at the University of North Texas in Denton. He is the author of *Vicente Blasco Ibáñez: Color Symbolism in Selected Novels* and *Conversar para aprender*, editor of *La barraca* and co-editor of *The Languages of Addiction* and *Eduardo Mendoza: A New Look*. As well, he is author of various articles and presentations on naturalism and its manifestations in nineteenth- and twentieth-century peninsular Spanish literature.

Carey Snyder is an assistant professor of 20th century English literature at Ohio University. This article is part of a larger project that examines the role that ethnography played in the emergence of the modernist novel.

Birgit Spengler teaches American Studies at Johann Wolfgang Goethe University in Frankfurt am Main, Germany, and is currently working on her PhD thesis, "Gaze, Narration and Gender: Looking and Story-telling in Nineteenth-Century American Women's Writing."

Policy

Woolf Studies Annual invites articles on the work and life of Virginia Woolf and her milieu. The Annual intends to represent the breadth and eclecticism of critical approaches to Woolf, and particularly welcomes new perspectives and contexts of inquiry. Articles discussing relations between Woolf and other writers and artists are also welcome.

Articles are sent for review anonymously to a member of the Editorial Board and at least one other reader. Manuscripts should not be under consideration elsewhere or have been previously published. Final decisions are made by the Editorial Board.

Preparation of Copy

1. Articles are typically between 25 and 30 pages, and do not exceed 8000 words.

2. A separate page should include the article's title, author's name, address, telephone & fax numbers, and e-mail address. The author's name and identifying references should not appear on the manuscript.

3. A photocopy of any illustrations should accompany the manuscript. (Black-and-white photographs will be required for accepted work.)

4. Manuscripts should be prepared according to most recent MLA style.

5. Three copies of the manuscript and an abstract of up to 150 words should be sent to: Mark Hussey, English Dept., Pace University, One Pace Plaza, New York NY 10038-1598. Only materials accompanied by a self-addressed, stamped envelope (or international reply coupon) will be returned.

6. Authors of accepted manuscripts will be asked to submit two hard copies and an electronic version. Authors are responsible for all necessary permissions fees.

Please address inquiries to: Mark Hussey, English Department, 41 Park Row Rm. 1510, New York, NY 10038. Email: mhussey@pace.edu
Fax: (212) 346-1754.

www.ingramcontent.com/pod-product-compliance
Lightning Source LLC
Chambersburg PA
CBHW021815300426
44114CB00009BA/180